HEBREW RELIGION

HEBREW RELIGION
ITS ORIGIN AND DEVELOPMENT

BY

W. O. E. OESTERLEY, Litt.D., D.D.(Camb.)

AND

THEODORE H. ROBINSON, Litt.D. (Camb.),
D.D. (Lond.)

LONDON
S · P · C · K
1966

First published 1930
Second, revised and enlarged, edition 1937
Reprinted 1940
Reprinted 1944
Reprinted 1947
Reprinted 1949
Reprinted 1952
Reprinted 1955
Reprinted 1957
Reprinted 1961
Reprinted 1966

MADE IN GREAT BRITAIN

DEDICATED TO THE MEMORY OF

ARTHUR S. PEAKE

TEACHER, SCHOLAR, FRIEND

PREFACE TO SECOND EDITION

WE welcome the opportunity, which the publishers have afforded us, of revising, expanding, and, in large measure, rewriting our work. We have endeavoured to make use of the advance made in many directions by Old Testament studies during the last six years, and, we hope, to correct certain weaknesses of which we were conscious in the first edition. Thus we have greatly expanded what we had previously written on the Life after Death, dividing the subject between the chief stages in its history. We have also added a short discussion of the Messianic Hope, and have appended a new chapter, in which we try to express our conviction that the religion of Israel culminates in the Gospel.

Several chapters, especially in Part I, have been re-arranged, and all have been numbered consecutively throughout the book. Several have been considerably expanded, particularly in Part II, and we hope that this section has now attained its due proportion.

We take this opportunity of thanking the numerous reviewers, who, by their generous appreciation of our first edition, have encouraged us in the production of a second, and who, by their many valuable hints and comments, have suggested lines along which revision might proceed. We send out this volume, then, in the hope that it may be as acceptable and as useful as the former, apparently, proved itself to be.

In conclusion, we desire to express our gratitude to our friend, Dr. H. H. Rowley, for a number of valuable suggestions, and for having so generously undertaken the laborious task of reading through the proof-sheets.

W. O. E. OESTERLEY.
THEODORE H. ROBINSON.

CONTENTS

PREFACE TO SECOND EDITION vii

PART I

THE BACKGROUND

CHAP.
I. THE EARLIEST STAGES OF RELIGIOUS BELIEF . . 3
  1. Introductory.
  2. The Earliest Stage (Pre-Animistic).
  3. The Animistic Stage :
    (a) Trees.
    (b) Streams, Springs, etc.
    (c) Stones, Rocks, and Mountains.
    (d) Polydæmonism.
  4. The Polytheistic Stage.
  5. Totemism.
  6. Taboo.
  7. Magic.
  8. The After-Life.
  9. Ancestor-Worship, and the Cult of the Dead.
  10. Necromancy.

II. REMNANTS OF ANIMISM IN HEBREW RELIGION : SACRED
    TREES 23
  1. General Semitic Belief.
  2. The Old Testament.

III. REMNANTS OF ANIMISM IN HEBREW RELIGION : SACRED
    WATERS 33
  1. General Semitic Belief.
  2. The Old Testament.

IV. REMNANTS OF ANIMISM IN HEBREW RELIGION : SACRED
    STONES, ROCKS, AND MOUNTAINS . . . 41
  1. General Semitic Belief.
  2. The Old Testament.

V. POLYTHEISTIC TENDENCIES IN HEBREW RELIGION . 50
  1. General Semitic Belief.
  2. The Old Testament.
    (a) The 'Elim.
    (b) The Be'alim.

VI. REMNANTS OF TOTEMISM AND TABOO IN HEBREW
    RELIGION 62
  1. Totemism.
  2. Taboo.

CONTENTS

CHAP.   PAGE

VII.   SOME FURTHER ELEMENTS IN THE RELIGIOUS BACK-
       GROUND : MAGIC   71
       1. Technical Magical Terms.
       2. Magical Arts.

VIII. SOME FURTHER ELEMENTS IN THE RELIGIOUS BACK-
       GROUND : THE AFTER-LIFE : THE EARLIEST STAGE
       OF BELIEF   79
       1. Babylonian Beliefs and Customs.
       2. Ancient Arab Beliefs and Customs.
       3. The Old Testament.

IX.   SOME FURTHER ELEMENTS IN THE RELIGIOUS BACK-
       GROUND : ANCESTOR-WORSHIP; NECROMANCY   .   98
       1. Ancestor-Worship.
       2. Necromancy.

X.   SOME FURTHER ELEMENTS IN THE RELIGIOUS BACK-
       GROUND : DEMONOLOGY   108
       1. General Semitic Belief.
       2. The Old Testament :—
          (a) Theriomorphic Demons :
              i. The *Seraphim*.
              ii. The *Se'irim*.
              iii. *'Azazel*.
              iv. Some other Demons.
          (b) Anthropomorphic Demons :
              i. *Lilith*.
              ii. *'Aluqah*.
              iii. The " Night-terror."
              iv. Miscellaneous Demons.
              v. Protective Amulets.

PART II

ISRAELITE RELIGION

XI.   NOMADIC RELIGION : THE PRE-MOSAIC AGE   .   .   125
       1. Introductory.
       2. Objects of Worship.
       3. New-Moon Festivals.
       4. The Passover Festival.
       5. Further Festivals and Sacrifices.
       6. The Sabbaths.
       7. Other Ancient Institutions.

XII.   NOMADIC RELIGION : THE BEGINNING OF THE WORSHIP
       OF YAHWEH   140
       1. The Exodus from Egypt, and the Subsequent
          Events.
       2. Yahweh, the God of the Hebrews.

XIII. MOSAISM : THE RELIGION OF ISRAEL IN THE
       WILDERNESS   151
       1. The Exodus.
       2. Yahweh.

CHAP.   PAGE

    3. The Covenant.
    4. Sacred Emblems.
    5. Sacred Persons.
    6. Ritual.
    7. Ethic.

XIV. THE RELIGION OF CANAAN 170
    1. The Sources.
    2. Canaanite Objects of Worship.
    3. Sanctuaries.
    4. The Cultus.
    5. Sacred Persons.
    6. The Ethic of Ba'alism.

XV. THE EARLY RELIGION OF THE SETTLEMENT : APOSTASY 188
    1. Israel in Palestine.
    2. Israel and the *Ba'als*.
    3. The Lesson of the Judges.

XVI. THE RELIGION OF ISRAEL IN THE EARLY MONARCHY . 195
    1. Polytheism.
    2. Syncretism.
    3. Religion in Southern Palestine
    4. Religion in Northern Palestine.

XVII. THE YAHWIST REVIVAL 205
    1. Liberty and Autocracy.
    2. Jezebel and Melkart.
    3. The Yahwist Guilds.
    4. Elijah.
    5. The Prophetic Revolution.

XVIII. THE RELIGION OF ISRAEL AFTER JEHU . . . 216
    1. Archæological Discovery.
    2. Prophetic Denunciation.
    3. Evidence outside of Palestine.
    4. Religious and Social Corruption.

XIX. THE CANONICAL PROPHETS 222
    1. The *Nebi'im* and the Canonical Prophets.
    2. The Teaching of the Prophets :
        (a) Yahweh as Law.
        (b) Yahweh as the Lord of Nature.
        (c) Yahweh as Lord of History.
        (d) Yahweh as Lord of the End of Things.
        (e) Yahweh as Lord of Universal Morality.
        (f) Yahweh as the God of Israel.
        (g) The Nature of Punishment.
        (h) Yahweh makes no Ritual Demands.

XX. THE EIGHTH-CENTURY PROPHETS 233
    1. Amos.
    2. Hosea.
    3. Isaiah.
    4. Hezekiah's Reforms.

CHAP.   PAGE
XXI.   THE AFTER-LIFE : SECOND STAGE OF BELIEF   .   .   243
       1. Babylonian Belief.
       2. The Old Testament.

XXII. THE REFORMS OF JOSIAH   254
       1. The Reforms.
       2. Deuteronomy.

XXIII. THE SEVENTH-CENTURY PROPHETS   259
       1. Zephaniah.
       2. Jeremiah.
       3. Habakkuk.
       4. The Fall of Jerusalem.

PART III

EARLY JUDAISM

THE PERIOD OF THE EXILE

XXIV.   BABYLONIAN INFLUENCE ON THE JEWS   .   .   .   271

XXV.   THE EARLY YEARS OF THE EXILE   276
        1. The Records of the Deportations.
        2. The Religious Beliefs of the People :
           (a) Those in Babylon who were Deported in
               597 B.C.
           (b) Those who were left in the Homeland.
           (c) Those who had Settled Down in Egypt.
           (d) Those in Babylon after the 586 B.C. De-
               portation.

XXVI.   THE JEWISH COMMUNITY IN EXILE   283
        1. Communal Life in the Exile.
        2. Religious Observances among the Exiles.

XXVII. RELIGIOUS TEACHERS : THE PRIEST-PROPHET EZEKIEL   289
        1. Ezekiel's Doctrine of God.
        2. Superhuman Beings.
        3. Individual Responsibility.
        4. Regeneration.
        5. The Ceremonial Law.
        6. Eschatological-Apocalyptic Ideas.

XXVIII. RELIGIOUS TEACHERS : DEUTERO-ISAIAH   .   .   .   299
        1. The Conception of God.
        2. The Regeneration of the People.
        3. Universalism.
        4. The " Servant of the Lord " Songs.
        5. Other Teachers of the Exilic Period.
        6. Summary of the Development of Hebrew Religion
           during the Exilic Period.

THE PERSIAN PERIOD

CHAP.   PAGE

XXIX. PERSIAN INFLUENCE ON JEWISH BELIEF . . . 312

XXX. THE RETURN FROM THE EXILE 315
1. Particularism and Universalism.
2. The Returned Exiles.

XXXI. THE LAW 320

XXXII. WISDOM 325

XXXIII. GOD AND THE SOUL : WORSHIP ; PIETISM . . 328
1. The Universality of Yahweh.
2. The Worship of Israel.
3. The Development of the Sacrificial System.
4. God and the Individual.

THE GREEK PERIOD

XXXIV. THE INFLUENCE OF HELLENISM ON THE JEWS . . 340

XXXV. THE PROBLEM OF SUFFERING 344
1. The Problem Intensified by Prophetic Teaching.
2. The "Servant Songs."
3. The Book of Job.

XXXVI. THE AFTER-LIFE : THE FINAL STAGE OF BELIEF . 352

XXXVII. WISDOM AND ITS DEVELOPMENTS 366
1. The Semitic Mind.
2. The *Mashal.*
3. Wisdom and its Fuller Meaning.

XXXVIII. THE MESSIANIC HOPE 375
1. The Earlier Stages.
2. The Messiah in Apocalyptic.

XXXIX. ESCHATOLOGY AND APOCALYPTIC 386
1. Jewish Eschatology.
2. Persian Eschatology and Apocalyptic :
  (*a*) Dualism.
  (*b*) World-epochs.
  (*e*) The Judgement and the Destruction of the World by Fire.
  (*d*) The Resurrection.
3. Some further Marks of Persian Influence.
4. Jewish Apocalyptists and their Literature.

XL. THE LAW AND ITS DEVELOPMENTS 401
1. Some Books of the Apocrypha.
2. Some Events in the History of the Maccabæan Rising.
3. The New Testament.
4. The Mishnah.

XLI. CONCLUSION 411

INDEX OF MODERN AUTHORS 418

INDEX OF BIBLICAL AND POST-BIBLICAL REFERENCES 420

INDEX : GENERAL 428

PART I

THE BACKGROUND

B

CHAPTER I

THE EARLIEST STAGES OF RELIGIOUS BELIEF

1. INTRODUCTORY

THE Hebrews were Semites, and their religion, in its origin, did not differ from that of the Semites in general. In order therefore to distinguish clearly those elements which were common to all Semites, and those which in course of time came to be specifically Hebrew, it is necessary to have some knowledge of early Semitic religion, so far as this is obtainable.

Now, most authorities hold that the original home of the Semites was the great Arabian peninsula, whence, owing to the pressure of population and scarcity of food, they flowed out in successive waves into the lands north, north-east, and north-west, and formed, in course of time, the various Semitic groups known to us as Babylonians, Assyrians, Aramæans, Phœnicians, Edomites, Moabites, Ammonites, Hebrews, and Abyssinians (Falashas). Thus it is obvious, on the face of it, that the Semites were for many long centuries *nomads* before the various groups in turn became agriculturists and, later, dwellers in cities. And it is important to remember that the religion of nomads cannot be quite the same thing as that of men who have reached the more cultured stages; nevertheless, owing to the tenacity of religious belief and custom, we must be prepared to see the remnants of the nomadic religious stage in subsequent ages.

We have, however, to go back yet a further step. The Semites formed only a branch of the human family, and there were elements in their religious beliefs and customs which were, in their origin, common to mankind in the earliest stages of which we have knowledge. We have therefore to begin our inquiry by going back to times when man was in a very primitive stage of culture, in order to seek the origins of some beliefs and customs which appear in the religion of the Semites generally as well as in that of the Hebrews.

2. The Earliest Stage (Pre-animistic)

It is necessary to touch, though it be but cursorily, upon the subject of the earliest forms of religious beliefs among men, because Hebrew religion cannot be properly understood without some knowledge of these. The roots of religious belief go very deep, and to cut off the later growths and developed forms of belief and ritual which we meet with in the Old Testament from that out of which they emerged would result in frequent misunderstandings of the meaning and significance of the concepts and rites of the religion of the Hebrews. That the different stages of belief overlap lies in the nature of things.

It must be recognized at the outset that it is impossible to say what men believed in the earliest religious stage, because there is no means of ascertaining scientifically the original belief of mankind about anything. Certain deductions may be drawn, nevertheless, from the beliefs and rites and general mental make-up of the earliest representatives of the human race now living, and there is much evidence to support the view now widely held that the origin of religion is to be sought in the vague primitive emotion expressed by the phrase " the sense of awe." Early man was constantly being confronted with phenomena within himself, among his fellows, and in the natural world, which mystified him; what was uncanny generated fear; the mystery of the incomprehensible called forth the emotion of awe. " The sense of wonder," says James, " in the presence of the mysterious has been one of the primary impulses of religion, and it may well be that it played a prominent part in the earliest stages of spiritual apprehension." [1] This sense of awe is seen to have been deeply prevalent in every succeeding stage of religion, a fact which in itself goes to support the contention that it lies at the base of all religion. Emotions, with their resultant impulses, are the antecedent elements which originate ideas; it is the play of the emotions which first impels the mind to frame rudimentary ideas; and the evidence goes to show that the emotion of awe among primitive peoples is the prime antecedent of the supernatural. In speaking of writers on religious origins, Marett says that they " for the most part profess, though not always in very plain

[1] " Primitive Monotheism," in *The Sociological Review*, XXVII, p. 331 (1935); see also Clodd, " Pre-animistic stages in Religion," *Transactions of the Third International Congress for the History of Religions*, i. 33 ff. (1908).

or positive terms, to discern beneath the fluctuating details
of its efforts at self-interpretation, a certain Religious
Sense, or, as many would call it, Instinct, whereof the
component 'moments' are Fear, Admiration, Wonder,
and the like, whilst its object is, broadly speaking, the
Supernatural. . . . Thus we must, I think, in any case
admit the fact that in response to, or at any rate, in connexion with, the emotions of Awe, Wonder, and the like,
wherein feeling would seem for the time being to have
outstripped the power of 'natural,' that is reasonable,
explanation, there arises in the region of human thought a
powerful impulse to objectify and even personify the
mysterious or 'supernatural' something felt, and in the
region of will a corresponding impulse to render it innocuous,
or better still, propitious, by force of constraint, communion,
or conciliation." [1] This is in agreement with what Andrew
Lang contended in regard to All-Fathers or "High Gods"
among many savage races,[2] but which has been interpreted
in recent years by W. Schmidt in a sense which we find
difficult to accept.[3] As E. O. James says : "What he [W.
Schmidt] is really out to maintain is that the idea of God,
so far from being a product of development within an
evolutionary process, is the original belief of the human
race as a whole—in short, that it constitutes a primeval
revelation to mankind. . . . While the universal occurrence
of High Gods among low races suggests a probability in
favour of the concept being a part of the original substratum
of religious consciousness, to interpret it in terms of a primeval
revelation raises more problems for the theologian than it
solves, and it is certainly to go beyond the legitimate limits
of anthropological evidence." [4]

The belief in High Gods presupposes the feeling of the
mysterious and the awesome, and it is this latter which
was the first impulse to religion, resulting in the consciousness
of dependence on a supernatural power; and this must be
regarded as the first stage of religion.

3. THE ANIMISTIC STAGE

"In the language of philosophy, Animism is the doctrine
which places the source of mental and even physical life

---

[1] *The Threshold of Religion*, pp. 10 ff. (1909).
[2] *The Making of Religion*, see especially pp. 173–253 (1900, 2nd ed.).
[3] *The Origin and Growth of Religion* (transl. by H. J. Rose), pp. 262–282
(1931).
[4] *Loc. cit.*, pp. 337 f.

in an energy independent of or at least distinct from the body. From the point of view of the history of religions, the term is taken, in a wider sense, to denote the belief in the existence of spiritual beings, some attached to bodies of which they constitute the real personality (*souls*), others without necessary connexion with a determinate body (*spirits*)." [1]

For purposes which will become clear as we proceed, it is necessary to consider very briefly the more outstanding objects with which Animism can best be illustrated. These comprise :

(*a*) Trees. (*b*) Streams, springs, etc. (*c*) Stones, rocks, and mountains.

(*a*) The movement of a tree when swayed by the wind made it one of the first things to be regarded by man in a very early stage of culture, first, as a living being, and later, as animated by a spirit. Cause and effect, as we understand them, not being recognized, the idea that the branches of a tree moved through the force of the wind did not occur. It was a spirit which occasioned this ; but here it must be remembered that the distinction between matter and spirit which is so obvious to us was unknown to man in undeveloped stages of culture. The primary point of importance suggested by motion in a tree was that it denoted the presence of life ; first, life inherent in the tree itself as a being much in the same sense that a man was ; and then, later, life as manifested by the presence of a " supernatural " being which took up its abode in the tree at certain times. An instructive example of the earlier stage of belief is given in the words of Porphyry : " They say that primitive men led an unhappy life, for their superstition did not stop at animals, but extended even to plants. For why should the slaughter of an ox or a sheep be a greater wrong than the felling of a fir or an oak, seeing that a soul is implanted in these trees also ? " [2] This we should describe as Animatism ; while as an illustration of animistic belief the following words of Pliny the Elder afford an example : in writing about trees he says that " these have been (in the past) temples of gods, and even now with ancient ritual the simple country folk dedicate a lofty tree to a god. Not more do

---

[1] Goblet d'Alviella, in *Encycl. of Religion and Ethics*, i. 535*b*. On the whole subject see Durkheim (Engl. transl. by J. W. Swain), *The Elementary Forms of the Religious Life*, pp. 48–70 (1926).

[2] *De abstinentia*, i. 6, quoted by Frazer, *Golden Bough*, " The Magic Art," ii. 12 (1911).

we adore images that shine with gold and ivory than sacred groves and the very silence in them." [1] A tree is dedicated to a god because it is believed that a shrine having been thus prepared for him, it will be utilized by him as a place of abode; and at such times as he sees fit to enter this it is, of course, expected that he will make his presence known. Pliny's words imply that the tree did not become a shrine until after it had been dedicated; but this would not have taken place unless there had been some reason for believing that the god would utilize the abode prepared for him. Trees must therefore have been looked upon as the abodes of spirits before some particular tree came to be dedicated to a god. As an illustration of this we are told, for example, that " when the missionary Jerome of Prague was persuading the heathen Lithuanians to fell their sacred groves, a multitude of women besought the Prince of Lithuania to stop him, saying that with the woods he was destroying the house of their god from which they had been wont to get sunshine and rain." [2] Very numerous examples of a similar character could be given.

If, then, a supernatural being takes up its abode in a tree, which is on that account sacred, it is easy to understand how in course of time it came to be believed that oracles were delivered by the indwelling spirit; examples of this have been noted in various parts of the world, both in ancient and later times. In the oracular shrine of Zeus at Dodona, for example, the oracles were given by sounds made by the sacred oak.[3] The ancient Prussians received audible answers from gods who were believed to inhabit oaks and other trees.[4] The heathen Lithuanians as late as the fourteenth century A.D. were in the habit of receiving oracular responses from oaks.[5] And, to give but one other example, among the natives of Uganda " the trees planted round the ancestral graves were sedulously tended by wise women, whose oracles, like those of the Pythian priestess, were taken as decisive in certain political crises." [6]

These few examples, out of many dozens which could be given, must suffice. Trees were thus regarded by man in

---

[1] Quoted by Baudissin, *Studien zur semitischen Religionsgeschichte*, ii. 184 (1878).
[2] Frazer, *op. cit.*, ii. 46.
[3] Farnell, *The Cults of the Greek States*, i. 38 ff. (1896-1909).
[4] Frazer, *op. cit.*, ii. 43.   [5] Frazer, *op. cit.*, ii. 9.
[6] Keane, in the *Encycl. of Religion and Ethics*, i. 164a. See further, Jevons, *Introduction to the History of Religion*, pp. 206-225, 242 f. (1904).

an early stage of culture, all the world over, as temporary or permanent places of abode of spirits, and later of gods. As a consequence they acquired a sacred character. Particular trees, owing to one or more of a variety of causes, would have a special sanctity attaching to them; such trees, as the evidence shows, became sanctuaries from which oracles were to be obtained.

(b) Since running water, rivers, streams, springs, and wells were objects which had activity enough to affect man, these, too, were believed to be animated by a life and will like his own. And as in the case of trees, the belief concerning these developed from Animatism to Animism. Running water must have appeared to early man, as soon as he became mentally of sufficient development to think about it, as extraordinarily mysterious. Its movement would convince him that it was living; its force and power were immeasurable; there would be something terribly awesome in a raging torrent which swept away rocks and trees in its rushing course; it uttered deafening sounds, as it would seem to man in the dawn of understanding; it engulfed man and beast like some hungry monster. No wonder that rivers and streams and the sea itself were believed to be living beings like men. And although in course of time, a spirit animating the water, and not the water itself, came to be thought of as the cause of movement, it is noteworthy that the tendency to the animatistic conception regarding water continued side by side with the animistic much longer than was the case with trees. Thus, the ancient Peruvians who lived on the coast looked upon the ocean itself as a powerful goddess, whom they called *mamacocha*, "mother-sea"; [1] to her they were indebted for their food in the shape of fish, one of their staple means of living; on the other hand, her power must sometimes have been exhibited by engulfing men.

As distinct from this animatistic conception there is, for example, the belief in the water-spirit who inhabited the sacred hot springs of Hierapolis.[2] Other illustrations are to be found in the legend of Heracles and Hersione, and in the better known one of Perseus and Andromeda; [3] and one has only to think of the Nereids and Nymphs to

---

[1] Payne, *History of the New World called America*, i. 451 (1892).
[2] Frazer, *G. B.*, "Adonis, Attis, Osiris," i. 208 (1927).
[3] Hans Schmidt, *Jona, eine Untersuchung zur vergleichenden Religionsgeschichte*, pp. 3 ff., 12 ff. (1907).

realize the beliefs in ancient times about rivers and springs. Such ideas, one may confidently assert, have a long history behind them, and have been handed down for untold centuries, since similar ones exist among races in a low stage of culture. For example, " the Tarahumares (Central America) place their houses at a distance from the water and never sleep near it when on a journey lest they should be molested by the indwelling spirit." [1] To go still lower in the scale, Tylor, in writing about savage tribes in Africa, says that " in the east, among the Wanika, every spring has its spirit, to which oblations are made; in the west, in the Akra district, lakes, ponds, and rivers receive worship as local deities. In the south, among the Kafirs, streams are venerated as personal beings, or the abodes of personal deities." [2]

The best illustrations of oracle-giving springs occur in classical writers and ancient historians; but these must be taken as showing how primitive ideas persist. Thus, to give but one or two examples : from the murmurous flow of the spring which is said to have gushed forth from the foot of the great oak at Dodona, the priestess drew oracles.[3] The oracle of Daphne, near Antioch, was obtained by dipping a laurel leaf into the water, though " we cannot take seriously the statement that the response appeared written on the leaf." [4] And, once more, " at Delphi the sacred spring may have been either Cassiotis or the more-famed Castaly, which issues from a narrow gorge, shut in by rocky walls of tremendous height, a little to the east of Apollo's temple. The waters of both were thought to be endowed with prophetic power." [5]

It will not be necessary to illustrate this further. Springs, streams, etc., like trees, were conceived of as spirits, or else as the abode of spirits, not only by men in a savage state, but also by races which had reached a high stage of culture; and it would be easy to show that this belief has persisted through the ages, and has probably not entirely disappeared in countries of the most advanced civilization even at the present day.

(c) While it is not difficult to understand that man in a primitive stage of culture should have had animistic ideas

[1] E. O. James, in E. R. E., xii. 708a.
[2] Primitive Culture, ii. 211 (1873).
[3] Frazer, G. B., " The Magic Art," ii. 172.
[4] Robertson Smith, The Religion of the Semites, p. 178 (1927).
[5] Frazer, G. B., " The Dying God," p. 79 (1911).

about trees and rivers on account of their movement, the case is somewhat different when it is seen that similar ideas were held in regard to stones of various kinds. The sight of a rolling stone might well have suggested life; but sacred stones were not as a rule such as moved or seemed to move. Yet stones were regarded both as living themselves, and as being the abode of spirits. The line of thought which suggested this to early man must have been different from that which led him to have the same belief about moving branches of trees and running water. Animistic conceptions about stones were prompted by a variety of things, not by the one guiding thought that movement meant life. " Wherever men have been struck by the appearance or position of a rock or stone, they have regarded it with awe as uncanny, and in innumerable cases they have ultimately erected it into a divinity, brought offerings, and put up prayers before it." [1] But in many cases the appearance of a stone might attract attention without necessarily inspiring awe; for example, among the Melanesians a stone in the shape of breadfruit is believed to effect a good crop of fruit; [2] this would be brought about by burying the stone at the foot of the tree in question. While originally it was, no doubt, believed that the stone itself had this power, in course of time it would come to be imputed to a spirit abiding in the stone; and one can understand how, by degrees, worship would be accorded to the stone as the embodiment or, later, the symbol of the spirit.

To take another instance, one which points to some development, and one in which the feeling of awe would certainly arise; Hartland refers to rocks and stones having natural depressions somewhat resembling a footprint, or the impression of what looks like a hand, knee, or head; this would naïvely, but quite naturally, be interpreted by savage man as the mark of the spirit whose abode the stone or rock was : " such a mark is looked upon with awe, and, if attributed to a sacred person, usually becomes the object of devout observance, if not of an actual cult." Thus, it is not difficult to understand that a standing stone should have suggested the idea of a man, and be looked upon as such, though of course a supernatural man; the modification

---

[1] Hartland, in *E. R. E.*, xi. 864a.
[2] Codrington, *The Melanesians*, p. 183 (1891). Hartland says that " among the Melanesians the shape of a stone rules the idea as to what kind of spirit dwells within it " (*Animism*, p. 78, 1905).

of regarding it as the abode of the spirit would follow in due course.

Among the Khasis of Assam, we are told, " the sacred upright stones, 'which resemble the Semitic *mazzĕboth* ('pillars '), are regarded as males, and the flat table-stones as females. . . . So in Nikunau, one of the Gilbert Islands in the South Pacific, the natives had sandstone slabs or pillars which represented gods and goddesses." [1] The anointing of stones was widespread; "it appears to have been customary to anoint the sacred cone with olive-oil at a solemn festival, in which people from Lycia and Caria participated—we learn this from an inscription found at Paphos. The custom of anointing a holy stone has been observed in many parts of the world; for example, in the sanctuary of Apollo at Delphi." [2]

Examples of holy hills and mountains whose sanctity is due to the presence of an indwelling spirit are very numerous; [3] the particular spot at which the spirit would be supposed to manifest himself would naturally be on the summit. Volcanoes would obviously suggest supernatural activity. [4]

Here again it is not necessary to multiply examples, for these can be found to any extent in books dealing with the beliefs of uncivilized man.

All that was necessary for our present purpose, so far, was to indicate by a few examples the fact that sacred trees, streams, and stones have played a very great part during the two stages of Animatism and Animism, stages through which all races have passed or are passing on their upward path towards higher forms of belief.

(d) Before we come to the next stage it is necessary to touch briefly on the subject of *Polydæmonism*.

Many authorities make a distinction between Animism and Polydæmonism, but others do not believe that any distinction can properly be made. While it must be admitted that it is not easy to distinguish between a spirit and a demon in the sense in which these words must be understood in the present connexion, we do nevertheless come across some creatures, at any rate in the Semitic area, which compel us to ask whether we must not postulate

---

[1] Frazer, *G. B.*, " Adonis, Attis, Osiris," i. 198 (1927).
[2] Frazer, *op. cit.*, i. 36.
[3] Baudissin, *op. cit.*, ii. 238 ff., gives many illustrations.
[4] Frazer, *op. cit.*, i. 216–222.

the existence of a belief in beings which cannot be said to come under the animistic category, and which are certainly not to be classed as gods.[1]

Two illustrations of what we mean may be given : the *Seraphim*, in the original, not in the developed, conception, and the *Se'irim*. What is said of these points to an advance beyond a merely animistic conception, but they are clearly of a very much lower order than gods and goddesses. A spring or a stream or a tree which is believed to move because it is animated by a spirit we understand as Animism ; but a *saraph* is not a serpent, nor is a *sa'ir* a goat, indwelt by a spirit or a demon—whatever the later beliefs may have been—but is itself a demon. The ordinary process of development through the three stages is, first the tree itself a spirit (Animatism), then the tree animated by a spirit (Animism), and then the spirit developing into a god or goddess (Polytheism). But in the case of the *Seraphim* and the *Se'irim* the process stops short; they do not develop into gods or goddesses, whatever they may have developed from.[2] So that from this point of view it would seem as though Animism in its development diverged in two directions, viz. on the one hand, into the Polytheistic stage, and on the other, into a stage in which the beings were of a more " concrete " nature than in the animistic stage proper, and never developed into anything further; they continued as they were, and ultimately died out—like the arrested development of a species, in another sphere. It cannot be objected that what has been said is an anachronism, because it is dealing with a stage of demonology which belongs to a later age, for we meet with the *Seraphim*, at any rate, as early as the Mosaic age, and nobody would suppose that they originated at that time; they must be much earlier.

4. THE POLYTHEISTIC STAGE

Polytheism, the belief in many gods and goddesses, has two points in common with the belief in spirits and demons : their multiplicity and the fact that they are unmoral. They may be harmful, or they may be beneficent, but they have no ethical attributes.

The first essential difference between a spirit or a demon and a god or goddess, is that the latter has individuality,

---

[1] See further T. H. Robinson, *Outline Introduction to the History of Religions*, pp. 65 f. (1926); and Chapter IX. below.
[2] See further Chapter VI.

the former has not. From this it follows that gods and goddesses have each some special attribute, which is not the case with the lower types of supernatural beings. Further, spirits, some harmful and some not, form a species, which is divided into varieties; therefore they have no names; but gods and goddesses have names. Another difference is that spirits and demons are not tied to any locality, but gods and goddesses are—at any rate in the early stage of belief in them. And lastly, there is this further difference, that spirits and demons are sexless—they are represented as hybrids or in the form of animals; but gods and goddesses, at any rate in the Semitic domain, are mostly conceived of as being in human form.[1]

The existence and character of Polytheism are so well known that it is quite unnecessary to give illustrations. But there are some further subjects to which a brief reference must be made.[2] While uncultured man was passing through the early phases of religious belief, certain institutions came into being which have played a part among many races. As remnants of these are found in the Old Testament, it is necessary that they should be mentioned; for if we are to study the origin and development of Hebrew religion, we must take all the facts and factors into consideration. A few words about these institutions must, therefore, find a place here.

5. TOTEMISM

The word *Totem* belongs originally to some of the North American Indian tribes. It is derived from the term *ototeman*, which means "his brother-sister kin." We shall not enter here into the much-discussed question of the origin of Totemism; the theory which seems to come nearest

---

[1] We have, it is true, the cow-divinity Astarte (see p. 36) and the bulls of Bethel and Dan; but these are symbols of the divinity, though actually worshipped. Babylonian and Hebrew figures of Astarte are always in female form; but some Babylonian deities are of hybrid form, partly human and partly animal. The Egyptian gods and goddesses were mostly animal representations; though the Egyptians did not belong to the Semitic domain, they belonged to the world that influenced the Hebrews. A Semitic strain may have entered in during the Hyksos domination, but this did not affect the Egyptian Pantheon. Barton, *Hamitic and Semitic Origins*, Chapter I (1934), argues in favour of the Egyptians being of Semitic origin; but this is questionable.

[2] We have advisedly omitted any discussion on Fetishism, partly because it does not exist among peoples of the lowest culture, and also because where it is found it often partakes of the nature of Magic, on which see below, pp. 16 f., 71 ff.

to the truth is that put forth by the Swedish scholar, Reuterskiold, which Hartland has summarized thus: " Totemism is connected with an impersonal conception of life. A group of men are allied with a group of animals. There is nothing personal, nothing individual, in their union. It is an association peculiar to the primitive mode of thought, which does not compare one thing with another : if it finds likeness between them, it identifies them. For primitive man the individual is nothing; the group or the species is everything. Man did not picture himself as lord of creation. He did not sever himself in thought from other living creatures; he was only a part of a great community. He felt himself closely united with a kind of animal living in his neighbourhood and coming in touch with him. It was no accident that he associated himself with one or other species. Totemism has its various sides—religious, magical, and social. These were in the origin undistinguished from one another. The distinction between them came later, with the development of individualism and analysis." With this Hartland largely agrees; without saying that this theory completely solves the question, he thinks that it envisages the conditions of primitive life and thought " sufficiently to define at all events some of the conditions to be fulfilled and so lead to a solution." [1]

While Totemism is widespread, there are various peoples which are non-totemic. Where it is found to exist it denotes a form of society in which the members of a clan believe themselves to be united by kinship to some animal or plant from which the clan has descended. The animal or plant, or whatever else it may be which is thus regarded as the tribal ancestor, is looked upon with profound veneration by all the members of the clan or tribe, as the case may be. It must never be harmed. In the case of an animal it may never be eaten excepting on very special occasions when the members of a clan feast on their totem animal; and this is a solemn religious rite. Though in its origin Totemism had nothing to do with religion, in course of time religion entered into it, and with it the supernatural element. Since a man was united by kinship to his totem he regarded it as his friend; and since it had something supernatural, and therefore powerful, about it, a man would look to it for help. So that here was a supernatural power

---

[1] *E. R. E.*, xii. 406*b*, 407*a*, and on the whole subject see Durkheim, *op. cit.*, 88–239.

distinguished from all others by the fact that it was in alliance with him; it became, as Jevons says, "a permanently friendly power; in a word, it became a god." [1]

With the subject of exogamy, i.e. the rule which does not allow a man to marry a woman of his own clan, an essential element of Totemism, we need not deal, as no signs of it occur in the Old Testament.

In studying the development of the early religious ideas of the Hebrews on broad lines the subject of Totemism cannot be ignored. Not that Totemism existed as an institution among the Hebrews, at any rate within the historical period, but the Old Testament has preserved some distinct traces of its former existence among the distant ancestors of the Hebrew race; hence the mention of it here. [2]

6. TABOO

Taboo, or *Tabu*, is a word borrowed from Polynesia, and means "marked off"; according to Marett it is perhaps derived from the Polynesian *ta* "mark" and *pu* "exceedingly." The term is applied to the institution, universal among all races in an undeveloped state of culture and even after, in which, for a large variety of reasons, contact with things and persons and even names (i.e. their utterance) is forbidden. Things or persons which are taboo are so because they are believed to be charged, either temporarily or permanently, with some supernatural influence. [3] Where it comes from or how it comes is not inquired into; it is *there*, that is the practical concern. This is always the underlying cause for the prohibition of contact, whatever other reasons may be added subsequently; for this supernatural influence is transmissible: "everything which comes in contact with a tabooed person or thing becomes itself as dangerous as the original object, becomes a fresh centre of infection, a fresh source of danger, to the community." [4] And it is just the unknown, the undefined nature of the danger which makes it so formidable and dreaded. Taboo postulates belief in something supernatural,

[1] *Op. cit.*, p. 104; and see further, Robertson Smith, *Rel. Sem.*, p. 54 (1927).

[2] On the general subject see McLennan, *Studies in Ancient History*, p. 491 ff. (1886), and Frazer, *Totemism and Exogamy* (1910).

[3] Marett remarks that "*Tabu* is the negative mode of the supernatural to which *mana* corresponds as the positive mode" (*op. cit.*, p. 127).

[4] Jevons, *op. cit.*, p. 161.

and in so far is connected with religious belief. " A primary source of fear," as Marett says, " is the unfamiliar or strange as such; and this kind of fear in varying degree is always present as an element in that complex emotion of awe or reverence which is the root of religion. Taboo, then, stands for the whole mass of such fear-inspired inhibitions in so far as they proceed directly from the religious emotion, as it regulates the social tradition in relative abeyance of reasoned direction." [1]

7. MAGIC

The word Magic connotes in the minds of most people something fraudulent or, at best, foolish; while " Black Magic " is supposed to involve having dealings with the devil. Of all such ideas we must divest our minds when thinking of Magic—the word is quite unsuitable—in connexion with men in a low stage of culture. To early man " magical " power was a supernatural energy inherent in inanimate matter. How the idea originated is a subject of much controversy among anthropologists; to go into the details of the various theories held by authoritative investigators is out of the question here; [2] but an indication of some of Marett's ideas on the subject is demanded because of their insight and cogency.[3]

First, it is to be noted that the primeval savage acted before he thought about his action; " correspondingly, therefore, in the sphere of nascent religion there must have been a stage of cult or ritual (if so it may be termed), the product of sheer unreflective habit, which preceded the growth of ideas concerning the how or why of what was being done. Certain recurrent situations in the social life . . . induce states of emotional intensity. The emotion must find a vent somehow. This they do either through activities directed to practical ends . . . or else through secondary activities such as are not immediately practical in their object, but serve simply as outlets of superfluous energy. . . . In either case habit entwines with the activities in question all sorts of more or less functionless accidents; and the presence of these unaccountable details helps to make the whole performance seem mysterious to the per-

---

[1] E. R. E., xii. 183a; there is much else in this interesting article regarding the religious element in Taboo which is noteworthy and instructive.

[2] See, e.g., W. Schmidt, op. cit., pp. 118-165.

[3] See The Threshold of Religion, pp. 33-84, and his article on " Magic " in E. R. E., viii. 245a—252a.

formers. . . . It is in regard to the 'secondary activities '—
of which examples are dances, playing at hunting, or at
fighting, or at love-making—that accretions in the way of
accidental features due to custom are likely to be more
pronounced. . . . Meanwhile, in proportion as these secondary activities conform to the same stimuli as the primary
activities of which they are the by-product, as, for instance,
when the hunting interest overflows into a pantomimic
rehearsal of the chase, they will wear an imitative appearance, though in reality being 'repercussions' rather than
imitations. When, however, an *ex post facto* justification
of them becomes necessary, it is quite natural that the
doctrine that they have 'power' should implicate the
belief that their seemingly imitative character has something
to do with their efficacy. . . . It is symbolical ritual—i.e. a
ritual that involves a more or less realistic reproduction
of some practical activity—that generates the doctrine of
'sympathetic' causation in one or another of its forms."
Thus, the magical quality is to be identified "not with the
imitativeness, which is a secondary feature, but with the
customariness, which is the real source of the value attaching to those non-utilitarian accompaniments of the more
exciting moments of the practical life. . . . For the rest,
in so far as these relatively unideated discharges of the social
energy need any supporting doctrine, they would find it,
not in any philosophy about like producing like, and so on—
ideas that appear quite late in the history of thought—
but in vague notions of the *mana* type. In other words,
the savage comforts himself with no theory of *how* these
ritual practices work, but is content to feel and know *that*
they work—that, despite all appearances to the contrary,
they have power and efficacy in them or behind them."

This, as it seems to us, gets to the roots of "magic";
and one can see how naturally from this the later developments of magic arose. We shall come across some of these
when dealing with the magical arts which are to be found
in some parts of the Old Testament.

8. The After-life

The belief in immortality, or at least in life of some kind
hereafter, seems to be ingrained in human consciousness;
it is doubtful whether any race of men, even the most
backward, are without some ideas of an after-life, which
is taken for granted. "If there is any natural knowledge

C

of human immortality," writes Frazer, " it must be acquired
either by intuition or by experience ; there is no other way " ;
and he shows that the savage " finds a very strong argument for immortality in the phenomena of dreams. . . .
When the images of persons whom he knows to be dead
appear to him in a dream he naturally infers that these
persons still exist somewhere and somehow apart from
their bodies, of the decay or destruction of which he may
have had ocular demonstration. How could he see dead
people, he asks, if they did not exist ? . . . Thus, arguing
from the real, but as we think misinterpreted, phenomena
of dreams, the savage may arrive at a doctrine of human
immortality. . . ." [1] Or, " to take a single example of
outward experience," he continues, " the resemblances
which children bear to deceased kinsfolk appear to have
prompted in the minds of many savages the notion that the
souls of these dead kinsfolk have been born again in their
descendants. From a few cases of resemblances so explained
it would be easy to arrive at a general theory that all living
persons are animated by the souls of the dead ; in other
words, that the human spirit survives death for an indefinite period, if not for eternity, during which it undergoes a series of rebirths or reincarnations." [2]

Be the reasons what they may, however, for belief in
life after death, its universality among all early races is
undoubted. To give illustrations of this is unnecessary,
since they are to be found in many volumes easily procurable.
One point, however, should be mentioned here, as it has a
bearing on what will be said later. Very widespread,
though probably not universal, among uncultured men is
the belief that death is not, properly speaking, the normal
lot of man. Why and how this belief arose is too large a
subject to consider here ; of its prevalence there is ample
proof ; the great number of myths explaining how it was
that death originated is sufficient to show that immortality
was believed to have been the original lot of man. This,
however, by the way. Death as a temporary, perhaps
only momentary, suspension of life, then, is universal
among all races of men.

In the Semitic area, therefore, with which we shall be
specially concerned, the After-life is taken for granted:

---

[1] *The Belief in Immortality*, i. 26 ff. (1913); J. S. Lincoln, *The Dream in
Primitive Cultures*, pp. 92 ff. (1935).
[2] *Ibid.*, i. 28 f.

this applies, of course, to the Hebrews. But what we find in the Old Testament regarding the earlier stages of belief was not indigenous to the Hebrews, and what we read there on the subject must be studied in the light of the general Semitic background. We shall, therefore, in due course, consider briefly the Babylonian and ancient Arab conceptions (see below p. 79, 88 ff., 243 ff.).

9. ANCESTOR-WORSHIP, AND THE CULT OF THE DEAD

Theories as to the origin of Ancestor-worship and the cult of the dead are various; but few people would agree with Spencer when he says: " Using the phrase Ancestor-worship in its broadest sense as comprehending all worship of the dead, be they of the same blood or not, we conclude that Ancestor-worship is the root of every religion "; [1] for this would make Ancestor-worship one of the oldest, if not the oldest, element in religion, which it certainly is not. To discuss all the various other theories which have been held would be out of place here; but to one other attention must be drawn. Jevons makes out a convincing case for his contention that the natural demonstrations of grief at the death of a relative were the original basis upon which, in course of ages, the superstructure of Ancestor-worship and the cult of the dead was raised. Having described the outbursts of sorrow among many savage races on the occasion of a death, Jevons continues: " While such spontaneous demonstrations of affection, grief, and desire for reunion with the departed do not amount to worship . . .", it is possible to trace from them the process by which they developed into Ancestor-worship. " . . . The first condition of any such development is that the demonstrations, at first spontaneous, should become conventional, and harden into custom. . . . When, then, it has become the tribal custom for relatives to perform certain acts, on the occasion of a death, which were originally spontaneous and now are the conventional expressions of grief, it becomes possible for fear to operate, in support of this as of other tribal customs, though it was not in fear that either it or they originated. . . . When this demonstration of grief and of affection has become conventional, the neglect of it inevitably comes to be regarded as a want of respect to the deceased, and the performance of it is regarded no

[1] *Principles of Sociology*, i. 411 (1877).

longer as a crude attempt to give fresh life to the deceased, but as something done to please him." Proceeding then to discuss the significance of offerings of food, hair, and blood, he points out that these are elements belonging both to the rites of what is due to the departed as well as to the worship of gods; but that they are the elements of Ancestor-worship—elements as yet held in suspension, however, and waiting for something to precipitate them. "In other words, worship in any proper sense of the word implies worshippers, united either by the natural bond of blood, or by the artificial bond of initiation. In the case of Ancestor-worship the body of worship is supplied by the family, and united by the natural bond of blood. . . . When the Ancestor-worship is established as a private cult, it, like other private cults, is steadily assimilated in form, in its rites and ceremonies, to the public worship of the gods. The animals which provided the food that the deceased was originally supposed to consume are now sacrificed according to the ritual observed in sacrificing animals to the gods. . . . When the assimilation of the rites for the dead to the ritual of the gods has proceeded thus far, it naturally happens that in many cases some superhuman powers are ascribed to the spirits of the dead. But it never happens that the spirits of the dead are conceived to be gods. . . . To speak of gods as ' deified ancestors ' is to use an expression which covers some ambiguity of thought. If what is implied is that in a community possessing the conception of divine personality, certain ancestors are, by some unexplained process, raised to the ranks of gods, the statement may be true, but it does not prove that the gods, to whose rank the spirit is promoted, were themselves originally ghosts— which is the very thing that it is intended to prove. What, then, are these gods? Either they are believed to be ancestors of some of their worshippers, or they are not. If they are believed to be the ancestors of the worshippers, then they are not believed to have been human; the worshipper's pride is that *his* ancestor was a god and no mere mortal. . . . If, on the other hand, a god is not believed to be the ancestor of any of his worshippers, then to assert that he was really a ' deified ancestor ' is to make a statement for which there is no evidence. . . . The fact is that ancestors known to have been human were not worshipped as gods, and that ancestors worshipped as gods were believed not to have been human. The last remark leads us to a generalization which, though obvious, is important : it is that wherever Ancestor-worship exists, it exists side by side with the public worship of the gods of the community. The two systems develop on lines which are parallel, indeed, and therefore never meet; whereas, if they had moved on the same line of development, one would have absorbed the other." [1]

We have given the salient features of Jevons' argument at some length both because it was demanded in order to make his position clear, and also because it explains some things in regard to the subject which might otherwise appear puzzling. Apart from the matters which, as we have seen, arise as soon as the subject is seriously considered, it may be said that the fundamental idea in Ancestor-worship is the keeping up of social relations with a dead ancestor. Just as, when living, the head of a family, clan, or tribe, acted as guardian and protector of his kin, who in turn honoured and served him as their head and benefactor, so this mutual relationship was intended to continue after death had removed the former from visible presence among the latter.

10. NECROMANCY

Necromancy is an essential part of the Cult of the Dead, and therefore demands a brief consideration. It has been practised among men from very early ages, and arose from the innate desire to know the future, though knowledge pertaining to present affairs was also sought. Those who were able, or who were supposed to be able, to give information, especially with regard to the future, must clearly possess powers denied to men of ordinary nature; they must, that is to say, be supernatural beings, with knowledge of, and interest in, men and affairs of this life, i.e., those who had once lived on earth. But the information they give is always conveyed by a medium who is believed to be endowed with the faculty of summoning the departed from whatever locality they may be supposed to inhabit, and of communicating with them. The assumption that a departed spirit continued to take an interest in the things of this world, and especially in those who had been known and loved during the earthly life, was prompted by natural feelings; but it is a striking fact that, so far as the evidence goes, the departed were not approached directly, but by

[1] *Introduction to the History of Religion*, pp. 189 ff. (1904, 3rd ed.).

means of a medicine man, a *shaman*, or what not. This might, at first sight, suggest the idea of charlatanism on the part of those who arrogated to themselves the power of approaching the departed spirits; but, while admitting the probability of chicanery on the part of some, it would be unfair to suggest that, given a real belief in an After-life, a man or a woman was necessarily a charlatan because he or she claimed to possess a faculty incomprehensible to the majority of mankind; it might, with almost equal injustice, be said that there was no reality in prophetic inspiration. Not that we would for a moment place the two on an equal footing; but to condemn wholesale, as is often done, an institution of almost universal prevalence, and by no means necessarily prompted by a bad motive, seems unjustifiable; unless belief in the reality of life hereafter be regarded as a baseless superstition, the denial of the possibility of the communion of spirits, whether embodied or disembodied, is a one-sided attitude; indeed, in view of such an occurrence as that recorded in Mark ix. 2–8 (cp. Matt. xvii. 1–8; Luke ix. 28–36), it is misguided.

Be that as it may, however, Necromancy was greatly in vogue among the Hebrews, for which reason it cannot be ignored in a general review of the background of Hebrew religion.

CHAPTER II

REMNANTS OF ANIMISM IN HEBREW RELIGION : SACRED TREES

1. GENERAL SEMITIC BELIEF

WE have seen that religious belief in its gradual development among early races passes through various stages. Since this is recognized as a universal rule among all peoples whose religion develops sufficiently, we may assume that the Hebrews, or their ancestors, were no exception. But something more than assumption is needed before this can be accepted as a fact, and therefore the evidence of the records must be examined. As a preliminary to this, however, it is quite necessary to glance, even though cursorily, at Semitic Religion in general, so far as the special points to be considered are concerned, for this will be of help in ascertaining, or at least of gaining some insight into, what the beliefs of the ancestors of the Hebrews were.

Therefore in studying the various indications of the existence of earlier animistic [1] beliefs afforded in the Old Testament we shall in each case begin with a brief consideration of general Semitic belief on the subject.

While not absent from other races, as we have seen, it was a specifically Semitic belief that trees, and above all evergreen trees, were regarded as the vehicles of the life-producing energy of spirits, and later of gods and goddesses. Animistic conceptions in connexion with them can be shown to have existed until comparatively late times. As Robertson Smith says : " Prayers were addressed to them, particularly for help in sickness, but doubtless also for fertile seasons and the like, and they were hung with votive gifts, especially garments and ornaments, perhaps also anointed with unguents as if they had been real persons." [2] Even at the present day in Syria there are many trees which are believed

---

[1] Indications of the pre-animistic stage are not to be looked for among people such as the Hebrews, who were already of a relatively advanced culture when we first hear of them.

[2] *Op. cit.*, p. 195.

to be possessed by spirits, to whom vows and sacrifices are made.[1]

In the main, the knowledge we have of the beliefs of the Babylonians and Assyrians dates from periods of such relatively advanced culture that bald animistic conceptions are hardly to be looked for. Nevertheless, it is certain that the ancient Babylonians believed that trees were inhabited by spirits;[2] moreover, the importance attached to sacred trees in their religion and the reverence with which they were treated necessitate the implication that we have here but the development of animistic conceptions. It is sufficient to point to the numerous inscriptions in which trees, in the more or less conventional style, are depicted;[3] worshippers kneel before these; in some cases gifts are being offered. The text on inscriptions of this kind does not suggest that the tree itself is being worshipped; it is either the symbol of a god or goddess, or else it is conceived of as a sanctuary of the deity, or as marking the site of a sanctuary. But, in any case, the existence of a tree in connexion with worship does not permit of any conclusion other than that of a development of some earlier animistic conceptions.[4]

Although the most frequently employed means of obtaining oracles—large numbers of which occur on Assyrian texts—was by the examination of an animal's liver (hepatoscopy), the tree oracles were far from being unknown; the cedar, cypress, and tamarisk are the trees which are most frequently mentioned in the ritual texts.[5]

As regards the Phœnicians and Canaanites, Robertson Smith refers to the testimony of Philo Byblius to the effect that " the plants of the earth were in ancient times esteemed as gods and honoured with libations and sacrifices, because from them the successive generations of men drew the support of their life. To this day the traveller in Palestine frequently meets with holy trees hung like an Arabian *dhāt anwāt* (tree for hanging things on), with rags as tokens of homage."[6]

Among the Phœnicians trees figured prominently in worship, especially in the cult of the goddess Astarte, to

---

[1] Curtiss, *Primitive Semitic Religion To-day*, p. 91 (1902).
[2] Jastrow, *Die Religion Babyloniens und Assyriens*, i. 48 (1912).
[3] Monuments of this kind can be seen in the British Museum.
[4] Further details will be found in Baudissin, *op. cit.*, ii. 189–192; Lagrange, *Études sur les Religions Sémitiques*, pp. 168–171 (1903); Jeremias, *Das Alte Testament im Lichte des alten Orients*, pp. 94 ff. (1904).
[5] Jastrow, *op. cit.*, ii. 200 ff.
[6] *Rel. Sem.*, p. 186.

whom the cypress was sacred. The myrtle and the palm were also associated with the worship of this goddess.[1]

In describing the festival of the Pyre or Lamp—to give a Syrian illustration—Lucian says : "They cut down tall trees and set them up in the court; then they bring goats and sheep and cattle and hang them living to the trees; they add to these birds and garments and gold and silver work. After all is finished, they carry the gods around the trees and set fire under; in a moment all is in a blaze. To this solemn rite a great multitude flocks from Syria and all the regions around." [2] This is, of course, a greatly developed form of cult, but from the present point of view the main importance is the hanging of offerings on the sacred trees; for these latter are not merely convenient objects upon which to suspend the offerings, they have a far greater significance than that; being sacred to different deities, they represent them; the offerings are made to the trees as representing the deities. The burning of the trees would not take place unless the gods they represented were present, as is the case here. The ceremony is clearly a development of the earlier practice of presenting offerings to trees, and this, in its turn, points to yet earlier animistic belief.

But the most instructive examples are to be sought among both ancient and modern Arabs. To quote our leading authority on Semitic religion once more, Robertson Smith says in reference to the ancient Arabs, that "while the supernatural associations of groves and thickets may appear to be sufficiently explained by the fact that these are the favourite lairs of wild beasts, it appears probable that the association of certain kinds of *jinn* with trees must in many cases be regarded as primary, the trees themselves being conceived as animated demoniac beings"; and again : "Primarily supernatural life and power reside in the trees themselves, which are conceived as animated and even rational." [3]

Oracles from trees were far from rare : "Sometimes the tree is believed to speak with an articulate voice, as the *gharcad* did in a dream to Moslim; but except in a dream it is obvious that the voice of the tree can only be some rustling sound, as the wind in the branches." [4]

[1] Baudissin, *op. cit.*, ii. 192–216, where abundant material will be found.
[2] *De Dea Syria*, § xlix.
[3] *Op. cit.*, pp. 132 ff., where illustrations are given; also in Wellhausen, *Reste arabischen Heidentums*, pp. 104 ff. (1897).
[4] Doughty, *Travels in Arabia Deserta*, ii. 209 (1888).

How these animistic conceptions have persisted up to the present day among the Arabs in Syria could be illustrated to almost any extent; but to give details, instructive as they are, would take up too much space. For these recourse must be had to such works as Burckhardt, *Travels in Syria and the Holy Land*; Doughty, *Travels in Arabia Deserta*; and Curtiss, *Primitive Semitic Religion To-day*.

2. THE OLD TESTAMENT

Having thus taken a bird's-eye glance at the subject of sacred trees among the Semites generally, we are in a better position to study some of the Biblical passages in which they are referred to. The question of the dates of passages to be quoted need not trouble us here; later it is one which becomes of importance; but in the present connexion, since the remnants of the early stages of belief linger on in ages long subsequent to those during which they formed the norm, it is immaterial for our purposes to what period a particular passage may be assigned provided it contains the echo or reflex of some " primitive " belief. At present we are concerned merely to show that the Old Testament itself gives indications that Hebrew religion passed through the Animistic stage of belief.

In Gen. xii. 6–8 mention is made of " the terebinth of Moreh " [1] (*'elon moreh*), translated literally this is : " the terebinth of the teacher," i.e. a tree at which divine teaching was given. What is meant is that the oracle was given there, so that it might well be rendered " the oracle-terebinth." This tree [2] stood in Shechem, and it was evidently thought of as extremely ancient, since it was there before Abraham came to Canaan. It was on this spot that Yahweh appeared to the patriarch, in consequence of which he built an altar to Yahweh. One cannot fail to recognize a connexion between the mention of a specific, and obviously well-known, tree and the divine appearance there. The tree was regarded as sacred. Abraham halts at it because he expects a divine manifestation there; and he is not disappointed. But why should the manifestation take place at the tree ? In the light of what has been said above about sacred trees there is no room for doubt that we have here an instance of the development of the belief

---

[1] In Deut. xi. 30 it is " the terebinths of M.," but it should be the singular as in the Septuagint.

[2] The terebinth is an evergreen.

that spirits took up their abode in trees. In other words, we have here an indication of the existence of an earlier animistic belief.

The same must be postulated of the terebinth of Mamre, in Hebron (Gen. xiii. 18, xviii. 1),[1] where Abraham again builds an altar to Yahweh. The spot must have been regarded as a holy one, otherwise it would not have been chosen as a site for this altar; but it was the presence of the terebinth that made it holy. That the site was a very ancient one is shown by the fact that Mamre is called "the Amorite" in Gen. xiv. 13, 24; the Amorites are spoken of as the pre-Israelite inhabitants of Canaan in Amos ii. 9, 10. In later days the personal name became a place-name, and was identified with Hebron (see Gen. xxiii. 19, xxxv. 27, belonging to the P document, where there is no mention of the tree).

In the case of the tamarisk tree in Beersheba which Abraham is said to have planted (Gen. xxi. 33) one might well ask, What was the point of his doing so? But this is in all probability a later tradition to explain the presence of an ancient tree-sanctuary. The verse must be read in connexion with Gen. xxvi. 23–35, which describes a theophany in the same place, but where the tree is not mentioned (cp. Gen. xlvi. 1). On Beersheba, see below, p. 39 f.

In Gen. xxxv. 4 occurs the curious episode of Jacob burying the "strange gods," together with the ear-rings of his followers, under the Shechem terebinth, which, as we have seen, was known as the "oracle-terebinth." As the context speaks of God's appearance to Jacob on the occasion of his fleeing from Esau, Jacob's action in burying these idols must be understood as meaning that, since he had accepted 'Elohim as his God, and thereby repudiated these other gods, the ill-will of these latter had to be provided against; there was no more efficacious means of achieving this than that of burying them under the tree-sanctuary of his God, because there they would be under the control of a more powerful spirit. The passage is, from our present point of view, a very instructive one, because it clearly implies that the terebinth was an abode of the deity; and thus it offers a clear indication of earlier animistic belief. There is an evident connexion between this passage and

---

[1] In both of these passages the Hebrew has the plural, but as in Deut. xi. 30, we must, following the Septuagint in each case, read the singular; note also that in Gen. xviii. 4 it is "the tree," not plural.

Joshua xxiv. 26, 27, for it is under this terebinth in Shechem that Joshua sets up a great stone as a witness lest the people deny God.

An interesting piece of evidence occurs in the isolated note in Gen. xxxv. 8 : " Deborah, Rebekah's nurse, died, and she was buried below Bethel under the oak (*'allon*), and the name of it was called *'Allōn-bakūth* " (i.e. the oak of weeping). Nothing is known of this Deborah, who is of course quite a different personality from the prophetess of the same name; but she must have played an important *rôle* for the tradition here mentioned to have been handed down. For the tree to have got this name must certainly mean that it was a sacred one; but we venture to think that it was not because Deborah was buried under it that it received its name. It is more likely that the statement that Deborah was buried under it was made in order to account for its name, the original reason for which was forgotten. It is not improbable that this tree was a spot where the annual " weeping for Tammuz " took place. Here it need only be said that this ceremony was a widely practised one, very ancient, and derived from the Babylonians; and as Tammuz was a vegetation god the " weeping " for him, which was always done by women, would appropriately be celebrated by a sacred tree.

The account of the divine appearance at the burning bush (Exod. iii. 2–5) is probably derived from two sources,[1] but in any case it contains two conceptions regarding the deity; fire as indicating the divine presence, and a tree as his abode. With the latter cp. Deut. xxxiii. 16, where it speaks baldly of Yahweh as of " Him that dwelt in the bush "; a more pointed illustration of an echo of animistic belief could not be given.

Joshua xix. 33 is a late passage—it belongs to the P document; but for present purposes that does not matter. Mention is there made of " the oak of Beza-'anannim," near Kadesh (cp. Judges iv. 11); the meaning of the name is too uncertain to draw any conclusions from it. Evidently it is mentioned only because it was a prominent landmark. But so conspicuous a tree, and, above all, one that had a name attached to it, must have had some further significance which has not been recorded. It is also interesting to note that the name still clung to it in late post-exilic times, as its occurrence in the Priestly Code shows.

---

[1] See, e.g., McNeile, *The Book of Exodus*, p. 16 (1908).

A highly instructive passage is Judges iv. 4, 5 : " Now Deborah, a prophetess, the wife of Lappidoth, she judged Israel at that time. And she sat [not ' dwelt,' see vi. 11, 1 Sam. xiv. 2, xxii. 6] under the palm tree of Deborah between Ramah and Bethel in the hill country of Ephraim ; and the children of Israel came up to her for judgement." Here we have another example of an oracle-terebinth like the tree in Shechem ; and we can see that the oracle might be given by a woman as well as by a man. The word " judgement " must, of course, not be understood in a modern sense : " decision " would far better express what is meant ; and that the people, as we should expect, came for the most diverse objects of inquiry can be seen from Exod. xxii. 7, 8. It is a divine oracle which is sought ; and the decision is given through a recognized expert. And when it is asked how the divine decision is communicated to the prophetess there can be only one answer : the rustling of the leaves of the sacred tree was believed to indicate the nature of the decision sought ; but this could, of course, be understood and interpreted only by one who was expert in such matters. Having then received this message, the prophetess was in a position to give the oracle inquired for. The passage is a striking confirmation of what has already been said as to the indications of earlier animistic belief.

A further indication of the same thing is to be found in the section Judges vi. 11-24. Here we read of the appearance of Yahweh (the " angel of Yahweh " was substituted later for reverential reasons ; see ver. 14 ff.) under the terebinth in Ophrah, " that pertained to Joash the Abiezrite," i.e. the terebinth, not Ophrah, belonged to Joash, indicating that it was a private sanctuary. The altar that is built marks the site as a permanent sanctuary, i.e. the tree was one in which it was believed that Yahweh was wont to take up His abode, and at certain times to issue from the tree and sit under it, thus " showing Himself," which is the literal meaning of the Hebrew word rendered " appeared " in ver. 12.

In Judges ix. 6 the Shechem terebinth is mentioned again. The solemn act of making Abimelech king is carried out at this sanctuary, presumably for the purpose of having the deity for witness. The Hebrew text, which says that they made Abimelech king " by the terebinth that was set up," is clearly corrupt, for trees are not set up ; on the basis of the Septuagint we must read " by the terebinth of the standing stone " (*mazzebah* for *muzzab*) ; this is the " great stone " mentioned in Joshua xxiv. 26 (see above, p. 28). The sacred standing stone by the side of the sacred tree is an interesting point, for, as we shall see (p. 43), it was in later times customary for a sacred pole (surrogate for the sacred tree) and the sacred pillar to be set up by the altar.

In the verses which follow occurs what is known as Jotham's parable ; we have a similar but much shorter one in 2 Kings xiv. 9 ; as Robertson Smith has pointed out, " the old Hebrew fables of trees that speak and act like human beings have their original source in the savage personification of vegetable species," [1] and he gives parallels among the ancient Arabs.

In the same chapter (Judges ix) ver. 37, reference is made to " the terebinth of Me'ōnenim," which means " the soothsayers' [or diviners'] terebinth " ; it is therefore another instance of an oracle tree mentioned in Gen. xii. 6 (see above, p. 26).

In Judges xx. 33 it is said that " all the men of Israel rose up out of their place and set themselves in array at Baal-tamar." This is presumably a place-name ; it is never mentioned elsewhere, and its locality is unknown. But, in any case, it was called after a baal who was believed to take up his abode in a palm-tree (tamar means " palm-tree "). That fact is sufficient for present purposes, as it is a clear instance of a somewhat developed animistic belief.

The terebinth of Tabor, close to Bethel, mentioned in 1 Sam. x. 3, must be identified with the terebinth of Deborah (Gen. xxxv. 8) : the latter stood " below Bethel," and the two names Tabor and Deborah are much alike in Hebrew ; we should undoubtedly read the latter here.

Another tree, the incidental mention of which without explanation shows that it was well known, was the pomegranate tree under which Saul sat (not " abode " as in the R.V., 1 Sam. xiv. 2). As king, Saul dispenses judgement, holding his court under this tree ; the significant point is that this takes place on such a spot. Whether or not the idea was that Saul was supposed to receive inspiration for his decisions from the indwelling deity cannot be said for certain, but there must have been some reason for this specific mention of the tree. Judging from the many references to sacred trees already dealt with, it can hardly

[1] *Op. cit.*, p. 133.

be doubted that this, too, was a sacred tree, and there could be only one reason for its sanctity.

In 1 Sam. xvii. 2 mention is made of "the terebinth valley" (not "the vale of Elah" as in the R.V.; the margin gives "terebinth"). Here the point of significance is that a valley should be known by the name of a single tree; it denotes that there was something specific about the tree, and being a terebinth (i.e. an evergreen) we may conclude that it was a sacred tree.

In 1 Sam. xxii. 6 we read : "Now Saul was sitting in Gibeah, under the tamarisk tree on the height." As is well known, sanctuaries were often situated on elevated spots, and as this tree stood in a sanctuary it was obviously a sacred one. Saul sits under it taking counsel with his followers, because he finds himself in a difficult position. No hint is given, it is true, as to the reason for this spot being chosen; but it is difficult to resist the conclusion that guidance was sought because of the presence of the deity there.

The burying of Saul's bones under a tamarisk tree (1 Sam. xxxi. 13), or under a terebinth (1 Chron. x. 12), in Jabesh, was done with the intention of according them the utmost reverence; there would be no point in making mention of this unless the tree had been regarded as a sacred one.

One of the most instructive passages is 2 Sam. v. 23, 24 (see also 1 Chron. xiv. 15). After David has inquired of Yahweh regarding his attack upon the Philistines, he is told that when he hears the sound of marching in the tops of the balsam trees it will be the time to bestir himself, "for then is Yahweh gone out before thee to smite the hosts of the Philistines"; marching in the tops of the trees is, of course, the sound of the rustling of the branches. It is quite clear from this passage that the belief was held that Yahweh entered the trees, His presence being indicated by the rustling. One could not have a more direct indication of animistic belief.

In 1 Kings xiii. 14 we read of a man of God sitting under a terebinth tree; as the context shows, this is the spot where he sought to give answer to inquiries made, but he is lured away by a false prophet. The fact that he is described as sitting under the terebinth would be pointless unless it were implied that this was an oracle-tree. As the scene is in Bethel, the tree is in all probability to be identified with the one mentioned in Gen. xxxv. 8, which was also in Bethel.

In later times worship under trees was condemned as heathen, but the passages in which such condemnation occurs show that trees were regarded as sacred in earlier times, and therefore indirectly witness to animistic conceptions; that this type of worship continued for so long only shows how deeply rooted these conceptions were.

CHAPTER III

REMNANTS OF ANIMISM IN HEBREW RELIGION : SACRED WATERS

1. GENERAL SEMITIC BELIEF

AMONG the Semites generally animistic conceptions in regard to water were at least as pronounced as in regard to trees. This applies, above all, to running water, rivers, streams, and springs. Lakes and the sea itself were also the abodes of supernatural beings, but with these we are not so directly concerned.

The ancient Babylonians believed that life was inherent in water; their water deities being, of course, a subsequent development.[1] Thus, the fact that Ea was the god of the deep permits the assumption that in an earlier stage of belief the sea itself was a living thing. In the ancient Babylonian Pantheon there were numerous water-gods, for every river and canal, great or small, had its special tutelary deity.[2] On the great Hammurabi inscription mention is made of the river-god Naru : the name itself probably means " river " (cp. *nahar*, the Hebrew word for " river "). A goddess named Ninakhakuddu is often mentioned in connexion with this god, from which fact Jastrow concludes that she was a river-goddess. Evidence of an earlier stage of belief may perhaps be discerned in the mention of water-witches. Jastrow quotes a magical text pronounced against a witch who had enticed a man into the water.[3] Belonging to later times, we are told that in the great temple of Marduk in Babylon there was a spring in which the gods, according to a Babylonian hymn, " bathed their faces."

Jastrow, in concluding his chapter on the remnants of Animism in Babylonian religion, lays emphasis on the close connexion that is seen to exist between gods and spirits in the popular forms of Babylonian religion. In the magical texts both of these belong to the Pantheon, and the same

---

[1] Jastrow, *op. cit.*, i. 48.   [2] *Ibid.*, p. 63.   [3] *Op. cit.*, i. 300, 310.

is the case in other branches of religious literature. Old-world traditional animistic conceptions dominate popular belief down to the latest times, and this in spite of the distinction that had been made between the higher and the lower powers, and in spite of the efforts of the learned classes to systematize and, so far as in them lay, to purify the ancient religious ideas. "Indeed," he says, "it must strike one as a satire on civilization that Animism, in the modified form (*in der abgeschwächten Form*) of Magic, is perhaps to be regarded as the most enduring heritage which Babylon has bequeathed to mankind. Among classical writers the representative of Babylonian culture, the priest, has become synonymous with magician." [1]

Regarding the Syrians, Lucian, in speaking of the sacred lake at Hierapolis, says that in the midst of it there stood "an altar of stone, which was always decked with ribbons; and many every day swim in the lake with crowns on their heads performing their acts of adoration." [2]

One of the most holy places among the Phœnicians was the pool of Aphaca at the source of the River Adonis.[3] Robertson Smith draws attention to the fact that temples were often erected near springs and rivers, and that while such a position was no doubt chosen partly on account of its convenience—water being required for ablutions and other ritual purposes—yet "the presence of living water in itself gave consecration to the place. The fountain or stream was not a mere adjunct to the temple, but was itself one of the principal *sacra* of the spot, to which special legends and a special ritual were often attached, and to which the temple in many instances owed its celebrity and even its name." [4] He gives various illustrations; but the most important point for our present purpose is expressed in the words: "The one general principle which runs through all the varieties of the legends, and which also lies at the basis of the ritual, is that the sacred waters are instinct with divine life and energy. The legends explain this in diverse ways, and bring the divine quality of the waters into connexion with various deities or supernatural powers, but they all agree in this, that their main object is to show how the fountain or stream comes to be impregnated, so to speak, with the vital energy of the deity to which it is sacred." [5]

[1] *Op. cit.*, i. 200.
[2] *De Dea Syria*, § xlvi.
[3] Baudissin, *op. cit.*, ii. 159 f.
[4] *Rel. Sem.*, p. 170.
[5] *Ibid.*, p. 173.

Regarding the ancient Arabs, the mention of sacred waters is comparatively rare—not to be wondered at in such an arid country as Arabia; but sufficient evidence exists to show without a shadow of doubt that their belief in this respect was identical with other Semites. In Mecca there was in the times of heathenism the holy well Zamzam into which gifts were cast; Wellhausen gives other instances of sacred waters at sanctuaries; he says that as a rule the spring or well lay at the foot of a hill or rock.[1] Robertson Smith says that " as healing springs and sacred springs are everywhere identified, it is noteworthy that the south Arabs regard medicinal waters as inhabited by *jinn*, usually of serpent form, and that the water of the sanctuary at the Palmetum was thought to be health-giving, and was carried home by pilgrims as Zamzam water now is."[2] He also gives instances showing that some holy wells become places of oracles and divination.

Abundant confirmation of the belief that springs and running waters are the abode of spirits is afforded by what can be observed at the present day in Syria, where the beliefs held millenniums ago are still in vogue. For illustrations of this see Curtiss, *op. cit.*, pp. 88 ff., 116 ff.

These few details are sufficient to show the ideas of the Semites in general regarding sacred waters, and will serve as a preliminary to our examination of what the Old Testament says upon the subject; to this we now turn.

2. THE OLD TESTAMENT

In Gen. xiv. 7 it is said that another name for *Kadesh* (" sanctuary ") was *'En-mishpat*, " the spring of decision." This name implies that it was a well to which men came in order to obtain a decision about some point of dispute; it was thus an oracle-well. It must therefore have been believed to be the abode of a spirit, a holy well, that is; and this is borne out by the name of the place in which it was situated, *Kadesh*, a " sanctuary." Naturally, the water of such a well was regarded as holy; and it was from a similar source that the " holy water " mentioned in Num. v. 17 was brought for use in the ritual for discovering the innocence or otherwise of a man's wife accused of adultery. The fact that the water is called " holy," as

---

[1] *Op cit.*, pp. 103 f.

[2] *Rel. Sem.*, 168, 178; further information is given by Lagrange, *op. cit.*, pp. 158–168. See also the very instructive example given by Frazer, *G. B.*, "Adonis, Attis, Osiris," i. 215 f.

well as the belief in its efficacy, means that it was believed to be impregnated by the nature and presence of a spirit.

The significance of such a name as *'En-mishpat* justifies the belief that in the case of other names compounded with *'En* there was originally a similar significance. Of course, this does not necessarily follow; but when it is realized how often supernatural powers were associated with springs and wells it will be seen that there is some justification for believing that place-names connected with *'En* do point to originally sacred sites. This is especially borne out by those cases in which the name of a god is attached to *'En*. Thus, we have *'En-shemesh* in Joshua xv. 7, xviii. 17, " the spring of the sun " ; if there were any doubt as to the significance of this name, it would be removed by the fact that in the latter passage the Septuagint renders it " the spring of *Beth-Shemesh* " ; for in place-names compounded with *Beth* the name following it is very frequently of a divine character, so that *Beth* in such cases means " temple." *'En-shemesh* was, therefore, a spring which at one time was connected with sun-worship.

There is mentioned also in Gen. xiv. 7 the place called *Chazazon-tamar* [1] which, according to 2 Chron. xx. 2, is the same as *'En-gedi* (" the spring of the Kid ") ; were it not for the other name by which *'En-gedi* was known, one would naturally assume that it received its name because it was situated in a spot where there was pasturage for flocks; but as it was marked by the presence of a sacred palm-tree the spring must have been a holy one. In the vicinity of *'En-gedi* there was another spring called *'En-'eglaim*, " the spring of the two calves " ; the mention of the *two* calves is interesting—it is not as though the plural did not often occur—for we naturally think of the two calves set up by Jeroboam I for worship (1 Kings xii. 29) ; and from 2 Kings x. 29 it looks as if two calves were set up both in Bethel and in Dan, not one calf in each; in Bethel (1 Kings xii. 32) and in Samaria also two calves were worshipped (2 Kings xvii. 16, though in Hos. viii. 5, 6, only one is mentioned). It is therefore quite possible that *'En-'eglaim* was at one time the sanctuary of a cow-divinity, viz. Astarte (cp. *Ashtoreth-Karnaim*, " Astarte of the two horns," Gen. xiv. 5) ; the large number of images of this goddess with two horns discovered during excavations in Palestine proves how prevalent this worship was.

[1] *Tamar* means a " palm-tree " ; it is not known what *Chazazon* means.

Another spring connected with the name of an animal but for an entirely different reason, was *'En-ha-Kore* (Judges xv. 18, 19); this has been wrongly interpreted in the Hebrew text as meaning " the spring of the caller," i.e. of one who calls upon God. That is folk-etymology. What it means is " the partridge spring "; it was the calling note of the partridge which gave it the name of " the caller " (see 1 Sam. xxvi. 20; Jer. xvii. 11). The reason why the spring was thus called is very interesting. There is another word for " partridge " in Hebrew, *Choglah*, or more probably *Chaglah*; this word comes from a root meaning to " hop," the cognate Arabic root is " to hobble " or " hop." The second name for a partridge was given to it because of the way in which it hops along. Now, in Joshua xv. 6, xviii. 19, 21, mention is made of a place close to Jericho which is called *Beth-Choglah* (*-Chaglah*), i.e. " the house, or sanctuary, of the hobbler," which must be in reference to a particular kind of sacred dance associated with the worship at this sanctuary. That this is not a fantastic idea will be seen by Robertson Smith's reference to Epiphanius : " The Syriac text of Epiphanius (*De pond. et mens.* § 62), tells us that 'Atad of Gen. l. 11. was identified with the spring and thorn-bush of Beth-hagla near Jericho, and the explanation offered of the name Beth-hagla seems to be based on a local tradition of a ritual procession round the sacred objects." [1] One can fully understand the identification referred to when reading in Gen. l. 11 of " the mourning (i.e. for Jacob) in the floor of 'Atad "; for a ritual dance as a mourning custom was widespread in antiquity.[2]

One other spring connected with the name of an animal may be mentioned, the *'En-ha-tannin*, or " Spring of the dragon," in Neh. ii. 13; there is good reason for identifying this with *'En-rogel*; both were in Jerusalem, and the latter was by the " serpent's stone " (" serpent " is used for " dragon " in Amos ix. 3). For a spring to be known by two names was evidently not uncommon, especially when, as in this case, there was a particular reason for it. That *'En-rogel* was a sanctuary is quite obvious, since it was a place of sacrifice (1 Kings i. 9).[3] It is well known that

[1] *Rel. Sem.*, p. 101, note 1. For other references to ritual dances in the Old Testament see the present writer's *The Sacred Dance*, pp. 50 f., 92 f. (1923).

[2] See *The Sacred Dance*, pp. 29 f.

[3] It is also mentioned in ver. 25 and in Joshua xv. 7, xviii. 16, 2 Sam. xvii. 17.

springs were often regarded as places of healing (see above,
p. 35), and, according to Num. xxi. 9, a serpent was the
emblem of healing. *'En-ha-tannin* may therefore well have
been originally a place for healing, the name having been
given to it because it was believed that it was the abode of a
spirit which appeared at times in the shape of a serpent;
damp spots are a favourite *habitat* for some kinds of serpents.
Then arises the question as to what *'En-rogel* means; it is
usually interpreted as meaning "the fuller's spring";
but this is questionable, and the word never occurs elsewhere
in Biblical Hebrew. But the root from which the word
comes means not infrequently to "search out" or "inquire"
about something (e.g. Judges xviii. 2; 2 Sam. x. 3 and elsewhere); and there is no reason why this should not be what
is meant here, "the well of inquiring," viz. about what one
should do to cure an ailment. In this connexion we are
reminded of *'En-harod*, "the well of trembling" (Judges
vii. 1), perhaps to be understood in the sense of the troubling
of the waters as in the case of the pool of Bethesda.

We have by no means exhausted the references to springs,[1]
but sufficient examples will have been given; moreover,
there is a further type of sacred waters to be considered.

So far we have been dealing with sacred *springs*, i.e.
waters which spring forth spontaneously; but the Hebrews
also attached great importance to sacred *wells*, i.e. waters
which had to be dug for before they came forth: in Hebrew,
Be'er. This distinction is, however, not always observed
in the Old Testament. A very instructive passage in this
connexion is Num. xxi. 17, 18, one of the oldest fragments
of poetry in the Bible, in which the well is addressed as
though it were a living being:

> Spring up, O well; sing ye to it:
> O well, which the princes digged,
> Which the nobles of the people delved
> With their sceptre, with their staves.

Such words, sung directly to the well, can only mean
that it was believed to be the embodiment of a supernatural
being who caused it to spring up. As Robertson Smith says:
"In Palestine to this day all springs are viewed as the
seats of spirits, and the peasant women, whether Moslem
or Christian, ask their permission before drawing water."[2]

---

[1] See, among others, Joshua xvii. 7, xix. 21, 37; 1 Sam. xxviii. 7; Neh.
xi. 29; Gen. xxxviii. 14, 21; Joshua xv. 32, 34, xix. 7; Num. xxxiv. 11.

[2] *Rel. Sem.*, p. 169, note 3. Other parallels, ancient and modern, are
given by Dalman, *Palästinischer Diwan*, p. 45 (1901); Gressmann, *Mose und
seine Zeit*, pp. 349 f. (1913).

The most important site of a sacred well was Beersheba (Gen. xxi. 22–23). Opinions differ as to whether we are to understand this name as meaning "the well of seven," i.e. spirits, or "seven wells"; von Gall argues strongly in favour of the former interpretation,[1] so too George Adam Smith;[2] but most others believe that it means "Seven Wells." Driver, e.g., says that "the stress laid on the number 'seven' in vers. 28–30 seems to show that the writer intends to explain 'Beersheba' as meaning 'Well of seven' (*sheba'* being 'seven' in Hebrew); but in ver. 31*b* it is explained expressly as meaning 'Well of swearing.' . . . But it is hardly doubtful that the real meaning of the name is 'Well of seven,' i.e. 'Seven Wells,' with allusion to the number of wells in the locality . . .";[3] and Robertson Smith points to the fact that "seven is a sacred number among the Semites, particularly affected in matters of ritual, and the Hebrew word 'to swear' means literally 'to come under the influence of seven things.' The seven ewe lambs figure in the oath between Abraham and Abimelech at Beersheba . . . the oath of purgation at seven wells would therefore have a peculiar force."[4]

However this may be, the main point is that the well, or wells, of Beersheba marked a sanctuary; and, like many another sanctuary, it had also its sacred tree, in this case a tamarisk (Gen. xxi. 33).[5] The deity which from time immemorial had been worshipped here was called 'El 'Olam, the "ancient 'El," or God, who was now identified with the God of Israel (cp. Gen. xxvi. 24). From Amos v. 5 we can see that the worship there was reprobated by the prophet.

Another interesting illustration is that of the well called *Be'er-lahai-roi*, situated between Kadesh and Bered (Gen. xvi. 14); the steps in the development of belief can be plainly discerned here. There was a very ancient well sacred to a local god, called 'El-roi; the belief being that the spirit whose abode this well was manifested himself at certain times; so that the well was called Be'er-'el-roi, i.e. a well

---

[1] *Altisraelitische Kultstätten*, pp. 44 ff. (1898).
[2] *Encycl. Bibl.*, i. 518*b*.
[3] *The Book of Genesis*, p. 215 (1904).
[4] *Rel. Sem.*, p. 182, where other instances are given. Cp. also the other form of the Beersheba tradition in Gen. xxvi. 23 ff., where in ver. 33 the name is interpreted as meaning "the well of the oath."
[5] Cp. also *Be'er-'elim*, "the well of the terebinths," in Isa. xv. 8, perhaps the same as that mentioned in Num. xxi. 16.

of an 'El apparition. This sanctuary became adapted
by the Israelites to Yahweh-worship, in consequence of
which the name underwent a change; and because it was
believed that no one could see God and live (see Gen. xxxii.
30), the name was altered so as to read " The well of my
seeing and (yet) living." [1] Then the final step was that for
reverential reasons the " angel of Yahweh " was substituted
for Yahweh Himself.[2]

In Joshua xix. 8 a place is mentioned called *Ba'alath-be'er*,
"the mistress of the well," showing that the belief in a female
spirit of a well also existed.

The sanctity of *running water* is well illustrated by the
ritual described in Deut. xxi. 4; one can, therefore, well
understand that certain rivers were looked upon as
sanctuaries of gods; probably this was the case with *all*
rivers originally. The Kishon (Judges v. 21, 1 Kings xviii.
40) is a case in point; in all probability the stream was called
after the god Kish, and conceived to be in some direct way
connected with him; so, too, with the rivers Belus and
Adonis. That the Gihon was likewise a sanctuary is clear
from the fact that Solomon was brought down to it to be
anointed king (1 Kings i. 33, 34).

Cases of this kind show that originally the river or stream
was regarded as sacred because of the spirit whose abode
it was.

We are, perhaps, apt to overlook the significance of
references to well-grown trees standing by waters (e.g.
Gen. xlix. 22; Isa. xliv. 4; Jer. xvii. 8; Ezek. xix. 10;
Ps. i. 3); in its origin this was because of the presence of a
spirit, primarily in the water.

---

[1] The Hebrew text of xvi. 14 can hardly be in order; see Driver's note
and his reference to Wellhausen's emendation (slightly different from that
here adopted), *op. cit.*, p. 183. It is referred to again below, p. 54.

[2] See further below, p. 155.

CHAPTER IV

REMNANTS OF ANIMISM IN HEBREW RELIGION: SACRED STONES, ROCKS, AND MOUNTAINS

1. General Semitic Belief

THERE are two points of difference between sacred trees, sacred springs, etc., and sacred stones, whether a rock, or a boulder, or a heap of stones, or a pillar. The first difference is that the former have, or were believed to have, independent life, while the latter were inanimate; and the second difference is that the former were natural sanctuaries, the latter artificial, at any rate as a general rule, among the Semites; instances of sacred natural rocks occur, but they are not frequent.

Whatever new conceptions, expressed by their ritual or otherwise, the Semites may have developed regarding the nature and meaning of stones as sanctuaries, it is certain that, like sacred trees and sacred springs, they were inherited by the Semites from man in the distant past.

Since a spirit, or later a god, was believed to take up his abode in the stone, it could make no difference, so far as its sanctity was concerned, what its shape or appearance was. Therefore we naturally ask, why, among the Semites, the stone sanctuary normally took the form of a standing pillar. Probably more than one answer must be given to this question since, in course of time, new ideas arose. Robertson Smith thinks that "it seems most probable that the choice of a pillar or cairn as the primitive idol was not dictated by any other consideration than convenience for ritual purposes. The stone or stone-heap was a convenient mark of the proper place of sacrifice, and at the same time, if the deity consented to be present at it, provided the means for carrying out the ritual of the sacrificial blood." [1] But the pillar or cairn as representing the spirit or the god, or

[1] *Rel. Sem.*, p. 212. He shows the fallacy of the opinion that sacred posts and pillars among the Semites were phallic symbols, on pp. 456 f.; not that these latter were wholly absent (see S. A. Cook, *The Religion of Ancient Palestine*, p. 32 [1908]).

later as constituting the place of abode of a god, must have existed long before the developed ritual of the sacrificial blood. It is therefore possible that originally there was something more significant about the standing stone than the mere question of convenience. One speaks tentatively here because, from the nature of the case, there can be no certainty; but the conjecture may be hazarded that the standing stone was originally chosen by the Semites as being the nearest approach to the human form (cp. what was said above, pp. 9 f.). This, however, is merely incidental; we are more concerned with the Semites within historic times.

Stone sanctuaries are not to be found among the Semites of comparatively advanced culture such as the Babylonians, Assyrians, and Phœnicians; among these we should not expect to find sacred stones or pillars in the primitive sense.[1] But it is possible that a survival of these is to be discerned in the pillars that stood at the entrance to temples. Thus, in the representation of a Babylonian temple dating from the third millennium B.C., two pillars stand at the entrance.[2] Another example is that of an Elamite temple which is depicted on a bronze slab belonging approximately to 1100 B.C.; this is a particularly interesting illustration, for what are quite evidently three tree-trunks and a standing stone are represented. It contains a short Babylonian inscription; the Elamites are known to have been influenced by the Babylonians, and this bronze slab illustrates the fact.[3]

To a later time, third to fourth century B.C., belongs a Punic votive tablet from Sicily on which three standing pillars are depicted; the middle one of these stands higher than those on either side of it. As Gressmann shows, these are supposed to be standing on, or beside, an altar.[4] Twin pillars stood also at the entrance to the temples of Paphos and Hierapolis; and Herodotus tells us that in Tyre he saw a temple dedicated to Hercules, " and in it were two pillars, one of fine gold, the other of emerald stone." [5] These were, of course, originally of stone. There is also plenty of evidence of single pillars standing within the precincts of a temple;

---

[1] The anointing of a sacred stone seems, however, to have been customary among the Assyrians, according to an inscription of Esarhaddon (Gunkel, *Genesis*, p. 290 [1901]).

[2] Gressmann, *Altorientalische Bilder zum Alten Testament*, p. 138 and Plate 476 (1927).

[3] Gressmann, *op. cit.*, p. 135, Plate 468.

[4] *Op. cit.*, pp. 126 ff., and Plate 437; for another example see Plate 438.

[5] Herodotus, ii. 44; see also Robertson Smith, *Rel. Sem.*, p. 208.

" A coin of the age of Macrinus shows the principal temple at Byblos; in the court is a conical stone upon an altar-like basis. Similar stones appear on many coins of cities in the Lebanon and on the Syrian coast." [1]

All these represent a great development in the history of the sacred stone. For the earlier phases among the Semites we must turn first to the ancient pre-Islamic Arabs. The sacred stone [2] was indispensable, and it was the most characteristic mark of the ancient Arab sanctuary. It represented the deity, not any particular one, but any god or goddess. Very often there were several of these in a sanctuary, even when only one god was worshipped there. Things were hung upon the sacred stone just as on the sacred tree; and it was smeared with blood, doubtless as an act of worship. Beside it a pit was often dug, called a *ghabghab*; into this the sacrificial blood was poured, and votive offerings were also thrown into it. [3] Sacred cairns, or stone-heaps, were also common. [4]

Still more instructive is the evidence afforded by excavation in Palestine. Thus, on the site of the ancient Megiddo, a high-place (*bamah*) was laid bare with its stone altar and two standing stone pillars. [5] Similar pillars were also found on the site of ancient Taanach; among them two which were scooped out for the purpose of offering blood or oil on them. [6] The most interesting, however, are the pillars which were found on the site of ancient Gezer in the temple there. This " superb megalithic structure consists of a row of seven monoliths, with an eighth standing apart, and flanked by stumps of two others at the northern end." One of these stands in a socket and has two cup-marks and grooves, probably for pouring in oblations; there is also a long socketed stone, clearly not an altar, in which in all probability the Asherah, or wooden pole, was placed. The smallest and most insignificant was probably the most important; its upper end has been worked almost to a point, and its polished

---

[1] G. F. Moore, in *Encycl. Bibl.*, iii. 2890. Cp. also the two pillars set up at the porch of the temple in Jerusalem, 1 Kings vii. 15, 21.

[2] Called *Nuzb*, it served as altar, and corresponds to the Hebrew *mazzebah* (" pillar ").

[3] For these and other details see Wellhausen, *op. cit.*, pp. 101 ff. (1897); Kittel, *Studien zur hebräischen Archäologie und Religionsgeschichte*, pp. 118 ff. (1908).

[4] Wellhausen, *op. cit.*, pp. 111 f.

[5] Jeremias, *op. cit.*, p. 209.

[6] Sellin, *Tell Ta'anek*, pp. 103 ff. (1904), where illustrations are given and many further particulars.

surface, quite absent from all the others, shows that it must have been kissed, or anointed, or otherwise handled by the worshippers; in fact, this little pillar was clearly the " bethel " of the temple.[1]

Evidence of this kind is highly instructive, and throws light on what we read on the subject in the Old Testament.

Finally, a brief reference must be made to holy mountains. After what has been said it needs no further words to show that holy hills and mountains witness to the existence of earlier animistic conceptions.

The best evidence regarding the sanctity of certain mountains among the Semites generally is offered in the Old Testament; therefore before giving examples of ancient Hebrew belief on the subject it will be well to mention some instances of sacred mountains situated in non-Israelite territory.

The sanctity of Mount Sinai, in Midianite territory, is too well known to need further discussion; it is sufficient to point to the name " the mount of Yahweh " being applied to it (Num. x. 33); a mountain on which a god is supposed to reside is obviously regarded as holy. The idea is extraordinarily *naïve*, but it must be remembered that even this is a development of an earlier animistic belief. Mount Sinai is an especially interesting instance, because the whole coast-land along the Ælanitic gulf is volcanic, and the mountain was certainly at one time a volcano.[2] A volcanic eruption would necessarily have been regarded by semi-cultured peoples as due to the spirit which made its abode there.

The heights of Nebo, Peʻor, and Pisgah lie in Moabite territory; the sanctity of the first is seen by the fact that it is the name of a Babylonian deity who must at one time have been worshipped there; and the city of Nebo, so named after the mountain, is mentioned on the Moabite Stone (cp. Num. xxxii. 38, Isa. xv. 2). According to Num. xxiii. 28–30, sacrifices were offered on Mount Peʻor, which shows it to have been a sanctuary; its possessor is spoken of in Num. xxv. 3 as the Baʻal of Peʻor," who was worshipped by the

[1] See the *Quarterly Statement of the Palestine Exploration Fund for* 1903, pp. 23–36. For sacred stones in Palestine at the present day see Curtiss, *op. cit.*, pp. 84 ff.

[2] The Old Testament, as against the later tradition, locates mount Sinai in Midianite or Edomite territory. See Exod. iii. 1, xviii. 1 ff.; Num. x. 29 ff.; Hab. iii. 7; and cp. Jer. xlix. 21; 2 Chron. viii. 17; and Exod. xxiii. 31; Num. xiv. 25, xxi. 4; Deut. i. 40, ii. 1. Sinai was originally the sanctuary of Sin, the Moon-god; as late as the sixth century A.D. the worship of the moon was still carried on there (see Baethgen, *Beiträge zur semitischen Religionsgeschichte*, p. 105 (1888).

Israelites. Pisgah is also shown to have been a sacred mount, because altars were erected and sacrifices offered on it (Num. xxiii. 14).

We now turn to examine Hebrew belief regarding sacred stones, etc. The presence of holy mountains in Israelite territory will be spoken of at the end of the next section.

2. THE OLD TESTAMENT

In the narrative of Jacob at Bethel (Gen. xxviii. 11–22) there are some instructive points. Jacob takes one of the stones of the place and uses it for his head to rest on while sleeping; it is owing to his contact with this stone that he dreams, and thus recognizes that it is the abode of a god, a *beth-el*. As a result he sets it up as the pillar (*mazzebah*), marking it as a sanctuary, and pours oil on it as an act of worship of the indwelling deity. From the sacred stone as a god's house the place receives the name of Bethel (cp. xxxv. 14, 15).

We have here the adaptation of an extremely ancient local tradition which is made to apply to the God of Israel; but the remnants of animistic conceptions are as plain as anything could be.

A stone of a different character, but in regard to which animistic conceptions are also to be discerned, is that spoken of in Joshua xxiv. 26, 27; here it is told how Joshua " took a great stone (*'eben*), and set it up there (i.e., in Shechem) under the oak that was in the sanctuary of Yahweh. And Joshua said unto all the people, Behold, this stone shall be a witness against us; for it hath heard all the words of Yahweh which He spake unto us; it shall therefore be a witness against you, lest ye deny your God." The presence of a sacred stone as well as a sacred tree in a sanctuary was the usual thing, and each denoted the presence of the deity; but as a symbol each was only a development of the more primitive belief of the actual indwelling of a spirit. The echo of animistic conceptions is discerned in the *naïve* belief in the stone, identified with the indwelling spirit, hearing what is said and being thought of as a witness.

A somewhat similar illustration occurs in Gen. xxxi. 44–48. The combination of sources in vers. 43–54 makes the passage a little difficult; but for the present purpose it is sufficient to note that in the two accounts of the covenant between Jacob and Laban, one speaks of a pillar (*mazzebah*) as the witness (ver. 45), the other of a cairn (*gal*), in the following verse; and one speaks of the common meal, following, of course, a sacrifice, as taking place by the side of the pillar (ver. 54), the other as partaken of *on* the cairn (ver. 46) —not " by " as the R.V. renders (for the covenant feast cp. xxvi. 30). We have thus another illustration of the way in which a pillar, or a cairn, is thought of as a witness, being in fact personified; and this can be understood only on the supposition that in more ancient times a spirit was believed to animate the one and the other (see further below, pp. 127, 159 ff.).

It is quite possible that some ancient tradition about a sacred cairn lies behind the narrative in Joshua iv. 1–14, where it is told of how, when the ark was brought across the Jordan, twelve stones were taken from the river and piled upon the bank as a " sign " (ver. 6) and a " memorial " (ver. 7). Presumably a cairn had stood here from time immemorial, and its presence was in later ages explained as in this passage. As this cairn stood in the middle of the river (ver. 9), it is permissible to suppose that it was originally set up in honour of the river-god. On the other hand, according to ver. 20, the stones were carried to Gilgal (stone-circle, or cromlech); clearly two traditions have again been combined.

Another indication pointing to originally animistic conceptions regarding sacred stones is to be discerned in the fact that certain important stones have names, though very few of these occur, and their meaning is not always clear. The best known is *'Eben-'ezer*, " stone of help "; two such seem to have existed, one near Aphek in the north of the plain of Sharon (1 Sam. iv. 1, v. 1), and the other near Mizpah, a little north-east of Jerusalem (1 Sam. vii 12). *'Eben-bohan* is mentioned as a boundary-stone (Joshua xv. 6, xviii. 17); *bohan* can hardly be a proper name, it may possibly mean the " stone of covering," in the sense of protection, and thus somewhat analogous to *'Eben-'ezer*. In 1 Kings i. 9 it is said that " Adonijah sacrificed sheep and oxen and fatlings by the stone of Zocheleth which is beside 'En-rogel "; the " stone of Zocheleth " probably means the " Serpent stone "; its sanctity is shown by the fact that animals were sacrificed beside it. Wellhausen suggests a connexion between this and the Arabic proper name *Zuhal*, the name for Saturn.[1] That this stone stood in a sanctuary

---

[1] *Op. cit.*, p. 146. The two pillars which stood in the porch of the temple (1 Kings vii. 21), called *Jachin* (" He that establisheth ") and *Boaz* (" In him is strength "), do not come under this category.

is seen by its proximity to the sacred spring (see above, pp. 37 f.).

In 1 Sam. xx. 19 the words " the stone 'Ezel " should be read " by this mound," following the Septuagint; the Hebrew text must be emended accordingly; [1] this passage therefore does not come into consideration here.

An instructive passage occurs in 1 Sam. vi. 14; here we are told that the kine which drew the cart bearing the ark " came into the field of Joshua the Bethshemite and stood there; and there was a great stone there; and they clave the wood of the cart and offered up the kine for a burnt offering unto Yahweh." Laconic as this passage is, it must be obvious that the reason why the kine came to this sudden halt was because of the " great stone "; it is implied that the power residing in the ark had expressly driven them to this spot that they might be sacrificed there. Robertson Smith points to the somewhat analogous instance of the ram which presents itself as an offering in lieu of Isaac (Gen. xxii. 13) : " Exactly this principle," he says, " was observed down to late times at the great Astarte temple at Eryx, where the victims were drawn from the sacred herds nourished at the sanctuary, and were believed to offer themselves spontaneously at the altar. This is quite analogous to the usage at the Diipolia, where a number of cattle were driven round the sacred table, and the bull was selected for slaughter that approached it and ate of the sacred *popana* " [2] (i.e. flat cakes which were sacred offerings). In the verse before us the sacrifice of the kine then takes place on the stone, which thus becomes an altar. But the deity is still thought of as abiding in the stone, because in ver. 18, where the corrupt Hebrew text must be emended on the basis of the Septuagint, it is said : " And a witness is the great stone, whereon they set down the ark of Yahweh, to this day " (cp. Joshua xxiv. 26, 27; Gen. xxxi. 45, dealt with above, p. 46). In 1 Sam. xiv. 33–35 we read also of a great stone being used for an altar, and although nothing is hinted at as to why this particular stone was used, it is extremely probable that it was chosen because it was regarded as a sacred one. See also 2 Sam. xx. 8.

To this ancient belief in the sacred character of certain stones was due the command recorded in Exod. xx. 24–25 :

---

[1] The Hebrew word, according to the emended text, means a mound of soil, not of stones; so it is not a cairn that is meant.

[2] *Rel. Sem.*, p. 309.

" An altar of earth shalt thou make unto me . . . and if
thou make me an altar of stone, thou shalt not build it of
hewn stones; for if thou lift up thy tool upon it, thou hast
polluted it " (cp. Deut. xxvii. 5, 6; Joshua viii. 31). The
idea was that if a stone was hammered the indwelling *numen*
would be driven out. It is, of course, not to be supposed
that this command was given with any thought of the old-
world conception; but it is a good instance of the persistence
of a custom long after its original significance has been
forgotten.

Before concluding, a few examples must be offered of holy
hills and mountains which lay in Israelite territory; for
these all owed their character, in the first instance, to a
spirit who was believed to have his abode in them.

The sanctity of Mount Carmel [1] is sufficiently illustrated
by what we read in 1 Kings xviii; altars are raised there
both to Baal and to Yahweh; the presence of an altar is
enough to prove that a site is holy. Its holy character
continued through the ages to very much later times;
it is spoken of by Tacitus as a sanctuary with its altar, but
where there was neither temple nor an image of a deity.[2]

Mount Tabor, on the border between the territories of
Issachar and Zebulon (Joshua xix. 22, 1 Chron. vi. 77),
was a holy mountain, since sacrifices were offered on it;
this may be rightly gathered from Hos. v. 1 : " Hear this,
O ye priests, and hearken, ye house of Israel . . . for ye have
been a snare at Mizpah, and a net spread upon Tabor."
There is an evident reference here to some illicit forms of
worship.

Gibeah, which means " hill," lay in the territory of Benjamin; its sacred character is very clearly seen by its being
called " Gibeah of God " (1 Sam. x. 5), and on account of a
holy tree there (1 Sam. xxii. 6). Geba, another name for
" hills," and a different place from the foregoing, though
also in Benjaminite territory, was also a hill sanctuary, as is
shown by 2 Kings xxiii. 8 : " And he brought all the priests
out of the cities of Judah, and defiled the high places where
the priests had burned incense, from Geba to Beersheba."

We have also clear evidence from 2 Sam. xv. 30–32 that
the Mount of Olives was a sanctuary in ancient Israel;

---

[1] Not to be confused with the Carmel in Judah, south of Hebron (see
1 Sam. xxv. 2 ff.).

[2] *Hist.*, ii. 78. See further G. A. Smith, *The Historical Geography of the
Holy Land*, pp. 337–341 (1910).

and it is evident that this is the mount referred to in 1 Kings
xi. 7 : " Then did Solomon build an high place for Chemosh,
the abomination of Moab, in the mount that is before
Jerusalem. . . ." The very frequent mention of " high-
places " (*bamoth*), which are always sanctuaries, shows how
numerous they were ; [1] their original existence was due to
the fact that in course of time hill and mountain sanctuaries
were insufficient for the growing population and the increase
of settlements ; " the high place " was thus an imitation of
the mountain sanctuary. But this belongs, of course, to
much later ages. The original sanctity of a mountain or
hill was due to the presence of a spirit ; and we must therefore see in the existence of such a thing as a sacred mountain
a remnant of very much earlier animistic conceptions.

We have dealt with many of the Old Testament passages
which support the contention that the ancestors of the
Hebrews passed through the Animistic stage of belief, the
marks of which were left even after Hebrew Religion had
reached a higher stage. The next step is the Polytheistic
stage ; but before we come to this it will be necessary to
show that the Old Testament gives indubitable indications
that at one time Totemism, Taboo, and Ancestor-worship,
as well as some other primitive beliefs, were in vogue among
the Semitic ancestors of the Hebrews, and that the marks of
this having been the case can be discerned in the Old
Testament.

<hr>

[1] On these see below, pp. 58 f.

E

CHAPTER V

POLYTHEISTIC TENDENCIES IN HEBREW RELIGION

1. GENERAL SEMITIC BELIEF

THE immense mass of Babylonian and Assyrian inscriptions, religious, historical and others, belonging to all ages, has furnished Assyriologists with ample material for acquiring detailed knowledge of the gods and goddesses worshipped by these peoples. Their names have been collected, and their functions defined, by Jastrow, who indicates also the different periods to which they belong. There is first the period preceding the confederation of the Babylonian states, i.e. before the time of Hammurabi (2300 B.C.). Among these the names of goddesses are comparatively few; from this it is not, however, to be concluded that goddesses were few in number; for it is evident that every god had his spouse, sometimes several; but, generally speaking, the *rôle* of the goddess was less important than that of the god, hence the smaller number of the names of goddesses which have been recorded. In this earliest period the deities may be divided into two classes; those of purely local origin who gradually attained to wider recognition as the locality in question rose to greater importance; and those, likewise originally local, who received more widespread veneration because they were regarded as embodying the forces of Nature.

The second period is that of the age of Hammurabi, who united under one rule the various hitherto independent Babylonian states. The gods are divided into the high gods (Marduk, Ishtar, Nabu, Ea, Shamash, Bel, Sin, Anu and others), and those of secondary power, whose names are less familiar.

Then we come to the third period, that of the Assyrian pantheon, which included most of the deities of the preceding period, though new ones were added (Asshur, Dagan, the healing goddess Gula, and a few others).

The last period is that of the Neo-Babylonian empire,

during which Marduk, who had been displaced by Asshur in the preceding period, assumed once more the position of supreme god. Practically all the gods and goddesses hitherto worshipped were recognized by the Babylonians, but in some cases a deity would be accorded a more distinguished place in the Pantheon.[1]

The names of the gods and goddesses of the ancient Arabs, together with their functions, have been collected by Wellhausen,[2] and also by Nielsen [3] in a later work. They are similarly many in number; but space forbids our giving details; the same applies to the deities of Syria, Phœnicia, Canaan, etc.[4] A few words must, however, be said about the Ras Shamra [5] tablets (belonging to about the sixteenth to thirteenth centuries B.C.), which have greatly increased our knowledge about the Phœnician gods and goddesses; of these more than fifty are named on the various inscriptions. " But two stand out from amongst the rest, and these two are precisely those whom one would expect to find holding higher rank in a document emanating from Phœnicia—El and Baal." The god El has his abode in a field, the *sad El*, " field of god," and his spouse is called *Asherat iam*, the Ashera of the sea, who exercises great influence over him. El is the supreme god over all other gods; but he has many opponents, the foremost of whom is Baal, against whom he incites fantastic creatures, whose description, summary though it be, recalls certain passages in Ezekiel. El and Baal have each a son, called respectively Mot and Aleïon, who are constantly struggling against each other; " when one disappears, the other supervenes; the newly arrived is regarded as having killed the departed. The life of the world, not that of men only, but also that of the gods, is bound up with alternating deaths and resurrections of Mot and Aleïon "; the ultimate conqueror is Aleïon, the son of Baal. It may be that this agricultural myth is an attempted explanation of the origins of society, for Mot is both the symbol or spirit of vegetation, a shepherd, and an agricultural labourer, living in the country; while Aleïon is a town-dweller.[6] Whether this theory of

[1] See Jastrow, *op. cit.*, i. 48–266.
[2] *Op. cit.*, pp. 1–68.
[3] *Die Altarabische Kultur*, pp. 197–250 (1927).
[4] See, e.g., S. A. Cook, *The Religion of Ancient Palestine in the Light of Archæology*, passim (1930).
[5] Situated on the coast of Syria facing the island of Cyprus.
[6] Virolleaud, "The Gods of Phœnicia," in *Antiquity*, pp. 405 ff. (1931); see also in the same journal, Schaeffer, " The French Excavations in Syria," pp. 460 ff. (1930); Dhorme, " Première traduction des textes

Virolleaud's is correct or not time will show. For our present purpose the importance of the Ras Shamra tablets lies in the abundant new evidence they offer regarding the polytheism of the Phœnicians.

2. THE OLD TESTAMENT

When the Israelites settled down in Canaan they came into contact with a people with whom they were racially closely connected. For the most part these people had for long been agriculturists; but in the south and south-east of the land there were those who were semi-nomads, people who lived on the edge of, or near to, the steppe-land, and who were, nevertheless, not wholly unacquainted with agriculture. As will be seen, the record suggests that the religion of these latter had been the worship of *'Elim*, " gods," which was, however, gradually merging into the religion proper to agriculturists. It is with the belief in these *'Elim* that we shall concern ourselves first.

(a) The 'Elim.

We have seen that the animistic stage of belief gradually developed into the polytheistic stage, and that no clear-cut line marks off one stage from another, but that earlier ideas persist on long after the more primitive stages have been passed. We find this, therefore, in what was the polytheistic stage, viz. belief in *'Elim*. They are gods, but there are indications of their having developed from beings of a lower order; indeed, according to a number of passages containing place-names (see below), it almost looks as though they had not reached the status of gods; in any case, these place-names point to a time when they were not gods. But before coming to the passages in which the *'Elim* are referred to, there are one or two preliminary remarks to be made.

It is uncertain what the root meaning of *'El* (plural: *'Elim*) is; that fact would seem to point to the antiquity of the idea expressed by the word, whatever its meaning may have been. Many scholars regard it as connected with a root meaning " to be strong "; but seeing that the *'Elim* were not always " gods," this is doubtful. In course of time it is likely enough that *'El* came to connote one who was strong, so that from the point of view of later times this

---

phéniciens de Ras Shamra," in *Revue Biblique*, pp. 32–56 (1931); and especially, Jack, *The Ras Shamra Tablets : their Bearing on the Old Testament*, pp. 13–26 (1935).

derivation would hold good. The words *'elah,* " terebinth," and *'allon,* " oak " (both from the same root as that from which *'El* comes), contain the idea of " strength," and they were regarded as the abodes of supernatural beings; but one cannot say for certain whether these trees were regarded as strong from their nature or from the believed connexion of an *'El* with them. It must be confessed that we do not know with any certainty what the root-meaning of the word is.

Secondly, it is to be noted that *'Eloah* and the plural form *'Elohim* are extended formations of *'El*; but though plural in form *'Elohim* is singular in meaning, when used in reference to Yahweh; hence the use of the article with it; in other cases it has the plural sense, viz. " other gods " in contradistinction to " the God," i.e. Yahweh; elsewhere the word means " angels " (Ps. viii. 5) [Hebr. 6]. But it is used also of a spirit of the dead (1 Sam. xxviii. 13), and even of a goddess, in 1 Kings xi. 33; in these latter cases the form is plural, but the sense singular.

And thirdly, *'El*, when used with the article, denotes, as in the case of *'Elohim*, the (only) God (e.g. Gen. xlvi. 3). Sometimes *'El* has this restricted sense even when written without the article; but this belongs to much later times (e.g. Isa. xl. 18, and elsewhere).

To come now to consider what we learn about the *'Elim* in the Old Testament.

There are a number of place-names connected with *'El* which are very ancient, having evidently been in existence long before the Israelites entered Canaan. Among these are the following (they are mentioned in the book of *Joshua,* excepting when otherwise indicated): Jabneel, " Let *'El* build " (xv. 11); Joqtheel, meaning uncertain (2 Kings xiv. 7); Jezreel, " Let *'El* sow " (xv. 56); Jiphtachel, " Let *'El* open " (xix. 14); Migdalel, " the tower of *'El* " (xix. 38); the well-known Bethel, " the abode, or sanctuary, of *'El* " (Gen. xxviii. 18, 19); and Penuel, " the face of *'El* " (Gen. xxxii. 31). An example of a different formation is Elteqeh (xix. 44), the meaning of which is uncertain; and there are others. Now, in regard to place-names like these, the *'El* is connected with the place, though for reasons which can now no more be determined; but the point is that, in a certain sense, in a modified sense, individuality is applied to him; yet the 'El has no name; the word is merely used as the title of a supernatural being; and therefore one

cannot say that he has yet reached the status of a god. In
other words, these place-names compounded with 'El point
to the transition stage of the spirit gradually developing into
a god.

But there are other instances in which something approaching a proper name is applied to an 'El; it will be well
to examine these.

When, in Exod. vi. 3, God is represented as saying that
by His name Yahweh He was not known to the patriarchs, a
fact is stated which all the evidence shows to have been true.
It is said in the same context that God was known to them
by the name of 'El Shaddai. Whatever the meaning of this
word may be (many theories are given by scholars), the
R.V. rendering " God Almighty " is, at any rate, quite misleading. But the form of the name, i.e. the combination
with 'El, gives an indication of what the religion of the
Hebrews in pre-Mosaic times was (cp. also 'El 'Elyon,
" the almighty 'El " (Gen. xiv. 18–20; Num. xxiv. 16).
The interest centres in the word 'El, " God." We are told
of quite a number of these gods in the Old Testament, and
doubtless there were many more than those named; in
nearly all the cases these gods are connected with a locality,
and even in the one or two instances in which the name of
the locality is not given, the analogy of the others suggests
that in these cases too the god was connected with a locality.
Let us enumerate some of these.

Very instructive is Gen. xvi. 13, 14. We will give the
R.V. rendering first, which is, however, again misleading :
" And she (Hagar) called the name of the Lord that spake
unto her, ' Thou art a God that seeth '; for she said, Have I
even here looked after him that seeth me ? Wherefore the
well was called Be'er Lahai-roi; behold it is between
Kadesh and Bered." The first part of this verse should run :
" She called the name of Yahweh who spoke unto her, Thou
art 'El-roi." The idea, and the text which expresses it, are
hardly possible; the name of Israel's God was Yahweh;
so how could He get another name ? It would be incompatible with Yahweh religion; and as the text stands the
name is : " Thou art 'El-roi," which as a name-formation is
impossible. It is quite obvious that the original text has
been, unskilfully, worked over in the supposed interests of
later religious belief. What stood there originally cannot
be said with certainty; but what seems fairly certain is that
there was a holy well here known as the well of " an 'El

apparition "—that is, in effect, what *'El-roi* means [1]—
because the *'El* to whom it belonged was believed to appear
there at certain times.[2] From our present point of view
the main thing is that the passage witnesses to what must
be called the " *'El* religion " of the immediate ancestors of the
Hebrews in pre-Mosaic times.

The next passage is Gen. xxi. 33; the R.V. reads : " And
(Abraham) planted a tamarisk tree in Beersheba, and called
there on the name of the Lord, the Everlasting God." Here
we have again a misleading rendering of a text which has
been manipulated in the interests of Yahweh religion.
From Gen. xxi. 30–33, and xxvi. 23 ff., it will be seen that
there was a holy well here in addition to the holy tree. In
the text before us we read : ". . . And called there on the
name of Yahweh *'El 'Olam*," as though Yahweh *'El 'Olam*
were all one name; but " Yahweh " is a later insertion. The
god, or *'El*, of Beersheba, to whom the tree and the well were
holy, was called *'El 'Olam*, " the ancient *'El*." So here we
have again an *'El* of a locality; upon him Abraham is
represented as calling, i.e. he offered him worship.

Further, in Gen. xxxv. 7 we read : " And he (Jacob) built
there an altar and called the place 'El-bethel." With this
must be read Gen. xxxi. 13, where " the angel of God "
(verse 11) says to Jacob : " I am the 'El of Bethel, where
thou anointedst a pillar," the reference being to xxviii.
10 ff. (esp. 18). Various points arise here with which we
cannot now deal; what especially concerns us is that
another local *'El* is spoken of. It was clearly a very ancient
spot, because the name Beth-el shows that an *'El* had already
been worshipped there : that must have been very long ago,
for another *'El* to come and take possession—*'El-Bethel* !
An interesting sign of developed belief, due to the working
over of the passage at a later period, is that " *the angel of
God* " (*'Elohim* with the article) says : " I am the *'El* of
Bethel "; this must have been done at a time when God
could no more be thought of as a local deity, hence the
substitution of the *angel* of God.

Another example is probably to be discerned in Gen. xxxi.
42, 53, where the curious expression " the Fear of Isaac "
occurs; as this is mentioned together with the " gods of my

[1] A. von Gall, *Altisraelitische Kultstätten*, p. 40 (1898) (the Septuagint
has " the well of the vision "). See further Gressmann, *Mose and seine
Zeit*, pp. 290 f. (1913); and the *Zeitschrift für die alttestamentliche Wissen-
schaft*, xxx. 8 (1910).

[2] See also above, pp. 39 f.

father, and the gods of Abraham " it must be the proper name of a god, as the R.V. rightly indicates by printing " fear " with a capital F. The Hebrew is *Pachad*, a word used in Job iv. 14 of " fear " as the result of a vision. It is not fanciful to see here the name of an 'El—'El-Pachad— whom Gunkel ingeniously identifies with the 'El who appeared to save Isaac from being sacrified.[1] The name " Fear of Isaac " is, in form, parallel to " Mighty One of Jacob " in Gen. xlix. 24.

An interesting instance, again, is the 'El-Berith of Sichem (Judges ix. 46), presumably an 'El who presided over covenants (*Berith* means " covenant "); in Judges viii. 33, ix. 4, he is called Ba'al-Berith; so that we have here an illustration of the influence of Canaanite religion on the early 'El-religion of the Hebrews. This is in the post-Mosaic period, which shows the old 'El-religion still persisting and coalescing with the Canaanite Ba'al-religion.

These examples must suffice; we have but to add such further indications as are afforded by " the company of Gods " (Gen. xxxii. 2) (3 in Hebrew), the " strange gods " spoken of in Gen. xxxv. 2, 4—to mention no others—in order to be convinced of the truth of the tradition that Yahweh was not known by that name by the pre-Mosaic Hebrew dwellers in Southern Palestine. Later religious authorities may have held the theory that 'El-Shaddai was another name for Yahweh, but the old records witness abundantly to the fact that 'El Shaddai was only one among many 'Elim. As Gressmann[2] says : " If it be asked what religion the patriarchs had, the answer cannot for a moment be in doubt, since the tradition knows only of the 'El-religion, but not of a Yahweh-religion, as in the time of Moses, nor of a Ba'al-religion, as among the Canaanites." [3]

It is very significant that not a single personal name in *Genesis* contains " Yahweh " in its formation; the ground-work of the patriarchal narratives must therefore belong to a time when the name of Yahweh was unknown to the Hebrews.

It would be too much to say that in the instances cited the name of the 'El was a proper name , but the names connected with it certainly seem to be on the way to becoming

[1] *Genesis*, p. 219 (1901).
[2] *Op. cit.*, pp. 426 ff.
[3] It is worth mentioning here that on a cuneiform tablet found by Winckler in Boghaz-keui, the ancient Hittite capital in Asia Minor, mention is made of the *ilani cha-ab-bi-ri*, the gods of the Chabiri (= Hebrews).

proper names. At any rate, they point to some of the *'Elim*
being singled out; so that the word *'El*, in such cases, is
something more than the generic term that it is in the place-
names.

The evidence seems, then, to point to the fact that the
'Elim form a development of the earlier spirits of the animistic stage pure and simple, and that they constitute a
transition from these to gods proper.[1] This was the type of
religion which existed among the more immediate ancestors
of the Israelites.

But side by side with this belief in *'Elim* there existed
among those Canaanites who were purely agricultural the
belief in *Be'alim*. When an *'El* became sufficiently individualized to be regarded as the one presiding deity of a
sanctuary, or a place, he came in course of time to be designated its proprietor or owner (*Ba'al*). While, speaking
generally, the *'Elim* belong to nomadic religion, and the *Be'alim*
to that of agriculturists, it is possible that one may discern
the transition gradually taking place in the existence of such
names as Jezreel, " let the *'El* sow," and Jabneel, " let the
'El build."

(b) The Be'alim.

Ba'al (plural : *Be'alim*) means " lord " or " owner,"
and Ba'alism, in its origin, centred in the belief that every
spot of fertile ground owed its fertility to the fact that a
supernatural being dwelt there and made it what it was.
The ground was therefore looked upon as the property of this
supernatural being, who was the owner of it, the lord or
mistress, the *Ba'al* or *Ba'alath*, according as to whether the
owner was a male or a female. How the owner came to
be regarded as the one or the other cannot, of course, be
said; all kinds of things would contribute to decide this;
uncultured and semi-cultured men are very *naïve* in their
reasoning.

According to early Semite belief, as we have seen, the water,

---

[1] A somewhat hazardous suggestion may be offered here. Among the
place-names compounded with *'El* there is *'Elealeh* (Num. xxxii. 3), which
means " *'El* doth ascend." This cannot refer to ascending heavenwards,
for the *'Elim* were never thus conceived of; it is, however, possible that
originally the ascending was from below. The root is the same as that used
in 1 Sam. xxviii. 13, of the shade of Samuel ascending from *She'ol*, though
there the word used in reference to him is *'Elohim*. We have no evidence
that the *'Elim* were ever believed to be departed spirits, but the possibility
of this having at one time been the case with some of them cannot be wholly
excluded.

whether spring, brook, or river, which makes a spot fertile, is the dwelling-place of a spirit; in course of time the spirit develops into a *Ba'al*; he has made the spot what it is.

The idea that *every* fertile spot or locality owed its fertility to one and the same *Ba'al*, or owner, never entered the mind of people; they would have argued on the analogy of what obtained among men; one human owner to a plot, therefore one *Ba'al* to each plot.

The ownership of the *Ba'al* of a locality was acknowledged and indicated by prefixing this word to the name of the place; as, for example, *Ba'al Me'on*, "lord, or owner, of the inhabited place" (Num. xxxii. 38); *Ba'al-Hermon*, "lord or owner of the sacred place" (Judges iii. 3); *Ba'al Pe'or*, "lord, or owner, of the chasm (or cleft)" (Num. xxv. 3), and others. But in such cases the name of the place is, strictly speaking, an abbreviation; for the word *Beth*, "house of" or "abode of" or "sanctuary of," is understood; so that the full name of the place would be *Beth-Ba'al Me'on*, etc., thus indicating that the place in question was the abode of the Ba'al, where he had his sanctuary.

Since the fertility of any locality was the work of its supernatural owner, anything that his land brought forth in consequence of that fertility belonged to him. If seed were sown in it, if vines or fig-trees were planted in it, whatever these brought forth was due to the power of producing fertility possessed by the Ba'al, and consequently belonged to him; therefore it would be an unheard-of thing for anyone to partake of the produce of the soil before due payment had been made to the *Ba'al*; hence the offerings of first-fruits. These consisted of a small, but choice, portion of the produce of the soil, which was "thrown down" (this is what the word for "heave-offering" implies) before the altar. It was not inquired how the *Ba'al* partook of the offering, such questions were not asked; that concerned the *Ba'al*, not the worshipper. What concerned the worshipper was that the *Ba'al* should be properly propitiated, otherwise he would be angry, which would mean a bad look-out for the harvest.

The place of worship was called a *bamah* (plural; *bamoth*) or "high-place"; that this means, in general, an elevated spot is proved by the fact that it is used as a parallel with "hill" (e.g. Num. xxi. 28; Deut. xxxii. 13 and elsewhere). Why such elevated spots were chosen for sanctuaries was presumably because they were a substitute for mountains; but there may well have been also the idea that the *Ba'al* liked to be high up, because he was there withdrawn from men. In later times, however, a *bamah* was not necessarily on an elevated spot; the word came to be used of a " sanctuary " (*miqdash*) generally (see Amos vii. 9, Hos. x. 8); and we read of a *bamah* situated even in a valley several times (Jer. vii. 31, xix. 5, xxxii. 35; Ezek. vi. 3), while in 2 Kings xvii. 9, xxiii, 5, mention is made of a *bamah* in the city.

The *bamah* was, however, not the only type of sanctuary. Worship was also offered under green trees; sometimes these stood in the *bamah*, though by no means necessarily. Green trees—strictly speaking evergreen trees—were believed to be the abodes of these fertility deities whose presence in them made them sanctuaries; one sees how near we still are to animistic belief ! In course of time, when sanctuaries were multiplied, and could not always be under green trees, a pole was set up, in place of the green tree, by the altar as a mark of the presence of the deity; this was called the '*Asherah*.

In the Old Testament '*Asherah* is used of the goddess of this name (Judges iii. 7; 1 Kings xv. 13; xviii. 19; 2 Kings xxi. 7, xxiii. 4, 7), as well as of the sacred pole representing her (Deut. vii. 5, xii. 3, where the command is given to burn such symbols; see also xvi. 21). The name of the goddess Asherah occurs in the Amarna letters, and on an inscription found in Tell Taanach,[1] also, as we have seen, on one of the Ras Shamra inscriptions. It is evident that Asherah and Astarte were two different goddesses.

Besides the wooden pole representing the goddess there was also the stone pillar, called *Mazzebah*,[2] which likewise stood beside the altar, and represented the *Ba'al*, i.e. the male deity. This upright stone pillar was the original form of the altar; and in nomadic times the blood of the sacrificial victim was poured down beside it; but when later, for a more convenient mode of offering the burnt sacrifices, the altar was placed horizontally, the stone pillar continued to be set beside it. Both the wooden '*Asherah* and the stone *Mazzebah* underwent development, becoming in course of time carved idols.

It is essential for the understanding of what we call the religion of *Ba'al* to realize why this presence in every sanctu-

---

[1] See Sellin, *Tell Ta'anek*, p. 113 (1904); on this inscription the expression " the finger of Asherah " occurs.

[2] From the root meaning " to set up."

ary of representatives of the male and female elements of
the deity should have been regarded as indispensable.

Baalism among the Hebrews originated with the agricultural stage of civilization; and its great importance lay
in the fact that to the people of those times it was inseparably
connected with what was, after all, the fundamental condition of life, viz. the obtaining of food : no fertility, no
corn; no corn, no bread; no bread, no life !

There can be no sort of doubt that at one time or other
the question must have presented itself to the minds of the
early Semites, when they entered upon the agricultural
stage, as to *how* the soil became fruitful and brought forth.
In the earlier nomadic stage the question would not have
presented itself in quite the same way. That flocks and
herds were endowed with fertility was easier to understand
than the process whereby the land could be made fruitful.
We are not told in the Old Testament how the ancient
Hebrews presented to themselves the way in which the
fertility of the soil was brought about; nor is this to be
expected; but certain rites which were practised make it
quite clear that they believed that the process whereby the
earth brought forth must be in some way similar to that
obtaining in other directions.

It is, no doubt, difficult to enter into the mental environment of men in a semi-cultured stage; but one can understand that with their extraordinarily limited knowledge and
naïve outlook they would argue on the analogy of themselves,
that, just as both men and their flocks increased by means of
natural generation, so the crops must somehow be produced
in a similar manner. It is well known that " among races
which have attained to a certain degree of culture the pre-
dominant conception of the gods is anthropomorphic; that
is, they are supposed on the whole to resemble men and act
like men." [1] It follows, therefore, that in the matter of
productivity the gods and goddesses were conceived of as
acting in the same way as human beings. It is a related
conception, and very instructive in the present connexion,
that the *Ba'al* is thought of as the husband of the land which
he fertilizes; this appears in Hos. ii. and underlies the figure
in Isa. lxii. 4, where the prophet contrasts the married land
(*Be'ulah*) with the wilderness : " Thou shalt no more be

---

[1] *Rel. Sem.*, p. 86; in his notes S. A. Cook refers to " the union of sky-god
and earth-mother," which " can be traced through the Mediterranean
area " (p. 537).

termed 'Forsaken'; neither shall thy land any more be termed 'Desolate'; but thou shalt be called 'Hephzi-bah' (= 'my delight is in her'), and thy land Be'ulah (= 'married'); for Yahweh delighteth in thee, and thy land shall be married." [1]

It is, furthermore, a belief universal among people in a semi-cultured stage, that the gods can, and should, be assisted in their doings by man's co-operation; and this is what lies at the base of, and is the meaning and purpose of, the widespread institution of sanctuary prostitutes, referred to in the Old Testament under the term Kedeshoth (Hos. iv. 14, Deut. xxiii. 17, 18 [in Hebrew 18, 19]), meaning "consecrated women," which shows that in its origin there was no thought of immorality.

This religion of *Ba'al*, then, was that which followed upon the belief in *'Elim*; and it was the religion with which the Israelites first came in contact when they entered Canaan. Since immediately prior to this, through the work of Moses, they had accepted Yahweh as their national God, it was inevitable that among the bulk of the people the worship of Yahweh should have been adapted to Baalism. In passing from the nomadic to an agricultural life, they learned, together with the arts of agriculture, the religion which was inseparably connected therewith. It is probable that at first the worship of Yahweh continued side by side with that of the *Ba'al*, but as the settlement proceeded Yahweh became the *Ba'al* of the land, and, though worshipped in name, the rites of His worship were those of Canaanite Baalism.

[1] S. A. Cook quotes one of the Amarna letters, in which Rib-Addi, lamenting the famine says : " My field is like a woman without a husband." In another of these letters the king of Byblos, whose land has been attacked by enemies, says that his fields are like a wife without a husband through lack of sustenance (see also Nielsen, *Handbuch*, i. 207 ff.).

CHAPTER VI

REMNANTS OF TOTEMISM AND TABOO IN HEBREW RELIGION

1. TOTEMISM

WE have seen that by Totemism is meant a form of society in which the members of a clan or tribe believe themselves to be united by kinship to some animal or plant, mainly the former, from which they are descended. We are not here concerned with the origin of this world-wide and extraordinary institution; various theories are held, but certain knowledge on the subject can hardly be expected, for it clearly goes back to an extreme antiquity—to a time, in fact, when man's reasoning powers were of so primitive a character that it is perhaps not possible for us to get down to his mentality. Even in the case of the most backward races among which the system is still in vogue it probably has a history of many millenniums behind it; but these more or less primitive institutions have an extraordinary way of leaving their marks for ages and ages after they have lost their meaning, and their remnants are to be discerned not only among the more cultured peoples of antiquity, but even at the present day in Europe. Therefore there it is not really at all surprising to find that in the Old Testament and in the religion of the Hebrews remnants of Totemism are discernible. Of course, as Robertson Smith says, " at the stage which even the rudest Semitic peoples had reached when they first became known to us it would be absurd to expect to find examples of totemism pure and simple. What we may expect to find is the fragmentary survival of totem ideas, in the shape of special associations between certain kinds of animals on the one hand, and certain tribes or religious communities and their gods on the other. And of evidence of this kind there is no lack in Semitic antiquity." [1]

While such evidence is to be found over the whole Semitic area, we shall, before coming to the Old Testament, confine

[1] *Rel. Sem.*, p. 444.

ourselves to the ancient Arabs, for in them and in their
stage of culture we find the closest parallel with the early
Hebrews; moreover, the available *data* are much greater
where they are concerned than among any other Semitic
people.[1]

In his *Kinship and Marriage in Early Arabia*, Robertson
Smith writes : " The complete proof of early totemism in
any race involves the following points : (1) the existence of
stocks named after plants and animals; (2) the prevalence
of the conception that the members of the stock are of the
blood of the eponym animal, or are sprung from a plant of
the species chosen as totem; (3) the ascription to the totem
of a sacred character, which may result in its being regarded
as the god of the stock, but at any rate makes it to be regarded with veneration, so that, for example, a totem animal
is not used as ordinary food.   If we can find all these things
together in the same tribe the proof of totemism is
complete . . . "[2]

In the pages which follow these words (220–281, and also
307–312) this proof is furnished; here it must suffice to give
just a few illustrations.   Under the first head eleven pages of
examples are given; among them we find such tribal names
as these : lion, ibex, wild cow, steer, serpent, sheep, wolf,
dog, panther, hyæna, etc.; and it is shown that these
various tribes are named after the animals.   "To students
of primitive society in general, who have learned what
animal stock-names habitually mean, the mass of such
names in Arabia must be highly significant; when very
primitive races call themselves dogs, panthers, snakes, sheep,
lion cubs, or sons of the lion, the jerboa, or the lizard, the
burden of proof really lies on those who maintain that such
designations do not mean what they mean in other parts of
the world.   That the names are mere accidents or mere
metaphors is an assumption which can seem plausible only
to those who do not know savage ways of thought."[3]

As to the conception that the members of a tribe were of the
same blood as the animal whose name they bore, and were
thus akin to it, we have such illustrations as that of a whole
clan mourning over a dead gazelle; if a serpent is killed, all
the members of the serpent clan are bound to avenge it;

---

[1] For Totemism among the Babylonians, see Jastrow, *op. cit.*, ii. 441,
896 f.
[2] *Kinship*, p. 219 (new edition, 1903).
[3] *Ibid.*, p. 237.

the *Hyrax Syriacus* was not eaten, because he was the brother of man, and " he who eats him will never see his father or mother again." Connected with this conception was also the belief that men could change themselves into animals ; some animals were not eaten because they were believed to be, in reality, men who had transformed themselves into such animals ; an idea of this kind would easily arise if men were convinced that there existed a physical kinship between them and the animal in question. Of a tribe living in Hadramaut, the land in the south-west of Arabia, it is related that in time of drought part of the tribe changed themselves into ravening were-wolves, and that they could change themselves back again into human shape. Others from the same district could change themselves into kites or vultures. In the Sinaitic Peninsula the hyrax and the panther are believed to have been men at one time. Muhammad would not eat lizards because he fancied them to be the offspring of a metamorphosed clan of Israelites.[1]

Thirdly, as to the sacred character of the animal chosen for the totem ; the most significant point here is that the animal may not be eaten as ordinary food, but only when sacrificed on special occasions. Thus, the camel was sacred to a camel clan—it was only eaten when offered in sacrifice ; [2] but to the Arabs in general the camel was common food.[3] Locusts were not eaten by all Arabs ; " in Islam they are lawful, but the copious discussions on the point by the traditionalists . . . show that in the prophet's time there was a doubt as to their lawfulness." [4] That there is not in *each* case evidence forthcoming of the sacred animal being eaten when sacrificed on special occasions is not to be expected. Again, to give an illustration from outside the Arab domain, the dove among the Syrians was not eaten ; it was sacred to Ashtoreth, and has all the marks of a totem : " The testimonies to this effect are collected by Bochart, and show that the bird was not merely a symbol, but received divine honour. In Arabia we find a dove-idol in the Ka'ba, and sacred doves around it." [5] Once more, there were several lizard clans among the Arabs, among them the *Dobaib* (" lizard ") ; this lizard was a sacred animal : " its flesh supplied the Arabs with medicines and antidotes to poisons, its bones and skin had magical virtues. Such

---

[1] For these and other illustrations see *Rel. Sem.*, p. 88 ; *Kinship*, pp. 238 f.
[2] For an interesting example see *Rel. Sem.*, p. 338.
[3] *Rel. Sem.*, p. 218.   [4] *Kinship*, p. 228.   [5] *Ibid.*, p. 229.

virtues are generally ascribed by rude nations to animals
that are not habitually eaten . . ." [1]

These few illustrations, out of a large number which could
be adduced, show that the animal after which the members
of a clan called themselves was regarded as sacred. But
when an animal is believed to be the ancestor of a clan, all
the members of which are his offspring, and, in consequence,
all the animals of the same kind as the ancestor are sacrosanct, it is a natural, one might almost say an inevitable,
development that the ancestor becomes a god, and all the
animals of his kind are thought of as his representatives.
That this was the actual course of development among the
Arabs has been shown by Robertson Smith in his *Kinship*,
pp. 240 ff. "There is abundance of independent evidence,"
he says, "that not only the Arabs, but all the Semites, often
spoke and thought of themselves as children of their
gods. . . .[2] We must therefore hold that it was because Arabic
tribes claimed to be the children of their tribal god that they
took his name. And when we find among such tribes cases
like the Banu Hilal, 'sons of the crescent moon,' or Banu
Badr, 'sons of the full moon,' where the divine being is at
the same time one of those heavenly beings which primitive
peoples everywhere have looked upon as animals, the
interval between divine tribal names and animal tribal
names is very nearly bridged over, and one is compelled to
ask whether both are not reducible to one ultimate principle
such as the totem theory supplies." [3]

Now, it is in the light of what has been said that we
must approach the subject of the remnants of Totemism in
the Old Testament.

It should be mentioned here that there are some prominent
Old Testament scholars, though their number is very small,
who deny altogether that there are any remnants of Totemism to be discerned in the Old Testament; among them,
notably, Lagrange, *Études sur les Religions sémitiques*,
pp. 112–118 (1903), and Ed. König, *Geschichte der alttesta-
mentlichen Religion*, pp. 72–78 (1924); but their objections

---

[1] *Kinship*, pp. 231 ff., where further illustrations will be found; cp.
Nielsen, *Handbuch der altarabischen Altertumskunde*, i. 206 (1927).

[2] How ingrained this idea was, and is, may be seen by the fact that a
missionary, in teaching a Mohammedan's children that they were descended
from Adam and Eve, was corrected by their mother who retorted : " No, the
moon is our father and the sun is our mother " (Nielsen, *Handbuch*, i. 211).

[3] See also *Rel. Sem.*, pp. 125 ff. For other animal names of gods among
the heathen Arabs, see Nielsen, *op. cit.*, i. 192.

F

do not carry conviction; one receives the impression that neither of them approaches the question with an unbiased mind, and in any case Robertson Smith's arguments are not seriously grappled with by either of them.

In the comparatively advanced stage of culture in which we find even the earliest Hebrews we should not expect to discern anything more in the records of their early beliefs than very faint remnants of such a primitive institution as Totemism; but that certain facts which will be pointed out are such remnants seems to be the most satisfactory and the most natural explanation of them.

We will take the steps of the argument in the order already followed, and begin by pointing out that just as among the early Arabs, so the early Hebrews had many animal clan names and tribal names. Thus Simeon means " hyæna "; Leah (= Levi) [1] means " wild cow "; Deborah means " bee "; Rachel means " ewe "; Caleb means " dog "; Shobal means " lion "; Epher means " young antelope "; Oren means " ibex." Other examples are place-names of animals, which, as Stade shows,[2] received their names from the clans inhabiting them, viz. Aijalon from Aijal, " stag "; Shaalbim, " foxes "; Ophra and Ephron, from Epher, " young antelope "; Eglon, from Egel, " calf "; Nimra, from Namer, " leopard "; and many others.[3] All these, it is to be noted, are clan or tribal, not personal names; and among the many animal proper names in the Old Testament by far the greater number are those of clans or tribes. The significance of this is that when an animal name is that of a clan it points to an original belief of kinship of all its members with the animal after which they are named; a *personal* animal name, on the other hand, might be, and is, given for a variety of reasons, but not because the bearer is believed to have kinship with the animal. But even personal animal names, according to Buchanan Gray, are indirectly explained by the totem theory. He explains them thus : " With the break-up of the totem clan system, the clan names became in certain cases personal, instances of which we perhaps find in Eglah, the name of David's wife, the two Deborahs, and other names of early individuals, though we have, it is true, no direct evidence that these were

---

[1] But see further on this Buchanan Gray, *Sacrifice in the Old Testament*, pp. 246 ff. (1925).
[2] *Geschichte des Volkes Israel*, i. 398, 409 (1886).
[3] See Buchanan Gray, *Hebrew Proper Names*, pp. 86 ff. (1896).

ever tribal. But the strictly personal character of many of the early names classified in the synopsis [1] is open to doubt. . . . It is certainly curious that so many of the early, and apparently individual, names turn out on closer inspection to be posssibly, or even probably, tribal. . . ." [2]

At any rate, there are a large number of certain cases, of which a few are given above, of clans or stocks named after animals.[3]

Cases among the Hebrews of the conception that the members of a stock are of the blood of an eponym animal are not forthcoming; that must be frankly acknowledged, nor is this to be expected [4]; but of animal cults which presuppose an earlier totemistic stage, there are indications. Thus, Ezekiel tells of how he saw in the sanctuary the worship of " every form of creeping things, and abominable beasts " (viii. 10); and in Isa. lxv. 4 reference is made to those who " sit among the graves, and lodge in secret places; which eat swine's flesh, and broth of unclean meats is in their vessels "; and again in Isa. lxvi. 3 there are references to animal cults : " He that killeth an ox is as he that slayeth a man; he that sacrificeth a lamb, as he that breaketh a dog's neck; he that offereth an oblation (as he that offereth) swine's blood; he that burneth frankincense, as he that blesseth an idol. Yea, they have chosen their own ways, and their soul delighteth in their abominations "; and also in Isa. lxvi. 17 : " They that sanctify themselves and purify themselves (to go) into the gardens after one in the midst (i.e. after the leader of the illicit ceremonies), eating swine's flesh, and swarming creatures, and the mouse." All the creatures mentioned in these passages and chosen for the sacrifices were " such as were unclean in the first degree, and surrounded by strong taboos of the kind which in heathenism imply that the animal is regarded as divine. . . . Here we have therefore a clear case of the re-emergence into the light of day of a cult of the most primitive totem type, which had been banished for centuries from public religion, but must have been kept alive in obscure circles of private or local

---

[1] Pp. 88–96 in his book.

[2] Op. cit., pp. 101 f

[3] The list in Gen. xxxvi. 20–30, containing the names of " the sons of Seir the Horite," has a very considerable proportion of animal names. See further Lods, op. cit., pp. 243–249.

[4] It is, however, possible that the conception expressed in Jer. ii. 27 goes back ultimately to totemism : " . . . which say to a stock, thou art my father; and to a stone, thou hast begotten us."

superstition." [1] It is not without significance that "the second commandment, the cardinal precept of spiritual worship, is explicitly directed against the worship of the denizens of air, earth, and water." [2]

It is further to be noted that, although the Old Testament offers little indication of the belief that the members of a clan with an animal name were the offspring of the totem animal, there are hints that worshippers believed themselves to be descended from a god; and, as we have seen, there are some grounds for holding that this is a development of the earlier belief. Thus, names compounded with a divine name, such as Abijah ("my father is Yah") or Ahijah ("my brother is Yah"),[3] and others, suggest the question as to whether or not they indicate a transition from the totem conception of kindred with a divine or totem animal to a conception of kinship with a personal God? To apply a spiritual interpretation to "father" in cases like these might be conceivable, but not so in regard to "brother"; but to do so even in the case of the former cannot be justified in view of the fact that "the name in question, together with those related to it in form, falls into disuse just when the deeper ideas of the fatherhood of God were developing." [4]

That the *conception* of a physical connexion between a god and his people was not unfamiliar to the Hebrews is evident from Num. xxi. 29 : "Woe to thee, Moab! Thou art undone, O people of Chemosh; he hath given his sons as fugitives, and his daughters into captivity, unto Sihon king of the Amorites." [5] It is significant that this downright expression of physical kinship to a god is toned down in later days when Jeremiah, in quoting this passage says : "Woe unto thee, Moab! the people of Chemosh is undone; for thy sons are taken away captive, and thy daughters into captivity" (xlviii. 46); and the significance is enhanced when it is seen how familiar Jeremiah was with the conception still in vogue among the idolaters. In the words already quoted he says : "Which say to a stock, thou art my father; and to a stone, thou hast begotten us" (ii. 27). It must be acknowledged, then, that there are good grounds for believing that some remnants of Totemism are to be discerned in the Old Testament; the case could be made

---

[1] *Rel. Sem.*, p. 357.   [2] *Op. cit.*, p. 625.
[3] For the same thing among the ancient Arabs, see Nielsen, *op. cit.*, i. 192.
[4] Buchanan Gray *op. cit.*, pp. 253 f.   [5] Cp. also Mal. ii. 11.

stronger if it could be more fully dealt with, but that would be out of place here; for this recourse must be had to the works cited.

2. TABOO

Closely associated with Totemism, indeed indissolubly connected with it in its origin, is *Taboo*. This prohibition to come into contact with certain things on account of their " holiness " is concerned in the first instance with various kinds of animals, the flesh of which may not be eaten because it is either " holy " or " unclean "; but it applies also to persons, especially those connected in any way with the deity and his worship, and to certain other persons and things with which we are not at present concerned; it applies also to ground dedicated to the deity. The apparent incongruity that under the term taboo are included both things which are holy and things which are unholy or unclean, is confusing; but what seems to be a contradiction may perhaps be explained by an analogy : the word " awe " expresses the two emotions of reverence and fear; reverence attracts, fear repels; and yet in both there is, if one may so express it, the element of " keep-at-a-distance." One may draw near to a holy thing, and yet refrain from touching it just because of its holiness, i.e. out of reverential awe; and one may keep from an unclean thing for fear of being harmed. The holy thing is awesome; the unclean thing is awful.[1]

Taboos among the Semites generally existed in plenty; just one or two instances may be mentioned. For holy animals among the Babylonians and Assyrians details will be found in Jastrow's work.[2] Among the Syrians Lucian tells us that fishes were deemed holy and were never touched; so too pigeons, while all other birds were eaten.[3] In the great court of the temple at Hierapolis he says that " oxen of great size browsed; horses too are there, and eagles and bears and lions, who never hurt mankind, but are all sacred, and all tame " (§ xli.). Elsewhere he says that " they sacrifice bulls and cows alike, and goats and sheep; pigs alone, which they abominate, are neither sacrificed nor eaten. Others look on swine without disgust, but as holy animals. Of birds the dove seems the most holy to them; nor do they think it right to harm these birds, and if anyone

---

[1] See further S. A. Cook's note in his *Notes to the Third Edition of the Religion of the Semites*, pp. 548-554.

[2] *Op. cit.*, ii. 874, 896 f., 933 ff., 943 ff.

[3] *De Dea Syria*, §§ xiv., xlv.

have harmed them unknowingly they are unholy for that day " (§ liv.). What is most significant from the present point of view is the mention of the animals that may not be eaten, specifically said of pigeons and pigs, though it is no doubt implied in the case of the others; for this prohibition was due to the fact that there was thought to be something divine about them, i.e. it was based on a religious taboo.

Among the Hebrews we find similar ideas. The corresponding term for taboo in the Old Testament is *tame*, " unclean," but not in the sense of disgusting or impure; it is simply a ritual term for something that must not be touched or, in the case of animals, eaten.

In Lev. xi. and Deut. xiv. 7–20 there are lists of animals which may not be eaten. As a large proportion of these are animals which nobody would think of eating, many of the prohibitions would appear utterly pointless, were it not that we know from similar prohibitions among other peoples the real reason why they were forbidden. " The most notable feature in the Levitical prohibitions is that they correspond so closely with those of the heathen Semites and yet are expressly set forth as belonging to Israel's peculiar consecration to Jehovah . . . The unclean creatures therefore are the divine animals of the heathen; such animals as the latter did not ordinarily eat or sacrifice. . . ." [1] Robertson Smith also mentions the significant fact that the Hebrew terms for " to have in abomination," and " an abomination," which constantly recur in Lev. xi. in reference to the prohibitions, " are indifferently applied to unclean beasts and to the gods of the heathen, but to nothing else."

There are a number of other taboos which, if broken, require a purificatory ceremony of one kind or another (see, e.g., Lev. vi. 27 ff., xi. 32 ff., 1 Sam. xxi. 4 ff.; 2 Sam. xi. 4, and others); the consideration of these would take us too far afield. It must suffice to have pointed out that the remnants of taboo are to be discerned in the Old Testament; and this is a further link in the chain of proof that ancient Hebrew beliefs go back to a great antiquity.

[1] *Kinship*, p. 311, and see further, *Rel. Sem.*, 218 ff.

CHAPTER VII

SOME FURTHER ELEMENTS IN THE RELIGIOUS BACKGROUND: MAGIC

1. TECHNICAL MAGICAL TERMS

SOME consideration of the subject of Magic is also demanded, for it has affinities with the institution of Taboos, as well as with Demonology,[1] and Necromancy.[2] Although, strictly speaking, outside the religious sphere, many magical rites verge so closely upon religion that they may justly be called magico-religious. It is quite certain that some forms of magic were not condemned by the official religious leaders of the Hebrews; but even in the case of the particular forms which were forbidden, the religious leaders did not regard them as mere imposture; indeed, it was just for this reason that they were forbidden; the supernatural agencies which were supposed to be controlled by magical rites were really believed to exist.

We will first examine the techical terms used in reference to the magic art, and then turn to some passages in which magical practices are described.

The usual words used in connexion with Magic come from the root *Kashaph*; its original signification is uncertain;[3] the words used in the Old Testament are: *Kesheph*, always used in the plural, " magic arts "; *Kashaph* and *Mekasheph*, " magician," of which the feminine is *Mekashephah*; and *Kisheph* " to practise magic."

In Mic. v. 11 (12 in R.V.) it is said in reference to Israel : " I will cut off thy magic arts (R.V. " witchcrafts ") out of thine hand." All that can be gathered from this passage is that what was done consisted of manual acts, and that it was abhorrent to Yahweh. In Exod. xxii. 17 (18 in R.V.) the

---

[1] See below, Chapter X.
[2] See further, Chapter IX, and for Babylonian Magic, Lenormant, *La Magie chez les Chaldéens et les origines Accadiennes* (1874, Engl. transl. 1877), passim.
[3] Robertson Smith, in the *Journal of Philology*, xiv. 125, 126 (1885), arguing from the cognate Arabic root meaning " to cut," holds that the noun *Kesheph* means herbs cut up, or shredded, into a magic brew.

command is given : " Thou shalt not suffer a sorceress to live "; and in Deut. xviii. 10–14 magic and other occult practices are forbidden because they are an abomination to Yahweh. In Jer. xxvii. 9 the prophet merely bids his people not to give heed to magicians any more than to the false prophets, diviners, and others. In Mal. iii. 5 magicians together with various other types of evil people are denounced; and in 2 Chron. xxxiii. 6 the practice of magic is mentioned among the other evils introduced by Manasseh. In the other six places in which the term in one or other of its forms is used, it is not in reference to Israel, viz. in Exod. vii. 11 to Pharaoh, 2 Kings ix. 22 to Jezebel (figurative use), Isa. xlvii. 9, 12 to Babylon, Nahum iii. 4 to Nineveh (figurative use), and Dan. ii. 2 to Nebuchadrezzar.

Wherever this term for magic is used, the practice is either directly or implicitly condemned, but nowhere is it hinted wherein the evil consisted. We can only assume, on the analogy of Babylonian magic, that the term [1] refers to magic in connexion with demons; this would account for its condemnation; for if the supernatural powers supposed to be controlled were believed to be demons, one can at once understand the condemnation of a practice whereby reliance was placed upon demons, and their help sought, instead of on Yahweh. Moreover, judging again from the analogy of Babylonian magical texts,[2] this type of magic would appear to have been practised mainly, if not wholly, for inflicting harm on people.

When we turn to the other terms used for practising magic we find that there is not necessarily any word of condemnation.

The term *lachash* means " to whisper " (an incantation) or " to mutter " (a spell);[3] this is probably the original meaning, as against Robertson Smith, who regards serpent-charming as the original connotation of the word (see Eccles. x. 11; Jer. viii. 17).[4] The classical passage is Ps. lviii. 3–9 (4–10 in Hebrew); this contains an incantation against the machinations of some evil-disposed persons; it is the innocent victim who has written down the in-

---

[1] The Assyrian word for practising magic is radically the same as the Hebrew term, viz. *Kashapu* (*Oxf. Hebr. Dict.*).

[2] Jastrow, *op. cit.*, i. pp. 373–92, and Weber, *Dämonenbeschwörung bei den Babyloniern und Assyrern*, in *Der Alte Orient*, VII, iv (1905).

[3] On some Babylonian magical texts there is the rubric : " Utter the spell in a whispering voice " (see, e.g., Weber, *op. cit.*, p. 28).

[4] *Journal of Philology*, xiv. 122 (1885).

cantation as a protective formula, but which his enemies
have tried to counteract, though in vain; they had tried to
make the formula ineffective (like a " deaf " [1] adder which
cannot hear the voice of the charmer) by seeking to avoid
hearing the incantation.   It is the term *lachash* which occurs
here of " whispering " the incantation.[2]

In Ps. xli. 7 (8 in Hebrew) the same term is used; but in
this case it is the wicked who compose the incantation against
a godly man; and the latter, instead of seeking to protect
himself by a counter-incantation, appeals to Yahweh.

In Isa. iii. 3 the R.V. rendering " skilful enchanter " means
in Hebrew literally, " experienced (in composing) an incantation," i.e. in writing magical formulas. It is instructive to note that the prophet here, so far from condemn-
ing the practice, mentions the judge and the prophet, with
others, in the same list, and regards the taking away of them
as a calamity.

In Isa. xxvi. 16 we should read, according to most commentators, following the Septuagint, instead of " they poured
out a prayer when the chastening was upon them," the words:
" a constraining magical formula (*lachash*) was the chastening
to them," i.e. the result of God chastening them was as
effective in its compelling force as an incantation. To
translate *lachash* by " prayer " is entirely without justification; the other alteration involves only the change of a
dot, which in any case did not figure in the original, con-
sonantal, text. The word occurs also in Isa. iii. 20 as a
woman's ornament; obviously an amulet is meant whereby
the evil eye was averted. The only other occurrence of
the term is in 2 Sam. xii. 19; [3] here it is used of David's
servants whispering together because his child had died.
The conjecture is perhaps hazardous, but when it is remembered that this term is used only in connexion with
magic, and when, as we shall see, the idea of raising the dead
by means of magic was not unknown to the ancient Hebrews,

---

[1] Baethgen points out that even at the present day in the East when a
snake-charmer fails in alluring a serpent away from a house he says it is
because the serpent is deaf (*Die Psalmen*, p. 169, 1904).

[2] For the justification of the interpretation given above one must consult
Nicolsky, *Spuren magischer Formeln in den Psalmen*, pp. 29–42 (1927); he
points to other psalms (vii., xxxv., lix., lxix., xci., cxli.) as containing remnants of magical formulas, but it would take us too far afield to deal with
these (see further *Church Quarterly Review* for April 1928, pp. 204 ff).

[3] Unless in Neh. iii. 12, x. 24 (Hebr. 25), we regard *Hallochesh*, not as a
proper name, but as "the whisperer (of incantations)"; the article is
certainly strange in a proper name.

it is possible that in this passage there is in reality a reference to an attempt to resuscitate David's child by means of an incantation.

The next term is that translated " charmer " in the R.V.; it occurs in Ps. lviii. 5 (Hebr. 6) as parallel with *lachash*, and, translated literally, means " one who ties knots " (*chober chabarim*). The very widespread use of knots tied or untied for magical purposes is too well known to need dilating upon.[1] The practice is forbidden, together with other magical arts, in Deut. xviii. 11; and in reference to Babylonian magic it is mentioned in Isa. xlvii. 9, 12 (rendered " enchantments " in the R.V.); the act is referred to in various Babylonian magical texts.[2]

In a passage already referred to—Isa. iii. 3—another term occurs; it is rendered " cunning artificer " (marg. " charmer ") in the R.V.; what it means is " skilled in magic arts " (*chakam charashim*), or perhaps, " in (making) drugs "; though in cognate languages the word means an " incantation."[3] The term does not occur elsewhere.

Then there is the term *nichesh*; in Gen. xliv. 5, 15 this word is used in reference to Joseph's silver cup whereby he " divined "—clearly an instance of hydromancy. In a different connexion it occurs in Gen. xxx. 27 in the sense of " observing the omens," but there is no indication of how the omens were observed; this is the case in 1 Kings xx. 33, where no details of the procedure are given. Although in these passages this form of magic is clearly not regarded as harmful, wherever else it is mentioned it is with condemnation, viz. 2 Kings xvii. 17, xxi. 6 (= 2 Chron. xxxiii. 6); Lev. xix. 26; Deut. xviii. 10.

Similarly with the term *'anan*, " to practise augury," which is mentioned side by side with the foregoing term. In such an early passage as Judges ix. 37 there is no condemnation of those who practise it, but elsewhere it is always either forbidden or condemned—Isa. ii. 6, lvii. 3; Mic. v. 11 (R.V. 12); Jer. xxvii. 9, and in the other passages above mentioned.

Finally, there is the term *qasam*, rendered " to practise divination," and the noun *qesem* " divination "; but, as Wellhausen has clearly shown,[4] this term is the equivalent

---

[1] For a full treatment of the subject see Frazer's *G. B.*, " Taboo and the Perils of the Soul," pp. 293–317 (1911).

[2] Jastrow, *op. cit.*, i. 285, 374 f.

[3] Robertson Smith, *Journal of Phil.*, xiv. 125 (1885).

[4] *Reste* . . . pp. 132 f.

of the Arabic *Istiqsam* which is used in reference to giving an
oracle by *lot*, and has nothing to do with magic; especially
instructive is Ezek. xxi. 26, 27 (21, 22 in E.V.), where we
are told of how the king of Babylon stood at the crossways,
and in order to be sure which road to take he consults the
oracle which is here of a threefold character : the throwing
of the arrows, the consulting of the *Teraphim*, and looking
into an animal's liver. The R.V. renders the Hebrew word
" to use divination " (*liqesom qesem*), it should, however, be
" to consult the oracle by lot " (cp. Prov. xvi. 10). Doubtless
it came to be connected with magic, otherwise it would not
have been condemned (Deut. xviii. 10; 2 Kings xvii. 17);
but it cannot, properly speaking, be classed under the terms
for magic.

2. MAGICAL ARTS

We cannot conclude this brief consideration of the prevalence of Magic among the Hebrews without making mention
of the fairly numerous descriptions of magical acts in connexion with which no technical term is used.

However one may seek to explain these things, the fact
remains that they are recorded, and the power of certain
people to perform them was evidently believed in.

The power of rain-making by magical means has been so
widely believed [1] in that it need occasion no surprise to find
it believed and practised among the Hebrews. Ultimately,
it is connected with animistic belief; for, according to old-
world ideas,[2] rain was " inspirited," like every other form of
water. In the Old Testament, it is true, the remnants of
this belief are few, and they offer but a faint reminiscence of
what must originally have obtained; but they are sufficiently
precise to preclude any doubt as to what is really meant.
Thus, in 1 Sam. xii. 16–18 Samuel is represented as bringing
rain, by calling unto Yahweh, at harvest time, i.e. during the
dry season. Elijah is said to have had the power of keeping
back the rain (1 Kings xvii. 1); but he could also bring rain,
and in 1 Kings xviii. 42–5, where no mention is made of
Yahweh, a kind of ritual is described whereby Elijah obtained
rain. Both Elijah and Elisha are credited with power to
control flowing water; in 2 Kings ii. 8 Elijah, by smiting the
water of Jordan with his rolled-up mantle, is able to keep it
parted while he and Elisha pass through on dry land; Elisha,

[1] See Frazer, *G. B.*, " The Magic Art," i. pp. 247–319 (1911).
[2] For the ancient Babylonians details are given by Jastrow, *op. cit.*,
i. pp. 48 f.

by using this magic mantle, is able to do so too (ver. 14).
Of the same prophet it is said that he was able to heal waters
which had hitherto caused death and miscarriage; he does
it by means of salt put in a new cruse; this he takes to the
" spring of the waters " and pours it in (2 Kings ii. 19–22).
One would expect some mention of an incantation; but if
this was ever part of the text one can well understand its
having been deleted by a later editor. There is another case
of waters being healed, in Exod. xv. 25; this is done by
Moses, who throws a piece of wood [1] into the water, which
immediately becomes drinkable.

An interesting instance of imitative magic occurs in 2
Kings vi. 5–7. Here it is related how a man dropped his
iron axe-head into the water; Elisha thereupon cuts a
piece of stick and throws it into the water at the spot where
the axe-head fell; then it is seen that just as the piece of
wood floats so the iron does the same. Another striking
piece of imitative magic is recounted of Elisha in 2 Kings
xiii. 14–19; he tells Joash, the king of Israel, to take bow and
arrows; then he lays his hands upon the king's hands (that
constitutes a magical act), and bids him open the window
eastward, i.e. in the direction of Syria, looking from Samaria,
where this takes place. Next, he tells the king to shoot an
arrow, which he does; thereupon Elisha utters an incantation: " A victory-arrow *from* Yahweh, a victory-arrow
against Aram (Syria)." That is the first part of the ritual.
Then follows the imitative magic. Elisha bids the king
smite the ground with the arrows; he does so three times,
but Elisha upbraids him for doing so only three times; he
ought to have done it five or six times, then he would have
wholly defeated the Syrians; since he has done it only three
times, he will gain only three victories over them.

Yet another instance of imitative magic occurs in 2 Kings
iv. 38–41, again performed by Elisha: a pottage is being
brewed by the prophet's followers, and one of them goes out
to gather herbs; among the herbs gathered there happens
to be a poisonous one, and this soon becomes apparent when
the company begin to partake of the pottage; but Elisha
calls for some meal and casts it into the brew, the immediate
effect of which is to make the poison innocuous. The idea
is parallel to that of the wood and iron; because the wood

---

[1] The R.V. has " tree "; but apart from the fact that one does not expect
a whole tree to be thrown into the water, the Hebrew word *ez* means
" wood " as well as " tree."

floats the iron will imitate it; so, too, because the meal is harmless will the poisonous herb become harmless. As in the former case, one expects a magical formula of some sort to be uttered, corresponding to the act of casting in the meal, and it is difficult to believe that something of the kind did not originally stand in the text.[1] Elisha's magical powers were very wide; in 2 Kings vi. 18–20 he is credited with the power of striking blind and giving sight again; in the text as it stands it is Yahweh, however, who actually does this, but at Elisha's bidding. Then, once more, Elisha is also represented as being able to raise the dead by means of a somewhat elaborate ritual (2 Kings iv. 32–5). This should perhaps come under the head of imitative magic; this is, at any rate, suggested by the ritual; for Elisha, the living, lays himself upon the dead boy, and puts mouth on mouth, eyes on eyes, and hands on hands; just as Elisha is alive, so the dead boy must become living. A similar story is told of Elijah, though with less detail (1 Kings xvii. 21, 22), and it is possible that the one is only an elaborated version of the other.

The subject of the magic rod offers some interesting points, but only in three cases can the references be regarded as coming strictly under the head of magic. One of these is in Exod. iv. 2 ff., where Moses' rod is turned into a serpent and back again into a rod. Another instance is when Moses, by holding up his rod, ensures success in battle to the Israelites (Exod. xvii. 8 ff.); and, once more, when Moses, with his magic rod, is able to draw water from a rock (Num. xx. 8 ff.). These are clear instances showing that the powers of the magic rod were believed in. The belief is, however, of animistic origin, though in the Biblical text this origin has been quite lost sight of; for it is, in reality, a spirit which is supposed to reside in the rod, and to effect what is required. An echo of this is to be seen in the fact that the rod is stated to be " the rod of God " (Exod. xvii. 9). The case of the " divining rod " for discovering water (Num. xx. 11), though doubtless of similar origin so far as the idea is concerned, comes under the head of divination rather than magic; and this is also true of Aaron's rod that budded (Num. xvii. 2–11 [in Hebrew 17–26]), which is a case of the flourishing or withering of a rod indicating the answer of the oracle.[2]

[1] It is possible that under the head of imitative magic we should class the looking at a bronze serpent on a pole, which had the effect of curing people bitten by a serpent, Num. xxi. 8, 9.

[2] For this widespread belief see Frazer, *G. B.*, "Adonis, Attis, Osiris," I., Chapters IX, X (1927); Bötticher, *Baumcultus der Hellenen*, xi (1856).

The remaining passages in which references to Magic occur deal with Egyptian magic and magicians (Gen. xli. 8; Exod. vii. 11, 22 ff., viii. 7, 18, 19 [in Hebrew 3, 14, 15], ix. 11), and in Dan. ii. 2 with Babylonian magic.

A great deal of what has been quoted here from the Old Testament is from passages of admittedly late date; but this in no way indicates that Magic does not belong to the most primitive elements of Semitic, and therefore of Hebrew, beliefs; very pointedly does Robertson Smith remark that " the savage point of view is constantly found to survive, in connexion with practices of magic, after it has been superseded in religion proper; and the superstitions of the vulgar in modern civilized countries are not much more advanced than those of the rudest nations. So, too, among the Semites, magical rites and vulgar superstitions are not so much survivals from the higher official heathenism of the great sanctuaries as from a lower and more primitive stage of belief, which the higher forms of heathen worship overshadowed, but did not extinguish." [1] Robertson Smith is referring to the Semites generally, but what he says applies, of course, to the Hebrews; we have only to substitute for " higher official heathenism " the " worship of Yahweh," and his words are literally true of the Hebrews. Therefore we are justified, when dealing with primitive forms of Hebrew belief, in illustrating this by practices which were still in vogue among them at a time later by untold centuries, it may be, than that of their origin.

[1] *Rel. Sem.*, p. 441; see further Lods, *Israel* (Engl. Trans. by S. H. Hooke [1932]), pp. 211–217.

CHAPTER VIII

SOME FURTHER ELEMENTS IN THE RELIGIOUS BACKGROUND: THE AFTER-LIFE: THE EARLIEST STAGE OF BELIEF

IF, in our treatment of this subject, we present a rather more detailed account than in that of those hitherto dealt with, the reason is that it is of gréater and more far-reaching importance. It may also be said that it possesses a deeper interest, which justifies more space being devoted to it. Moreover, for the earlier periods the archæological evidence is particularly full and instructive.

1. BABYLONIAN BELIEFS AND CUSTOMS

An important fact to be borne in mind here is that the gods of Babylonian worship were concerned mainly with the practical affairs of everyday life on this earth; so that the religion of the Babylonian priesthood was but little concerned with the Hereafter. The consequence of this was that ideas and speculations regarding what happened after this life were left to popular imagination—not that this was necessarily all to the bad, for popular instinct may sometimes come nearer to the mark than the wisdom of the wise; this being so, however, it will be realized that the *periods* to which the various relevant inscriptions belong are not of great importance from the present point of view; popular conceptions which are again and again reflected in the inscriptions persist through the ages, so that a relatively late document will often echo very ancient thought.

But belief in an After-life was not confined to the generality of the unlearned; the intellectuals also had their speculations on the subject of immortality. These, no doubt, belong to somewhat later times, but may nevertheless be mentioned here. Thoughts about the immortality of the soul and the union of the purified mortal with his god hereafter occupied many of the wise men of Baby-

lon; they recalled instances in the distant past such as of
the deities Ishtar and Tammuz having ascended from the
realm of the dead, of how Adapa, a mythical ancient hero,
by a mere oversight lost the gift of everlasing life,[1] how
Ut-napishtim (the Biblical Noah) actually obtained this
precious gift, and of how Gilgamesh very nearly succeeded
in acquiring the same. So that the theoretical possibility
of attaining to everlasting life was firmly believed in. How
widely this belief was held is proved by the many cylinder-
seals which have been excavated, and on which are depicted
a throned god bestowing on his worshipper a cup containing
the water of life, and the food of life.[2]

But whatever popular conceptions there might have been,
whatever speculations the intellectual classes framed, about
the life hereafter and about the attainment of immortality,
the official theology of the priesthood was directed sternly
against any idea of everlasting life. " When the gods
created men," it was taught, " they destined man for death,
but reserved life in their own hands." The official religion
recognized, it is true, a place whither all the departed
went; when man died, his body turned to clay, and his
soul was turned into a " spirit of the dead," " clothed in a
garment of feathers "; and the underworld remained his
abode; but this was a place of such a lugubrious nature,
and the feather-clad shade was so lifeless, that the continued existence of man could not be contemplated under
such conditions. In other words, the official religion of
Babylon had no belief in a life hereafter, nor, of course, in
immortality, in any real sense. It need, however, hardly
be insisted upon that the official religion marks a later
stage of belief; the popular conceptions go back to an
immemorial antiquity; nor were they ever eradicated. It
is, therefore, with the religious beliefs of the *people* that
we shall be concerned mainly.

We may begin with the custom of providing food and
drink, as well as a variety of useful objects, for the dead;
for this points clearly enough to the belief in the continued
life of the departed hereafter. For example, " at Ur brick
vaults of considerable size containing several skeletons were
excavated by Taylor. Ordinarily each skeleton is accompanied by jars, platters for bread and food, the deceased's
seal, combs, and, in the case of women, even brushes (for

---

[1] See below, p. 86.
[2] Meissner, *Babylonien und Assyrien*, ii. 140 (1925).

colouring the eyes?). . . ." It was the kinsmen of the dead who "provided the soul with food and raiment in the grave. There are remnants of an ancient belief," Langdon continues, "that the soul actually consumed the elements and wore the raiment left for his use." Langdon maintains that the food and drink became, still in very early times, symbolic, and that "behind the symbolic bread and drink lay the mystery of communion with the deified souls and with divine life itself. Each family seems to have made monthly offerings to the shades of its ancestors, which consisted in a communion meal at which images of the departed were present. . . ." An inscription of the high-priest of the temple of the moon-god at Harran runs : "Fat sheep, breads, date wine, cypress oil, fruit of the garden . . . I broke unto them. An incense offering, the choice incense as a regular offering, I fixed for them, and placed before them." The high-priest here performs for the kinsmen that sacred ceremony of breaking bread for the souls of the dead. "The expression 'placing incense before them' refers to the statues of the departed whose souls are thus represented at the communion meal, and whose portion is the incense. . . . The repose of the soul, we may say even its immortality, depends upon the communion sacrifice performed monthly for it by its kinsmen." [1] It was the duty of the son of the departed to "pour out water" for him, and to bring offerings, otherwise the departed spirit would inevitably roam about restlessly. The idea of communion seems also to have been connected with the funeral feast after a burial; the remains of the offerings to the departed furnished the funeral feast which was partaken of both by the mourners and also by the *Anunnaki* (demons of the underworld, see below) and the gods who were about the tomb.[2]

These facts show clearly that belief in the continued existence hereafter was very real among the Babylonians.

But to return for a moment to the deposits in the tombs placed there for the use of the departed. At Tell el-Obeid, in Babylonia, near the temple, a burial site dating from early Sumerian times (the Sumerians were a non-Semitic people who inhabited Babylonia before the advent of the Babylonians) was excavated. Here in the tombs in which women were buried, necklaces of lapis-lazuli and pearls

[1] In Hastings' *Encycl. of Rel. and Ethics*, iv. 445b, 446a.
[2] Meissner, *op. cit.*, i. 428 (1920).

G

were found; in other graves copper daggers and axes had
been placed beside the bodies; also many vessels made of
clay and ornamented with black and white geometrical
figures; these were all food and drinking-vessels.[1] Again,
in a burial-place on a hill close to Ur, the soil had been to a
large extent washed away by rain, revealing the contents of
tombs; here a large find was made of terra-cotta figures and
cylinder seals; among the former were women playing the
tambourine, heads and busts of gods holding axes and
clubs, nude females, worshippers with sacrificial animals in
their arms; also clay masks, and figures of animals, horse,
monkey, lion, pig, and tortoise. The date of this burying-
place was definitely fixed as about 2400 B.C.[2]

In another tomb were found lying beside the departed a
number of clay figures representing his occupations; these
were doubtless intended to help the departed to continue
his calling in the next world.[3] Once more, on another site
in Babylonia (Charsagkalama), further finds were made in
tombs belonging to about B.C. 2900; these consisted of a
great mass of ancient Sumerian articles: seals, copper
implements, pearls, gold and silver ornaments, and many
vessels made of clay; in one tomb three cylinder seals were
found; in other tombs also these were found; they were
made of shells, hæmatite, lapis-lazuli, and limestone; on
the same site a number of ostrich eggs were found; these
were often cut in two and used as drinking-vessels. In
many graves in Kish necklaces of cornelian and lapis-lazuli,
the former both red and white, had been deposited; also
numbers of other necklaces made of precious stones, together
with a delicately formed golden chain.[4] These examples
must suffice, but they could be greatly multiplied.

We naturally ask ourselves how the Babylonians conceived
that the departed could make use of these articles placed
alongside them in their graves? The reply is that they
simply did not frame any theories about that; when the
departed were alive they used these things; therefore they
must require them in their new life. And if they were not
supplied with them they would be angry, and then woe
betide their relatives whose duty it was to see that their
departed kinsmen were furnished with their requirements.
We have, therefore, to see a twofold object in these grave

[1] Langdon, *Ausgrabungen in Babylonien seit* 1918, in *Der Alte Orient*,
xxvi. 18 (1928).
[2] *Ibid.*, pp. 34 f.   [3] *Ibid.*, p. 52.   [4] *Ibid.*, pp. 63 f.

deposits : primarily, likely enough, affection prompted the desire to see that the departed got all they wanted; but fear also entered in, for it was firmly believed that the spirits of the departed had power to wreak vengeance on negligent relatives. This brings us to another, but closely connected subject—namely, exorcism formulas.

These were used, and recited, for the purpose of banning the spirits of the departed who had come up from below with some sinister object against the living in view.

The many specimens of these formulas which have been unearthed belong to comparatively late times; but, as Jastrow has pointed out,[1] formulas which had been proved by practice to be efficacious were copied out and handed down from generation to generation, and kept in the temple archives; so that a formula found, for example, among the collections in the library of Asshur-bani-pal in the seventh century B.C. might in reality have come down from an immemorial antiquity.

The spirits of the departed, or many of them, who came up from the nether-world, were looked upon with fear and horror on account of the harm they were believed to be capable of inflicting on the living; they are described as blood-sucking monsters harming mortals, even going so far in their reckless wickedness as to damage the images of the gods. Like snakes, they slid into the houses of people; it is said of them that "they entice a wife away from her husband, snatch the child from the father's knee, drive the householder from the family circle." [2]

Hence it is commanded that the entry to the sepulchre, the place of rest, be secured with a strong bronze bar, and that a compelling incantation be pronounced over it, so as to prevent the spirit of the departed from issuing forth.[3]

The spirits of the dead are thus believed to be able to wander about on the earth, if, having once been called up from the under-world, they are unwilling to return there; and their activity is mainly directed against luckless mortals. In one text, for example, a sick man complains that he is held in the power of a wandering spirit from the realms of the dead; in this case, apparently, it is not a question of the spirit having been called up. he has simply left the abode of the dead of his own free will. Another similar

---

[1] Op. cit., i. 269.

[2] Jeremias, Hölle und Paradies bei den Babyloniern, in Der Alte Orient, p. 86 (1900). [3] Meissner, op. cit., i. 428.

text records the case of a man, dangerously ill, who declares that his illness is due to an evil-disposed spirit who has come up from the realms of the dead. Another tablet contains the prayer of a man who is convinced that he is " possessed " by the spirit of a departed mortal.[1] And there are many others to the same effect.

That in all the cases of this kind it is not a question of ordinary demons whose *habitat* is in waste places, ruins, and the like, and who are incarnate in various animals, seems certain; they belong to a different category, though it is likely enough that in course of time the two categories became mixed up. Exorcism formulas were thus recited to ban the evil-disposed spirit of the departed who had returned. Then we have a further object of these exorcism formulas :

While there are a good number of cases on record in which the departed spirit seems to act on his own initiative in leaving the abode of the dead, generally speaking it was necessary for the spirit to be called up by competent necromancers. Among the priests were various categories who performed this ceremony—they are described under such titles as " conjurors of the dead," they who " bring up the dead," " questioners (or inquirers) of the dead "; the terms may be comparatively of late date, but the offices are certainly very ancient.

The object of this consulting of the departed spirits was, obviously, because they were believed to have knowledge not possessed by mortals on this earth, especially with regard to future events, thus showing that the spirits of the departed were thought of as knowing all about what was going on in the world.

That there was a more or less stereotyped ritual in calling up the spirits of the dead stands to reason. In the " Gilgamesh Epic " there are many details of such ritual : Gilgamesh describes very fully the various acts, and especially prohibitions, in connexion with the calling up of the spirit of his friend Engidu; thus, he may not anoint himself with sweet-smelling oil, lest he should attract the spirits of the dead in too forcible a manner. He may not have his bow with him, lest he should be incommoded by the crowd of those spirits who had met their death by means of it. He may not hold a sceptre, for that would frighten away the spirit; and he must be careful not to have on creaking footwear, lest he should scare away the spirit by the un-

[1] Meissner, *op. cit.*, p. i. 89.

seemly noise. The proper thing in approaching the spirits of the dead is to come naked, for both the deity Ninazu who commands them, and the spirits themselves, are nude. At first, the Epic tells us, Gilgamesh, in spite of all his efforts, failed in his attempt to bring up the spirit of his friend; but, at last, Ea intercedes with Nergal, who thereupon " opens the hole of the underworld and causes the spirit of Engidu to rise up out of the earth like a wind." [1]

Again, in the closing lines of the poem known as " The Descent of Ishtar," we have one or two further details of the ritual : " In the days of Tammuz," it is said, " play to me upon the crystal flute, play to me upon the [word obliterated] instrument, his dirge, ye mourning men and women, in order that the dead may ascend, and smell the incense." [2] This points to the belief that the spirits of the departed could be induced to ascend from their abode by the sound of the flute and the smell of incense.

In this " Descent of Ishtar " occur some further ideas concerning the dead, and, as this poem reflects ancient conceptions, these are worth mentioning. Reference is made to a spring containing the water of life; this spring is situated under the " eternal palace," i.e. the holy of holies in the underworld; it is guarded by the demons of the underworld called the *Anunnaki* (the meaning of the word is uncertain),[3] beings wholly distinct from the ordinary inhabitants of the underworld; this water of life can be obtained only by pronouncing a magic word, known to none but the god Ea, one of the greatest of the Babylonian gods. So that here we have the idea expressed, though in a *naïve* and very old-world form, of the possibility of rising from the underworld by means of the water of life obtainable through the use of a magic word.

In this connexion it may be pointed out that in the account of the annual Tammuz Festival beliefs are expressed both of liberation from the realm of the dead, as well as that of resurrection; true, there is here no reference to departed spirits of men, but only to a *divine being*; nevertheless, it seems certain that the Tammuz precedent was applied to the spirits of men in the underworld, for the term " awakeners of the dead " is used of a number of Babylonian deities; originally, no doubt, this awakening had reference to the " resurrection of Nature " in the spring,

[1] Meissner, *op. cit.*, ii. 148 (1925).
[2] Jeremias, *op. cit.*, p. 88.   [3] Jastrow, *op. cit.*, i. 197.

but the conception is also at times used directly in reference to departed mortals in the underworld; thus, of the sun-god Shamash it is said : " It is in thy power to make the dead alive, and to release those who are bound"; the god Nabu is praised as being one " who can lengthen the days of life, and who can awaken the dead "; similarly it is said of Marduk that he is " the merciful one, who loves to awaken the dead"; his spouse, Gula, has the same power, she is called " the Mistress, the awakener of the dead"; and Nergal himself, the god of the underworld, has the name Nergal-uballith, " Nergal, the quickener " (i.e. of the dead).[1]

It may be added here that in the " Gilgamesh Epic," referred to just now, it is recorded how Ut-napishtim (the Biblical Noah), a *mortal*, attained immortality. Moreover, the possibility of a *mortal* gaining everlasting life is entertained in the " Adapa Myth "; in this poem it is described how Adapa was deceived by Ea; he is told by Ea that when he appears before Anu, the great god, he will be offered the food of life and the water of life, and he is warned not to partake of them. So when he appears before Anu, the great god commands " food of life " and " water of life," which will give immortality to Adapa, to be set before him; but Adapa, acting on the warning he had received from Ea, refused to eat and drink of these. Then said Anu to him : " O Adapa, wherefore didst thou not eat, didst thou not drink ? Now will immortality not be thy lot." So that, according to this myth, the possibility of a mortal attaining everlasting life is recognized; it was only by deception that Adapa, an ordinary mortal, was deprived of it.

Another point about Babylonian belief regarding the After-life is of great interest and importance. Mention has been made of the *Anunnaki*, demons of the underworld who guard the spring containing the water of life; they had other functions as well; and among these was that of judges in their court of judgement, before which every spirit that entered the realm of the dead had to appear and be judged; in fact they are sometimes reckoned among the gods who decide the destiny of men;[2] so that here there is clearly the idea of a differentiation in the fate of the departed in the After-life. And this is definitely brought out on a tablet published by Ebeling; it is a Sumerian tablet, a fact which witnesses to the great antiquity of the conception (although

[1] Jeremias, *op. cit.*, pp. 90 f.   [2] Jastrow, *op. cit.*, ii. 40.

the present form of the text is much later, belonging, Ebeling thinks, to the time of the Kassites; the Kassite dynasty of Babylon was founded about 1750 B.C. [1]); part of this text runs as follows : " . . . they come to the place of the decision of destiny, to the underworld river; he separates the good from the bad; the righteous man lies down in peace; he who is evil . . . his spirit will abide in the depth of the Ocean. . . ." At the end of the text the god says : " The breath of life is in my hand, the righteous shall continue to exist, the wicked shall not escape from my arm." [2]

It will be agreed that this idea of the separation of the good from the bad in the After-life at such an early period (about 4000 B.C.) is very remarkable, even though the " good " and " bad " might not have the meaning that we attach to the words.

Another tablet, which speaks of the court of judgement in the underworld, is worth quoting; though found in a tomb in Elam, it came, according to Ebeling, from Babylon originally; it is a kind of *Vade Mecum* which was placed beside the body in the tomb. The words are supposed to be uttered by the departed spirit; he expresses his readiness to be brought before the *Anunnaki*, the deciders of destiny, in order to hear their verdict. He prays to his god to be with him and to keep him from harm : " Come, I will go, O my god, into the presence of the *Anunnaki*; I will pass from the tomb (?); I will take hold of thy hand; before the great gods I will hear the verdict, clasping thy feet. Thou enlightenest the house of darkness, O my god; thou wilt deliver me from the entanglement (lit. " thicket ") of weakness and weariness. In the land of dire distress thou wilt look upon me, thou wilt refresh me with water and oil in the thirsty land." [3] This touching expression of trust in his god reminds one irresistibly of the 23rd Psalm : " Yea, though I walk through the valley of the shadow of death, I will fear no evil, for Thou art with me, Thy rod and Thy staff, they comfort me; Thou preparest a table before me in the presence of mine enemies; Thou hast anointed my head with oil; my cup runneth over."

Finally, as illustrating the fact that the Babylonians, at

---

[1] See *Camb. Anc. Hist.*, i. 363 (1923).

[2] Ebeling, *Tod und Leben nach den Vorstellungen der Babylonier*, i. 22 f. (1931).

[3] Ebeling, *op. cit.*, i. 19 ff.

any rate during the earlier periods, did not regard existence
in the hereafter as blankly hopeless, we may mention two
expressions; one of these is, " he ascended his mountain, he
passed through the sea," in reference to one who has died;
whatever may be meant by this—and into that we cannot
go now—it does not give the impression that death was
thought of as something terrible. The other is : " His god
called him away," [1] which implies that the deceased believed
in his god; so that to be called to him would express comfort
rather than fear.

2. Ancient Arab Beliefs and Customs

In common with what we have seen to have been the
case among the Babylonians, indirect evidence for belief in
the After-life on the part of the ancient Arabs is afforded by
the numerous articles placed in tombs by the side of the
departed; [2] these are not offerings to the dead, but gifts of
things which it was believed the departed one would require
in his life in the other world. Most important among these
is his horse, or camel; sometimes the camel, with its saddle
and other belongings of the departed, was burned by the
grave-side; or else it was placed in a pit dug out by the
grave and left to die. But the most usual procedure was
to cut its tendons, so that it could not run away. Mention
is also made of the deceased's horse being slaughtered on
the grave; this proves that in that matter there was no
idea of sacrifice, for the horse was not a sacrificial animal
among the Arabs.

A very frequent custom was the pouring out of water or
wine on the grave, for the spirit of the departed was believed
to be very thirsty. A constant prayer for the departed was
that it might rain upon the grave. Here again there was
no question of offering a sacrificial libation; the idea was to
keep up a relationship with the departed; the friends would
call out to him : " Be not far from us." Another way in
which this relationship was kept up was by pitching a tent
on the grave; in this the relatives would dwell for a considerable time. When anybody passed near the grave of a
friend they would always greet him or her, and it was
believed that he returned the greeting. An instance is
recorded of one who told his lady-love that if she greeted
him in this way after he was dead he would not fail to

---

[1] Jeremias, *Das alte Testament im Lichte des alten Orients*, pp. 570 f. (1930).
[2] See Wellhausen, *op. cit.*, pp. 177 ff.

acknowledge the greeting; when he was dead his beloved came to his grave, and as she greeted him an owl flew from the grave; but she expressed a doubt as to whether her lover had really greeted her from his grave in the shape of this owl; whereupon she died; the reason being, of course, that the lover was displeased at her for doubting his word. It was a widespread belief among the Arabs that the spirits of the departed appeared in the shape of birds, especially owls.

In addition to graves for individuals there were family tombs in which the members of a family were laid, generation after generation; it was believed that in this way the family was reunited after death. Large family tombs have been discovered in Petra and Ezra. On the other hand, the dead were often buried either in or near their houses in order that they might be near their relatives; an interesting ancient Arab poem bears witness to this, though it seems to lament that the custom was dying; part of it runs thus :

The people have a burying-place around the court-yard square;
The graves increase in number, but the living get more rare.
The dwelling-place may ancient grow, in ruins it may fall,
Still grows the number of the dead beside the court-yard wall.
The living as their neighbours have the spirits of the dead,
But intercourse with them is rare, since far away they've sped.[1]

What has been said points clearly to the fact that the ancient Arabs believed in a continued existence after death; their ideas as to the conditions under which the departed lived were very vague, nor is it at all clear that in the early times they had formed any conceptions as to *where* the abode of the dead was; for the most part they were thought to be confined to the grave; yet that they could leave the grave was certainly believed. But however all this may be, the main point is that these ancient Arabs cherished a profound belief in an After-life.

So far we have dealt only with what may be called the " primitive " stage regarding the belief in immortality of the ancient Arabs; there is another point of view, held by many of the more cultured, about the next world of which a word must be said, because this other view came in course of time to exercise a profound effect; the parallel to it is, moreover, found in Babylonian and Israelite belief.

In ancient Arabic writings it is insisted again and again

[1] Quoted in a German translation by Bertholet, *Die israelitischen Vorstellungen vom Zustand nach dem Tode*, p. 13.

that death is the end of all things; the thought that death will come some time or other is an incentive to make the most of this life, for there is no glimmer of hope, it is said, when once a man has closed his eyes in death. Death is viewed with horror; the one comfort is that everyone has to die, so that all the world is in the same plight. It is said that to salute the dead in passing by graves is nonsense; the dead have ceased to exist.

Now, it will be realized at once how utterly incongruous all this is in view of what was said previously. We have here two entirely different conceptions regarding the After-life, and both are represented in the same early Arabic literature. The explanation of this is that both the " primitive " and the " advanced " views are represented in these writings. The former was the popular belief of the bulk of the people, the latter was the official orthodox view. That the popular belief was never eradicated is proved by the fact that it still exists at the present day. Illustrations of this will be found in plenty in Curtiss' *Primitive Semitic Religion To-day* (1902).

3. THE OLD TESTAMENT

It has been pointed out that among the Babylonians and ancient Arabs there were two sets of conceptions regarding the Hereafter which, in many particulars, were contradictory. We are now to see that a precisely similar phenomenon is to be observed among the Hebrews.

For convenience' sake we have called these two conceptions the " popular " and the " official." The popular conception dated from time immemorial and continued throughout the ages; it would be difficult to say to how late a date. As to the " official " teaching, there is reason to believe that it arose in Israel somewhere about the eighth century B.C.; the evidence for this we shall come to later.

The " popular " view is, as one would expect, by far the more interesting, and there is much more to be said about it than about the " official " teaching; moreover, as we shall see finally, the " popular " belief, in spite of a great deal that was false, came much nearer to the truth than the " official " view.

We will begin, then, with the popular conceptions about the departed; and the first matter to be dealt with is that of *consulting the dead*; for obviously this presupposes the belief in the continued conscious life of the departed hereafter. Most of the references in the Old Testament to this practice consist of prohibitions, to these we shall come in due course, but they are all late passages. The earliest reference to the practice is, however, fairly full, and is not a prohibition. It is contained in 1 Sam. xxviii. 3–25, the narrative about Saul and the Witch of Endor. To this we must devote a little detailed attention. It is necessary to point out, first, that in verse 3 there is a later insertion; the words, " and Saul had put away those that had familiar spirits and the wizards from the land," do not belong to the original text. Why should these words be a later insertion? For two conclusive reasons : (1) the words break the sequence of the text; this will be seen at once by reading verses 3 and 4 without the words in question, thus : " Now Samuel was dead, and all Israel had lamented him, and buried him in Ramah, even in his own city. And the Philistines gathered themselves together, and came and pitched in Shunem . . .," meaning that as soon as Samuel was dead the Philistines plucked up courage again, because previously it had been the anointing of Saul by Samuel which had entailed their defeat (1 Sam. ix. 16 and xiii. xiv.); now that Samuel was dead they determined to attack the Israelites again. It is right in the middle of this sentence that the words about Saul putting away those that had familiar spirits, are inserted. So that obviously they do not belong to the text in its original form. (2) The other reason why these words belong to a later time is even more convincing; the Hebrew word for " one who has a familiar spirit " is *'Ob*; but this word is used in two senses : the early meaning is a " departed spirit," the later meaning is " one who consults, or has, a departed (or familiar) spirit "; in our passage the word is used in the *later* sense, which proves that it belongs to a later time; in the other part of the narrative it is used in the early sense. The account then goes on to say that Saul, owing to his fear regarding the impending battle with the Philistines, had sought the guidance of Yahweh by means of dreams, Urim, and prophets, but in vain, hence, as a last resort, he comes to consult the dead. That certainly suggests that the consulting of a departed spirit was resorted to only in cases of dire necessity, and therefore not of frequent occurrence; but this would be a wrong conclusion, because the number of prohibitions against consulting the dead proves its prevalence; and that these prohibitions were not put forth until the seventh century only shows for how long a time no objection was urged against the practice.

To continue the narrative, then : Saul disguises himself and goes to the witch of Endor by night ; he disguises himself because (as is often held) he does not want to be recognized by the witch ; it is, however, more likely that he does not want to be recognized by the *spirit* ; it was a world-wide belief that the spirits of the departed were harmful, so that it was best to preserve one's incognito. He comes by night because the spirits of the departed do not like the light. Saul then says to the witch : " Divine unto me, I pray, by means of the *'Ob*, and bring up to me him whom I tell thee " ; here *'Ob* is used in its early sense of a departed spirit.[1] The witch then says to him : " Whom shall I bring up unto thee ? And he said, Bring me up Samuel " (verse 11 ; verses 9, 10 and 12 are a later insertion, we need not trouble about them) ; it then continues : " And the king said unto her, Be not afraid, but tell me (so the Septuagint) what thou seest " ;—the point is this : Saul is a firm believer in necromancy ; the whole narrative makes that clear ; his one object in coming to the witch, in whose power of divination he believes, is in order to consult the spirit of Samuel ; so he *expects* Samuel to appear ; but he quite realizes that when he says " Bring me up Samuel," this would come as a shock to the witch, for Samuel was not an ordinary person ; so Saul says : " Be not afraid, but tell me, what seest thou ? " " And she says : I see a god coming up out of the earth." That the witch speaks of the figure rising out of the earth—i.e. a cavern—as a god is quite natural ; the word *Elohim*, " god," is used of superhuman, but not divine, beings several times in the Old Testament.[2] Saul then says to her : " What is his appearance ? "—i.e. what does he look like ? The description given by the witch is precisely as Samuel is described during his life-time, viz. " an old man," and " covered with a robe " ; in the same way, in 1 Sam. xii. 2 Samuel says : " I am old and grey-headed " ; and in 1 Sam. xv. 27 reference is made to the " robe " he wore ; in each case the words are the same as in our passage. This agrees with what we find elsewhere in the Old Testament, that the appearance of the departed spirits is similar to that of their earthly life ; thus, according to Isa. xiv. 9, the departed spirit of a king continues to sit on a throne ;

---

[1] See further on this subject below, pp. 105 f.
[2] Exod. xxi. 6, xxii. 8, 9 (7, 8), 28 (27) ; Judges v. 8 ; 1 Sam. ii. 25 ; Ps. xlv. 6 (7), lviii. 1 (2).

according to Ezek. xxxii. 27, the departed spirits still carry their weapons of war and their swords, just as during their earthly life. So that we can understand why it was that Saul at once recognized that the figure arising from the earth was the spirit of Samuel : " And Saul perceived that it was Samuel, and he bowed with his face to the ground, and did obeisance."

With the further part of the narrative we are not here concerned, excepting to say that Samuel—speaking of course through the witch—tells Saul of his impending death, which soon came to pass.

Now, whatever opinion may be held about this narrative, nobody will deny that it is an important illustration of the belief of the early Israelites concerning the departed. They continue to live, they remember, they foresee; they can leave whatever place it is in which they abide; and they can return to the world, in a certain sense.

One other matter connected with the " popular " belief must be dealt with, although it takes us away from the Old Testament to some degree; that is, *the archæological evidence.* We have said something about the Babylonian customs as illustrated by archæological finds : let us do the same with regard to the Hebrews.

We have already referred to the subject of food and drink being placed on graves as gifts to the departed, and have shown how such customs witness to a belief in the continuance of life hereafter. We will now describe some of the results of more or less recent excavations in so far as they touch upon our present subject, restricting ourselves to Palestine, as we are dealing with the Israelites.

On the site of ancient Gezer, in southern Palestine near the Philistine border, a burial cave belonging to the early Israelite period (Patriarchal period) was examined; in one part of the cave was a paved platform on which was laid a large jar of coarse brick, red porous ware; stones were built up round it to keep it in position. This jar " contained a few bones, sufficient to show that the body of an infant, at birth or immediately after, had been deposited in it. It is difficult to avoid the conclusion that we have here the remains of the victim of an infant sacrifice. On no other hypothesis can the special treatment of this individual infant—one of many of the same age whose remains were found in the cave—be accounted for." [1] Similarly, on special occasions, children were offered up in sacrifice to a god,

[1] *P.E.F.Q.S.*, 1902, p. 352.

according to various passages in the Old Testament, viz.
Gen. xxii. 1 ff.; Judg. xi. 31 ff.; 1 Sam. xv. 3, 33; 2 Kings
iii. 27, xvi. 3, xxi. 6, xxiii. 10; Jer. vii. 31, xxxii. 35; Ezek.
xxiii. 39; Hos. xiii. 2. In the case before us the sacrifice
was offered to the departed; the idea was to offer of one's
best, thereby to propitiate the dead. In this burial cave
were also found numerous vessels, cups, bowls, platters, of
various shapes and sizes; "these were found lying about
all over the floor; others were built into crevices of the
grave enclosures, always in groups of at least two, a jug and
a bowl." [1] Naturally enough, nothing was found inside
these vessels; but there can be no doubt that when they
were first deposited by the side of the dead they contained
food and drink. Of other objects this burial cave contained
but few—shells and enamelled beads made of agate and
carnelian. As these things were deposited for the benefit
of the departed spirits, it is clear that it was believed that
they could make use of them, and this shows a belief in
the continued life hereafter.

Of still greater interest was the second burial cave discovered, belonging to much the same period. In this
burial-place no food vessels were found; stones were laid
under, round, and sometimes above the bodies—skeletons
as they are now; and other objects had been placed by
them—spears, knives, needles, axeheads, all bronze, and a
three-legged stone fire-dish for cooking. This was frac-
tured in accordance with the usual custom of fracturing
objects deposited in graves in order that their spirits may be
released and minister to the needs of the spirits of the
departed. Animistic ideas of this kind are world-wide.

In this burial cave fifteen persons had been laid, fourteen
of these were males and one a female; their ages ranged
from about 16 to 50; the female was about 14 years old.
"The chief problem presented by the cave," says Macalister
who discovered it, "lies in the extraordinary circumstances
attending the single female interment; the body had been
cut in two just below the ribs, and the upper half was alone
deposited in the cave . . . the lower half was not to be
found anywhere in the burial chamber." [2]

There cannot be any doubt that we have here another
instance of human sacrifice, and that it was in some way
connected with the departed stands to reason, since it was
offered in or by the burial cave. That no traces of the

_____

[1] *Ibid.*, p. 358.   [2] *Ibid.*, 1903, pp. 12 ff.

lower part of the body were found suggests that it was ceremonially eaten at a sacrificial funeral feast, with the object of effecting union with the departed; the object of this would be to prevent the departed from harming the living, because, obviously, the departed would not harm those who were united with them. But in any case, it points to conceptions about the dead which regard them as very much alive; and that is our main point. In this connexion another interesting point may be noted : " In a number of tombs, all about 1200 B.C., there were found with the vessels containing food exactly identical vessels containing one or more human bones. In one, for instance, was a small earthenware jug containing the finger-bones of an infant "; elsewhere a bowl with part of a skull fitted into it, but mostly they are finger-bones, both of infants (mainly) and adults.[1] That this curious custom must have had relationship with the departed stands to reason seeing that the bones are placed in tombs. Now, seeing that bones were regarded as synonymous with the individual itself—and that would, of course, apply equally to even a fragment of bone—the object of placing these bones in the tombs was probably to continue the companionship of those who had lived together on this earth in the Hereafter.

In passing, we might mention a custom which used to be in vogue among the Déné Indians of the Hudson Bay Territory; one of their tribes is known as the " Carriers " because the widows used to carry about with them the bones of their dead husbands.[2] What was a comfort to the living, might well have been so to the departed.

However crass the idea may be, this custom of placing finger-bones in tombs is important from our present point of view because it illustrates the belief that life continued in the next world and that the departed not only retained consciousness and memory, but also affection for those whom they had loved on earth.

What has been said so far regarding archæological finds has reference to Gezer. Just a few words may be added about similar things on the site of ancient Taanach, in northern Palestine. Here, too, numerous utensils were found in the tombs, but above all eating and drinking vessels, many of them beautifully shaped. In one of the tombs, described by Sellin, the excavator, there was placed at the head of

---

[1] *Ibid.*, 1905, pp. 32 f.
[2] Frazer, *Golden Bough* : Balder the Beautiful, i. 91 (1913).

the skeleton a very large bowl, and similarly at its feet; by its side was a platter full of quite small bones—not human ones; together with a long spear-head of bronze. All the remains of human bodies found on this spot were of men, and as the burying-place was situated close to the ruins of what had been a strong fortress, it is likely that the bodies were those of warriors who fell in defence of it. Food and drinking-vessels were supplied to all of them.[1] So that here again we have the concrete proof of the belief that the life of the departed continued hereafter, since their requirements were the same as on this earth.

Similar evidence is forthcoming from other ancient sites in Palestine : Tell Duweir (Lachish), Tell Zakariya (Azekah), Tell es-Safi (Gath, or Libnah), Tell Sandahannah (Moresheth), Tell el-Mutesellim (Megiddo), 'Ain esh-Shems (Beth-Shemesh), and some others; but space would fail us to deal with these.[2]

There is another kind of grave-deposit found in great numbers of which a word must be said, namely, little lamps placed in tombs and also apparently on graves. Macalister suggests that these lamps may be a remnant reminiscent of a funeral sacrifice involving fire which was at one time in vogue, and is typified by the lamp; the objection to this theory is that we have evidence of funeral sacrifices in times quite as late as these lamp deposits, so that there would really be no point in having them if they symbolized a rite still in vogue. The explanation may be much simpler, and more realistic; tombs are dark, the underground was dark, what more necessary than to have lamps to see one's way about ? They stand in the same category as food and drinking-vessels—what men had required on this earth they would require in their new life. Thus, another illustration of the ingrained belief that life did not end with the death of men in this world.

That no indication of the things referred to should be mentioned in the Old Testament need not cause surprise; the Old Testament has been edited, worked over, and corrected by the priestly scribes of later times; and from their point of view much which originally stood in the text has rightly been eliminated; the wonder is that they overlooked so many things.

---

[1] *Tell Ta'annek*, pp. 51 ff. (1904).
[2] See further Vincent, *Canaan d'après l'exploration récente*, pp. 205-296 (1907).

Belonging to the "popular" conceptions of the After-life was one expressed by such phrases as that occurring, e.g., in Gen. xxv. 8 : "And Abraham gave up the ghost, and died in a good old age . . . *and was gathered to his people,*" see also verse 17 and xxxv. 29; or, as in Gen. xv. 15 : "Thou shalt go to thy fathers in peace"; and Gen. xlvii. 30, "When I sleep with my fathers"; Gen. xlix. 29 : "Bury me with my fathers"; in these and many another passage what is meant is that a man should be buried in the same sepulchre as his fathers (see further 2 Sam. xvii. 23, xxi. 14 and others); that is to say, it was believed that there was a gathering together again of the clan in the family burying-place, and this is clear evidence of the belief that the departed recognized one another and enjoyed one another's companionship in the After-life.

It will now be fully realized that according to the "popular" belief among the Israelites, life after death was a very real thing; and this belief was not the less real for being indefinite as to the How and Where; the "Where" was sometimes thought of as beneath in the earth, at other times in the tomb; the "How" was doubtless thought of as being similar to life on this earth; but what element of man it was that lived so could be only vaguely conceived of. This vagueness and indefiniteness did not, however, affect the real conviction that the departed lived.

For the Old Testament belief in later times, the "official" as distinct from the "popular," see Chapter XXI.

H

CHAPTER IX

SOME FURTHER ELEMENTS IN THE RELIGIOUS BACKGROUND: ANCESTOR-WORSHIP; NECRO-MANCY

1. ANCESTOR-WORSHIP

IT is not difficult to trace the steps whereby it can be seen that there is a connexion between Totemism and Ancestor-worship. Totemism, as already pointed out, explains clan or tribal animal names; and we have also seen how divine tribal names arise through heavenly beings having been looked upon as animals (see above, p. 65). The two processes of a totem-ancestor gradually developing into a human ancestor, and of a human ancestor gradually becoming divine, are not necessarily successive steps, and may well have often proceeded concurrently; in that case Ancestor-worship would at a certain stage arise quite naturally.

But however it may have actually come about,[1] of its existence there is no sort of doubt. In the Semitic domain the subject is a highly controversial one, and to enter upon a discussion of it here would take up a disproportionate amount of space. The difficulty does not lie in the *data*, which are abundant, but in their interpretation. Many facts which appear to some scholars to point to Ancestor-worship are held by others to admit of a different explanation. It must therefore suffice if we refer to some writers on the subject, and then give some of the passages in the Old Testament which, in the light of extra-Biblical evidence, must be looked upon, according to the opinion of the present writer, as containing remnants of Ancestor-worship among the Hebrews, or their forebears, of earlier ages. So far as the Semitic area is concerned, and it is with this alone that we are dealing here, the following works contain important material: Goldziher, *Culte des Ancêtres chez les Arabes*, *passim* (1885); Stade, *Geschichte des Volkes Israel*, i. 387 ff.

[1] See the present writer's *Immortality and the Unseen World*, pp. 95 ff. (1921).

(1886), *Biblische Theologie des alten Testaments*, i. 104 ff. (1905): Wellhausen, *Reste Arabischen Heidentums*, pp. 183 ff. (1897). Hölscher, *Geschichte der Israelitischen und Jüdischen Religion*, pp. 24 ff., 30 ff. (1922); S. A. Cook in Robertson Smith's *Religion of the Semites*, pp. 508 ff., 544 ff. (1927). Representing a rather different standpoint are : Lagrange, *Études sur les Religions sémitiques*, pp. 269 ff. (1903); Vincent, *Canaan d'après l'Exploration Récente*, pp. 288 ff. (1907); Margoliouth in Hastings' *Encycl. of Rel. and Ethics*, i. 444 ff. (1908); Lods, *Israel* (Engl. ed. by S. H. Hooke), pp. 113 ff., 227 ff.[1]

"Even on general principles, the cult of sacred beings who were regarded as ancestors, and of ancestors who were gods or heroic beings, is only to be expected in ancient times and among the Semites. The evidence has no doubt been exaggerated. To Vincent the archæological *data* suggest care for the dead, rather than a cult. But there was evidently a belief in their continued existence, and the denunciation of mourning customs by the Israelite reformers is highly significant." These mourning customs to which S. A. Cook refers in these words constitute one of the strongest arguments in favour of Ancestor-worship being in vogue at one time among the ancient Hebrews. We cannot deal with these here in detail,[2] but they may be briefly enumerated : the rending of the garments which was a palliative of the laceration of the body, cutting off the hair, putting on sackcloth, sprinkling ashes on the head, fasting, wailing, baring the feet, and possibly one or two others. To regard these as remnants of Ancestor-worship may be thought by many to be fantastic; but conclusions must not be drawn before the subject of their origins is investigated in the light of comparative religion; and even so there are considerable differences of opinion among scholars; but a strong case can be made out in favour of the view here represented. This is stated in the present writer's book already referred to.

There are other *data* in the Old Testament which point to the fact that Ancestor-worship was at one time in vogue among the forebears of the Hebrews.

Gad, meaning "fortune," is a divine name; this is

[1] For Ancestor-worship among the Babylonians, see the relevant chapter in Jastrow, *op. cit.*; Jeremias, *Bab.-Assyr. Vorstellungen vom Leben nach dem Tode* (1887); and *Hölle und Paradies bei den Babyloniern*. See also S. A. Cook, *The Religion of Ancient Palestine*, pp. 57 ff. (1921).

[2] They are dealt with in *Immortality and the Unseen World*, pp. 141–189.

proved not only by such names as Baal-Gad (Joshua xi. 17, xii. 7, xiii. 5), Migdal-Gad (Joshua xv. 37), but by the definite assertion in Isa. lxv. 11, " . . . that prepare a table for Gad, and that fill up mingled wine unto Meni." [1] Gad was also the name of one of the Israelite tribes. A tribal name which is known to be a divine name points indubitably to Ancestor-worship at some time, since an ancestor who is believed to be a god obviously receives worship.

Then, once more, the whole subject of the sanctity of the graves, or reputed burying-places, of ancestors is clearly bound up with that of Ancestor-worship. Here again we must content ourselves with a few allusions without going into the subject. Thus, the grave of Sarah, the cave of Machpelah (Gen. xxiii. 1 ff.), is shown by Gen. xiii. 18, xviii. 1, to have been a sanctuary; this is also true of the graves of Deborah, Rebecca's nurse (Gen. xxxv. 8), of Joseph (Joshua xxiv. 32; for Shechem as a sanctuary see Gen. xii. 6, xxxv. 4), of Miriam (Num. xx. 1; the name Kadesh, "holy," marks it as a sanctuary), and of Rachel (Gen. xxxv. 20; cp. 1 Sam. x. 2). No argument is needed, it may be hoped, to establish the fact that among ancient peoples, if the grave of an ancestor, or reputed ancestor, is a *sanctuary*, it means that that ancestor is worshipped. In the instance referred to the worship had been transferred from an ancestor to that of Yahweh, the God of Israel.[2]

It is held by many modern authorities that the existence of *Teraphim*,[3] mentioned in certain passages, is an indication of a remnant of Ancestor-worship; this is denied by other authorities, owing, they maintain, to lack of evidence. It must be conceded that actual proof is not forthcoming. The real difficulty lies in the uncertainty regarding the derivation of the word *Teraphim*. The bulk of opinion inclines to the belief that the word comes from the root meaning " to nourish," or " to maintain," and they point to the cognate Arabic word *tárifa*, " to have abundance of goods." Others, following Schwally,[4] hold that it is radically connected with *Repha'im*, " shades " of the departed [5] (cp.

---

[1] Further details are given by Siegfried, in *Jahrb. für protestantische Theol.*, pp. 361 ff. (1875).

[2] For further details see the present writer's *Immortality* . . . pp. 101 ff.

[3] The word is plural in form, but singular in conception, like Elohim; cp. 1 Sam. xix. 13, where it is spoken of as " it." See also for the view that Elohim means originally the spirits of the dead, 1 Sam. xxviii. 13.

[4] *Das Leben nach dem Tode*, pp. 35 ff. (1892).

[5] On the meaning of *Repha'im* see, however, below, pp. 249 ff.

54392

the Assyrian word *tarpu*, " spectre "). What the Old Testament says upon the subject is as follows, put very briefly :
from Gen. xxxi. 19, 30–35, Judges xvii. 5, 1 Sam. xix. 13,
16, it may be gathered that a household god is meant; it
appears to belong especially to the head of the family, it is
kept in houses, and it is spoken of as a god. From Judges
xviii. 14, 17, 20, 1 Sam. xv. 23, 2 Kings xxiii. 24, Hos. iii. 4,
Ezek. xxi. 26 (21 in E.V.), Zech. x. 2, it is quite clear that
the *Teraphim* was used for divination. These are the outstanding facts, and while they offer no proof, they certainly
suggest the possibility that the *Teraphim* was a remnant of
Ancestor-worship.

In the light, therefore, of what has been said it must be
recognized that the remnants of Totemism, and of Ancestor-
worship, are to be discovered in the Old Testament; and
that these old-world institutions, therefore, played their part
in the early background of Hebrew religious belief.

2. NECROMANCY [1]

As will be seen, there is a close connexion between this
subject and Demonology on the one hand, and with Ancestor-
worship and the Cult of the Dead on the other.

In all that concerns the primitive beliefs of the Hebrews
there can be no doubt that material common to the Semites
in general is involved; it will therefore be instructive to
begin by taking a glance at the practice of Necromancy
among the Babylonians.

" Necromancy," says Margoliouth, " which is an essential
part of the cult of the dead, and which must also have been
connected with the presentation of offerings to the shades
consulted, undoubtedly held a prominent place among the
magic arts of the Babylonians." [2]

As mentioned in the preceding chapter, among the various
categories of Babylonian priests we read of " conjurors of
the dead "—that is, " priests who bring up the spirits of
the dead "; mention is also made of the " questioner of the
dead," [3] the reference being obviously to one who would
presumably be what is called a " medium " nowadays, and
who was believed to have the faculty of receiving messages
from the spirits of the departed. The procedure seems to
be referred to in the closing lines of the " Descent of Ishtar,"

---

[1] For this subject see also the present writer's *Immortality and the
Unseen World*, pp. 125–140, where further details will be found.
[2] In *E. R. E.*, i. 439. [3] Jeremias, *op. cit.*, p. 288.

quoted above in a different connexion; it is said there:
" In the days of Tammuz, play to me upon the crystal
flute, play to me upon the [text mutilated] instrument, his
dirge, ye mourning men and mourning women, in order that
the dead may ascend, and smell the incense." [1]

From this we may gather that the spirits of the departed
were believed to be induced to rise up from their abode by
the sound of the flute and the smell of the incense.

In the " Gilgamesh Epic " there is an account of the hero
communicating with his dead friend Engidu; this he does
by the help of Nergal, the god of the underworld, who
makes an opening in the earth and causes the spirit of
Engidu to come forth " like a breath of wind." [2] Here it
is the god Nergal who acts the part of the " medium."

But although the authorities on the subject are agreed as
to the prevalence of Necromancy among the Babylonians,
there are otherwise scarcely any examples, which have come
down to us, of that particular department of the subject
with which we are here specially concerned, viz. the consulting of departed spirits regarding the affairs of men and
especially about future events.[3] In the great mass of cases
recorded in which mention is made of any relationship
between men and departed spirits the main thing is to
counteract the harmful activities of the latter. It was
believed that for one reason or another many spirits of the
departed left their abode in the underworld and roamed
about on the earth to the detriment of men; and it was to
combat these untoward activities that the services of the
magician were employed (see further Chapter VIII).

Now, in the Old Testament, while we have next to nothing
told us about the spirits of the departed harming men, there
is a considerable amount of evidence to show that the
departed were consulted either for guidance in the ordinary
affairs of life or in regard to future events. The most
obvious illustration is, of course, that of the Witch of Endor
(1 Sam. xxviii. 3–25). This has already been dealt with
(p. 91); here it may, however, be added that the somewhat
full account of the *procedure* given must be regarded, more

---

[1] Jeremias, *Hölle und Paradies bei den Babyloniern*, p. 20 in *Der Alte
Orient* (1900).

[2] It is on the twelfth tablet; a translation is given by Ebeling in Gressmann's *Altorientalische Texte zum Alten Testament*, pp. 150–198 (1926).

[3] Jeremias, however, mentions among the different orders of priests the
" exorcist of the spirits of the dead," " he who raises the spirit of the dead,"
and " the inquirer of the dead," called *Sha'ilu* (*Hölle* . . ., p. 28).

or less, as that implied in the other references to the consulting of departed spirits where the details are not given. The following points are to be noted : there is clearly a firm belief in the literal reality of what is recorded. The note in ver. 3 about Saul having put away those who had familiar spirits is a later insertion, both because it is incongruous in view of Saul himself going to consult one, and also because they were still flourishing in the days of the prophets (see below), but chiefly because the words of ver. 7 show that their continued presence in the land is taken for granted by Saul; when he asks where a woman who has a familiar spirit is to be found, his servants know at once; there is no need to seek for her. Another point to notice is that the consulting of the dead is regarded as a last resort; the other methods of learning about the future were by dreams, by *Urim* [1] and by prophets. As these had failed, this last means was employed.

But since the normal methods are spoken of as the way in which men enquired of Yahweh, to have recourse to the departed meant an act of disloyalty to the national God; it is here that we must see the real reason for the later prohibitions regarding necromancy. It is true, the prophet (Isa. viii. 19) shows that there is some chicanery about the business, but it is not that that troubles him; the real evil that he sees in it is that it draws people away from God. His words are worth quoting : " And when they shall say unto you, Seek unto them that have familiar spirits and unto the wizards, that chirp and that mutter; should not a people seek unto their God ? On behalf of the living should they seek unto the dead ? " But while he sees both the folly and the evil of it, his words show that it was greatly in vogue. It is similar in Isa. xxix. 4, where the prophet compares the humbled Mount Zion (" Ariel," see ver. 7) with one who has a familiar spirit : " And thou shalt be brought down, and shalt speak out of the ground, and thy speech shall be low out of the dust; and thy voice shall be as one that hath a familiar spirit, out of the ground, and

---

[1] *Urim* and *Thummim* were the sacred lots used by the priests for giving oracles; whether they were of stone or of wood cannot be said with certainty. The most important passage is 1 Sam. xiv. 41; the Hebrew text is corrupt, but, emended on the basis of the Septuagint, it should be rendered : " And Saul said : O Yahweh, God of Israel, wherefore hast thou not answered thy servant this day ? If this iniquity be in me, or in Jonathan my son, then, Yahweh, God of Israel, give *Urim*; but if it be in thy people Israel, then give *Thummim*."

thy speech shall whisper (marg., ' chirp ') out of the dust."
Here again it is taken for granted that the necromancers
are busy in the land. In Isa. xix. 3, although the note of
contempt is again sounded it is recognized that they are
present and resorted to : " . . . And they shall seek unto
the idols and to the charmers (marg. ' whisperers '), and
to them that have familiar spirits, and to the wizards."

Such passages witness to the wide prevalence of Necromancy, and although it is looked upon with contempt by
the prophet, it is only implicitly, not directly, that he condemns it; and were it not that it became a mark of disloyalty to Yahweh, it is probable that the prophet would
have regarded it as foolishness rather than as moral evil.
But that it was widely prevalent there can be no doubt,
so that when a little later it is said of the King Manasseh
that he " practised augury, and used enchantments and
dealt with them that had familiar spirits, and with wizards "
(2 Kings xxi. 6), we must see in this not the resuscitation
of practices which had fallen into desuetude (in spite of
earlier reforms), but rather the official recognition of what
had been done by the people all along.

It is, further, instructive to note how this subject is dealt
with in the various codes of laws preserved in the Old
Testament. The earliest, " The Book of the Covenant "
(Exod. xx. 22–xxiii. 33) [1] contains no prohibition against it,
the reason being that at the time Necromancy was regarded
as a natural and legitimate practice, as among the rest of
the Semites. The prophets, however, gradually came to
realize that it was incompatible with the worship of Yahweh;
hence we find that in the Deuteronomic legislation it is prohibited; in Deut. xviii. 10–12 it is said : " There shall not
be found with thee . . . one that useth divination, one that
practiseth augury, or an enchanter, or a sorcerer, or a
charmer, or a consulter with a familiar spirit, or a wizard,
or a necromancer. For whoso doeth these things is an
abomination unto Yahweh "; see also 2 Kings xxiii. 24 (the
Josianic reformation). The prohibition can have had but
little effect, for in the next code (the " Law of Holiness,"
Lev. xvii–xxvi), condemnation is added to prohibition :
" The soul that turneth unto them that have familiar spirits,
and unto the wizards, to go a whoring after them, I will
even set my face against that soul, and will cut him off from
among his people " (Lev. xx. 6; see also ver. 27). The

_____
[1] The oldest part of the combined documents J and E.

subject is not mentioned in the Priestly Code, but the Chronicler accounts for the death of Saul by saying that it was because of " his trespass which he committed against Yahweh, because of the word of Yahweh, which he kept not; and also for that he asked counsel of one that had a familiar spirit, to enquire thereby, and enquired not of Yahweh; therefore he slew him. . . ." (1 Chron. x. 13, 14). But in spite of prohibitions and in spite of the death penalty pronounced against those who practised it, we find that long after the Exile Necromancy was still prevalent in Judæa; for a late writer speaks of a " rebellious people," which " walketh in a way that is not good, after their own thoughts; a people that provoketh me to my face continually . . . which sit among the graves, and spend the night in vaults " (Isa. lxv. 2–4). The reference here is, in all probability, to what is known as " incubation "; by resorting to a grave or a sepulchral vault, and spending the night there, it was believed that the departed spirit would appear to the sleeper in a dream, and that the desired information or guidance would be imparted in this way. That this was one of the ways whereby Yahweh was believed to indicate His will may be seen from such passages as Gen. xx. 3, xxxi. 11; Num. xii. 6; 1 Sam. xxviii. 6, 15, and others.

In the Old Testament three expressions are used in reference to this subject. The first of these is what is called the 'Ob; this is translated by " familiar spirit." What is implied by this expression 'Ob, in other words, what its derivation is, cannot be said with certainty. According to some scholars, the root-idea is that of something hollow, on account of the hollow tone of the voice that a spirit may be supposed to utter; others explain the hollowness in reference to the hole in the earth from which the voice of the departed proceeds; others, again, hold that it came to be applied to a spirit or ghost because it was believed to appear in bodily form, but was hollow inside. This last seems to be the most probable; but if so, it implies that a real apparition was seen; nor need one doubt that this was so sometimes; and it is interesting to note that the cognate word in Arabic means a " revenant."

The word, in connexion with Necromancy,[1] is not always used in quite the same sense. In 1 Sam. xxviii. 7 it is said : " Seek me a woman that doth possess (or, ' is mis-

[1] In Job xxxii. 19, the same word is used of a " wine-skin."

tress of ') an *'Ob* " : the distinction between the woman
and the *'Ob* is clear here. So, too, is ver. 8 : " Divine
unto me, I pray thee, by the *'Ob*, and bring me up whom-
soever I shall name unto thee." [1] So that the woman is
the " medium," the *'Ob* is what spiritualists would call the
" control," and the apparition would presumably be called
a " materialization." This distinction is also clearly
shown in Deut. xviii. 11, where the phrase occurs :
" One that consulteth " (lit. " asketh ") an *'Ob*; so, too,
in Lev. xx. 27 : " A man or a woman in whom is an *'Ob*."
In other passages, however, the *'Ob* is used in reference to
the " medium " himself or herself (1 Sam. xxviii. 3, 9;
2 Kings xxi. 6, xxiii. 24; 2 Chron. xxxiii. 6; cp. also Isa.
viii. 19, xix. 3, xxix. 4).

Whatever deductions are to be drawn from this, of one
thing there is no doubt, viz. that up to the time of the
Deuteronomist the consulting of departed spirits was
regarded as something that really took place; it was not
looked upon as a piece of mere chicanery.

Then there is the term *Yidde'oni*, from the root meaning
" to know "; but whether this is in reference to the
" medium " who knows how to get into communication
with departed spirits, or in reference to the spirit itself who
knows, and can therefore give, the information sought,
cannot be said with any certainty.

There is also the term *'Ittim*—" whisperers," or " mutterers "—used, however, only in the three Isaiah passages
referred to as a parallel to the *'Ob* and the *Yidde'oni*; but
whether these formed another class may be doubted;
probably it is descriptive of one part of the method of
procedure followed by the *'Ob*, in the later sense of the
term.

Finally, the possibility must be recognized of the *Teraphim*
belonging to the subject of Necromancy, at any rate in the
earlier stage of belief; for if we are to understand by this
term a household god (see above, p. 100) which was used
for giving oracles, then it must be regarded as at one time
having been connected with Necromancy, and as parallel
with the *Manes*-oracle, the earliest known form of oracle
outside the Semitic domain.[2]

In all that has been said in this and in the preceding
chapters it has not been a question of folk-belief as distinct

---

[1] The whole passage is discussed above, p. 91.
[2] Stade, *Geschichte des Volkes Israel*, i. 467.

from the official religion. We have simply taken passages both early and late in which reference is made to the various subjects considered because they afford indications of " remnants "; for this affords proof that animistic conceptions, and the rest, were in full vogue among the forebears of the Hebrews, and therefore formed the background of their religion. When we come to consider the later stages of religious development, then of course it becomes necessary always to make a clear distinction between the popular religion and that of the religious leaders.

CHAPTER X

SOME FURTHER ELEMENTS IN THE RELIGIOUS BACKGROUND: DEMONOLOGY

1. GENERAL SEMITIC BELIEF

CHARACTERISTIC of all Semitic belief in demons is their multiplicity; on one of the many Babylonian texts which refer to demons it is said that they cover the world; another text says that " they cover the earth like grass." [1] Similarly among the ancient Arabs; their names for the various categories of demons, as well as the more general term *Jinn*, which is a collective word, points to their great numbers. Among the Babylonians the connexion between demons and the spirits of the departed is strongly marked; the demons were held to be the messengers of Ereshkigal, queen of the realm of the dead. Namtaru, one of the most dangerous demons, issued, it was said, from the netherworld. Utukku, who harms those who sojourn in the wilderness, is also a spirit of the dead; and closely connected with him is Ekimmu, " the departed soul," as he is called, who can find no rest, and wanders over the earth injuring men wherever he can. The anger of this demon is specially directed against those with whom he had had any relations while he lived on earth, and it is supposed to be partly their fault that he is unable to re-enter the realm of the dead and find rest. [2] If for any reason the spirits of the departed are unable to enter the realm of the dead, they are compelled to wander about the earth until the hindrance is taken away; while thus banished from their rightful abode they make it their business to harm all those with whom they had been in company when on earth, especially relatives; for, according to Babylonian belief, it is owing to the neglect of those who are left behind that the departed spirits are unable to obtain

---

[1] Jastrow, *op. cit.*, i. 355 ff.
[2] Nöldeke, in *E. R. E.*, i. 669 f.; Baudissin, *Studien zur semitischen Religionsgeschichte*, i. 279 ff. (1876); O. Weber, *Die Literatur der Babylonier und Assyrier*, pp. 148, 167 (1907).

rest. Among the causes which hinder departed spirits from entering into rest is neglect of the prescribed burial rites, and, above all, when a body remains unburied, or lies in foreign soil; neglect to bring the proper offerings to the dead would also, doubtless, have been considered another cause for the restlessness of departed spirits. This identification between departed spirits and demons is found also among the ancient Arabs, according to whose teaching the *Jinn* (the " dark " or " concealed " ones) were " the ghostly shadows of nations that have perished. . . . Certain ruined sites, too, such as Higr and Niçibin, were pointed to as being inhabited by the spirits of those who in days gone by had lived there. All burial-places, apart from the tombs of the saints, were believed to be infested by demons." [1] Desert places are also favourite haunts of demons.

All sickness was ascribed to the harmful action of demons; the Babylonian pest-demons were Labartu and Namtaru, chiefs of hordes of minor demons; Ashakku was the demon of burning fever, and Dimetum was " the evil curse "; another, but unnamed, demon was the cause of headache. So, too, among the ancient Arabs, fainting fits, epilepsy, gout, fever, and epidemics of every kind were the result of the harmful activity of demons; madness is described as being the after-effect of a demon taking up his abode in a man and " possessing " him.

The power of demons is greatest at night-time; the Babylonian Alu is a special night-demon; he is to be found especially in ruined places, where he hides, waiting to fall on any luckless passer-by; he also creeps into bedrooms and robs the weary of their sleep; he is described as running about at night " like a dog." In a similar way the demon named Gallu sweeps through the streets after dark, making every place insecure.[2] The ancient Arabs, it is said, always covered up the children's faces at nights lest the night-demons should molest them; doors were locked as helping to keep out demons, every vessel was covered to preserve it from pollution; lights were lit, not so much to give light, as to keep demons at bay. It was only with the rising of the morning stars that these demons withdrew.

Demons, according to ancient Semitic belief, had the power of making themselves invisible; Ashakku, it is said, " places himself by the side of a man, but nobody sees him "; [3] the

---

[1] Wellhausen, *op. cit.*, p. 150.   [2] O. Weber, *op. cit.*, p. 148.
[3] O. Weber, in *Der Alte Orient*, VII. iv. 16 (1906).

Arabs held the same belief in this power of demons being able to become invisible.

The relation between certain animals and demons is another characteristic common to Semitic demonology. The demons of one class were conceived of as always taking up their abode in animals; it was one of the ways in which the Babylonians explained to themselves whither demons withdrew when not occupied with their normal business of injuring men; this was why it was thought that many of the demons appeared in the shape of animals, birds, scorpions, and also as hybrid monsters, such as birds with the heads of lions or donkeys; but, above all, in the form of serpents.[1]

According to Semitic Demonology, then, the demons were divided into certain types or classes, though this kind of systematization was, of course, a development; this applies especially to the names given to particular demons; originally they were all nameless. In the Babylonian system there are different categories, the members of which are the followers of a head, who is a named demon, e.g. Utukku, Ekimmu, and others, though it is by no means clear that the different categories restricted themselves to particular spheres of activity; a demon of sickness might also be a night-demon, and so on. Among the Arabs the *Jinn* had no individuality, but they, too, were of different classes, some of which were more harmful than others.

This short *résumé* must suffice, as there is a good deal to be said about the demonology of the Old Testament.

2. THE OLD TESTAMENT

Most of the passages in the Old Testament in which demons are referred to belong to comparatively late times; but this is no argument against the belief in their existence in the earliest times. On the analogy of all that has been hitherto said, the presumption is that the Hebrews, being Semites, shared with the rest of the race, in the earliest stages of its history, *all* the beliefs which the evidence shows to have been

---

[1] Jastrow, *op. cit.*, p. 281. Regarding Babylonian Demonology a good deal of information will be found in Lenormant, *La Magie chez les Chaldéens et les origines Accadiennes* (1874, Eng. trans. 1877); see especially pp. 1–62. The scribes of Ashurbanipal made several copies of a large work of great antiquity in the library of the famous priestly school of Erech; this work was called *The Evil Spirits*. It is from this, to a great extent, that our knowledge of Babylonian Demonology is derived; only part of it has been preserved; it contains a great number of magical formulas used for averting the malignant attacks of evil spirits, etc.

common property. But, further, it must be remembered
that even in some of those books of the Old Testament which
in their present form are demonstrably late, a considerable
amount of very early material has been preserved. And when
it is realized that the editors of the Old Testament books,
from the Exile onwards, had reached a religious development
enormously in advance of their distant forebears, the
wonder is that they permitted *any* reference to beliefs which
must have been abhorrent to them. Indeed, so far as
necromancy is concerned, the only reason for its mention
was that it might be condemned as incompatible with the
worship of Yahweh. Nevertheless, as we shall see, it is not
wholly in the later books that references to these subjects
occur.

We do not propose, on account of the extensiveness of the
subject, to deal with the belief in demons among the Semites
generally,[1] but shall restrict ourselves here to the Old
Testament, though a few references to the wider sphere will
occur. As we study this subject in detail it will soon become
apparent that belief in demons is a development of animistic
conceptions. And in order to embrace the whole subject as
it appears in the Old Testament, it will be necessary to go
beyond the stage of primitive belief to which we are otherwise restricting ourselves at present.

In the forms in which demons appear in the Old Testament
they may be divided into two classes : (1) Theriomorphic
(Animal form), and (2) Anthropomorphic (Human form).

(a) THERIOMORPHIC DEMONS

i. *The Seraphim.*

The word comes from the root meaning " to burn," in a
literal sense; the *Seraphim* were therefore the " burning
ones." In the present connexion, however, this does not
refer to the burning of fire, but to the " burning " occasioned
by the bites which these demons, who are in serpent-form,
gave. Thus, in Num. xxi. 6 it is said : " And Yahweh sent
fiery-serpents (lit. *seraphim*-serpents) among the people,
and they bit the people; and much people of Israel died."
In ver. 8 of the same chapter it continues : " And Yahweh
said to Moses, Make thee a seraph, and put it on a pole;
and it shall come to pass that everyone that is bitten, when

[1] A good deal of evidence will be found in *Immortality and the Unseen World*, pp. 24–34.

he seeth it, shall live." This is a kind of imitative magic which shows the antiquity of the belief in this type of demon. That it was regarded as a true " demon of the waste " is seen from Deut. viii. 15 : ". . . Who led thee through the great and terrible wilderness wherein were seraph-serpents and scorpions " (see also Isa. xiv. 29, xxx. 6). The generally held Semitic belief that serpents were the incarnation of demons makes it certain, apart from other reasons, that the Israelites regarded these *Seraphim* as demons of the waste. In one direction they developed into angelic beings, as we see from the prophet's description of his vision in the well-known passage in Isa. vi. ; but their original character also persisted, as we can see from the *Deuteronomy* passage already cited. This incongruity need not occasion surprise ; there are other instances of the same kind of thing.

ii. *The Se'irim.*

This word, the " hairy ones," comes from a root meaning " to be hairy," and obviously they must have been so called on account of their appearance. Let us first quote the passages in which they are mentioned :

Lev. xvii. 7 : " And they shall no more sacrifice their sacrifices unto the Se'irim (R.V. ' he-goats', marg. ' satyrs '), after whom they go a-whoring. This shall be a statute for ever unto them throughout their generations."

2 Kings xxiii. 8 : In the account of Josiah's reforms occurs this meaningless passage : " . . . And he brake down the high places of the gates that were at the entering in of the gate of Joshua the governor of the city . . ." ; " the high places of the gates " should, it is recognized on all hands, be " the high place of the *Se'irim* " (reading *ha-se'irim* for *ha-she'arim*). This is borne out by 2 Chron. xi. 15, where it is said that Jeroboam had " appointed him priest for the high places, and for the *Se'irim*, and for the calves which he had made."

Isa. xxxiv. 14 tells of the desolation of Edom, and it is said that in the ruins of the land " the *sa'ir* shall cry to his fellow " (this time the R.V. has " satyr " in the text and " he-goat " in the margin). We shall return to this passage later. And, lastly, we have another passage from *Isaiah* which will also occupy us again presently, where it says that in the ruins of Babylon the *Se'irim* shall dance (Isa. xiii. 21) ; in this passage the Septuagint renders the word *Se'irim* by " demons."

From these passages we learn the following points about the *Se'irim* : They were worshipped in high places (i.e. they had their own sanctuaries), sacrifices were offered to them there, special priests performed the ritual; they were quite obviously visible, not only because they were called " hairy ones," but also because the worship of them is paralleled with that of the calves. It is also said that they inhabit ruined sites. To translate the word by " satyrs " is misleading, because the satyr was a purely imaginary creature, a hybrid, partly man, partly goat; whereas the *Se'irim* were real. There is no doubt that they were he-goats in the ordinary sense (*sa'ir* is the usual word for " he-goat "). From the Lev., 2 Kings and 2 Chron. passages it can hardly be doubted that at one time the Israelites worshipped these animals, either as gods, or as representing gods, just as in the case of the calves. Then, in later days, when, through the work of the prophets, the worship of Yahweh had become such that no other form of worship could be tolerated, these gods were degraded to demons. The connexion between demons and goats in Semitic belief has been shown by such writers as Baudissin, Wellhausen, and Robertson Smith; there is no need to enlarge further upon the point. It is to be noted that these *Se'irim* were just as real as *demons* as they had been as *gods*; that is clear from the Isaiah passages.

Thus, we have in the case of the *Se'irim* the converse of what happened in that of the *Seraphim* : the latter developed from demons to angels; the former were degraded from gods to demons.

Although we are dealing at present with theriomorphic demons, it is appropriate to discuss here *'Azazel*; he began and ended by being a person, but went through an intermediate demonic stage.

iii. *'Azazel*.

The form of this word in Hebrew (*'Aza'zel*, meaning " complete removal ") has caused difficulty; its formation is certainly unusual. Cheyne's solution, both on account of its simplicity, as well as on account of its intrinsic probability, is the most acceptable. He believes that in its present form it was a deliberate corruption, undertaken no doubt from reverential feelings; the original form was *'Azaz'el*,[1] which

---

[1] It is difficult, in transliteration, to make the difference of the two forms clear; in Hebrew they are עֲזָאזֵל and עֲזַזְאֵל.

I

means "God strengthens," constructed like the name
'*Azaziah* in 1 Chron. xv. 21, "Yahweh is mighty."

The passage about '*Azazel* is Lev. xvi. 7–28 : two he-goats
are taken from the congregation of Israel for a sin-offering;
these Aaron sets before Yahweh "at the door of the tent of
meeting." Then it is said that "Aaron shall cast lots upon
the two goats; one lot for Yahweh, and the other lot for
'*Azazel*. Clearly, from these words, '*Azazel* is regarded as a
personal being like Yahweh. Therefore to make '*Azazel*
equivalent to the scapegoat is doing violence to the text.
It then goes on to say that the goat upon which the lot for
'*Azazel* fell was to be sent away "for '*Azazel*" into the
wilderness, meaning that it was an offering to '*Azazel*.
From this we also see that '*Azazel* dwelt in the wilderness like
the *Se'irim*. Without going into details, for which we have
not space, the *data* suggest that '*Azazel* was originally a god
of the flocks—just as Astarte was a cow-deity—and that this
'*Azazel*-ritual was a development and adaptation of what
at some early period was an offering to a god of the waste.
Then '*Azazel* became degraded to a demon of the waste,
possibly being thought of as the head of the *Se'irim*.
Finally, he became identified with the author of all evil, i.e.
Satan; for in the *Book of Enoch* vi. 7 it is said : "Thou seest
what '*Azazel* hath done, who hath taught all unrighteousness
on earth . . ."; see also ix. 6, x. 4–6.

iv. *Some other Demons.*

In Isa. xiii. 21, 22, already referred to, there occur, in
addition to the *Se'irim*, some other types of what were also
undoubtedly looked upon as demons of the waste. A word
or two about these must be said.

First, the *Ziyyim*, translated "wild beasts"; in Jer. l. 39
they are called "the wild beasts of the desert." The word
comes from a root meaning "to be dry," and the noun would
therefore presumably imply connexion with a dry place, an
inhabiter of the waste; it stands, thus, in the same category
as *Se'irim*, thus bearing out the *Jeremiah* reference. While it
does not seem possible to identify the animal referred to, it
may be taken for granted that it was a real animal of some
kind which was believed to be the incarnation of a demon,
not an imaginary creature. It is therefore to be reckoned
among the demons of the waste.

In the same passage we have what are called '*Ochim*,
translated "doleful creatures"; it is parallel with the last

type, and, like it, is used in the plural; therefore they, too, congregate in numbers. The word comes apparently from a root meaning "to howl," and, according to Delitzsch, the cognate Assyrian word 'ahu means a "jackal"; we are thus justified in assuming that jackals are meant; and they would be regarded as animals in which demons took up their abode.

Then there are mentioned some creatures called Benoth Ya'anah, also in the plural, which the Revised Version translates "ostriches"; this is probably right; but the term means "daughters of greed." The Septuagint renders the term "Syrens," and makes them parallel with "demons." The Arabs say that demons have the hunger of lions; it is possible that the idea may have something to do with these "daughters of greed," and perhaps it was the voracity of the bird which suggested the connexion with demons. In any case, the Arab said that demons used ostriches to ride upon; and they also believed that demons appeared in the form of ostriches. At the present day ostriches are not seen in Palestine, but there is historical evidence that they were formerly more widely spread in Asia; besides, there are quite a number of references to them in the Old Testament. In Job xxxix. 18 it is said that "she scorneth the horse and his rider," so that evidently they were hunted in Palestine in days gone by.

Another type of what were regarded as demons, and which is also mentioned in Isa. xiii. 22, is described as 'Iyyim; it comes from a root meaning "to screech," and the word for "hawk" comes from the same root. In view of the fact that many birds were regarded as the incarnations of demons it may be that a bird of prey of some kind was meant. The parallel word in our passage, Tannim, another family of demons, and translated "jackals," would favour the R.V. translation "wolves" for 'Iyyim; but the meaning of Tannim is quite uncertain, and we have already had "jackals"; a bird of prey therefore seems more likely.

These exhaust the types of theriomorphic demons mentioned in the Old Testament, and, as will have been noticed, they are all demons of the waste, a fact brought out in the context in every case, and they are always mentioned in the plural. These animals were really believed to be closely associated with demons, and were, no doubt, often identified with them; and they were feared just because harmful supernatural beings were believed to take up their abode in them.

Before we come to demons in human form there is one
which must be briefly referred to here because it seems to
occupy a position, so far as one can judge from the very
meagre *data*, between the animal and the human. In
Gen. iv. 7 we have a difficult, and often misinterpreted,
passage; the R.V. translates : " If thou doest well " (it is
the Lord speaking to Cain) " shalt thou not be accepted ?
and if thou doest not well, sin coucheth at the door; unto
thee shall be his desire, and thou shalt rule over him."
Readers of *Genesis* in Hebrew will know that this is somewhat
in the nature of a paraphrase of an ungrammatical and un-
translateable passage.   Gunkel [1] says that the total corruption of this passage must be explained on the supposition
that, the text having become illegible—whether through
obliteration of the writing or mutilation of the manuscript—
it was reconstructed by a copyist to the best of his ability,
on the basis of Gen. iii. 16*b* (" And thy desire shall be to thy
husband, and he shall rule over thee ").   With this most
scholars will agree.   But in the R.V. rendering there is one
phrase meriting special attention—"sin coucheth at the
door."   This is an impossible rendering of the Hebrew,
because " sin " is feminine, and " coucheth " is masculine.
This can, however, be satisfactorily explained as Duhm [2]
points out, by regarding " sin " as a marginal gloss to
" coucheth "; from the margin it was somewhat thought-
lessly put into the text by a later copyist.   The words will
then run : " . . . But if thou doest not well (there is) one
that coucheth at the door."   Who coucheth at the door ?
Why does he couch there ?   And what door does he couch
at ?   And what has it to do with the context ?   It is well
known that Assyro-Babylonian demonology had a considerable influence on Jewish belief in demons.   Now, the Babylonians and Assyrians had a horrible demon called *Rabitzu*;
he is mentioned, e.g. on a magical text translated in Jastrow's
Die Religion Babyloniens und Assyriens, ii. 765 (1192).
He is called the lord of the underworld,[3] and, moreover, a
whole class of demons is called after him.[4]   The name comes
from a root meaning " to lurk " or " couch."   *Rabitzu* is
thus a proper name, and means the " lurker " or " coucher."
In the text which we are considering the Hebrew word for
" one coucheth " is *Robetz*, the consonants of which correspond with the Assyrian *Rabitzu*; and therefore *Robetz*,

[1] *Genesis*, p. 39 (1901).   [2] *Die bösen Geister des A.T.*, p. 9 (1904).
[3] Duhm, *ibid.*   [4] Lenormant, *La magie* . . ., pp. 24, 47.

like the Assyrian equivalent, should be regarded as a proper name, and the text should read : " . . . But if thou doest not well *Robetz* is at the door " ! It is not for a moment suggested that that was the original form of the text, but only that it was the form of some copyist's emendation. The Babylonians believed that *Robetz* lurked at the threshold of people's dwellings, and was ready to spring on a man if he came out unwarily ; the Hebrew writer adapted this belief, and spiritualized it by identifying *Robetz* with Sin ; so that he interpreted this passage as meaning that God said to Cain, " If thou does not well, remember, *Robetz* is at the door " ; or, in other words, if a man is inclined to do what is wrong, there is an evil demon always lurking at hand to aid and further him in his evil intentions.

Robetz is thus an animal in that he lurks or couches as animals do, but he approximates to the anthropomorphic form of demon in other respects.

This brings us, then, to anthropomorphic demons proper.

(b) ANTHROPOMORPHIC DEMONS

There are not many references to these in the Old Testament, but when considered in the light of Babylonian parallels, they will be found to be significant.

(i) First we have *Lilith*. In Isa. xxxiv. 11–15, where the prophet speaks of the devastation of Edom, he says, in ver. 14 : " And the wild beasts of the desert (*Ziyyim*) shall encounter the wolves ('*Iyyim*), and the *sa'ir* (" he-goat ") shall meet his fellows ; there, in truth, shall *Lilith* repose, and shall find a resting place for herself." The R.V. translates *Lilith* by " night-monster," but it is a proper name. The fact that *Lilith*, represented now as a female demon, and now as a male one, was well-known among the Assyrians supports the belief that *Lilith* played a part in Hebrew Demonology in pre-Exilic times. The Assyrian beliefs regarding this demon appear in later Babylonian belief in a greatly developed form, for here we have a demon-triad *Lilu*, *Lilitu*, and *Ardat Lili*—the male, the female, and the handmaid ; the Old Testament *Lilith* would correspond to the second of these, *Lilitu*. They are spoken of as flying, so that they were conceived as of having wings, as in later times.

The way in which *Lilith* is mentioned in the Isaiah passage, without explanation, shows that the name was familiar. According to later Jewish teaching, which may well, however, have been handed down for centuries pre-

viously, *Lilith* was a night-hag, and got her name from
Layelah, "night." The etymology was false, but *Lilith*
was, nevertheless, the night-demon *par excellence*. There
is an evident reference to this demon, though her name is not
mentioned, in Ps. xci. 5 : "Thou shalt not be afraid because
of the night-terror nor because of the arrow that flieth by
day." In the *Midrash* to the Psalms (*Midr. Tehillim*), the
comment on this verse says : "There is a harmful spirit
that flies like a bird and shoots like an arrow "; while it is a
mistake to suppose, as the Rabbi does, that only one demon
is spoken of in this verse, he is no doubt right in picturing
Lilith as one who flies, for the Jewish conception regarding
this demon is likely to have corresponded with the Babylonian, which, as we have seen, also described her as flying at
nights. In this later Jewish belief, which is, however, largely
traditional, *Lilith* appears as the head of one of the three
great classes into which developed Jewish Demonology
divided the demons, viz. the *Lilin*, who take their name from
her. They are described as of human form, and have wings;
they are all females, and children are their chief victims.
Lilith herself is conceived of as a beautiful woman, with
long flowing hair; it is at nights that she seeks her prey.
She is dangerous to men because of her beauty; but she does
not appear to molest women.[1]

(ii) A female demon of a different character is *'Aluqah*,
mentioned in Prov. xxx. 15. It is true that, according to
many commentators, this is from one of the latest portions
of the book of *Proverbs*, belonging to the third century B.C.,
but even if this should be the case, the fact that *'Aluqah* is
mentioned without explanation shows that the name was
familiar, and therefore traditional. But more significant
is the further fact that *'Aluqah* is only the Hebrew form of the
demon *'Aluq*, who figures in ancient heathen Arabian
demonology;[2] she was a flesh-devouring ghoul, according to

---

[1] It may be of interest to point out, in passing, that this form of the
Lilith-myth was borrowed and adapted (unless all the forms of the myth go
back to a common ancestor) in a variety of ways in the Middle Ages. It is,
conceivably, the source of the "Frau Holde" legend, the beautiful woman
who dwelt in a great mountain at the entrance to which she appeared on
moonlight nights; and woe to the luckless man who caught sight of her
and became fascinated by her beauty, for, being lured by her into her mountain home, he was never seen to issue forth again. One form of the Tannhäuser legend, as also that of Peer Gynt, possibly have a similar origin; and
the same may be true of the Loreley story, however much it may have been
transformed by Teutonic poetical genius.

[2] Wellhausen, *op. cit.*, pp. 149 ff.

the early Arabs. Her mention here is a good illustration of the fact that the occurrence of the name of a demon in a late passage (if this one is a late passage) does not necessarily mean that the belief in the demon is late. Ingrained ideas often persist through untold numbers of generations, and their non-appearance in earlier writings does not necessarily imply that they were not in existence previously. In this particular case we fortunately have external evidence to show that the demon 'Aluqah had long been believed in. That this demon was not sexless, and that she had a proper name, is, of course, a development; but that only proves that something corresponding to her existed previously. This may be further illustrated by the mention of some other demons which are referred to in the Old Testament.

(iii) In Ps. xci. 5, 6, it is said to him who trusts in Yahweh, that he need not fear the " night-terror," nor the " arrow that flies in the daytime," nor the " pestilence that goes about in the dark," nor the " destruction that wastes at noonday." Here are four things to which action is imputed; and, at the first glance, one might well argue that they are all merely metaphorical expressions. But in the light of comparative demonology this is extremely improbable. Moreover, on general grounds, there would be more point in the passage if the writer had in mind certain harmful beings, belief in whose existence was universal, but whose power for harm was curtailed when the help of God was sought against them. That this is the case in this passage is very likely.

The first is the " night-terror "; the very expression suggests a spiritual power, for what human power would be likely to be so described ? Mention has already been made of Lilith, the night-hag, who would be very appropriately described as the " night-terror," for so she was regarded; it seems therefore highly probable that Lilith is referred to here. That her name is not expressed is easily understood; for according to antique ideas the mention of the name of a demon was dangerous because it might result in bringing its bearer near.[1]

Then we have the " arrow that flies in the day-time." That this cannot refer to an arrow shot by a man is evident, for in that case it would not be spoken of as something of general occurrence, as is here implied. What is meant is the scorching ray of the sun, the result of which, sun-stroke, headache, or faintness, was believed to be due to a demon,

---

[1] This would not necessarily apply to all demons.

like all sickness. But what especially compels the conviction that demons are here referred to is the " pestilence that goes about in the dark " and the " destruction that wastes at midday." As to the first of these, we have an instructive parallel in the Babylonian pest-demon, *Namtar*; he is often spoken of as " violent *Namtar*," and he is said to come among men as the pest-bringing envoy from the realms of the dead like a " raging wind." His action is described in a Babylonian magical text in this way : " Wicked *Namtar*, who scorches the land like fire, who approaches a man like Ashakku (another Babylonian demon), who rages through the wilderness like a storm-wind, who pounces upon a man like a robber, who plagues a man like the pestilence, who has no hands, no feet, who goes about at night. . . ." [1]

Regarding the second, the word for " destruction " is *Qeteb*; if this was not a proper name when this psalm was written, it became so later (see below). But that a demon is referred to may be gathered for several reasons : the word occurs in Deut. xxxii. 24, where the context clearly refers to the activity of demons (see also Isa. xxviii. 2); it occurs also in Hos. xiii. 14—an instructive passage because *Qeteb* is brought into connexion with *She'ol*, the underworld; and in Babylonian demonology there is a parallel to this demon, namely Nergal, who is, on the one hand, "ruler of the great abode" of the dead and, on the other, the blazing midday sun [2] (it is in this latter that he offers a parallel); and lastly, the Septuagint rendering of " that wastes at noon-day " is : " the midday demon." [3] It may be added that in Rabbinical literature *Qeteb* is used as the proper name of a demon. In the *Midrash* on the Psalms the comment on the word *Qeteb* is : " Our Rabbis said, 'It is a demon (*shed*).' . . . Rabbi Huna, speaking in the name of Rabbi Jose, said, 'The poisonous *Qeteb* is covered with scales and with hair, and he sees only out of one eye, the other one is in the middle of his heart.' . . ."

It would seem therefore that we have in Ps. xci. 5, 6, four demons referred to, all of which were perfectly familiar to readers; and though this psalm is an admittedly late one, it has preserved traces of early belief in this particular.

---

[1] O. Weber, " Dämonenbeschwörung bei den Babyloniern und Assyrern," in *Der Alte Orient*, VII. iv. 16 (1906); Jastrow, *op. cit.*, i. 287, 385.

[2] Jastrow, *op. cit.*, i. 65, 66.

[3] It is also probable that the Hebrew word for " that wasteth " (*yashod*) is intended to be a word-play on *shed* (" demon ") at the back of the writer's mind.

(iv) A few other references, indirect or implied, may be added. In Gen. xiv. 3 mention is made of "the vale of Siddim"; the place is unknown, and the renderings of the Versions show that the translators were mystified; hence most commentators make the emendation, involving only a change in vowel-points, *Shedim*, "demons," and read "the demon-valley." If this emendation is correct, which is highly probable, we have here reference to a spot which, for what reason is not known, was believed to be the resort of demons.

(v) As is well known, amulets were originally worn in order to ward off the attacks of evil spirits, and there are a number of passages in the Old Testament in which, therefore, the mention of an amulet implies the belief in demons. Thus, in Gen. xxxv. 4, the ear-rings worn by Jacob's followers are, like the strange gods, hidden away as something unlawful; this can only have been done because the rings were regarded as superstitious objects. The point of view is a later one, but witnesses to the belief in demons.

Again, the "fringes," spoken of in Num. xv. 38, were knotted cords, and all folklorists know that knots were protective amulets against all kinds of evils; [1] in the first instance these "fringes" were worn as a protection against evil spirits. For further examples see Gen. xxxviii. 18, 25; Exod. xxviii. 33; Deut. xxii. 12; Judges viii. 24; Isa. iii. 20 ff. In course of time these protective amulets became, probably enough, ornaments pure and simple.

Most of the passages which have here been referred to belong to the later periods of Israelite history; but this only shows how persistent ingrained superstitions are; there can be no kind of doubt that belief in demons is an offshoot from Animism, and belongs to the very early beginnings of Hebrew belief.

[1] See Frazer, *G. B.*, "Taboo and the Perils of the Soul," pp. 306 ff. (1911); cp. also Deut. xviii. 11, where the expression *chober cheber* means, in all probability, "he who ties a (magic) knot."

PART II
ISRAELITE RELIGION

CHAPTER XI

NOMADIC RELIGION : THE PRE-MOSAIC AGE

1. INTRODUCTORY

SINCE in the Old Testament there are various beliefs and practices to be observed which were handed down from the time when the ancestors of the Hebrews were nomads, it will be necessary to deal shortly with these. It stands to reason that the form of these beliefs and practices will have undergone considerable modification in the course of their history, and that therefore their original form will have been somewhat different from that in which they appear in the Old Testament.

The history of Israel begins with Moses. He was the originator alike of her national unity and of her religion, and it is not surprising that later generations attributed to him the whole fabric of her social and ecclesiastical organization. Before his time, we find a group of tribes, possibly recognizing their common kinship, but with little else to hold them together. After him, though we should be wrong if we assumed that the national growth was complete, there was at least a nucleus round which other elements could gather, and a continuity of national life which enables us to speak of a real history. No doubt centuries passed before the various sections of which the whole was ultimately composed were fashioned into a single entity, but with Moses began the process which ended in the appearance of a race which hitherto no hostility or persecution had robbed of its sense of nationality or of its faith—the most durable people in human history.

Tradition stated that the ancestors of Israel were nomads, and this stage in the social order was not passed till after the death of Moses—even then, as we shall have occasion to insist, there were sections of the people who did not rise to the agricultural and civic plane. Since in the Old Testament there are various beliefs and practices to be observed which were handed down from this early, pre-Mosaic, time, it will

125

be necessary to deal shortly with these. We should, if possible, form some idea of the objects worshipped by the nomad ancestors of Israel, difficult as it may be to reach any sure conclusions on this head. We should also glance at certain features of the religious life of Israel in later days, which seem to have their roots in these early times. It stands to reason that some of these beliefs and practices will have undergone considerable modification in the course of their history, and that, therefore, their original form will have been somewhat different from that in which they appear in the Old Testament.

2. Objects of Worship

One element in the traditions of Israel (J) speaks as though Yahweh were known to the Patriarchs from Abraham onwards, and that it was in pursuance of His command that the original migration from Mesopotamia was undertaken. But in Exod. vi. 3, while Yahweh, the God who called Moses, is identified with the deity of the Patriarchs, it is expressly stated that the name of Yahweh had not been known to them. Further, in Exod. iii. 15 the communication of the name Yahweh seems to be a complete novelty to Moses. There is, also, other evidence to be drawn from the Old Testament which suggests that Moses was the first to recognize in Yahweh the true national God in whom the whole people might be united and redeemed.

Thus the narrative of Gen. xxxv. tells us in v. 2 that, as Jacob approached the site of Bethel (whose sanctuary probably claimed him as its founder), he "said unto his household, and to all that were with him, Put away the strange gods that are among you." And in v. 4 we read that "they gave Jacob all the strange gods . . . and Jacob hid them under the oak which was by Shechem." Whether this incident is rightly connected with Jacob or not, it is clear that the writer believed that the religion of Israel's ancestors, at one stage, and in some quarters, included a number of deities. Of the various objects of worship, however, we hear nothing, unless we are to include the *Teraphim* stolen by Rachel from her father.[1] We are thus forced back on conjecture, and must rely on such evidence as can be supplied from comparative religion and from philology. Now, it is an interesting fact that the names of some of the Israelite tribes appear elsewhere as those of

[1] Gen. xxxi. 19, 30, 35.

gods. Gad is a well-known Semitic deity, a god of luck, identified in Mesopotamia with the planet Jupiter. Asher may well be a slight modification of the name of the great god of northern Mesopotamia, Ashur, after whom a city and a people were named. Two place-names which occur on an inscription of Thothmes III (circa 1500 B.C.) have been read as Jacob-el [1] and Joseph-el (though the identification, especially in the second case, has been disputed), forms which imply that the first element in each is the name of a god. A deity named Laban was known in Cappadocia, and in the Ras Shamra tablets we meet with a god bearing the name of Terah, identical with that of Abraham's father. Further, the common word for " god " in Hebrew is 'Elohim, a plural form of which the singular, 'Eloah, appears only in later parts of the Hebrew Bible. It is commonly explained as a "plural of majesty," but in 1 Sam. xxviii. 13 we seem to have a glimpse of its primitive meaning. Here the "medium" consulted by Saul says "I see a god (R.V. margin " Or gods " [Hebrew 'Elohim]) coming up out of the earth, and the apparition is identified as the ghost of Samuel. This suggests that the word was practically equivalent to the Latin Manes—likewise an animistic plural with no singular—and was applied to the spirits of the dead worshipped by so many primitive peoples.[2] Such evidence as is available, then, suggests that, in pre-Mosaic days, some, at least, of the ancestors of Israel worshipped the individuals from whom the tribes derived their names. If that be so, then it is clear that, as a result of the work of Moses, they sank back to the human level, and resumed their original status as the eponymous ancestors of the Israelite tribes.

At the same time, many other objects of worship were recognized, each in his own place, and the records indicate that such beings as the river-spirit of Peniel, the stone-spirit of Bethel (Bethel itself later became the name of a god), the well-spirit of Beer-lahai-roi, and many another, were venerated at the spots where they had manifested their presence. This ritual, such as it was, probably varied, each tribal and local " demon " demanding a separate formula and ceremonial. At the same time, it seems likely that there were certain modes of worship and certain religious customs which might be regarded as common to all the tribes, though

---

[1] Appears also as the name of one of the " Hyksos " (Semitic) kings of Egypt, cf. C. A. H , i 313.

[2] The word seems to be used in the same sense in Isa. viii. 19.

especially characteristic of none, and we must now turn to the more prominent of these.

3. New-Moon Festivals

Lunar festivals were common to all the peoples of antiquity, but they were more especially observed among the Semites; so far as these latter are concerned the earliest form of worship of the Moon is to be sought among the ancient nomadic Arabs. For peoples who had reached an agricultural stage of culture the sun necessarily played the leading *rôle*; but not so for those who were still in the nomadic stage. Owners of flocks and herds, who wandered over the measureless tracts of steppe-land, moved mostly by night because of the heat during the day; to them, therefore, the moon was of paramount importance; [1] and since all the Semites were at one time nomads, the moon was originally their chief deity. Further, as a god, whenever the moon first appeared in the skies (i.e. at every " new-moon ") its appearance was hailed with joyful shouts; it is significant that the Arabic word *hilal* means both " new-moon " and " festal shout." There are numerous indications pointing to the fact that from the earliest times the appearance of the new moon was celebrated as a great festival in Arabia,[2] the reason obviously being the desire to do honour to the god on his reappearance. But the most important of all the new-moon festivals was that which fell in the month *Ragab*, equivalent to the Hebrew month *'Abib*, for this was the time when the ancient Arabs celebrated the Spring festival after the casting of their young among the flocks and herds.[3]

On the analogy of the ancient Arabs, therefore, there is every reason to believe that the new-moon feasts, and the sacrifices offered on these occasions, among the Hebrews go back to nomadic times. They are frequently mentioned in the Old Testament, but it is significant that the object of their celebration is never hinted at; they are holy days and,

---

[1] Hommel, *Der Gottesdienst der alten Araber und die israelitische Ueberlieferung*, pp. 8, 9 (1901); Weber, *Arabien vor dem Islam*, in *Der alte Orient, dritter Jahrgang*, p. 19 (1902). Nielsen, *Die alte arabische Mond-religion*, pp. 33, 34 (1904); *Handbuch*, i. 198, 213 ff.

[2] Meinhold, *Sabbat und Woche im Alten Testament* (1905); Nielsen, *Handbuch*, pp. 49, 50.

[3] Further details are given by Wellhausen, *op. cit.*, Nielsen, *Mondreligion*, p. 92. Robertson Smith (*Rel. Sem.*, p. 406) says : " In pastoral Arabia domestic cattle habitually yean in the brief season of the spring pasture, and this would serve to fix an annual season of sacrifice." See also pp. 641 f.

like the Sabbath, days of rest (Amos viii. 4, 5), not because work was forbidden on them, however, but because they were days of worship, to which they were devoted. It is note-worthy that these festivals are not mentioned in the Book of the Covenant nor in the Deuteronomic law, doubtless on account of their connexion with lunar worship; but the observance of them was too ingrained to be eradicated, and they continued down to Christian times (see Col. ii. 16).

4. The Passover Festival

The history of the development of this feast, as described in the Old Testament and later Jewish writings, presents us with various features which do not belong to its original form. After tracing this history back and denuding the celebration of the feast of those parts which can be proved to be later developments or modifications,[1] we are able to indicate those elements which, even though they may not all have belonged to the feast as originally celebrated,[2] can with certitude be stated to have been its essential features at the period when it formed one, and probably the most important, of the religious observances of the Hebrews in the nomadic stage. These features are as follows :

(1) *The sacrifice of a victim.* This was taken from the flocks or herds, i.e. either a sheep, or a goat, or one of the larger animals; even as late as the time of the Deuteronomic legislation the choice is left open (Deut. xvi. 2). The age of the victim is not mentioned before the time of the Priestly Code (Exod. xii. 5), where it is said that it must be " of the first year "; this, however, was an extension of the original custom, as we shall see. The victim was eaten at a *sacrificial meal*, which was held in the dwellings of the various wor-shippers; it had to be entirely consumed before the morning, since—

(2) It was a *night celebration*, which took place between sunset and sunrise; the earliest laws do not define the time more closely than this, but it was clearly after darkness had set in.

The night on which the celebration took place was that of the *full moon of the month nearest the Spring Equinox.*[3] It is true, the earliest direct evidence of this is in Deut. xvi. 1 :

---

[1] The subject is admirably dealt with by Benzinger in the *Encycl. Bibl.*, iii. 3593–3600; and especially by Buchanan Gray, *Sacrifice in the Old Testament*, pp. 337–382 (1925); (see also Driver, *Deuteronomy*, pp. 190–193 (1902)).

[2] Its real origin must lie far back in prehistoric times.

[3] Nielsen, *Handbuch*, i. 244.

K

" Observe the month of Abib (the later name is Nisan, see Neh. ii. 1, equivalent to the month of April), and keep the Passover unto Yahweh thy God "; but in so ancient and important a feast as this it may rightly be assumed that the Deuteronomic law prescribed traditional use; there is nothing in the whole of the Old Testament that points to any other time.

(3) *The blood of the victim* was smeared on the outside of the dwelling-places of the worshippers.

Those are the outstanding features of this feast as it appears after the demonstrably later accretions have been eliminated. We have also to remember that the explanations as to the origin and meaning of the Passover given in the Old Testament are of a late date, when its significance had either been forgotten or, if known, had to be reinterpreted for reasons which are fully comprehensible. Moreover, it must be noted that these explanations, when examined, are really no explanations; thus, Deut. xvi. 1 explains it by saying that " in the month Abib Yahweh thy God brought thee forth out of Egypt by night "; but the mention of which night of the month it was on which this happened is studiously avoided in the whole section, vers. 1–8; and in ver. 2 : " Thou shalt sacrifice *Pesach* [there is no article in the Hebrew] [1] . . . of the flock and the herd," is distinctly ambiguous; it does not explain why a sacrifice should be offered; and when, further, it is said in reference to the blood on the lintel that " Yahweh will pass over the door, and will not suffer the destroyer to come in unto your houses to smite you " (Exod. xii. 23), it does not explain who the destroyer was, nor yet why he should want to smite the people.

What the feast originally was, and what its object was, and what the blood-smearing on the lintel meant are all obvious to the folk-lorist and to the student of primitive Semitic religion, but it may be well to say something in explanation of them here.

The first thing to note is the time of the year at which this festival was celebrated : it was, as already pointed out, in what we call the month of April, i.e. in the spring; so that it was a *Spring Festival*. As is well known, it was a world-wide custom among uncultured and semi-cultured peoples to offer the firstlings of the flocks and herds, later the first-

---

[1] For the contention that the name of the feast " Pesach " (Passover) was derived from the sacred dance performed during its celebration, see the present writer's *The Sacred Dance*, pp. 50 f.

fruits of the produce of the soil, to the deity, in order to ensure the increase of these during the coming year.[1] In the nomadic stage it was the increase of the flocks and herds which was of paramount importance ; but the revival of the vegetation in the steppe-lands, through which the nomads roamed with their flocks and herds, was also a matter of real importance.   Their main concern, however, would naturally be the former ; hence the offering to the fertility-deity the firstlings of the flocks and herds.[2] In the Old Testament accounts only one victim is mentioned ; this, it may safely be affirmed, was not the original custom ; *each* head of a family or more properly of a clan, would have made his offering.   And therefore it may be surmised that the offering was made either before each tent of a nomad encampment, or before the chief tent of a group belonging to a clan.[3]

Then as to the victim.   In Exod. xii. 9 and 46 there are two prohibitions in regard to it : " Eat not of it raw, nor sodden at all with water, but roast it with fire " ; and : " Neither shall ye break a bone thereof."   These prohibitions would have no force unless intended to put an end to customs still in vogue.   They can only mean therefore that originally the victim was eaten raw,[4] and the bones pounded up and also consumed ; and this, indeed, is precisely what one would expect to have been the case, because, according to early Semitic belief, the life resided in the blood [5] and in the bones,[6] and the object of the sacrificial meal at which the victim was eaten was to absorb the divine life conceived to be present in the sacred victim, and thus to become united with the deity.   This in no way detracts from the primary object of the feast.   Further, the command in Deut. xvi. 4 : " Neither shall any of the flesh which thou sacrificest the first day at even, remain all night until the morning," becomes quite intelligible when the sacred character of the moon, as pointed out above, is remembered ; the sacred feast takes place in the presence of the deity, and must be concluded before he retires.

That the fourteenth day of the month, i.e. full-moon day,

---

[1] For many illustrations see Frazer, *G. B.*, " The Dying God," pp. 246–285 (1911).

[2] For the Moon as a fertility-god, see Nielsen, *Handbuch*, i. 213 ff.

[3] The flocks and herds were the common property of the clan.

[4] This was also done in much later times ; see 1 Sam. xiv. 32 ; Ezek. xxxiii. 25 ; Lev. xix. 26 ; Isa. lxv. 4, lxvi. 3 ; Zech. ix. 7.

[5] See, e.g., Lev. xvii. 11, 14.

[6] See, e.g., Isa. lxvi. 14 ; Ecclus. xlvi. 11, 12, xlix. 10.

was that on which the festival was celebrated was obviously because it was then that the deity showed himself in his full glory.

A more difficult question arises when we seek the meaning of the blood ritual. A variety of explanations have been offered,[1] but it is impossible to deal with these here. We believe the reason of the blood-smearing to have been similar to that for which the Jews in later days fixed on their door-posts what is now called the *Mezuzah*, i.e. a small tube made of wood, metal, or glass, in which is rolled up a piece of parchment containing the *Shema'* (Deut. vi. 4–9 and xi. 13–21); the custom is at least pre-Christian; it is referred to by Josephus (*Antiq.* IV. viii. 13); the Rabbis in Talmudic times attributed to it a protective power against demons, and this doubtless was the original purpose of it. The Mohammedans have a similar custom of inscribing verses from the Qoran on their doors and at the entrances to their houses, with a like object. This seems likely to have been the reason for smearing the blood of the sacred victim on the tents of nomads, for not only were the hours of darkness always believed to be the time when evil spirits were particularly active, but on this special occasion there were reasons for more pronounced virulence than usual on their part.[2] With this view Buchanan Gray, among others, agrees. He says: "What the ancient Hebrews endeavoured to repel from their houses were spirits, demons of plague, or sickness and the like, much as the modern Bedawy or Syrian peasant." [3]

5. FURTHER FESTIVALS AND SACRIFICES

Besides the Moon festivals and the Passover festival with the sacrificial celebrations proper to all festivals, there may well have been other occasions on which sacrifices were offered, though it must be confessed that the evidence for these is largely inferential. Lods believes that among the nomad Hebrews there must have been, " even if in a somewhat barbarous and elementary form, the greater part of the rites which were later codified in the levitical law." [4] If a little over-stated, there is perhaps some truth in this, though the supposed ancient Arab analogies are not always

[1] Curtiss, *Primitive Semitic Religion To-day*, pp. 226 f. (1902); Trumbull, *The Threshold Covenant*, pp. 203 ff. (1906); Frazer, *G. B.* "The Dying God," pp. 174 ff. (1911).
[2] See Frazer, *G. B.*, "The Scapegoat," esp. chapters ii. and iv. (1913), and "The Dying God," pp. 246–271.
[3] *Op. cit.*, p. 364.   [4] *Op. cit.*, p. 277.

convincing. The sacrifice accompanied by a meal (*Zebach*), as we have seen in the case of the Passover, was certainly in vogue; so, too, covenant sacrifices; and the evidence of a prototype of the *Kalil*, the whole burnt-sacrifice, is supported by the Ras Shamra tablets; [1] but that there was anything in the shape of atoning sacrifices is very improbable. So that when Lods says that " it is evident that nearly all the forms of sacrifice which we find practised by the Israelites of the historical period, must have existed, at least in germ, among the pre-Mosaic Hebrews," the statement can be accepted only with an emphasis on the words " in germ."

One other festival, with its sacrificial element, belonging to the nomad period, may be mentioned before we come to deal with the Sabbaths; this is the feast of sheep-shearing.

The term is more strictly " Flock-shearing "; and the Hebrew word for " flock " (*zon*) includes goats as well as sheep. Moreover, the Hebrew word for " wool " (*zemer*) is used of the wool of both sheep and goats. The *shearing* of animals of the flock belongs to agricultural times; the earlier custom was to pluck off the wool with the hands.

Although this feast is referred to only three times in the Old Testament (Gen. xxxviii. 12, 13; 1 Sam. xxv. 2 ff., 36; 2 Sam. xiii. 23, 24), it must obviously have been celebrated at regular intervals. There can be no doubt that it went back originally to nomadic times, for the clothing of nomads was made of the wool of sheep and goats as well as from their skins. Like all the ancient feasts, it was a joyful time, the technical term *yom tob*, " a good day," is applied to it in 1 Sam. xxv. 8, and that much eating and drinking took place is seen from ver. 36. But, none the less, it was a religious feast. This will be clear when it is remembered that the deity was looked to for the increase of the flocks, so that the wool would also be regarded as his gift; this was so in later days too (see Hos. ii. 5 [7 in Hebrew]).

The details of this feast which have come down to us are very scanty; no mention is made of any sacrifice, but it is difficult to believe that any feast among the ancient Semites lacked this. The main thing, however, from our present point of view, is that this feast belonged originally to nomadic times, and was brought from their nomad life by the Hebrews into Canaan.

[1] Wellhausen, *op. cit.*, p. 121, gives an isolated piece of evidence, and see Jack, *The Ras Shamra Tablets*, p. 30 (1935).

6. The Sabbaths

As a preliminary it is interesting to note the various reasons given in the Old Testament as to why the Sabbath was to be observed; taking the several legal codes in the chronological order generally accepted, this is what we find :

In the *Book of the Covenant* it is in order that the beasts may rest and that slaves and strangers may be refreshed; so far as the Israelites in general are concerned, it is only said that they are to " keep Sabbath "; there is no command given to them to rest (Exod. xxiii. 12).

In the code of *J*, no reason is given for its observance, nor is there any command to rest; it is only commanded that " thou shalt keep Sabbath," with special reference to ploughing and harvest time (Exod. xxxiv. 21).

In *E* it is because God rested on the Sabbath (Exod. xx. 8 ff.).

In *D* it is because God brought the people out of the land of Egypt, i.e. it was to be observed in memory of that event (Deut. v. 12–15).

In the " Code of Holiness " (Lev. xvii.–xxvi.), belonging to a time soon after D, no reason is given; there is only the command to keep the Sabbath and to refrain from work (Lev. xxiii. 3; cp. xix. 30).

In *P* it is because it is a sign between Yahweh and His people (Exod. xxxi. 12–17).

So much for the mention of the Sabbath in the legal codes.

In the earliest passage—that in which the Sabbath is mentioned for the first time—it is seen that the Sabbath, like a new-moon day, was a day on which one could travel on a beast because on that day the beasts rested from their ordinary labour (2 Kings iv. 23).

Three conclusions may be justifiably drawn from these *data* : (1) the real origin of the Sabbath was unknown; (2) it originated, in any case, before the entry into Canaan; its unknown origin suggests this; (3) it was not originally a day of rest from labour.

That the Israelites did not adopt the observance of the Sabbath from the Canaanites seems certain, inasmuch as there is absolutely no trace of its existence among them. Had it ever been an institution among the Canaanites it is hardly likely that it would have died out; but, as Budde has pointed out, Nehemiah had to take proceedings against the Canaanite tradesmen who brought their wares into

Jerusalem on the Sabbath (Neh. xiii. 17-21); clearly they knew nothing about Sabbath observance. Though we have, as he says, little information available as to the *ancient* Canaanites, " yet we have abundance from the contemporary Phœnicians, their kinsmen, over the whole of the Mediterranean coastal area as far as Carthage, Gaul, and Spain, but nowhere is there the slightest trace of the Sabbath; on the contrary, Israel justly feels conscious that no parallel for it is to be found in the whole of her environment." [1]

Further, that the Israelites did *not* get the Sabbath from the Babylonians seems likewise certain for three reasons : (1) the latter observed a five-day, not a seven-day week; [2] (2) with them the Sabbaths were evil days, days of ill-omen, on which it was unlucky to do certain things; (3) there is good reason for believing that among the Babylonians themselves the word *shapattu* (= Sabbath) was a loan-word borrowed from the ancient Arabs. To deal with these points in any detail would involve a good deal of discussion which would take us too far afield. [3]

Mainly on negative grounds, therefore, it may be concluded that the Sabbath did not originate among the Hebrews, and that they borrowed it neither from the Canaanites nor from the Babylonians. Thus we are forced to the conclusion that they brought it with them from their nomadic life. For our present purpose that is sufficient; for with the very complicated and still unsettled question as to the real origin of the Sabbath we cannot concern ourselves here beyond saying that, from the nature of the case, it seems highly probable that it originated among the ancient nomadic Arabs; [4] we say from the nature of the case, because the close connexion between new-moons and Sabbaths, so frequently bracketed together (2 Kings iv. 23; Amos viii. 5; Hos. ii. 11 [13 in Hebrew]; Isa. i. 13, lxvi. 23; Ps. lxxxi. 3 [4 in Hebrew]; Ezek. xlv. 17, xlvi. 1, 3; Neh. x. 33 [34 in Hebrew]; 1 Chron. xxiii. 31; 2 Chron. ii. 4 [3 in Hebrew], viii. 13, xxxi. 3; cp. Ezra iii. 5), shows that the

---

[1] *The Journal of Theological Studies* for Oct. 1928, p. 5.

[2] As S. A. Cook, among others, points out, there were special *taboo* days for the King in Babylonia, on which certain things were forbidden him; these days were " the 7th, 14th, 21st, and 28th day of each month, also the 19th (the 49th from the beginning of the preceding month) " (*op. cit.*, p. 89). But this is a different matter from that of the five-day week.

[3] The subject is dealt with by Budde in his article, already referred to, pp. 6, 7; and more especially by Hommel, *Die altorientalischen Denkmäler und das alte Testament*, pp. 18, 19 (1902), and Nielsen, *op. cit.*, pp. 87 ff. 153 ff.

[4] Nielsen, *Handbuch*, i. 244 ff.

latter was a lunar feast in its origin; and this being so, it would originate among nomads; as we have seen, the moon played the leading *rôle* among them.

So far, then, as religion is concerned—and it is only with this that we are dealing—we have seen that belonging to the religious observances of the Hebrews during the nomadic period, there were the new-moon festivals, the Sabbaths, the feast of Passover, and the feast of sheep-shearing, indissolubly connected with all of which sacrifices were offered; in how far, apart from these sacrifices, sacrificial worship obtained is not altogether easy to determine; that offerings, e.g. those of a private character, were made, apart from those mentioned, may be taken as highly probable; but the lack of sufficient evidence makes it difficult to indicate these with certitude.

Before we come to what is by far the most important element in the nomadic religion of the Hebrews, namely, the beginning of the worship of Yahweh, there are some other institutions belonging to the nomadic stage which were of a quasi-religious character, though at one time, no doubt, wholly religious; these must be briefly dealt with, for they appear in the later history of Israel.

7. OTHER ANCIENT INSTITUTIONS

The rite of *Circumcision* is claimed in the Old Testament as of Hebrew origin, but the accounts of its institution are wholly at variance; one account describes it as having originated with Abraham (Gen. xvii. 1–14, *P*); another points to Joshua as having introduced it (Josh. v. 5 ff.), while the oldest account connects it with Moses (Exod. iv. 25 ff., *J*). The rite was, however, common to most of the Semites (although it was not practised by the Babylonians), as well as to the Egyptians and many other non-Semitic peoples.[1] Interesting is the statement of Herodotus that "the Colchians, Egyptians, and Ethiopians, are the only nations of the world who, from the first, have practised circumcision. For the Phœnicians, and the Syrians in Palestine, acknowledge that they learned the custom from the Egyptians . . . but of the Egyptians and Ethiopians I an unable to say which learned it from the other, for it is evidently a very ancient custom." [2]   It is possible that the

---

[1] Ploss, *Das Kind in Brauch und Sitte der Völker*, i. 342 ff. (1882).
[2] Herodotus, ii. 104.

rite came from Africa to Arabia, and spread among the tribes of the steppe-land.[1] Of its great antiquity there can be no doubt, though as to its original purpose scholars differ; inasmuch as the rite was performed on both males and females, it is possible that it denoted the consecration of the reproductive organs to the deity in order to ensure offspring; in which case it was from its origin a religious rite. Its antiquity is further shown by the fact that the rite was performed with a flint (Exod. iv. 25; Josh. v. 2, 3).

Another institution of immemorial antiquity, and likewise religious in its origin, was that of *Blood-revenge*. " Among the ancient Arabs the tribal bond was conceived of as a bond of kinship, and all the members of a clan or tribe were of one kin with the tribal god, and therefore of his blood; if one member of the tribe were killed, it was an offence not only against all the other members, but also against the god of the tribe; his honour and rights therefore demanded revenge, and it was a sacred duty laid upon every member of the tribe to exact this." " If a man kills one of his own kin he finds no one to take his part. Either he is put to death by his own people or he becomes an outlaw and must take refuge in an alien group. On the other hand, if the slayer and slain are of different kindred groups a blood-feud at once arises, and the slain man may be avenged by any member of his own group or by any member of the group of the slayer. This is the general rule of blood-revenge all over the world, and with certain minor modifications it holds good in Arabia at the present day, in spite of Islam, as it held good in the oldest times of which we have record." [2]

There can be no doubt that among the nomadic Hebrews the unwritten law of blood-revenge held good; and this is borne out by the numerous references to it in the Old Testament (see Gen. iv. 14, 15, 23, 24; Judges viii. 18–21; 2 Sam. xiv. 7, xxi. 1–14, and elsewhere).

Mention must be made next of what is termed the law of *Cherem*, or the " Ban," i.e. " devoted " to the deity, to utter destruction; this, too, was therefore a religious institution, and was doubtless observed as such by the nomadic Hebrews, though originally it may have been magical rather than religious.[3] The *Cherem* was carried out primarily in con-

---

[1] Hölscher, *Geschichte der israelitischen und jüdischen Religion*, p. 25 (1922).
[2] Robertson Smith, *Kinship and Marriage in early Arabia*, pp. 25 f. (1903).
[3] Lods, *op. cit.*, pp. 213, 289.

nexion with war. The enemies of a tribe, or later, of a
nation, were the enemies of the tribal or national god; a
battle was, therefore, fought either by the command of the
god, or at any rate in his name; in the former case he might
demand as a condition of victory that the entire booty should
be devoted to him (*Cherem*); in the latter case, prayer might
be made to him for victory with the promise that everything
should be devoted to him in recognition of his help. An
instance of the former occurs in 1 Sam. xv. 2, 3 : "Thus
saith Yahweh of hosts . . . Now go and smite Amalek
and utterly destroy ('devote') all that they have, and spare
them not; but slay both man and woman, infant and
suckling, ox and sheep, camel and ass"; the latter is
illustrated by Num. xxi. 2, 3 : "And Israel vowed a vow
unto Yahweh, and said, If thou wilt indeed deliver this
people into my hand, then I will utterly destroy ('devote')
their cities. And Yahweh hearkened to the voice of Israel,
and delivered up the Canaanites, and they utterly destroyed
them and their cities, and the name of the place was called
Hormah ('devoted')." A precisely parallel case to the
former is recorded on the Moabite Stone where Mesha, the
king of Moab, says : "Chemosh said to me, Go and take Nebo
from Israel; and I went by night, and assaulted it from day-
break till noon, and I took it, and massacred all the inhabitants, seven thousand men and (boys), and women and
(girls), and slave-girls, because I had vowed to destroy it
utterly ('devote it') in honour of Ashtor-Chemosh." Lods
pointedly remarks that "the effect of *Cherem* is to release
a fatal power. But the blind working of this force, which
may destroy friends as well as foes, suggests that originally
it was not conceived of as personal. The *Cherem*, no doubt,
was at first regarded as a particularly efficacious curse,
which, like the other curses, entered into the people and
things against whom it was directed, and by its own power
brought about their destruction; after the completion of
the seventh magic circle drawn round Jericho—the city
which had been devoted to the *Cherem*—the wall fell of
itself. The deity, who derived no profit from this vow, only
appeared at first when the narrator brought him in, as a
means by which the curse was rendered effectual." [1] For an
illustration of the automatic working of a curse, see Zech. v.
1–4. Hence, as Lods says, "the *Cherem* seems to have been
originally a magical rite, one of the many forms of war-

[1] *Op. cit.*, p. 289; see also Loisy, *La religion d'Israël*, pp. 134 f. (1908).

magic." But among the Israelites the ban was the carrying out of vengeance on Yahweh's enemies (Jer. l. 15). Since all that comes under the ban is Yahweh's property, it is *taboo* for men, and therefore both presumptuous and dangerous for them to touch it, so that it must be destroyed (Deut. vii. 16, Isa. xxxiv. 2, 3, 6; Jer. xlvi. 10, l. 25, Mic. iv. 13). Not to carry out the ban was to sin in the sight of Yahweh (1 Sam. xv. 22 ff.; 1 Kings xx. 42).

In connexion with the ban there occurs the expression " sowing with salt " (Judges ix. 45); the actual term, " ban," is not used, but the context makes it clear that it is a question of the " ban "; there are differences of opinion as to what precisely the expression " sowing with salt " connotes; probably, however, it indicates that the land or city devoted to the ban is to be made arid and waste; and therefore becomes the abode of the demons of the desert (cp. Ps. cvii. 34; Zeph. ii. 9). A mitigated form of the " ban " is commanded in Deut. xx. 14; Josh. xi. 14 (the latter doubtless reflects Deuteronomic influence). Originally the ban was inflicted on enemies of the Israelites only; where it is carried out within Israel it is exceptional (e.g. Deut. xiii. 12–17, Josh. vii. 1 ff.).

One other matter may be briefly referred to, viz. fasting before a battle; in 1 Sam. xiv. 24 Saul says : " Cursed be the man that eateth any food until it be evening, and I be avenged on mine enemies. So none of the people tasted food "; as all war was conceived of as a religious act (cp. the phrase " to sanctify war," Josh. iii. 5, Isa. xxxiv. 5, cp. Deut. ii. 34, Jer. vi. 4, Mic. iii. 5), the purpose of the preliminary fast was meant to be an appeal to Yahweh whereby his sympathy would be aroused, and his help accorded. In this connexion it should also be mentioned that it was customary to sacrifice burnt-offerings before the opening of a campaign (Judges vi. 20, 26, xx. 26; 1 Sam. vii. 9, xiii. 10). But sacrifices were preceded by a fast; " there are very strong reasons for believing that, in the strict Oriental form in which total abstinence from meat and drink is prescribed, fasting is primarily nothing more than a preparation for the sacramental eating of holy flesh." [1] Two distinct ideas thus come into consideration here; our *data* are, however, insufficient to indicate whether the primary idea of the fast was to evoke Yahweh's sympathy or to fulfil the obligation of the pre-sacrificial fast. Nevertheless, in either case, war was preceded by fasting.

[1] Robertson Smith, *Rel. Sem.*, p. 434.

CHAPTER XII

NOMADIC RELIGION: THE BEGINNING OF THE WORSHIP OF YAHWEH

To the nomadic religion of the Hebrews belongs, in their beginnings, the knowledge and acceptation of Yahweh, through Moses, as the God of Israel.

We are not concerned here with the work of Moses as the founder of the religion of Yahweh among the Hebrews; nor yet with the religious teaching of Moses and his presentation to the people of Him whom they ultimately came to recognize as the one and only God; this will all be dealt with in subsequent chapters. Our object at present is to point to two outstanding events which, under God, were the immediate causes of the recognition and acceptation of Yahweh by the Hebrew people themselves, after the revelation accorded to Moses. This belongs, therefore, if not to the actual background of Hebrew religion, at least to the threshold of that faith.

The great prophets insisted again and again on the truth that Yahweh was the God of Nature; [1] they also constantly emphasized the truth that God was "from everlasting." [2] On the very threshold of their entry into the wilderness and of their taking up the nomad life once more, the Hebrews had such a signal illustration of the truth that Yahweh was the God of Nature that it never lost its hold on them, however much other currents of religious belief may have swept them from the main stream of true faith. They also received such a striking illustration of the further truth that in every age Yahweh was revealing Himself to men in accordance with their capacity of apprehension, that through the long years of their history which followed, the echo of how this truth was exemplified at this early period resounded again and again in the records of the nation.

The two outstanding events (more strictly, the two series of events) with which we are about to deal belong closely

[1] See p. 225.   [2] See, e.g., Hab. i. 12.

together, but they can be treated separately. For most of what follows we are indebted to two notable Old Testament scholars. Regarding the first event we make our acknowledgements to the late Prof. Gressmann; [1] the interpretation which he was the first to offer of what is often called " the passage of the Red Sea," with its accompanying events, may in some respects be open to criticism, since it may not always be possible to reconcile it with the conflicting statements found in the different sources containing the records; but there is so much in what he says which conforms to the probabilities of the case, and which appeals to common sense, that his interpretation of the events well deserves consideration. In some details we have been led to make modifications, and in some respects we have been able to confirm his view independently; but for the main thesis we have to express our indebtedness to him.

Regarding the other event, which deals with the existence of the worship of Yahweh before Moses established it as the religion of the Hebrews, we are wholly indebted to Prof. Budde.[2]

1. THE EXODUS FROM EGYPT, AND THE SUBSEQUENT EVENTS

In Exod. xiii. 18, it is recorded : " And it came to pass, when Pharaoh had let the people go, that God led them not by the way of the land of the Philistines, although that was near; but God said, Lest peradventure the people repent when they see war, and they return to Egypt; but God led the people about, by the way of the wilderness by the Red Sea; and the children of Israel went up armed out of the land of Egypt." The passage is instructive from several points of view. It belongs to the " Elohist " document— that is recognized by all critics; and this means that a tradition, oral or written, but more probably the latter, was used by a compiler in the middle of the eighth century B.C. in writing the history of his people. That he was really utilizing ancient material will be evident from the following considerations : In going from Goshen to Palestine there are two available routes; one runs north-east along the coast through what in the compiler's time was the land

---

[1] *Mose und seine Zeit*, pp. 108–121 (1913); there is, unfortunately, no English translation of this work.
[2] *Die Religion des Volkes Israel bis zur Verbannung*, pp. 9–31 (1900); an English translation, published in New York, forms vol. iv. of the *American Lectures on the History of Religions*.

of the Philistines—that was the direct and obvious route to take; the other led south-east through the desert, via Akaba, and then almost due north—a very roundabout way, and quite unnecessary unless there were special reasons for it. Now, in the source used by our compiler (as will be obvious in a moment) it is simply stated that the Israelites went by the longer route, without giving the reason for this, which we know, however, from another source. The compiler of this Elohistic document therefore added what he believed must have been the reason, and from his point of view it would have been a sufficiently strong reason—namely, the fear on the part of the Israelites that they would be attacked by the Philistines. But the fact is that at the time of the exodus from Egypt and for a considerable period of time after, the Philistines were not yet in possession of the land which they conquered later, and in which they settled down.[1] The passage under consideration therefore offers a good illustration, many of which are to be found in the Old Testament, of a genuinely ancient historical detail being expanded for the purpose of explanation by a later compiler. The explanation was thoroughly *bona fide*, but nevertheless a mistaken one.

The Israelites, then, took the south-eastern route, not the north-eastern one; and they did this for the simple reason that Palestine was not their objective. The most reliable sources[2] for the history immediately following the exodus, discrepant though they are in some particulars, make it clear that the objective of the Israelites on leaving Egypt was not Palestine, but Kadesh; but for special reasons they made a stay first at Mount Sinai, involving a journey still farther south-eastwards. Where Mount Sinai lay will be considered presently; it is necessary first to say a word about the position of the " Red Sea " (as it is called in the English Version), mentioned in the passage referred to above.

The fact must be recognized that there is no authority for bringing the Red Sea into the narrative at all if by the Red Sea is meant what it means nowadays. The Old Testament speaks of the *Yam-Suph* as the waters in which the Egyptians were overwhelmed; that means either the " Reed Sea," or

---

[1] The Philistine invasion did not take place until about 1194 B.C.; for the evidence see H. R. Hall in the *Cambr. Anc. Hist.*, ii. pp. 283 ff. (1924).
[2] JE : Num. xx. 1, xiii. 26; cp. xxxii. 8 ff., xiv. 33; also Judges xi. 16.
D : Deut. ii. 4.
P : Num. xx. 1a–13, 22, xxvii. 14; Deut. xxxii. 51.

perhaps more correctly, the " Sea of Weeds " ; [1] and in the Old Testament we are told quite distinctly where this lay : in 1 Kings ix. 26, for example, it says : " And king Solomon made a navy of ships in Ezion-geber, which is beside Elath, on the shore of the *Yam-Suph*, in the land of Edom." Elath lay at the extreme northern part, on the eastern side, of the Ælanitic Gulf, or the Gulf of Akaba, the long narrow arm north of the Red Sea, and running from this sea to a distance of about 125 miles ; it is on the eastern side of what is now known as the Sinaitic Peninsula. In Jer. xlix. 21 it is clearly indicated that the *Yam-Suph* lay in Edomite territory, which touched on that of Midian to the south.[2] When, therefore, the Old Testament speaks of the *Yam-Suph* as the waters in which the Egyptians were overwhelmed, it has no doubt about the exact spot where this happened.

Coming now to Mount Sinai, it is to be noted first, that in reading the various forms of the narrative, in whatever sources they are contained, it comes out clearly enough that Mount Sinai cannot have been very far distant from the scene of the Egyptian catastrophe. Mount Sinai has usually been located in the south of what is now called the " Sinaitic " Peninsula, which takes its name from the supposed position of Mount Sinai. But the fact is that there is absolutely no evidence for locating Mount Sinai here ; in the Old Testament everything points against it ; for it is there asserted quite clearly that it was situated in Midianite territory.[3] It was only in Christian times that the tradition arose about Mount Sinai being situated in the south of the " Sinaitic " Peninsula. Again, we shall see in a moment that there is every reason to believe, from the Old Testament descriptions, that Mount Sinai was a volcano ; but geological experts who have carefully examined the country assure us that the " Sinaitic " Peninsula is not volcanic. On the other hand, the entire eastern coast of the Ælanitic Gulf, right up to where the Old Testament places Mount Sinai, i.e. into Midianite and Edomite territory, *is* volcanic, according to these experts. So that this further supports the Old Testament indications that Mount Sinai was not far distant from the *Yam-Suph*, or rather that part of it at which the Egyptian catastrophe occurred.

Next, it is interesting to see how very clearly the Old

---

[1] Cp. Jon. ii. 5 (Hebr. 6): "The weeds (*suph*) were wrapped about my head."
[2] Cp. also 2 Chron. viii. 17, and Exod. xxiii. 31 ; Num. xiv. 25, xxi. 4 ; Deut. i. 40, ii. 1.
[3] Edomite and Midianite territory ran into one another ; there was no clear-cut boundary.

Testament descriptions of Mount Sinai show that it was a
volcano. In Exod. xix. 18 we read : " And mount Sinai
was altogether on smoke, because Yahweh descended upon
it in fire ; and the smoke thereof ascended as the smoke of
a furnace, and the whole mount quaked greatly." Again,
in Deut. iv. 11, 12, it is said : " And ye came near and stood
under the mountain ; and the mountain burned with fire
unto the heart of heaven, with darkness, cloud, and thick
darkness. And the voice of Yahweh spoke unto you out
of the midst of the fire . . ." Once more, in Judges v. 4, 5,
the reminiscence of what happened at Mount Sinai finds
expression thus :

> Yahweh, when thou wentest forth out of Seir,
> When thou marchedst out of the field of Edom,
> The earth trembled, the heavens also dropped,
> Yea, the clouds dropped water.
> The mountains quaked at the presence of Yahweh,
> Even yon Sinai at the presence of Yahweh, the God of Israel.

So, too, in Ps. lxviii. 7, 8, similar language is used in
referring to the same event : " the earth trembled," " the
heavens dropped," " even yon Sinai (trembled) at the
presence of Yahweh." Without quoting other passages to
the same effect, it is abundantly clear that whatever else
may have happened at the time of the escape of the Israelites
from the Egyptians, expressions such as " the mountain
burned with fire," " the smoke thereof ascended as the smoke
of a furnace," " the mountains quaked," " the earth
trembled," etc., point to a volcanic eruption of a severe
character, accompanied by an earthquake ; this will be
further illustrated presently.

Bearing in mind, then, the two facts that the Old Testament places Mount Sinai at the extreme north of the Ælanitic
Gulf, and that it clearly represents Mount Sinai as a volcano,
which was in eruption just at the time of the Egyptian
pursuit of the Israelites, and that an earthquake, as so often
during volcanic eruptions, took place at the same time, we
can picture to ourselves the course of events somewhat as
follows :

The Hebrews, during their flight from Egypt, have reached
the coast on the west of what we know as the Gulf of Akaba,
the northern extremity of the *Yam-Suph*. Their way is
therefore barred. Evening is not far off, when they suddenly
realize that in the far distance the Egyptians are following
them. A great expanse of water in front and a powerful
enemy behind—what chance of escape is there for the more

or less defenceless multitude, with women and children, and encumbered with baggage, to say nothing of flocks and herds which, as nomads, they must have had with them! Short of a miracle they are doomed. At this moment occurs what must naturally have appeared to the Hebrews as the miraculous intervention of some supernatural being. A volcanic eruption, accompanied by earthquake, shakes the land, and the fire and smoke emitted from the mountain cast a lurid light upon the darkening landscape; above all, the immense cloud formed by the volumes of smoke rising from the mountain-top, being permeated with incandescent gases, glows with unspeakable majesty; and, slowly wafted by the wind, comes towards them. Then occurs one of those terrible cataclysms which have happened again and again in the case of volcanoes situated near the sea-coast (two other notable instances will be given presently): the sea-bottom is raised over a large area by the underlying explosion of pent-up gases, and land appears where a few moments before there was but the dark surface of water. The Hebrews seize their opportunity, and with one accord make for the newly appeared land; over this they speed and gain the farther side of what had been the sea. But on looking back they perceive that the pursuing enemy has followed their example, and is likewise passing over the land in their wake. But once more there occurs what also has happened time and again since: the sea-bottom, which had been forced upwards, being unable to bear its own weight when the underlying pressure is withdrawn by the gradual dispersal of the gaseous vapours underground, collapses! The waters which had receded now return with incredible roar and overwhelm the whole body of the pursuing Egyptians.

The picture drawn of what happened at the time of this landmark in the history of Hebrew Religion might well appear fantastic were it not that, so far as the physical cataclysm is concerned, similar occurrences have been recorded at different times since. Two of these may be briefly recounted. On September 29th, 1538, of our era, Monte Nuovo, close to Naples, came into existence; immediately prior to its appearance the sea at Puzzuoli suddenly receded; numberless fish, it is told, lay about on the now dry land, and were carried off in wagon-loads by the inhabitants. After some hours the sea returned as suddenly; then the earth rose and the mountain was formed; at the same time, amid terrific thunder, an immense pillar of fire was shot out, together with glowing stones, an enormous cloud of

L

eam, and ashes. As there was no lava-stream very few
eople perished. The cataclysm lasted altogether two days
and two nights. This is an outline of an eye-witness'
account, named Simone Porzio, published at Florence in
1551.

The other happened as recently as 1902, when there
occurred the appalling eruption of Mont Pelé,[1] on the island
of Martinique. One of the most remarkable things about it
was the moving incandescent cloud which the mountain
belched forth. Simultaneously with the eruption there was
a fearful gale; at the same time, too, there was an earthquake which had an extraordinary effect upon the sea; an
eye-witness tells of how it suddenly became rough, it rose
higher and higher, and immense waves came sweeping over
the city and the surrounding country, and then receded.
It has been observed that during volcanic eruptions the sea
is often affected in this way, volcanoes being, in very many
cases, situated near the sea-coast.[2]

In view, then, of what the Old Testament records tell us,
and in view of subsequent occurrences of a somewhat similar
character, the belief is justified that the account of the
" Red Sea Catastrophe " is based on an actual occurrence.
More than one account, as already pointed out, has been
incorporated in the Old Testament, which easily explains
the inconsistencies which are found in the narrative. One
must also make allowances for additions and embellishments,
as well as for what are intended to be explanatory comments,
due to later scribes—an entirely natural proceeding. But
in its essence the story tells of an actual historical fact;
and what is of special importance is that it had a most
profound effect upon the development of Hebrew Religion.

2. YAHWEH, THE GOD OF THE HEBREWS

Inseparably connected with this providential deliverance
of the Hebrews was the founding of what was in effect a
new religion; for the experience at Sinai was what one might
call the coping-stone of the edifice of which Moses was the
builder. That is to say, the beginning of the religion of
Yahweh among the Hebrews centred in Moses; and it was
the Sinai revelation to which was primarily due the acceptation of Yahweh as their God by the Hebrew people.

[1] Pelé is the name of the Hawaiian volcano goddess.
[2] For the account given above the writer is indebted to Gressmann,
op. cit., pp. 116, 117.

We have seen what the religion of the Hebrews was before the time of Moses; we have now to inquire by what means it was that Moses came to the knowledge of Yahweh. Exod. iii. gives us an account of this. Moses was on Mount Horeb, another name for Mount Sinai, in Midian, where he was keeping the flock of Jethro his father-in-law, " the priest of Midian," and where Yahweh revealed Himself to him. Moses had fled to this country, which was situated to the east of the northern extremity of the Gulf of Akaba, to escape the consequences of murdering an Egyptian (Exod. ii. 14, 15). Now, if he was tending the flock of Jethro he was within the district belonging to Jethro's tribe, of which, as priest, he was in all probability the patriarch; and, according to Judges i. 16, this Midianite tribe, or rather clan belonging to the tribe, was that of the Kenites. It is well to bear in mind that there is, and always has been, a strict unwritten law of the desert in regard to the tracts of land belonging to the different tribes among nomads. The division of the land of Canaan in later times among the Israelite tribes was but the adaptation of this tribal law of the wilderness to new conditions. Moses, then, was feeding Jethro's flock in the territory belonging to the Kenite clan. Further, as is well known, among nomadic tribes there were tribal gods; each tribe had its own god, and the god held sway within the limits of the tribal territory; just as in later days there were national gods whose power was restricted to the country of the nation. It follows, therefore, that Mount Sinai, close to which, according to Exod. iii. 1, Moses was feeding Jethro's flock, was within the Kenite territory of the Midianite land, and that Yahweh, Who is described as dwelling on Mount Sinai, was originally the tribal god of the Kenites, and Jethro was His priest. This explains the revered and authoritative position which Jethro occupies in the sight of Moses. In Exod. xviii. 15 ff.[1] we read of how Jethro instructs Moses in the ways of administrating justice; and in ver. 24 it is said: " So Moses hearkened unto the voice of his father-in-law, and did all that he had said." Again, according to Num. x. 29 ff., Moses says to him: " We are journeying unto the place of which Yahweh said, I will give it to you; come thou with us, and we will do thee good; for Yahweh hath spoken good concerning Israel." At first, Jethro hesitates, and Moses urges him further:

---

[1] The fact that these two passages come from different sources (E and J respectively) is interesting as showing that, on this point of the position of superiority ascribed to Moses' father-in-law, they are in agreement.

"Leave us not, I pray thee; forasmuch as thou knowest how we are to encamp in the wilderness, and thou shalt be to us instead of eyes. And it shall be, if thou go with us, yea, it shall be, that what good soever Yahweh shall do unto us, the same will He do unto thee."

It must strike one as somewhat remarkable that Moses, the leader, the law-giver, and the religious head of his people, should pay such deference to his father-in-law, and be guided by his counsel, and be so loth to lose his company. There must have been very special reasons for this. But still more striking is that which we find recorded in Exod. xviii. 8 ff.; after Moses has told Jethro about the deliverance of the Israelites, it continues : " And Jethro rejoiced for all the good which Yahweh had done to Israel, in that he had delivered them out of the hand of the Egyptians. And Jethro said, Blessed be Yahweh, who hath delivered you out of the hand of the Egyptians. . . . Now I know that Yahweh is greater than all gods. . . . And Jethro, Moses' father-in-law, took a burnt-offering and sacrifices for God; and Aaron came, and all the elders of Israel, to eat bread with Moses' father-in-law before God." This action is incomprehensible except on the supposition that Yahweh was the God of Jethro and his tribe, the Kenites, and that Jethro himself was Yahweh's priest.

There is a good deal in the later history of the Israelites which bears out the contention that Moses adopted the worship of Yahweh from the religion of the Kenites; but with these details we cannot deal here.[1]

Since, then, as we have seen, Mount Sinai was believed to be the special abode of Yahweh, we can fully understand that the volcanic eruption, the earthquake, and its effects upon the waters of the *Yam-Suph*, resulting in the destruction of the Egyptian pursuers, were all ascribed to the direct action of Yahweh, the God of Sinai. The incandescent cloud blazing, as it seemed, with fire, was believed to be the manifestation of the deity; a belief natural enough to semi-civilized nomads.

It must, therefore, be recognized that the new religion which Moses founded was adopted from the Kenite tribe of the Midianite people. But this statement demands a little further consideration.

From the account in Exod. iii. 1 ff. we have been taught to believe that Moses first came to the knowledge of Yahweh through the divine manifestation at the burning bush.

---

[1] See further, Budde, *op. cit.*, pp. 41 ff.

Now, when these verses are carefully examined it will be seen that there are two passages in them which require to be accounted for. The first is in ver. 1, already quoted, which says : " Now Moses was keeping the flock of Jethro his father-in-law, the priest of Midian." One naturally asks, what is the point of prefacing the account of the burning bush with this reference to Jethro, the priest of Midian, when it has no connexion with what follows ? As we have seen, in the light of other passages we are able to discern the significance of the mention of the priest of Midian ; but as the text stands there is no connexion. But this want of connexion with the context suggests that the passage of which this verse is part is not in the form in which it appeared originally ; the assumption is not unjustified that when this verse was first written down it stood in a different context from that in which it now appears ; in other words, the passage is not in the form in which it stood originally. And this is borne out by the words of vers. 7, 8 : " And Yahweh said, I have surely seen the affliction of my people which are in Egypt . . . and I am come down to deliver them from out of the hand of the Egyptians, and to bring them up out of that land unto a good land and a large, unto a land flowing with milk and honey. . . ."

Apart from some other points in these verses which might be commented on, it must be asked : How can Yahweh speak of the Hebrews while still in Egypt as " My people " when they had not yet accepted Him as their God, nor even heard of Him ? We must beware of reading into these words modern ideas which they cannot bear ; we might say that Yahweh could speak of the Hebrews in Egypt as His people before they had heard of Him because He had accepted them as His people even though they knew nothing about it. But that will not do. That is not the ancient way of thinking, whether of the Hebrews or of any other people of antiquity. In those far distant times a people did not accept a new God unless they knew something about him first. Moses accepted Yahweh because he had learned about Him from His priest Jethro ; the Hebrews accepted Yahweh because, as they believed, He had shown forth His power and delivered them. The fact is that this passage in which Yahweh is made to speak of the Hebrews while still in Egypt as " My people," belongs to a time centuries later than the Mosaic age ; and the whole account is coloured by the point of view of later thought. And therefore, while ancient material lies embodied in the record, we must not look upon the episode of the burning bush as historical in the way that a later writer intended. The revelation of Yahweh to Moses was very real, but it was accorded by means of the instrument which He chose.

Finally, the objection may, quite naturally, be urged that if the religion of the Hebrews was merely borrowed from that of the Kenites, how can the *uniqueness* of the Hebrew Religion be maintained? The answer is simply : in the use made of opportunity. To both, to the Kenites as well as to the Hebrews, was accorded the light of revelation according to their capacity of apprehension. The Kenites had worshipped Yahweh as their tribal God from time immemorial; and in course of time the Hebrews came to worship Him too. But what a profound difference there was between the two in the use of the germ of revelation ! In the case of the Kenites no religious development took place because the human response was wanting. In the case of the Hebrews how different ! First through Moses, and later through the prophets, they gradually came to realize more and more fully the Personality and Character of Yahweh, and thus to apprehend, in some measure, the Being of God. All through their history there was, in spite of setbacks, the slow yet continuous increase of this apprehension because of the human response to the divine prompting. True, it was never the nation as a whole that responded; that is always so. Elect instruments of God first come into touch with Him; and they are the means of disseminating the knowledge of Him. Moses, with all his limitations— and the Old Testament makes no secret of them—was one of those elect instruments, perhaps the greatest in pre-Christian times; for his stupendous importance in the history of religion is seen in that he took the first and greatest step towards monotheistic belief that the world had known.

For untold centuries among all nations, tribes, and kindreds, religion had flourished, but belief and practice were *naïve*, crude, crass. Then an insignificant man, belonging to an insignificant people, in an insignificant corner of the world, received through human means the divine spark of revelation; but he not only received it, he accepted it and responded to it; and, like St. Paul to the Athenians long after, he said to his people, in effect : " Whom ye ignorantly worship, Him declare I unto you."

CHAPTER XIII

MOSAISM: THE RELIGION OF ISRAEL IN THE WILDERNESS

1. THE EXODUS

THE historicity of Moses and of his work has never been seriously doubted.[1] Indeed, if we had no record of Moses, it would have been necessary to invent him, for such a work as that ascribed to him demands the genius and inspiration of an individual almost unique. It may well be that as the story has been handed down from generation to generation it has received modifications, and we may feel ourselves disinclined to accept all the details, but a personality and a series of events which have loomed so large in the imagination of a people as Moses, the Exodus, and the Sinai covenant, must have a secure basis in actual fact.[2]

The name of Moses is Egyptian, and forms an element in more than one of the royal names of the eighteenth dynasty, 1600–1350 B.C.[3] Hebrew tradition held that he was of Hebrew blood, adopted by the royal house, and compelled for some crime to flee beyond the borders of civilization. He took refuge with the Midianites, a pastoral tribe whose grazing lands lay to the south of Palestine, married into the family of a Midianite (or Kenite?) priest, and received a special revelation at a sacred mountain. Here there appeared to him a God named Yahweh;[4] he was bidden to lead out of Egypt his kinsmen, the Hebrews,

[1] In view of the statement so frequently made, that the "Higher Critics" deny the historicity of Moses and of his work, it may be as well to insist that only two scholars of repute, Winckler and Cheyne (see especially articles in the *Encycl. Bibl.* signed T. K. C.) have adopted this position, and that it has found no acceptance either among their contemporaries or among their successors. It is utterly untrue to attribute this view to the "Higher Critics" as a body.

[2] See McNeile, *The Book of Exodus*, pp. cix–cxviii (1908).

[3] E.g. Ahmose, Tutmose.

[4] This, apparently, is the original form of the Hebrew personal name represented in our English Bibles by the word LORD.

who had been subjected to forced labour by the Egyptian
Government. The occasion was to be the celebration of a
festival at a spot three days' journey from Egypt in the
wilderness—presumably the mountain on which the revelation had been made (Exod. iii. 18). Moses is expressly told,
according to one ancient account (Exod. iii. 6), that Yahweh
may be identified with the God of Israel's remote ancestors,
though it is clear that the name will be strange to the present
generation.

Moses carries out his instructions, and finds that the
Egyptian king refuses to permit the expedition. Egypt
suffers from the wrath of Yahweh; but the Government is
obdurate, and at length, since Israel cannot go to Yahweh's
home for the celebration, Yahweh is forced to come to
Egypt. The ritual is there observed as well as conditions
allow, and Yahweh's presence proves disastrous to the
Egyptians. Israel is thus enabled to escape, and an
Egyptian force which pursues them is caught by the returning tide as it follows the fugitives across an arm of the sea.[1]
Moses then leads the people to the sacred mountain, variously
called Sinai and Horeb,[2] and there the union between
Yahweh and Israel is brought about.

Unless we accept the conjecture of Josephus (followed,
among modern scholars, by Dr. H. R. Hall) that the story
of the Exodus is an account of the expulsion of the Hyksos
seen from the Semitic side,[3] we have as yet no reference to
these events in Egyptian records. To the Pharaoh and to
his people it seemed but a small thing. Yet to the world it
was the most important occurrence that ever took place on
Egyptian soil. It made an ineradicable impression by the
Hebrews, and it is not surprising that the whole series of
events was interpreted as a miraculous intervention by the
God of Sinai, and that this view found expression in many
of the details of the story as it now lies before us. Later
Israel saw in the Exodus an authentication of Yahweh's
call of the people, and we can hardly doubt that the same
feeling worked still more effectively in the generation which
experienced it. When therefore they reached the sacred
mountain, they were ready to accept the God who was
offered to them.

[1] Another interpretation of this episode is given by Gressmann, *Mose
und seine Zeit*, pp. 108 ff. (1913). See also Chapter XII, § 1.
[2] According to the varying traditions; see below.
[3] This is not accepted by most modern scholars.

2. YAHWEH

Two traditions have survived as to the location of the sacred mountain. That which was current in northern Israel, introduced into the south apparently only at the end of the seventh century, identified it with Horeb, which seems to have been to the north-east of the Gulf of Akaba. The other, that better known in Judah, placed it at Sinai,[1] probably in the neighbourhood of Kadesh-barnea, the modern 'Ain Qadis. But if there is a divergent tradition as to the locality there is none as to the God who met Israel. In all forms of the story He is Yahweh, and the essential features of His relation to His people are always the same.

It is clear that Yahweh had been recognized and had been worshipped before Israel came into contact with Him.[2] We have, of course, no details as to the earlier cult, and we are entirely dependent on Israelite records for the picture that men formed of Him. We may, however, be fairly sure that Israelite theology in Moses' day did not differ materially from that of other peoples at the same stage of development. The meaning of the name has evoked a good deal of discussion. The ancient Hebrew derivation suggested by Exod. iii. 14—" I AM THAT I AM "—has been suspected, as implying too advanced a metaphysical conception of God for an early nomad people. Other explanations deriving the name from the substantive verb are less open to this objection, and roots suggesting " falling " and " blowing " have been cited as possible derivations.[3]

We have a certain amount of evidence which suggests that Yahweh was known outside those circles from which His worship must have reached Israel. In various forms the syllable Yah appears in a number of Mesopotamian names, though none of these can be assigned to a period earlier than the ninth century B.C. But in northern Palestine there was a god Yeuo, who was worshipped at Byblos from the beginning of the first millennium B.C., and the Ras Shamra tablets mention " a god called Yav or Yo (in the combination Yo-Elath), a name which may have some connexion with Yahweh." [4] This carries us back to the

[1] It is also possible that both names refer to the same place. See above, p. 143.

[2] Cp. Wheeler Robinson, *The Religious Ideas of the Old Testament*, p. 53 (1926).

[3] Stade, *Biblische Theologie des Alten Testaments*, i. 29 (1905); Hastings, *D.B.*, art. " GOD," by A. B. Davidson, ii. 199b.

[4] Jack, *The Ras Shamra Tablets*, p. 23 (1935).

fourteenth century B.C., i.e. to a time nearly as early as that of Moses. Since we have suggestions elsewhere in the Ras Shamra documents that there is some curious link between northern Syria and the south (cf. the references to the Negeb), we may suspect that a knowledge of Yahweh had penetrated to this distant spot at a period long before the time of Moses. It is worth noting, too, that this deity occupies a quite subordinate position in the Pantheon, as would probably happen in the case of one imported through a somewhat insignificant tribe. We have, further, a king named Azriau of Ja'udi, a state in the neighbourhood of Mt. Amanus, ,mentioned on an inscription of Tiglath-pileser III (738 B.C.) and it seems likely that the second part of the name is that of Yahweh. In the form in which it is familiar to us it occurs first on the well-known inscription of Mesha, king of Moab (ninth century), and is there the name of the God of Israel. All the evidence points to a widely-known, though generally insignificant, deity, who might well have been worshipped by some ubiquitous but comparatively unimportant tribe or other group.

Biblical references give us clearer light on the character assigned to Yahweh. It goes without saying that He is a mountain 'El, and later generations thought of His proper home as being in Sinai or Horeb, even after His dwelling had been established in Jerusalem. Thus, in the early days of the settlement in Palestine, the poet to whom we owe the Song of Deborah can speak of His coming from Edomite territory—from Sinai. And though Amos in the eighth century hears Yahweh roar from Zion, Elijah, a hundred years earlier, goes to Horeb, to the mount of God, in order to get into direct contact with Him.

The descriptions which we find in *Exodus* suggest that Yahweh's original home was in a volcanic region.[1] Now Palestine proper—especially the country to the west of Jordan—has no volcanoes, the rocks being practically all

---

[1] This is the strongest justification for Gressmann's view, for which see (presented even more effectively than was done by Gressmann himself) pp. 143-146. There appears, however, to be some doubt as to the geological facts. That the whole region to the immediate east of the Gulf of Akaba was volcanic may be accepted as certain, but it is less clear that there has been actual eruptive activity there in the most recent geological time. " Modern " deposits of lava are found in the Hauran to the north and in the Harras to the south, and we may have to assume either that Yahweh was first recognized in one of these, or in some similar, district, or that the narratives have been coloured by later knowledge of volcanic action. (T. H. R.).

of some form of limestone, but the Hebrews recognized the presence of Yahweh in the storm. After all, to the primitive mind, an eruption and a storm are not unlike; volcanic action is, as it were, a subterranean tempest. It was in the storm which swept away Sisera's troops that Israel saw the coming of Yahweh, and the same conception is to be seen in such later passages as Ps. xxix, while His character as a fire-god is attested by the ancient tradition which spoke of His presence in the pillar of cloud and fire. Other references imply that Yahweh was a warrior.[1] Wars, to the ancient Semitic mind, are not merely, not even principally, a question of human armies; the deities themselves play a leading part.[2] Such accounts as we have of the early battles of Israel suggest that there was little hand-to-hand fighting. The two armies would be drawn up face to face, each would start moving in a charge against its foe, but, before the shock of contact came, one side or the other would, as we should say, lose its nerve, and turn in flight. When our records speak of one or the other being " smitten before their enemies," the stroke is not that of material weapons, it is the panic sent by the more powerful of the two contending deities on the troops of the other.[3] It is only then that men begin to fall; the slaughter takes place in flight and pursuit, and when the two armies stand face to face and fight at close quarters, the fact is thought worthy of special mention. Israel believed that Yahweh was pre-eminent in His power of instilling this panic into the hearts of their enemies. Further, it is clear from the earnestness with which Moses pleads that Yahweh will go with Israel (cp. Exod. xxxiii. 15), that Yahweh is recognized as a guide through the wilderness.[4] He knows the safe trails, the rare wells, the spots where vegetation may be found for the cattle, and can guide His people without danger to themselves. This combination of mountain spirit, storm and volcanic deity, and wilderness guide, clearly goes back to the nomad period of Israel's history. That Yahweh was more, much more, than this, was a lesson which Israel learnt slowly through the centuries.

We do not know who it was that worshipped Yahweh

---

[1] See, e.g., Judges v. 23.

[2] See, e.g., a passage as late as Zech. ix. 13, 14.

[3] For this the Hebrew uses the word *nagaph*, while actual blows are described by the root *nakah*.

[4] It should be remembered that the " wilderness "—Hebrew *midhbar*— is not the absolutely waterless desert, but the region of scanty vegetation and poor rainfall over which the pastoral nomad ranges.

before He became specifically the God of Israel. We may
assume that He was in some way connected with the family
into which Moses married during his exile, but here we seem
to have two different traditions. On the one hand his
father-in-law is called either Reuel or Jethro, and is a
Midianite priest. If this be the original form of the tradition,
we may reasonably suppose that Yahweh also was a Midianite
deity. But in Num. x. 29 the father-in-law (or, perhaps,
the brother-in-law) of Moses is called Hobab, and in Judges
iv. 11 this Hobab is stated to have been a Kenite. Now the
Kenites were the smith clan, and seem to have lived a wandering life like that of the curious smith tribes described by
Doughty in modern Arabia. The temptation to regard
Yahweh as originally a Kenite God is strengthened by the
fact that He is so frequently conceived as a God of the
celestial fires manifested in the thunderstorm, and of the
terrestrial fires appearing in the earthquake and the volcano.
But, probable as this last suggestion may be, it still remains
a conjecture, and all we know for certain is that Yahweh
had an independent existence before His adoption of Israel
as His people.[1]

3. THE COVENANT

The task of Moses was to bring together the tribes under
his leadership and this God, so welding the former into a
single people. As we have seen, the circumstances of the
Exodus were likely to help him, but this must not be allowed
to detract from the supreme genius of the man who carried
into effect the great religious partnership. The story is
described in the opening verses of Exod. xxiv, though it
would seem that either the tradition or the actual text has
received accretions in process of transmission. The main
outlines of the original rite, however, seem to be beyond
dispute. On the one side stand the people, on the other
the God, the latter represented by an " altar." Victims
are slain, and their blood is drained off into bowls. Half of
it is then thrown over the altar, the terms on which the
covenant is to be made are read before the people, and, on
their consenting to observe them, the remainder of the
blood is flung over their heads.

The meaning of this ritual is not far to seek. The blood
is the life (Lev. xvii. 11, 14), the vital essence. Two parties,
at present independent one of another, are to be united in a

---

[1] Details are given by Budde, *Die Religion des Volkes Israel bis zur
Verbannung*, pp. 1–35 (1900). See also pp. 147 ff.

single whole, and, to secure the desired union, a third party is introduced. Its life is taken from it and made available for the other two. Both come under it, both are included in it, the same vital essence now covers and embraces the two. They are thus no longer independent entities, they are one, finding their unity with each other in their unity with that third party whose blood now covers them both. Till this point is reached, however near they might have been brought one to another, they are merely contiguous; now they are continuous, and form parts of a single indivisible whole. We might almost say that now Yahweh is Himself included in the term Israel; henceforward it will connote not merely a human community, but one of which He is a member.

Thus from the outset the religion of Israel was marked by a unique feature whose importance it is impossible to exaggerate. The principle of one tribe, one tribal god, may have been fairly well accepted among ancient Semitic communities. But elsewhere the god is a natural member of the people to whom he belongs, and is inconceivable apart from it. If through the disappearance of his tribe or from some other cause he loses his people, he ceases to rank as a god, and descends to the level of that intermediate class to whom the Arab theologian gives the name of *Jinn*—a wild god, a masterless and isolated spirit, retaining some of his powers, but practically none of his prestige.[1] As long as his people exists, his position is secure, but he is as dependent on the human members of his clan as they are upon him; in the nature of the case each is indispensable to the other.

The early Israelite may have thought of Yahweh much as the Moabite thought of Chemosh, but the relationship rested on a different basis. Chemosh always had been a Moabite and never could be anything else; Yahweh had existed as a God independently of Israel, and, if need be, could so exist again, or could, on the other hand, extend His interests and His influence to others than the original Israel. The connexion between God and people was not " natural " but (if we may use the word without being misunderstood) " artificial." It had a definite beginning at a definite point in time, and might equally well have a definite conclusion. It depended on a " covenant "—a deed of partnership, and if at any time either party violated the terms originally laid down, it was within the right of the

—————
[1] Part I, Chapter X.

other to declare the agreement and the partnership at an end. It is true that we do not meet with the actual formula, " I will become their God and they shall become my people," in so many words till the end of the seventh century, but the essence is implied from the first.[1] This aspect of the religion of Israel was never wholly lost, and while Israel, all through her history, was guilty of repeated breaches of the terms, she was forced to admit that they had never once been broken on the divine side. What Yahweh had said, that He did : His word stood ever sure.

What the terms of the Covenant were we do not know. The passage which precedes the account of the ceremony, Exod. xxi–xxiii, forms a short code of laws, to which the name " Book of the Covenant " is now frequently applied. But this is simply an Israelite form of the type of code common to practically all the ancient East, known to have existed, with local and national variations, in Babylonia, Assyria, and Anatolia, as well as in Israel. It is essentially the code of an agricultural and commercial people, and has little that can apply at all to a community still on the nomad stage. Even if we could suppose that it was Mosaic in origin, we should have to admit that it was given for a future age, and that it had little practical meaning for the generation which was actually a party to the Covenant itself. This seems so unlikely that it is now widely held that the Code was formulated in a later age, long after Israel had made its home in the promised land. Some have found the basis for the Sinai Covenant in the familiar Decalogue of Exod. xx, not, indeed, in the exact terms in which it has been preserved, but in a more concise form. To this the objections raised against the next three chapters do not apply, but, on the other hand, we can hardly say that the evidence for this view is definite enough to justify a dogmatic conclusion. Another Decalogue—mainly concerned with ritual—appears in Exod. xxxiv, but this, again, is applicable to the settled farmer rather than to the wandering shepherd. Of one thing we may be sure, that the Covenant demanded that the worship of Israel should be paid to Yahweh alone, and that the Israelite should use no other divine name in taking an oath. There may also have been an insistence on the Passover—essentially a pastoral festival [2]—and it is not impossible that a form of the Sabbath in which the use of fire was prohibited on the seventh day was imposed. Beyond

---

[1] But cp. Gen. xxviii. 20–22.   [2] Cp. Part I, pp. 129 ff.

these points it is hardly possible even to hazard a conjecture.

There were, we may be sure, obligations on the divine side also.[1] These are not clearly stated, but we may assume that Yahweh stood to Israel in the relation normal among such peoples. He was their guide in the desert (cp., e.g., Amos ii. 10) and their inspiration in war (cp., e.g., 1 Sam. iv. 3). Though a member of the community like the men composing it, He had special powers, and was not subject to the laws of decay and death. He was especially the guardian of the blood of the tribe and the supreme judge in cases of dispute between its human members. He had means of making His will known to His people, and could be consulted in times of difficulty, uncertainty, or danger. He would see that vengeance was taken for wrongs inflicted on any member of His community, whether the criminal were an Israelite or a stranger, and would jealously punish any infringement of an oath taken in His name. To His own people He was Lord and King.

4. SACRED EMBLEMS

It is possible, though not probable, that through the wilderness period Israel may have had no material object particularly associated with Yahweh round which such cultus as there was might centre. As a matter of fact, all tradition points to the presence of certain things which accompanied the people through their wanderings, and were taken by them into Palestine during their invasion of the country. Three sacred emblems were worshipped in later days, for which it was claimed that their peculiar cult originated in the wilderness. These were the Bull, whose most important sanctuary was at Bethel; the Snake, which had its home in Jerusalem; and the Ark, which, after being located in different temples, at last found a home also in Jerusalem.

Of these the first two seem to have been objects of worship in Palestine before the Israelite conquest. Archæological research has revealed numbers of figures both of bulls and of snakes from *strata* which must be earlier than the advent of Israel.[2] It is, however, not quite certain that these

---

[1] Cp. Gen. xxviii. 20, 21.
[2] Details are given by Sellin, *Tell Ta'anek* (1904); Macalister, *Bible Sidelights from the Mount of Gezer* (1906); *Excavations at Gezer* (1912); cp. also S. A. Cook, *The Religion of Ancient Palestine in the Light of Archæology*, pp. 27 ff., 82, 98 f.

represent objects of worship—a difficulty which frequently attaches to archæological discoveries. But both were familiar in the cults of the ancient agricultural world, inasmuch as both were regarded as symbols of fertility, and the known facts are against rather than for their claim to be objects of Israelite cults dating from the nomadic age. Yet each had traditions surrounding it which took it back to that early period.

Bull-worship in Israel is first mentioned as an act of apostasy which took place at Sinai itself. The story, as recorded in Exod. xxxii, tells how the people grew anxious at the prolonged absence of Moses on the mountain, whither he had ascended to receive instructions from Yahweh. They had been brought out of Egypt by Moses in order to come into contact with Yahweh, and they had lost their leader without finding their God. Accordingly they applied to Aaron, who bade them bring their golden jewels, which he melted down and made into a calf, telling Israel that this was the God who had brought them out of Egypt. While the revelry in connexion with its worship was at its height, Moses returned, investigated the facts, and strongly condemned the action of Aaron, who defended himself by throwing the blame on the people, and suggesting that the calf form taken by the molten metal was not deliberately planned by him, but was the result of chance.[1] He himself seems to have escaped punishment, but numbers of Israelites fell by the hand of the Levites, who took the sword to avenge the insult put upon Yahweh.

Now we may suspect that at the great bull sanctuaries, such as Bethel, a story rather like this was told to explain the origin of the cult. But it would have been Moses, not Aaron, who was its author, and the pouring of molten metal into water would be a method whereby men could ascertain the exact form under which Yahweh preferred to be worshipped. A later generation, with the prohibition of images in mind, could not endure the slur on Moses, and while they could not eliminate the tradition, they transferred the odium of it to Aaron, a man who elsewhere is little more than a lay figure with no independent personality of his own. Possibly we have a relic of a cult connected with Horeb and transferred to northern Israel. It is significant that

---

[1] For the justification of this interpretation see the present writer's article in the *Expositor*, "The Golden Calf," Series VIII, Vol. XXIV, pp. 121 ff. (T. H. R.).

Elijah, for whom Yahweh's dwelling was in Horeb, made no protest, as far as we know, against the cult of the bull.

The construction of the bronze snake was attributed directly to Moses, but the tradition recorded in Num. xxi. 4–9 stated that he made it at the command of Yahweh Himself, in order to cure those who were bitten by snakes on the road between Hor and the Red Sea. It is significant that the species of snake which attacked Israel there is described by the same name as that which is applied to the superhuman attendants of Yahweh seen by Isaiah in his inaugural vision. It will be remembered that it was not till some years after the call of the prophet that the bronze snake was destroyed by Hezekiah. But, apart from the narrative in Num. xxi, we do not hear of the snake till the suppression of its worship.

With the Ark the case is very different. Tradition said that it was carried with Israel through all the wanderings, that it entered the promised land with the people, and that it had a series of resting-places, finding its last home in the Temple of Solomon at Jerusalem. It is true that it received no attention during the reign of Saul, but both Samuel and David are connected with it. Now the Ark was simply a box, and it does not seem likely that such an object would have been revered if it had been supposed to be empty. There was, it is true, a divine power within it, and Israelite history told of its prowess when confronted with Dagon, the god of Ashdod (1 Sam. v. 1–5), and of its power to drive cows ruthlessly away from their calves in spite of their lowing protests (1 Sam. vi. 7 ff.). It seems likely therefore that there was some object within the Ark which represented the deity. Tradition stated that the stones bearing the Law were placed in it, together with a pot of manna and the rod of Aaron. The theory of divine residence in stones is familiar to every student of ancient Semitic religion,[1] and it is easy to guess that the stones were originally taken from the sacred mountain, and held to contain the very essence of Yahweh Himself. Again, a later age has so modified the story as to eliminate the suggestion of idolatrous worship, but of the three objects suggested, the stone (or stones) is by far the most likely to have dated from the wilderness period.

In further support of this view we may refer to the traditional Israelite attitude towards the worship of images.

[1] See Part I, Chapter IV

M

It is sometimes claimed that from the first the Hebrew cultus was purely spiritual, that it set before men no material object of reverence. On *a priori* grounds this appears to be unlikely, and the early stories of the Ark show that there, at least, was a venerated object which was held to embody a supremely powerful personality. But we do find a strong feeling against the worship of *artificial* objects. Two very primitive codes have come down to us, one of which includes, the other almost entirely consists of, ritual prescriptions. These are found in Exod. xx. 2–17, and in Exod. xxxiv. 14–26. Both seem to have undergone a process of expansion, especially the latter, but a number of primitive " commandments " may easily be crystallized out from each passage. The former seems to have been handed down in northern Israel, while the latter bears the stamp of Judaic tradition. In Exod. xx it will be noted that the " graven image " is strictly prohibited; in Exod. xxxiv. 17 the " molten image " is forbidden. The bull at Bethel—if we are right in regarding the narrative of Exod. xxxii as a modified form of the tradition of that sanctuary—was a " molten image," and would not be excluded by the law of Exod. xx. 4.

No details are given us in Num. xxi as to the construction of the bronze snake, but it is quite possible that this was a carved figure, which would thus avoid the condemnation of Exod. xxxiv. But the more primitive feeling, expressed in the altar law of Exod. xx. 24, 25, is that there must be no human workmanship in any object closely associated with Yahweh. Of course, the receptacle in which any sacred emblem was placed must be manufactured, but the emblem itself must be free from human contamination. We may suspect that it was only after the entry into Canaan and the adoption of certain forms of cultus existing there already that in each case the rule was so modified as to permit the use of an object sanctified by ages of worship. The primitive feeling is undoubtedly better represented by the stone than by either of the other objects.

It remains to mention the Tabernacle. It goes without saying that the deity must have his home. We need not accept the elaborate picture of the tabernacle drawn in *Exodus* which is clearly a reflection back into an earlier period of Solomon's Temple. But we may be sure that there was a special tent, wherein dwelt the very presence of Yahweh, where men might meet Him, and where, from time to time, there appeared manifestations of the divine glory.

5. SACRED PERSONS

The allotment of certain persons to the special service of the deity is a feature common to practically all known forms of religion. Particularly in a more primitive stage of religious development, men feel that the beings whom they worship are peculiar people; there is, as Otto has insisted, an awful sense of the " numinous." [1] To the undeveloped mind gods are dangerous, for they are whimsical and capricious, to be approached only by those who fully understand their ways and their tastes. Thus in our Old Testament we have the story of Nadab and Abihu, who were struck dead for daring to offer " strange fire " to Yahweh (Lev. x. 1–7), and Uzzah meets with a like fate for the impulse which leads him to steady the Ark as the oxen which draw it stumble (2 Sam. vi. 6–8). Further, the shrine of the deity, with all that belongs to it, needs special care. In a nomad people, who carry the divine emblems with them, there must be those whose duty it is to attend to the movements of the sacred objects. The will of the god is made known in obscure ways, and an interpreter is necessary to declare the meaning of the signs to the lay world. There is always an intermediary between the object of worship and the great mass of human worshippers.

A priesthood of a kind was, then, a necessity in early Israel as elsewhere. We have, however, a variant tradition as to the actual person or persons who fulfilled this office. The official and generally accepted theory of the writers of the Old Testament was that the priesthood was in the hands of the family of Moses. He himself is, indeed, the first priest, and his successors derive from him their authority. It is true that he exercises ecclesiastical functions only for a short time, and that one of his first acts is to consecrate his brother Aaron, from whom the later Jerusalem priesthood traced its descent. But he always stands even between the priests and their God, for all instructions are conveyed through him, and though he is permitted to delegate to his brother's family the special duties of the sanctuary, he has free access thereto in a fashion denied to all others. For practical purposes it is Aaron and his sons who are the legitimate priests.

[1] Rudolf Otto, *The Idea of the Holy*, pp. 7, etc.

We have, however, traces of another tradition which assigned this position not to Aaron but to Joshua. It is said in Exod. xxxiii. 11 that while Moses lived in the camp, i.e. amongst the people, " his minister, Joshua, the son of Nun, a young man, departed not out of the Tent." Here we have a form of the tradition—surely current in Ephraimite northern Israel—according to which the priesthood, while primarily still vested in Moses, is delegated, not to any member of his family or clan, but to a subordinate person in his own household.

The questions raised by the priesthood in ancient Israel are too numerous and too complicated to be discussed except in an extensive monograph. We do not know whether the name " Levi " applied originally to a clan or to an office—there is evidence for both views.[1] We do not know when the tradition which assigned the first place to Aaron was fully accepted in Israel. We do not know how the priesthoods of the various ancient sanctuaries of Israel were related one to another. But of two facts we may be certain. One is that there must have been a priesthood of some kind from the earliest times, to tend the shrine and its contents, to regulate the human approach to Yahweh, and to interpret the will of Yahweh to men. The second fact is that originally this priesthood was in some way connected with Moses, and that there were thus concentrated in him all the functions of a leader, civil and ecclesiastical. From the start Israel recognized divine leadership in all matters, though it was communicated through a human intermediary.

6. RITUAL

A large proportion of the books of *Exodus, Leviticus,* and *Numbers* is occupied with prescriptions for the ritual to be employed in the service of Yahweh. This is primarily sacrificial, and every event in the life of the individual or of the community, every special season or occurrence, even every day, had its own appropriate offerings. We find other references in the exilic and post-exilic prophets, especially in *Ezekiel,* and in the historical books, all showing that in its final form the ceremonial of Israelite worship was elaborate and costly. But we may doubt whether we are justified in accepting the tradition which ascribed the establishment of this whole system to Moses. The pre-exilic prophets, who represent rather the older traditions of nomadic Israel, seem without a dissentient voice to deny

[1] See Buchanan Gray : *Sacrifice in the Old Testament,* pp. 241-255 (1925).

that sacrifice was enjoined on Israel in the wilderness. It may be, however, that they did not intend to include the Passover [1] (as distinct from the Feast of Unleavened Bread), which was much older than Israel. And when we come to examine the ritual as described for us, we see that it embodies an ecclesiastical year centring round three main festivals. These are even mentioned in one of our oldest ritual codes, that of Exod. xxxiv, and are (1) Unleavened Bread (ver. 18); (2) the Feast of Weeks, the firstfruits of the harvest; (3) the Feast of Ingathering at the " year's end " (ver. 22).[2] These are clearly agricultural festivals, and have little or no relation to the pastoral life of the wilderness. Apart from any question as to the date of this passage, it is obvious that it had no bearing, and could have had no bearing, on the actual life of Israel till they had settled down in Palestine.

This does not mean, however, that we must necessarily deny all ritual of every kind to the early days of Israel's history. At first sight it seems as if the Sabbath also must have been introduced into Israelite life after the Conquest, but it has been pointed out that possibly this institution was taken over with the primitive Yahwism from Kenites, who, as smiths, may well have observed a *taboo* on fire for one day in every seven.[3] As we have seen, the celebration of the Passover was older than Israel, being, indeed, the festival which served as the occasion for the Exodus. There is nothing in it which is inconsistent with the nomad life, and its combination with the days of Unleavened Bread may be due to the fact that both were, in Palestine, spring festivals. But it is improbable that there was much more than these, and we are forced to admit that the observance of even the Sabbath and the Passover in the wilderness is largely a matter of conjecture.[4]

---

[1] See Part I, Chapter XI, § 4, and cf., e.g., Am. v. 21 ff., Hos. vi. 6, Isa. i. 11 ff., Jer. vi. 20, vii. 21 ff. There is, however, a growing body of opinion, shared by Dr. Oesterley, which holds that, even in the nomadic period, there was a fairly extensive sacrificial system. The main grounds for this view are to be found in the practices of other nomad peoples, ancient and modern. If it be correct, then it will be necessary either to suppose that the prophets mentioned were mistaken as to the historical facts, or that some other interpretation must be given to their language. Their primary purpose was to insist that no sacrifice, whatever its origin, could be a substitute for the right conduct and attitude which Yahweh required of Israel.

[2] The Hebrew term is literally " the turn of the year," and other references lead us to think of it rather as the beginning than as the end of the year.

[3] See Part I, Chapter XI, § 6.   [4] See, however, Part I, Chapter XI.

It is clear that if there was no sacrifice (except at the Passover, where, to judge from the narrative in *Exodus*, various tribes assembled at the sacred mountain), there was no need of an altar proper. There are instructions for making a primitive altar of earth or of unhewn stone in Exod. xx. 24, 25, but in view of what we have already seen, this must relate rather to the worship of the Palestinian community. But we may, perhaps, include among forms of ritual the methods adopted for ascertaining the divine will. Here again, while we know a good deal about the practice of later Israel, we cannot assert with confidence that the means used in after days were inherited from the primitive period. Several methods were in use in the ancient East, particularly those of the inspection of the entrails of victims and the sacred lot. The former is clearly out of the question in an age in which sacrifice was infrequent; we are left therefore with the latter. In Palestine we hear of two objects used for this purpose : (1) the *Ephod*, and (2) the *Urim and Thummim*. We are not certain what either was; the first name seems to have been used both for a garment and for an image,[1] and may have been a sort of waistcoat with pockets in it where the other articles were kept. These, the *Urim and Thummim*, were, possibly, flat stones, white on one side and black on the other. If both fell white side upwards the answer was in the affirmative, if black side upwards then a negative; if they differed, no reply was vouchsafed to the question. This is one of the suggestions made as to their use, but, once again, we have no certainty either that these objects can be traced back to the wilderness period or that they were employed in this manner. We should note also in this connexion the use of oracular wells and trees.[2] All we know is that nomadic Israel must have had some mechanical means of ascertaining the will of Yahweh.

7. Ethic

The life of the pastoral nomad is extremely simple. He has little or no private property, for the flocks belong to the community as a whole, while his work demands little apparatus, and leaves small room for articles of comfort. Even the tent in which he lives may belong to the whole family, and all he can call his own will be a few weapons, simple clothes, and cooking vessels. He is thus free from

[1] Hölscher, *Geschichte der israelitischen und jüdischen Religion*, pp. 20, 72 (1922).

[2] See further, Part I, Chapters II, III.

many of the complications and temptations which beset
people living under the more advanced agricultural and
civic system. On the other hand, the conditions are such as
to lay the greatest stress on the value of personality. It is
true that there are " sheikhly " families, but their position
entitles them to no more than a certain social respect;
their members have no authority beyond that which their
individual wisdom, age, or prowess gives to them. Tribal
decisions are commonly taken in an informal assembly,
where every free man is at liberty to have his say, and where
the collective opinion alone can override the wishes of any
individual. In all matters which do not affect the well-
being of the group (though the range of these subjects is,
necessarily, somewhat limited), each free member of the
community has the right to do as he thinks fit. At critical
moments or in hazardous undertakings, when travelling
through difficult country or engaging in war, it may, and
commonly does, happen that one man will come to the front,
and, by his sagacity and courage, lead his fellows to success.
But even so, his prominence may be only temporary, and, in
any case, it gives him no authority to control the actions of
his fellows, to make personal demands on them, or to issue
orders to them. There are many limitations on the power
of the nomad to do exactly as he pleases, without reference
to his neighbours, but they are imposed by the general will
and by the common interests of the community as a whole,
and not by the superior authority of another individual.
An intense passion for personal liberty, and for a sense of
equality as between the persons composing the group, is
one of the outstanding characteristics of the " wilderness "
tribes, and it is a factor in the spiritual heritage of the later
Israel which must always be taken into account. In the
early days it may not have been consciously expressed; it
is rather one of those basic assumptions of the social life of
the people which are so whole-heartedly assumed as to need
no formal statement. Only when the rights of the individual
are challenged will it become necessary to insist that all free
Israelites are brethren.

Another feature of the wilderness is that the conditions of
the nomad life are hard. " In the day the drought consumed me and the frost by night; and my sleep fled from
mine eyes," says Jacob in justifying himself to Laban
(Gen. xxxi. 40); and he is clearly giving a picture of the
normal shepherd life. There is constant danger from
enemies, animal and human, and the flocks can be preserved

only at the price of relentless vigilance. There is no room
for the leisure and enervating luxury which give so much
occasion for selfishness and vice in other spheres. The
nomad thus has commonly a fairly high moral standard,
especially in sexual matters. African travellers assure us
that nomad peoples such as the Masai maintain an ethical
level considerably above that of the agricultural peoples of
the continent.

It is significant that a man like Jeremiah could look back
on this period of Israel's history as that which attained more
nearly than any other to the ideal (cp. Jer. ii. 2, 3). It is
equally significant that when, in the time of the monarchy,
the corruption of national life reached its height, the first
protests made in the name of Yahweh came from two men
of the wilderness or semi-wilderness community, Elijah
(1 Kings xvii. 1) in the ninth century B.C. and Amos in the
eighth (Amos i. 1). All through the history of Israel there
persisted the tradition of a high moral standard demanded
by Yahweh, and, indeed, it was this influence which in the
end proved to be the decisive factor in making Israelite
religion unique in the ancient world.

It is sometimes held that the familiar ethical Decalogue
of Exod. xx. 3–17, at least in a simpler form, was the work
of Moses himself.[1] It is true that the commands have undergone modification, and some of them have been expanded.
The second commandment, for instance, probably ran
simply : " Thou shalt not make unto thee a graven image " ;
the fourth : " Remember the Sabbath day to keep it holy " ;
and the fifth : " Honour thy father and thy mother." We
may suspect that originally the commandments took some
such form, whatever be the date of their formulation, but
we cannot say definitely that even thus abbreviated they go
back to Moses. While there is nothing in them which
prohibits a wilderness origin, the evidence is hardly strong
enough to justify us in being dogmatic either for or against
their Mosaic authorship.

This much, however, we can say. Whether these commandments are the work of Moses or not, they do represent
very fairly the general moral standard which we may ascribe
to Israel in the days preceding the Settlement. There are
two matters which are vital to the existence of a pastoral
clan, that which finds expression in the laws of marriage and
that which is covered by the law of murder. The purity of
its blood and the sanctity of the life of its members are

[1] Cf. above, p. 158.

matters which are fundamental to the tribe, and the most stringent regulations have to be adopted in order to guard them. The practical needs of the community are, no doubt, reinforced by feelings and theories in these matters which come down to us from very early times. The beginning and the end of life are both surrounded with that kind of mystery which arouses the fear and the respect of primitive man, and wherever we go amongst early peoples we find that each is the centre of a number of beliefs and practices. There seems always to be something strange about blood, which is, indeed, not merely a " giver of life " but is endowed with a personality of its own. Thus we hear of the blood of Abel " crying out from the ground," [1] and the primitive law of blood revenge was based not on mere vindictiveness but on the fear that blood unsatisfied might prove an appalling peril to the living.

In addition to the two subjects already mentioned, we must recognize a very strong respect for tradition, for antiquity, and for the standing and authority of the older members of the tribe. Long after they have passed the climax of their physical vigour, the " elders " are of value because of their experience of life, and the leadership of the clan commonly devolves on them as individuals or as a group. It is true that they can no longer protect themselves against violence, but they certainly have a right to be heard in the counsels of their people. Hence the respect paid to a man's parents, a respect which again is strengthened by the facts of birth. We need not doubt that the fifth commandment was recognized and observed from the days when Israel first became a nation, and possibly from still more ancient times.

There is thus no reason to doubt that the ethical standard of primitive Israel stood high. The fact is of the greatest importance in the history of the nation, because in Israel, almost alone of ancient peoples, much of the tradition and outlook of the primitive days was preserved, at least in a section of the community. The time was to come when, amid the breakdown of the social and political order, there was to be a revival of the old views. The men who, more than any others, gave to the religion of Israel that peculiar position which made it of supreme significance in the spiritual history of man were the prophets of the eighth and seventh centuries, and the moral passion which inspired them was a direct inheritance from the days of Moses.

[1] Gen. iv. 10.

CHAPTER XIV

THE RELIGION OF CANAAN

1. THE SOURCES

IN considering the religion of the Hebrews before their entry into the Promised Land, we found ourselves frequently forced back on conjecture. Our sources of information were scanty, and we were compelled to admit that such records and traditions as have been handed down from that age have suffered a certain amount of modification at the hands of the generations through which they have passed. We had help from the comparative study of religions, but archæology gave us even less than tradition, and the result was a wide margin of possible error. With the period that follows, while there are many points that are far from clear, we are on much firmer ground. There are passages in our Old Testament (e.g. the Song of Deborah in Judges v) which we all recognize as going back to a very early stage in the history of the settled community, and the light they throw on the faith and practice of Israel, even before the establishment of the monarchy, is of the highest value. Further, the evidence of archæology is comparatively extensive. Several sites of ancient Canaanite worship have been investigated; some of them, such as Gezer, Jerusalem, Jericho, Taanach, and Megiddo, dating from a time anterior to the Hebrew occupation of the spot in question; others, such as Shechem, Samaria, and Lachish, clearly belonging to the monarchy. The combination of our various sources of information gives us a tolerably reliable picture of the conditions and of the course of events.

Our knowledge of Palestine goes back to centuries before the Hebrew conquest of the country. We have, in particular, a series of documents in the Tell-el-Amarna letters,[1] dating from the fourteenth century B.C., which may allude to

---

[1] An admirable and popular account of these letters is given by Niebuhr, *Die Amarna-Zeit*, in *Der Alte Orient*, i. 37 ff. (1900), and the English reader may be referred to J. Baikie, *The Amarna Age*, 1926.

the Aramæan invaders whom we call Hebrews, and certainly
depicts conditions before their occupation. This corre-
spondence reveals to us a country already at a comparatively
advanced stage of political and social development, corresponding fairly exactly with that which we glean from the
stories of the Conquest preserved in the books of *Joshua* and
Judges. The land contained many cities, some of them
apparently very strong, but most of them independent one of
another. Some were ruled by native princes, some by
foreign governors, but all were nominally subject to the
court of Egypt. The authority of the African state,
however, was challenged from several quarters, and was in
danger of being overthrown. On the one hand, we have
the growing Hittite power in the north, gradually expanding under that master of subtle intrigue, Shubiluliuma.
On the other hand, we have a series of invasions from
the wilderness by groups of tribes whom modern opinion
tends more and more to identify with the Hebrews. The
type of civilization was that generally characteristic of
the peoples of Western Asia, and it is noteworthy that
Mesopotamian culture had so strong a hold on the land that,
while the native speech was an early form of Hebrew, the
Palestinian chiefs and governors corresponded with their
overlord neither in that language nor in Egyptian, but in
Babylonian, even though there are occasional signs that
neither writer nor reader was wholly familiar with it.[1]

In the period which followed that of the Tell-el-Amarna
letters, these Aramæan invaders made good their footing
in the land and gradually settled down. Probably they
never formed a very large proportion of the population,
but they were much the strongest element, and the necessities
of external pressure, culminating in the Philistine invasions,
gave them a position of leadership and authority. They
entered the land with the faith and cult (such as it was) of
the wilderness, and to appreciate the history of Hebrew
religion we must study the reaction on one another of the
two types of social order and of belief.

Our knowledge of pre-Israelite religion in Palestine is
based on two types of evidence. On the one hand, we have
the discoveries made by archæology, which has made very
great progress in the nearer East during the last twenty
years, and will, probably, throw even more light on the
subject in the future than it has done in the past. The great

---

[1] See further, *The Cambridge Ancient History*, ii. 260 ff., 330 ff. (1924).

difficulty presented by this kind of material lies in its exact interpretation.[1] We have numerous buildings—or rather the lower portions of buildings—and a mass of smaller objects, many of which are simply fragments, but we cannot always be certain as to their primary significance and actual use. Sometimes we find that archæologists themselves differ on these points, or they may change their opinion, especially when fuller knowledge reveals similar objects elsewhere. At one of the best-known sanctuaries, for instance—that of Gezer—there is a line of upright stones standing on a platform. These used to be explained as "*mazzeboth*," or sacred "*menhirs*," but they are now "regarded by some scholars as a line of pillars, mere memorials, devoid of sacred significance."[2] Nevertheless, from some points of view, the evidence supplied by archæology is the most reliable that we have, for it gives us the very sites, buildings, and objects which were familiar to the people whose religion we are trying to understand.

On the other hand, we have a valuable source of information in literature. Unfortunately we have very little indeed written in Palestine before the advent of Israel. By far the most important body of material is to be found in the Tell-el-Amarna letters, to which allusion has already been made.[3] Their subject, however, is almost invariably political, and references to religion occur only sporadically and casually. A certain amount of help is given by inscriptions, including the numerous seals which have survived. Two of our most important series of documents come from outside Israel, the one from northern Syria and the other from Egypt. The former were found at Ras Shamra, the ancient Ugarit, and include, not only business and official documents, but also sacred poems, describing the myths which, presumably, were associated with the festival of the New Year.[4] There is ground for supposing that similar ritual myths were current further south also. In the other case, that of the Elephantiné papyri, we have documents which date from the fifth century B.C., and are, therefore, very much later than the Israelite conquest of Palestine. Yet they reflect features of religion which must have been handed down from a time anterior to Joshua.

[1] Cf. S. A. Cook, *The Old Testament : A Reinterpretation*, p. 79 (1936).
[2] S. A. Cook, *Rel. Pal.*, p. 88 (1930).
[3] P. 170.
[4] Cf. *Myth and Ritual*, pp. 76 ff. (1933), and J. W. Jack, *The Ras Shamra Tablets* (1935).

But our main literary source is the Bible itself, and its evidence is invaluable. Even here, however, we need to be on our guard, for there is no doubt that the narratives have undergone very considerable modification in the course of transmission, in order to adapt them to the growing moral and religious sense of Israel. There was much in the life of the people at an early stage which was intolerable to the later writers, and, accordingly, it was either glossed over or eliminated. Even within the pages of the Old Testament we have clear indications of this process; to some writers, for instance, the use of the *mazzebah* appeared innocuous, while to others it was a direct violation of the divine will. In spite of this difficulty, however, the Old Testament is our most reliable source of information as to the general character of religion in Pre-Israelite Palestine.

In various portions of the Old Testament, especially in books like *Deuteronomy* and the Prophets, we meet with denunciations of various forms of cultus which the true Israelite regarded as heretical, i.e. as being inconsistent with the genuine Yahwism handed down from the time of Moses. The tone of the protests makes it clear that the evil was a living and pressing spiritual danger, and that the practices condemned formed a part of the current popular cultus. It is clear that these were elements which were either in the land when the first conquests took place, or that they were introduced from abroad through commerce or war. Instances of the latter type are to be found in the cults introduced by Solomon [1] and, probably, by Ahaz,[2] while a very striking illustration of an unsuccessful attempt to import a foreign deity is to be seen in the story of Jezebel.

Prophetic and legal denunciations, however, do not exhaust our sources of information as to the religious practices of early Palestine. As we have already seen, it is possible to form a fairly reliable conception of the nature of the religion of nomad Israel; the fully developed cultus, however, with which we meet in the ritual portions of the Old Testament presents us with a very different picture. The comparative study of religions shows us that many of the new features belong to the common stock of agricultural, civic, and imperial religions, and we are fairly safe in assuming that these were adopted by the invaders, perhaps only after some centuries' residence in the land, as

[1] Cf. 1 Kings xi. 1–10.   [2] Cf. 2 Kings xvi. 10 ff.

a part of their general assimilation to their predecessors.
We shall certainly find no suggestion of the acceptance of
any deity other than Yahweh; that was the point on which,
above all others, the later official religion most strongly
insisted. But we shall, equally certainly, find elements in
the method of Yahweh-worship which we cannot trace back
to the nomad stage, while they have numerous parallels
among the more developed civilizations. Nowhere is the
protest against Canaanite cults stronger than in *Deuteronomy*,
yet even in *Deuteronomy* we meet with cultic practices—e.g.
the offering of firstfruits—which could not possibly have
belonged to the old Mosaic religion of pastoral tribes wandering in the untilled lands. It is hardly possible to doubt the
ultimate Canaanite origin of these features of the later
official Judaism. Bearing these facts in mind, we may
proceed to glance briefly at the Canaanite objects of
worship, sanctuaries, cultus, sacred persons, and religious
ethic.

2. CANAANITE OBJECTS OF WORSHIP

Canaanite religion shared with that of the Hebrews the
general characteristics of Polydæmonism.[1] That is to say,
there were a number of spirits worshipped, many of which
were of the same type, though, instead of being merely the
" group-spirits " characteristic of a pure animism, they were
individualized and isolated. It was not necessary that
they should have separate names; it was enough that they
were confined, more or less, each to his own sphere of influence. But there were several striking differences between
the *numina* venerated in Palestine and those which claimed
the allegiance of the pastoral tribes.

In the first place, while all classes of animistic spirits
probably received attention (and particularly the spirits
of the departed), the outstanding deities belonged, not
to the *'El* class but to that of the *Ba'als*.[2] That is to say,
they were not primarily spirits of the open country, but
rather of the arable land, and their chief business was the
promotion of agriculture. They were thus essentially
fertility spirits, such as are found almost everywhere among
early farming peoples. They were local deities rather
than tribal spirits, attached to the soil rather than to the
clan. Their authority was territorially limited, and one
of the most impressive of the exploits of Elijah was his

---

[1] Part I, Chapter I, § 3.   [2] Part I, Chapter V.

proof of the fact that the writ of a foreign *Ba'al* did not run on Israelite soil.[1]

It goes without saying that the presence of the *Ba'als* was indicated by some material objects. The excavator not infrequently discovers whole or broken snake-heads or bull-heads in stone or bronze. These may have had a special place in the cultus, and the examples of Bethel and of Jerusalem in Israelite days lend probability to the suggestion. But we cannot be certain of the fact, while we have direct evidence as to the presence of two other objects, the *Mazzebah*, an upright natural stone, and the *'Asherah*, a wooden pillar. There is some reason to suspect that the latter sometimes represented a goddess, though the reference in Jer. ii. 27 shows that the stone might be feminine and the wood masculine. Specimens of the *'Asherah* have, naturally, not survived, but every pre-exilic sanctuary which has been excavated contained monoliths, sometimes singly, sometimes in variously arranged groups. There can be no doubt that, whatever else the sanctuaries may have contained, these two objects were in practically universal use as emblems of the local deities.

Generally speaking, it may be said that the *Ba'al* took much the same place in the life of the local agricultural community as that filled by the tribal god of the pastoral group. He is the king, the father, the leader in war, the guardian of the locality, and the final judicial authority for his city or village. Apart from his help there is no hope of success in the production of the annual crops; he controls the rain (an especially important function in Palestine) and causes the seed to germinate. To his bounty are due the products of the soil, especially those three most necessary means of civilized livelihood, corn, wine, and oil. If his worship be not properly carried out, he can and will withhold these things, and in an extreme case he may go yet further and bring on the erring community more positive disasters, foreign enemies, or wild beasts. Israel was not the only people which believed that defeat in the field was the direct result of the anger of the national god.

The natural and original religion of Palestine, then, seems to have been a Polydæmonistic Baalism, which persisted through every stage of the history of the land to a com-

---

[1] This is the real meaning of the trial scene on Mount Carmel, and of the slaughter of the prophets of *Ba'al* which followed it. See 1 Kings xviii, and below, pp. 211–213.

paratively late period.   But cults of this kind are far from
exhausting the religious phenomena of pre-Israelite Palestine.
From the dawn of history, the country has been exposed to
foreign invasion, and has suffered from foreign domination.
Each wave of invaders may be expected to leave a more or
less permanent mark on the religious life and thought of the
people, and we have abundant evidence as to the worship
of great gods and goddesses, who stand on a very different
plane from the local fertility spirits, and in some cases seem
to have absorbed or superseded them.

In this connexion it is interesting to observe how slight
was the influence of Egypt.   From the middle of the fifteenth
century B.C. to the end of the tenth—possibly later also—
Egypt claimed suzerainty over Palestine.   Her rule was not
always effective, and towards the end of the period degener-
ated into spasmodic raids, like that which destroyed Gezer
in Solomon's time and that which desolated Judah under
Rehoboam.   During the period of her real ascendancy
(which probably came to an end with the Philistine invasions
at the beginning of the twelfth century) she governed mainly
through native subject princes, but there were certain strong
points, e.g. at Bethshean, where she posted her own officials
and established some kind of garrison.   In such places—
and, indeed, in many others—we find unmistakable
evidence of Egyptian occupation, such as scarabs bearing
Egyptian names, and various inscriptions showing royal
cartouches of the XVIIIth and XIXth dynasties (roughly
1450–1200 B.C.).   But, strangely enough, there is little to
show that the cult of the Egyptian gods ever gained a real
hold on the people in general.   Even the temples excavated
at the sites where Egyptian influence is most prominent are
of a Semitic type, and the chief deities worshipped there
seem not to have been Egyptian.   It is true that there may
have been some identification of gods and goddesses; it was
easy, for instance, to regard Astarte and Hathor as being
one and the same person under different names.   But the
cultus, in all its features, seems to have been rather that of
the former than that of the latter.   There were features
of the religion of Palestine which were imported into Egypt,
and left some mark on that country, but the reverse process
was far less significant, and the direct influence of Egyptian
religion on that of Canaan was hardly greater than the influence of Christianity on Hinduism would have been if
there had been no Christian missions in India.

It seems clear that the great deities of Palestine came almost entirely from the east and from the north. The country itself gives us comparatively little information, but we know more of the religion of Damascus and of Phœnicia, and it seems almost certain that the deities known and revered in these countries would have spread southwards also, especially since we find many of them mentioned in Egypt and in the Ras Shamra tablets.[1] A list of over twenty gods and goddesses could be compiled, most of them being familiar elsewhere also. Thus we hear of Resheph, of Sutekh and Shamash, of Sin and of Nergal. The composite deity Hadad-Rimmon seems to have been worshipped in Palestine proper; Gad certainly had at least one shrine in the country. It has been plausibly conjectured that both Salem and Zedek were divine names connected with Jerusalem, and in Dagon—or, more properly, Dagan—we have a corn-spirit who has become a full god. The Elephantiné papyri attest the presence of gods named Herem and Bethel alongside of Yahweh, and, since these deities bear Semitic, and not Egyptian, names, they must have been imported by the colonists themselves. A curious feature of the Elephantiné Pantheon is the fact that the subordinate gods are usually paired,[2] either with each other or with Yahweh. We have further definite evidence from the Old Testament itself. Ezekiel speaks of the cult of Tammuz, and down to Isaiah's time there was a serpent-god in Jerusalem known as Nehushtan. Amos refers to Kewan and Sakkuth; both are well-known Mesopotamian divine names, and, since Israel had not yet come seriously into contact with Babylonia, we are justified in assuming that these were gods whose residence went back to the early days of eastern influence in Palestine. It is even possible that David was a divine name, though, more probably, it was an epithet applied to various deities, or perhaps some cultural object.

The list of goddesses is somewhat shorter, though some of them attained to very great importance. Nikal—not mentioned in the Old Testament—was a Sumerian goddess, and it is sometimes supposed that the term Kadesh was the proper name of another, though the word may have been a mere epithet. A goddess Ashimah seems to have been known to Amos, and she appears again in the Elephantiné papyri. Three great goddesses were known and revered in Israel.

---

[1] Cf. p. 172.

[2] E.g. 'Anath-Bethel, 'Ishumbethel (Cowley, 22[123-125]), 'Anath-Ya'u (44[3]), Herem-Bethel (7[7]), cf. Hadad-Rimmon (Zech. xii. 11).

N

One of these bore the name Asherah, a term also used for the sacred wooden pillar. It is not clear what place she held in Palestine, but she was a prominent figure in the mythology of nothern Syria. The most lofty and dignified of all was Anath, the "queen of heaven," who has left her name at several places in Palestine, and was, apparently, the consort of Yahweh in Elephantiné. Best known, however, was Ashtoreth, or Astarte, the western form of the greatest of all Mesopotamian deities, Ishtar. In her and in the other goddesses, we have forms of the mother-goddess whose cult was practically universal in the agricultural communities of western Asia. This may explain the fact that her name sometimes appears in a plural form. Again, we find her to the east of Jordan in Ashtoreth-Karnaim, and recent excavation has unearthed a great temple consecrated to her at Tell-el-Nasbeh, the ancient Mizpah. Here she was worshipped alongside of Yahweh till at least the end of the eighth century.

We have thus a picture of an extraordinary medley of religious beliefs and objects of worship. We need not suppose that every one of the great gods and goddesses had a shrine in every city; probably there was room for only two or three in each place. Palestine was essentially a land divided into small communities, and we may conjecture that each place had its own peculiar deity, while offering hospitality to others. In the country, in the small towns and the villages, the old Baalism remained supreme; the polytheistic cults belonged to the cities. But Israel was to come into contact with both, and neither can be neglected when we are trying to sum up the religious forces which met the Aramæan invaders on their settlement in the promised land.

3. SANCTUARIES

Just as the dweller on the soil has a more solid and permanent home than the nomad, so the god of the latter is better housed than in a mere tent. It may be taken for granted that the sanctuaries were among the most stable buildings in ancient Palestine, though the materials used were probably the same as those employed in the houses of the wealthier citizens. The foundations and lower courses of the walls were usually constructed of stone or of burnt brick, the upper portions being of sun-dried mud. The latter has, of course, perished, with the result that it is possible to see little more than the ground-plans of the ancient edifices. These, however, make it clear that the whole might have been somewhat elaborate, as it must have been in the greater shrines to meet the complicated demands of the cultus.

The site chosen was not infrequently a hill-top. The city might be at the foot of the hill or on the slope, and the sanctuary outside its walls above it. This, at least, seems to have been the situation at Ramah, at Gibeah, and at early Jerusalem, and the name *Bāmāh*, " high place," applied to these sanctuaries in the Old Testament, suggests some elevation. The site covered a fairly large area, and included places where the victims might be sacrificed, a room or a series of rooms where the worshippers might consume the sacrificial flesh, apartments for the priests, and even spots where the remains of victims wholly offered on the altar might be disposed of. A large part of the space was open to the sky, especially a court where the main altar probably stood in front of the actual shrine itself.[1] This latter was the apartment of the god; here were placed the symbols most sacred to him; entry was possible probably to none but priests, and the threshold was carefully guarded by a series of *taboos*. Possibly, as in Mesopotamian and Egyptian palaces and temples, the entrance was flanked by figures representing guardian spirits, and similar objects might be found even inside the shrine. We hear little of images within the inner building, and others beside Israel may have dispensed with artificial figures. But archæological evidence shows that in some sanctuaries, at all events, images existed; thus, in many places representations of the nude mother-goddess of Asia Minor have been discovered.[2] They may have been used as amulets or charms; or they may have been votive offerings connected with the sacrifice of virginity, there are so many that they can hardly have been temple cult-objects. The only certain reference, however, in our Old Testament is to the image of Dagon at Ashdod, and this may have been due to ideas imported with the Philistines. At the same time, as we have already seen, the figures of the snake and the bull, worshipped in Israel during the monarchical period, may be relics of a Canaanite cult.[3]

[1] For an interesting and very informing account of the altar in Israel see Kittel, *Studien zur hebräischen Archäologie und Religionsgeschichte*, pp. 97–158 (1908); also J. Battersby Harford, *Altars and Sanctuaries in the Old Testament* (1929).

[2] *Quarterly Statement: Palestine Exploration Fund*, 1903, p. 36; and see further, S. A. Cook, *The Religion of Ancient Palestine in the Light of Archæology*, pp. 123 ff. (1930).

[3] The model of a cobra in bronze was found on the site of the Gezer temple; an illustration is in the *Quarterly Statement (Palestine Exploration Fund)*, 1903, p. 222.

4. THE CULTUS

The whole aim of an agricultural religion is to secure the hearty co-operation of the deity in the production of the various crops. For this reason he needs to be kept in a favourable mood, and he requires the assistance of certain types of ritual which resemble sympathetic magic. All the efforts of the worshippers will be unavailing unless the close bond between the god and his people be constantly maintained and renewed. There are the occasional, often personal, forms of ritual, achieving atonement for ceremonial sins, but the two main items in the cultus were the festivals and sacrifice.

(a) The principal festivals were three in number. Over the whole of the nearer East, the greatest agricultural festival in ancient times was that which took place in the autumn, at the end of one year and the beginning of the next. It is true that we have no record of the ceremonial observed on Palestinian soil before the Hebrew conquest, but there seems no reason to doubt that the same kind of ritual was observed there as in other parts of the ancient East. The whole centred round the marriage and death of a vegetation god, and one of the best accounts we have comes to us from Theocritus, who describes the rite as performed in Egypt in Ptolemaic times. An element of sympathetic magic is clearly present, and the ceremony is evidently intended to help the fertility spirits to perform their annual tasks.[1]

The next critical point in the farmer's calendar comes with the beginning of the harvest, which takes place in Palestine in spring. Bread was leavened with sour dough, a small piece from each baking being left to ferment and used for the next batch. There is thus a continuity in the successive generations of the bread, and it goes without saying that some contamination may be transmitted throughout the year. The ill-effects of this can be avoided only by breaking the chain, and so for the first days during which the new crop is being used leaven is prohibited, being resumed only when the new dough has begun to ferment of itself. The cutting of the first sheaf and the eating of unleavened bread are the outstanding features of this ritual.

The third of the three great feasts falls at the end of the wheat harvest, roughly some seven weeks later than the

[1] Cf. *Myth and Ritual*, pp. 68–86 (1933).

second. It is less critical than either of the other two, and is mainly a festival of thanksgiving to the god for the crop that he has once more supplied.

(b) Sacrifice [1] is of two kinds, with two fundamentally distinct ideas and aims underlying it. One type is essentially a gift made to the deity,[2] the other is a common meal in which the god and his worshippers share.[3] The two types are very widely spread, and it may even be asserted that one or the other, usually both, may be found in the ritual of practically every religion known to us. The difference of purpose produces differences in the ritual, and the two are very easily to be distinguished.

Gift sacrifices depend on the worshippers' view of the personality and claims of the deity. He is the lord of the land, and as the king of the community he can claim a certain proportion of the produce of the soil. We should therefore include under this head the offerings of tithes and first-fruits. The latter are especially stringent; the first-born of every animal is sacred, the first year's fruit borne by a tree may not be touched by man. To bring the fruit into common use is to " profane " it, and the same may be said of the produce of new fields. From time to time land had to lie fallow, and though the practice was necessitated by the demands of agriculture, the original reasons for it were religious rather than scientific. Even when land had been long worked, the god as the king claimed his tribute, and this took the form of tithe, payable in kind at stated intervals. But the most obvious form of gift, indeed perhaps the commonest, consisted of the bodies of slaughtered animals.

No doubt this practice goes back to an age when the god is supposed to be in need of the same kind of sustenance as men, and to eat and drink as they do. But it was realized at a comparatively early stage that the divine essence was even more attenuated than the human, and that the presentation of food in its simplest form would not be acceptable. The god might, nevertheless, delight in the smell of the victim, and if it could be transformed into a " soothing savour " it would give him both satis-

---

[1] We are not dealing here with the origin of sacrifice, which would involve too intricate a discussion. We would only point out that the evidence suggests to many scholars that in their origin sacrifices were a development of magical rites, or an attempt to maintain the life of the deity. See further, Oesterley, *Sacrifices in Ancient Israel* (1937).

[2] See especially Buchanan Gray, *Sacrifice in the Old Testament*, pp. 1–95.

[3] This is worked out in much detail by Robertson Smith, *Rel. Sem.*, pp. 244–352.

faction and maintenance. So it was burnt on the altar, and the ascending smoke carried the essence of the victim to the god in a condition in which he could readily assimilate it.[1] The gods gather like flies to the scent of the Babylonian sacrifice,[2] and even in Hebrew tradition Yahweh is presented as so delighted with the offering of Noah that He made a solemn promise never again to drown off a race which could afford Him so much pleasure (Gen. viii. 20, 21).

Such a sacrifice might be offered in normal times as a regular gift or tribute, but it had a special place in the elimination of sin. Every religion recognizes and allows for the fact of sin, knowing that there is always something arising from the nature or from the life of man which interrupts the ideal relationship between the worshipper and the object of his worship. The deity will be offended, and something must be done to restore him to a good humour. The obvious method is to make him a gift, and, while other ideas may at times be involved, the conception of a fine or bribe which will restore the divine favour is almost universal.

It goes without saying that the species of animals which might be offered in sacrifice was limited. There were always those which were held to be especially suitable, normally those which man himself used, for food, though there were notable exceptions. But the great majority of sacrifices consisted of the domestic animals, goats, sheep, and oxen. Since man enjoyed their flesh, it was natural to suppose that the deity would take equal pleasure in eating them, and they must be supplied to him. The great exception is human sacrifice. It seems not unlikely that in comparatively early days all the first-born of men as well as of beasts were consecrated in this way. But for the general application of the principle of human sacrifice there is no evidence in historic times in Palestine. At the same time, it certainly existed, though it was subsequent to animal-sacrifice. Among the objects discovered at the great sanctuary at Gezer were a number of jars containing the bones of infants, and one skeleton at least suggested that the rite had been postponed to a later age of the victim.[3] We hear of Mesha, king of Moab, offering up his

---

[1] The root-meaning of *'olah* (" whole burnt-sacrifice ") is " to ascend," i.e., in reference to what goes up on to the altar.

[2] See further Ball, *Light from the East*, p. 40 (1899).

[3] See *Quarterly Statement: Palestine Exploration Fund*, 1903, pp. 17–19, where an illustration of the skeleton found *in situ* may be seen. For the best concise account of Gezer, see S. A. Cook, *Religion of Ancient Palestine in the Light of Archæology*, pp. 78 ff. (1930).

eldest son on the wall of his city (2 Kings iii. 27). He was reduced to the last extremity, and assumed that his danger was due to the wrath of Chemosh his god. His only chance was to recover the favour of the god, or rather to turn the anger of Chemosh on Israel by the gift of his choicest possession, his own son, and the Hebrew record states that in this he was successful, and that the armies of Israel were compelled to return to their own land.

It was, however, not only in such extremity as this that men resorted to this practice. There is reason to believe that the widespread custom of offering a " foundation-sacrifice " was prevalent also in ancient Palestine. It has been conjectured that such a custom lies ultimately behind the story of Cain and Abel, in Gen. iv., though this is now generally held to be an unlikely explanation of the narrative. But it is clear that the curse pronounced by Joshua on the site of Jericho [1] and its fulfilment by Hiel [2] involve a sacrifice of this kind. Here the object may have been to guard the house or city against the intrusion of hostile spirits. Superstitions connected with the threshold seem to have been strongly held in ancient times, and it was commonly believed that it was a place of peculiar danger, either to those who lived in the house or to strangers who entered it.

The *communion* sacrifice involved a very different ritual. Its aim was to renew or to strengthen the natural bond between the god and the community. To this end both partook of the flesh of the same victim; in certain instances, especially where Totemism was prevalent, the worshipper may have felt that he was actually eating the god, and so absorbing his being in a most practical way; as its essence entered into both, they were once more united into a single whole. It is to be noted that in early times the flesh of the domestic animals, which belonged to the community and therefore to the god, could be eaten by men only under the auspices of religion. Slaughter involved sacrifice to the ancient mind, and wild game alone was exempt from this rule. The ritual seems to have been much as follows. The worshipper would bring his victim to the sanctuary, present it before the god and slaughter it. Certain parts of it were reserved for the altar fire, and these were first removed and burnt. This was the share especially appropriate to the god. The worshipper, with his family or other group, retired to one of the chambers in the sanctuary, and there began to cook the remainder of the carcass. A portion was necessarily

[1] Josh. vi. 26.   [2] 1 Kings xvi. 34.

to be given to the priest as the human proxy of the god, and this might be determined by chance or it might be a fixed part of the animal. The latter practice probably grew up when it was found that methods of chance might possibly be controlled by the priest.[1] Thus god, priest, and worshipper all shared in the meal, and the bond between them was renewed and strengthened.[2]

5. SACRED PERSONS

If a priestly order is a necessity to the comparatively simple nomad religion, it is still more so to the elaborate cultus of the agricultural community. The essential functions of the priesthood will, of course, be the same at all stages, but a larger establishment will be needed for the many duties which have to be performed. The sanctuary itself needs attention; the extensive buildings must be kept in a state of comparative cleanliness. The worshippers who come to offer sacrifice have to be guided and instructed in their ritual, for it goes without saying that an offering must be presented in the right way and with appropriate words. The altar must be constantly tended, its fire must be kept alight, and the portions reserved for the exclusive use of the god must be burnt. It is true that the actual slaughter of the victim was carried out by the worshipper himself except when the sacrifice was offered on behalf of the community as a whole, but the presentation of the blood and fat was probably to be performed only by duly qualified persons. Moreover, animal sacrifice is a disgusting affair, and it was necessary that something should be done to keep the premises fairly clean, while the ashes of the altar itself had to be removed at frequent intervals if the fire was not to be choked by them. And to the duties about the sanctuary must be added the responsibility for interpreting the sacred lot, or whatever means was adopted for ascertaining the divine will.

The priests naturally tended to form close corporations' and the succession was maintained either in the same family or through a process of adoption. The duties were required to be learnt, and involved the knowledge of a store of tradition handed down for generations. But in addition to these " regular " cultic persons, whose functions were professional, there rose from time to time individuals whose relation to their deity was directly personal. Any

[1] Cf. 1 Sam. ii. 12–17.
[2] For the later development of the sacrificial system see **Part III,** Chapter XXXIII, § 3.

abnormal state of mind is in the ancient world attributed to
direct divine agency, and phenomena like those of second
sight, epilepsy, and even insanity, are attributed to possession
by some *numen*. There had been a " breathing " which had
entered into the subject and transformed him. For the time
being he was not himself, and the experiences through which
he passed were held to be a direct manifestation of the deity.

The phenomena of this possession have a double aspect.
In the first place, there is the experience of the subject to
consider; he becomes conscious of another world than that
in which men ordinarily live, and in which he himself normally
dwells. He is still aware of the familiar objects of daily
life, but in addition to this he is conscious of sights and sounds
which those about him cannot appreciate. It is as though a
veil had suddenly been withdrawn from a whole universe
which is just as real as that so familiar to all men, but which
is hidden from them. The man's eyes are " opened," his
ears are " uncovered," and the secret world of the gods is
available for him also. These phenomena are to be found in
many places and under many forms of religious belief, and
they are characteristic of the type of person to whom the
name " seer " is commonly given.

The outside world, of course, does not share this inner
experience, but there are usually signs which show to
the observers that the person affected is in an abnormal
condition. In Asia Minor and in Palestine these took
the form of what is often called *ecstasy*. The muscles
might be constricted and the limbs stiffened, the subject
remaining motionless and speechless in a trance-like state.
On the other hand, there might be the wildest activity,
arms and legs being flung about and the movements being
apparently quite uncontrolled. The condition was in some
measure infectious, and when a group of persons in a state
of ecstasy acted together, their movements tended to become
rhythmical—formed, in fact, a " dance." Pain was no longer
felt, and men in this state might lash themselves or their
fellows with whips or gash themselves with knives. We have
in the Old Testament a vivid account of the " ecstatic " in
the description of the prophets of *Ba'al* on Mount Carmel.[1]

These phenomena at a later time were spread over
the whole of the Mediterranean world, and one of our
best accounts of them comes to us from Apuleius.[2] But

[1] 1 Kings xviii. 26–29.
[2] *The Golden Ass*, xi. 8–17. The date of Apuleius is the second half of
the second century A.D. (see also Herodotus, ii. 61 ff.).

they can always be traced back either to Asia Minor or to
Palestine; they do not appear in Egypt till near the fifth
century B.C., and there seems to be no trace of them either
in early Arabia or in Mesopotamia.   Except for Moses himself, who seems to have been possessed of second sight,
though probably without the wilder manifestations of the
ecstatic proper, the only persons of whom such activities
are recorded in the wilderness period are the seventy elders
mentioned in Num. xi. 25–29, and this story may well be a
reflection back into the nomad age of phenomena belonging
to a later time.   We certainly have evidence from an early
period of the presence of the ecstatic in Syria, and of the
recognition of his activities as directly inspired by a *Ba'al*.[1]

6. The Ethic of Ba'alism

We have seen that the moral standard of a pastoral people
is commonly high, and that there is reason to believe that
the Aramæan ancestors of Israel were no exception to this
rule.   But the life of the agriculturist, especially when it
is combined with a developed commercial system, is far
more complicated and difficult.   The institution of private
property on a large scale, the presence of a number of
different professions side by side, the traditional occupation
of a particular piece of territory, the greater stability of
society, the gradual raising of the standard of comfort
to a point where it becomes luxury—all these facts (and
others also) present the more advanced community with
problems which are unknown to the more primitive stage,
and expose men to temptations previously non-existent or
almost negligible.   At the same time, the demands of the
deities become more elaborate in matters of ritual, and it is
almost inevitable that religion should develop mainly along
this line.   The moral requirements of the wilderness stage
are not forgotten; there is still the same insistence on certain
types of sexual purity and on the sanctity of human life, but
the moral law does not extend the sphere of its application,
and a large area of life remains outside its influence.   This is
not to say that men were unconscious of the ethical demand;
on the contrary, they realized even more clearly than before
the difference between right and wrong.   But the human
conscience grows apart from religion, and it is one of the
tragedies of the spiritual life of man that his faith is so often

[1] See further T. H. Robinson, *Prophecy and the Prophets in Ancient
Israel* (1923).

below his private moral standard.   The religion of the ancient agricultural world is a signal illustration of this divorce of morality from religion.   An act might be universally recognized as a vice or a crime; it did not follow that it was a sin.   Except in so far as religion insisted on the observance of certain primitive *taboos*, it was indifferent to the treatment accorded by a man to his neighbours, and left the vindication of moral and social right either to the individual wronged or to the civil heads of the community.

There is a still graver charge to be brought against the religion of ancient Palestine.   It was not merely indifferent to the claims of simple ethics, it even condoned and authorized direct violations of the moral law.   No one would justify murder in ordinary civil life, yet there were times— rare, it is true—when human sacrifice was practised.   Sexual irregularity was condemned by the common feeling of the western Semites, but sacramental fornication was a regular feature of the religious life, clearly appearing at other times as well as at the autumn festival.   Indeed, it may well have been that this vice was practically confined to the " high places."   And the great festivals, especially that of the autumn, seem to have been times of riotous licence, when free rein was given to human passions.

In one way, and in one only, does the ancient religion of Palestine appear to have imposed a moral restraint, and this was due, not so much to any ethical character of the *Ba'als*, but to their demand for personal respect. If a man bound himself by an oath, he broke his word at his own peril, and was sure to suffer from the vengeance of the god.   By its very nature the oath is an attempt to secure a divine sanction.   The formula is: " May the god do so " (probably accompanied by a gesture implying ruin) " to me, and so again, if I do . . ." or some similar phrase which invites the deity to take vengeance if the oath is broken.   When this has been said the very pride of the god demands that he shall punish perjury, and so strong was the fear of vengeance that a solemn oath taken by one party or the other in the presence of the god was sufficient to settle any dispute.   If a man swore that he was not guilty of an offence, it was assumed that he was innocent, for none would dare so to flout the god as to " take his name in vain." But while the oath did undoubtedly have a moral value, its very existence testified to the ethical deficiencies of the religion which required it.

CHAPTER XV

THE EARLY RELIGION OF THE SETTLEMENT: APOSTASY

WE have seen in Chapter XIII something of the general character of the religion of the Hebrews in the wilderness, and in Chapter XIV we have glanced at the religion of Canaan. We have now to see the effect of the impact of a higher civilization, with its more elaborate life and ritual, on the faith of the Hebrew invaders who overran Palestine at some time between the end of the sixteenth century B.C. and the beginning of the eleventh. It was inevitable that contact with the more advanced people, and a change from the social order of the wandering shepherd to that of the settled farmer and trader, should have a profound influence on the whole outlook of the people, and that their religion should be affected as well as other sides of their life. In order to appreciate this we must briefly consider the actual situation of the Hebrews during the centuries which immediately followed the conquest and preceded the establishment of the monarchy.

1. ISRAEL IN PALESTINE

The conquest of Palestine was neither sudden nor complete, as we learn from the book of *Judges*. The Aramæan invaders at first were able to make good their footing only in the wilder parts of the country, the hills in the centre of the land, and the grazing country to the east of Jordan and to the south. The fertile lands, such as the maritime plain and the plain of Esdraelon, remained in the hands of their former possessors, and there were two belts of unsubdued Canaanites who cut the Israelite settlements into three main divisions. Between those who found a home in the south, with their centre at Hebron,[1] and those who established themselves in the centre, in the Bethel district, lay Jerusalem, which became Israelite only when captured by David. Another group in the far north was again cut off from its fellows by a

---

[1] This group seems to have entered from the south, and it is possible that the name Judah originally belonged to a Canaanite group, later absorbed by the invading Yahweh-worshippers. Cf. T. H. Robinson in *Amicitiae Corolla*, pp. 265 ff. (1933).

line of fortresses stretching from Megiddo on the slopes of the Carmel range to Bethshean, which guarded the chief ford across the Jordan, just south of the Sea of Galilee. Even Saul's kingdom never included the plain of Esdraelon, though he was able to cross it by night, in order to consult the necromancer of Endor.[1] His northern frontier was Mount Gilboa, and it was there that the Philistines, after a long series of fruitless attacks on him from the west, made their final and successful attempt to overthrow him, using the valley of Jezreel and the city of Bethshean as their base. But, in those districts which they did occupy (especially the Ephraimitic hills) Israel brought a new vigour into the country, and as they gradually spread into the arable districts, largely through peaceful penetration and intermarriage (Abimelech is a case in point, Judges ix. 1 ff.), they provided an element which successfully resisted attacks made from the outside. The book of *Judges* is largely a record of these assaults, and it is significant that Deborah and Barak are the only " judges " who have to meet a Canaanite foe. The others fight the battles of the older inhabitants as much as those of Israel, and the process of welding together the two elements in the population reaches its climax in the resistance made to the Philistines.

The Hebrew invaders thus formed but a comparatively small element in the population, and though their military prowess enabled them to take and to hold a leading position, their general culture was below the level of that of their new neighbours. It was only gradually that they took to the operations of agriculture, and they must have been generally impressed by the superiority of their predecessors. It seems, in fact, that they simply adopted the culture of Palestine *en bloc*. Their original language was, presumably, a dialect of Aramaic; in Canaan they used Hebrew, the old speech of the people in the Tell-el-Amarna age. The civil law which we find embodied in Israel's earliest codes is a form of that common to all the peoples of Western Asia, and resembles the type represented in the law of the Hittites, the Babylonians, and the Assyrians. Strangely enough, the Old Testament appears to offer us the most primitive form of that law which has come down to us, suggesting that it was current in Palestine even before the age of the great Hammurabi [2] (c. 2000 B.C.). We may observe, too, that the folk-lore and mythology, including the cosmology, of Israel,

[1] 1 Sam. xxviii. 4 ff.
[2] Cf. Jirku: *Das weltliche Recht im Alten Testament* (1927).

while presenting us with significant and indeed unique features, have parallels with Mesopotamian literature, and we gather from occasional hints in the Old Testament that if the popular tales, as they were told among the common folk, had been preserved, we should have found the resemblance greater still. We need not doubt that, just as the Teutonic invaders of the fourth century A.D. adapted themselves in large measure to the culture of imperial Rome, so these new conquerors of Palestine inherited with the land they occupied much, if not all, of the existing mode of life. And to carry the parallel a step farther, just as the northern invaders of the ancient Mediterranean world accepted, in the main, the religion of the land which they entered, so, too, Israel went far in accepting the deities and the cultus which they found already in the country. It is true that no new people can adopt a religion without importing something into it, and that they may in the long run have a profound influence on its nature; but for some generations we must expect to find little difference, if any, between the faith of the older inhabitants and that of the new-comers.

2. ISRAEL AND THE BAʻALS

We have already glanced in brief outline at the religion of Palestine before the entry of Israel into the land.[1] In addition to the natural respect which even a victorious race feels for the higher culture of its defeated enemy, there were strong reasons which predisposed the new-comers to adopt the cultus and belief of their predecessors. The tribal conception of deity which prevailed in the wilderness was exchanged for a theory of territorial dominion. The land belonged to the deities long worshipped there, including both great gods and goddesses such as those already mentioned,[2] but also the local *Baʻals*, who seem to have assumed an even greater importance in the mind of the people than the better-known deities. While these older objects of worship might differ among themselves in importance and power, the locality in which each made his home owed allegiance to him and to no other. The national gods—and there were *Baʻals* with a wider authority than the village or city—exercised supreme control over their own land, and their worshippers never admitted that they were conquered by other powers. If, in later times, Moab suffers from an invasion of Israel, or Israel is laid waste by a foreign

[1] Cf. Chapters V and XIV.   [2] See pp. 177 f.

army, the calamity is due to the anger of the national god manifested against his own people; if and when he can be appeased, the enemy will be expelled as a matter of course. When Naaman the Syrian, in gratitude for his cure, decides that he will worship no god but Yahweh, he can solve the problem of territorial dominion only by taking two mules' burden of earth with him (2 Kings v. 17). It is a piece of Yahweh's land, and on it he can erect an altar to Yahweh and offer Him due service. Even the writer of Ps. xlii–xliii, though his date can hardly be earlier than 597 B.C., counts it his greatest sorrow that he is leaving his God behind him as he goes into exile.

These illustrations are all derived from a period later than that which we are now considering, but we may safely assume that the ideas which they manifest are survivals from the earlier stage. In the first generations of the settlement men still thought of Yahweh as being no permanent inhabitant of Palestine, but as dwelling in the far south, whence He would come in times of special need to serve His people against their enemies (cp. Judges v. 4 and 1 Kings xix, where Elijah has to go to "Horeb" to meet Yahweh). The deities on the spot were the Ba'als, and they must be taken into consideration. If they did not receive due reverence and tribute, their anger would be aroused, and they would exhibit their displeasure by bringing calamity on the land. Centuries later Israel suffered from foreign invasion, and a part of her population was deported. The place of the exiles was partially filled by settlers from distant parts of the Assyrian empire, and the new-comers found themselves plagued by lions. Instead of attributing their troubles to the scanty population, which failed to check the increase of wild beasts, they ascribed their difficulties to the anger of the god of the land, i.e. Yahweh, and were not relieved till a priest of Yahweh was sent to teach them how He should be worshipped (2 Kings xvii. 24–28). The narrator of the story fully shares the beliefs which he describes, and here again we need not doubt that we have a survival of a very ancient idea. When they made their home in Palestine, the Israelites must have been in fear lest they should incur disaster by the neglect of the established Ba'als, the divine owners of the soil.

Even if they had felt reasonably secure against such disaster—and they may have held that Yahweh could, after all, protect them against the anger of these objects of local worship—there was still another consideration which weighed with Israel. Yahweh was their national God, though He still dwelt in Sinai or Horeb. He had served them well, led them through the wilderness, brought them into the land, given them direction when they needed it, fought their battles for them. But He was essentially an *'El*, a wilderness god, and they had no experience of His ability to handle the new problems with which they were faced. They were now undertaking gradually the operations of agriculture : could Yahweh help them ? Did this southern storm- and mountain-God know how to grow corn ? Did He understand the culture of the vine and the olive ? Was He able to supply flax and other products of the ground so necessary for the new life on which they were entering ? This is not a fancy suggestion; even as late as the time of Hosea there were men in Israel who did not know that it was Yahweh who supplied them with the produce of the soil (Hos. ii. 5, 8). It was almost inevitable that Israel should turn from Yahweh to the *Ba'als* to secure, not merely freedom from danger, but also prosperity in the new venture.

3. The Lesson of the Judges

It was through the bitter experiences of the centuries which elapsed between the conquest and the establishment of the monarchy that Israel learned her mistake, and the story of the lesson is told us in the book of *Judges*. As it stands, that book consists of a series of narratives dealing with the " Judges " of Israel, compiled in its present form by a writer, or a school of writers, who used the incidents recorded to illustrate a particular philosophy of history. The whole is a repetition of a regular cycle of events, and may be stated in a formula : " And the children of Israel forgot Yahweh their God, and served the *Ba'als*, and Yahweh sold them into the hand of A (an oppressor), and they served A so-and-so many years. And they repented and cried unto Yahweh their God, and Yahweh raised up for them a Judge, B, who delivered them out of the hand of A. (Then follows the detailed account of the exploits of B, taken from much older sources.) And the land had rest so-and-so many years. And it came to pass that the children of Israel served Yahweh all the days of B, but after the death of B they forgot Yahweh their God . . ."; and so the cycle is renewed, with its succession of apostasy, oppression, repentance, and deliverance.

Now this is not a piece of arbitrary punishment, but a very sound interpretation of history. Powerful as a *Ba'al* might possibly be in his own locality, he asked for no allegiance from without, and exercised no authority save in his own limited area. *Ba'alism* was thus necessarily a disintegrating force, separating city from city and village from village. In face of an enemy, be he a Palestinian dynast such as Sisera, or a foreign invader such as the other oppressors, there was in *Ba'alism* nothing that would unite the people against him and so create an effective resistance. The hordes that swept in from the desert in search of plunder and the more systematically organized armies of imperially-minded kings alike found an easy prey in the disunited communities into which Palestine was split up, and plundered or destroyed their victims piecemeal.

Before the entry into Canaan, Israel was a loose confederacy of tribes, held together by a sense of common blood and the common worship of Yahweh. It was inevitable that the former of these two bonds should be slackened as between the isolated communities in Palestine after the Conquest; and *Ba'alism*, with its village patriotism, offered no cohesive influence. The only unifying force which Israel possessed lay in her worship of Yahweh, and if she once lost her grip on that, she fell an easy prey to the oppressor. It is significant that when the need arose and the appeal went out to the scattered clans, it was sent in the name of Yahweh, and failure to respond brought down a condemnation, based not on national but on religious grounds. The Judges themselves were men and women inspired by Yahweh, and having something of the character of the ecstatic prophet.[1] They were recognized as the means and instruments whereby the national God worked salvation for His people, and it was in Him and in Him alone that the armies of Israel could unite and achieve their triumphs. It was not an accident that apostasy meant oppression, and fidelity brought deliverance; it arose out of the very facts of the situation.

But Israel was slow to grasp the lesson, and some centuries passed before it was fully learned. The country suffered from the domination of Moab and from the invasions of the tribes akin to the Bedawin—Ammonites, Midianites,

---

[1] Cf. Judges vi. 34, where it is said that the spirit of Yahweh " put on " Gideon as a garment, i.e. entered into him and used him as its material instrument.

O

" Children of the East,"—and was freed each time by the action of a Yahweh-inspired Judge. Finally, the struggle against the Philistines, more severe and lasting than any earlier conflicts, brought matters to a head, and, under Saul and David, produced a genuine unity of the inhabitants of Palestine for the first time in the history of the land. Both men were devotees of Yahweh. Saul was a typical " Nabi," or prophet of the older type, and was, throughout his life, subject to the onrush of the divine Spirit. David, while less obviously ecstatic, made it his aim to secure the unity of his people in a common faith, and established at Jerusalem a centre not only of the political life of Israel but also of its cultus. Other sanctuaries certainly remained, and received honour, but that which sheltered the Ark (like Shiloh in an earlier generation) had a special pre-eminence, and served as a symbol, both of the royal power, and still more of the oneness of Israel in the worship of her God.

CHAPTER XVI

THE RELIGION OF ISRAEL IN THE EARLY MONARCHY

THE establishment of the Monarchy in Israel proved in a certain sense to be the victory of Yahweh. The nation now recognized definitely and finally that for them He was the supreme God.[1] Others might and did exist, and could be worshipped each in his or her own sphere. But any city which was within the community and recognized that it formed a part of the political and national whole, accepted Yahweh as at least one of the beings who must be worshipped within his own bounds. And we may add that in most cases, if not in all, He was held to be the greatest and the most powerful of all. He had shown by His prowess and by His gifts in Nature (though this last point was slow in achieving full recognition) that the land did, as a matter of fact, belong to Him. He was no longer a mountain-God with His home in the far south; He dwelt in Palestine, among His own people, and men could there enter directly into communion with Him.

But this recognition of Yahweh as the supreme God of Israel, even in Palestine, did not necessarily mean the triumph of the old religion of nomadic Israel. Forces were at work in the new home which tended profoundly to modify both the theory and practice of Yahwism, and we may suspect that Moses and his immediate successors would have failed to recognize in the popular worship of Solomon, Ahab,

---

[1] Important evidence is to be derived from the personal names used at various periods in Israel. G. B. Gray has shown conclusively (*Hebrew Proper Names*, esp. pp. 158 ff., and the tables on pp. 281 ff. [1896]), that the use of names in which Yahweh formed an element grew rapidly during the period of the Monarchy; six persons only before the time of David bore names of this type, while they predominate in the eighth and seventh centuries B.C. This fact is not inconsistent with the worship of other deities, as is shewn by the Elephantiné papyri, where the great majority of the names are Yahweh-formations, though other gods are recognized. But it does prove the *supremacy* of Yahweh, and points to a state of religious thought in which He was regarded as the great object of national worship.

and Manasseh, the faith which had inspired them in the
wilderness. We must, then, glance briefly at the general
characteristics of religion in this period, and then at such
features as may have been peculiar in different parts of the
country.

1. POLYTHEISM

It was supposed, until comparatively recent years, that
during the monarchic period Yahweh was the only God
worshipped normally in Israel, and that the apparent
references to other cults are to be explained as emphatic
condemnation of the form which Yahwism took in the civic
and agricultural life of Israel. While this explanation must
be admitted to be partly correct, we know now that the
veneration of other deities was a frequent, perhaps a normal,
feature of Israelite life practically down to the time of the
Exile. We have frequent mention of strange gods in the
Old Testament. In Deut. xiii there is a passionate condemnation of heathen worship, whose intensity surely points
to the existence of the evil it seeks to uproot. The great
prophets from time to time speak of the rivals of Yahweh;
according to Hosea, Israel did not know that it was He who
gave her her corn and her wine and her oil (ii. 8), while the
protest against heathen cults is one of the outstanding
features of his message. In Amos we even have the names
of Kewan and Sakkuth, both Mesopotamian names for Saturn
(v. 26), and possibly also of Ashimah (viii. 14), a goddess found
also in the Elephantiné community. It was left to Josiah
to eradicate from Jerusalem the cult of Asherah, and it is
certain that all the gods of the Elephantiné community must
have been brought by them from Palestine, since their
names are Semitic and not Egyptian.

2. SYNCRETISM

" Syncretism " is a term used in the historical study of
religion to indicate a mixture of two or more religions,
especially where the objects of worship proper to the one
are adored with a form of cultus derived from another.
This type of religious hybridism is very common where a
higher religion has nominally conquered and ousted a lower
faith, and instances may be seen in the history of Buddhism,
Christianity, and, to a lesser extent, in Islam. In the
history of Israel we have, perhaps, the best illustration of
all; and we shall do well to remember that even though

Yahweh was superimposed on the *Ba'als*, it by no means followed that the resultant Yahwism was in any sense pure.

We have already seen something of the influences and beliefs which tended to draw the early Israelite settlers towards the worship of the *Ba'als*. While Yahweh was now recognized as the supreme God of Israel, these forces had by no means lost their power. What had happened was, in effect, that as Israel had taken to the life of the farmer, her God had done likewise, and must henceforward be regarded as a fertility deity. His task with Israel was no longer that of guidance through the paths of the wilderness, though He retained the character of rain-giver. But His function was now less the production of occasional fodder for the wandering flocks than the regular supply of the crops. And the worship of Israel was intended in no small part to give Him such help as He might require. For Yahweh the character of a fertility God was new, but there had been others long in the land. If He was to take the place and perform the duties of the old *Ba'als*, it was only natural that men should assume that they could best serve Him (and so, indirectly, themselves) by offering to Him a worship like that which had been paid to His predecessors. While, then, the name used in worship was often that of Yahweh, the details of the cultus were, we may believe, very much what they had been in Palestine from time immemorial.

It would seem that many of the old sanctuaries, perhaps all,[1] were devoted to Yahweh instead of to the local *Ba'al*. In some instances we have narratives which suggest that an entirely new type of cultus with a fresh altar was introduced. Such are the stories of Manoah at Zor'ah,[2] and of the origin of the sanctity of Jerusalem in the time of David. It has been suspected that the story in Judges xiii is intended to explain the sanctity of the rock-altar still to be seen at Zor'ah, and that the account of the meeting of David and the angel of pestilence at the threshing-floor of Araunah gives the reason for the use of the great rock near by as a holy place. But both rocks, though certainly used as altars in ancient times, show cup-marks and channels which are

---

[1] It should be remarked that recently Dr. A. C. Welch (*The Code of Deuteronomy*, 1924) has asserted that the old *Ba'al* sanctuaries retained their original purpose, and a few great Yahweh sanctuaries were set up. Recent research has justified the theory, at least as far as it maintains that the old cults survived.

[2] See further, Kittel, *Studien zur hebr. Arch.*, pp. 104–108.

probably far older than Israel,[1] and even if the theory as to
the source of the narratives themselves be correct (and this is
by no means certain), it seems fairly clear that the places in
question were holy long before the Israelite occupation of
Palestine, and that they are to be classed among the
sanctuaries adapted to Yahwism.

It is probable that most of the literature containing the
ritual prescriptions comes to us in its present form from after
the Exile and that it has been subjected to drastic purification.   Even if that be so, it must contain a very large pre-
exilic element, and though we must allow for the development
of the forms, we may suppose that many primitive features
have been preserved. These belong, not merely to early Israel,
but even to the older Canaanite worship. From this source
were derived the three great agricultural festivals to which
allusion has already been made,[2] much of the popular mythology of Israel, the general type of building proper to the cultus,
and, above all, the institution of sacrifice on a large scale.[3]

We may note some of these features in rather more detail.
The study of comparative mythology shows us that a story
of creation was told almost everywhere in the ancient Semitic
world, and that it was associated with the annual return of
Nature to life in the spring.   It took various forms, of which
the best-known is that preserved in the Babylonian Epic of
Creation. The narrative opens with a rebellion of the
powers of Chaos against the gods, under the leadership of a
great monster named Tiamat. The gods are in a state of
anxiety approaching panic, until one of them, a young god
named Marduk, undertakes to conquer the enemy. He goes
out to war against her, defeats and destroys her, and from
the remains of her body creates the earth and all that is in
it. A very different type of myth was current in northern
Syria, where it was held that every year there is a struggle
between the powers of fertility and those of barrenness, in
which the great god of life is temporarily overthrown and
killed, only to be restored again with the opening year.
Similar myths were current both in Egypt and in Greece,
and it is possible that we have some conflation of myths
derived from different sources.   There is abundant evidence
to the existence of some myth of this kind in ancient Israel,
though it seems probable that it varied with different

---

[1] See Buchanan Gray, *Sacrifice in the Old Testament*, p. 121 (1925);
Kittel, *op. cit.*, pp. 131 ff.
[2] See above, pp. 165, 180 f.   [3] But see above, pp. 132 f.

localities. It appears to have resembled the Mesopotamian form in the defeat of the great Chaos-monster, which, however, was sometimes cut in pieces, sometimes burnt, and sometimes merely imprisoned. It is also probable that the Israelite myth resembled that of northern Syria in speaking of the marriage of the god—in this case Yahweh—and of the consequent fertilization of the soil. In this form of the story, the consort of Yahweh was probably Anath.

It may be taken for granted that this and other myths were connected with the cultus, and, indeed, owed their preservation to that fact. In particular, the great New Year festival probably involved in Israel (as it certainly did elsewhere in the ancient world) a dramatic representation of the myth of Creation in one form or another. We may suppose that the divergent references which have come down to us are to be explained by local variations. The story as enacted at Bethel may have been quite different from that which was performed in Samaria, and there may have been other forms of it in the southern sanctuaries. But we may take it for granted that it included nearly everywhere a representation of the marriage of Yahweh with the " Queen of Heaven," i.e. Anath, and so gave ground for the charges of immorality which the pre-exilic prophets so often brought against the cultus. There may have been centres of worship where these rites were not performed, but we do not know where they were, for every sacred site mentioned, e.g. by Amos and Hosea, falls under the prophetic condemnation.[1]

Equally important with these developments of the cultus is the attitude adopted by His worshippers to Yahweh, and their altered conception of Him. This may be summed up by saying that from being an *'El* He had now become a *Ba'al*. Indeed, there is reason to believe that the word " *Ba'al* " was actually applied to Him as a descriptive title, and that it was not till after Hosea's day that the term fell out of use. If ever there were two men in the history of Israel who were devoted Yahweh enthusiasts, they were Saul and David. Yet the families of both contained persons whose names were compounded with the word *Ba'al* in such a fashion as to show that he was regarded as a deity.[2] This

---

[1] For the whole subject, see *Myth and Ritual*, especially Chapters VI and VIII.

[2] Ishba'al, son of Saul, 1 Chron. viii. 33, and Meriba'al, son of Jonathan, 1 Chron. viii. 34, seem to have been the original forms of the names found in *Samuel* as Ishbosheth and Mephibosheth, while Be'eliada, son of David, is mentioned in 1 Chron. xiv. 7, but appears in *Samuel* as Eliada.

can mean only that Yahweh Himself was intended and, in fact, He was probably indistinguishable from the older *Ba'als* save by His name.

One other most important feature of the older Canaanite religion must be mentioned. This was the presence of ecstatic prophecy. As we have already seen,[1] there is reason to believe that this was an element in the religious life of Palestine and of Syria before the coming of the Israelites, and that among them it was unknown or hardly known till after the Conquest. But Yahweh enthusiasts appeared as well as *Ba'al* enthusiasts, and they played a prominent part in the politics as well as in the religion of Israel. By the end of the ninth century they had evidently attained some sort of organization, and formed regular communities. The number of them seems to have been large, for we hear of communities outgrowing their homes and being compelled to migrate, while no less than four hundred are said to have been included in the company that attended the court of Ahab (1 Kings xxii. 6). Their social standing seems to have been low, and their methods questionable; but they did at least stand for Yahweh, and were recognized as being the *media* through whom He made His will known. The civil code and ecstatic prophecy existed as regular elements in Palestinian life before the Hebrew Conquest; Israel inherited both the Law and the Prophets from her predecessors in Palestine.

A prophet was a person " possessed " by the deity to whom he was consecrated. That is to say, as has already been suggested, his own personality was for the time in abeyance, being superseded by that of the inspiring power. Judges and kings, as well as professional prophets, manifest the same phenomena. " The spirit of Yahweh clothed itself in Gideon " (Judges vi. 34)—the man became, as it were, merely the garment of the God; Saul " became another man " (1 Sam. x. 6) while he was under the influence of the prophetic spirit. It was natural that such persons should be held to be *media* of divine communication. For in the quest of the message and instruction of a deity, it was essential that some means should be employed which were outside human control. It is this feeling which lies behind the lot as a method of ascertaining the divine will. It is assumed that no man can so manipulate the machinery as to produce an effect which he himself desires. Every event is

---

[1] See above, pp. 185 f.

the direct result of an act of will; if that will be not human it must be divine, and all that is necessary is to perform the ritual in circumstances which ensure the presence and activity of the right superhuman person. The ecstatic condition of the prophet might, it is true, be induced by artificial *stimuli*, but when once it had been induced, the possessing power took absolute control and no man could foresee or decide what the message would be.

It is, then, easy to understand how groups of prophets came to be attached to many, perhaps all, of the sanctuaries of Israel. The answering of questions was no small part of the function of sacred persons and sacred places, and, in addition to the priests, whose enquiries were conducted through the lot, there were the prophets, who could speak with more direct inspiration on a wider range of subjects. The lot could answer only Yes or No; the prophet (or, indeed, the seer) could give detailed instructions if need be. As time passed, it seems that there grew up a more or less elaborate ritual in which the prophet played a part as the mouthpiece of God. It is possible, even probable, that such formal liturgies are to be found in our present Psalter,[1] and these must date back to comparatively early pre-exilic days, though they have doubtless undergone more or less extensive modifications before reaching their present form. It is true that, before a liturgical formula could be evolved, the spontaneity of prophecy, originally essential, must have been largely forgotten, but that is the kind of process which is constantly to be found in the development of ceremonial and ritual. In the early monarchy, we may be reasonably sure, men still regarded the prophetic word as a reliable indication of the divine will as applied to each particular occasion on which it was sought. It is, indeed, possible that the demand of Amos, "Seek me, and ye shall live" (Amos v. 4), was intended to draw the contrast between the formal and stereotyped message which would be delivered at a recognized sanctuary, in accordance with an established ritual, and the uncontrolled, spontaneous utterance of the "free" prophet.

The contrast between the two types is well illustrated by Elijah and Micaiah, prophets who belong to the next period in the religious history of Israel, though it is convenient to consider this aspect of them here. Both are isolated;

[1] For a concise and clear statement of the whole position, see A. R. Johnson, "The Prophet in Israelite Worship," *Exp. Times*, XLVII (1936), pp. 113–119.

unlike Elisha, Elijah is independent of the prophetic guilds established at the sanctuaries, though these latter recognize his inspiration and authority (cp. 2 Kings ii. 3, 5, 7). Micaiah, on the other hand (1 Kings xxii. 7 ff.), is definitely contrasted with the court prophets—presumably also cult-prophets— whom Ahab consults. The narrative is of great importance for the history of prophecy, inasmuch as it shows that, alongside of the cult-prophets, there were men who relied purely on spontaneous inspiration and could stand alone against the infective influence of the ecstatic group. It was to this class that the canonical prophets belonged, and they are the legitimate successors of Elijah and of Micaiah, not of those who played a definite and formal part in the ritual of the sanctuaries. Here we have the culmination of a process which must have started early in the history of the monarchy, if not before.

3. RELIGION IN SOUTHERN PALESTINE

The comparatively close association of Judah with Israel begins with David. The tribe is not mentioned, either for praise or for blame, in the Song of Deborah, and the belt of unsubdued Canaanites whose centre was at Jerusalem made communication between the two sections difficult. It is even possible that the southern settlements were made at a different time and under different sets of leaders from those in the centre and the north of Palestine. And through all the history of the monarchy there was division between the two sections, manifesting itself after the death of Solomon in the great disruption of the kingdom. Yet the kinship between the south and the north was strongly felt, at least in religion, for both parts of the country recognized Yahweh as their God.

The principal difference during the period of the monarchy seems to have been in the form under which Yahweh was worshipped. In pre-monarchic days the chief sacred symbol had always been the Ark—so tradition held—and there seems no reason to doubt it. After the disastrous battle of Aphek (1 Sam. iv), in which the Ark was captured by the Philistines, and which resulted, as it seems, in the destruction of the old sanctuary of Shiloh, the Ark nearly disappeared, and came into prominence again only with David. After his conquest of Jerusalem, and even before his building operations were complete, David brought the Ark to Jerusalem and set it up for worship there, probably on the hill to the north of the

Ophel, where the original Jebusite city had been established. There, on a site close to the great altar of natural rock over which the so-called Mosque of Omar now stands, Solomon built the Temple, as a home in which the Ark should be placed. It is clear that while the king himself held other sanctuaries in reverence (for he sacrificed not only at Jerusalem but also at Gibeon), that of Jerusalem was intended to be the centre of the worship of Yahweh. This meant a definite settlement in the land; Yahweh dwelt between the Cherubim. A hundred years later it was necessary for Elijah to go to Horeb, the mount of God, to get into close personal touch with Yahweh; but in the eighth century Amos could speak of Yahweh as " roaring from Zion." [1]

Of the Jerusalem cultus we have few details which can be traced with absolute certainty to the period of the early monarchy. We know practically nothing of the worship of the snake, to which reference has already been made; [2] we do not even know whether this object found a place in the Temple precincts or whether there was a separate shrine in another part of the city. But the great sanctuary of the Ark continued to be the chief centre of worship down to the time of the destruction of Jerusalem in 586 B.C., and sacrifices were offered at the spot even after that time (cp. Jer. xli. 5). Though the northern kingdom far exceeded the southern in extent and power, there was no other sacred place which challenged the supremacy of Jerusalem.

4. RELIGION IN NORTHERN PALESTINE

In the south of Canaan during the monarchical period we hear of several sanctuaries, e.g. of Beersheba, but none that in any way approached the importance of the Temple at Jerusalem. In the north there was none which could claim quite the same pre-eminence. It is true that Jeroboam and his successors gave the old high place at Bethel a special position, in the hope that it might rival Jerusalem, but the attempt does not seem to have been wholly successful; Gilgal and Dan also claimed the allegiance of northern Israel, in spite of the prestige afforded to Bethel by the presence of the royal sanctuary. Unless we are to suppose that there are elements in the traditional ritual which originated in Bethel rather than in Jerusalem, we have no trace of the type of cultus practised there, but we may fairly assume that it did not differ greatly from that of other sacred places

---

[1] Amos i. 2. [2] See above, pp. 159 ff.

in Palestine. It seems fairly clear that there were somewhat elaborate buildings, and that the priesthood of Bethel enjoyed the special patronage and protection of the king. But our records were all collected or edited at a period when worship at Bethel was held to be an act of apostasy, and practically no references remain.

It seems, however, to be clear that Bethel contributed less, if possible, than Jerusalem to a high moral and social standard in Israel generally. In the eighth century we hear of complaints made by Amos, and suggested by Hosea, of iniquities associated with the northern sanctuaries. Yahweh was worshipped as a fertility God under the form of a bull, and this in itself would seem to imply a sexual element in the cult. Further, northern Israel was comparatively rich and prosperous : her soil was fertile and her opportunities for trade extensive. Social corruption of many kinds flourished, and if we cannot claim that the Temple at Jerusalem exercised a strong influence in favour of the higher morality, we know positively that the tendencies of the northern religion were still more discordant with recognized moral principles. It seems to be clear that here the " *Ba'alization* " of Yahweh was complete, and when Hosea inveighs against the cult of *Ba'al*, he probably means, not only that other deities were worshipped, but also that Yahweh, as interpreted in the northern kingdom, was not the true Yahweh at all, but only *Ba'al* under another name. The type of religion presented at Bethel was a syncretism, in which the later, superimposed religion had little part except in the name of the deity worshipped.

CHAPTER XVII

THE YAHWIST REVIVAL

THE conditions depicted in the last chapter were those of the agricultural and commercial portions of the community, in other words, those that were settled in western Palestine, perhaps to some extent affected by proximity to Phœnicia. But it must never be forgotten that there was another Israel, and this fact of the social and economic division of the people is of the highest importance for the understanding of Israelite history, both in politics and in religion. There were certain tribes which had never made their home on the west of the Jordan, though they were recognized as forming a part of the true Israel, owed allegiance to her kings, and were expected to take their share in fighting her battles.[1] In Num. xxxii we are told that the reason for this eastern settlement was that on the far side of Jordan the land was a " land for cattle," i.e. grazing country.[2] In the south of Judah, too, the soil and climate are unsuited for the production of crops, and we are all familiar with the fact that David in Bethlehem lived as a shepherd, while one of the most beautiful stories of his life deals with a great shepherd chieftain of the southern Carmel, south of Hebron.

Side by side, then, with the agricultural community we have groups in the country abutting on the " wilderness " which still lived on the pastoral, if not on the nomad, plane of social order, yet recognizing a common kinship and worshipping a common deity with their more " advanced " brethren. It was only to be expected that the tribes of the east and south should thus preserve, far more completely than the rest, the ancient traditions, outlook, and mode of worship which had characterized the Aramæan tribes before their entry into Palestine. We shall not greatly err if we ascribe to them a religious and political life not far removed

[1] Cp. Judges v. 14 (Machir), 15, 16 (Reuben), and 17 (Gilead, i.e. Gad).
[2] Cp. also Amos iv. 1.

from that of all the tribes in the wilderness period, and, as has already been said, this double standard in Israel is, in a certain sense, the key to the history of the middle and later monarchy. In particular, it was from this element in the population that there came first a protest against that declension from primitive Yahwist principles in Church and State which marked the syncretism of agricultural Palestine.

1. LIBERTY AND AUTOCRACY

Politically, Israel, perhaps alone among the nations of the ancient East, preserved much of the " democratic " spirit which marked the shepherd tribes of western Asia.[1] While the earlier stage probably did not specifically recognize the principle of equality as an element in religion, yet the whole of the tradition inherited from Israel's nomad ancestry formed a real and indivisible entity. In the days of the original and pure Yahwism, no man had a right to exercise authority over his fellows. It was not unnatural that Yahweh Himself should be held to be the final guardian of the rights of personality, and that any attempt to impose a personal will, as distinct from that of the community or of the Deity, should be condemned as a breach of religious, as well as of social, law. Reduced to its simplest terms, it implied that no man could give orders to his neighbour, except in circumstances where he was the representative of the whole community. Israel admitted no distinction in status as between one freeman and another; all were " brethren." We have no trace of a noble order or caste here, such as we find in Mesopotamia and in Egypt. Nomad Israel did, to a large extent, succeed in imposing this " democratic " principle on the land she conquered, and the constant interaction of the " wilderness " and of the more settled communities of western Palestine, meant that true Yahwism was a religion which demanded, first and foremost, a recognition of the place due to the free individual.

In direct opposition to this democratic spirit stood the ordinary Oriental conception of royal authority. Elsewhere in the ancient world the phrase " limited monarchy " would have seemed a contradiction in terms. Society formed a pyramid, at whose base were the lowest of the people, who had the right to command none, and to whom all others could give orders. Above them stood the smaller class who could demand their service, but also owned the domination

[1] Cf. p. 166.

of other and higher social strata.   At the very summit stood
the king, bound by no law except that of his own will, owing
allegiance to no superior power except that of the gods,
claiming as a right the obedience and service of every other
member of the community.   His powers were uncontrolled
and his authority above all challenge; he rendered account
to no human individual or group, and only divine prerogative
could impose limitations on his actions.

Monarchy in Israel was an attempt at a compromise
between these two incompatible types of social theory.
Political necessity and the appearance of two strong per-
sonalities brought about the concentration of national
authority in the hands of a single individual.   Saul's kingship was essentially " charismatic "; he was a " Nabi'',"
and it was his direct inspiration, resulting in military
triumph, which gave him his position.   In some respects
he more closely resembled his predecessors, the Judges, than
his successors, the kings.   In his accession there was nothing
which challenged the familiar principles on which Israelite
polity had always been traditionally based.   But his
constant struggle against the Philistines led to a more complete organization than any of his predecessors had achieved,
though it was to be completely overshadowed by that which
David established.   Further, no Israelite leader had ever
included so great an area under his sway.   While his own
home was in the south of the Ephraimite hills, his exploit
at Jabesh-Gilead gave him a firm footing to the east of the
Jordan, and, since this part of the country was never subject
to Philistine attacks, it was here that he and his house found
their most secure stronghold.   He was vaguely accepted as
king far to the south of Jerusalem, and the northern limit
of his power was the plain of Esdraelon.   If he began his
public life as a Judge, he ended it as a true king of Israel.

David, on the other hand, though a passionate Yahweh
enthusiast, lacked the divine authorization afforded to Saul
by his prophetic inspiration.   His outstanding military
abilities, his political wisdom, and his personal charm,
however, sufficed to raise him from the leadership of a brigand
company to full royalty, and he was the only king who
handed on to his successor a united realm which stretched
" from Dan to Beersheba."   But his sovereignty was based
on a " covenant," [1] and, though we are not told its terms,
it must have imposed mutual obligations and restraints on

[1] 2 Sam. v. 3.

both king and people. There is ground for believing that
the precedent was normally followed in later days, and that,
at any rate after the death of Solomon, every king of Israel
was compelled to grant a " charter " of some kind on his
accession. Again, we are uncertain as to its terms, but the
records justify us in assuming that to some extent the
rights of the individual were secured against the exercise
of arbitrary royal authority. The king must recognize that
his fellow-countrymen were his " brethren," not his
slaves.[1]

The accession of Solomon was the result of a palace
revolution, achieved through the presence of the royal
bodyguard—the most undemocratic of all David's institutions. It was a victory for " prerogative " over " privilege,"
and his reign was a swift declension both in politics and in
religion. Of all the claims made by Oriental monarchy,
that which was most revolting to the free Beduin spirit was
the system of forced labour, the *corvée*. Solomon has won
a great reputation for his magnificent buildings, but it must
not be forgotten that their erection was made possible only
by the iniquitous use of his people's labour and time. He
organized the nation for service in Lebanon and elsewhere,
and claimed no less than four months of every man's time.
Such a proceeding was a glaring violation of the rights of
man, as understood by the average Israelite, and it is clear
that their discontent found point and expression in the
prophetic party, the permanent repositories of the true
nomad tradition. Solomon himself was too strong to be
overthrown, but on his death a revolution, inspired by the
prophet Ahijah, excluded Rehoboam from the throne, and
confined him to Judah, which had enjoyed preferential
treatment under his father. The principle had been strik-
ingly vindicated, and, through all the vicissitudes of the
northern kingdom, it seems to have been unnecessary to
insist on it again until the marriage of Ahab with a Phœnician
princess once more introduced the foreign conception of
kingship into Israel.

In religion, too, Solomon's policy was obnoxious to the
true Israelite. It would have been bad enough, from their
point of view, that the older cults should be maintained, but
Solomon went further, and his foreign alliances all meant the
introduction of new deities into the land. In this respect
the north seems to have maintained a purer standard than

[1] Cf. Deut. xvii. 20, Jer. xxii. 13.

the south, for it was about Jerusalem that the greatest mass of strange deities was to be found. Apart from the bull-and other cults which were, doubtless, inherited from pre-Israelite days, we have little reason to believe that the northern kings introduced the gods of the peoples about them, until the wider policy of Ahab once more brought Israel into the circle of the nations.

2. Jezebel and Melkart

In the middle of the ninth century B.C., Omri succeeded in raising his kingdom to the position of one of the minor powers of the East, and northern Israel was known to the Assyrians after his day as " Bit Humri." [1] One sign of his position was the alliance with Sidon, and, just as the marriage with an Egyptian princess gave prestige to Solomon's court, so the wedding of Jezebel and Ahab attested the high place that Israel now held among the nations. But the alliance meant the introduction of ideas and tendencies against which the spirit of Israel, still affected by its nomad tradition, utterly rebelled. It is clear that the queen tried to suppress the cult of Yahweh altogether, or, at least, to reduce the national God of Israel to a level below that of her own deity, the Phœnician *Ba'al* whose proper name was Melkart. She may well have seen in the Yahweh cult, especially as represented by the Prophets, an insurmountable obstacle to the realization of her political aims, and a wholly effective check on the absolute power of the Crown. She may, on the other hand, have been actuated purely by the desire to secure the predominance of her own god. But, whatever her motive may have been, it is clear that she made the prophets and their adherents objects of special attack. The great mass of the people were induced to conform to the worship of Melkart, and 7000 is the figure given as the number of those who had not surrendered to him. [2] Further, she is said to have organized massacres of the prophets [3] so complete that one of them could lament that he was the only survivor. [4] Her action probably had a double purpose, for, not only did she rid herself of that element in the people which provided the stoutest resistance to her schemes, but she challenged Yahweh by showing that He was unable to

---

[1] On an inscription of Tiglath-pileser III, *circa* B.C. 734 —the " House of Omri."
[2] 1 Kings xix. 18. [3] *loc. cit.*, and 1 Kings. xviii. 4.
[4] 1 Kings xix. 10, 14.

P

defend His own devotees in His own land. If He could neither protect nor avenge them, then He was obviously inferior to the deity in whose interests they had been slaughtered.

On its political side, the conflict is illustrated by the story of Naboth's vineyard. When the little freeholder refuses to surrender his ancestral property, it never occurs to Ahab to try to impose his own will on his subject, either by force or by guile. He does not like the situation, but he has to accept it. But his Sidonian wife has been bred in other theories of the royal prerogative, and if the subject will not yield to her, so much the worse for him. Yet even she is compelled to proceed by the recognized forms of justice; she dare not flout popular opinion utterly.

3. THE YAHWIST GUILDS

From the religious point of view, there were still forces which maintained the old tradition, and among the groups which stood for Yahweh as against all other objects of worship, it is usual to enumerate three, the Prophets, or *Nebi'im*, the Nazirites, and the Rechabites. As we have already seen, the first class consisted of ecstatic devotees, whose wild behaviour testified to their possession by Yahweh, and who stood for Him against all rivals. It is clear that by the middle of the ninth century they had attained to some kind of organized and communal life, and, as we shall have reason to see later, they were in a position to exercise no small political influence. In a very real sense they represented the national God, and made an irresistible appeal to the great mass of the people.

The subject of the Nazirites is obscure. In later times the Nazirite took a temporary vow of abstention from certain practices, notably the cutting of the hair and the drinking of wine. In earlier days, however, the vow seems to have been taken for life, and the Nazirite stood as a permanent protest against certain aspects of the higher social order. The type of the ancient Nazirite is Samson, and as late as the days of Amos the class was closely connected in men's minds with the *Nebi'im*.[1] The ancient Israelite who was devoted especially to Yahweh would use no razor—the opening phrase of the Song of Deborah (Judges v. 2) is best rendered " When the long locks in Israel streamed free "— and would drink no wine. For the vine was one of the

[1] Cp. Amos ii. 11.

typical products of the agricultural life, and was even more closely identified with it than corn.   Cereals can be grown by the semi-nomad, who may spend a few months from autumn to spring in a comparatively fertile spot, sowing and reaping his crop.   But the vine takes some years of careful cultivation before it yields its fruit at all, and only those who have some prospect of an extended residence in the same spot will undertake its culture.   The Nazirite stood for the old ways, and by his existence protested against the un-Israelite character of the settled life.

This feature is even more obvious when we look at the Rechabites.   The founder of the group, Jonadab, the son of Rechab, is first mentioned in connexion with the revolution of Jehu, which took place some ten years after the death of Ahab.   But the way in which he is introduced into the narrative [1] makes it clear that the Rechabite was already a well-known and significant figure in the life of Israel.   Like the Nazirite he eschewed the use of all products of the vine; his protest was not so much against drunkenness as against civilization.   This is clear from the second outstanding feature of the class—their refusal to live in any house other than a mobile tent.   Here again we see the protest of the nomad against the farmer.   The houses of the Eastern peasantry are often no more than mud and reeds, poor enough and flimsy enough to Western ideas, but they do at least indicate a permanent settlement on the land, for they cannot easily be taken down, transported, and erected elsewhere.   To the mind of the Rechabite, the representative of the true Israel, the Aramæan nomad, must have no home on the land.   His is essentially a life of movement, and he must be free to pull up his tent-pegs and go elsewhere at the behest of his God.   To both Nazirite and Rechabite the settlement of an agricultural community was in itself an act of apostasy, a surrender to the *Ba'als*.   While it seems probable that both classes were small in numbers, their influence must have been considerable, and their presence and testimony served to form a nucleus of discontent which readily broke into more open and obvious action at the stimulus of the new conditions.

4. ELIJAH

The various tendencies and feelings which made for a reversion to the older conception of Israel's religion found

[1] 2 Kings x. 15.

their medium of expression in Elijah. He is one of the most clearly marked figures in the whole of the Old Testament, and his personality made such an impression on his own and subsequent generations that he became the typical prophet to the mind of later Israel. His figure, perhaps owing in part to the striking story of his disappearance, became almost an apocalyptic symbol, and the last of the great prophetic order definitely adopted his style. He stands out before us as a man of intense feeling, a child of his own time in his comparative indifference to the claims of compassion, but possessed by a courage and a fiery enthusiasm able to carry him through difficulties which might well have daunted a lesser man.

With these personal qualities it is important to note his political and religious position. He comes from the east of Jordan, from that section of the people which had never made agriculture its staple occupation, and he carried on in a very real sense the old traditions of early Israel. It is not a mere accident that men associated him in their minds with Moses; it is possible to assert that there was a gap in the religious history of the people between these two great men. We may well feel that if Moses founded the religion of Israel, it was Elijah who first called the people effectively back to the ideals of his greater predecessor, and thus made possible that further advance which the next two centuries were to witness.

The protest of Elijah was a double one. The first element was moral and political, and manifested itself most strongly in the case of Naboth. The new ideas of the social order which Jezebel championed were inconsistent, not merely with Israelite political tradition, but also with the fundamental ethical principles of the old wilderness Yahwism. The judicial murder of the small farmer was not only a crime, it was a sin, a violation of the well-established laws of Yahweh. The religious authorities of the city community might lay the entire stress on ritual, and in this respect Melkart and the Ba'al-Yahweh of Bethel might be at one, but the true God of Israel, the 'El-Yahweh, held different ideals and made other demands on men. In a very real sense Elijah was a forerunner of the great ethical prophets of the eighth and seventh centuries B.C.

It was with the worship of Melkart that these new and dangerous principles had entered the land, and Elijah fully realized that the real enemy of his people and of their faith

was the Sidonian *Ba'al*. It was his task to convince men
that Melkart had no standing in the land of Yahweh, and
that for Israel the only valid form of worship was that of
Israel's own God. The great trial scene on Mount Carmel
will stand for all time as one of the most dramatic events in
history.[1] There it was shown that, in spite of every
advantage, the prophets of the *Ba'al* were unable to summon
their god to their help. Elijah did not deny the existence
of Melkart, or challenge his claims to adoration in Phœnicia,
but he did insist, and prove, that his power did not extend
to Israel. The sequel to the trial makes this yet clearer.
The prophets of *Ba'al* were taken and slain—a cruel act,
judged by modern standards, but quite in accord with the
spirit of the times. We shall make a serious mistake if we
imagine this to have been nothing more than a piece of
brutal vindictiveness. It is the act which sets the seal on
the verdict of the previous scene. The prophet is sacrosanct,
and any act of violence done to him is bound to be resented
and terribly avenged by the god who is insulted in his person.
The slaughter of the prophets of *Ba'al* is a proclamation to
the world, uttered in compelling and overwhelmingly convincing language, that *Ba'al* is helpless in the land of Yahweh; whatever his power may be in Phœnicia, in Israel his
writ does not run. By no other course of action could
Elijah possibly have brought home to the people the utter
helplessness of Melkart and the futility of offering him
worship. That was Elijah's task, and seldom has such a
duty been performed with more drastic thoroughness.

5. THE PROPHETIC REVOLUTION

The temptation to a national apostasy seems to have
ceased, at any rate for a time, with the slaughter of the
prophets of *Ba'al*. But it is most unlikely that Jezebel's
own private establishment suffered further attacks, and
within Israel there still remained the actual sanctuary of
Melkart—and would remain as long as the dynasty of Omri
sat on the throne of Samaria. Still more impelling was the
memory of the murder of Naboth. As Elijah had implied,[2]
this crime had left the guilt of blood attached to Ahab.
Elsewhere there was none who could take vengeance against
a king, and no kinsman of Naboth's would have felt himself

---

[1] While the narrative in 1 Kings xviii may have been " embellished
in later ages," we cannot doubt that it contains an historic kernel.
[2] Cf. 1 Kings xxi. 17 ff.

in a position to satisfy the demands of the blood-feud. In a certain sense it was all Israel who should have risen up to avenge the dead man; as a matter of fact it was to be left to Yahweh and to Yahweh's instruments, the prophets and their adherents. When Ahab died, the blood of Naboth was still crying out from the ground. It was true that the king himself had not committed the deed, and that he was unaware of it till all was over, but he had entered into possession of the vineyard, and the whole ground was tainted with the appealing blood. So the guilt fell on all the king's family, and atonement could be made only by the extermination of all the royal house. To the danger that Jezebel might make a fresh attempt to restore the cult of Melkart was added the claim of the blood-feud, and the genuine Israelite spirit had already condemned the house of Ahab to extinction. It was not Elijah, however, who carried out the full prophetic programme; the completion of his work was left to other hands. The accomplishment of the task was reserved for two men, Elisha, the follower of Elijah, and Jehu.

We possess a number of stories about Elisha, but they have little or no bearing on the development of the religious life of Israel, since most of them record miracles performed by him in one of the prophetic companies and elsewhere. His importance for our present study lies in the fact that he stood behind Jehu, and inspired him to the act of usurpation which ended the rule of the house of Omri. The new king was simply a tool in the hands of the prophetic party, and he stood, like them, for the old isolation of Israel from her nearer neighbours.

The story of the revolution is too familiar to need extended comment. After the elimination of the royal house, Jehu, with the approval and support of Jonadab ben Rechab, proceeded to destroy all traces of the cult of Melkart. The narrative shows that the worshippers of *Ba'al* were few in number, since they could all be crowded into a single building. This is strong testimony to the effectiveness of Elijah's work, for prior to this, and even in his day, it could be said that only seven thousand had not bowed the knee to *Ba'al* (1 Kings xix. 18). But by now the devotees of Melkart seem to have included little more than the official establishment of the Sidonian sanctuary maintained by the house of Omri in Samaria. To them may have been added Phœnician merchants and other temporary residents or visitors, but it is clear that the Israelite element in the group was negligible.

Judah, like northern Israel, had been affected by the cult of the Phœnician *Ba'al*. The two kingdoms were now in close alliance, and Jehoram, son of Jehoshaphat, had married Athaliah, daughter of Ahab. She brought with her the worship of Melkart, and a shrine was set up in Jerusalem to the Phœnician god.[1] Ahaziah, son of the Judahite Jehoram, and, therefore, grandson of Ahab, was included in the ban against the house of Omri, and he shared his uncle's fate. When the news reached Jerusalem, his mother, Athaliah, seized the throne, murdering all the members of the royal family on whom she could lay her hands. One was saved, however, a baby named Joash, and, six years later, the priest Jehoiada carried out a successful revolution, killing Athaliah, destroying the shrine of Melkart, and putting its priest to death. It seems, however, that the Phœnician cult had never taken so strong a hold on the south as it did on the north, and we hear of no lives lost except those of the queen and her priest. The work of Jehoiada was but a minor detail, completing that of Jehu, and it was in Israel that the real defeat of Melkart was achieved.

We may, from our own standpoint, condemn in un-measured terms the bloodthirsty cruelty of the prophetic revolution. It did, indeed, call forth the strongest censure from Hosea [2] a century later. But it did its work, and never again was the supremacy of Yahweh within His own land challenged, as far as we know. He had shown Himself to be supreme; His rivals had been unable to prove their right to a place in His territory, and had been shown to be utterly powerless to vindicate themselves against the deadliest insult. It is true that Jehu's action meant a break with his immediate neighbours, and compelled him to seek for Assyrian protection. The Assyrians, no doubt, followed their usual practice and insisted on the establishment of some sort of ritual which typified their authority. But there was never any danger that Ashur would oust Yahweh from the affections, or in the devotion, of Israel; the danger would naturally come only from her immediate neighbours. In tremendous language the enthusiasts of Yahweh had told the world that Israel must have no other gods before Him.

[1] Cf. 2 Kings xi. 18.   [2] Cf. Hos. i. 4.

CHAPTER XVIII

THE RELIGION OF ISRAEL AFTER JEHU

WHILE the movement which first showed itself under Elijah, and found its completion in the prophetic revolution, settled once and for all the question as to whether any other god than Yahweh should hold sway in Israel, it made, as far as we can tell, comparatively little difference to the syncretistic religion of the country. Elijah raised no protest against the established sanctuaries, sacrifice continued to be offered as of old, and no objection was made to the veneration paid to the sacred bulls at Dan and Bethel. It was necessary first that the absolute devotion of Israel to Yahweh should be secured, before the manifestation of those unique features which distinguished the later Judaism could be made.

It has, however, become clear in recent years that this whole-hearted consecration of the people to Yahweh was far from being complete, even after the violent extinction of the cult of the Phœnician Melkart. Jehu paid tribute to Assyria in 841 B.C., and it is almost certain that his submission involved the establishment of some kind of Assyrian cult. But it does not seem to have taken any serious hold on the people, and no attempt was made to challenge the superiority of Yahweh, or His claim to be the true national God of Israel. During the first half of the eighth century the power of Assyria greatly declined, and, since Egypt was equally weak, Palestine was virtually free from foreign interference. Damascus had been reduced to practical impotence by Assyria, and the reigns of Jeroboam II (788–747 B.C.) of Israel and Uzziah (786–744 B.C.) of Judah marked the last peak of Israelite political power. There was thus little or no temptation to introduce fresh deities from abroad, and we have no ground for supposing that the Hebrew people deliberately went in search of other gods.

There is, however, abundant evidence to show that the older, pre-Israelite, deities of Palestine maintained their position. The facts have already been stated,[1] but it will be convenient to summarize them once again. Our Bible has been carefully edited, and much has been eliminated from the historical records which would have painted too dark a picture of the popular religion. But we have other sources of information, of which we may mention three in particular : archæological discovery in Palestine itself, the denunciations of the eighth- and seventh-century prophets, and references found in documents outside Israel.

1. ARCHÆOLOGICAL DISCOVERY

In recent years the excavators have unearthed a number of sacred sites, some of them being temples of considerable extent. We may mention especially the well-known cases of Gezer, Megiddo, and Lachish. In all these places, however, the sites consecrated to other deities than Yahweh may belong to periods during which the cities in question were not under Israelite control, and they do not really affect our present subject. But excavations at Tell-el-Nasbeh (Mizpah), undertaken in 1935, have revealed the existence of a temple to Astoreth contemporary with that of Yahweh in the same place.[2] Here the evidence is beyond dispute, and removes all doubt as to the polytheism which was to be found in Israel during the eighth century B.C. We may regard it as being highly probable that further discoveries will be made on other sites.

2. PROPHETIC DENUNCIATION

A large part of what the prophets have to say in condemnation of the religion of their contemporaries is directed against the worship of Yahweh Himself, and the false ideas and undesirable practices which men connected with it. Hosea, it is true, speaks as though the normal faith of his time was a species of Ba'alism,[3] but this is commonly, and perhaps rightly, interpreted as meaning that Israel degraded Yahweh to the level of a Ba'al, and, while claiming to worship Him, really adored the old fertility spirits under His name. But both Hosea and Jeremiah [4] seem to have had more than this in view, and their denunciations of Israel's apostasy may be regarded as evidence of a persistent polytheism. In 2 Kings certain of the sovereigns of Judah

[1] See pp. 174 ff., 196.
[2] Cf. Badé, in *Werden und Wesen des Alten Testaments* (1936).
[3] E.g., ii. 8, 13, 17; xi. 2.   [4] Cf., e.g., ii. 23.

are commended as having done " that which was right in the eyes of Yahweh," with the reservation that " the high places were not taken away."[1] These were the sites of the old local cults, and while many of them had been converted to the use of Yahweh, at least nominally,[2] we may suspect that others retained also the names of their Canaanite occupants. The language used by Amos [3] suggests that he did not regard the cults of Bethel and of Gilgal as true Yahwism, though, as with Hosea, we may explain his words as a condemnation of syncretism, not of apostasy. But he certainly alludes to the Mesopotamian deities Kewan and Sakkuth,[4] and to the old Canaanite goddess Ashimah,[5] while with the latter he couples gods of Dan and (following the LXX to correct an obscure text) the " gods " or " the beloved " [6] of Beersheba.[7]

In this connexion we may also adduce the curious collection of strange cults which Josiah eliminated from the Temple of Jerusalem in 621 B.C.[8] Here were to be found emblems of *Ba'al*, Asherah (she is very prominent), and the " host of heaven "—an astral cult. There were horses and chariots dedicated to the Sun, while Chemosh, Melek, and Ashtoreth all had shrines in the immediate neighbourhood. Some of these cults are traced back to Solomon, others to Ahaz and Manasseh ; the former class were clearly maintained throughout the whole history of the monarchy, in spite of the reforming zeal of men like Asa [9] and Hezekiah.[10] The failure of the latter king to remove these cults is the more remarkable, inasmuch as it was he who destroyed the bronze snake which was almost certainly a Yahweh symbol. If he found the other deities so strongly entrenched that it was not safe to remove them, it is clear that the old polytheism must have had a firm hold on the popular mind.

[1] So Joash, 2 Kings xii. 4; Amaziah xiv. 4; Azariah xv. 4.
[2] This was certainly true of the high place at Gibeon, 1 Kings iii. 4, and we can hardly suppose it to have been the only instance.
[3] E.g., v. 5.   [4] v. 26.   [5] viii. 14.
[6] This term seems to have been used of an idolatrous emblem of more than one deity. It occurs on the inscription of Mesha as one of the objects sacred to Yahweh which were carried away and presented to Chemosh on the victory of Moab over Israel.
[7] Mention might be made here of a theory propounded by Nyberg, who believes that our texts of Hosea have frequently disguised the divine name 'Al, a synonym of 'Elyon. See *Studien zum Hoseabuch*, esp. pp. 58 ff. (1935). The theory, as Nyberg expounds it, has, however, certain improbabilities, and is seldom the best explanation of the passages to which he refers it.
[8] 2 Kings xxiii. 4 ff.   [9] 1 Kings xv. 10-12.
[10] 2 Kings xviii. 4.

3. Evidence from Outside of Palestine

It is not to be expected that foreign records should have much to say about the religion of Israel. Great conquerors enumerated the spoil they took, but were comparatively indifferent as to the deities whose temples they plundered. When they mention the gods of other peoples, they do so in general terms, without giving names or other details. An exception is to be found in Mesha, king of Moab, who says that he dragged the " altar-hearth " (evidently some cumbersome piece of ritual furniture) " of its Beloved," when speaking of the sack of the Israelite city of Ataroth. As we have seen, the " Beloved " may well be a divine name or, more probably, epithet, and there is ground for supposing that it was regarded by Amos as a symbol of apostasy. In describing the capture of Nebo, Mesha says that he carried away the vessels of Yahweh, this being the first time that the Tetragrammaton is found outside the Bible. From this it is clear that, though other deities might have a place, yet Yahweh was still prominent to the east of the Jordan.

Our strongest evidence under this head, however, comes to us from the Elephantiné papyri.[1] We have already glanced at the various deities therein mentioned, and it remains only to make a few comments. The names of the gods and goddesses are all Semitic; therefore they were not adopted from their Egyptian neighbours. They must have been brought into Egypt with the immigrants, who were obviously unaware of any impropriety in associating these other objects of worship with Yahweh. They claim themselves that they had settled in Elephantiné before the Persian conquest, and we may be fairly sure that they had migrated from Palestine before the days of Josiah. The circumstances of their coming to Egypt, however, must remain a matter of conjecture. They may have been descendants of northern Israelites carried away by Tiglath-pileser and his successors.[2] They may have been the result of a general drift of fugitives who sought to escape from the advancing Assyrians in the last years of the northern kingdom,[3] or they may have been deliberately sold as mercenaries by kings of Israel and Judah. Her man-power was almost the only export of value that Palestine possessed

---

[1] See Cowley, *Aramaic Papyri of the Fifth Century, B.C.* (1923), and *Jewish Documents of the Time of Ezra* (1919).

[2] Cf. Oesterley, *History of Israel*, II. 160 f. (1932).

[3] Cf., e.g., Hos. viii 12, ix 3, 6.

in ancient times, and there is only too much reason to suppose
that this was the price paid for the royal horses, if for no other
commodity. The condemnation of the practice in Deut.
xvii. 16 can be explained only on the ground that it was a
real and pressing grievance. But, however they reached
Egypt, it is clear that their advent thither is to be placed
somewhere between the middle of the ninth century B.C.
and the reform of Josiah, and that their Pantheon was that
of Israel, or of a portion of Israel, during the latter half of the
monarchical period.

4. RELIGIOUS AND SOCIAL CORRUPTION

As we have already seen, we have in reality two Israels,
that of the settled community, and that of those sections,
mainly to the east and south, who still continued more or
less on the pastoral plane. While, then, on the one hand, we
have the maintenance of the polytheism and syncretism of an
earlier stage, on the other hand, the purer, more primitive
tradition, with its stress on ethics and its comparative indifference to ritual and especially to sacrifice, maintained
itself in the east of Jordan and in the extreme south. There
was thus ready to hand a source whence a fresh revival of
the older faith might spring. Elijah had been a product
of the former district, and, nearly a century after his time,
there came from the south the first of the line of the canonical
prophets, Amos.

As to other aspects of the religion of Israel—its ritual and
its ethical content—we have little direct information in the
period that elapsed between Jehu and Amos—roughly
between 840 B.C. and 760 B.C. There are references
in the book of *Kings*, but, except for the numerous stories
of Elisha, these deal mainly with political events, and record
little more than the successive kings of the two realms. But
we can see what must have been the general character
assumed by the religion of Israel during the period. We
have an established priesthood, an elaborate ritual, meticulously observed, a wealth of sacrifice, and an eschatology
which taught that in His own time Yahweh would appear to
take vengeance on the enemies of Israel and to set her up as
supreme. At the same time, religion had little or no moral
content. Provided men paid their dues, offered their
sacrifices, and observed their *taboos*, Yahweh would not
interfere with their treatment one of another. Not only so,
but religion was held to override the claims of the ordinary

moral life.   The common law of Israel, for instance, forbade a moneylender to keep during the night the garment taken in pledge.[1]   The borrower must be allowed to have it back, for it was his one covering, and without it he was in danger of suffering severely from the cold.   But if the creditor could claim that he needed it for some ceremony in the temple— some form of "incubation," perhaps—he was under no obligation to return it.   Sexual irregularities [2] were at all times abhorrent to the true Hebrew genius, yet there is evidence which shows that ritual fornication was a regular practice at the sanctuaries.   This was the general condition with which men like Amos and Isaiah were faced, and it corresponds so closely with what we know from other sources of the religion of the nearer East that we can hardly doubt that the conditions were those inherited from the old *Ba'alism*, and generally retained throughout the period of the monarchy.

[1] Cp. Exod. xxii. 25–27 ; Amos ii. 8.

[2] These, of course, do not include polygamy or concubinage, which were regarded as legitimate.

CHAPTER XIX

THE CANONICAL PROPHETS

PROPHETS—*Nebi'im*—were, of course, a familiar feature in the life of Israel. The ecstatics, either in companies or singly, were a well-recognized class, and were accepted as men inspired by Yahweh. It did not follow that what they said was true. Men had not yet learnt to think of Yahweh as moral, and they believed that, in order to entrap to their ruin men whom He would destroy, He might inspire His prophets to utter falsehood. The best known illustration is that of the lying spirit seen in Micaiah's vision, who entered into the prophets of Ahab to induce him to go up against Ramoth Gilead where he would fall (1 Kings xxii. 19–23). Hebrew had even a technical term for such a divine deceit [1] mediated through a prophet, and though the theory underwent certain slight changes, it remained at least till the time of Ezekiel.

1. THE NEBI'IM AND THE CANONICAL PROPHETS

The prophets of Ahab were accustomed to deliver a popular message, or at least one which should be satisfactory to their king. But those whose words are recorded for us in the Bible were men of another stamp. They were actuated by a passion for Yahweh no less than their contemporaries, but their thought went deeper, and they conceived of Yahweh in terms very different from those which would have been employed by the earlier *Nebi'im*. Yet to outward appearance there seemed to be no essential difference between the two classes. It is now generally agreed that the canonical prophets were ecstatic, though the extent to which they were subject to this condition is still disputed. There are those who hold that every utterance found its occasion, its form, and its authentication, in an access of the ecstasy, while others believe that while the prophet must have had at least one such experience at the

---

[1] 1 Kings xxii. 20, 21, 22; Jer. xx. 7; Ezek. xiv. 9.

beginning of his ministry, his later utterances were consciously composed and delivered in a normal state of mind. But, since in abnormal psychological states it is a man's real nature and opinions that are expressed, it makes little or no difference whether and to what extent men like Hosea and Micah were ecstatic; in any case, they believed profoundly in the truth of what they said, and they were impelled to speak by their own intense convictions.[1]

2. THE TEACHING OF THE PROPHETS

The result of their thinking and of their strong convictions was that the prophets of Israel offered men a new doctrine. They varied, of course, among themselves, and each had his own clearly marked individuality and message. Yet the differences depend rather on stress than on any real variation of opinion as between them. All were alike in certain broad outlines of truth, and in these they differed from their contemporaries, and, indeed, from practically all other religious teachers. Outside Israel the tendency has always been for the man interested in morals to turn away from religion, believing (and a study of the world's religions gives him some justification) that it had no ethical value, and might even be opposed to the human conscience. If Israel had had nothing better to offer the world than the syncretistic worship of Bethel, then she would have disappeared and her name would almost have perished—and rightly so. Any impulse in favour of moral reform would have found itself opposed to established religion, and the ethical teachers of Israel would have been compelled, as were Siddhartha, Euripides, Lucretius, and perhaps Confucius, to choose between religion and goodness, between God and righteousness. The supreme place which must be ascribed to the Israelite prophets is due to the fact that they dared to identify God with the good, and asserted that His character was at least as high as that of man. It was here that the ancient tradition of nomadic Israel had its effect. In early days Yahweh had been the guardian of the simple ethic of the wandering tribe, and the prophets insisted that He would retain this function, and apply to the far more complicated life of the settled agricultural community those moral and social principles which, on the more elementary plane, had commended themselves alike to the religious instinct and to the conscience of man. The two social orders existed

[1] See T. H. Robinson, *Prophecy and the Prophets*, pp. 44 f.

side by side, and, perhaps, men were hardly conscious of the division. Israel was one in religion and possessed a common inheritance, for her historians traced all the tribes back to a common stock, and though the actual blood of the Palestinians may have been very mixed, the tradition which survived was largely derived from the Aramæan element. While we must not in any way detract from the moral and religious greatness of the canonical prophets, we cannot blind ourselves to the circumstances which facilitated their unique contribution to human thought about God.

There are certain features in the teaching of the prophets common to them all, of which the most important must be enumerated.

(a) In the first place, the prophets saw *Yahweh as Law.* The normal Oriental conception of deity is of beings who are extraordinarily powerful but are almost wholly capricious. The attitude is best represented for us in Islam, and it is impossible to read the *Qoran* without feeling that in his anxiety to maintain the omnipotence of God, Muhammad was in some danger of depreciating His moral character. We get the impression of a benevolent despot whose will is absolute and above any challenge. There are no standards by which to judge Him, for He recognizes none save His own imperial will. His actions are arbitrary, uncontrolled by any principle, and unchecked by any external power. Such a view is far below that of Amos and his successors. Though they do not use the term, they might have described Yahweh as omnipotent, but they would have said that omnipotence was limited by self-consistency. It was possible to know what Yahweh would do, for He could not be false to Himself. His will might be absolute, but it was reliable; He did not change, and what was good in His sight to-day would not appear evil to-morrow. He was not a man that He should repent, and His treatment of His subjects was invariable. If a man or a nation sow the wind it must reap the whirlwind, for no other crop could spring from such a seed except through the violation of the law of consistency.

It is true that this doctrine is never expressed in so many words, but we must remember that the ancient Semite thought in other categories than ours. Yet it is always present, and forms a very real basis for all that these men had to say. They could predict the divine action in the sphere of personality because they knew Yahweh, just as a scientist can predict the behaviour of the bodies and substances with which he deals if he is sufficiently acquainted with the principles that govern their reactions. The prophets were in this sense spiritual scientists; their study was, however, not the structure of the physical world, but the nature of God and man, and the principles on which the interaction of the two was based. Knowing Yahweh, they knew what He would do in any given set of circumstances, for they saw Him as Law.

(b) Further, the prophets saw Yahweh as the *Lord of Nature*. Here they were fully in accord with the popular belief of Israel. From the first Yahweh had appeared to men as a deity who had some connexion with the weather, and was especially a mountain God. But by the middle of the eighth century, probably much earlier, the belief in Yahweh as the Master of the physical universe had greatly developed, and found expression in the myths of Creation to which allusion has already been made.[1] Every people which adopted such a myth made its own national deity the hero. Thus in its Sumerian form it is Enlil who destroys the Chaos-monster, in Babylonia it is Marduk, and in Assyria it is Ashur. We need not doubt that in Israel it was Yahweh who was held to be the conqueror of darkness. But the myth, along with its ritual presentation, was inherited from Israel's predecessors, and the divergences which we find in the Old Testament references may be due to variant forms of the story as told at different sacred sites. As Yahweh nominally superseded each divinity, the myth would be attached to Him in its local form. The prophetic protest against the immoral accompaniments of the ritual was so far effective that the story was eliminated almost entirely from the official theology of Israel, and the narrative of Gen. i (the other creation-story, Gen. ii. 4 ff., seems to have an independent origin) contains only faint hints of connexion with the general myth. But there are occasional references, especially in the *Psalms* and in the book of *Job*, which make it clear that the story, in several forms, was current in Israel, and even the prophets could use its language to express their thought. They accepted the central doctrine, and, as against all other nations, claimed Yahweh as the Creator-hero.

Along with creation went also control, and the prophets, like all other Israelites, held Yahweh to be the Master of all natural phenomena. Palestine is a country which is

[1] See pp. 198 f.

Q

almost entirely dependent on the rain for its fertility, and it is Yahweh alone who can give or withhold it.[1] He also controls the pests of the farmer's life, the swarms of locusts, and the more insignificant parasites which bring destruction on the crops. Israel is threatened with these as a punishment for her sins, a method which looks arbitrary, but is, nevertheless, subject to rigid moral laws, for the ethical and the physical are not sharply divided from one another. On the other hand, if Israel is faithful, and obeys the commands of Yahweh, crops will be abundant, for it is He and no other who is the giver of all the products of the cultivated land. Nothing happens in nature, great or small, except by His will, and that will follow the definite laws of Yahweh's own self-consistent being.

(c) *Yahweh as Lord of History.*—It is not only the world of physical nature, but also the world of human relations, which is under His complete control. The polytheist has in all ages represented the struggles of man as bound up with the gods' jealousy of one another, and has thought of them as fighting on different sides. Even the monolatrous Semite thought of war as a conflict between national gods as well as between national armies, and it is interesting to find that while Israel was compelled to admit disastrous defeat at the hands of the Philistines, she was careful to add that this did not mean the defeat of her God. On the contrary it gave Him an opportunity of showing His superiority to the gods of the Philistines, insomuch that the people were only too glad to be rid of their divine captive (1 Sam. vi. 1 ff.).

But the peculiar claim of the Hebrew prophet is that Yahweh is concerned to control not merely the fortunes of his own people but the destinies of all nations. The Assyrians may believe that it is by their own military prowess that they have conquered the world; Isaiah knows better, and sees that Assyria is but the rod of the anger of Yahweh. She is an instrument in His hand, and has been used by Him to vindicate on His own people, and elsewhere, His own laws and character. As soon as Assyria loses sight of this fact, and claims to have achieved her triumphs purely in her own strength, she in turn will fall. As long as she can be useful to Yahweh she stands, but when her task is done she can be discarded and destroyed (Isa. x. 5–19). Even the great

---

[1] For stress on this point, especially in comparison with Egyptian life, cp. Deut. xi. 10–12.

racial migrations are the work of Yahweh : He has brought
Israel out of Egypt—that is natural, but He also brought
the Philistines from their early home, and the Syrians from
Kir (Amos ix. 7).

Within the nation itself, of course, Yahweh's power is
absolute. But it is always governed by principles. There
are certain types of polity and particular modes of treatment
which must inevitably lead to disaster. A social and
political order, on the other hand, which gives free play to
the rights and privileges of personality, will bring safety and
prosperity with it. Though the agents of reward and punishment may be foreign powers, they are all controlled by
Yahweh, and history is neither the result of the conflict
between divine whims nor the outcome of human ambition;
it is the development of a single great purpose.

(d) *Yahweh as Lord of the End of Things.*—It is by no
means easy to define the marches between eschatology
and prophecy, for the same essential doctrines, the lord-
ship of Yahweh over nature and over history, are involved
in both. Perhaps the nearest approach we can make to a
distinction is to suggest that in prophecy in the narrower
sense Yahweh brings about the end in what we may call
normal ways, i.e. through events which are of a familiar
type, though their particular manifestation may be abnor-
mally powerful. In eschatology, on the other hand, that
which ends the age is not normal, and the events predicted
are altogether outside human experience in the past.
Eschatology is much older than the canonical prophets, and
they found it necessary to correct men's ideas on the subject
(Amos v. 18–20), but they insisted with equal stress that
Yahweh could and would make an end of things. Indeed,
an eschatology is an inevitable corollary of a doctrine of
creation, for as soon as men have made up their minds as to
how the world began, they will begin to speculate on how it
must end.

The great prophets of Israel certainly shared with their
predecessors and with their contemporaries the belief
that Yahweh would interfere to put an end to the existing
order. To some extent their views were apocalyptic
in the strictest sense of the term, and there are passages
which suggest that they looked forward to the great day
when the heaven should fall and the earth be shattered,
that a new world might be born from the ruins of the old.
But there was a fundamental difference between the two

points of view. The popular eschatology was political and national, while the prophetic was primarily ethical and religious. The people in general held to the doctrine that when matters reached their worst, when Israel was overwhelmed and oppressed by her enemies and was at the very last gasp, the great Day of Yahweh would suddenly dawn, Israel's God would appear in all His splendour and His might, to destroy the old universe of men and things and create a new one in which Israel and Yahweh should have sole pre-eminence. It was a part of the prophetic message to insist on the fundamental mistake of this view. Amos and his successors did not deny the coming of the Day of Yahweh, but for Israel it would be a day of darkness, rayless gloom, not a day of light and glory.[1] For when Yahweh came it would not be to avenge His people on their foes, it would be to vindicate His own moral character by taking a final vengeance on His own people for their apostasy and immorality; it would mean the ruin of Israel, not her salvation. He who had revealed His Law in Nature and in History, in the beginning of things and in the progress of events, would still more terribly show Himself in the End, when all that neglected or resisted His will should be made to cease from being.

(e) *Yahweh as Lord of Universal Morality.*—The prophetic doctrine was sufficiently novel and significant in that it proclaimed the supreme place given to the moral element in Yahweh's demands on His own people. But it did not cease there. He was concerned to note the behaviour of other nations as well as that of Israel. Wherever wrong, moral wrong, was done, whether it be to Israel or by Israel or by another people to a third, it was a violation of the Law of Yahweh, a contradiction of His glorious will, and must meet with His punishment. It is true that the geographical and political horizon of Israel in the eighth and seventh centuries was limited, and embraced few peoples outside the immediate environs of Palestine, but the principle was of universal application. Wherever cruelty and injustice were found, there Yahweh sat in judgement, and sooner or later His vengeance would fall. Amos condemns Damascus, Philistia, Phœnicia, Edom, and Ammon for injuries inflicted on Israelites (Amos. i. 3–15). Any Hebrew patriot would have endorsed the prophet's denunciations. But few would have shared in the indignation Amos expressed at the

[1] Cf. Amos v. 18–20.

atrocities perpetrated by Moab on Edom, or have recognized that the God of Israel was interested in the relations between these two peoples (Amos ii. 1–3). Yet such a doctrine is the logical and necessary deduction from the prophetic premises. Yahweh is a moral being, and He is supreme over all races and lands, hence it follows as a matter of course that He must take their general behaviour into consideration and call them to account. It is true that He will not be so strict with those whom He has not " known " (cp. Amos iii. 1, 2), but they are morally responsible to their own conscience, and since no other deity in the world takes cognizance of their conduct from a purely ethical standpoint, He will take matters into His own hands and vindicate His claim.

(f) *Yahweh as the God of Israel.*—The danger of a universalism is that it may obscure the position, rights, and duties, of the individual, whether it be one person or a small national group. The time came, indeed, when Israel, far away from her own land, and set in the midst of the great peoples of the world, was tempted to doubt Yahweh's special care for His own people.[1] But the thought does not seem to have entered the mind of the pre-exilic prophets, and, while they recognized Yahweh as the Master of the physical and personal universe, they also insisted on His special relation to Israel. He had chosen her to be a peculiar and holy people. His power had been manifested, as nowhere else, in her redemption from Egypt and in the conquest of Palestine. He had given to her groups and classes of men through whom His nature and will could be made known in unique fashion. He had bestowed on her a friendship which He had offered to no others, and, in spite of her apostasy, He still pleaded with her in tones of loving tenderness which no others could ever hear. But her special privileges involved her in special responsibility. Much had been given to her, and of her much would be required. She could, and should, have known Yahweh thoroughly, and should have followed Him with changeless fidelity. Yet she had rejected all that He had had to offer her, had refused to " know " Him, and had turned to the debased and debasing forms of belief which were current about her. It was, then, inevitable that her punishment should match her offence; because she had sinned against a purer light than others, she must suffer a heavier penalty. Her task in the divine plan had been to cultivate and to manifest the peculiar

[1] Cf. Is. xl. 27 f.

character and demands of her God; when she turned aside to lower ideals, she brought upon herself a doom from which there was no escape.

(g) *The Nature of Punishment.*—It is characteristic of the prophets—as, indeed, of the Old Testament in general—that they do not regard the penalty of sin as being merely the expression of an arbitrarily vindictive spirit. Yahweh was a God of Law, a God of Nature, a God of History, a God of Israel. But, even so, there were spheres which seemed to be outside His control. Theoretically, no doubt, He could still have done as he pleased in the face of Israel's transgression, and more than once the prophets represent Him as "repenting" of a punishment which He had threatened, and even as struggling against the penalty which He Himself must inflict. But, though He might postpone the final doom, even He could not avert it, without being false to His own nature. A man or a nation which violated His laws thereby let loose into the world an evil force, a living and deadly thing, which no power, whether human or divine, could stay from its ultimate fulfilment. Sooner or later it must recoil, and find its home with the author of its being. To man, limited in perception and experience by categories of time and space, sin and punishment are two different events; seen (as the prophets saw them) *sub specie æternitatis*, they are one and the same thing, presenting two different sides, but no more separable than the two sides of a piece of paper. It may not be untrue to say that Yahweh punishes, but His action is negative rather than positive; He leaves the sinner to his sin, as, being self-consistent, He must do, and the disaster in which sin culminates is the inevitable and inexorable issue of man's own action and thought.

It is true that there are grades and stages in the progress of evil. For long there remains open the possibility that repentance may avert further suffering, and make possible a restoration. Hence the prophets are full of appeals, sometimes based on love and sometimes on fear, calling the nation to turn from their ways before it is too late, and to find that pardon which Yahweh longs passionately to grant. Some of the most terrible of threats are conditional, and that which they hold out before men may be avoided if the right action be taken. But there is a limit, and, unless human repentance intervene, the final blow must fall, though the very heart of God be broken with the stroke.

(h) Yahweh makes no Ritual Demands.—It is, perhaps, here that we see more clearly than anywhere else the inheritance of the pastoral religion. The syncretistic cultus of the Ba'al-Yahweh was largely based on sacrifice, and its performance was inconceivable apart from the great sanctuaries. It was held that His delight was in the offerings that were made to Him, and that His vengeance would fall most surely on the man who neglected to pay due homage at His shrine. This was fully in line with the accepted beliefs of most religions in the ancient world, and has not altogether faded even in modern times. But the pre-exilic prophets with one voice declare that it is not thus that Israel can win the favour of her God. Some go so far as to deny categorically that sacrifice was ordained at all in the nomadic period, and they seek to revert to the principles and practices of those early days. All are agreed that Yahweh does not want these things, that He is sated with the blood of bulls and goats, that the music of the assemblies is noxious to Him, and that He will have no respect to the offerings that people make (cp. Isa. i. 10 ff., Jer. vii. 21, Hos. vi. 6, viii. 11 ff., Amos v. 21–23).[1] We need not assume that all the prophets thought that animal sacrifice was positively wicked; probably they might have acquiesced in its practice, if they had not found that men were offering ceremonial worship as a substitute for those spiritual and moral qualities on which the demands of Yahweh really centred. The slaughter of the victims in a religion which requires sacrifice is, as already pointed out, a disgusting business from the æsthetic point of view, but we cannot assume that the ancient prophets were actuated by considerations of this kind. Their objection was rather that it served as a moral opiate, and dulled the consciences of men to the reality of true spiritual values. It has been the practical experience of the noblest spirits in all sacrificial religions that the blood of animals can never take away sin, perhaps because such persons feel that sin is more than a matter of ritual and can therefore never be met by mere ceremonial.

To the ordinary Israelite sin was a neglect of ritual regulations; to the prophets it was a violation of the moral law. The two were in spheres between which there was no point of contact, and there could be no valid connexion

---

[1] Possibly (cf. p. 165) the prophets were historically inaccurate on this point, or the passages cited may be capable of other explanations.

between them.   It followed that no ritual within the area
of sacrifice could possibly atone for sins committed in the
region of conscience.   A piece of ceremonial might put the
worshipper right with a god whose ceremonial demands he had
neglected, but it could not possibly affect a relation between
man and God which was based on morality.   The atonement
must be moral, and even the costliest of sacrifices was utterly
futile in the effort to recover the favour of Yahweh.   The
God of Israel, alone among the deities worshipped by
men, made no ritual demands; to Him sacrifice was always
a weariness, and, when substituted for morality, an abomination (cp. Isa. i. 11-15).

CHAPTER XX

THE EIGHTH-CENTURY PROPHETS

It was the eighth century which witnessed the last revival of the Assyrian empire, and between 750 and 650 B.C. the power of Nineveh reached its zenith. Never before had the authority of the Assyrian king spread so far; his conquests in the west began with the subjugation of Damascus in 734 and did not cease till the end of the century, when his armies had penetrated to the very borders of Egypt. The conquest of that country was the final goal on which the Assyrian kings fixed their eyes, but this was not achieved till well on in the seventh century, and even then was neither complete nor permanent. But the little states, including the two Hebrew kingdoms, which lay on or near the route, were thoroughly subdued; Samaria was taken and the northern kingdom brought to an end, while the southern kingdom became a vassal of Nineveh. When Hezekiah, at the very end of the century, allowed himself to be drawn into the general rising of Assyrian subjects which took place with the accession of Sennacherib, the land was overrun and plundered, Jerusalem besieged, though not taken, and the country so thoroughly cowed that it never again revolted against the Assyrian king.

In Palestine itself the social and religious declines which had their origin in the foreign influence of Jezebel had reached the point of maximum danger. In 760 B.C. Assyria was still suffering from the temporary eclipse which ended with the accession of Tiglath-pileser III in 745 B.C., and under Jeroboam II northern Israel had attained a prosperity which the country had never enjoyed since the days of Solomon. Military victory had restored the old ideal borders to the land, while successful trade poured wealth into the country. But the tendency was for power of all kinds to be concentrated in the hands of the few,[1] and the

---

[1] It is worth noting that, while earlier prophets, such as Ahijah and Elijah, had attacked the royal tyranny, Amos and his successors were much more concerned with a wealthy class of agrarian and financial magnates. Jehoiakim (cf. Jer. xxii. 13 ff.) is the only conspicuous example, in the canonical prophets, of a king who violated the principles of social justice.

poor grew poorer yet. In particular, a complete social and economic change had passed over the country. The old type of small peasant farmer, the independent crofter, represented by Naboth in the ninth century, had practically disappeared, and the land was now divided up into large estates, worked chiefly by serf or even slave labour. Such a condition is perilous in the extreme, for if the lower classes have lost the manliness which would impel them to rise against their oppressors they will no longer have the strength to resist the encroachments of foreign enemies. In either case the country is doomed. If we would understand the prophets of the eighth century, we must see them against this double background of rotting social order, and of the advancing Assyrian power.

The prophets whose activity is to be placed in this period are four : Amos (c. 760 B.C.); Hosea, a generation later; Isaiah, whose ministry covered approximately forty years (740–701 B.C.), and Micah, who was a contemporary of Isaiah. The work of the first two lay wholly in the northern kingdom, while Isaiah, though a southerner, had something to say about Samaria as well as about Jerusalem. Micah had little to contribute to the development of Hebrew religion; his attitude and teaching were those of Amos, though with a deeper bitterness, since he himself was among those who suffered from the evils he denounced. But each of the other three has his own stress, and merits special attention.

1. Amos

Like Elijah, Amos was a foreigner to the agricultural community of central and northern Palestine. His home was in the far south, in the neighbourhood of Tekoa, and he was brought up among the shepherd community, adding to his livelihood what he could earn by tending a species of coarse fig. Such a man could enter the community of Samaria and Bethel with a complete detachment. He was in no way implicated in the evils of the social order, and he spoke as one who need not share in the doom he pronounced. Such a man could see with great clearness the sins that were rife among the northern people, and could form an estimate of the moral and religious condition of Israel on the basis of the purer life and faith of the semi-pastoral south.

The message of Amos included all those features which we have seen to be characteristic of the prophetic teaching in general.   He saw Yahweh as Law, as one who could not be inconsistent with Himself.   His close and intimate knowledge of the world of nature helped him to stress the control of Yahweh over the physical world.   More than once we meet with snatches of doxology in the book which bears his name,[1] and these leave the impression of having being drawn from some great hymn of praise to the Creator.   Further, when he envisages the calamities which are to fall on Israel as a result of her sins, he sees, more often than other prophets, disasters in the world of nature—famine, drought, blight, mildew, pestilence, earthquake [2]—as the means whereby Yahweh seeks to bring His people to repentance.   The God of Israel is, too, the Lord of History; and controls the great racial migrations; not only did He bring Israel out of Egypt, but He was responsible also for the wandering of the Aramæans from Kir, and for the breaking up of the old Ægean cultures, which ended in the establishment of the Philistines in Palestine.[3]   His denunciation of Moab for the desecration of royal graves in Edom [4] is striking testimony to Yahweh's claim to be Lord of universal morality.   The cultus, as he saw it, met with uncompromising condemnation.   It was not at the great sanctuaries that Yahweh was really to be found,[5] and the normal ritual roused only his scorn.[6]   Sacrifice did not belong to the true religion of Israel, that of the nomad age,[7] and the great festivals, with their elaborate ceremonial, were hateful to Yahweh.[8]   Among other evils Amos denounced the utter lack of any real ethical quality in the worship of Israel, and condemned the immoralities and illegalities, not merely countenanced, but actively endorsed and imposed by the current theories of religious duty.[9]   While he bitterly attacked the popular eschatological beliefs of his time, he proclaimed a "Day of Yahweh," which should mean the ruin of the evil-doers in Israel,[10] and deplored the failure, both of Yahweh's benefits and of His punishments, to recall the people to a sense of the real demands of their God.

The point, however, on which Amos fastened with clearest insight was the unfair dealing of man with man. He found the trader, while meticulously observing the regulation taboo on the Sabbath, planning how he could on

---

[1] Amos iv. 13, v. 8 f., ix. 6 f.   [2] Cf. especially Amos, iv. 6–11.
[3] Amos ix. 7.   [4] Amos ii. 1.   [5] Cf., e.g., Amos v. 5.
[6] Cf. Amos iv. 4 f.   [7] Amos v. 25.   [8] Amos v. 21 ff.
[9] Cf., e.g., Amos ii. 7b–8.   [10] Amos v. 18 ff.

the morrow cheat his customers in every possible way.[1]
Still more terrible was the maladministration of justice.
This is a standing social evil in the East, but it seems to have
reached its height in eighth-century Israel. The smallest
bribe offered by an influential person was sufficient to win a
case, and it seems probable that the economic change already
mentioned had been brought about in part by the illicit
use of the processes of law. The precedent set by Jezebel
had been only too freely followed, and men had lost their
freedom through the decisions given against them by corrupt
judges. It was enough, says Amos with bitter scorn, to
give the judge a pair of shoes, and the defendant would be
handed over as a slave—they sell the poor for a pair of shoes.[2]

Hence the supreme demand of Amos is for fair dealing
as between man and man. Justice, equity, honesty[3]—
these are the qualities which Yahweh demands of Israel.
There is hope, but not much, of a reform which will lead to
safety. But, if Israel will not seek Yahweh, abandoning
the vain quest at the sanctuaries, and will not look for Him
in righteous act, her doom is certain. There are those who
hold that Amos could already see the Assyrian threat in the
distance, though he does not expressly mention it, but
whether he realized the means that would be used or not is a
matter of small importance. He knew Yahweh, and he knew
the state of Israel; he knew, then, that destruction was the
only possible issue (cp., e.g., vii. 9).

2. Hosea

Hosea offers in many ways a strong contrast to Amos.
His work is probably to be dated some twenty years
after the time of his predecessor, for there are signs of
the collapse of the monarchy through frequent revolution,[4]
and one or two references suggest that Samaria had
already fallen before his ministry was ended. He is a
native of the north, and cannot contemplate the sins of his
people with any abstraction or detachment. He is that
truest of patriots, the man who identifies himself with his
country, feels her calamities as though they were his own,
and repents with bitter tears for her sins as if he had himself
committed them. He is a man of intense passions, feeling
strongly, yet thinking clearly, and his very style breathes his
whole fervent nature.

[1] Cf. Amos viii. 5.   [2] Amos ii. 6, viii. 6.
[3] Amos v. 24.   [4] Cf., e.g., Hos. vii. 7, viii. 4.

We cannot think of Hosea apart from the tragedy of his marriage, told to us by the historian in the first chapter of the book that bears his name, and by himself in chapter three. It was from the agony of his own experience that he learnt his lesson and received his message. If he could so love a woman who was probably from the first unworthy, and certainly showed herself faithless, how much greater would be the love of Yahweh for His people !

The sexual metaphor as an expression of the relation between the worshipper and the object of his worship was only too common in the ancient East. In Hosea it was purified and ennobled, being delivered from the grosser elements which have thrown so black a shadow on much of the religious life of the agricultural world. It seemed to him that Yahweh's attitude to Israel was that of a loving husband to his wife. Sin was the rejection of that love, the surrender to another of something most precious which belonged to the great Lover alone. On Israel Yahweh had lavished every sign of His tender affection, yet when she had given thanks for the benefits she had received, her gratitude had been paid, not to Yahweh, but to the *Ba'als*. The marriage metaphor is not the only one he uses to express the ideal relation between Yahweh and His people, and the Bible contains few more tender passages than that which draws the picture of the divine Father teaching the infant feet to walk.[1] But the end of this passage is that of the others; Israel fails to recognize Yahweh as He really is. The *Ba'als* were still freely worshipped in the land, and even the nominal cult of Yahweh was but a thin disguise, easily penetrated by the keen sight of the prophet, under which the old deities were revered. Men must abandon the official sanctuaries and the official ceremonial if they would win the favour of Yahweh. Hosea is, in fact, as far as we know, the first explicitly to condemn the bull-cult of Bethel.[2]

Hosea felt, as did Amos, the commercial and social iniquity of his people.[3] But, as a citizen of the northern kingdom, he was interested in political matters to an extent which we should not expect of Amos. In him we meet, perhaps for the first time,[4] with a strong protest against the institution of monarchy, and a feeling that human kingship was inconsistent with the true principles of Yahweh. The kings

---

[1] Hos. xi. 1–4.   [2] Cf., e.g., Hos. viii. 5 f. xiii. 2.   [3] Cf., e.g., Hos. iv. 2.
[4] The date of the second account of the establishment of the monarchy, 1 Sam. viii., x. 17–27, xii., is uncertain, and may be later than Hosea.

whom he knew were unworthy of their office, and failed in their duty.[1] But Hosea went further than mere denunciation of individuals; he felt that Israel had sinned in anointing kings at all.[2]

Amos, too, had little interest in the foreign politics of Israel; his nearest approach to an utterance on the subject is his condemnation of the short-sighted, jingoistic patriotism which could exult over the victories of Jeroboam to the east of the Jordan.[3] Twenty years later, the relations of Israel with the great powers had become one of the burning questions of the day, and Tiglath-pileser was already beginning his brilliant career of conquest. The weakness of Egypt was not quite as obvious as it became at the end of the eighth century B.C., but even before the fall of Samaria, Hosea had cause to denounce the uncertain, wavering, foreign policy of his Government, which fluttered fitfully from Assyria to Egypt, and back again.[4] The appeal to Assyria, indeed, is an act of apostasy—possibly a reference to the tribute paid by Menahem in 738 B.C. Israel is Yahweh's and Yahweh is Israel's; let that be enough. She has nothing to do with any foreign power, whether of gods or of men.

Yahweh's supreme demand from men, as Hosea understood Him, was for a quality expressed in the Hebrew word *chesed*, quite untranslatable in English. It means love, but more than love, for it always implies the obligations imposed by a definite relationship, and thus carries with it something of the content of duty. Even so, it is not merely an attitude adopted by one person to another, but that essential quality of the soul from which love, sympathy, pity, devotion, all spring. It may produce an attitude of the inferior to the superior, of man to God. It may imply the attitude of the superior to the inferior, of God to man. Or, again, it may be the attitude of equals to one another, of man to man. In any case it implies a full appreciation of, and a complete devotion to, a personality.

Hosea thus goes deeper than Amos. Where the latter lays the stress on the external conduct, the former searches the inner springs of action. It is not enough to demand of men that they should behave themselves; they must have that deep within them which will compel them to upright and loving conduct. It is this which Yahweh Himself has exhibited in His dealings with Israel, and she

---

[1] Cf., e.g., Hos. v. 1. [2] Cf. Hos. vii. 3, viii. 4, 10, xiii. 10 f.
[3] Cf. Amos vi. 13. [4] Cf., e.g., Hos. v. 13, vii. 8, 11, viii. 9–11, ix. 6.

can fulfil His demands only by giving Him her answering love. If that fails—and Hosea saw little hope of repentance —the doom of the people is certain, for it was better for Israel to perish as a nation than to continue as she was, and Hosea ascribed to Yahweh a love which could inflict the last penalty, though at appalling cost to Himself.

Yet there is a love so great, passionate, and intense, that it cannot abandon the hope of restoration, even when men and nations have reached the limits of sin and suffering. It was incredible to Hosea that Yahweh should be defeated in the long run. His love was bound up with a patience which could endure to the uttermost, and still would leave room for a fresh start. Israel might be so shattered as to be reduced to her old status of a little nomad tribe, but, even so, she would once more be wooed and won by her God. Yet again would she be brought to the promised land, and, crossing the Jordan where Joshua had crossed it, would stand facing the great rampart of cliff which fronted the river valley. Again she would explore the entrances to the land, up the gorges which led to the people's true home, and she would find in the valley of Achor a door of hope.[1] Love is stronger than death, and St. Paul, in one of the most glorious of his utterances, falls back on the language of Hosea in order to describe the supreme triumph.[2] Though the babe perish in its mother's womb, and come still-born into the world, yet will Yahweh ransom it from *She'ol*, and give it new and valid life.[3] Never in the history of man's thought has the boundless optimism of love found more striking expression than in Hosea.

3. ISAIAH

Isaiah stands in a position different both from that of Amos and from that of Hosea. While Samaria was included in the range of his prophecies until the fall of the northern kingdom, he lived and did his main work in Jerusalem. He dealt, it is true, with much the same evils in Judah as those which Amos denounced in the north. His anger was aroused by the absence of true justice, and by the oppression of the poor and lowly by the wealthier classes.[4] He recognized the *latifundia* which had produced so great a change in the social and economic life of Israel, and appreciated the magnitude of the danger which it involved. It meant the ultimate desolation of the countryside, and the

[1] Hos. ii. 14 f.
[3] Hos. xiii., 13 f.
[2] 1 Cor. xv. 55, cf. Hos. xiii. 14.
[4] Cf., e.g., Is. iii. 12, 15, v. 7, 23, x. 1 f.

disappearance of the freeman, who might have fought in the defence of the land.[1] He held the women to be responsible for much that was amiss in the life of Israel,[2] and condemned those who should have been the leaders of the people and their protectors.[3] [He denounced the cultus in unmeasured terms,[4] and attacked the worship of other deities than Yahweh, giving them the contemptuous name " godlings." [5] He counted necromancy among the dangerous forms of apostasy, and insisted that it was but a futile refuge in time of trouble.[6] Like Hosea, he shared with the Rechabites a detestation of wine, though not because it was a symbol of the agricultural life, but because it was morally and spiritually destructive.[7]

The great contribution of Isaiah to the developing picture of Yahweh and Yahwism was his insistence on the *holiness* of Yahweh. This was by no means a new idea, for the conception of holiness in one form or another is necessarily almost as old as religion itself. As applied to human affairs it indicates a separation from the ordinary and the secular, a thing set apart for the sole use and enjoyment of the deity. But with Isaiah this conception had gained a moral content too often wanting elsewhere. Since Yahweh was supremely good, it followed that any thing or person set apart for Him must also be good, and the nation especially consecrated to Him must justify its position by a high moral standard.

The effect of Isaiah's conception of holiness on his view of the moral demands of Yahweh is obvious. But it also affected his attitude in politics. He seems, according to tradition, to have played a larger part in the public life of his time than any other prophet of the eighth century. He has been classed among the great statesmen of the ancient east, and it has been held that he, almost alone of the men of his day, appreciated the position of Judah, and therefore urged that she was safe as long as she refrained from meddling with the great world powers and their quarrels. But, if that were his real reason, he was singularly successful in concealing it. It seems much more certain that his policy of isolation was dictated by his conviction that foreign politics involved a spiritual danger, that Yahweh and Israel were holy to one another, and must keep apart from the world. The prophet's ground of complaint against Ahaz was not, as far as we know, based on the king's introduction

---

[1] Isa. v. 8 ff.
[2] Isa. iii. 16 ff.
[3] Cp., e.g., Isa. iii. 14, ix. 14 (Hebr. 13).
[4] Cp., e.g., Isa. i. 10–17.
[5] Isa. ii. 8.
[6] Isa. viii. 19 ff.
[7] Isa. v. 11 ., 22, xxviii. 7 ff., cf. Hos. iv. 11.

of foreign elements into the cultus,[1] though his action would
have lent point to the warnings of Isaiah, but on the conviction that Yahweh would not, and could not, surrender a
city which was faithful to Him. The Syro-Ephraimite
confederacy was foredoomed to failure in its attempt on
Jerusalem,[2] and when, under the greatest provocation,
Sennacherib threatened Jerusalem, Isaiah was confident that,
however the country might suffer, the city itself was safe.[3]
Egypt was a particular danger, not only on general grounds,
but especially because of her weakness and ineffectiveness.
If Judah must plunge into the vortex of international
politics, let it be on the side of Assyria, not on that of Egypt.[4]
Even Assyria, whose conquests are certain, is but an instrument in the hand of Yahweh, who controls all the peoples
and their movements,[5] and will be employed to vindicate the
holiness of Yahweh. When that purpose is accomplished,
then the rod itself may be broken and discarded. Judah
was safe, because she was in the hands of a greater than
Assyria, and His will must at last be done.

It is characteristic of Isaiah that he seems to have thought
of Yahweh as being " holy " to Israel, as well as of Israel
as being " holy " to Yahweh. That is to say that the
consecration was mutual. Israel could not dispense with
Yahweh, but Yahweh needed Israel for His self-expression.
Israel was His people; therefore He could not suffer her to
be utterly destroyed; Jerusalem was the spot where He had
chosen to set His name; therefore the city could not be
polluted by the entry of a foreign enemy.

Yet the sin of Israel must meet with punishment, and
Isaiah saw clearly enough that foreign invasion must come.
But this did not mean, as it meant to Hosea, a destruction
practically complete. However much Judah suffered for
her sins, there must always be a remnant,[6] who should be
ready to start a new life in a better community and a more
perfect order. At its head would be a king who should be
the ideal of human monarchy, the perfect ruler.[7] It is with
Isaiah that we find the beginning of that conception which

[1] 2 Kings xvi. 10 ff. [2] Isa. vii. 1 ff.
[3] Isa. xxxvii. 6 f., 35. Though not included in the strictly "prophetic"
portion of the Book of Isaiah, these utterances are in complete harmony
with all that Isaiah had to say elsewhere, and there is no reason to doubt
the tradition which ascribes them to him.
[4] Cp. Isa. xxx. 1 ff., xxxi. 1 ff. [5] Isa. x. 5 ff.
[6] Cp. Isa. vii. 3 (the name Shear-jashub="a remnant shall return "),
x. 20 ff.
[7] Cp. ix. 1 ff. (xi. 1 ff. is probably the utterance of an exilic prophet),
xxxii. 1 ff.

later ripened into a full Messianic doctrine,[1] and we shall not
greatly err if we trace it back to the prophet's conception of
the mutual holiness of Yahweh and Israel.

4. HEZEKIAH'S REFORMS

In 2 Kings xviii. 4–6 we have an appreciation of Hezekiah,
largely from the pen of the editor of the book, which speaks
of him as the most perfect king who ever sat on the throne of
Judah, with the one exception of David. This is based, as
it seems, on a reform which he carried through, destroying
the local sanctuaries or " high places," those old seats of
Ba'al-cults but imperfectly turned to the service of Yahweh,
and breaking in pieces the bronze serpent which tradition
carried back to the days of Moses.

We know also that on the death of Sargon in 705 B.C.,
Hezekiah and the other western princes joined in the
general revolt against Sennacherib engineered by Marduk-
apal-iddina (the Biblical Merodach-baladan), king of
Babylon. One element in the revolt was almost certainly
the elimination of the Assyrian cult imposed by Tiglath-
pileser on Ahaz in 734 B.C., and the removal of the " pillars "
and " asherim " probably included the destruction of a
symbol of the supremacy of Assyria. Further, in the few
details which are given to us, we seem to have an adumbration of the reforms carried out nearly a century later by
Josiah. Is it possible that the account is in some measure a
reflexion back into the eighth century of events which were
properly confined to the seventh ? The historian or compiler
of the books of *Kings* wrote under the stress of the influence
of Josiah's reform and the principle of the centralization of
sacrifice which was its outstanding feature. Hezekiah's
interest in the national worship, and his undoubted attempt
to introduce a purer form of it than had been current, may
well have led this writer or school to believe that he must
have gone farther than he actually did, and to ascribe to
him a measure which was not taken, as a matter of fact, for
three-quarters of a century after his time. In any case,
even if the record in 2 Kings xviii. be historically accurate, no
permanent effect was produced by the reforms, for Hezekiah's son and successor, Manasseh, reverted to the old ways,
and re-established the local sanctuaries. That there was
some purification of the worship of Israel we need not doubt,
and we may be sure that it had its influence in preparing
the way for yet more complete reformation.

[1] See below, Chapter XXXVIII.

CHAPTER XXI

THE AFTER-LIFE: SECOND STAGE OF BELIEF

1. BABYLONIAN BELIEF

In an earlier chapter [1] we dealt with the Semitic belief regarding the After-life as held in the most remote times of which we have information; and it was pointed out that the conceptions in vogue in those early days persisted in spite of the teaching of the religious leaders of later times, who saw that there was much in those early beliefs, and the practices to which they gave rise, which was incompatible with the worship of Yahweh. We have now to consider this later teaching which was put forth by the religious leaders.

As in the earlier chapter, we shall begin by drawing attention to Babylonian teaching, which, like that of the Hebrews, entered upon this second stage.

In comparing the belief of this second stage with that of earlier times, it will be seen that the two are incompatible with one another. Perhaps this is to be accounted for in two ways: the varied and contradictory ideas found in the inscriptions may be due to the amalgamation of conceptions belonging to different ages; even when a development of thought—or what is held to be a development—has taken place, the old ideas are impossible to eradicate. It is also doubtless due to the various illogical trains of thought on the subject which is characteristic among so many ancient peoples. Nothing moves people more deeply, nothing excites their speculations more vividly, than thoughts of death and the Hereafter; naturally enough they think differently according to the variable character of temperament. There is no occasion for surprise, therefore, when we find incompatible and contradictory thought and teaching on the subject among the Babylonians. It has already been pointed out that the religion of the Babylonian priesthood was but little concerned with the Hereafter, and that, in

[1] Chapter VIII.

consequence, ideas and speculations regarding this were left to popular imagination. It is, therefore, true to say that those early ideas represent the popular point of view. But obviously, an official priesthood cannot wholly ignore a subject which exercises popular thought and imagination, and which greatly affects their lives.

It would seem, therefore, that an *official* doctrine regarding what happened after death was put forth; for it is impossible to believe, in view of what we have seen to be the popular conceptions, that this other picture of the After-life can have arisen among the generality of men. Some ideas, it is true, were common to both, but the differences were greater. Hence what is now to be described may be designated the official doctrine.

According to this doctrine—and here, as in some other details, the popular view concurred—there were special gods of the underworld; they were subordinate to the great gods of the Babylonian Pantheon, but they were nevertheless gods. These netherworld gods had their palace in the abode of the dead. Foremost among the rulers of the underworld was the goddess Erishkigal, "The Mistress of the great place" (i.e. of the dead); she is also known as Allatu, "The mighty one." Together with her is her husband, Nergal, called "Lord of the great land" (i.e. of the dead); their wedding is referred to on one of the Tell-el-Amarna tablets. The Sumerians, who lived in the country of the Babylonians before these latter drove them out, also had their ideas about the departed and their abode; and the Babylonians evidently borrowed from them some of their ideas. The Sumerians called the place of the departed *Kurnugea*, which means "the land without return," and this name figures in Babylonian poetry, showing that the Babylonians were in some respects indebted to the Sumerians for their ideas on the subject. Thus, in the account of Ishtar's descent into the realm of the departed this place is spoken of as "the abode which whosoever enters never leaves again; the path from which there is no return"; it will at once be realized how entirely incompatible this is with the popular view about the spirits being able to leave their abode. While this place is sometimes conceived of as a great hollow mountain, it is more usually thought of as an immense city which could not be measured for size. The way to it was across the ocean, westward, towards the sinking sun, for it was situated beyond the waters that are beneath the earth. This great city of the dead is described as being enclosed by seven walls, and there are seven double gates with ponderous bolts; and when a newcomer has entered one of these gates the guardian who keeps watch by it closes it again and makes it secure with bolts and bars. It is said that this city is " a house of darkness," and they who live there are shut out from the light. They who enter this dark city must divest themselves of all clothing before assuming the " garment of wings "; it is described very graphically in the poem already spoken of, *The Descent of Ishtar*, where it tells of how this goddess, daughter of the Moon-god, had, on entering, to submit to the decrees of this realm; at the first gate she removed her diadem from her head, at the second her ear-rings, then her necklace, then the ornament adorning her bosom, then her bejewelled girdle, then the bracelets on her feet and hands, all of which she had to leave behind, until finally, at the seventh gate, she slipped off the robe which covered her beautiful form, and stood naked before the queen of the underworld.

No ranks are recognized in the realm of the dead; there all are equal. And in that place of darkness dust overspreads all things; dust on the gates, dust on bolt and bar, dust on the shades of men and women as they silently glide along the dust-laden streets of this city of the dead. The food of these weird inhabitants is dust; and black, murky, dust-mixed water is their drink. In that place there is neither love nor hate, only sorrow and wailing; monotonous moaning echoes through the streets of dust; that is the only sound in the surrounding silence, the only occupation of the dusty shades of men.[1] The following quotation from *The Descent of Ishtar* gives a graphic picture :

> Ishtar, the moon-god's daughter,
> Bethought her of the ' Land without Return ' . . .
> The daughter of the moon-god bethought her
> Of the house of darkness, the abode of Irkalla (= Nergal),
> Of the house which whosoever enters never leaves again,
> Of the path from which there is no return,
> Of the house which whosoever enters is taken from the light,
> Of the place where dust is their food, and soil their nutriment,
> Where they behold no light, but dwell in darkness,
> Where they are clad like birds in garments of wings,
> Where dust is spread on door and bolt.[2]

[1] Cp. among others, Delitzsch, *Das Land ohne Heimkehr*, pp. 14 ff. (1911).
[2] Jeremias, *Hölle* . . . p. 15; Jastrow, *op. cit.*, ii. 958. For further names of and ideas concerning the world of the dead, see Tallquist, *Sumerisch-Akkadische Namen der Totenwelt* (1934).

It will thus be seen that while in some particulars the popular conceptions agree with the "official" ones, in fundamentals the two are very different; and it is a matter of particular interest that, as we shall see, the Old Testament presents us with a precisely similar phenomenon.

2. THE OLD TESTAMENT

According to the official teaching, the place of the departed was called *She'ol*; there is no certitude as to the meaning of this word; by some scholars it is held that it means "the place of inquiry"; this is unlikely because nowhere in the Old Testament do we find anything to support the idea that, according to this official teaching, the departed were subjected to an inquiry of any kind. Again, the argument put forward that *She'ol* was a place of inquiry because necromancers inquired of the dead is not valid, because that, too, would apply to the *dead*, not the place of their abode. More likely, but still uncertain, is the theory that the word is connected with a root meaning " to be hollow," *She'ol* being thought of as a deep hollow place; the Babylonians, as we have seen, pictured *She'ol* as a huge hollow mountain; in this connexion it is worth mentioning that our word Hell, and the German Hölle, mean in their essence a " hole." The simplicity of this explanation is in its favour, because, whatever developments took place, in its origin we naturally look for a simple idea in connexion with such a subject.

We will now consider what the Old Testament says about this place. So far as possible we will take the passages chronologically, but one has always to bear in mind the possibility that a later scribe may have added something to a passage in accordance with his ideas.

It is to be noted, first of all, that in the pre-exilic literature the references to *She'ol* are very scanty; its existence is taken for granted, showing that by the time the pre-exilic books were written the official *She'ol* doctrine had already been put forth, though the popular conceptions regarding the After-life continued to be held.

The pre-exilic passages may be divided into two categories : those which merely make mention of *She'ol*, and those which give some details in regard to it. Thus, Gen. xlii. 38, xliv. 29, 31 (all belonging to the J document), Gen. xxxvii. 35 (belonging to the E document), 1 Kings ii. 6, 9, merely refer to *She'ol* without saying anything further about it.

The remaining pre-exilic passages give details; but it

must be remembered that in some cases it is probable that there has been some working over on the part of later editors. In Num. xvi. 20 ff. (J document), we have the account of the deaths of Korah, Dathan, and Abiram and their company; it is said (verses 31–33) that " the earth opened her mouth, and swallowed them up, and their households. . . . So they, and all that appertained to them, went down alive into *She'ol*; and the earth closed upon them, and they perished from among the assembly." Doubtless, some actual occurrence lies behind the narrative; but what concerns us here is the idea that *She'ol* is situated under the earth which " opens its mouth " to receive those who go down to it; the same quaint thought occurs in Am. ix. 2, where the prophet speaks of those who flee from the wrath of God, but will be unable to escape though they dig down into *She'ol*; the words, it is true, are meant figuratively, for the prophet goes on to say that even if they climb up to heaven they will be brought down; but the idea of *She'ol* being deep down in the earth echoes the current belief. Parallel with this passage is Isa. vii. 11, where the prophet bids King Ahaz ask a sign from God; he says: " Ask it either in *She'ol*, or in the height above," meaning that wherever in the whole universe the sign is sought it will be forthcoming; the words are, of course, again meant to be understood figuratively. There is also a parallel to the Korah episode of people going down alive to *She'ol* in Isa. v. 14 : " Therefore *She'ol* hath enlarged her desire, and opened her mouth without measure; and their glory, and their multitude, and their pomp, and he that rejoiceth among them, shall descend into it." A very curious superstition, referred to by Isaiah, is that of men thinking by magical means to prolong their lives, and thus avoiding, or at least postponing, their descent into *She'ol*; the passage is Isa. xxviii. 15, where the prophet quotes these people as saying: "We have made a covenant with death, and with *She'ol* we are at agreement." Death as a synonym for *She'ol* occurs also in Hos. xiii. 14, where the words are put into the mouth of God : " Should I ransom them from the power of *She'ol*; should I redeem them from death ? " The R.V. translates this, wrongly, as though it were a statement: " I will ransom them . . ."; but it is a question expecting the answer No; the reference being to the iniquitous men of Ephraim. That, however, by the way; the passage is mentioned only to show that Death and *She'ol* are synonymous. This is found once more in Hab. ii. 5, where the prophet inveighs against the drunkards, and says that wine is a treacherous dealer " who enlargeth his desire as *She'ol*, and he is as Death, which cannot be satisfied. . . ." See also Deut. xxxii. 22 (probably pre-exilic).

These are all the passages belonging to pre-exilic times, and it will be realized that they are comparatively few in number. In passing, attention may be drawn to the fact that the R.V. is somewhat inconsistent in the way it renders the Hebrew word *She'ol*; in the pre-exilic passages mentioned, it translates the word in four different ways; presumably there must have been some reason for this; but it is not easy to discern what the reason was; it is, however, only fair to add that in every case the right translation is noted in the margin. The renderings are these :

In Gen. xliv. 29, 31; xlii. 38; xxxvii. 35; 1 Kings ii. 6, 9; Hos. xiii. 14, it is " grave " : in Deut. xxxii. 22, Num. xvi. 29–33, " pit "; in Am. ix. 2; Isa. v. 14, xiv. 11, xxviii. 15, xxxviii. 18; Hab. ii. 5, " hell "; and in Isa. viii. 11, " depth."

Now it is clear that these pre-exilic passages tell us very little about the place of the departed or about their state; but there can be little doubt about the reason of this. The object of the official teaching regarding the After-life was to counteract the popular beliefs, because those popular beliefs had led to practices which were incompatible with the worship of Yahweh—we shall return to this later. The period during which the official teaching about *She'ol* and the After-life arose was the *prophetical period*, beginning, roughly, early in the eighth century B.C.; for this official teaching to have its effect among the generality of the nation would obviously take time; and it would take more time for ideas about *She'ol* to develop. We can, therefore, understand easily enough that during the earlier stages of the *She'ol*-belief it did not greatly occupy the minds of people; it ran counter to the traditional beliefs; so that the comparatively rare mention of *She'ol* in the pre-exilic literature is natural enough.

As we have now examined all the pre-exilic passages in which reference is made to *She'ol*, our next step should normally be to examine the post-exilic literature in order to see what, if any, developments took place. But before we come to this,[1] there is something of much interest which must first occupy us; the reason being that this subject cuts across the pre- and post-exilic periods; it is a popular

[1] See Chapter XXXV.

belief which held its own in spite of the official doctrine; and we find it dealt with in early and late literature.

The subject is that of what are called the *Rephaim*. The meaning of the word will become clear as we proceed. In dealing with this subject there is no need to distinguish between pre- and post-exilic passages because the beliefs about the *Rephaim* are all ancient, and when referred to in late passages it is always old-world ideas which are re-echoed.

In the Old Testament *Rephaim* means two things: it means an ancient race of giants, and it means the departed; nevertheless, in reality, as will be seen, it means the departed only.

We will first take the passages in which *Rephaim* refers to an ancient mythical race of giants. They are mentioned for the first time in Gen. xiv. 5 (this chap. contains old material, but stands outside any of the ordinary Pentateuchal documents); here it is said that among those who were overcome by Chedorlaomer and the kings that were with him, were "Rephaim in Ashtaroth-Karnaim" (cp. Gen. xv. 20, where they are mentioned again); they lived in the forest land, according to Josh. xvii. 15. In the very early history of Israel they were looked upon as a "remnant" of the original inhabitants of Canaan. Josh. xiii. 12 ff., though a late passage, echoes an old tradition to the effect that in the time of Moses these people, among others, were driven out of the land: "All the kingdom of Og in Bashan, which reigned in Ashtaroth and in Edrei (the same was left of the remnant of the Rephaim) for these did Moses smite, and drave them out" (cp. Deut. ii. 20). In Deut. iii. 11, similarly, it is said: "For only Og the king of Bashan remained of the remnant of the Rephaim" (cp. Deut. iii. 13). Another ancient notice is preserved in Deut. ii. 10, 11: "The Emim dwelt there aforetime, a people great and many, and tall, as the Anakim; these also are accounted Rephaim, as the Anakim; but the Moabites call them Emim." Once more, it is said in Deut. ii. 20, 21, regarding the land of Amon, "that also is accounted a land of Rephaim; Rephaim dwelt there aforetime; but the Ammonites call them Zamzummim; a people great, and many, and tall, as the Anakim."

Now, it may be thought that these details are uninteresting and beside the point; but that is not so, as will be seen presently. The first thing to note is that of the twenty occurrences of this name *Rephaim* in the Old Testament, it is written fourteen times without the article; normally they

were spoken of as *Rephaim*, not as " the " *Rephaim*; the
addition of the article seems to belong to a later time when
it was thought that once a race existed who were called " the
Rephaim "; so that in its origin *Rephaim* was not a gentilic
name, not the name of a people; peoples are usually spoken
of with the definite article when referred to as a race—*the*
Egyptians, *the* Ammonites, *the* Philistines, and so on.   Then
we note, further, that there are some other names which
usually have not the article (in one or two instances the
article is added), and which, therefore, are not the names of
peoples, although they were regarded as such by the Biblical
writers; these are : Anakim, Emim, Zamzummim, Zuzim,
Nephilim; they are all either other names for *Rephaim*,
or else in some way connected with them; that is proved
by examining the various passages in question (Gen. vi. 4;
Num. xiii. 33; Ezek. xxxii. 27, etc., as already quoted).
The little that is known about these names is interesting :
Anakim (or " sons of Anak ") means " long-necked ones,"
probably in reference to serpents; [1] *Emim* means, in all
probability, serpent spirits; [2] in the singular it is used in
Ezek. xxi. 26 (R.V. 21) as " crossways," the point at which
two roads cross each other, therefore a knot; [3] that means to
say that the word is connected with magic—for, as is well
known, knots played a great part in the magic art, with
which evil spirits were often connected.[4] Then, as to
Zamzummim (of which *Zuzim* is probably a shortened
form), this is an onomatopoetic word connected with a
Semitic root meaning " to hiss," used of the hissing, whistling
sound made by the *Jinn*, or evil spirits, of the desert in the
night.   Finally, the *Nephilim* are mentioned in connexion
with the myth, referred to in Gen. vi. 4, of " the sons of the
gods who came in unto the daughters of men, and they bare
children unto them."   We may therefore regard the *Nephilim*
as mythic semi-divine beings, but of questionable birth, and
therefore of evil repute.   All these names, then, have something mysterious about them, and it seems certain that, in
their origin, they were beings *not* of this world; they are all,
as we have seen, included under the name *Rephaim*.   More
than a century ago it was held by Herder [5]—and time has
shown the correctness of his view—that the term *Rephaim*

---

[1] *Anak* also means a "necklace," something which coils around the neck.
[2] Schwally, *ZATW*, p. 135 (1918).
[3] König, *Hebräisches und Aramäisches Wörterbuch*, s.v.
[4] See above, pp. 111 ff.   [5] *Vom Geist der hebräischen Poesie* i. 368.

referred to the giants (equivalent to " the sons of the gods,"
and the *Nephilim* in Gen. vi. 1–7), who were destroyed by
God from the earth and cast down into the underworld.[1]
Then, in course of time, when the ancient myth had been
gradually toned down, the name *Rephaim* came to be used
as a general designation of *all* those in the underworld,
among whom were, of course, included the departed from
this world.

This leads us to examine the passages in the Old Testament in which *Rephaim* is used of the *departed*. That all
such passages are post-exilic bears out what has just been
said, namely, that the term *Rephaim*, as applied to the departed, is a comparatively late usage. We will quote the
passages first; they are seven in number :

Job xxvi. 5 : " The Rephaim tremble beneath the waters
with the inhabitants thereof." Ps. lxxxviii. 11 (R.V. 10) :
" Wilt thou show wonders to the dead ? Shall Rephaim
arise and praise thee ? " Isa. xiv. 9, 10 : " Sheol from
beneath is moved for thee to meet thee at thy coming; it
stirreth up Rephaim. . . . All they shall answer and say
unto thee, Art thou also become weak as we ? Art thou
become like unto us ? " This is said in reference to the king
of Babylon who is mockingly greeted as he enters the realm
of the dead by those, i.e. Rephaim, who are gathered there.
In Isa. xxvi. 14 it is said : " They that are dead, they shall
not live; Rephaim shall not rise." And three times in the
book of *Proverbs*, *Rephaim* are referred to : ii. 18, 19 :
" For her house (i.e. the house of the strange woman)
inclineth unto death, and her paths unto Rephaim. None
that go unto her shall return . . ."; ix. 18 : " But he
(i.e. the man without understanding) knoweth not that
Rephaim are there (i.e. in the house of folly) that her guests
(i.e. the guests of the foolish woman) are in the depth of
She'ol "; and, lastly, xxi. 16 : " The man that wandereth
out of the way of understanding shall rest in the congregation
of Rephaim."

All these passages, as we have said, are post-exilic; they
are the only ones in the Old Testament in which the *Rephaim*
are referred to by name when this term is intended to apply
to the departed. Let us examine them a little more closely
to see what they tell us about the beliefs regarding these
Rephaim. " They tremble beneath the waters "; why do

[1] This is dealt with in the Book of Enoch, viii–xvi; Book of Jubilees, v,
and elsewhere.

they tremble? The context would suggest that they tremble at the presence of God; if that is so, it points to a great development of conception regarding those in the After-life, for as we shall see, the normal belief is that God has no concern at all with the departed; the thought that He is interested in the departed belongs to a late period. Further, when it is said that they tremble " beneath the waters," we have a reference to the ancient Babylonian cosmology, according to which the earth is cradled on the ocean, so that " beneath the waters " refers to a realm outside the created world. Then again, according to the *Psalms* passage (lxxxviii. 11 10 [R.V.]), the departed cannot arise and praise God; on the other hand, they recognize the king of Babylon who comes into their abode, and are able to speak to him. Once more, according to Prov. ii. 19, it is said that there is no return from the place where *Rephaim* abide.

Next, we must examine one or two passages referring to the departed, in which *Rephaim* are obviously in the mind of the writers, though not mentioned by name.

Isa. xxxviii. 18 : " For She'ol cannot praise thee, death cannot celebrate thee ; they that go down to the Pit cannot hope for thy truth "; here *She'ol* and Death are used collectively of those in the abode of the departed. An important passage is Job iii. 11–19; it is too long to quote in full, but the salient parts are these : " Why died I not from the womb ? . . . For now should I have lien down and been quiet; I should have slept; then had I been at rest with kings and counsellors of the earth. . . . There the wicked cease from troubling, and the weary are at rest. There the prisoners are at ease together; they hear not the voice of the taskmaster. The small and the great are there; and the servant is free from his master." Another important passage is Ezek. xxxii. 17–32, from which a few quotations may be given; it is a prophetic denunciation telling of the coming woe upon Egypt : " The strong ones of the mighty (i.e. the gods who are thought of as consigned to the realms of the departed) shall speak to him (the Egyptians collectively) out of the midst of She'ol with them that help him; they are gone down, they lie still, even the uncircumcized, who went down to She'ol with their weapons of war; and they laid their swords under their heads, and their shields are upon their bones. . . . Pharaoh shall see them, and shall be comforted over all his multitude." [1]

---

[1] The passages in the *Psalms* referring to the After-life will be dealt with in pp. 357 ff.

Now, in these passages we have to note some ideas which are quite incompatible with one another; this is instructive because it witnesses to the mingling of older and newer thought on the subject. In the *Isaiah* passage the dead are thought of as pitiable, leading a silent, aimless existence; they have no relationship with God, they cannot praise Him, there is nothing to hope for from Him. But in the *Job* and *Ezekiel* passages, while there is no reference to God, it is clear that the condition of the departed which is contemplated is quite different. The place where the dead are is a place of rest, where the ordinary man is in the company of kings, who nevertheless retain their rank there; in that place there is no annoyance; the prisoners are at ease; though master and servant are there, the "small and the great," there is no oppression. From Job xxxviii. 17, on the other hand, it is evident that God knows all about the place of the departed, and therefore, presumably, about them too. The *Ezekiel* passage is very striking; it represents the dead as recognizing new-comers into their abode, and as speaking to them. From xxxii. 27 we gather that the prophet recognizes a kind of aristocracy in the abode of the dead; and he describes how that in *She'ol* the mighty heroes of old still have their swords and shields.

The point of special importance about these passages is that, while they reflect some popular ideas, they witness in some respects to a development of belief regarding the state of the departed. And this in spite of the fact that the official teaching about *She'ol* seems to have continued much the same for long after the Exile. The fact is that as among the Babylonians, so among the Hebrews, there were thinkers among the people who realized, on the one hand, that though there was truth, there was also much superstitious folly, in the popular beliefs; but that, on the other hand, the official belief was unsatisfying.

This official *She'ol* belief is, then, the second stage in the Old Testament doctrine of Immortality. The third, and final, stage is dealt with in Chapter XXXV.

CHAPTER XXII

THE REFORMS OF JOSIAH

THE long reign of Manasseh, extending, according to 2 Kings xxi. 1, for fifty-five years, i.e. from 696 to 641 B.C., was held by later Israel to be the worst period in the religious life of Judah. All that which Hezekiah had achieved was undone; the successors of Isaiah, if they attempted any public work, were suppressed—tradition even tells us that in this reign Isaiah himself was put to death by being sawn asunder [1]— and Jerusalem was deluged with innocent blood. Human sacrifice was offered, and various forms of necromancy were resorted to—an act of apostasy, since the spirits of the dead were illegitimate objects of worship. At the same time, Manasseh remained a faithful vassal of the court of Nineveh; and, save for a late tradition in *Chronicles* (2 Chron. xxxiii. 11), we hear no more of foreign invasion. The period was one of comparative prosperity, which remained undisturbed until the break-up of the Assyrian empire and the brief re-crudescence of Egypt at the end of the seventh century. It seemed as if the work of the prophets, especially of Isaiah, had been undone, and his threats remained unfulfilled except in the ravaging of the land by Sennacherib in 701 B.C.

1. THE REFORMS

In the reign of the grandson of Manasseh, Josiah, there came a change. The old Assyrian empire was crumbling, the last of her great kings, Ashurbanipal, died in 626 B.C., and the shock of the Scythian invasions prevented her from recovering herself in time to resist the combined forces of the Babylonians and Medes. In 621 B.C. Josiah undertook repairs to the Temple, which, presumably, had been neglected during his minority. In the course of the work a book was found claiming to be the law of Moses, laying down pre-scriptions for the establishment of a single sanctuary where

---

[1] In the apocalyptic book, called *The Ascension of Isaiah*, v.; the earliest portion of this composite work belongs to the first half of the first century A.D.

sacrifice and tithes might be offered. On the basis of this law a thorough reform was undertaken throughout the whole land. First the Temple itself was purified, and the motley collection of strange cults, gathered from almost every known people, was flung out and destroyed. Then the king and his emissaries toured the whole country, destroying the local sanctuaries, and paying particular attention to that which still existed at Bethel. Henceforward the great altar at Jerusalem was the one spot on which sacrifice could be legitimately offered to Yahweh.

Obviously the concentration of sacrifice in a single spot, and its restriction to a single altar, demanded the readjustment of various practices. Attention may be called to three of these, prescribed by *Deuteronomy* (see below), and presumably carried into effect by Josiah. In the first place, the distance of the central sanctuary made it difficult for men to slaughter all their animals there. In the old days, beef, mutton, and goat's flesh, could be eaten only when the creature had been ceremonially killed, and portions offered in sacrifice (see p. 183 f.). But now the flesh was secularized, and men were free to eat it when and where they would, only taking care that the blood of the animal was drained on the ground (cp. also Jer. vii. 21). Another special regulation was the provision of some form of sanctuary for the man who had unintentionally exposed himself to the guilt of blood. Formerly this had been the altar of Yahweh; now this was often too far away, and accordingly " cities of refuge " were established, in which the man in this kind of danger could be safe while his case was being considered. Finally there were numbers of priests, formerly attached to the old sanctuaries, and living largely on the sacrifices offered there; though some of them (e.g. the family of Jeremiah, cf. Jer. xxxii.) had land, the abolition of the sanctuaries must have left many destitute. They were to be permitted to migrate to Jerusalem and share in the gifts offered there—a provision which was never actually carried out, owing, probably, to the opposition of the Jerusalem priests.

We may suspect that, as in the case of Hezekiah, the reform had a political aspect, and was to be regarded as a gesture of independence. Certainly thirteen years later Josiah lost his life at the hands of the supporter and friend of the falling Assyrian power, Necho, king of Egypt. Yet we need not suspect Josiah's motives, and we shall find it

difficult to overestimate the importance of the step which
he took. On the one hand, it may be regarded as the
completion, in a practical way, of the work begun by Elijah.
Whatever the *Ba'alistic* associations of the local sanctuaries
may have been, Jerusalem was now, at least, free from them,
and there was no other place where they could be revived.

Moreover, the concentration of sacrifice in one place made
it essential that the piety of Israel should find some other
means of expression. It is true that it was not till after
the Exile that this result manifested itself, but in the end it
led to the establishment and growth of the worship of the
synagogue, a cultus which required neither priest nor altar
nor temple, and which has therefore survived to the present
day in spite of all the vicissitudes that the people of Israel
have suffered, and in spite of the fact that they have had no
place of sacrifice for eighteen hundred and fifty years, and
no independent native government in a land of their own for
twenty-five centuries.

2. DEUTERONOMY

It is usual to identify the Book of the Law found by
Hilkiah in the Temple with *Deuteronomy*, or with an original
draft of that book.[1] The position has been challenged in
recent years, one or two scholars seeking to place it later
than the exile, others carrying it back to the early monarchy.
Neither position, however, has yet found general support,
and what Dr. Welch calls the " regnant hypothesis " still
holds the field for practical purposes.

Deuteronomy is an expanded edition of the so-called
" Book of the Covenant " (Exod. xxi–xxiii), rewritten from
a nobler and more humane standpoint, and containing a
great deal of material not found in the earlier code. It has
been provided, possibly by later hands, with hortatory
introduction and conclusion,[2] and it is possible that in its
pre-exilic form it was a good deal shorter than it is to-day.
But its outstanding characteristic is its tone, which is
strongly reminiscent of the outlook of the eighth-century
prophets. It is generally held to be a compromise between
the ideals of Hosea and Isaiah, and the priestly establishment, an attempt to attain the moral aims of the prophets
without abandoning the institution of sacrifice and all that

---

[1] It is generally held that the book in its earliest form comprised Chapters
v–xxvi, xxviii.

[2] Chapters i–iv, xxvii, xxix–xxxiv.

it implied. If this be so, then it holds a very important place in the religious history of Israel, as an effort to translate into terms of practical life the ideals which the eighth-century prophets held before their people, and it has made the civil and ecclesiastical law of Israel unique. Nowhere else do we find the humanitarian atmosphere, the care for the weak and the helpless, the consideration shown to those who are unable to defend themselves—aliens, women and slaves, the constant demand for love with and behind the ritual, the stress on motive and character rather than on actual deeds; and it is not surprising that men have believed it to have been compiled by the prophetic school, driven underground by persecution, and preserved till a better day should dawn.

But there is another aspect of the case. Whether or not *Deuteronomy* was the book found by Hilkiah, some book was found, and that book was immediately accepted as having divine authority. Hitherto the will of Yahweh had been made known through His chosen instruments, priests or prophets; now Israel began to feel that this was unnecessary. Jeremiah attests the reverence that was paid to this or some other code, and insists that, in the form in which it was made known among the people, it was largely the work of the priests. He was faced with disbelief and rejection. Men said that they now had the will of Yahweh before them in black and white, and had no more need of prophet and priest to interpret it.[1]

In this feeling there was much truth. For neither priest nor prophet was to endure indefinitely, and it was well for Israel in later days that she had some spiritual support so concrete and indestructible as a book. The influence of the idea of revelation through literature has been incalculable, and, as far as we know, the eighteenth year of the reign of Josiah was the first occasion on which the conception emerged in human religion. For the first time we have *Scripture*, and though there is much in the Old Testament which is certainly earlier than the end of the seventh century, it was only after the acceptance of *Deuteronomy* that the rest took similar rank. It is with Josiah's book that the history of the Bible begins.

Finally, the importance of *Deuteronomy*—or at least of the book which was responsible for the centralization of worship —is to be seen in its effect on other portions of the Old

---

[1] Jer. viii. 8.

Testament.   There grew up a school, which seems to have been most active during and after the Exile, which collected, transcribed, and " edited " the traditions, laws, and history of Israel.   The men who were chiefly responsible for this work wrote in the spirit of *Deuteronomy*.   Their judgement was framed on its provisions, and they saw all history in its light.   In the book of *Kings*, for instance, which is one of their compilations, every monarch of Israel and Judah is either commended or condemned, and the ground on which sentence is recorded is his adherence to, or his neglect of, the law of the central sanctuary.   It is sometimes a little difficult for us to allow for the Deuteronomic element in reading our Old Testament, but the fact is unmistakeable.   The reforms of Josiah had an effect reaching far beyond their own day, and one of the most fruitful results of the teaching of the eighth-century prophets was the construction and appearance of this great Book of the Law.

CHAPTER XXIII

THE SEVENTH-CENTURY PROPHETS

THE last forty years during which the kingdom of Judah existed form one of the great critical epochs in history. The ancient kingdom of Assyria came to a violent end, not merely losing its imperial authority, but ceasing for ever to exist as an independent entity. Its capital, the great and famous Nineveh, was left a heap of blackened ruins, whose very site was forgotten for two and a half millennia. For nine centuries the supremacy of the civilized world had lain between the great empire on the Tigris and that which lay along the Nile. The power of the latter had steadily weakened, but there was always the hope of a revival until the final defeat of Necho at Carchemish in 605 B.C. Egypt never again stood in a position to make a bid for the hegemony of the world. Babylon, for many a century a nominal vassal of Assyria, achieved under the new Chaldæan dynasty both freedom and empire, and the ninety years which followed the accession of Nabo-polassar were the most brilliant in her whole history. Judah, crushed between the two great world-powers, saw her Temple destroyed, her capital laid in ruins, the best elements in her population deported, and her independence so completely eclipsed that, save for a short period in the late second and early first centuries B.C., it has never since been restored.

Excluding Ezekiel, whose work lay entirely in Babylonia, though he was born in Jerusalem and may have performed the functions of the priesthood at the old Temple, there are four of our canonical prophets whose activity is to be placed in the last forty years of the kingdom of Judah. The work of Jeremiah covers the whole period : his ministry began in 626 B.C., and did not cease with the fall of Jerusalem in 586 B.C. Contemporary with his earlier utterances are those of Zephaniah, who seems to have been roused to prophecy by the same series of events with which Jeremiah first dealt. Nahum must be assigned to the years immediately preceding the fall of Nineveh; and while the exact date of Habakkuk's work is less certain, it probably lay between 608 and 600 B.C. Of the four, Nahum is negligible for our present purpose, since he deals solely with the ruin of Nineveh from the standpoint of an Israelite patriot.[1] The book which bears his name is unique in the prophetic literature, and its chief value—apart from its magnificent style—lies in the illustration it affords of the popular prophecy of Judah in this period. But the other three are important, Jeremiah and Habakkuk pivotal.

1. ZEPHANIAH

One of the world-shaking events of the latter part of the seventh century was a series of invasions or raids by peoples inhabiting the unknown north and north-east. Throughout ancient history the civilized world that bordered on the Mediterranean was subject to such invasions, and in the end it was the irruption of " barbarians " which brought the Roman world to destruction. The tribes who made themselves felt during our period were known to the Greeks by the collective names of Scythian and Cimmerian. Herodotus tells us that they dominated Western Asia for twenty-seven years, which must be taken as indicating the time over which their raids extended, for they do not seem to have made any permanent settlements in the south. They overran the whole of the fertile crescent, being checked only on the borders of Egypt, and their interference contributed materially to the downfall of the Assyrian empire and the destruction of Nineveh. It would seem that in 626 B.C. (though the facts are disputed in some quarters) hordes of these people poured into Palestine, ravaging and destroying where they could. They even, it seems, besieged Jerusalem; but they were ill-equipped for operations against strong fortifications, and the city itself remained unhurt.

Whether we are right or not in maintaining the historicity of this series of raids, it was in the year 626 B.C. that both Zephaniah and Jeremiah began their ministry. The former was probably of the royal house, for his genealogy is traced farther back than that of any other prophet, and the highest name is that of Hezekiah. Zephaniah is fully in line with his

---

[1] The Psalm with which the book opens, i. 1–11, is probably not to be included in the actual work of Nahum.

predecessors of the eighth century in his denunciation of Israel's sin, but he brings out an element in the prophetic teaching which was little stressed by them. That is eschatology. His picture of the Day of Yahweh is thoroughly apocalyptic,[1] and in the third chapter we have set before us a great gathering of the nations which ends in the triumph and final supremacy of Judah. We cannot suppose that he was alone in his expectation, and certainly among those who came after him, especially in times of distress, there were many to take up and complete the picture which he sketched in outline.

2. JEREMIAH

We know more of Jeremiah than of any other Old Testament character. We have a larger amount of prophetic utterances from him than from any other prophet except Ezekiel; we have a number of records describing events in his life written by some sympathetic associate, possibly Baruch; and he has also left us detailed accounts of some of his own experiences, particularly in his direct dealings with Yahweh. The figure revealed by this material is singularly attractive, and never fails to call forth the sympathy and admiration of every serious student. Except Hosea, whom in temperament and outlook Jeremiah somewhat closely resembled, no other Hebrew prophet suffered so terribly in the course of his service, and it was this very pain and struggle which gave him his supreme value and unique place in the history of religion.

In theology, Jeremiah had little to add to the work of his predecessors. We find in him all the familiar denunciations of moral and social evil. Like Amos, he was disgusted with the dishonesty of the common tradesman [2] and with the lack of justice in the courts.[3] He had learnt much from Hosea, and there are constant reminiscences of the earlier prophet in the utterances of the later. In particular he thought of the relation between Yahweh and His people as a marriage, and of apostasy as adultery.[4] This was a natural view for a man who had been brought up in a priestly family, and, perhaps, had witnessed, and even shared in, the cult of Anath. He did not follow Hosea in his condemnation of the monarchy as an institution, though no other canonical

---

[1] Cf., e.g., Zeph. i. 14 ff. [2] Cf. Jer. v. 1 ff.
[3] Cf., e.g., Jer. v. 28, vii. 5.
[4] Cf., e.g., Jer. ii. 1 ff., 20 ff., iii. 6 ff., iv. 30.

prophet spoke of individual sovereigns as Jeremiah did.[1] He could look back over the ruin of the north, even to the days preceding the monarchy, and felt that Judah was even more deserving of punishment than Israel had been.[2] Much of his surviving work, however, is neither warning nor denunciation, but simply the expression of deep and heart-rending sorrow over calamities which actually befel his country. This element appears in other prophets,[3] but is nowhere else so prominent. Jeremiah's pain is all the keener because he knows that the suffering of Judah is simply the inevitable result of her infidelity. Yet, like Hosea, he clung to the hope of restoration, and expressed it in a doctrine of which we must speak later. Indeed, his very appeals for repentance imply the possibility of a return and a reconstruction of the ideal relations between Judah and her God.

In all this there is nothing in which Jeremiah's thought cannot be paralleled from that of the other prophets. But his actual relations with Yahweh were very different from theirs. Though he was shy and retiring, yet he loved human society, and would have sought nothing better than a quiet home in his native village of Anathoth. Yet all his life he had to stand alone, never knowing the responsibilities of family life, and excluded even from the simple festivals of the home. He was filled with a double passion, a patriotism like that of Hosea which meant an overwhelming love for his people, and an equally overwhelming devotion to his God. The consuming desire of his soul was to see the two united in a valid and permanent bond which no human sin could break; but all his life, save perhaps for two short intervals under Josiah and Gedaliah, he was doomed to disappointment. He knew only too well that the sole hope of salvation for Judah lay in this close association; for while Yahweh did not need Israel, the nation was lost unless it could find its safety in a firm association with its God. For forty years he saw and proclaimed the coming doom. Many times it seemed as if his threats were on the verge of fulfilment, but always the danger passed, and those who placed a superstitious trust in the mere physical presence of the Temple and of the Ark seemed to be justified.

This experience had its reaction on his own soul. It was always difficult to distinguish between the prophet who

---

[1] Cf. the series of oracles against the kings of his time, preserved in Jer. xxii. Josiah alone is commended, and that in a way which contrasts him with his successors.

[2] Cf. iii. 6 ff., vii. 12 ff. [3] Cf., e.g., Is. i. 4-9.

spoke the truth and the prophet whom Yahweh was using to entrap some poor victim to his ruin.[1] In Jeremiah's day the authenticity of the prophet was attested mainly by the fulfilment of his predictions, and if they remained inoperative it was assumed that the speaker was one whom Yahweh had sought to destroy. Jeremiah, conscious of the reality of his own call and experience, saw his words returning void, and had to endure the mockery of those about him as a man seduced by Yahweh. Indeed, he shared the belief himself, and human literature holds few more awful expressions of poignant agony than Jeremiah's remonstrance with Yahweh in Chapter xx. 7 ff.

But it was just this bitter pain of spirit that gave to Jeremiah his importance in the history of religion. The older thinking of Israel, in every sphere, was largely conditioned by a conception of corporate personality.[2] It was not merely, or even primarily, the single human or divine individual who was regarded as the true spiritual unit. Before the emergence of the later attitude, it was the whole group that was conceived as a " person," and the isolated individual had no standing apart from the larger body. Hence a nation could be treated as an individual; if Achan, the Israelite, was contaminated by appropriating that which lay under the *taboo*, it could be said that " Israel hath sinned "[3] and the penalty must be paid by the whole people. So, also, especially in the patriarchal narratives, we have reason for supposing that we have tribal history disguised under the language of personal adventures.

This does not mean that the individual had no standing in the political and religious life of ancient Israel. It is obvious that every man had his own place, and we can see in what survives to us of the pre-exilic ritual of Israel (especially in many of the " cult-Psalms ") that he was held responsible, within the community, for his own acts. If he offended, he either placed himself outside the pale of his group, or he involved it in his guilt. In the first case his primary duty was to procure restoration, in the second he must so purify himself as to remove the stain from the whole community. Careful study of the ritual, even in its late form, shows that conceptions of this kind underlie much of the ceremonial. When we speak of religion as being communal, and not

[1] Cf., Ezek. xiv. 9.
[2] For a classical exposition of this doctrine, see H. Wheeler Robinson, in *Werden und Wesen des alten Testaments*, pp. 49 ff. (1936).
[3] Josh. vii. 11.

individualistic, we do not mean that the individual had no place within the community, and so no standing whatever.

What we do mean is that a man's religion was always mediated through the community. The true human unit was always the group, and it was as a sub-unit within the group that the Israelite could approach Yahweh. David, forced by slander to take refuge outside Israel, could say of his enemies " they have driven me out this day from abiding in the inheritance of Yahweh, saying, Go, serve other gods." [1] Even the prophetic experience, striking as it was, did not make earlier prophets feel independent of their fellows; men are slow to realize the implications of their own beliefs and experiences. But the facts of Jeremiah's life were so impressive as to make it inevitable that he should, even though but dimly, become conscious of a relation to his God which was independent of Judah, and which, from time to time, left him standing, as it were, wholly apart from and even opposed to the people to whom he belonged. Shut out as he seems to have been, at any rate for some portion of his career, from the general worship of the people in the Temple,[2] he was forced back on his own personal relations with Yahweh, and discovered his God for himself. Fully to appreciate the heroism of the man, we must remember that he had no thought of a doctrine of religion after death. The whole drama of his relations with Yahweh must be played out on the stage of this life, and it was a drama of two characters only in the last resort. First of all men, as far as we know, Jeremiah lived alone with his God, the world shut out, and he is in a very real sense the father of all individualism in religion, the founder of personal faith.

One actual doctrine remains to be noted. It was during Jeremiah's early ministry that the reforms of Josiah were carried through, based on the book of *Deuteronomy*. The prophet seems to have accepted the situation, but as time passed he realized that a religion dependent merely on a book was as futile as a religion dependent merely on sacrifice. Yet, from the start the relation between Yahweh and Israel had been of the nature of a covenant, a voluntary agreement resting on the deliberate choice of the people by the God and the equally deliberate acceptance of the God by the people. Again and again had the terms of the agreement been broken on the human side, though never on the other, and again and again had it been restored. What was

---

[1] 1 Sam. xxvi. 19.   [2] Cf. Jer. xxxvi. 5.

needed was some form of covenant which would enter so deeply into the heart and mind of man as to make a breach as impossible for man as for God. Jeremiah saw that even a written covenant, as long as it was that and nothing more, was practically worthless, even though it were graven on the solid stone. To be valid it must be set in men's inward parts and written on their hearts, and nowhere is the grand optimism of the prophet more completely illustrated than in his prophecy of the *New Covenant*.[1] Yet there was one feature of the ideal agreement which even Jeremiah did not see. A covenant, as the writer of the Epistle to the Hebrews so well knew, was valid to the ancient mind only when it was made through the life-blood of a third party, when the two contracting sides had found their common unity by absorption in the vital essence freely available in the very life of a third. So, for the fulfilment of the greatest word ever spoken by a prophet the world had to wait six hundred years, till that night when Jesus, gathered with His disciples in an upper room, took a cup, and when He had given thanks, gave it to them and said : *This is my blood of the Covenant, which is shed for many.*

3. HABAKKUK

Amos and his successors had proclaimed that Yahweh was both omnipotent and righteous, that He punished sin and rewarded goodness. It was inevitable that men should look on the world about them in order to test the theory of the prophet. And it must be admitted that the facts do not at first sight endorse the doctrine. It does not follow that the unjust man meets with calamity and perishes in shame and despair; nor does it always happen that the righteous has a prosperous life and a happy death. And the clash between the hypothesis and the fact necessarily produced a problem. It could not have been raised as a problem till the righteousness of God was a recognized element in men's creed; but when that was once accepted, the question was bound to arise and demand at least some attempt at a solution.

A century and a half had passed since Amos delivered his message at Bethel; that, however, is but a short period in which men may see something of the implications of their own theories and beliefs. Jeremiah felt the urgency of the question, but it did not take the place in his thinking

[1] Jer. xxxi. 31–34.

that it did in that of Habakkuk, and when he propounded it he was told not to trouble himself about a theoretical question, since more difficult practical problems were awaiting him. It is the centre of the thought of Habakkuk. The death of the honest, democratic king Josiah had roused doubts in his mind, and he was smarting, along with others in Israel, under the despotic rule of Jehoiakim, a prince who sought to revive the glories and the monarchic absolutism which had not been known in Israel since the days of Solomon, and rested his power on the support of Egypt. It was not enough for Habakkuk to know that the Chaldæan armies would take vengeance on the oppressor; the mere fact that the righteous could suffer any undeserved pain was problem enough for him. " Thou that art of purer eyes than to behold evil, and that canst not look on perverseness, wherefore lookest thou upon them that deal treacherously, and holdest thy peace when the wicked man swalloweth up the man that is more righteous than he ? " (i. 13.)

There was the problem. The only answer Habakkuk received was that the righteous should live by his fidelity, a reply which may form a contribution to the solution, but can hardly be taken as a solution itself. It is, indeed, not too much to say that this question has agitated the minds of thoughtful men ever since, and that no complete answer has ever been found. It may well be that the answer is finally beyond the grasp of human finite intelligence, and that its communication or discovery would raise further questions that would yet more bewilder the mind of man. It has exercised already the most profound influence on human thinking, and may in the long run prove to be the most important question that man has ever asked. Various attempts were made at a solution in ancient Israel, but these belong to the exilic and post-exilic periods, and cannot be discussed here.[1] It is enough to note that it was Habakkuk who asked it, and left the age to close with the great problem propounded, but unsolved.

4. The Fall of Jerusalem

We have traced in severest outline the story of Israel's religious life. We have seen how through Moses she was first led into communion with that deity whom she came to

[1] See Part III, Chapter XXXV.

know as her own peculiar possession and privilege. We have noted the comparative simplicity of Israel's religion in her national childhood, and observed the syncretistic corruptions into which her adolescence fell. We have watched the growth of a nobler standard, due to the contact between the two widely sundered elements in her population, we have heard the voice of the prophet thundering his essential principles, the moral nature and demands of Yahweh, and we have glanced at the way in which successive prophets each in turn threw a characteristic of the religion of Yahweh into prominence until the picture grew more and more complete.

There was yet much that Israel had to learn. There is nothing in the pre-exilic prophets and writers which we can call unmistakable monotheism, though we shall agree that their doctrines must lead logically to the conviction that there is but one living and true God. There was as yet no valid doctrine of a future life. Men did not believe, it is true, that the dead ceased to be, but they either lay crumbling in the grave or else passed to the joyless gloom of *She'ol*. In either case they were cut off, not only from man but also from God, for Yahweh had no place or part with those beneath. Philosophy, even such philosophy as that of which the Semitic mind was capable, was not yet born, and centuries were to pass before the Jew, in contact with the Greek, ventured on the ocean of metaphysical speculation.

Yet the prophets had taught her enough for her own immediate safety, and none can say what might have been the issue had their precepts been accepted and followed by the nation at large. But the nation did not follow. Except for sporadic movements, such as the reform of Josiah, the great mass of the people went on their old, evil, and dangerous ways. It was not by mere preaching, however completely inspired, that the great lessons of the Kingdom of God could be brought home to them, and they could grasp the truth set before them only when it was presented with the super-logic of facts. So Israel refused to accept the hope offered to her, and went on the way that led to destruction. The monarchy, an isolated phenomenon in the long history of Palestine, had served its turn; in no other *milieu* could the doctrines of the great prophets have been adequately proclaimed or illustrated. But Israelite independence was no longer necessary; it had become indeed a snare, and the nation must be taught by sterner methods. So when the

Chaldæan armies surrounded Jerusalem, broke down its walls, laid its houses in ruins, and burnt its temple, they were but fulfilling unconsciously the purpose of the God of Israel, who had to inflict upon His people this last of human calamities that they might learn as a whole the essential principles of the Kingdom of God.

PART III
EARLY JUDAISM

THE PERIOD OF THE EXILE

CHAPTER XXIV

BABYLONIAN INFLUENCE ON THE JEWS

It is a necessary preliminary to the study of the condition, religious or otherwise, of the Jews in exile, to consider very briefly the question as to whether, and if so how far, they were affected by Babylonian influences. We are thinking here, of course, primarily, of religious influences; but since, to the Hebrew, every department of life had from time immemorial been connected with religion, even the purely secular and cultural spheres of Babylonian life may have indirectly contributed in affecting the Jews religiously, as they must certainly have done in other respects. To take but one example : it is no exaggeration to say that contact with the mercantile life of Babylon (see Ezek. xvi. 29, xvii. 4; cp. Nahum iii. 16) originated the trading habits of the Jews which became later characteristic of them; [1] that this had a detrimental effect upon their religious life seems to be clear from Ezek. xvi. 29.

But it is with religious beliefs and practices that we are specially concerned now. There are plenty of indications showing that before the Exile Assyrian religion, which was largely identical with that of Babylonia, greatly influenced the Hebrews (see, e.g., 2 Kings xxiii. 11, 12; Zeph. i. 5;

---

[1] During the excavations undertaken by the Pennsylvania University in Nippur, which was situated on the river (properly canal) Chebar (Ezek. i. 3), a great number of tablets containing business transactions were unearthed, showing that Nippur was a great mercantile centre. On many of these tablets the names of Jews occur, such as Hananiah, Gedaliah, Pedaiah, Benjamin, and others; these Jews appear to have carried on business transactions with the leading mercantile house of the city, Murashu Sons. The tablets, it is true, all belong to the reigns of Artaxerxes I and Darius II (465–405 B.C.), which is, of course, rather later than the period under consideration; but the Jews mentioned on these business documents are not likely to have been the first among their people to conduct mercantile pursuits. See, on this subject, Hilprecht, *The Babylonian Expedition of the University of Pennsylvania*, vol. ix, pp. 28, 76 ff. (1898).

Jer. vii. 17, 18, cp. xliv. 17–19, 25 (Ishtar); Ezek. viii. 14–17
[Tammuz]); but the Jews were now to come into direct
contact with these and other forms of Eastern religion;
and we know from such a passage, e.g., as Ezek. xiv. 1 ff.,
that many of the exiles were deeply influenced by them.
We are not without definite knowledge regarding the details
of Babylonian religion at this time.

In Babylon itself was the great temple E-Sagila of Marduk,
"Lord of Heaven and earth "; this temple had been built
on a grandiose style by Nebuchadrezzar. The most imposing ritual in connexion with his worship took place on
Nisan 10, New Year's Day. On this occasion a great procession, in which the king took the leading part, was formed,
and the god Marduk was taken from his temple and placed
on his ship; this was then drawn to his sanctuary outside
the city, where prayer was offered to him; on the following
day the procession returned to the temple of the god.[1]
Great multitudes thronged the whole way along which the
procession passed, and there can scarcely be a doubt that
many of the Jewish exiles witnessed this imposing ceremony.
They could hardly fail to contrast it with the humble and
comparatively simple worship to which they had been
accustomed in their own land. It is well within the bounds
of possibility that the prophet had this great annual procession in mind when he wrote : " They have no knowledge
that carry the wood of their graven image, and pray unto a
god that cannot save " (Isa. xlv. 20); the very fact that he
utters a polemic against the Babylonian god suggests that
among his people there were those who were in danger of
being drawn into worshipping him. A still more pointed
passage is that in which the prophet claims for Yahweh, the
God of Israel, the victory in the combat with the primeval
monster Tiamat, which, according to Babylonian mythology,
had been achieved by Marduk : " Awake, awake, put on
strength, O arm of Yahweh; awake as in days of old, as in
ages long since past. Art not thou that which clave in
twain Rahab, that pierced the Dragon ? Art not thou that
which dried up the sea, the waters of Tehom Rabbah ? "
(Isa. li. 9–10.) It is impossible not to see what the prophet's
object was here, viz. to set against the Babylonian deity
the superiority of Yahweh; but he is writing for his own

[1] See Zimmern, *Das babylonische Neujahrsfest*, in *Der alte Orient*,
xxv., Heft 3 (1926); Hans Schmidt, *Die Thronfahrt Jahves* . . . (1927);
Myth and Ritual, passim (ed. S. H. Hooke, 1933).

people, and therefore there would be but little point in his words unless he saw that many of the exiles were being attracted by Babylonian worship.

Again, Nippur, near which was situated Tel-abib on the great canal Kabari (Chebar), was the centre of the worship of Bel (= Enlil), called the " lord of lands," who dwelt on the " great mountain," the summit of which reached to heaven. We know from Ezek. iii. 15, viii. 1, that a colony of the exiles was settled in Tel-abib; they were therefore in close proximity to the temple of Bel, and must often have been witnesses of his worship, judging by the prophet's words in Isa. xlvi. 1: " Bel boweth down, Nebo stoopeth . . ."; his contemptuous irony may well have been intended to counteract a tendency on the part of some of the exiles to partake of the worship of these gods.[1] It is very necessary to remember what is pointed out elsewhere that, according to the ideas of the times, the gods of Babylonia had proved themselves stronger than the God of Israel; this afforded an additional inducement to offer them allegiance; the exiles were outside of Yahweh's land.

A further mark of the influence of Babylonian religion is to be discerned in Isa. lxv. 11: " But ye that forsake Yahweh, that forget my holy mountain, that prepare a table for Gad, and that fill up mingled wine unto Meni." Gad, the god of Fortune, occurs on Assyrian tablets;[2] Meni is not mentioned elsewhere; both were evidently worshipped by the Babylonians, but Gad was widely venerated in Syria too. It is quite possible that these were astral deities, as the destinies of men were believed to be influenced by the stars; if so, the passage is an illustration of what is said in Isa. xlvii. 13, where, in reference to Babylon, the prophet says: " Let now the astrologers, the star-gazers, the monthly prognosticators, stand up, and save thee from the things that shall come upon thee."

How strong Babylonian influence is likely to have been upon the exiles may be gathered from various passages in the book of *Ezekiel*, in which we find a great familiarity with Babylonian mythology and religion. A brief reference to these will be of interest.

In i. 4 the prophet tells of how in his vision Yahweh

[1] The centre of the worship of Nebo was Borsippa, the sister-city of Babylon.

[2] Zimmern's edition (third) of Schrader's *Keilinschriften und das alte Testament*, pp. 479 f. (1903). Gad has been identified with the planet Jupiter (see *Encycl. Bibl.*, ii. [1557]).

T

appeared to him in a great cloud driven by a stormy wind "out of the north"; according to Babylonian belief the abode of the gods was in the north; here in the north lay the "holy mountain" of the gods (xxviii. 14, 16; and see Isa. xiv. 13; Job xxxvii. 22), as well as "the garden" of the gods (xxxi. 8, 9). Again, a very pronounced Babylonian *trait* occurs in the description of the "four living creatures" (i. 5 ff., especially ver. 10); the "face of a man" refers to Nebo, the "face of a lion" to Nergal, the "face of an ox" (i.e. bull) to Marduk, and the "face of an eagle" to Ninib; these are the astral gods of the four corners of the earth, who, according to the prophet, are the ministers of Yahweh. Once more, in ix. 2–11 we read of the seven avengers who take vengeance on the idolaters in Jerusalem; they come from the north, and are messengers of Yahweh : " And behold, six men came from the way of the upper gate, which lieth toward the north . . . and one man in the midst of them, clothed in linen, with a writer's inkhorn by his side. . . ." The prototype of these seven were the seven planets, gods of the Babylonian pantheon; the man with the inkhorn by his side clearly represents the god Nebo, who was the writer of the Book of Fate. In each case the prophet adapts Babylonian beliefs to the religion of Yahweh. Finally, in chapter xl, where the plan of the new temple is described in a vision to the prophet by a man "whose appearance was like the appearance of brass," we have a procedure which is paralleled in Babylonian literature; one of the inscriptions of Gudea, for example, tells of how Gudea in a vision sees a divine figure who bids him build a house; heavenly beings appear with stylus and tablet who show him the plan. The idea, common to the ancient East, is that everything on earth has its corresponding pattern in heaven.[1]

The prophet himself was not affected by these things so far as his belief in fundamentals was concerned; but the allusions he makes without a word of explanation show that he spoke of things with which his hearers were familiar. The exiles were living in surroundings in which they constantly witnessed the celebration of Babylonian religious rites; they were thus familiar with these as belonging to a people far more highly cultured than themselves; it is, therefore, difficult to believe that such things were

[1] Jeremias, *Das alte Testament im Lichte des alten Orients*, pp. 361 f. (1904).

without effect upon them. The probability is that an appreciable number of the exiles gave up the religion of the fathers and became worshippers of the Babylonian gods.[1] But while in some respects Babylonian culture influenced the Jews, it is certain that Babylonian religion did not affect the bulk of the exiles; it would be difficult to point to any essential doctrine or religious practice of Judaism of which it could be said that it was the result of Babylonian religious influence.

It is true that in some respects affinities between the religions of the Babylonians and the Hebrews are to be discerned, such as the *She'ol* belief, the sense of sin which appears in both Babylonian and Hebrew psalms, and others; but in none of these can it be proved that Babylonian influence affected Hebrew religion; it is far more likely that both can be ultimately traced back to a common origin. The name of Yahweh (though not in this form), it is well known, appears [2] on some Babylonian inscriptions; but there is nothing to show that, apart from the name, there was anything in common between the Babylonian deity and the God of Israel.

Again, some of the *Genesis* narratives were in all probability indebted to a Babylonian prototype, but so far as religious ideas are concerned the far more spiritual tone of the Hebrew forms proves that in this respect Babylonian influence was non-existent.

It has been claimed that the monotheistic belief of the Hebrews is to some extent indebted to Babylonian religion; a true comparison between the two shows the complete untenability of the claim.

It is granted that Babylonian demonology left permanent marks on Jewish demonology; but this does not come under the head of religion, in the true sense.

The conclusion is that while during the Exile Babylonian influences in many directions strongly affected many of the Jews, and in a certain number of cases fatally, where religion was concerned, yet the Jewish religious leaders saw to it that the essence of Judaism was untouched by those influences.

[1] Cp. also such Babylonian theophoric names as Sheshbazzar and Zerubbabel.

[2] But not before the ninth century B.C. (see G. R. Driver, in *Old Testament Essays*, p. 20 [1927]).

CHAPTER XXV

THE EARLY YEARS OF THE EXILE

1. The Records of the Deportations

ALTHOUGH we are dealing exclusively with the religion of the Hebrews, it is essential that at times the historical background should be taken into consideration in so far as this tended to affect religious conditions. We must therefore begin by quoting the records which tell of the leading away of the people from Palestine to Babylon. There were three occasions on which this happened; the first was in 597 B.C.

" And he (i.e. Nebuchadrezzar) carried away all Jerusalem, and all the princes, and all the mighty men of valour, even ten thousand captives, and all the craftsmen and the smiths; none remained, save the poorest sort of the people of the land. And he carried away Jehoiachin to Babylon, and the king's mother, and the king's wives, and his officers, and the chief men of the land carried he into captivity from Jerusalem to Babylon. And all the men of might, even seven thousand, and the craftsmen and the smiths a thousand, all of them strong and apt for war, even them the king of Babylon brought captive to Babylon " (2 Kings xxiv. 14–16; in 2 Chron. xxxvi. 9, 10, the account is extremely meagre).

The repetition in this passage, with the variation in the number of the exiles, is perhaps due to a combination of excerpts from two different sources. But in any case, the number was comparatively small; and this is borne out, moreover, by the further variations in numbers given as three thousand and twenty-three in Jer. lii. 28.

It should be noted that the renderings " captives," " carried into captivity," and " brought captive " of the Revised Version are somewhat misleading. In the original the idea is that of leading away,[1] not captivity. The point is not unimportant, as will be seen later.

Another thing to note is that the statement that only

---

[1] The technical terms for the " leading away " and therefore of the Exile, are *golah*, *galuth*.

the poorest sort of the people of the land were left, is not
quite accurate in view of what is said about the second
deportation, eleven years later: "And the captain of
the guard took Seraiah the chief priest, and Zephaniah
the second priest, and the three keepers of the door; and
out of the city he took an officer that was set over the
men of war; and five men of them that saw the king's
face, which were found in the city; and the scribe, the
captain of the host, which mustered the people of the land;
and three score men of the people of the land, that were
found in the city" (2 Kings xxv. 18, 19). It is difficult
to believe that the poorest sort of the people could have
been found capable of bearing the load and responsibility
of the important post here mentioned. The passages
2 Kings xxv. 23–26, Jer. xl. 7–12, should also be consulted
in this connexion.

The second deportation took place in 586 B.C.; it is
recorded in 2 Kings xxv. 1–22, especially vers. 11, 12:
"And the residue of the people that were left in the city
. . . did Nebuzaradan the captain of the guard carry away
captive. But the captain of the guard left of the poorest
of the land to be vine-dressers and husbandmen" (cp.
2 Chron. xxxvi. 17–20); the number of the exiles in this
case is not given; but according to Jer. lii. 29 it was eight
hundred and thirty-two.

Yet a third deportation is referred to in Jer. lii. 30, in
the year 581 B.C. (i.e. the twenty-third year of Nebuchadrezzar), when seven hundred and forty-five more exiles
were led away. Possibly it is to this that Josephus refers
when he says that in this year, the twenty-third year of
Nebuchadrezzar, the king "took those Jews that were
there (i.e. in Egypt) captives, and led them away to Babylon"
(*Antiq.* x. ix. 7); but it must be granted that if the same event
is referred to one would expect some mention of Egypt
in Jer. lii. 30.

One other episode must be noted. A body of Jews
under the leadership of Johanan the son of Kareah, fearing
the wrath of the king of Babylon on account of the murder
of Gedaliah, fled to Egypt, compelling Jeremiah to go with
them, and settled down in Migdol, Tahpanhes, Noph, and
in the country of Pathros (i.e. Upper Egypt) (see 2 Kings
xxv. 25–26; Jer. xli.–xliv.).

So much, then, for the records which tell of the deportations from the homeland.

2. THE RELIGIOUS BELIEFS OF THE PEOPLE

From what has been said it will be seen that we must
consider the religious condition of four different bodies
of Jews during this early period of the Exile :

(a) Those in Babylon who were deported in 597 B.C.
(b) Those who were left in the homeland.
(c) Those who had settled down in Egypt.
(d) Those in Babylon after the 586 B.C. deportation.

(a) The exiles who were led away in 597 B.C. could take
comfort in the knowledge that Jerusalem still stood intact,
and, even more important, in the thought that the Temple,
the dwelling-place of the God of Israel, though despoiled
(2 Kings xxiv. 13), was still in existence. Their belief was
strong in the inviolability of the city of God, proclaimed
by Isaiah long since (2 Kings xix. 34), as well as in that of
the Temple (Jer. vii. 4). This meant for them that Yahweh
was still in the midst of His people, mighty to save. The
downfall of the great Assyrian empire, of but recent date,
had signally proved that Yahweh's will must prevail (cp.
Nahum i. 1 ff.). There was, indeed, much reason for the
exiles to believe that an instrument was being raised up to
smite Babylon (Jer. xxviii. 1–4). What their God had done
before He would do again, before long; such was their
belief, though falsely inspired : there would be a return to
the homeland.

The faith in Yahweh of these first exiles, then, was un-
diminished in spite of His having permitted them to be
carried away into a heathen land; so that Jeremiah could
liken them to the good figs in his vision of the two baskets
of figs (Jer. xxiv. 5). True, their inability to worship God
as they had been accustomed to would be bitter to them;
but they could comfort themselves with the thought that
this was only a temporary hardship. Though their hopes
were founded on the misguided teaching of false prophets
(Jer. xxix. 8, 9, etc.), yet for the time, at any rate, their
belief was real and their trust genuine.

(b) If our knowledge of the religious condition of the
first exiles is to some extent based on inference, we have
abundance of detail regarding those, the great bulk of
the nation, who had been left in the homeland. Both
morally and religiously things could hardly have been
worse; religion was practically the same as it had been

in earlier times among the mass of the people; the Josianic reform might never have been instituted, the prophets with their teaching might never have existed. The ancient Canaanite *Ba'al* cult was still practised (Jer. vii. 9; Ezek. vi. 13); the centralization of worship, with its primary object of doing away with the false worship in local sanctuaries, was a dead letter (Jer. ii. 28, vii. 17–19; cp. Ezek. xxxiii. 25); alien cults of all kinds were shamelessly observed: the worship of Ishtar, "the queen of heaven" (Jer. vii. 18); Sun-worship (Ezek vi. 4–6); Tammuz-worship, and other Babylonian cults (Ezek. viii. 9–18); still other forms of worship are also referred to in Ezek. v. 11.

Frequent stress is laid on the ominous part played by the leaders of the people, both priests and prophets; a few years before the first deportation Jeremiah says in reference to the former: "Woe unto the shepherds that destroy and scatter the sheep of my pasture! saith Yahweh. Therefore thus saith Yahweh, the God of Israel, against the shepherds that feed my people: Ye have scattered my flock, and driven them away, and have not visited them; behold I will visit upon you the evil of your doings, saith Yahweh" (Jer. xxiii. 1, 2). Of the prophets he says: "Both prophet and priest are profane; yea, in my house have I found their wickedness, saith Yahweh." Here in Judah things are just as bad as they had been in the northern kingdom: "And I have seen folly in the prophets of Samaria; they prophesied by Baal, and caused my people Israel to err. In the prophets of Jerusalem also I have seen a horrible thing; they commit adultery, and walk in lies, and they strengthen the hands of evil-doers, that none doth return from his wickedness; they are all of them become unto me as Sodom, and the inhabitants thereof as Gomorrah" (Jer. xxiii. 11–14; see also the rest of this chapter).

A picture of hopeless immorality is drawn by Ezekiel in reference to Jerusalem, the "bloody city," the details of which must have been described to him by those who had come from there (Ezek. xxii.; see, too, Ezek. xxxiii. 21–29, and v. 5–10). And Jeremiah draws attention to the melancholy fact that the people seem to have no sense of their sinfulness; they are quoted as saying: "Wherefore hath Yahweh pronounced all this great evil against us? or what is our iniquity? or what is our sin that we have committed against Yahweh our God?" (Jer. xvi. 10).

In contemplating this picture of religious and moral depravity of priests, prophets, and people, one realizes the superb individuality and strength of character of such men as Jeremiah and Ezekiel, who in face of overwhelming odds not only stood firm, but by their predominating influence and exalted teaching preserved the knowledge of God among men and handed on the torch of revelation. Though clearly in a small minority, they must have had their followers; true, nothing is said of these, but *somebody* must have preserved the records of the teaching of these inspired teachers.

(c) The little that we are told about the Jews who went to Egypt at this time is but a further illustration of the falling-away from the worship of Yahweh which was so pronounced in Judah. We read of Jeremiah rebuking the people in Pathros, and especially the women, for their worship of the " queen of heaven "; they refuse to give up this form of worship : " We will certainly perform every word that is gone forth out of our mouth, to burn incense unto the queen of heaven, and to pour out drink offerings unto her, as we have done, we and our fathers, our kings and our princes, in the cities of Judah, and in the streets of Jerusalem; for then we had plenty of food, and were well, and saw no evil. But since we left off to burn incense to the queen of heaven, and to pour out drink offerings unto her, we have wanted all things and have been consumed by the sword and by the famine . . ." (Jer. xliv. 15–19). That other cults were also practised is clear from the words " burning incense unto other gods in the land of Egypt, whither ye be gone to sojourn " (Jer. xliv. 8; cp. ii. 16–19). As a result, the destruction of all the men of Judah in the land of Egypt is prophesied (ver. 27), as well as the downfall of Hophra king of Egypt (ver. 30). It is interesting to note that Ezekiel, in making a similar prophecy, mentions Seveneh, i.e. Syene or Assouan, in Upper Egypt, where, as we have learned from the Elephantiné papyri, there was also a Jewish colony. As the Jewish Temple belonging to this colony was standing in 525 B.C., when Cambyses conquered Egypt, it is quite possible that Jews were already settled there in Jeremiah's time. They worshipped Yahweh (which they pronounced Yahu). The fact that Jeremiah makes no reference to these Jews (on the assumption that this colony was already in existence in his day) need not cause surprise, for Pathros was a district which covered a very large area.

(d) Lastly, we turn to the exiles again, reinforced now by those of the deportation of 586 B.C.

As long as the monarchy existed, i.e. as long as the nation, as such, was in being, even though subject to a suzerain power, as long as the Holy City stood firm in her glory, and above all, as long as the Temple remained inviolate, belief in Yahweh, the God of the people, was justified; hope and the eager expectancy of deliverance from exile would animate the hearts of the people. But this was now all past. Yahweh had forsaken His land (Ezek. viii. 12, ix. 9), and therefore His people; so it was interpreted both by those in the homeland and by those in exile. The God of Israel had succumbed before the gods of Babylon; Marduk and Ishtar had proved themselves stronger than Yahweh! They would not wholly forget Him; but they were now in a land belonging to other gods to whom they believed worship was due. This is all graphically described by Ezekiel: "Then came certain of the elders of Israel unto me, and sat before me. And the word of Yahweh came unto me saying, Son of man, these men have taken their idols into their hearts, and put the stumbling-block of their iniquity before their face; should I be enquired of them at all? Therefore speak unto them, and say unto them, thus saith Yahweh: Every man of the house of Israel that taketh his idols into his heart, and putteth the stumbling-block of his iniquity before his face, and cometh to the prophet, I, Yahweh, will answer him therein according to the multitude of his idols, that I may take the house of Israel in their own heart, because they are all estranged from me through their idols . . . " (xiv. 1–11). It was a kind of syncretistic worship such as had been practised in connexion with *Ba'al* worship in Canaan.[1] Nevertheless, among many of these there was yet the possibility of their being kept from the allurements of the Babylonian temples, hence both the prophet's warning as well as his words of encouragement in ver. 11, " that the house of Israel may go no more astray from me, neither defile themselves any more with all their transgressions; but that they may be my people, and I may be their God, saith Yahweh." And, doubtless, among these waverers many remained true to their God, but there will have been many others who believed the gods of their conquerors to be more powerful than Yahweh, and who transferred their allegiance altogether,

[1] See pp. 57 ff.

thus losing their religious identity, and becoming absorbed by the people of their new surroundings.[1]

But we know that there were yet others who had come wholly under the influence of the teaching of Jeremiah and Ezekiel, and whose faith had never wavered. To these exile was a bitter experience; they longed for the land of their fathers, and the sad memory of days gone by would be reflected in their psalmist's words :

How shall we sing the Lord's song in a strange land?
If I forget thee, O Jerusalem, may my right hand forget (her cunning);[2]
May my tongue cleave to the roof of my mouth if I remember thee not.

(Ps. cxxxvii. 4-6.)

This clinging in affectionate remembrance to their God and to the homeland marked the true servants of God, and their loyalty to their ancestral religion was only intensified in face of surrounding opposition.

We have been concerned so far with the state of religion among the Jews during the first ten years or so of the Exile. We shall have to consider next the course of religious development during the succeeding years of exile.

[1] Tobit i. 10 may well be an echo of actual fact, the memory of which had been handed down; it is said there : " And when I was carried away captive to Nineveh, all my brethren and those that were of my kindred did eat of the bread of the Gentiles."

[2] The reference is to the use of the right hand in playing the harp as an accompaniment to the singing; the verbs in vers. 1-3 of the psalm are in the perfect, so that this psalm does not belong to the Exile, but echoes the frame of mind of the faithful among the exiles.

CHAPTER XXVI

THE JEWISH COMMUNITY IN EXILE

1. Communal Life in the Exile

There are some clear indications in the Old Testament records that the communal life of the Jewish exiles in Babylon was similar to that to which they had been accustomed in their own land. This, as we shall see, had a direct bearing on the continuity of religious belief.

Our first indication as to the conditions of life of the exiles is to be sought in Jeremiah's letter sent " to the residue of the elders of the *golah*, and to the priests, and to the prophets, and to all the people." As this letter was sent from Jerusalem, it must have been sent before the destruction of the city, and therefore before the second deportation. It runs as follows : " Build ye houses, and dwell in them; and plant gardens, and eat the fruit of them; take ye wives and beget sons and daughters; and take wives for your sons, and give your daughters husbands, that they may bear sons and daughters; and multiply ye there, and be not diminished. And seek the peace of the land (so the Septuagint instead of " city " in the Hebrew text) whither I have caused you to be carried away, and pray unto Yahweh for it, for in the peace thereof ye shall have peace " (Jer. xxix. 1–7).

The mention of the building of houses and the planting of gardens implies liberty to move about within areas of settlement; so that there were *colonies* of Jewish exiles. But this implies, further, that the exiles had complete freedom in the exercise of their religion; indeed, there is nowhere any hint that they suffered any disabilities in this respect. Jeremiah clearly takes this for granted; for when he bids the exiles marry and beget children he knows that Jewish fathers bring up their children in their ancestral faith.

Again, in Ezek. viii. 1, the prophet says : " As I sat in my house and the elders of Judah sat before me, the

hand of the Lord God fell there upon me "; see also xiv.
1, and xx. 1 ff. That gatherings of this kind could take
place in the prophet's own house shows that a good deal
of freedom of action was permitted to the exiles. It is
also of interest to note that the ancient position of the elders
as leaders of the community reappears. It was the disappearance of the monarchy that brought this organization,
originally characteristic of nomadic times, into being once
more. But it meant, and this is the important point, that
families and clans were permitted to dwell together. What
a boon this was to the exiles will at once be realized when
it is remembered that there were very large and widely
separated tracts of country over which they might have been
indiscriminately scattered. In this connexion we find
that in the lists of the returned exiles (Ezra ii. 3 ff., 20 ff.,
36 f., viii. 1 ff., 16 ff.) these are enumerated not only according to heads of families, but also according to the districts
in which their families had lived *before* the Exile; thus,
there are mentioned the children of Pathah-moab, of
Bethlehem, of Anathoth, of Kiriath-jearim, of Beeroth,
of Ramah, of Geba, of Bethel, of Ai, of Nebo, and of Jericho
—to mention the best known place-names; and clearly,
if they are enumerated in this way as returned exiles it
must have been under such designations that the various
communities were known in the land of exile, otherwise
such an enumeration would be entirely pointless.[1] And
thus the conclusion is obvious that in Babylonia the Jews
were allowed to live together just as they had done in
Palestine. From this there follows the important fact
that in this community-life not only was the sense of
nationality upheld, but, more important, the Jews in exile
were able to practise their religion with the traditional
customs and usages in connexion therewith, as far as it
was possible.

2. RELIGIOUS OBSERVANCES AMONG THE EXILES

In Ezek. xi. 16 it is said: "Thus saith the Lord God,
whereas I have removed them (i.e. the exiles) far off among
the nations, and whereas I have scattered them among
the countries, yet have I become unto them a sanctuary

---

[1] Kittel, *op. cit.*, iii., pp. 113 f. It is, of course, possible that in these
Ezra passages the chronicler is transferring the conditions of his own time
to earlier times; but, upon the whole, the view given above seems the more
likely one.

only to a small extent in the countries where they are come."[1]
The meaning of this last sentence is that the important
externals of the worship of Yahweh, as it had been in the
past, were now wanting, and therefore the form of worship
was insignificant as compared with what they had been
accustomed to in the Temple. This raises therefore the
important question as to what kind of substitute for the
Temple services was adopted by those among the exiles
who were loyal to their ancestral religion, and intended to
remain so.

Jeremiah, and other spiritually-minded prophets, had
already contemplated the possibility of a non-sacrificial
worship;[2] this was now to become a reality. But it was
only the compelling force of circumstances that could have
induced the people to remain content with a form of worship
alien to tradition and practice. For the relationship
hitherto conceived to exist between them and their God
had been exhibited in such numberless ways; no animal
was killed for food but that part of it was dedicated to
Yahweh as His due; no bread was eaten of which in some
form the first-fruits had not been offered to Him; no feast
was inaugurated without bringing to Him the gifts due.
The sacrificial system had touched the people in endless
ways in everyday life, as well as in their worship proper.[3]
And now this had all ceased. To substitute a new form
of worship must at first have presented real difficulties.
Kittel suggests,[4] with much probability, that since the
regular feasts could not be observed as in the past, the seasons
at which they had been kept were celebrated as *memorials*.
At such gatherings what more likely than that the mercies
accorded in the past by the God of Israel to His people should
be the subject of commemoration ? The exodus from Egypt,
the deliverance from the pursing Egyptians, the revelation
at Sinai, the entry into the promised land and its final
possession. Such commemorations would keep the thought
of divine mercies before their minds, and kindle hopes for the
future; for what God had done in the past He could do
again. True, we have no proof that such commemorative
substitutes actually took the place of the earlier festal

[1] The Revised Version rendering : " . . . Yet will I be to them a sanctuary for a little while . . .," does not represent the Hebrew; it also obscures
the meaning of the passage.

[2] See, e.g., Jer. vi. 16, 20, vii. 21, 22; Mic. vi. 6, 7.

[3] Stade, *Geschichte des Volkes Israel*, ii. 9 (1888).

[4] *Op. cit.*, iii. 125.

celebrations; but there is much in Deutero-Isaiah's outlook and prophecies [1] somewhat later that suggests the
probability of this. We have direct evidence, moreover, of
the institution of annual fast-days, which were, however,
abrogated after the Return (Zech. vii. 3, 5, viii. 19); if,
therefore, fasts were observed it is impossible to believe
that this should not also have been the case in some form
with feasts. Further, the Sabbath, though now without
its prescribed sacrifices, became the chief and regular
day of worship. This may be seen, for example, by the
stress laid on the Sabbaths, and the denunciation against
their non-observance, in Ezek. xx. 12–24. As a day set
apart for congregational worship every week the Sabbath
became supremely important during the Exile; and it is
not difficult to indicate, in the light of later evidence, what
the main elements at these weekly assemblies for worship
were. Not infrequently mention is made of both priests
and prophets among the exiles—obviously they would
have been the leaders in worship; the reading of the
prophetical books and of such a book as *Deuteronomy* will
have been an important element; the presence of prophets
would make the spoken word a notable part of the service;
sacred songs, sung during the Temple worship, and therefore
very familiar, would be sung; and doubtless other psalms
would have been composed and used. Nor can it be doubted
that public prayer soon became a prominent feature. These
are all among the earliest elements of the Synagogue liturgy;
and all authorities are agreed that the origins of the synagogal
worship must be sought in the period of the Exile.

Together with the Sabbath great stress came to be laid
upon the rite of Circumcision; though, of course, familiar
in pre-exilic times, it had not been emphasized before as
it was during this period; the uncircumcized were, it is
true, spoken of with contempt, but, with the exception
of the Philistines, few such existed among the nations in
the surroundings of Canaan; so that it could not have
been the special mark of a true son of Israel.[2] But conditions in exilic times were different. The Jews now
came into contact with peoples of another kind who knew
nothing of such a custom, and thus Circumcision became
one of the *distinctive* marks of a Jew. It was during the
Exile that there arose among the Jews, as never before,

---

[1] E.g. li. 1–3, 7.
[2] The oldest legal code makes no mention of it.

the consciousness of being different from other peoples; the conviction of superiority over others began to assert itself, and not without reason; for their grasp of the truth of the ethical righteousness of God, together with the corresponding demands made upon them as the people of God, marked them out as standing, in a religious sense, on a much higher plane than any other people. They felt the need therefore of adopting an attitude of aloofness towards all who stood on a lower religious plane.[1] One special means, as Kittel has shown,[2] of emphasizing the separation between themselves and others was in the more strenuous observance of the ancient laws regarding purification and forbidden food. As in the case of the Sabbath and Circumcision so with these; they had all been known and to a greater or less extent observed in pre-exilic days; but they had not been, as they now became, of fundamental importance, for they now assumed a new significance. It is for this reason that in the Priestly Code [3] much emphasis is laid upon these laws, as on certain others; though quite out of harmony with the spirit of the time and the advance of religious thought, they were nevertheless taken up as part of the Law, not for what they had originally meant— for the original meaning was for the most part quite forgotten—but simply with the object of making the separation of the Jews as obvious and ostentatious as possible. As an illustration of this we may instance the laws regarding clean and unclean animals in Lev. xi; this is an expansion of the Law of Holiness (Lev. xvii–xxvi), which itself embodies some things of immemorial antiquity. That the compilers of the laws which ultimately took the form of the Priestly Code had any knowledge of the original reason why certain animals were *taboo* is extremely unlikely; nor was this knowledge necessary, for the fact that some foods were prohibited and therefore not eaten by Jews differentiated them from their Gentile neighbours; that was the main point.

One important consequence of this elaboration of the Law was a great increase of priestly activity, though of a kind very different from that of earlier days. The Temple,

---

[1] Jewish exclusiveness had, it is true, already been emphasized in *Deuteronomy*, but it was during the Exile that this became accentuated (see Lev. xix. 2, xx. 22–6, xxii. 31–2).

[2] *Op. cit.*, iii. 127.

[3] It is not intended to imply that the Priestly Code *as we now have it* was a product to the Exile.

with its sacrificial system and cultural rites, was for the
present non-existent; but the priesthood now found scope
for its energies in framing multifarious precepts for the
regulation of the everyday life of the people in accordance
with an elaborated legal code; new cases were constantly
arising as to the bearing of the Law on particular acts.
For example, in view of the prominence given to the observance of the Sabbath on which all work must cease, it became
necessary to define with exactitude what constituted work;
this raised many nice points, the settling of which called forth
the exercise of much ingenuity. Then there arose, too, the
question of what work on the Sabbath might be regarded
as permissible because necessary, and since every act of
labour was prohibited much casuistry came into play,
which, judging from the records of later times, did more
honour to mental acumen than to honesty.[1] In short,
the priests had plenty to occupy them.

The development of all this took time; but it was during
the Exile that the elaboration of the Law began; and
however much, in process of time, it tended into directions
detrimental to true religion, it must in fairness be recognized
that in its origin the motive was entirely good. The priesthood was actuated by the desire to make their flock realize
at every step that as the people of God they must by act
as well as by word prove to themselves, as well as to the
world of their surroundings, that they were different from
others, different in religion, different in morals, different in
manner of life.

What has so far been said has been mainly concerned
with the externals of religion; we have to deal next with
the more important subject of religious teaching.

---

[1] The Mishnah tractate *Shabbath* contains later developments, but it
will not be questioned that it has preserved much traditional material.

CHAPTER XXVII

RELIGIOUS TEACHERS: THE PRIEST-PROPHET EZEKIEL

THE externals of religious belief which, as we have seen, were prominent during the exilic period, were the outcome of the teaching of the religious leaders. Important and indispensable as such externals must always be, they are nevertheless of value only in so far as they represent the outward expression, necessarily inadequate, of underlying religious truths. To discern and to grasp these religious truths we must go to the teaching of the religious leaders who expounded them. Just as in the earlier history of Israel the prophetical teachers were men whose ideals soared far above the thoughts of the mass of their contemporaries, so during the exilic period the teachers put forth truths which few of their followers could assimilate. In dealing therefore with the religion of the Hebrews during this, as during any other period, it must necessarily be the teaching at its best. And this is as it should be; only it must be realized that the people in general did not (nor were they capable of doing so) grasp to the full or assimilate the truths which their religious teachers put before them.

The first of these teachers so far as we know, was Ezekiel; and it is to his writings that we must go first to see what Hebrew religion at its best was at this time.

1. EZEKIEL'S DOCTRINE OF GOD

In one respect Ezekiel's experience of God differed from that of any prophet before him. He had known Yahweh as the God of Israel in the land of Israel; he had also come to know Him as the God of Israel in a foreign land. True, other prophets, such as Amos, Isaiah, and Jeremiah, had taught that Yahweh was more than a national God, and that His power was equally manifested in other lands; but Ezekiel was the first to have the proof of this by actual experience.[1]

---

[1] Jeremiah, it is true, had this personal experience when he had been carried off to Egypt (Jer. xliii. 6, 7), but this happened late in his life.

It cannot be doubted that this fact had a real influence upon his conception of God. Further, it seems certain from some of the mental pictures which he presents that he was not unfamiliar with the elaborate ritual wherewith the Babylonians worshipped their gods; if heathen conceptions of their gods were such as to necessitate the worship of them on so grand a scale, how infinitely greater must be the one and only God, who, unlike those gods, was a reality. To this must also be added the remarkably vivid powers of imagination possessed by Ezekiel; these worked upon his mental vision when his thoughts were occupied with the greatest and most sublime theme of the Personality of God. And, finally, the contrast between the mighty and merciful and pure God, with the age-long ingratitude and unfaithfulness of His chosen people, placed in vivid and terrible relief the immeasurable distance between the divine Creator and the pitiable insignificance of created mortals.

Thus it came about that Ezekiel's outstanding conception of God was that of the *divine transcendence*. How this is illustrated by his frequent endeavour to express his sense of the divine majesty will be seen from the following words : ". . . And above the firmament that was over their heads was the likeness of a throne, as the appearance of a sapphire stone; and upon the likeness of the throne was a likeness as the appearance of a man upon it above. And I saw as the colour of amber, as the appearance of fire within it, round about, from the appearance of his loins and upwards; and from the appearance of his loins and downward I saw as it were the appearance of fire, and there was brightness round about him. As the appearance of the bow that is in the cloud in the day of rain, so was the appearance of the brightness round about. This was the appearance of the likeness of the glory of Yahweh. And when I saw it, I fell upon my face " (Ezek. i. 26–28). Very significant here is the way in which the prophet shrinks from a direct mention of the Almighty—" the likeness as the appearance of a man "; to Ezekiel the holiness of God is such that He is enveloped in light and fire, unapproachable, and very far distant from man; and the utmost that man can do at the thought of His presence is that he should fall upon his face. And even when, in the spirit, Ezekiel receives a divine communication, his first act is to fall down and hide his face in the presence of the glory which indicates the divine presence.

This teaching of Ezekiel on divine transcendance is one aspect of the conception of God which is balanced by that other aspect, so characteristic of Jeremiah, of His condescension. Jeremiah, in his doctrine of God, lays emphasis on His nearness; but Ezekiel is overwhelmed by His transcendent holiness and greatness, and therefore in a real sense His far-offness from man. These two aspects of the conception of God were held in wonderful balance, as we shall see, by another exilic prophet. The twofold truth has rarely been more exquisitely expressed than in Dryden's words :

> Thy throne is darkness in excess of light,
> A blaze of glory which forbids the sight.
> O teach me to believe Thee thus concealed,
> And search no farther than thyself revealed.

But in the further history of Jewish religion this " proportion of faith " seems, with the one exception, to be referred to, to have been incapable of achievement.

2. SUPERHUMAN BEINGS

Of angelology in the strict sense of the term Ezekiel has but little to say; but he refers to other superhuman beings, and this demands a little attention in view of later developments. It can hardly admit of doubt that what Ezekiel has to say of these intermediate beings between God and man was an outcome of his doctrine of divine transcendence.

While normally Yahweh speaks directly to the prophet, there are quite a number of passages in which intermediate supernatural beings are mentioned. Thus, in xl. 3 f., it is not Yahweh but " a man, whose appearance was like the appearance of brass," who speaks to the prophet. In xi. 1–6 it is a spirit that speaks to him; in ii. 2 the spirit sets him on his feet (see also iii. 14, viii. 3). This may be a development of the idea of the spirit mentioned in such passages as Judges xiv. 19; 1 Kings xxii. 21; 2 Kings ii. 16; but it is clear from the way in which Ezekiel speaks of this being that in his thought it is of a much higher order than in the earlier conception.

But another type of supernatural being mentioned in various passages points to Babylonian influence. The ancient conception of the Cherubim—in all probability of non-Israelite origin—meets us here; and again, there is a development, and their hybrid forms, lion, bull, eagle,

with four wings and hands beneath, but all having the
faces of a man, point very clearly to Babylonian influence
(i. 5–10, and cp. x. 1 ff.).   Due to the same influence is the
reference to the seven destroying angels, of human appearance, in ix. 1–11.   These are probably seven planets, who
were Babylonian deities, but the prophet subordinates them
to Yahweh—a clear indication of his monotheistic belief—
and they act as His instruments in carrying out His purpose.

3. Individual Responsibility

Perhaps nowhere in the book of *Ezekiel* is the teaching
on this subject set forth more tersely than in the words :
"The soul that sinneth it shall die;   the son shall not
bear the iniquity of the father, neither shall the father
bear the iniquity of the son;   the righteousness of the
righteous shall be upon him, and the wickedness of the
wicked shall be upon him " (xviii. 20;   the whole of this
chapter deals with the subject).   Most striking here is
the contrast between this teaching and the authoritative
words put forth not much more than a generation before
of "visiting the sins of the fathers upon the children,
and upon the third and upon the fourth generation of
them that hate me " (Deut. v. 9).   The difference between
these two points of view was a result of the Exile.   Previous
to this, belief in the solidarity of the nation, and in earlier
days the solidarity of the tribe, carried with it the conviction
that individuals necessarily shared in the prosperity of the
nation as a whole;   so that if the ancestors did what was right,
or, on the contrary, what was wrong, every member of the
nation partook of the resulting prosperity or misfortune.
The individual was considered only in so far as he was one
of the items that went to make up the nation.   But when
the nation, as such, ceased to exist, and Israel consisted
merely of scattered individuals far from their homeland,
it followed in a very natural course that the importance
and significance of the individual came to the fore.   Each
individual, Ezekiel teaches, is responsible for his own acts;
for the evil that he suffers if he has sinned, he has nobody
but himself to blame;   while, on the other hand, he cannot
rely on the good deeds of his ancestors to stand him in stead
if he himself is lacking in these.

It is instructive to compare again Ezekiel's teaching
on this subject with that of Jeremiah.   The earlier prophet,
as we know, was the first to teach that man, the individual,

not the nation, was the unit,[1] and it is very remarkable that even before the Exile he should have taught what in effect constituted a fundamental change in the conception of religion. The difference in the teaching on Individualism between these prophets is briefly this : Jeremiah's individualism centres in man's close relationship with God, and he is thus the earliest exponent of *personal religion*; Ezekiel's individualism emphasizes man's own responsibility for his deeds, and he is thus the first to teach *personal responsibility*. One can easily see how from these respective points of view two differing ideas regarding the individual in the sight of God arose; for, according to Jeremiah's teaching, man feels that he is precious in the sight of God; while, according to Ezekiel's teaching, man feels his insignificance and unworthiness in the sight of God; for the sense of responsibility, whatever else it may do, reveals his shortcomings to man. Thus the teaching of these two prophets on Individualism touches closely upon their respective teaching on the divine Personality; for it follows naturally that Jeremiah's conception of God envisages pre-eminently His nearness to the creature; but Ezekiel, with his conception of the divine transcendence, feels how great is the distance between the Holy One and sinful mortals.

4. REGENERATION

Whatever specifically characteristic points in his teaching a prophet may have, it will always be found that they are dependent upon, or the outcome of, his conception of God. In chapter xxxvi. 16 ff. the word of Yahweh comes to Ezekiel, remind him of the past ingratitude and unfaithfulness of his people; but in spite of this, it goes on to say : " I had pity for mine holy name, which the house of Israel had profaned among the nations whither they went. Therefore say unto the house of Israel, Thus saith the Lord God : I do not this for your sake, O house of Israel, but for mine holy name, which ye have profaned among the nations whither ye went. And I will sanctify my great name. . . . And I will sprinkle clean water upon you, and ye shall be clean; from all your filthiness, and from all your idols will I cleanse you. A new heart also will I give you, and a new spirit will I put within you. . . ." (vers. 16–30). The prophet here teaches—and it is a necessary outcome of his belief in the holy all-power of God—that the divine

[1] See p. 263.

purpose, however thwarted by a renegade people, will ultimately prevail. For the honour of his holy name, He will see to it that the people, in spite of themselves, will accomplish their destiny as pre-ordained by God. The first step in the process of their regeneration is the divine cleansing, followed by the creation of a new spirit within them. This, as the words of ver. 31 show, brings about the true condition of repentance—self-loathing because of past sin : "Then shall ye remember your evil ways, and your doings that were not good; and ye shall loathe yourselves in your own sight for your iniquities and for your abominations." Ezekiel follows Jeremiah here to some extent; but he goes his own inimitable way in the remarkable picture contained in chapter xxxvii, in which he sees the valley full of dry bones, representing Israel dead in sin, and through the action of the divine spirit the dead bones become clothed with flesh, and live, quickened to a regenerate life.

Ezekiel's teaching on divine forgiveness, cleansing, and consequent regeneration of His people, reaches a religious stage which transcends anything hitherto existent in the religion of the Hebrews.

5. The Ceremonial Law

The teaching of Ezekiel about the ceremonial law and the importance he attaches to its observance, and further, his idealization of the Temple and its services—all these are the logical outcome of his conception of the majesty and holiness of God. As a priest he sometimes over-emphasizes the priestly point of view; that, perhaps, was inevitable; but zeal for the glory of God in things external as well as spiritual was the real motive-power in all his teaching.

As an illustration of the importance he attaches to the ceremonial law we have his words in iv. 14 : "Then said I, Ah, Lord God! behold, my soul hath not been polluted; for from my youth up even until now have I not eaten of that which dieth of itself, or is torn of beasts; neither came there abominable flesh into my mouth." In chapters viii–x he makes it clear that the most abominable sin of the people is the way in which they have dese-crated the Temple by the introduction of alien cults. It is noteworthy that in these chapters there is placed in contrast to these debasing rites some of those passages in which the transcendent glory of God is described (viii. 2, x. 1, 4 ff.), showing that it is his conception of the divine transcendence which calls forth his abhorrence of everything that is not in accordance with what the worship of God should be.

Then, to turn to another side of Ezekiel's teaching on the ceremonial law,[1] the directions which he gives regarding the dress of the priests, and the need of the priests keeping separate from the people, may well strike us as *naïve*, for the primitive idea of *taboʋ* comes to the fore again (xliv. 17–19); and it is not to be denied that old-world ideas do assert themselves here; but it must be remembered that this is not peculiar to Hebrew religion—it is a phenomenon which appears again and again in the history of every religion; human nature is thus constituted. The fact must, however, be registered here because Ezekiel's insistence on ceremonial observances was not without its effect on succeeding ages. It is fully in accord with Ezekiel's priestly point of view that he regards the sons of Zadok as the representatives of the true priesthood, before which the idea of a temporal ruler recedes into the background, and the Levites as a subordinate order (xliv. 10–27; cp. xliii. 19, xlviii. 11); in *Deuteronomy* all the Levites were priests.[2]

Thus to the prophetic activity of Ezekiel, already referred to, we must add the priestly point of view; so that in spite of a somewhat narrow view in some directions a broader outlook is to be discerned in others.

6. Eschatological-Apocalyptic Ideas

What Ezekiel says about this subject is in the main the current material of which the earlier prophets had made use;[3] but he adds some apocalyptic *traits* which occur in his book for the first time, though there can be no doubt that here, too, traditional material has been utilized.[4]

The ideas regarding the final catastrophe which will overtake the sinners in the last day are briefly as follows : the day itself is spoken of in vii. 7 ff. : ". . . The time is

[1] We must, however, confess that we are in considerable doubt as to whether chapters xl–xlviii really belong to Ezekiel.

[2] In the Priestly Code, however, priests and Levites appear as distinct orders; this is what one would expect after what Ezekiel had taught.

[3] See Chapter XIX.

[4] Chapters xxxvii–xxxix are those especially, though by no means exclusively, concerned; but the authenticity of xxxviii and xxxix is denied by a number of scholars.

come, the day is near; a day of tumult, and not of joyful
shouting, upon the mountains. Now will I shortly pour
my fury upon thee, and accomplish my anger against
thee, and will judge thee according to thy ways . . ."
(see also xiv. 19, xxii. 22). The terrors of that day are
mentioned again and again : they will be seen in the natural
world, darkness, and cloud (xxxiv. 12), storm and tempest
(xiii. 11), drought (xxx. 12), and fire (xx. 47, 48 [in Hebrew
xxi. 3, 4]), etc.; further, famine and evil beasts, pestilence
and blood, and the sword (v. 15–17); and the most terrible
of all, the sword of Yahweh (xxi. 3–5 [in Hebrew 8–10]),
and the cup of destruction from Yahweh (xxiii. 31–4).
In that day Yahweh will be king, but He will reign in fury
(xx. 33, 34). This last point illustrates the variety and
not always consistent character of eschatological thought in
the prophetical books—a mark of the different traditions
current. It is said in this last passage that Yahweh Himself
will be king; but elsewhere when the future is spoken of it
is one of the house of David who will be king : " And I
will set up one shepherd over them, and he shall feed them,
even my servant David; he shall feed them, and he shall
be their shepherd. And I Yahweh will be their God, and
my servant David prince among them. And I will make
with them a covenant of peace . . ." (xxxiv. 23 ff.; see
also xxxvii. 24–6). The term " shepherd," applied to the
Messianic ruler, becomes from now onwards a constant
trait in eschatological thought.

The blessedness of the Messianic times finds frequent
mention : the cleansing of the people from sin is, of course,
a necessary preliminary (xxxvi. 33); the ingathering of
Israel, from all the lands in which they are dispersed, will
then follow (xi. 17; cp. xx. 34); and the remarkable thought
that even those will be gathered who are in their graves
occurs in xxxvii. 12–14. In that day, further, the land will
be very fruitful (xxxvi. 34, 35), and there will be peace
and plenty (xxxiv. 25–7). A large amount of space is taken
up with the account of the destruction of Israel's foes;
this, of course, was one of the oldest popular traditional
ideas regarding the Day of Yahweh (xxv–xxxii, xxxv).

Expecially characteristic of Ezekiel's thought regarding
the Messianic era is his emphasis on the cult (xx. 40, 41);
in xxxvii. 26–8 he says : " . . . And I will multiply them,
and will place my sanctuary in the midst of them for evermore. My tabernacle shall also be over them; and I

will be their God, and they shall be my people. And
the nations shall know that I, Yahweh, am he that sanctifieth
Israel, when my sanctuary shall be in the midst of them
for evermore." The very great importance attached to
worship in the Messianic times is seen by this prophet's
description of the Temple (xl–xlviii).[1]

A marked inconsistency is that long after the Messianic
time has been inaugurated and the people are dwelling
securely, the great foe Gog, at the head of Israel's enemies,
will come to destroy the land of Palestine. Gog seems
to have been the name of a legendary people living in the
far north, and it is evident that the prophet, whether
Ezekiel or another, was utilizing some traditional material
in writing about them in xxxviii, xxxix; but he is doubtless
applying the mythical names of Gog and Magog to some
actual enemies whom he has in mind.[2] Some, at least,
of the apocalyptic pictures presented point to the utilization
of extraneous ideas; thus, in xxxviii. 18–23, we have a
curious mixture of Hebrew and non-Hebraic thought;
the passage is a remarkable one, and therefore worth quoting
in full : " And it shall come to pass in that day, when Gog
shall come against the land of Israel, saith the Lord God,
that my fury shall come up into my nostrils. For in my
jealousy and in the fire of my wrath have I spoken; surely
in that day there shall be a great shaking in the land of
Israel; so that the fishes of the sea, and the fowls of the
heaven, and the beasts of the field, and all creeping things
that creep upon the earth, and all the men that are upon the
face of the earth, shall shake at my presence, and the
mountains shall be thrown down, and the steep places shall
fall, and every wall shall fall to the ground. And I will call
for a sword against him unto all my mountains, saith
the Lord God; every man's sword shall be against his
brother. And I will plead against him with pestilence
and with blood; and I will rain upon him, and upon his
hordes, and upon the many peoples that are with him,
an overflowing shower, and great hailstones, fire and brim-
stone. And I will magnify myself, and I will make myself
known in the eyes of many nations; and they shall know
that I am Yahweh."

[1] There is, however, considerable doubt among some scholars as to
whether these chapters are Ezekiel's.

[2] Hölscher favours the theory that Gog represents Gyges, king of Lydia,
who reigned about 660 B.C. (*Hesekiel, der Dichter und das Buch*, p. 189
[1924]).

This is not the place to deal with the many points of interest arising out of this passage; one has but to read it to realize that it contains diverse elements. It offers one of the best illustrations of the fact that the eschatological and apocalyptic ideas in the prophetical books are largely drawn from extraneous sources. This will be further dealt with in Chapter XXXIX.

CHAPTER XXVIII

RELIGIOUS TEACHERS: DEUTERO-ISAIAH

THE latest record that we have of Ezekiel belongs to the year 571 B.C.; whether he lived and taught after this we have no means of knowing.

From the writings which have been preserved of the great prophet whom we designate Deutero-Isaiah,[1] it is evident that his ministry began at a time when the menace to the Babylonian empire had become serious. In a passage from another part of *Isaiah* which clearly belongs to this period the coming doom is foreseen : " Behold, I will stir up the Medes against them, which shall not regard silver, and as for gold, they shall not delight in it. And their bows shall dash the young men in pieces; and they shall have no pity on the fruit of the womb; their eye shall not spare children. And Babylon, the glory of kingdoms, the beauty of the Chaldeans' pride, shall be as when God overthrew Sodom and Gomorrah " (Isa. xiii. 17–19). This points, in all probability, to the time when Cyrus, after his conquest of the Lydian kingdom, 546 B.C., was in a position to begin his campaign against the Babylonian empire of Nabonidus. Thus the Deutero-Isaianic writings may be assigned to the period between 546 B.C. and 538 B.C., the year of the first return of Jewish exiles to Palestine.

1. THE CONCEPTION OF GOD

With the teaching of this prophet on the nature and personality of God we reach the zenith of Hebrew religious belief. Monotheism had, indeed, been implicit in the teaching of earlier prophets; but never before had it been explicit, never before had there been the reiterated insistence upon the truth as expressed by this prophet. God is the Creator from everlasting, the eternal and only One:

---

[1] Isa. xl–lv.

" Before Me there was no God formed, neither shall there
be after Me. I, even I, am Yahweh; and beside me there
is no saviour " (xliii. 10); " I am Yahweh, and there is
none else; beside me there is no God . . . I am Yahweh,
and there is none else. I form the light and create darkness;
I make peace, and bring calamity; I am Yahweh that doeth
all these things " (xlv. 5–7). " For thus saith Yahweh
that created the heavens; he is God, that formed the earth
and made it; he established it, he created it not in vain,
he formed it to be inhabited; I am Yahweh, and there is
none else " (xlv. 18). As the Creator of all, the cosmic
forces are to Him but small and insignificant : " Who hath
measured the waters in the hollow of his hand, and meted
out the heavens with a span, and comprehended the dust
of the earth in a measure, and weighed the mountains in
scales, and the hills in a balance ? . . . Behold, the nations
are as a drop of a bucket, and are counted as the small dust
of the balance; behold, the isles are as the fine dust that is
lifted up " (xl. 12–15). And once more : " Hast thou
not known ? Hast thou not heard ? Yahweh is the
everlasting God, the Creator of the ends of the earth;
he fainteth not, neither is he weary; there is no searching
of his understanding " (xl. 28; cp. also ver. 8).

Passages like these show to what a sublime height of
conception this prophet had attained; no doubt there
were things happening in the world which may have contributed to this—the fall of nations and the impotence
of Babylonian and other gods; but there was something
more and something deeper than this that gave to this
prophet such an insight into and apprehension of the nature
and personality of God. The natural evolution of ideas
does much to deepen and enlarge men's thought of God;
but there come moments when to such development there
is needed the self-revelation of God Himself (we may not
know how or by what means) and without which development alone merely disperses itself and becomes thin air,
or else degeneration supervenes, of which the history of
religion has offered many illustrations. Here was one of the
men to whom God vouchsafed to reveal Himself in a very
special way, and there are not many to whom such revelation
has been accorded, but when there is response, as in the case
of Deutero-Isaiah, they become landmarks in the history of
religion. This prophet could say with truth in the name of
God, " My thoughts are not your thoughts, neither are your

ways my ways"; but at times he himself was the mouthpiece whereby the thoughts of God were proclaimed.

It is instructive to see how this prophet, with all his insight into the greatness and omnipotence of God, was not unmindful of that other aspect of the divine character, of which he speaks, for example, in such words as these: "He shall feed his flock like a shepherd, he shall gather the lambs in his arm, and carry them in his bosom, and shall gently lead those that give suck" (xl. 11), thus combining the characteristic teaching of Jeremiah on the divine condescension with that of Ezekiel on the transcendental character of God.

2. THE REGENERATION OF THE PEOPLE

The deeply religious character of this prophet was such that in whatever direction his teaching tended, his Godward thought always predominated. This is well illustrated in the words of comfort and encouragement to his people, in which he tells them of how God will deal with them in the time that is to come. In the restoration of the nation which he portrays and which is about to take place in the near future, the first condition must be a people purified from sin, and therefore he cries in the name of the Lord: "I have blotted out, as a thick cloud, thy transgressions, and, as a cloud, thy sins; return unto me, for I have redeemed thee" (Isa. xliv. 22). It is the first act of divine mercy; a regenerated people, ready therefore and fit, as God's chosen servants, to welcome the divine presence in their midst: "But thou, Israel, my servant, Jacob whom I have chosen, the seed of Abraham my friend; thou whom I have taken hold of from the ends of the earth, and called thee from the corners thereof, and said unto thee, Thou art my servant, I have chosen thee and not cast thee away; fear thou not, for I am with thee; be not dismayed, for I am thy God; I will strengthen thee; yea, I will help thee; yea, I will uphold thee with the right hand of my righteousness" (Isa. xli. 8–10). There are many other words to the same effect; and what is very noteworthy is the fact that the prophet fully realizes that nothing which the people have done has called forth these marks of divine pardon and loving protection; the nature of God as love impels Him to be true to Himself, and therefore for His name's sake His mercy is shown forth: "For mine own sake, for mine own sake, will I do it; for how should my name be

profaned? and my glory will I not give to another " (Isa.
xlviii. 11). Both Jeremiah and Ezekiel had uttered a
similar thought. And the sequel, the prophet teaches,
shall be a worthy response on the part of the people : " All
thy children shall be taught of Yahweh, and great shall be
the peace of thy children. In righteousness shalt thou be
established " (Isa. liv. 13, 14). Regeneration is thus
prominent in this prophet's thought; and while in this he
follows Ezekiel (cp. Ezek. xxxvii), he handles the subject
quite independently, and develops it in his own way with a
warmth of feeling and a depth of apprehension of the love
of God which is unrivalled elsewhere in Hebrew religious
teaching.

3. UNIVERSALISM

With his exalted conception of the unity and all-power
of God it followed that Deutero-Isaiah could not be content
with the restrictive idea of Yahweh as a national God.
He speaks therefore in the name of God, saying : " Look
unto me, and be ye saved, all the ends of the earth; for I
am God, and there is none else. By myself have I sworn,
the word is gone forth from my mouth, and shall not return,
that unto me every knee shall bow, every tongue shall swear "
(xlv. 22, 23). " The God of the whole earth shall he be called "
(liv. 5).

And it is in accordance with this universalistic idea
that the prophet points to Cyrus as God's anointed, called
forth to do His will : " Thus saith Yahweh to his anointed,
to Cyrus, whose right hand I have holden, to subdue nations
before him " (xlv. 1); " My counsel shall stand, and I will
do all my pleasure, calling a ravenous bird from the east,
the man of my counsel from a far country " (xlvi. 10, 11).

As the instrument for the conversion of the Gentiles
it is but natural that Israel should be regarded as pre-
eminent; hence those passages which, on the one hand,
speak of the nations as joining themselves to Israel, and,
on the other hand, those which describe them as subservient
to Israel : " Thus saith Yahweh, The labour of Egypt,
and the merchandise of Ethiopia, and the Sabæans, men
of stature, shall come over unto thee, and they shall be
thine; they shall go after thee; in chains they shall come
over; and they shall fall down unto thee, they shall make
supplication unto thee, saying, Surely God is in thee, and
there is none else, there is no other God " (xlv. 14). And

again, in the well-known passage, xlix. 22, 23 : " Behold, I will lift up mine hand to the nations, and set up mine ensign to the peoples, and they shall bring thy sons in their bosom, and thy daughters shall be carried upon their shoulders. And kings shall be thy nursing fathers, and their queens thy nursing mothers; they shall bow down to thee with their faces to the earth, and lick the dust of thy feet; and thou shalt know that I am Yahweh, and they that wait for me shall not be ashamed." [1]

The final conception, however, is that of the leadership of Israel among the Gentiles, without any thought of subserviency on the part of the latter : " Behold, I have given him for a witness to the peoples, a leader and a commander to the peoples. Behold, thou shalt call a nation that thou knowest not, and a nation that knew not thee shall run unto thee, because of Yahweh thy God, and for the Holy one of Israel; for he hath glorified thee " (lv. 4, 5). In this passage it is noteworthy that the thought of God again predominates; it is because Yahweh is their God that this nation will join itself to Israel.

It is impossible to over-emphasize the importance of this universalistic teaching, and of Israel being designated the instrument whereby the conversion of the Gentiles was to be brought about, for quite evidently in the mind of *Deutero-Isaiah* there was the thought of the religion of the Hebrews becoming a world-religion. Doubtless there was in the teaching of some of the earlier prophets that which logically tended in the same direction; but it is in *Deutero-Isaiah* that this becomes a concrete expectation. Two things were primarily responsible for this : the Exile, with the wider outlook upon the world which it offered; but still more Deutero-Isaiah's conception of God. With his apprehension of Yahweh as the God of the whole world, there followed of necessity that He should be thought of as the God of all men, and that the worship of Him should become world-wide.

4. THE " SERVANT OF THE LORD " SONGS

Though there are some notable exceptions, the majority of modern scholars regard these four songs (Isa. xlii. 1–4, xlix. 1–6, l. 4–9, lii. 13–liii. 12) [2] as not belonging to Deutero-

---

[1] This passage and the next are regarded by some commentators as of different authorship, but this is not necessarily the case.

[2] According to some scholars the first three songs should respectively comprise xlii. 1–9, xlix. 1–13, l. 4–11.

Isaiah. The difficult problem need not trouble us, as we are dealing with religious teaching; who gave the teaching is of less importance than the fact that it *was* given. One thing, however, seems certain : the spirit and style of these songs are so reminiscent of Deutero-Isaiah, and some of their outstanding thoughts are so similar to his, that if this prophet was not the author it must have been somebody very much under his influence and wholly imbued with his spirit who wrote them.[1] But there is justification in either case for treating them separately, because there can be no doubt that they were originally independent pieces, and did not stand in the text as they do now.

Nor are we, for the moment, concerned with the question as to who the " Servant of the Lord " was (see below); one thing only we would wish to state with emphasis : the contention that Israel as a nation is meant seems to us quite out of the question; only a forced and unnatural exegesis can give such an interpretation to passages like xlix. 1, 5, 6; and if Israel is the " Servant," how are we to understand liii. 4–6? Who is the " he " and who the " we " in such words as : " Surely *he* hath borne *our* griefs and carried *our* sorrows; yet *we* did esteem *him* stricken of God and afflicted. But *he* was wounded for *our* transgressions . . ." ? In xlix. 3, it is true, Israel is definitely mentioned as the servant; but it must be obvious that in face of vers. 5, 6, " Israel " is a gloss; for if Israel is the servant, how can it be said that he is " to bring Jacob again to him, and that Israel be gathered unto him (Yahweh) " ? How is Israel " to raise up the tribes of Jacob, and to restore the preserved of Israel " ? [2]

Who the " Servant " was we are not prepared to say, other than that he was a real, not an idealized, man (see below).

What is of greater importance than these controversial questions is the teaching contained in these songs. This is of the deepest significance, as will be seen.

First, as to the vocation of the " Servant." The words, " I have put my spirit upon him " (xlii. 1) can be interpreted

---

[1] The present writers find it difficult to resist the conclusion that they were written by Deutero-Isaiah.

[2] It is also worth pointing out that the rhythm (three strokes to each half-verse) is broken if " Israel " is inserted. For a very sane presentation of the " Servant " representing the collective nation (though the present writer finds himself unable to accept this interpretation) see Wheeler Robinson, *The Religious Ideas of the Old Testament*, pp. 202 ff. (1926).

as marking him out as the Messiah, or as in reference to the divine gift to enable him to fulfil his calling as prophet. For the present let us leave it open as to which is meant. Then there is the universalistic teaching which we have seen to be so characteristic of Deutero-Isaiah. In xlii. 1 it is said : " He shall bring forth judgement to the Gentiles " : judgement here means the righteousness and justice of divine principles; this, together with ver. 4 and xlix. 6, " I will also give thee for a light to the Gentiles, that my salvation may be unto the end of the earth," show that, as Deutero-Isaiah teaches elsewhere, the religion of the Jews was to become a world-religion.

One other subject, the teaching of which is the same as that found elsewhere in this book, is the conception of God; this will become clear as we proceed.

But now we come to deal with teaching which belongs specifically to these songs. The " Servant," in spite of his high calling, is subdued, humble, and of extreme gentleness : " He shall not cry nor lift up, nor cause his voice to be heard in the street. A bruised reed shall he not break, and the smoking flax shall he not quench " (xlii. 2, 3). It is difficult to see how or why the " Servant " should be thus depicted unless it portrayed an actual person. But what was to be gained by describing the Messiah [1] or a prophet in this way? It was not such a figure that would appeal to the people. Had the writer intended to present an *ideal* man, he would, one feels, have constructed a different picture. But he could not help himself, because his hero was one whom he saw as he was; it was, in any case, going to be a difficult thing to account for the facts of the life and sufferings and death of this chosen instrument of God; but the writer was dealing with things as they were, not as he would have wished them to be.

He sees, further, that this " Servant " was in personal appearance unattractive; he was the victim of some scourge, so that men turned from him as from some unclean person (lii. 14, liii. 2, 3). Here, if anywhere, according to the belief of the times, was the case of one suffering calamity and disease because he had sinned : " We did esteem him stricken, smitten of God and afflicted " (liii. 4). Yet it is perfectly clear to the writer that this " Servant " was a righteous man : " He had done no violence, neither was any deceit

[1] The portraiture would be still more difficult to account for if the idealized nation were meant.

x

in his mouth " (liii. 9).   So that here was the problem of a
righteous man suffering.   How was it to be accounted for ?
The writer of these songs teaches—and he was the first to
put forth the doctrine—that since sin must be atoned for,
and since the " Servant," as a righteous man, cannot be
atoning for his own sins, therefore he is atoning for the
sins of others :   " He was wounded for our transgressions,
he was bruised for our iniquities;   the chastisement of
our peace was upon him, and with his stripes we are
healed " (liii. 5; cp. ver. 8).

Now there are some reasons, in spite of what was said
just now, for holding that the writer of these songs believed
the " Servant " to be the expected Messiah; this is denied
by many modern scholars; but there are the following points
to be considered :

There is no doubt that one of the functions of the Messiah
was to lead back the people from captivity and rule over
them in their own land, if not as king, at least as prince;
this is clearly seen in the case of Zerubbabel, whom these
prophets regard as the Messiah (Zech. iv. 11, 14, vi. 12;
Hag. ii. 1–9 and 23).   Similarly in xlix. 5, 6, the " Servant "
is described as one who is to bring back the people and restore
them to their own land.   This is further emphasized if vers.
7–9 of this chapter be regarded, as they may well be, as
belonging to the second song.

Then again, the way in which the spirit of God is said to
rest upon Zerubbabel (Zech. iv. 6, 14; Hag. ii. 4, 5) is
paralleled by xlii. 1; and further, Zerubbabel is spoken
of as " My servant " (Hag. ii. 23; cp. Isa. xlii. 1, xlix. 3, 6,
lii. 13, where the hero of these songs receives a similar title).

Leader of the captives to their native land, one on whom
the spirit of God rests, one who receives the title of " My
Servant "—to Zerubbabel, who is admittedly regarded as
the Messiah, these things apply; so that if they are also
all applied to the " Servant " of these songs, the fact is a strong
argument in favour of the contention that the " Servant "
was thought of as the Messiah.

There is a further consideration which points in the
same direction : in xlix. 7 it is said in reference to the
" Servant " :   " Kings shall see and arise; princes, and
they shall do homage," and in lii. 15 : " So shall he startle [1]
many nations; kings shall shut their mouths because of

---

[1] The text can hardly be in order; the Septuagint has : " So shall many
nations marvel at him "; we should probably read : " So shall many nations
be perturbed (concerning him)."

him." There would not be much point in these words
if the "Servant" were thought of as an ordinary ruler;
but they are very significant if he was intended to be thought
of as the Messiah. And if the idealized nation were meant
there would be a mixing-up of the ideal and the real; but
this is not the way of the writer of these songs.

But if this is so we are confronted with the difficulty
of the death of the Messiah under conditions which are
wholly inappropriate (liii. 9); the "Servant" witnesses
for Yahweh and His truth, he suffers for this, and bears
the sins of others; ultimately he dies a martyr's death.

This is not the kind of Messianic picture that is to be
expected; nor, as we shall see, was the writer of the songs
satisfied with it, extremely beautiful as his whole conception is. There is, however, another and supremely important matter in connexion with the "Servant" which
must be referred to, and it is concerned with what is, after
all, the fundamental teaching of the whole of this book—
the conception of God, a conception which, as we have
seen, reaches the summit of Hebrew religion. Nothing is
more significant in all these songs than the intimate and close
relationship of the "Servant" with God—incidentally
this might well be urged as a further indication of the Messiahship of the "Servant";—thus in xlii. 1: "Behold; my
servant, whom I uphold; my chosen in whom my soul
delighteth; I have put my spirit upon him"; in xlix.
1–3: "Yahweh hath called me from the womb . . . and
he said unto me, Thou art my servant in whom I will be
glorified"; in l. 4 ff.: "The Lord God hath given me the
tongue of them that are taught . . . the Lord God hath
opened mine ear . . . the Lord God will help me . . .";
in liii. 6: "Yahweh hath laid on him the iniquity of us all."
This intimate relationship between the "Servant" and
God must be thought of in connexion with the enlarged and
exalted conception of God which is peculiar to this book.
In particular, it must be recognized that in this book there
is a constant emphasis laid upon God as the Everlasting:
"The Everlasting God, Yahweh, the Creator of the ends
of the earth, fainteth not, neither is weary; there is no
searching of his understanding" (xl. 28); in one form or
another this thought of God as eternal finds expression
again and again (see xl. 8, xli. 4, xliii. 10, xliv. 6, xlviii.
12, li. 6, 8, lv. 13). Is it too much to believe that to a
man like Deutero-Isaiah, with his deep apprehension of

the spiritual nature and majesty of God, this conception of the eternity of God should have suggested the possibility of His being concerned with the spirits of men after death? The current *She'ol* belief did, at any rate, recognize the continued existence of the shades of men in the Hereafter; it was a nebulous and unsatisfying belief; and in the mind of Deutero-Isaiah, who believed in the divine eternity, may there not have been an incongruity in the thought that the interest of God, the Creator, in man, created in His own image, should be restricted to the short span of this life? It can hardly be denied that with a developed conception of the Personality of God, with a deeper apprehension of His spiritual nature, and with a fuller realization of His creative power, there must necessarily, sooner or later, have arisen a doubt as to the correctness of a belief that God was only concerned with men in this world. With his sublime conception of God, to Deutero-Isaiah the traditional belief that God was concerned only with men in this life must have been agonizing when he had before him the picture of the righteous chosen " Servant " ending in death that intimate relationship with God which had been so marked all through his life. So the conviction came upon him that death was not the end; for what else can the words mean : " Therefore will I divide him a portion with the great, and he shall divide the spoil with the strong, because he poured out his soul unto death, and was numbered with the transgressors " (liii. 12)? How, after being dead, can it be said that he shall have a portion with the great, unless he was to rise from the dead to take the part assigned him by God? Ezekiel had already formulated the conception of the nation dead in sin rising to righteousness through the action of the divine spirit. Deutero-Isaiah's adaptation of this conception in a higher sense was made easier, seeing that he had the figure of the *righteous* " Servant " before him. Thus, there is some justification for believing that Deutero-Isaiah was the first to adumbrate, if nothing more, a doctrine of the resurrection among the Jews.[1] Such a conception would naturally, at first, be only of a tentative character; many years too would pass before it could become a generally accepted belief. But such a thought, however inspired, could only arise in the minds

---

[1] Persian influences regarding the doctrine of Immortality may well have been exerted as early as this time (see, further, below, Chapter XXXIX, pp. 393 f.).

of the people's most advanced thinkers; and among these Deutero-Isaiah stood out pre-eminent.

Our conclusion, therefore, is that the "Servant" was an actual person who, on account of his pre-eminent righteousness, was believed by the prophet to be the Messiah. He suffered in a "naughty" world because of his righteousness; but his suffering was to the prophet of comparatively small moment, because he was convinced that the "Servant" would rise from death to complete his work; and it was the "Servant's" close relationship with God, and the prophet's profound belief in the righteousness and eternity of God, that compelled this conviction.[1]

5. OTHER TEACHERS OF THE EXILIC PERIOD

In addition to the great outstanding teachers already mentioned there were many others, fragments of whose teaching have come down to us, e.g. Lamentations; Isa. xiii. 1–xiv. 23; Obad. 1–14; Lev. xvii–xxvi, and some of the Psalms. As compared with Ezekiel and Deutero-Isaiah, however, there is nothing of sufficiently outstanding importance to demand separate treatment.

Then, further, there was the Deuteronomic circle of teachers whose interpretation of the past history of the people is indelibly impressed on the historical books. These were men of deep piety and religious feeling, and their influence is to be seen in all the writings of this period; but their contribution to the development of Hebrew religion was not equal to that of the two great prophets mentioned.

Finally, there was the very important priestly school whose influence upon the formulation of the Law was profound and very far-reaching; but while we know that their activity was already exercised during the exilic period, it is not until we study the post-exilic literature that we come to the details of their teaching. To this we shall devote our attention in Chapter XXXV.

6. SUMMARY OF THE DEVELOPMENT OF HEBREW RELIGION DURING THE EXILIC PERIOD

The profound and far-reaching developments in Hebrew Religion during the Exile may now be summarized. At the base of the teaching of the exilic prophets lay that of the great prophets of the preceding centuries, so that a

---

[1] On the subject of vicarious suffering, see below, Chapter XXXV.

great deal of the religious teaching of this period was not new; as this has already been dealt with we are not now concerned with it; the developments from this earlier teaching is what we must keep before our minds.

The external religious observances which during the Exile assumed a prominence and importance never previously accorded to them were the rite of Circumcision and the Sabbath. Owing to the inevitable absence of the sacrificial services worship took the form of assemblies of the faithful, primarily on Sabbaths, at which there are reasons for believing that the main elements consisted of the reading of the prophetical writings and *Deuteronomy*, preaching, the singing of psalms, and the offering of prayer.

Both at such assemblies and in all probability at other times the great religious truths connected with belief in Yahweh were put forth.

The chief inspirers here were Ezekiel and the prophet we speak of as Deutero-Isaiah. The former's teaching on divine transcendence surpassed all that had hitherto been taught. His doctrine of man centred in individual responsibility. Further, as an outcome of his conception of God he looked for the regeneration of his people; this culminated in his picture of the resuscitation of the people from death in sin to a new life through the action of the divine spirit; a thought which contained the germ of belief in resurrection. As a priest, Ezekiel insisted upon the need of the observance of the ceremonial law; and his ideal picture of the renovation of the Temple and its services preserved among the exiles the hope of its realization in a happy future in their own land.

In Deutero-Isaiah the conception of God reached its highest and final development in Hebrew Religion. He conceives of Yahweh as the God of the universe, and therefore the God of all peoples; with him the truth of the unity of God is reiterated, and becomes explicit as never before. He teaches, too, that God is from everlasting to everlasting. The religion of the Jews was to become a world-religion. While thus fully in accord with Ezekiel's conception of the divine transcendence, he balances this truth with what he teaches on the divine condescension, comparing God's love and care for men with a shepherd's solicitude for his flock. Ezekiel's teaching on regeneration is continued by Deutero-Isaiah, but he emphasizes more fully the divine mercy in blotting out the sins of the people.

A special importance attaches to the religious teaching contained in the " Servant of the Lord " songs; whether Deutero-Isaiah was the author of these, as we hold, or another, is a matter of less importance than the teaching contained in them. The writer's universalistic teaching is in entire agreement with what is taught on this subject in the rest of the book.

There are reasons for believing that the " Servant " was, in the mind of the writer, the Messiah. As the chosen of God and a righteous man his suffering cannot have been for sins which he had committed, according to the traditional belief; therefore, the writer teaches, his suffering is for the sins of his people; it is the first time that the doctrine of vicarious suffering is put forth. The suffering " Servant " ultimately dies a martyr's death; but to the writer, with his sublime conception of the eternal and righteous God, this cannot be the end; and he therefore teaches, implicitly it is true, that God will raise up His " Servant " from death to complete the work He gave him to do.

Teaching of another kind was given during the Exile, but as the details of this occur only in post-exilic writings, they are not dealt with here.

CHAPTER XXIX

PERSIAN INFLUENCE ON JEWISH BELIEF

WHILE the antecedents of the religion of Persia (Zoroastrianism) [1] go back to the fifteenth century B.C., when Iranian influence can be traced in Syria and Palestine, it was not until the time of Cyrus, probably a little earlier, that the Jews, coming into contact with the Persians, had an opportunity of learning about their religion.

The question as to how far the religion of the Jews was influenced by that of Persia is a very controversial one; some scholars deny any Persian influence, others see a good deal of it. Both extreme positions are probably exaggerated. In one direction it seems quite impossible not to see that strong Persian influences had been at work, viz. in the domain of Eschatology and Apocalyptic; but as we are dealing with this in Chapter XXXIX we shall not refer to it further here.

But in other directions it is recognized that there is a great difficulty in deciding whether or not Persian influences are to be discerned. What cannot but strike even a superficial observer in comparing Zoroastrianism with Judaism is the existence of some remarkable parallels; not that these necessarily denote the influence of either on the other; but even assuming that there was *no* influence (apart from Eschatology) it is impossible not to recognize that the Jewish religious leaders must have felt considerable sympathy with much that they saw in Zoroastrian belief and practice.

We will enumerate the more prominent parallels between the two religions in order to show that there was much similarity of thought between them.

---

[1] Zoroaster is the Græcized form of the Persian Zarathustra. There is uncertainty as to when he lived; most authorities give his date as *circa* 1000 B.C.

Zoroaster appeared as a reformer and spiritualizer of a religion which had been in existence long before his time. His rejection of the gods of this earlier religion and his teaching that there was only one God, must have appealed to the monotheistic belief of the Jews.

Ahura Mazda ("Wise Lord"), he taught, was the one God and All-Father of the world, who dwells in light, Creator of the sun, moon, and stars, of light and darkness, of the earth and all on it. This teaching suffered deterioration afterwards; but so far as Zoroaster himself was concerned he was a monotheist.

Nobody, of course, would for a moment suppose that the monotheistic belief of the Jews owed anything to Persian religion here; but the parallel is worth mention if for no other reason than that it must have commended Zoroastrianism to them; and this would make it easier to understand Persian influence in other directions. But even here it is possible that in a small but interesting particular, Persian influence may be discerned. Ahura Mazda, as we have just seen, was said to dwell in light and to have created light and darkness; an act of praise in which this belief is expressed was said daily at dawn. One of the oldest pre-Christian Benedictions in the Jewish Liturgy, which was also said at dawn, begins with the words : " Blessed art thou, O Lord our God, King of the Universe, who formest light and createst darkness." It may be merely a coincidence, but if so it is certainly a very striking one. The Jewish Benediction was, no doubt, based directly on Isa. xlv. 7; but that Deutero-Isaiah may have adapted extraneous beliefs to the religion of Yahweh, as Ezekiel had done, is not an unreasonable supposition.[1]

Again, apart from Judaism, no religion laid such emphasis on moral living as Zoroastrianism did. The great reformer declared his task to be the setting-up of a kingdom of God on earth; his adherents must be pure in body as in mind. Many of the Zoroastrian laws are puerile, and sometimes repulsive; but the high ethical ideal which was set must have appealed to the Jewish religious leaders as entirely in accordance with their Law.

Arising out of this there is the further point of parallelism that Zoroastrianism was a book-religion just as Judaism

---

[1] Gen. i. 1–5 belongs to the Priestly Code, and therefore does not come into consideration here.

had come to be. Each had its Law; and what may conceivably have influenced the Jews was the fact that the Persians believed in the pre-existence of the divine Law which they personified. The Jews identified their Law with Wisdom, which they personified; and, as we see from Prov. viii, they believed in the existence of Wisdom before the creation of the world.[1] And finally, it is probable that the Angelology and Demonology of the Persians directly influenced Judaism; in these things the earlier form of Iranian religion persisted in spite of Zoroaster's teaching. This is true also of the Dualism of the Persians, which, however, was never accepted by the Jews.

Our main conclusion therefore is that while there was much in Persian religion which would have been regarded with sympathy by the Jews, they were influenced but little directly thereby. The great exception to this was in the domain of Eschatology; but as this requires more detailed examination, a separate chapter must be devoted to the subject (see Chapter XXXIX).

---

[1] Prov. viii belongs to the latest portion of the book of *Proverbs*, probably the third century B.C.; but this is not to say that it may not in some respects reflect earlier thought.

CHAPTER XXX

THE RETURN FROM EXILE

1. PARTICULARISM AND UNIVERSALISM

THE difference in mental outlook between priest and prophet was age-long. Fundamentally, it is engendered by tendencies which are inborn in man; but it is fostered by the difference of calling and function as between priest and prophet. The two points of view were already in evidence long before the Exile, and although they did not necessarily cause a cleavage between the priesthood and the prophetical office, yet signs were not wanting which pointed to the fact that difference in aim and method made a fusion of the two mental attitudes characteristic of them respectively difficult, at times impossible. That the priestly and the prophetical points of view were in evidence during the exilic period is certain, though the actual proof of this only emerges fully later. Nevertheless, the diverging tendencies are already clearly discernible in the mental attitudes of Ezekiel the priest and Deutero-Isaiah the prophet respectively.

These tendencies we express, in one main direction at any rate, respectively by the terms Particularism and Universalism. In the present connexion the former term connotes, in general, a somewhat restricted nationalistic point of view, while the latter denotes a wider mental outlook. The particularistic attitude conceives of God as the God of Israel, the universalistic attitude would express itself in such words as : "Look unto me, and be ye saved, all the ends of the earth" (Isa. xlv. 22). The former would regard Israel as alone worthy of divine consideration, the latter would include the Gentiles within God's scheme of salvation.

We draw attention to these tendencies here because they are discernible in this period; they come to grips in subsequent periods, and the conflict becomes a death-struggle.[1]

2. THE RETURNED EXILES

It was not until the period of the Exile was drawing to a close that, as we have seen, Deutero-Isaiah arose as a teacher of his people. During most of the exilic period, therefore, the dominant influence had been exercised by the circle of priestly teachers whose interest centred in the study and elaboration of the Law and its observances. Thus it is that we are confronted by the ironical fact that to Deutero-Isaiah the misinterpretation of his own words which we find in vogue in the time of John the Baptist, became applicable : " The voice of one crying in the wilderness "; instead of : " The voice of one crying : In the wilderness. . . ." For the voice of Deutero-Isaiah, as the sequel shows, proclaiming the most sublime teaching the world had ever heard, made little appeal. The earlier priestly influence and teaching had taken root too deeply. Concentration on the *minutiæ* of legal observances was having a narrowing effect upon the mind; to the priestly teachers the Jews were the people of the Law, and therefore they had no interest in Gentiles. As it was Yahweh who had given the Law, His pre-eminent demand must be the observance of His Law. As the Jews were His chosen people they must be His chief concern. And thus the universalistic teaching of Deutero-Isaiah did not bear fruit; some there were who followed in his steps, and later the spirit of his teaching emerged; but for the present their influence, with one exception to be referred to in the next chapter, so far as we can gather from the records, was negligible. From now on belief and practice narrowed down, in the main, into nationalistic grooves; and the religion which the greater prophets, and especially Deutero-Isaiah, would have made a world-religion, assumed of set purpose a form which excluded non-Jews.

Before we come to deal with the great thought-movements the seeds of which, though taking root during the Exile, did not come to full fruition until rather later during the post-exilic period, we must take a brief glance at the more prominent points of teaching of which we have records

---

[1] As outstanding illustrations of the particularistic and universalistic attitudes respectively, we may point to Joel iii. 9-14, and the book of *Jonah*; both belong to the Greek period.

during the few years immediately following upon the Return. This is advisable because, so far as our present knowledge goes, there is a gap in the history after the time of Haggai and Zechariah—perhaps Malachi should also be included; so that the few years from the Return to the building of the Temple, 538–516 B.C., are cut off, as it were, from the subsequent history, which is not taken up again until more than half a century had passed.

In 520 B.C. we find a considerable community of returned exiles settled in Jerusalem and the vicinity; their chief leaders and teachers are Haggai and Zechariah, though there are indications that priestly influence was dominant.[1]

The exiles had returned with the ostensible purpose of rebuilding the Temple; but they were in no hurry to undertake the task. Material conditions were dispiriting : most of the people depended upon agriculture for gaining a living; but the seasons were bad, crops were poor, harvests were delayed; there was a dire struggle for existence. Haggai taught that this was all due to God's anger because they had not built the Temple—a not very inspiring conception. Zechariah joined with Haggai in urging the people to build the Temple, for this was an indispensable condition for the coming of the Messiah. Indeed, Messianic expectation forms the central point of Zechariah's teaching. His " Night visions " are all concerned with the preparation of the people and the land for the coming Messiah and the Messianic era. Both Haggai and Zechariah point to Zerubbabel as the coming Messiah, who is for them, therefore, a purely temporal ruler. These points must be considered a little further. There is no need to insist here upon the close connexion, from post-exilic times onwards, between Messianic teaching and the " Day of the Lord " ; it is brought out clearly by Haggai and Zechariah.[2] The former gives utterance to the traditional ideas regarding the " Day of the Lord " in ii. 6, 7, of his book : " Yet once, it is a little while, and I will shake the heavens, and the earth, and the sea, and the dry land; and I will shake all nations, and the desirable things of all nations shall come, and I will fill this house with glory, saith Yahweh of hosts." This world-cataclysm is to herald the coming of the Messianic era; for this prophet's main concern is the rebuilding of the Temple in view of the advent of the Messiah, i.e. Zerubbabel,

[1] See, e.g., Hag. ii. 11 ff.
[2] Only Zech. i–viii come into consideration here.

according to Haggai (see ii. 20–23)—it is to be made glorious through the offerings which are most prized by the nations, i.e. silver and gold, which, however, in reality belong to Yahweh (ver. 8). Zechariah's teaching is entirely in accordance with this; for him, too, a world-cataclysm, with the destruction of the nations, is to herald the opening of the Messianic Era with the advent of the Messiah (Zerub-babel, see Zech. iii. 8, 9, iv. 10, vi. 9–15 [1]); this is not stated in definite terms by Haggai, but is clearly implied in i. 11–15. Zechariah, however, though also anxious for the building of the Temple, is far more concerned with the preparation of Jerusalem (ii. 1–13 [in Hebrew ii. 5–17]), the purification of the people (v. 1–4), and the removal of wickedness from the land (v. 5, 11); all of which are preparatory to the Messiah's advent (cp. Mal. iii. 1–6).

The main points to be noted here are that the Messiah is thought of as a purely human ruler, that his advent is to be marked by a world-cataclysm, the "Day of the Lord"; and that the Gentiles are either to become subservient to Israel, or to be destroyed. The last two points are important to bear in mind in view of later apocalyptic teaching.

Then, prominent in the very meagre literature belonging to these years is the reference to angels. Noticeable in the book of *Zechariah* is the frequent mention of an angel as intermediary between God and the prophet. It must be evident from the way in which this is represented as the normal way of divine communication that belief in these intermediate beings had become a fixed element in the religion not only of the leaders but also of the people them-selves. In all his visions the prophet tells of an angel who is the mouthpiece by means of which God speaks (i. 19 [in Hebrew ii. 2], and often); this is very different from the direct intercourse which is invariably found among the earlier prophets; but we must doubtless see here the outcome of Ezekiel's teaching on divine transcendence. A somewhat different conception regarding the superhuman being is observable as between Ezekiel and Zechariah; the former, who speaks of this intermediate being as a "spirit," seems to think of it as more closely associated with the personality

[1] In vi. 11 we must read "crown" for "crowns," and the name of Joshua was inserted in place of Zerubbabel at a later time when the Priest was at the head of the theocratic government. The Hebrew text of vi. 9–15 is in considerable disorder, and shows clear marks of having been tampered with.

of God than is the case with Zechariah; for this latter always speaks of a "messenger," usually translated "angel," and this gives the impression of being intended to express more pronouncedly the distinction, or separation, between God and His supernatural instrument. If we are correct in this, it points to a further step in the teaching of the wide distance between God and man.

In *Zechariah* we meet for the first time with the word "Satan" as applied to a superhuman person; he is represented as "*the* adversary," [1] the word occurring with the definite article. Satan appears here as one of the angels; he is not yet an evil spirit, but a superhuman being whose special function is that of accusing men before God (Zech. iii. 1–2).

During those few years, then, which followed immediately upon the return of the exiles to the homeland, the thought of the building of the Temple, together with the Messianic Hope with which it is so intimately connected, fills the foreground; and the messages regarding the coming of the Messiah which the prophet receives are all given through the intermediary of an angel. So that Messianism and Angelology are really the only two subjects which occupy the mind of the one true successor of the prophets, at this time, namely, Zechariah. That the seeds of thought-movements which were to reach great developments were already beginning to germinate we know from the subsequent literature and history; and faint signs of them are to be discerned in the books of *Haggai* and *Zechariah*; and, doubtless, during the seventy years of silence which followed the completion of the Temple these movements were proceeding apace; for when the curtain rises again we find that considerable development has taken place. But this leads us to subjects which demand, each of them, special and individual attention.

[1] As a proper name "Satan" occurs for the first time in 1 Chron. xxi. 1.

CHAPTER XXXI

THE LAW

WE have seen that during the period of the Exile and immediately following upon the Return, the interest of the Jewish religious leaders was centred, first on the written Law, mainly the book of *Deuteronomy*; but it is highly probable that the Oral Law had already begun to take shape; secondly, on the Temple; and thirdly, on the Messianic Hope. These three—the Law, the Temple, and the Messianic Hope—are the foundations upon which the religious superstructure of post-exilic Judaism was built.

The clearest way in which to discern the steps in the development which now takes place will be to study the four following subjects, dealing with each separately, though, as is only to be expected, each will to some extent encroach upon the others. These subjects are : the Law, Wisdom, and Worship; and Apocalypse, to be considered later. Why Wisdom is assigned the second place will be explained when we come to deal with it. Worship will naturally include the subject of Pietism, and out of this there arises inevitably the problem of suffering; and the connexion between the Messianic Hope and all that is included under the term Apocalypse will become sufficiently clear when the latter is studied. For reasons which will be explained later, the Law and Wisdom are each dealt with under two periods.

The dating of the literature which comes into consideration offers considerable difficulties, for opinions differ regarding the dates of the books; for our purpose, however, precise dating is not a *sine qua non*; what is demanded is that the Biblical books, or parts of them, to be utilized shall belong to the period to be studied; and in regard to this there is a fairly general consensus of opinion.

We start with the Law. The first beginnings of what came to be the religion of the Law of post-exilic Judaism are to be sought in the time of the Josianic reform, when the book of *Deuteronomy* was adopted as that which gave the norm of religious observances and practice. From this time the religion of the Hebrews began to become the religion of a book.

The combination of the prophetic and priestly ideals characteristic of *Deuteronomy* is to be found in the teaching of Ezekiel; but the tendency for the priestly ideals to predominate began already during the Exile; and this, as we have seen, is emphasized by Haggai and Malachi, and to a somewhat less extent by Zechariah. The tendency becomes more pronounced in some parts of chapters lvi–lxvi of the book of *Isaiah*.

Very instructive are the two phrases with which these chapters begin : " Keep judgement," and " Do righteousness." The former means : Observe the Law; and it is interesting to note that in *Deutero-Isaiah* the corresponding phrase is : " Seek judgement " : the Hebrew word for " judgement " (*mishpat*) would be better rendered " justice " or " equity." When used with the verb " to keep " the meaning of *mishpat* undergoes a change, and connotes legal ordinances. The second term means : Do the righteousness of the Law. Thus the two terms are parallel, and they show that emphasis was laid on the observance of legal precepts. This is borne out and illustrated by much that is written in these chapters (Isa. lvi–lxvi) as well as elsewhere in the literature of this period. Thus, much stress is laid on observing the Sabbath, and this primarily in a negative direction, i.e. by not doing anything that might profane it : " Blessed is the man . . . that keepeth the Sabbath from profaning it " (Isa. lvi. 2; cp. ver. 6); this is more fully illustrated in Neh. xiii. 15–22, where Nehemiah takes drastic measures to prevent the Sabbath from being desecrated. The prominent place which Sabbath observance had now come to occupy may be seen further from, eg., Isa. lviii. 13, lxvi. 23; Neh. ix. 14, x. 33; and another indication of the importance of the Sabbath is to be gathered from the fact that a proper name, *Shabbethai*, is formed from it (Neh. viii. 7, xi. 16; Ezra x. 15). But it is in the Priestly Code, which belongs to this period, that the development of Sabbath observance is seen most clearly; in Exod. xxxi. 12–17, for example, it is to be observed as a " solemn rest," and " everyone that profaneth it shall be put to death."

Besides the stringent law regarding the Sabbath, a new

Y

importance is attached to the festivals and especially the new-moon festival, because all the other feasts were regulated by it; they are dealt with especially in Num. xxviii. 11–31.[1]

The law regarding sacrifices also underwent development during this period and what is most important here is the prominence of the element of atonement, owing to the deeper sense of sin, a result of prophetical teaching, and the experiences of the Exile.

One other matter, so far as the law regarding sacred observances was concerned, was the importance attached to the sacred dues; nowhere does this come out more clearly than in Mal. iii. 8–10 : " Will a man rob God ? Yet ye rob me. But ye say, Wherein have we robbed thee ? In tithes and offerings. Ye are cursed with a curse; for ye rob me, even this whole nation. Bring ye the whole tithe into the storehouse, that there may be meat in mine house . . ." (cp. Neh. x. 37, 38).

The development of the priesthood is seen primarily in two directions, the distinction between the Levites and the priests (Num. xvi. 10, 18–23), and the position of the High-priest, who tends to become a civil ruler as much as the holder of the chief sacred office.

All that has been said refers to specifically sacred matters; but the many ordinances in the Law dealing with other things show that it affected the people in multifarious ways in ordinary life.

It will be well now to consider quite briefly some of the effects which Legalism had on the religious life of the people.

That its observance was a source of joy to many a devout soul goes without saying; but a subtle danger lay in the fact that the diligent carrying out of legal precepts might have the effect of engendering self-righteousness, and of making a man think that because he kept the divine law, therefore God was, as it were, placed under the obligation of rewarding him for this. There is a passage, for example, in Ps. xix. 7–11 (8–12 in Hebrew), which, while showing how a godly man rejoiced in the Law, contains some thoughts which might easily suggest self-righteousness in the heart of one less spiritually-minded :

---

[1] Fasting came into prominence during this period; but with the exception of the Day of Atonement (Lev. xvi. 29–31), it is not dealt with in the Law.

The Law of Yahweh is perfect, restoring the soul :
The testimony of Yahweh is sure, making wise the simple.
The precepts of Yahweh are right, rejoicing the heart;
The commandment of Yahweh is pure, enlightening the eyes.
The fear of Yahweh is clean, enduring for ever;
The judgements of Yahweh are true, and righteous altogether.
More to be desired are they than gold, yea, than much fine gold;
Sweeter also than honey and the honeycomb.
Moreover by them is thy servant warned,
In keeping them there is great reward.

The psalmist is speaking of his personal experience in saying that the Law makes wise and enlightens the eyes, and though there is nothing to suggest that in his case this conviction engendered a sense of superiority, it cannot be denied that the danger of this was present, and might well manifest itself in the case of others, as indeed we know happened in course of time. So, too, in the matter of reward for keeping the ordinances of the Law; with the psalmist it is likely enough that all that was meant was delight in doing what was right, which is its own reward; but there are passages elsewhere which certainly express the feeling that he who keeps the Law has a claim on God to receive reward (see, e.g., Ps. cxix. 17, 22, 94, 121, 173); and there is plenty of evidence in later times to show that he who kept the Law felt that he had a right to expect reward from God.

The importance of this subject, in view of later developments of Judaism, justifies a further illustration, which may be seen in the contrasted points of view between *Deutero-Isaiah* and the later chapters of the book of *Isaiah* (lvi ff.), i.e. between the prophetic and the priestly ideals. Both these writers describe the means whereby the coming deliverance and salvation, upon which they both lay stress, is to be attained. In the former we have, for example in lv. 1, these words : " Ho, every one that thirsteth, come ye to the waters; and he that hath no money, come ye, buy and eat; yea, come; buy wine and milk without money and without price." Here, in figurative language, the people are bidden to take what is *freely* offered them, i.e. the blessings of the Messianic time. Simple acceptation is all that is required. In lvi. 1, on the other hand, the coming salvation must be *acquired* by the fulfilment of legal ordinances : " Observe (or, Keep) the Law," i.e. do what you ought to do in obeying legal ordinances, and thereby acquire, as of right, reward. It is not fanciful to see here the beginnings of what in later Judaism developed into the doctrine of works, i.e. that the works of the Law are meritorious and demand reward *per se*. The efficacy of works and the claim of reward for doing them are doctrines which appeal to men as being no more than what bare justice demands; and because that is true between man and man, it is also assumed to be true as between God and man. In later Judaism, where the doctrine of divine grace plays a relatively subordinate part, this doctrine of the merit of works and therefore the right to claim reward is naturally somewhat prominent. It is not contended that during the period with which we are dealing there was any formulated doctrine on this subject; but there are indications of the existence of the new trend of thought; they are but the beginnings from which, in course of time, large developments grew. It is for this reason that attention to the subject is drawn here; it will be more fully dealt with in Chapter XL, § 3.

CHAPTER XXXII

WISDOM

THE golden age of Hebrew Wisdom belongs to a later period (see below, Chapter XXXVI); but inasmuch as the roots of the Wisdom literature proper are to be discerned in much earlier days, it is well that something should be said on the subject here, especially as there are strong reasons for believing that the pursuit of Wisdom, in the Hebrew sense, occupied the minds of some of Israel's thinkers during the Persian period, the material of still earlier times being the basis of this. It is worthy of note that as early as the time of Jeremiah the " wise man," or *Chakam*, occupies a recognized position side by side with priest and prophet : " For the law shall not perish from the priest, nor counsel from the wise, nor the word from the prophet " (Jer. xviii. 18). Equally pointed is a passage in *Isaiah* where, because of the people's insincerity of worship, the prophet says : " The wisdom of their wise men shall perish, and the understanding of the prudent men shall be hid " (Isa. xxix. 14). So that it is evident that already in the eighth century B.C. the wise men were known as a class; and since they were also scribes,[1] there can be no doubt that they wrote down their wise sayings; in a word, Wisdom as part of Hebrew literature was in existence in the eighth century B.C., and therefore the supposition is a reasonable one that both during the Exile and the Persian period collections of wise sayings were being composed as well as collected, thus forming the basis for the future development of Wisdom writings to be discussed later.

The earlier Hebrew Wisdom literature was largely influenced by Egyptian and Babylonian thought; but, however great their indebtedness to external influences, the Hebrew Wisdom writers had an individuality of their own, and created a type of Wisdom literature distinct from that of any other nation. What is specifically Hebrew here is the religious connotation of Wisdom; not that

---

[1] For the proof of this, as well as for the pre-exilic Wisdom literature, see Oesterley, *The Book of Proverbs*, pp. 20–26, 68–73 (1929).

this is absent from Egyptian and Babylonian Wisdom writings,[1] but among the Hebrews it is the wholly predominating element.

In the Hebrew literature Wisdom is not used in the sense of pure knowledge; at first it meant the faculty of distinguishing between what was useful or the reverse, and between what was beneficent or harmful; but an ethical element soon entered in, and then it came to mean the faculty of distinguishing between what was good and what was bad. This faculty was, however, believed to be a divine gift; and to use this gift in the right way was to establish a true relationship between a man and his God. And since the faculty to distinguish between what was good and what was evil was a divine endowment, it followed that *every* form of Wisdom was from God. And, further, as in its widest sense Wisdom can be exhibited in a variety of ways—forethought, foresight, discernment, carefulness, skill, etc.—all of these were the gifts of God; and thus Wisdom in a religious sense was brought into the everyday affairs of men. But while there were many forms of Wisdom, the highest form, the zenith, was the fear of the Lord; hence the frequent phrase : " The fear of the Lord is the beginning (or zenith) of wisdom."

During the Exile the Jews were brought into close touch with Babylonian thought and culture, and the result of this is to be seen in the later literature. One example of this may be given as appropriate in the present connexion. According to the Babylonian cosmology, Wisdom dwelt in the depths of the sea with Ea, the creative deity. Apsu, " The Deep," is called the " house of Wisdom," because out of it came forth the wisdom of Ea and the word of Ea; one of the epithets applied to the god Ea is : " Lord of Wisdom." [2] The thought of Wisdom having been in existence before the Creation evidently influenced the later Jewish sage who wrote Prov. viii. 22, 23 :

> Yahweh begat me at the beginning of his ways (i.e. his acts of Creation),
> The first of his works, of old (he begat me); [3]
> I was set up from everlasting, from the beginning,
> Or ever the earth was.

[1] In the Egyptian Wisdom book, *The Teaching of Amen-em-ope*, for example, the religious element is very prominent.
[2] Jeremias, *Das Alte Testament im Lichte des alten Orients*, pp. 29, 80 (1904).
[3] For this rendering of the verse, see Oesterley, *Proverbs, in loc.*

and the idea of the deep being the original *habitat* of Wisdom seems to be reflected in Ps. xxxvi. 6 (7 in Hebrew) :

Thy judgements are (like) the great deep.[1]

where the Hebrew has for " the great deep " *Tehom Rabbah*, the ancient proper name for the ocean. Thus the Hebrew belief regarding the origin of Wisdom is, in all probability, from Babylonian thought.

It can be shown that of the various collections of wise sayings which have been incorporated in the book of *Proverbs*, some are pre-exilic, others are late post-exilic; [2] this being so, it is difficult to believe that between the dates, say 700 B.C. and 300, there should have been an entire suspension of the work of the Sages; [3] and therefore although one cannot definitely assert that any particular collection or collections in the book of *Proverbs* belong to the exilic or Persian period, yet the probabilities of the case point to this having been so. That the Sages, in their oral teachings as well as in their writings, did a great work in bringing religion into the everyday life of the people is certain; and this is the justification for the brief mention of the subject here.

[1] The content of this psalm, viz., the problem of the wicked in prosperity, shows that it is post-exilic.

[2] See Oesterley, *Proverbs*, pp. 20–26.

[3] The interest in Wisdom literature is illustrated by the fact that the Babylonian " Wisdom of Achikar " circulated in an Aramaic translation among the Jewish colonists in Elephantiné (middle of the fifth century B.C.).

CHAPTER XXXIII

GOD AND THE SOUL: WORSHIP; PIETISM

In dealing with this subject, which covers the whole area of devotional and practical religion, it is impossible to observe the bounds of any period; we shall therefore treat it as it is presented in the whole post-exilic period, referring also to earlier times where the consideration of a particular thought or practice is made clearer by referring to its earlier history. Some incursion into subjects already dealt with or which will come before us again later is inevitable; but it will be readily understood that the slight repetitions involved cannot well be avoided.

1. The Universality of Yahweh

No nation has ever undergone so striking a spiritual experience as that which befell Israel during the Exile. She had been brought up on the old territorial conception of religion, which confined a deity and his worship to a limited area, save and in so far as it might be formally transplanted with all the paraphernalia of the *cultus* to some other spot. She was steeped in the same kind of theology which made Naaman take with him two mule-loads of Yahweh's land in order that he might be able to worship Him; and though at different times and in different circles the home of Yahweh was assigned to various sites, it was generally felt that His dwelling was not far from the land of Israel, even though it might be in Sinai. Even that saint to whom we owe Ps. xlii–xliii [1] was not free from this idea. It is true that he feels terribly the disaster which has befallen his country, and the jeers of his captors, but the thought that overwhelms him is the conviction that in the land to which he is journeying through affliction and peril he will be separated from his God; [2] we may fairly assume

[1] The definite dating of psalms is always a matter of uncertainty, but this psalm (for the two are surely two parts of one whole) seems to have as its author one of the exiles carried away with Jehoiachin in 597.

[2] Ver. 6 (7 in Hebrew) shows that he has reached the northern part of the land, Mount Hermon, where the Jordan rises, hence "the land of Jordan." That the psalm cannot belong to the Exile itself is clear from xliii. 3, 4, i.e. the Temple is still standing; it was not destroyed until 586.

that he did not stand alone. The testimony of Jeremiah may be cited to prove that some at least of the exiles of the 597 deportation were men of deep religious faith, who sympathized with the prophetic ideals (cp. Jer. xxiv). But these men of faithful soul went into Mesopotamia believing that they had left Yahweh behind them. Their great discovery was to be that they were mistaken. They had not left Yahweh behind them; He was with them in Babylonia.

There may have been several causes which contributed to this conclusion, and probably it did not come home to exiled Israel at once. We may conjecture that the most powerful influence was the continuance of prophecy among the deported Judeans. The belief of Israel, however, went farther than this. It is quite possible to hold that a god may manifest himself in more than one spot, even though the sites of his revelation may be as distant as Palestine and Mesopotamia, and still to admit the existence of other deities valid enough for other nations and races.

But this new discovery, that Yahweh had not been left behind, was reinforced by much of the teaching of the pre-exilic prophets. They had held that Yahweh was the Lord of the physical universe, the Lord of all human history, the Lord of universal morality.[1] The final conclusion of such doctrines could be nothing but an absolute monotheism. Yet men are very slow to realize the implications of their own beliefs, and but for the experience of the Exile, Israel might have postponed the final step for some centuries. The speed with which great souls among them attained a monotheistic conclusion (and a couple of centuries is a very short time in which to develop a wholly new idea such as this) was in part due to the circumstances of the fall of the Chaldæan empire. The gods and goddesses of Babylonia were powerless to control or to foresee events; the God of Israel could predict them because he ordained them. We must not suppose that ancient Mesopotamia actually worshipped objects of wood, stone, or metal, in the sense that they attributed to the material things a personal divinity; such a belief would be pure animism. They did believe, however, that these things had some special connexion with the great deities, and truly represented their presence. Men believed that the image was, in a certain sense, the portable home of Ishtar or of Marduk

[1] See Part II, Chapter XIX.

or of Nebo. What the Israelite prophet realized by the
end of the Exile was that there was no personal, spiritual
reality behind these objects. The great gods simply did
not exist, they were nothing beyond the images (cp. Isa.
xliv. 9, 18); there was only one living and true God,
Maker of heaven and earth, and Lord of all things—Yahweh,
the God of Israel.

2. THE WORSHIP OF ISRAEL

In pre-exilic Israel worship was limited to certain spots.
The old patriarchal stories spoke of Abraham as " calling
upon the name of Yahweh," and made special mention
of the place where this was done. Thus, we have in Gen.
xiii. 4 one account of the origin of the sanctuary at Bethel;
at other spots also Yahweh appeared to him, in consequence
of which he built an altar and offered sacrifice. But it
would seem that even the patriarchs could enter into
communion with their God only where He chose to meet
with them; and throughout the earlier history of Israel,
that is, until the recognition of the great sanctuaries such
as Jerusalem and Bethel, we have occasional theophanies
which testified to the fact that worship might be offered
in the place where they occurred. Originally, no doubt,
these places had been consecrated to different *numina*;
probably early tradition located different " *'Els* " at Bethel,
Peniel, 'El-lahai-Roi,[1] etc., but in process of time Yahweh
alone was accepted, and all local objects of worship were
absorbed into His own *cultus*.

This still left a large number of sanctuaries, and it is
unlikely that any Israelite in the cultivated portions of
the country had very far to go to find a place of sacrifice.

But the reform of Josiah concentrated sacrifice in Jerusalem, and made its temple the one spot where worship
could be duly paid. For it must be remembered that,
to the ancient world, worship always meant sacrifice.
Prayer was, of course, employed, but it was normally an
accompaniment of sacrifice. We hear, it is true, in the
patriarchal traditions and elsewhere of prayer being offered
where sacrifice is not mentioned; but it was generally
before the altar that men made their requests to God.
Had Israel been confined to the older methods and ideas
of communion with God, even the evidence of His presence
in Babylonia would have helped them little unless they had

[1] See Part I, Chapters IV, V.

been free to do as the Egyptian Jews of the fifth century did, and build a temple where they could offer sacrifice with their prayer.

It was but a single generation that could have lived under the *régime* inaugurated by Josiah, yet the time seems to have been long enough at least to suggest the possibility of worship apart from the Temple. For it was obviously impossible for people living in distant parts of the country to appear as regularly at Jerusalem as they had done at the old local shrines. Indeed, in the Deuteronomic law itself provision was made for this in more than one way,[1] for its promoters clearly recognized that a fundamental change in outlook was involved in the centralization of sacrifice. In particular the ritual provisions of *Deuteronomy* permitted the eating of domestic animals apart from sacrifice. Hitherto every meal of meat had been, as it were, a " communion service "; it was now transferred from the sphere of religion to that of secular life (Deut. xii. 20-28).

Here, then, we have a significant illustration of the great change which necessarily took place with the reforms of Josiah, though it is but one symptom of a modification which must have made itself felt in every department of life. In the old days the line between secular and sacred was closely drawn, it is true, but almost every act of man's life had its cultural affiliations. Now, with the sanctuary far away, the religious aspect but seldom obtruded itself on men's consciousness. Attendance at the three great festivals was still enjoined, but even if this prescription were rigorously enforced, many Israelites would necessarily spend months together without any religious exercise apart from the weekly abstention from labour on the Sabbath.

No religion can live on a negation, and those to whom active observances of some kind were a necessity of the religious life were compelled to find their exercise in new ways. Here the experience of the Exile was of profound value. Even if sacrifice could not be offered, prayer was possible to a God who was really everywhere. The sense of the universality of Yahweh alone made it possible for any Jewish religion to continue in Mesopotamia; and, comparatively scanty as it was, the exiles clung to it with determination.

[1] Cf. p. 255.

It must be at once admitted that evidence for the growth of details in the new form of worship which Israel developed is greatly lacking. It is not till the beginning of the fourth century that we find anything like an organized *cultus* accepted; but then, in Ezra, we have the traditional founder of synagogue-worship. Yet it must surely be clear that he, in so far as he may have organized the worship of the community, was relying on tendencies and practices which came into being before his time. Of these the most important was the Law; in its general aspect this has already been dealt with (Chapter XXXI); but it is necessary to call attention to it here in order to emphasize the unique place which it took in the worship of Israel.

The Law lay at the heart of all the thinking of the later Judaism, and in a very real sense the worship of the synagogue was, and is, the cult of the Law. There were, of course, other elements; prayers were recited and hymns were sung, and instruction of various kinds was given both to children and to adults; but the centre of the whole was the reading of the Law, followed by exposition and comments from those best able to expound and apply it. There grew up thus a class of men whose whole time was given to its study, those to whom the name of "Scribes" is especially applied in New Testament times. While the official religion of Israel centred in the Temple with its sacrificial system (see next section), it was the Law which formed the basis of worship for the average Israelite, and constituted his weekly, even his daily, study.

The practical value of this element in worship is too obvious to need special emphasis. The time was to come when Israel was to lose all the external paraphernalia of worship, when her Temple was to be destroyed, and sacrifice was to cease. But for the Law her faith and her nationality would have perished; but for the Synagogue her religion would have ceased to be. These were things which she had already carried wherever she had gone. In every city where the Jew was established there was at least a "place of prayer"; and the larger cities contained synagogues. In Palestine itself there were many such institutions which survived the destruction of the Temple, and such a form of worship as this could be destroyed only with the extermination of the Jewish race.

As compared and contrasted with all other faiths in which the element of ritual is strong, Judaism offered, and offers, a standing protest against materialism in religion. There is room, no doubt, for that form of misguided worship which we call bibliolatry, but its temptations are less subtle and pressing, less general in their application, than those of any other form of the cult of a material thing. The worship of the Synagogue, followed in this respect by that of the Christian Church, stands as a testimony to the pure spirituality of true religion, and echoes that greatest of all sayings on the subject of the human approach to God : " God is a Spirit, and they that worship Him must worship Him in spirit and in truth " (John iv. 24).

3. THE DEVELOPMENT OF THE SACRIFICIAL SYSTEM

But side by side with this gradually developing spiritual worship there was the official religion which centred in the Temple with its sacrificial system. It is therefore necessary that something should be said about the development of this which took place after the Exile.

That the reason for this development was the growth of a deeper sense of sin is evident from the type of sacrifices, as will be seen presently. If it be asked why the realization of sin should have been one of the results of the Exile, the answer is that it was due to several factors; thus, the teaching of both Ezekiel and Deutero-Isaiah on the transcendental character of God, with the inevitable recognition of the insignificance of man in His sight must have generated the sense of unworthiness. Then, again, is it not natural to believe that the exaltation of the divine Law with its ever-increasing demands tended to make many feel their inability to fulfil its requirements adequately ? In later times, it is true, the observance of legal precepts had just the contrary effect and occasioned spiritual pride; but at first this was not so; the spirit engendered was rather that illustrated by Neh. viii. 9, where it is said that " the people wept when they heard the words of the Law."

But, above all, it was the fact of the Exile itself which contributed to a deepened sense of sin; for the spectacle of the exiles, representing the whole nation, banished from the centre of their worship, was the most signal mark of divine disfavour, which could only be explained by the recognition of national sin; and this, we can well understand, would be retrospective.

In any case, whatever the causes, the fact is quite obvious that during the post-exilic period a deeper sense of sin prevailed. And nothing witnesses to this so clearly as the development of the sacrificial system. Thus, we have, to begin with, two types of sacrifice, the " guilt-offering," called *'asham*, and the " sin-offering," called *chattath*; both terms are pre-exilic, and their earlier connotation is that of compensation for injury (e.g., 2 Kings xii. 17, in E.V. 16); but as applied to animal victims presented on the altar they occur only in exilic and post-exilic literature.[1] It is not always easy to see what the difference between the two offerings was; but regarding the guilt- or trespass-offering (*'asham*) the ideas seems to have been that the guilt incurred through a trespass was atoned for by it, and it was offered concurrently with the restoration of something to a fellowman; while the " sin-offering " (*chattath*) was thought of as a means of the removal of sin. In both the idea of expiation is suggested.

Then we have the Incense-offering spoken of in the Priestly Code (Exod. xxx. 34–8); this is never referred to. by Ezekiel, and though there is a reference to it in Jer. vi. 20, xli. 5, he evidently regards it as a foreign custom; otherwise it is not mentioned in pre-exilic literature; it must therefore be regarded as specifically post-exilic. Whatever symbolic significance this may have come to have (see Ps. cxli. 2; Rev. v. 8, viii. 3, 4), its original intention is perhaps to be sought in the parallel of the ascending smoke of the burnt-offering, though the sweet smell would, no doubt, have been thought of as in some sense pleasing to the deity.

Of special importance was the *Tamid*; this was the daily morning and evening burnt-offering (Num. xxviii. 3–8; Exod. xxix. 38–42), which was a development of the pre-exilic morning burnt-offering and evening meal-offering (2 Kings xvi. 15). In its developed form its importance was emphasized by having the meal-offering and a wine-offering as its adjuncts (Num. xv. 4, 5). The continuous burning of the altar-fire was a result of this twofold daily burnt-offering, and it is not improbable that the idea of the fire being never quenched was due to Persian influence. The term *Tamid* means " continuous " here [2] (cp. Num. xxviii. 3, " a continual burnt-offering "); the abbreviated

---

[1] That in Hos. iv. 8 *chattath* does not mean " sin-offering," but simply " sin," is clear from the parallel word "iniquity," which occurs in the second strophe of the verse.

[2] The adverbial use is earlier and more frequent.

form, "the *Tamid*," in reference to this sacrifice belongs to later usage, and occurs first in Dan. viii. 11–14, xi. 31, xii. 11.[1] It came to occupy the central position of the Temple *cultus*; the feelings aroused by its cessation in the reign of Antiochus Epiphanes can be seen from the *Daniel* passages referred to.

Of less importance, but worth a passing mention, were the libations; wine has taken the place of water in the Priestly Code (Exod. xxix. 40), and both wine and oil offerings have lost their independent character, and are only used as accompaniments to the more important sacrifices.

In regard to all the sacrifices the ritual tends to become more elaborate (as an example see Lev. iv. 15–21 in connexion with the *chattath*); and their main object centres in their atoning efficacy, thus they were means of becoming reconciled to God. *All* sacrifices, whether bloodless or bloody, effect reconciliation (cp. Ezek. xlv. 15, 17); i.e. they are the means of obtaining divine forgiveness. The term *le-kapper*,[2] "to effect atonement," expresses the basic idea, and the sin-cleansing power of blood becomes very marked (see, e.g., Lev. iv. 5, 7, 16–18). It is nowhere explained why blood should atone for sin; it was a divine ordinance, and that sufficed. When, in Lev. xvii. 11, the expiatory efficacy of blood is ascribed to the "life" that is in it, this is no explanation, but only the expression of an accepted fact. To discuss the reason or reasons why blood should have been thought of as of atoning efficacy would take us too far afield; it must suffice to say that, like so many religious ideas, there is a long history behind it.

The idea reached the zenith of its expression in the institution of the Day of Atonement (Lev. xvi); [3] its object is stated clearly enough in Lev. xvi. 33, where it is said that the priest shall " make atonement for the holy sanctuary, and he shall make atonement for the tent of meeting and for the altar; and he shall make atonement for the priests and for all the people of the assembly." It was thus an annual complete atonement for all sin; whatever sin had been unatoned for during the past year, or whatever sin had been unconsciously committed, or forgotten, all were atoned for

---

[1] The R.V. renders "the continual burnt-offering," but in the original it is a proper name, "The *Tamid*."

[2] The noun *kappara* is post-biblical.

[3] For an admirable and convincing presentation of the reasons why the Day of Atonement must have been instituted in post-exilic times, see Kennett, *Old Testament Essays*, pp. 105–118 (1928).

on this great day; it gave assurance of reconciliation with God, and of a renewed right relationship with Him.

A word must here be added regarding the thought of some of those deeply spiritual minds which contemplated the entire absence of sacrifices in worship. It is possible, however, that in regard to some of the earlier pre-exilic passages which have been sometimes held to advocate the abolition of sacrifices, there has been something of an overstatement of the case. For example, the passage Amos v. 21–5 is sometimes interpreted in the sense that the prophet was advocating the abrogation of the whole sacrificial system as it existed in his day; this passage runs: "I hate, I despise your feasts, I will take no delight in your solemn assemblies; for though ye bring me burnt-offerings— [1], and your meal-offerings, I will not accept, neither will I regard the peace-offerings of your fat beasts. . . . Did ye bring unto me sacrifices and offerings in the wilderness forty years, O house of Israel?"

These words were a rebuke against a developed form of sacrificial worship which had become debased through contact with Canaanite religion; but that Amos contemplated the entire abrogation of the sacrificial system at the time at which he lived, i.e. before, as yet, prophetical teaching had had time to make itself widely felt, is difficult to believe; for one thing, he must have known that during the nomadic period of the wanderings in the wilderness sacrifices were offered (see above, Part II, Chapter XX, § 3), though not of the agricultural type to which he refers; moreover, what would he, as one who faced realities and knew that the people were not yet capable of offering purely spiritual worship, have suggested as a substitute if *all* sacrifices were to be abolished? Or again, when it is said in Isa. i. 10–17, "To what purpose is the multitude of your sacrifices unto me? saith Yahweh . . .," the denunciation is not against the sacrificial system, as such, but against the particular sacrifices of those to whom the words were addressed; evil living made insincere worship. Had the lives of the worshippers been in accordance with the teaching of the prophets, his words would not have been necessary.

Not until there was some definite form of worship to take the place of the sacrificial system would its needlessness, and therefore its entire abolition, be contemplated; and this was not the case until the Exile had taught the

---

[1] Something has fallen out of the Hebrew text here.

possibility of a purely spiritual worship. Then the thoughts expressed in such passages as Mic. vi. 6–8, generally acknowledged to be a late passage, and Ps. l. 8–15, became very significant, and show the exalted trend of thought among Israel's most spiritual teachers. But this by the way.

The impression gained that there *was* a certain element of mechanical religion in connexion with the sacrificial system is balanced by reading the psalms of the post-exilic period. It is not to be expected that in what is somewhat of the nature of a legal code, i.e. the P document, a true insight into the mind and emotions of the worshippers is to be gained; for this, in addition to the psalms mentioned, one must look to the best religious instincts of the people as handed down and embodied in the writings of the later Rabbis. No greater wrong has been done to the religion of the later Judaism than the ignoring of their teaching on sin and atonement, as it appears in the earliest years of the Christian era, but which reflects earlier teaching. The difficulty here has been that this teaching is largely obscured by a mass of other material in Rabbinical writings. This has, however, now been remedied, and in a recently published volume, *Studies in Sin and Atonement in the Rabbinic Literature of the First Century* (1928), Dr. A. Büchler has provided us with all that can be desired to gain a clear and unbiased estimate of what Judaism teaches on these important subjects. We cannot do better than close this section with some words from the Introduction to this work : " The extent to which the relation of the Jew to his fellow-man and the social duties generally expressed themselves in obedience to the Torah or in sin, and how far they influenced Rabbinic ethical legislation and determined its standard, can be learned from the relevant statements and the decrees of the Rabbinic authorities of the first century. . . . The actual practice of sacrificial atonement for social sins as recorded in the Rabbinic literature, and the religious conception of atoning sacrifices, the preliminary essential acts of repentence, restitution, conciliation, and confession preceding the sin offering, and their religious and moral values, give insight into the Rabbinic concepts of sin and sacrificial atonement."

4. GOD AND THE INDIVIDUAL

The religion of the ancient world was primarily concerned with communities rather than with individuals; and this

z

is true of the religion of Israel. But with Jeremiah, as
we have already seen,[1] the individual human being begins
to take on a new importance. The community as a whole
is still, of course, the more prominent; but one man may
reach God apart from his fellows; he is no longer dependent
on or wholly linked up with the community in his dealings
with Him whom he worships. This has a double aspect.
In the first place, Yahweh may come into contact with and
control the religious experience of a man by himself. In
Jeremiah's struggles there is no thought of Israel as a whole;
the rest of the world seems shut out, and the man stands
alone with his God. But on the other side we have the
doctrine of individual responsibility. It is this latter which
is especially emphasized by Ezekiel. Indeed, Ezek. xviii
might almost be a commentary on Jer. xxxi. 29, 30. And
to Ezekiel this teaching was fundamental. He held to a
rigid theory of divine retribution, and while we may feel
that the picture he draws of Yahweh is harsh, inhuman,
and mechanical, we must admit that he fully realized the
truth that " whatsoever a man soweth, that shall he also
reap."

On the old " communal " view of religion, insisting as
it did on the absolute solidarity of the race, the sins of the
generation which preceded the Exile could be met only
by the complete destruction of the whole nation; but
Ezekiel, following Isaiah here, could not believe that
Yahweh would destroy the people who represented Him
to the world, and thus believed profoundly in their ultimate
restoration. A new start was possible, and was possible
only because with the destruction of the actual sinners
the sin was wiped out. Each generation, each individual,
could begin life afresh, and could lay the foundations of a
new order, in which Israel could achieve the great purpose
for which she had been chosen and maintained in the world :
the proclamation of Yahweh as the Lord of all mankind.

The old view did not die; there was too much truth
in it. It has always lived on, although some forms of
Judaism, and of its daughter faith, Christianity, have
tended to obscure or even to lose sight of it. Yet it maintains itself in such great utterances as the Pauline : " No
man liveth unto himself "; " Ye are members one of
another "; and the more complicated human society
grows, the more obvious does the truth become. But the

[1] Chapter XXIII, § 2.

other aspect, the importance of the individual in religion and in human life, received, and must continue to receive, due attention, and is unmistakably in evidence in the history of post-exilic Jewish thought.

It is, above all, in the *Psalms* that we naturally look for at least one element in this new doctrine. Opinions as to the dating of the *Psalms* have undergone considerable changes in the twentieth century, and most scholars to-day would attribute a much larger number of the psalms to the pre-exilic period than did their predecessors. Many of these have the appearance of being the utterance of individual souls, the plea of the oppressed righteous against the wicked oppressor, the cry of the victim for vengeance on the tyrant. Yet the view is rapidly gaining ground that where such "individualistic" psalms are to be assigned to the pre-exilic age, they either present the community under the guise of an individual, or they form part of the regular ritual carried out in certain forms of legal process whereby Yahweh was invoked.

In other psalms, however, we may assert without possibility of error that we have the cry of a single person. Some of these are among the richest literary fruits of men's spiritual experience, and are as valid for us to-day as when they were first penned. One feature of these expressions of the inner life of men is that they are dateless, meeting the needs of saints and sinners in all ages and of all races. Among such psalms we may instance xi, xxiii, xxv, li, and many others.

THE GREEK PERIOD

CHAPTER XXXIV

THE INFLUENCE OF HELLENISM ON THE JEWS

THE Greek period may be reckoned as beginning about 300 B.C. and lasting to the time when the power of Rome began to extend its influence eastwards, i.e. until about 100 B.C.[1]

After the death of Alexander in 323 B.C., a period of great turmoil followed, during which his leading generals fought among themselves, each trying to secure some portion of the dismembered empire for himself. The battle of Ipsus, 301 B.C., was, for the time being, decisive; a settlement was reached, the empire of Alexander being divided as follows: Lysimachus ruled in Asia Minor, Demetrius Poliorketes in Greece, Seleucus in Syria and farther eastward, and Ptolemy in Egypt; to the kingdom of the latter belonged also Jerusalem and the southern part of Palestine. We are concerned here with the last two only.

Alexander's ideal had been to create a world-empire which should be not only a political unity but the component parts of which should be welded together by the unifying influence of Greek culture.

One of the most potent means whereby this was achieved was by founding cities on the Greek model and peopling them with Greeks, and in the case of already existing cities by forcing them to adopt the pattern of the Greek city-state, i.e. the city was governed by a council (*Boulé*), elected annually by the people, instead of the earlier senate (*Gerousia*), which consisted of representatives of the aristocracy.

The successors of Alexander were his zealous imitators in this, and a great part of the East was soon dotted with numerous centres from which Hellenic culture, language,

---

[1] Not that Greek influence ceased at this date; but at its best it was during the period indicated that Hellenic influence was exercised.

and customs radiated. Palestine was included in this; among the Hellenized cities here may be mentioned Joppa, Gaza, Askelon, Dora, Apollonia, Ptolemais, and Scythopolis, on the west of Jordan; and Hippus, Gadara, Pella, Dium, and Philadelphia, on the east of Jordan, and others.

Judæa, being thus surrounded by a network of Greek cities, could not fail to be influenced by the Greek spirit, and it must have been at work for some time previously when we find that early in the second century B.C. both the leaders and a large section of the people were eager to welcome Greek customs; thus, in 1 Macc. i. 11–15 it is said: " In those days came there forth out of Israel transgressors of the law, and persuaded many, saying, Let us go and make a covenant with the Gentiles that are round about us; for since we were parted from them many evils have befallen us. And the saying was good in their eyes. And certain of the people were forward herein, and went to the king, and he gave them licence to do after the ordinances of the Gentiles. And they built a place of exercise in Jerusalem according to the laws of the Gentiles; and they made themselves uncircumcized, and forsook the holy covenant, and joined themselves to the Gentiles, and sold themselves to do evil." It should be noted here that the words, " since we were parted from them," whatever it may be to which reference is made, point to the fact of still earlier contact with and influence of Hellenism on the part of one section of the Jews of Jerusalem.

It is important, further, to note that in this passage, which is a crucial one, there is, with the exception of the mention of the Abrahamic rite, no reference to religion. These words were written at the very least fifty to sixty years later than the beginning of the reign of Antiochus Epiphanes, when the champions of orthodoxy and the Law had won the day, and when everything contrary to the Law, or what was considered as contrary to the Law, would have been emphasized; but in spite of this, with the exception mentioned, there is no question of Hellenic influences having affected the religion of the Jews. This point needs emphasis.

By the end of the fourth century B.C. Greek thought was not what it had been a century earlier; it was not the spirit of the culture of Athens of the fifth century that influenced the Oriental world of the third and following century; by this time the enlightenment of those earlier days had resulted in the decay of the popular religion and the sovereignty of Individualism and Intellectualism of which the ultimate outcome was Scepticism and Positivism. " There remained a civilization dominated by art and science; this alone, and not the spirit of ancient Greek culture is what permeated the East from the time of Alexander . . . the Forum, the theatre, the gymnasium, the public baths, were built in the Greek architectural style; the cities received their democratic constitution; commerce and the army, bibliography and art, brought various loan-words into the Oriental languages. At the most all this affected merely the surface of things. Of a deeper spiritual Hellenic influence during the third and second centuries on the educated classes there can be no question, let alone the bulk of the people." [1]

This being so, we must realize that that considerable section of the Jews which was attracted by Hellenism, such as it now was, did not become renegades to their own religion because they were offered what they conceived to be a more enlightened religion, but, firstly, because the external allurements of Greek civilization fascinated them, and secondly, because political considerations made it worth their while. They did not accept a new religion; they merely became atheists. This explains the fact that in spite of Greek environment, in spite of their being the subjects of an alien Greek sovereign, in spite of the influence of the Greek language, Greek ways of thought, Greek customs, etc., the *religion* of the Jews remained quite unaffected by Greek ideas or Greek philosophy.[2] Upon the Jews themselves there is no doubt that Hellenism had effects in a large variety of ways, especially upon the Jews of the Dispersion, as witness, e.g., the existence of the Greek Old Testament, necessitated by the fact that the Jews outside Palestine could understand

[1] Hölscher, *Geschichte der israelitischen und jüdischen Religion*, p. 163 (1922).

[2] The conception of Wisdom personified is no doubt in part due to the influence of Greek thought, but that approximates to philosophy rather than to religion; see, further, below, p. 340; and in any case such a book as *The Wisdom of Solomon*, like *Ecclesiastes*, only represents individual thought, not that of any large section of the Jews. Doubtless, one can point to Philo, on whom Greek philosophy, methods of thought, and general world-outlook exercised a profound influence; but Philo was very exceptional. It is difficult to believe that many Jews, even of the Dispersion, were similarly influenced; for had that been the case would not some more manifest signs of it have been preserved? Philo's guiding principle, the essence of his intellectual and religious thought, was the contrast between the spiritual and the material; but could this be said to be characteristic of orthodox Judaism of the last century B.C. and the first century A.D.?

their Scriptures in no other language; but in whatever directions this influence manifested itself orthodox Judaism as it existed during the Greek period, and as it has existed ever since, was unaffected.

Schürer believes that the influence of the Greek spirit was so strong among the Jews of Judæa by the beginning of the second century B.C. that had the process of Hellenization been allowed to continue, without the drastic intervention of Antiochus Epiphanes, the Judaism of Palestine would presumably, in course of time, have assumed a form in which it would have been no more recognizable, a form much more syncretistic than that of a Philo.[1] We believe this estimate to be erroneous; for even the Jews of the Dispersion, living in the midst of Greek influences of every conceivable kind, without the hold that Jerusalem and the Temple would naturally have upon those within their sphere —even those Jews of the Dispersion as a whole remained loyal to the religion of their fathers.

[1] *Geschichte des Jüdischen Volkes*, i. 189 f.

CHAPTER XXXV

THE PROBLEM OF SUFFERING

LIKE every new truth, the doctrine of individualism brought new problems with it. Chief of these was the problem of suffering, which, though not created by the teaching of Jeremiah and Ezekiel, was yet terribly reinforced thereby; and it has troubled the mind of man without intermission from the last days of the kingdom of Judah. We are forced to admit that, though we may have light on the problem, and though for many its pressure is no longer crushing, we have as yet found no answer which we can regard as finally valid and satisfying to the human mind. Nevertheless, even if a conclusive answer to the great question has not been suggested, by grappling with it much light has been thrown on the relation between man and God; and this we must briefly trace out.

1. THE PROBLEM INTENSIFIED BY PROPHETIC TEACHING

An earlier age might have thought of the distribution of good and of ill as due to the divine whim, irrespective of the character of the recipient. But from the day when Amos first proclaimed the double doctrine of the righteousness of Yahweh and His supremacy, such a view became impossible. The pre-exilic prophets taught of Yahweh as one who was perfectly just, and at the same time ruled the universe alike of nature and of man. It would seem to follow from these premisses that goodness would always be rewarded with earthly prosperity, and that sin must be punished with material disaster.

Men are slow to realize the results of their own thinking. A century and a half after the days of Amos, Habakkuk asked the age-long question: " Thou that art of purer eyes than to behold evil, and that canst not look on perverseness, wherefore lookest thou upon them that deal treacherously, and holdest thy peace when the wicked swalloweth up the man that is more righteous than he ? " (Hab. i. 13). Such a question could not have arisen save on the basis of the teaching of the eighth-century prophets. The fact of the inequalities of life was always obvious; the problem arose when the fact had to be reconciled with the doctrine of divine justice. So that when once that doctrine had been accepted Habakkuk's question became inevitable.[1]

In so far as he himself attempted a solution, it was expressed in the obscure phrase : "The just shall live in his faithfulness" (see the R.V. marg. of Hab. ii. 4). The prophet's meaning cannot be said to be clear; most probably it suggests that virtue is its own reward, and that a man who really is faithful can have no higher gift or benefit bestowed on him. Goodness is so good that it cannot be recompensed save by itself; sin is so terrible that no punishment can be adequate. But even if this be the prophet's meaning, which is by no means certain, it is not an answer which will satisfy everyone.

Jeremiah was faced with the same question, but he found no answer at all.

It was, naturally enough, in exilic and post-exilic times that the pressure of the question became most severe. It was handled by such writers as the author of Ps. xxxvii, who reached the conclusion that the adversity of the righteous, and the prosperity of the wicked are alike evanescent, and that before death each will reap the due reward of his deeds. This became, in fact, the orthodox view of post-exilic Judaism, in spite of numerous apparent exceptions. Where it did not fit the obvious facts, it was assumed that the sufferer who seemed to be righteous was in reality guilty of some terrible secret sin for which he was being punished by Yahweh, and thus to disaster was added the cruel and doubtless often unjustified suspicion of wickedness.

2. THE "SERVANT SONGS"

A real advance in the thought about this problem was contributed by the thinker and writer to whom we owe the so-called "Servant Songs" embedded in Isa. xl–lv. In the best known of these, lii. 13–liii. 12, we have a picture of the final calamities which overwhelm the faithful "slave of Yahweh." This is no place to discuss the authorship or the original application of this and its companion passages. It would seem, however, that no one individual sat for the

[1] Cp. pp. 265 f.

ideal portrait, but that the writer draws on the experiences of at least two different men.[1] The Servant is one who suffers from physical pain, " a man of pains, and known unto sickness." For this or for some other reason his face is veiled, " as one who hid his face from us, he was despised." [2] In the terrible word " stricken " the truth is brought home; the man is a leper. But in some strange way his sufferings are redemptive for others, and bring to those who survive him forgiveness and peace. They, however, do not understand until it is too late, and the Servant has to endure persecution, a false charge, a tyrannical sentence, and a criminal's death and burial. It is a dark picture, yet there are moments of vision when he realizes the meaning of his own agony : " away out of the agony of his soul shall he look, and shall be satisfied by his knowledge." [3]

It is here that we have light on the problem immediately before us. For a man who has fully and perfectly surrendered himself to the will of his Master, Yahweh, for a man who knows to the uttermost the meaning of self-denial, it is enough to understand that his own suffering will win something of incalculable value for others,—he is " satisfied by his knowledge." He who has really " poured out his soul unto death " will not seek or demand reward for himself, for in the certainty that others are blessed through his pain he finds his heart's desire.

Such a solution may be satisfactory for the sufferer himself, if he be fully surrendered, but to the more contemplative mind it fails to justify God. The man himself may have no complaint to make, but is it fair that Yahweh should make the agony of one person the indispensable condition of the happiness of another ? Abstract justice would seem to require that pain and pleasure should at least balance one another in the experience of one and the same individual; absolute equity might conceivably accept an atonement vicariously offered, but it could hardly demand it, still less assume that this was to be the normal means whereby the sinner should be restored.

---

[1] The difference of view taken by my collaborator in Chapter XXVIII and my own here does not affect the teaching of the Song, which is our main present concern. It will be well to compare what is said there with what is written here; for taking our respective views as a whole they are complementary rather than opposed (T. H. R.).

[2] This rendering involves a very slight change in the vocalization of the Hebrew, the omission of a single dot, reading *mastir* for *master*.

[3] So, probably, liii. 11a should be rendered.

3. THE BOOK OF JOB

It is in the book of *Job* that we find the most thorough, frank, and honest discussion which the subject has ever received. This is not the place in which to enlarge upon the qualities of a book which may reasonably claim to be the finest piece of literature that the world has yet seen. Its central problem is the question which we now have under consideration, the problem of suffering in relation to the goodness and the omnipotence of God.

The poet had before him an old story, told in prose, of the sufferings which befell Job, of his patience under his afflictions, of his conversation with his friends, and of his final restoration. The beginning and end of this he has taken for his own purposes, accepting as the basis of his discussion the account of the successive misfortunes which fell on the hero, and accepting, too, the view that in the first instance they were due to the jealous zeal of Satan, the official Accuser-General attached to the divine court. But instead of retaining the central portion of the narrative he has inserted his own poem, placing himself in the position of Job, and speaking through his mouth.

The poem is a record of the conflict between the old orthodoxy and the relentless quest for truth. The former is represented by the three friends, the latter by Job. Eliphaz, Bildad, and Zophar all accept the current view, which we have noted as being that of Ps. xxxvii, namely, that all suffering is punishment for sin, and that a man's misfortunes prove that he must have done wrong in the sight of God. They therefore urge Job to confess and repent, and promise him that if he does so, he will be restored to his former prosperity. While the three friends are skilfully differentiated, they all present the same general point of view; and when this has once been stated in the first speech of Eliphaz, no further advance whatever is made by any of them. Each speaks in turn, and there are three series of speeches. In our present text there are only two speeches in the third series, Zophar remaining silent; but it is probable that this is due to textual corruption, and that part, at any rate, of Zophar's third speech is now included in one of Job's.

Job opens the debate, and speaks after each of his friends, appealing in the last speech to God to appear and justify His actions. A fifth character is introduced, Elihu by name, but there are good reasons for believing that his speeches, which are neither answered nor noticed by Job, are the insertion of a later poet, who was not satisfied with the book as it stood. Finally, in answer to Job's appeal, God appears, and by His words reduces Job to humble submission to the divine will.

The heart of the book lies in the progress of Job's thought as he struggles for a solution of his difficulties. He has two problems, distinct, yet closely interrelated. The first is that of God's own attitude towards himself, and he has to find out for himself whether God is his friend or his enemy, for him or against him. The second is the wider, more general question of the justice to be found in the Divine government of the universe as a whole, and of human life in particular. The answer to the first will be a personal faith, the solution of the second will be a theodicy. The consummate art of the poet is nowhere better illustrated than in the fact that while the friends never make the slightest movement from the position they have originally taken up, the advance Job makes is from time to time based on remarks that have fallen from them.

Job's first speech in chapter iii is simply a cry of pain. Would that he had never been born! If he must be born, would that he had perished at once and never reached years of self-consciousness! If he must live his life and suffer, would that he could die now and end his pain! In all this there is no *problem*; there is intense suffering, but no real question as to his relation with God. Eliphaz replies, however, that God must be punishing him for some secret sin, and that if he will but humble himself and repent, all will yet be well. The effect on Job is to raise the problem of his relations with God. He knows that he has not sinned in such measure as to deserve what he endures, and he will not confess to crimes which he has not committed. It must be an arbitrary love of torture, or hatred of the victim, which rouses God to inflict such agony on His creature. Can God not leave Job alone for a moment? He is doomed to die, but—and here we have the first faint glimmering of a ray of light—God will realize His mistake, and will seek for His servant, only to find that it is too late : Job will have passed out of God's reach into *She'ol*.

Bildad reminds Job that God is righteous, and raises a new train of thought. " Righteous " is a term with more than one meaning. It may imply moral justice, or it may be used in its primitive sense of a man who wins his case

in a court of law. In the second sense, Job says, God is
" righteous," for no power can overcome Him, no argument
can prove Him wrong. If a man were to come into conflict
with Him, He would be at once accuser, jury, judge, and
executioner. Yet he toys with the idea of a meeting in
which he might lay his whole case before God. But he puts
it from him for the time; there seems no hope that way.
It is God who tortures him, behaving to him like an omnipotent demon. He is God's creature, and God has absolute
power over him. Were they to meet, the infinitesimal
could only be crushed utterly by the Infinite. After all, the
best for which he can hope and plead is that God will leave
him alone till nature and disease bring him to the grave.

Zophar has nothing to add to his predecessors, but his
speech is a more pointed personal attack than theirs, and
Job is aroused to a more direct complaint of the " comfort "
which they all have to offer him.

Eliphaz speaks yet more strongly than before; he is
convinced that Job is one of the worst of sinners. Job
sees the futility of hoping for any help from his friends;
the tension becomes stronger; his anguish of spirit becomes
more poignant; he must have a refuge; and he turns to
God. He appeals from the God of conventional theology to
God as He really must be :

> O earth, cover not my blood,
> And let my cry have no resting place.
> Even now, behold, my witness is in heaven,
> And he that voucheth for me is on high.
> My friends scorn me;
> But mine eye poureth out tears unto God;
> That He would maintain the right of a man with God,
> And of a son of man with his neighbour (Job xvi. 18–21).

So nearly has he found a rock on which to plant his feet.
But the wave of despair returns, and sweeps him back with
it; he is doomed, and must die. What hope is there then,
he asks, that even God will justify him ?

Again Bildad speaks, more sharply than ever rebuking
the sinner before him; and once more Job is convinced
that he has nothing to look for from his friends. In frantic
distress he turns now to them, now to God, until, at the very
last gasp, he makes the great leap of faith and finds that he
has passed that barrier of threatening death against which
he had hitherto beaten himself in vain. The text of xix.

25–27 is obscure and almost certainly corrupt in parts, but
on this we may rely :

> But I know that my redeemer liveth,
> And that he shall stand up at last upon the earth.
>
> . . . . . .
>
> Yet without my flesh shall I see God,
> Whom I shall see for myself,
> And mine eyes shall behold, and not another.

There is no general or formulated doctrine of the resurrection of the dead here. Yet there is the conviction that,
for Job at least, death is not the end; there will still be
possible some kind of valid relationship between himself and
his God. There is no thought of eternal life, no suggestion
of heaven, but there is an assurance which will inevitably
lead to these doctrines.

This, of course, does not solve the problem for Job;
but it does enable him to approach it in a calmer spirit.
He knows now that God is on his side, and he dare with
greater freedom claim to enter the divine presence and
utter his complaint. But his difficulty is that he does not
not know where he may find Him, for though the evidence
of his power is everywhere, He Himself remains concealed.
Finally, Job stakes all on one great challenge to God, and
appeals to Him to reveal Himself. And God answers. And
then there follows an exposition of the greatness of God in the
works of creation. True, Job's questions are not answered,
but for him it is enough, for in the presence of God they are
forgotten. It is, after all, here that the final message of the
book lies. Questions may agitate the mind of man, problems
may torture his spirit, but when once he has seen God, when
once he has stood before Him, and begun to know Him,
the questions and the problems vanish. There is something deeper than reason, more convincing than logical
argument, and in the light of experience others may cry
with Job :

> I have heard of thee with the hearing of the ear,
> But now mine eye seeth thee,
> Therefore I abhor myself and repent
> In dust and ashes (Job xlii. 6).

That the writer here implicitly expresses his belief in life
after death can hardly be doubted. But as this subject is
dealt with in Chapter XXXVI, we say nothing further
about it here.

The problem of suffering was not solved; but this whole-hearted grappling with it brought to the minds of the writers of this book the realisation of some vital truths. Suffering may be a mystery, but the true believer in God will not be alienated from his faith thereby; it may test the faith of the pious, but it will show that his *piety is disinterested* : " Though he slay me, yet will I wait for him " (Job xiii. 15). Suffering may be a bitter, painful experience; but when the sufferer has passed through the fire of affliction he will come to the realization that *suffering has strengthened his character* :

> He delivereth the afflicted by his affliction,
> And openeth the ear by adversity (Job xxxvi. 15).

The suffering of the righteous may raise the question of the justice of God's government of the world; but the contemplation of the divine creative work brings man *to a deeper apprehension of God*, and he comes to see that God is concerned with something more than the mere punishing and rewarding of men; and thus there is generated a clearer *sense of the proportion of things*. The psalmist's words compress much that finds expression in the book :

> When I consider thy heavens, the work of thy fingers,
> The moon and the stars which thou hast ordained,
> What is man that thou art mindful of him?
> And the son of man, that thou visitest him?
>   (Ps. viii. 3, 4 [4, 5 in Hebrew]; cp. Job vii. 17, 18.)

CHAPTER XXXVI

THE AFTER-LIFE: THE FINAL STAGE OF BELIEF

WE have seen from certain passages in the Old Testament that the ideas about the state of the departed were undergoing change in spite of the official *She'ol* doctrine. These passages were post-exilic; but stress must be laid on the fact that though it is in post-exilic passages in which signs of development are to be discerned, it by no means follows that they did not exist previously; indeed, it is perhaps not too much to say that when a particular belief is found in *written* form it almost compels the assumption that it had been current for some time beforehand. However, we will not dogmatize upon that point. What we shall now do is to examine some further passages which throw light on this question of the development of belief; the dates of these passages are in some cases uncertain, but for present purposes that does not greatly matter, because we are more concerned with the *fact* of development than with the time at which it took place.

In any case, a new idea is not generally accepted when first put forth.

We deal first with [Isa. liii. 8–12]; the passage is one of the most difficult in the Old Testament; the Hebrew text is very corrupt, and demands considerable emendation; and, as is almost inevitable, the opinions of experts differ a good deal. The reconstruction of the text, however, proposed by Duhm,[1] based partly on the Septuagint and partly on the phraseology of other Old Testament passages, reveals so much insight, and is so admirably in accordance with what even the corrupt text seems to suggest, that we have no hesitation in adopting it. It should also be pointed out that Duhm's emendation is metrically in entire agreement with that of the rest of this " Servant of the Lord " song; and in the other verses of this song the Hebrew text offers no

---

[1] *Das Buch Jesaia*, pp. 371 ff. (1914).

difficulties. An English translation of Duhm's emended text is as follows :

From oppression and condemnation he was delivered,
And his dwelling-place who considers?
For he was cut off from the land of the living,
Because of the transgression of my people he was smitten to death:

And they made his grave with the wicked,
And with the wrong-doers his burial-mound;
Yet he had done no violence,
And there was no deceit in his mouth.

And it pleased Yahweh to purify him,
To renew his old age;
The delight of his soul shall he see,
A seed, and length of days.

And Yahweh's purpose is in his hand,
He will deliver his soul from harm,
Will show him light, and make him satisfied,
And pronounce him guiltless as to his suffering.

Contemptible was his servant to many,
Yet their iniquities he bore;
Therefore shall he receive the inheritance of many,
And with many shall he divide the spoil.

For he laid down his life.
And was numbered among transgressors;
But he bore the sin of many,
And for transgressors he made intercessions.

To justify the details of this rendering would involve a lengthy discussion, which would be out of place here. But the main point is that we have here the thought of life after death; the Servant was " smitten to death," as the Septuagint reads; and yet he renews his old age, has children,[1] lives for long after, and fulfils the purpose of God by bearing the sin of many, and by his intercession for sinners.

In this connexion it is worth referring to such a passage, among others, as Luke xviii. 31 ff., where our Lord says to His disciples : " . . . we go up to Jerusalem, and all things that are written by the prophets shall be accomplished unto the Son of Man "; these things are then enumerated, ending with the words : " and the third day he shall rise again." There is no passage in the prophetical books, apart from Isa.

---

[1] The Hebrew expression (a textual emendation) translated above by " the delight (lit. ' burden ') of his soul," in reference to offspring, the joy of every Hebrew, occurs also in Ezek. xxiv. 25.

A A

liii. 8 ff., where the thought of resurrection occurs; it is true that there is no mention of the third day in this passage; but that cannot be pressed; the important and central element is that of resurrection. If, as seems likely, our Lord has this passage in mind, it substantiates the contention that Isa. liii. 8 ff. contains the thought of the After-life in a very developed form.

We turn next to some points of far less importance, but inasmuch as they indicate a development, small though it be, in the conception of the After-life, they must find mention here. It is a question of the modification of the *She'ol* conception. In certain passages in the Old Testament it will be seen that three other terms are used in connexion with it. The first of these is *Bor*, meaning "Pit"; thus, in Isa. xiv. 15 [1] it is said: "Yet shalt thou be brought down to *She'ol*, to the uttermost parts of the *Bor*"; this does not read as though the term were synonymous with *She'ol*. It suggests rather that in the mind of the writer there was the idea of there being a particularly deep locality in the abode of the dead reserved for the worst enemies of Yahweh. That is also the impression gained from Ezek. xxxii. 23, 25, 28-30. In this case the conjecture may be hazarded that the use of the term *Bor* may point to the beginnings of the idea of some differentiation between the dwellers in *She'ol*, i.e. the idea of a difference of condition there corresponding with the kind of life men had lived on earth. We have seen that in much earlier times the belief was held in some circles among the Babylonians that in the Underworld there was a separation between the good and the bad. In so many other respects there are parallels between the Babylonian and Hebrew ideas concerning the Hereafter that Babylonian influence may perhaps be discerned here too.

Then there is the term *Shachath*, "corruption," or "destruction," used for the place of the departed (Job xvii. 13-16; Isa. xxxviii. 17; Ezek. xxviii. 8; Jonah ii. 6 [7 in Hebr.]). Synonymous with this is the expression *'Abaddon*, from the root meaning "to perish" or "to destroy" (Job xxvi. 6, xxviii. 22; Prov. xv. 11, xxvii. 20). These two terms are mentioned for completeness' sake; if the idea of total annihilation was regarded as a development (cp. Eccles. ix. 1-11), it was a development in the wrong direction.

A development of vastly greater importance is seen in the passage Isa. xxvi. 19; this is a difficult verse, the Hebrew

[1] Belonging to a section of the book much later than the time of Isaiah.

text of which seems to have undergone some revision; it should be read thus : " Thy dead men (i.e. of Israel) shall arise; the inhabitants of the dust shall awake, and shout for joy; for a dew of lights is thy dew, and the earth shall bring forth Rephaim." The Targum emphasizes the belief in the resurrection of the body by adding after " thy dead men,"— " the bones of their corpses," implying that the flesh went to corruption, but that the bones were the nucleus of the resurrection body; great importance was attached to the bones of the human body in Hebrew thought. The latter part of the passage means that just as the dew at nights comes down to refresh and give renewed life to the vegetation of the soil, so a heavenly dew will descend to re-animate the bodies of the dead lying in the earth; it is a " dew of lights," because it comes from the heavenly sphere illumined by the stars.

Here we have, then, although intermixed with one or two quaint ideas, a definite belief in the resurrection of the body set forth.

The abrupt assertion of the resurrection contained in this passage, without any explanatory words, shows that the belief was generally accepted when it was written. Some commentators date the section to which it belongs (Isa. xxiv–xxvii) to the period 200 B.C. onwards; and this is justified by its Apocalyptic character.

The only other passage in the Old Testament in which belief in the resurrection of the body is definitely expressed is Dan. xii. 2, belonging approximately to the middle of the second century B.C.: " And many of them that sleep in the dust of the earth shall awake, some to everlasting life, and some to shame and everlasting contempt." The general resurrection of both the good and the evil, with a definite differentiation between their respective states in the next world, marks a developed stage of belief; but we begin to enter here into the domain of Apocalyptic, and with this we shall be more particularly concerned in Chapter XXXIX.

Before we come to deal with what is, in reality, the most important part of our subject, there is a passage of deep interest which must be briefly discussed : viz. Job xix. 25–27, beginning with the familiar words : " I know that my Redeemer liveth." It will be best if we give the R.V. rendering sentence by sentence, and add a more literal translation of the Hebrew, thereby seeking to bring out somewhat more fully the meaning of the original :—

But (R.V. marg. " For ") *I know that my redeemer liveth*:
the Hebrew has: "But I know that my vindicator so
(R.V. marg.) liveth "; [1] the words are a profession of faith in
God, Who will declare that it is not because of sin that Job is
suffering, as his friends have maintained; God will vindicate
his innocence.

And that he shall stand up at the last upon the earth (lit.
" dust," so R.V. marg.) : [2] this does not accurately represent
the Hebrew; the order of the words in the original is
significant: "And (as the last one) upon the earth will he
stand up "; emphasis is laid upon " the last one," the
meaning being that God will have the last word in affirming
Job's innocence. It is a forensic picture, God will be the
final witness. The rendering of the Prayer Book version
" at the latter day " gives an entirely wrong meaning; there
is no reference to any " day "; when this vindication will
take place is left indefinite.

And after my skin hath been thus destroyed : this, with a
slight emendation, represents the Hebrew. The speaker is
referring, and pointing to the ravages of the disease from
which he is suffering; this disease, described elsewhere in
the book, is represented as the worst form of leprosy, known
as Elephantiasis; the skin becomes black, and folded,
resembling the hide of an elephant, and, together with the
flesh, gradually falls off from the bone. This is what is
referred to in the text. There is no mention of " worms "
which occurs in the Prayer Book version.

Yet from my flesh shall I see God : the R.V. marg. has
" without " for " yet from "; the general sense would suggest
rather : " away from," or " apart from "; and " flesh " is
often used for " body " (vi. 12, xiii. 14, and elsewhere).
The reference is to the vision of God which Job is convinced
will be accorded to him, and which is, in fact, vouchsafed to
him; it is recorded in xlii. 2 ff. To see God in ecstatic
vision is to see Him " apart from the flesh," or body. We may
recall St. Paul's words in 2 Cor. xii. 2, 3, when, in describing
his vision of the Lord, he says : " Whether in the body, I
know not, or whether out of the body, I know not—God
knoweth."

Whom I shall see for myself, and not another : the R.V.
marg., rightly, renders : " on my side," for " for myself."

---

[1] The Hebrew for this, *go'el*, means literally " one who acts as Kinsman."
[2] " Dust " in the sense of " earth " occurs also in Job xli. 33 (25 in Hebr.):
" Upon earth there is not his like."

The force of the words is that Job, even Job, incredible as it may seem, will see God taking Job's part, and affirming his innocence.

And mine eyes shall behold, and not another : the R.V. marg. renders, more correctly : " . . . and not (as) a stranger "; the meaning is that when he is vouchsafed the vision of God, he will behold the Almighty as his friend, because he is innocent : " I had heard of thee by the hearing of the ear; but now mine eye seeth thee " (xlii. 5).

My reins are consumed within me : the meaning is that his innermost being is overwhelmed with the yearning to see God.

It will, therefore, be realized that as it stands in its original form this beautiful passage contains no reference to life beyond the grave. Attention is drawn to it here, however, for two reasons; first, because it has, in the Christian Church, always been interpreted as referring to the After-life; and secondly, because, although according to the interpretation here offered, the passage does not refer to the Hereafter, it does, nevertheless, speak of something which is indissolubly connected with belief in immortality in its truly developed form. By saying this we do not mean to imply that the writer himself realized what was involved in that close relationship with God—the vision of God—to which he refers more than once. He had not quite reached the point—though he was getting very near it—at which the great truth dawns upon the mind, that the fuller conception of God, of His power, and eternity, and love, *necessitates* belief in immortality. To this we shall now come.

It will have been noticed that, so far, no reference has been made to any passage in the *Psalms*; this has been done of set purpose because it will be found instructive to treat these separately. The fact is that the full development of belief in Immortality, so far as pre-Christian times are concerned, is found only in the *Psalms*. This is easily accounted for by the fact that personal religion, the relation between God and man, without which a developed belief in Immortality is impossible, is nowhere so much in evidence as in the *Psalms*. Belief in the resurrection, which is expressed in the two passages last dealt with, does not constitute the most developed form of belief in Immortality in pre-Christian times; this will become clear in discussing the salient passages in the *Psalms*.

In examining the belief in Immortality in the *Psalms*, we are confronted with the interesting and important fact that, in them, all the stages of this belief are found, from the earliest to the latest; true, regarding the earliest stage, the references in the *Psalms* are very few and vague; but that is natural enough because the *Psalms* have, for liturgical purposes, undergone a great deal of revision and adaptation. Nevertheless, inasmuch as the *Psalms* cover a period of something like eight centuries, it is clear that the earliest stage of belief must have been in vogue at the time that the earliest psalms, *in the original form*, were composed. What the Hebrews believed about the Hereafter during, say, the Davidic period, about 1000 B.C., and for at least a couple of centuries after, was different from what they believed during the prophetic period, from about 800 B.C. onwards; and what they believed during the Greek period, from about 300 B.C. onwards, was different from what they believed during the prophetic period. That is putting it quite generally; because, obviously, it is quite impossible to give definite dates; for where religious beliefs are concerned one can never say: From such a time to such a time this was believed, and from then onwards something was believed, and so on—for the simple reason that development of belief is always gradual, and it always overlaps periods; no belief becomes universal at once; the old and the new continue to intermingle for long.

In the *Psalms*, then, references to all the stages of belief regarding the Hereafter are to be found; of the first stage we need say but very little; of the second somewhat more, in order to supplement what has already been said in Chapter XXI; the final stage is what will mainly concern us. We have seen that the first stage of the Hebrews' belief about the Hereafter contained an important element of truth in that the reality of life beyond the grave was recognized; but fears, crass and superstitious, and cruel practices connected with that first stage of belief, and above all, the fact that it cut at the root of a true belief in God— impelled the religious leaders to combat this form of belief, and to put something in its place. One illustration from the *Psalms* in which the earliest stage of belief is referred to will suffice: in Ps. cvi. 28 the psalmist recalls how in earlier days the people " ate the sacrifices of the dead." That, and many another evil practice, undermined trust and belief in God; therefore the *She'ol* belief was put forth by the religious leaders. The first essential was to teach the people that the departed did not go on living the same kind of life that they had lived here on earth; they became mere shades, according to this *She'ol* doctrine. And the second essential was to teach the people that the departed had not the power and the knowledge which had been imputed to them, and that to have recourse to them in trouble was folly, to worship them was worse; in this way alone could the people be brought to look to their God as the only true Help and Guide in their daily life (see Isa. viii. 19).[1]

But excellent as the intentions of the religious leaders were, their *She'ol* doctrine led them into some grievous errors; these appear very clearly in some of the psalms; for example, in order to combat the belief that the departed had knowledge and foresight, for which reason they were consulted, it is said that when men go down to *She'ol* they forget everything; thus in Ps. lxxxviii. 13 (R.V. 12) *She'ol* is called " the land of forgetfulness "; the same teaching, somewhat differently expressed, occurs in Ps. cxlvi. 4 : " His breath goeth forth, he returneth to his earth; in that very day his thoughts perish "; it means that the thinking powers cease to function, and therefore he forgets everything. But a far more serious error about the *She'ol* doctrine was that it taught that the presence of God was entirely excluded from the abode of the departed; in other words, that the departed have nothing to do with God, nor God with them. That indicates an extraordinarily circumscribed conception of the power of God, an incredibly inadequate belief in the love of God. And when we think of the exalted thoughts and sublime ideas expressed about the Personality of God by both prophets and psalmists, it becomes very difficult to understand how they could reconcile their *She'ol* doctrine with their belief in God. But that kind of incongruity has been characteristic of men's religious beliefs in all ages.

Further, one of the most striking passages in the *Psalms* in this connexion is in Ps. vi. 6 (R.V. 5) : " For in death there is no remembrance of thee, in *She'ol* who shall give thee thanks ? "

Again, in Ps. xxx. 10 (R.V. 9) : " What profit is there in my blood (blood being thought of as the seat of life) when I go down to the Pit ? Shall the dust praise thee, shall it declare thy faithfulness ? " Similarly, in Ps. xxviii. 1 the psalmist says : " Unto thee, Yahweh, do I call; my Rock, be not deaf unto me; lest, if thou be silent unto me, I be

---

[1] " Should not a people seek unto their God? On behalf of the living should they seek unto the dead? "

compared with them that go down into the Pit." And
there are a number of other passages to the same effect. They
all imply, or state definitely, that when once a man has
passed from this life he is unable to pray to, or to worship
God; death sunders all relationship between a man and his
God. But the *She'ol* doctrine teaches something even
worse; not only is it taught that the departed lose all power
of communion with God, but also that God utterly disregards
them; they are of no concern whatsoever to God! What
could be more painful in this connexion than the whole of
Ps. lxxxviii, especially verses 5 and 6 (R.V. 4, 5): "I am
counted with them that go down into the Pit, *I am become as
a man without God.* Cast off among the dead, like the slain
that lie in the grave; *whom thou rememberest no more,* for
they are cut off from thy hand." It is these last words,
especially, which reveal the essence of this dreadful belief:
"*whom thou rememberest no more,* for they are cut off from
thy hand." In Ps. xxxi. 13 (12 in R.V.), again, it is said:
"I am forgotten as a dead man out of mind, I am like a
broken vessel."

Thus, there can be no shadow of doubt that, according to
this official *She'ol* doctrine, God had no interest in, no relationship with men in the land of the Hereafter. Once dead, and
a man had not only nothing more to do with those whom he
loved on earth, but his whole knowledge of, hope in, trust in,
relationship with, God Almighty, Immortal, Omnipotent,
Omniscient, came to an end!—attributes of God which
prophets and psalmists believed in!

That was the *normal* belief of the Hebrews from the
prophetical period (roughly 800 B.C.) to within a couple of
centuries or so before the beginning of the Christian era.
We say the *normal* belief because there were some—isolated
thinkers—who were beyond their age, and who, by divine
inspiration had come to learn more of the truth. To two or
three of these we have already referred; that there were
some others we shall see presently.

What is of the highest importance to bear in mind in
connexion with what has been said is that to think that God
has no relationship with, no interest in, the spirits of the
departed, involves a very inadequate conception of God.
So far as the Personality of God was concerned—His
righteousness, justice, loving-kindness, and mercy—nothing
could exceed the prophetical ideals; but their thoughts were
always centred on the *present,* on the affairs of *this* world,

on the demands of the Almighty on the *living*. That was inevitable, because the prophets strove to make men lead better lives. Therefore their thoughts were not directed towards what happens hereafter. So that the prophets' conception of God was undeveloped, inadequate, in so far that they had not yet realized that, since God is a Spirit, it cannot make the slightest difference to Him whether the spirits of men are clothed with a body or not, whether they are living on this earth or in the great Hereafter. That was a truth that most of the prophets and most of the psalmists did not grasp. We repeat, therefore, that the kind of belief which men have about the Hereafter *must* depend upon the kind of belief they have about God. There could be no true development of belief concerning the Hereafter until the spirituality of the Divine Nature was more fully apprehended. It was a developed belief in God which *necessitated* a developed belief in the Hereafter. And of this we have sure signs, few though they be, in the Psalms.

Let us first of all take a passage in which the writer expresses the old *She'ol* conception with its mournful outlook for the world to come; he says (Ps. lxxxviii. 11–13 [R.V. 10–12]): " Wilt thou do wonders among the dead ? Shall the dead arise and praise thee? Shall thy loving-kindness be declared in the grave ? And thy faithfulness in the place of corruption? Shall thy wonders be known in the dark ? And thy righteousness in the land of forgetfulness ? " In the mind of the psalmist the answer to all these questions is : " No," as their form in the original Hebrew shows ; but one can see at once that only one thing was wanted to change each answer into a " Yes." And that one thing was— a fuller realization of God ! Now let us turn to another passage, not a great deal later, but certainly later, than the one just quoted (Ps. cxxxix. 7–12) : " Whither can I go then from thy spirit? And whither can I flee from thy presence? If I ascend up into heaven thou art there ; and if I make my bed in *She'ol*, behold, thou art there ! And if I lift up my wings towards the dawn, if I dwell in the farthest sea, even there thy hand will take hold of me, and thy right hand will grasp me. . . ." These two passages bring out in a wonderfully clear manner the two notes, respectively, of despair and hope regarding the future life, which belong, on the one hand, to an inadequate, on the other, to a fuller, apprehension of the Personality of God. But there is something more than must be said about this very instructive

139th psalm. After the psalmist has shown, through his fuller apprehension of God, that in the life on the other side of the grave the divine presence will not be wanting, he goes on to speak of what he conceives to be the nature of the body that man will have hereafter. He gives expression to what must appear to us a most extraordinary idea, though his conceptions are still tinged with materialism—not that *that* can really occasion surprise when we think of the material-istic conceptions people have even at the present day. The passage to be considered is Ps. cxxxix. 7–18; all com-mentators are agreed that this is one of the most difficult passages in the whole of the Psalter, though every one recognizes that the psalmist is speaking about the future life. There can also be no doubt as to what he is referring to in verses 13, 14, where he says: "For thou didst form my inward parts. Thou didst cover me in my mother's womb. I thank thee for thy marvellous works; thou art wonderful, and thy works are wonderful; and my soul knoweth that right well." Here there is a clear and unambiguous reference to the formation of the material body preparatory to its appearance on earth; this is declared to be the creative act of God; the passage closes with an acknowledgement of the wondrousness of this act. But now, in the next four verses, there is a further reference to the formation of the body; only this time the body is not spoken of as being formed in the womb, but in the "lowest parts of the earth," that is, in *She'ol*; and the component parts of the unformed substance are written down in God's book. The passage closes with the affirmation that, when he (the Psalmist) awakes from the sleep of death, he will find himself in the presence of God. Before discussing the meaning of this passage it will be well to quote it in full; the verses are 15–18:

> My frame was not hidden from thee
> When I was made in secret,
> And curiously wrought in the lowest parts of the earth.
> Thine eyes did see mine unformed substance,
> And in thy book hath it all been written.
>   Days were ordained
> When as yet there were none of them.[1]
> How precious to me are thy thoughts, O God,
> How great is the sum of them.
> Should I count them, they would be more in number than the
>   grains of sand;
> When I shall have awakened I shall still be with thee.

[1] I.e., there was a time when none of the parts of the "unformed sub-stance" were yet in existence.

The whole passage means that just as God prepares the body in the womb for life on this earth, so does He also prepare, in the womb of the earth, another body after death for the life that is to be. The psalmist, it is true, conceives of this future body as material, but that does not affect the main thought; materialistic as the conception is, it witnesses nevertheless to a great development of thought. One has only to think of how the existence in *She'ol* was conceived of to realize what a stupendous advance is contained in the belief of a *living* body in the word to come, and in the conviction that in that day man will have uninterrupted communion with God. *She'ol* is no more a mere abode where the shades of the departed congregate in dark forgetfulness, and without any knowledge of God; but a place where God prepares men for the glorious consummation which is to come.

But we have yet to follow out a still further step in the development of belief in Immortality in the *Psalms*. The highest point reached in this belief is found in Ps. lxxiii. It is a long psalm, and cannot be quoted in full, but we will give the salient passages :

In conscious innocence the psalmist says, in verse 2 :

" And as for me my feet were almost gone, my steps had well-nigh slipped "; in spite of his conviction that he is a righteous man, he sees that misfortune has overtaken him; and then he goes on to contrast his sorry plight with the much more fortunate lot of the wicked (verses 3–5) :

> For I am envious at the arrogant, when I see the prosperity of the wicked;
> For they have no worries, but perfect and settled is their strength;
> They are not in trouble as other men are; neither are they plagued like others.

The wicked and their ways are then described up to the end of verse 12, concluding with the words : " Behold, these are the wicked, and, being always at ease, they increase in wealth."

Upon this follows a hypothetical statement; that is to say, the psalmist, for the purpose of his argument, *assumes* a wrong attitude; he says : " Surely in vain have I cleansed my heart, and washed my hands in innocency ! For all day long have I been plagued, and chastened every morning "; and then he makes it quite clear that this attitude has been taken up only for argument's sake; for he goes on :

" If I had said, I will speak thus, Behold, I should have dealt untruly with the generation of thy children." And he proceeds to describe the utter destruction of the wicked at their latter end; while, in regard to himself, who has sought to lead a godly life, he says (verses 23–25) :

> Nevertheless, I am continually with thee,
> Thou holdest me by my right hand;
> Thou guidest me by thy counsel,
> And afterward thou wilt take me to glory.
> Whom have I in heaven but thee?
> And having thee (i.e. being with thee) I desire nought else on earth.

Here, then, we reach a beautiful height in the conception of Immortality. And this passage is the more striking in that the thought-development manifests itself in three directions. First, regarding the belief in God; for it will have been noticed at once that God is apprehended in a far fuller way than in earlier days; it is realized that His power and activity among men are not restricted to this earth, as in the old *She'ol* belief, but that His interest in man is just as great in the Hereafter as in this life, and that in His love and mercy He receives men in a celestial abode. Then, as to the belief concerning the future life, the passage witnesses to the conviction that it is a glorious life, for in the Hereafter God is man's portion for ever. And finally, the psalmist is brought to understand that the solution of the perplexities, and of what seemed to be the inconsistencies and incongruities of the divine rule on earth, is to be seen in the reward laid up for the righteous in the world to come.

This, then, is the final stage of the belief in Immortality as taught in the Old Testament; and we see that here, as in other directions, various stages of belief precede the fuller apprehension of the truth.

The doctrine of Immortality seems to have been accepted by the bulk of the people but slowly in Israel; and even down to the time of the destruction of the Temple it was denied in the prominent and powerful Sadducæan circles from which the priestly leaders of the people were mainly drawn. One characteristic piece of literature belonging to this school survives; it is what we call the book of *Ecclesiastes*. This is a very extraordinary work, and its inclusion in the Canon of the Jewish Scriptures can only be explained by the tradition which ascribed it to Solomon; even so, its canonicity was disputed as late as the second century A.D. Its prevail-

ing note is that of disillusionment. The writer has looked at
and studied human life from many points of view, and all he
finds in the end is " vanity." He knows that men think of
God as rewarding goodness and punishing wickedness, yet
he does not see that there is any practical difference between
them in the end (cp. Eccles. viii. 10, ix. 1–3). All paths
lead to one end—the grave, and there men share the same
lot, and have no memory of what their life has been. The
writer is aware of the doctrine of human immortality, but he
cannot accept it; there is no proof of it : " Who knoweth
the spirit of man whether it goeth upward, or the spirit of the
beast whether it goeth downward into the earth ? " (Eccles.
iii. 21).

Again, in the *Wisdom of Ben-Sira* (*Ecclesiasticus*), which
contains indications of having issued from Sadducæan
circles, and belongs approximately to 200 B.C., there are
similarly no signs of a fuller belief in Immortality, the standpoint being the traditional *She'ol* doctrine.

The Sadducæan position, however, failed to maintain its
hold on the mass of the people, and, as a serious element in
Jewish thought, did not survive the destruction of the
Temple in A.D. 70. It was always more closely bound up
with the priestly caste, and so connected with the religion of
the Temple. The popular creed, on the other hand, of the
Scribes and Pharisees was that most common in the synagogues; and it is interesting to note that in one of the pre-
Christian elements of the Jewish synagogal Liturgy, the
prayer called *Shemoneh 'Esreh* (the " Eighteen Benedictions "), belief in the resurrection finds explicit utterance :
" Blessed art thou, O Lord, that quickenest the dead." It
was this fuller belief that survived, and it has continued up
to the present day to be an integral part of the Jewish faith.

CHAPTER XXXVII

WISDOM AND ITS DEVELOPMENTS

1. THE SEMITIC MIND

IT is commonly said that the Semitic races have no gift for philosophy, and that for a thorough discussion of metaphysical questions it is necessary to turn to the Indo-European mind. It is pointed out that the Semite feels very strongly, but is not given to abstract speculation. He is intensely sensitive to personal appeals, sees quickly and clearly in pictures—so quickly and clearly as to pass from one metaphor to another with a speed which bewilders the pedestrian Aryan mind. But he does not reason consecutively or follow a complicated train of thought. The forms of literature most character-istic of the Hebrew genius are the lyric and the short prophetic oracle, instinct with life, throbbing with emotion, but rarely the product of deep and conscious reflexion. Among such a people we must not look for any elaborate or deeply conceived metaphysic, unless and until they come into contact with some other race to whom philosophical speculation is more natural. We may then find a combina-tion of the old and the new, the native and the foreign, especially when the Semitic people has a deep respect for the intelligence of its new acquaintance.

There is, furthermore, a fundamental difference in out-look between the Semitic and the Indo-European mind. The latter, in that quest for unity which is the mainspring of all metaphysic, has invariably tended to become pantheistic, reducing all the objects of experience to a single whole, and assuming that every appearance of separate identity, whether of person or of thing, is illusory or transient.[1] The Semitic mind, on the other hand, laid intense stress on

[1] An apparent exception is presented by Zoroastrianism, though there are indications which suggest that this faith would have had a history similar to that of Indian religion if it had been able to develop without interference.

personality. Its exponents would not have used the expression; it was so fundamental to all their thinking
that it never occurred to them to formulate it in so many
words, and we may doubt whether they even had a term
corresponding to our word. Yet their conception of the universe was based on what we call personality, and though
in religion they thought of the community as the human
unit, that community was commonly described in terms
which suggest that it was personified in their thought.
To the Jew men were persons, and God was a person; no
explanation of their thought can be valid unless it is based
on this fundamental presupposition.

2. THE MASHAL

The aim of all science and philosophy is the unification of experience, the reduction of all phenomena to a
single rule, the discovery of a single fact of principle with
which all the varied manifestations of the universe can be
brought into accord.   Its earliest effort at expression is
normally in the epigram or proverb, a short saying in
which a number of different facts are brought together,
a generalization which shall include the results of a number
of different observations.   The wise man is he who has
so observed life and the inter-relations of man and man,
of man and nature, or of man and God, that he is able to
group them, or many of them, under a single general
" law."   Such a law may be either descriptive of experience in the material world, when it will be an elementary
form of natural science, or it may be normative of conduct,
when it will be a moral precept, or it may go deeper into the
nature of reality, when it will be classed as metaphysical.

We find this tendency showing itself in the thought of
Greece, especially at that comparatively early stage
which is represented to us in the older Ionian philosophy,
and remained to some extent the popular conception.
We are all familiar with the old story of how the seven
sages came together to formulate the world's wisdom in a
series of short, pithy sentences.[1]   The famous " Know
thyself," and " Nothing too much," are ethical generalizations by which their authors sought to reduce to a common

---

[1] It is perhaps unnecessary to remark that this story has no historical
value whatever; the sages concerned were not contemporaries.   But it
does illustrate the love of early Greek thinking for this type of generalized
statement.

law all rules of conduct. "All things are in a state of
flux " is primarily an attempt to state the laws of the
physical universe, but is capable of being extended into a
metaphysical generalization. These efforts after unification
of experience are genuinely scientific and philosophical,
though the science and the philosophy are still on a very
elementary plane.

Such statements of life are common to practically all
nations and types of mind at a particular stage of their
development, and it is impossible not to feel that even
to-day the epigram is a far more powerful instrument of
conviction than logic. Millions who know nothing of
meteorology will quote and believe :

> A red sky at night
> Is the shepherd's delight ¡
> A red sky in the morning
> Is the shepherd's warning.

Many peoples, on reaching a stage at which literature
becomes possible, have formed collections of these sayings ;
Martin Tupper has a long pedigree. We find these collections in Egypt in such works as the well-known *Teaching
of Amen-em-ope* and other books, and in Mesopotamia in
the *Sayings of Achikar*, of which a fifth-century copy in
Aramaic has recently come to light.[1] In Hebrew and
Jewish literature they are chiefly concentrated in three
books, *Proverbs, Ecclesiastes*, and the *Wisdom of Ben-Sira*
(*Ecclesiasticus*). All three were originally written in Hebrew,
and the Hebrew text of the two former survives complete,
but the third is best known to us in the Greek translation, though some portions of the original Hebrew text
have been recovered among Egyptian papryi. Though
this last is the latest of the three, it has much closer
affinities with *Proverbs* than with *Ecclesiastes*, and it will
be convenient to glance at the books in this order.

The Hebrew title of the book of *Proverbs* is *Mishlê*.
The singular of this word, *mashal*, is used in a wide variety
of meanings. Its root signification seems to have been
" comparison," and the analogous root is used in Arabic to
this day almost in the sense of the preposition " like."
But it is used of such different pieces as the oracles of
Balaam (Num. xxiii, xxiv), the great taunt-song over
the fall of the tyrant in Isa. xiv. 4–21, and the short epi-

---

[1] See especially Oesterley, *Commentary on Proverbs*, pp. xxxiii–lv (1929).

gram in Ezek. xvii. 2. It is clear that it is in the same
sense as in the last-mentioned passage that the word is
used in the title of the book of *Proverbs*. For that book is,
in the main, a collection of these generalizations, short
and memorable, on life and conduct. In form each is
usually a distich, or line in two well-divided parts,
manifesting that parallelism which is the outstanding
feature of Hebrew and of some other early poetry. The
book professedly contains several collections, and tradition ascribed the earliest work of collection to Solomon,
and certainly one aspect of his renowned wisdom was
supposed to lie in his ability to produce such sayings.

Many subjects are covered by these *Meshalim*. Some
of them deal with human relationships, some are simple
comparisons or metaphors, some are concerned with
religious matters. It is now fairly clear that the collection drew on similar documents found in other literatures,
and not a few of the utterances can be paralleled in many
parts of the world. It is impossible to assign any specific
date to them : some may be very ancient, and others
comparatively modern. The collections, as collections,
are hardly likely to have been any earlier than the middle
monarchy, though there is no reason to doubt the tradition which links them with Solomon. He may quite well
be responsible for the form which some of them take.
The book in its final form is almost certainly post-exilic,
and throughout breathes a high moral tone. At the
same time we miss, inevitably, some of the features
which make the religion of the prophets so valuable.
The moral precepts enjoined are reinforced, not by an
appeal to the will of God, nor to an absolute standard of
ethics, but by purely material and prudential considerations. "Be good because if you are you will be happy;
refrain from sin because you will suffer if you commit it"
is the usual burden of the speakers.

Ben-Sira presents us with much the same quality, but
is more ambitious, and the book includes several well-
known passages, particularly the great panegyric on the
heroes of Israel. But both are marked with one feature
which strikes every reader who compares the Hebrew
wisdom with that of Egypt. While the resemblance
between the two is at times so close as to make an independent origin impossible, the whole of the Egyptian
thought is oriented to a doctrine of a future life. This

B B

has no place whatever either in *Proverbs* or in *Ben-Sira*, and both contemplate the life of man on this earth and consider nothing further. This is readily comprehensible in the book of *Proverbs*, which probably reached its present form before the development of the doctrine of the resurrection, but we are compelled to regard *Ben-Sira* as a typically Sadducæan work.

Ecclesiastes has already been mentioned, and attention has been drawn to its categorical rejection of a belief in life after death. In other respects it resembles to some extent the collections of the *Meshalim*. It is, however, the work of one author. He is a man who has studied human life through many years, and in old age finds himself disillusioned. All is hollow, empty, vain. His first sentence, " Vanity of vanities, saith the preacher, all is vanity," is his thesis, and he proceeds to develop it by reference alike to the world of nature and to that of human life. Here is a generalization which is necessarily philosophical, though pessimistic. Yet, paradoxically enough, his is a much more deeply religious mind than that of the *Meshalim* composers. They deal throughout with human life and with that alone—or almost alone. *Ecclesiastes*, on the other hand, always has God in the background of his thinking, and it is striking testimony to the intense hold that religion had on the Jewish mind that even so hopeless a writer can still retain his personal faith in God. God cannot do much for him, it is true, but God is there, and must not be neglected.

3. Wisdom and its Fuller Meaning

Hebrew philosophy could not and did not stop short with the construction of epigrams. It was compelled to look further into reality and to attempt a deeper analysis of experience. There was never any inclination to doubt the being of God, or of trying to explain Him as an Indo-European philosopher might have done. But there were two main problems which needed to be discussed, two outstanding questions to which an answer was slowly evolved. These we may call the problems of creation and of revelation; the questions: " How did God make the world ? " and " How can and does God communicate with man ? "

Neither problem presented any real difficulty to the rather more primitive Hebrew of pre-exilic days. His conception of God was anthropomorphic, and he thought of Yahweh as possessing a physical body, not unlike that of man, though with much greater powers. The creation of the world, then, was accomplished just as a human artificer would construct a work of art. The story told in Gen. ii assumes the existence of the world, and offers no speculation as to how matter came into being. It tells of Yahweh modelling the moistened clay to make first man, then the animals, and speaks of His planting the garden in which His man is placed. The heavens are the work of His fingers, and His hands have fashioned the earth.

A more sophisticated age could not be content with such a position, and as the conception of Yahweh grew more spiritual and less material, it became necessary to look for some other explanation of the Universe. The outlook of the first centuries after the Exile is represented in Gen. i.[1] The contrast with the older narrative is very striking. All the anthropomorphism has vanished, and in its place we have a stately, scientific, almost evolution-ary process. There is no longer any suggestion of a human frame or of mechanical measures for the construction of the Universe; God speaks, and it is done. If we had been able to cross-examine the writer we should probably have learnt that when he used the phrase " God said," he was not thinking of actual utterance. Hebrew has a very limited and a very concrete vocabulary, and the thought of the passage would be more faithfully represented by saying " *God willed.*" But the metaphor of speech is there, and was destined to have an important effect on the development of Jewish theology.

Men looked farther. In all the arrangement, the ad-justments, the regularity of the world and its working they recognized the expression of a mind, immeasurably greater than their own but like it in nature. It seemed to them that, just as a piece of man-made machinery could be adduced as evidence of a mind which had planned and produced it, so the Universe betrayed at every moment the activity of a supreme Intelligence, and they spoke of " Him that by wisdom made the heavens." Thus wisdom became the highest of all personal qualities, and began to receive special attention, and the Wisdom of God became almost an object of adoration. In Job

---

[1] In its present form this passage dates from the fifth century, though it is almost certainly a modification or an adaptation of a far older narrative.

xxviii we have a passage which is hardly original in that book, but which is of great importance for the development of Jewish thought, inasmuch as it confines true wisdom to God ; men may search for it where they will, but God alone knows where it is and how it may be found. And in such a passage as Prov. viii we have a personification of Wisdom which may have been poetical in origin, but is on the verge of becoming a philosophical doctrine.

The problem of communion has a similar history. In pre-exilic days it was held that Yahweh could and did appear to men in human form. Often they did not recognize their visitor until some superhuman act betrayed His divinity. As time passed, this simple theophany gave place to other theories. Men sought to discover communications from God in mechanical ways such as the casting of the sacred lot, or through other methods by which He could be put to the test and so declare His will. Should He desire to enter spontaneously into men's lives, He took possession of some man or woman, "breathed" into them, and through them uttered His message.[1] The medium of communication was thus the breath or "spirit" of God. But in post-exilic years this source of knowledge failed, and men were compelled to look for less startling modes of revelation. Again the divine intelligence made its appeal to men, and they recognized in all human thinking the impact of the divine mind. So here also men were led to the same conclusion as in seeking an answer to the other question. In Prov. viii the personified Wisdom is the vehicle of the divine message to men, and the two problems find a single solution in later Jewish thought.

The doctrine is stated more completely than elsewhere in the book which passes under the name of the *Wisdom of Solomon*, and it is here that we have its fullest development on purely Jewish soil. The great passage vii. 22–viii. 1 may be regarded as the kernel of the book for our present purposes. Wisdom is personified even more completely than in Prov. viii, and the personification has risen beyond a poetical metaphor to a philosophical doctrine. She is the agent of creation, the artificer of all things. It is she who brings man into contact with God : "In all ages entering into holy souls, she maketh them friends of God, and prophets "—note the identifica-

_____
[1] Cf. pp. 200 f.

tion of Wisdom with the prophetic spirit of old time. So
much we might have deduced from earlier Jewish thinking, but in one point a striking advance is made. This is
in the conception of Wisdom in her relation to God Himself. " She is the breath of the power of God, and a pure
effluence flowing from the glory of the Almighty . . . the
brightness of the everlasting light, the unspotted mirror
of the power of God, and the image of His goodness "
(Wisd. vii. 25, 26).

Here we have the elements of a philosophical theology,
a speculation on the very being of God. Wisdom is at
once a quality of God and a Person within the divine
personality—in technical theological language, a hypostasis.

It seems hardly possible that this doctrine should be
wholly independent of Greek thought. But the evidence
of Hellenic influence is most in evidence when we study
the work of Philo of Alexandria. This is no place to
discuss the history of Greek philosophy ; suffice it to
say that there the same problems had exercised men's
minds, and that by the beginning of the Christian era
men had come to believe in the " Logos "—" Word "
or " Reason "—as the ultimate principle that lay behind
all the universe. Needless to say, in the Greek thinkers
this philosophical conception had little room for religion,
and could not rank as theology. But in Philo we have a
Jew who was also a Greek philosopher. Few, if any,
have ever understood or expounded Plato better, and yet
his primary interest was to expound Moses. He identified
the Wisdom of Jewish theology with the Logos of Greek
philosophy, and, like the writer of the book of *Wisdom*,
held her to be a divine hypostasis. To him the *Logos*
(this is the term he prefers) is the divine agent alike in
creation and in communion, that through which alone
God comes into contact with man and makes and sustains
the universe. Yet the influence of Greek thinking has
had one interesting effect on Philo. He does not seem to
be quite sure whether the *Logos* is really personal or not.
We are left uncertain as to whether we are considering
one so completely individual as the Wisdom of the Jewish
philosopher or an abstraction like that of the Stoic.
Nevertheless, it is in Philo that we have the confluence
of the two great streams of thought, Hebrew and Jewish ;
and in a very real sense both find, not only their union,
but also their highest point, in him.

One further step remained. The *Logos*-Wisdom, however firmly believed in, was a philosophical conception, the produce of metaphysical speculation. Men reached the idea by argument, and must inevitably be left with some uncertainty on the whole subject. At any point men might break away and evolve a new theory altogether. Certainty could be attained only by experience, and this was not to be had within the bounds either of Judaism proper or of Greek thought. The climax, the final certification, was reached outside the borders of the Jewish faith when the evangelist, summing up the result of all that was best and truest in the thought of the two civilizations, placed the coping-stone on men's philosophy with the words, " The Logos became flesh and dwelt among us, and we beheld his glory, glory as of the only-begotten of the Father, full of grace and truth."

CHAPTER XXXVIII

THE MESSIANIC HOPE

1. THE EARLIER STAGES

KINGSHIP and deity are often found in close association. There are, indeed, many early forms of religion in which the "king" is the principal god of the tribe or locality, and the welfare of the whole community is thought to be centred in him.[1] Thus he must be protected from every form of evil, for, if disaster befall him, the whole body must suffer.[2] It often happens that if the king grows weak or old, he is violently removed, and a younger or stronger person is installed in his place.[3] In the higher cultures of Egypt and Mesopotamia, the theory was not carried to quite the extreme at which it appears among some more primitive peoples, but in Egypt the king was the son of a god, while in Babylonia he stood in a special relation to the deity. It has been supposed that a similar theory of the king as being divine was to be found also in Israel, but direct evidence is lacking, and the intensely strong "democratic" instincts of the Hebrew people make it improbable that this view was ever seriously held. It is, however, not impossible that the king played the rôle of the deity in certain types of dramatic ceremonial, and the fact that he had been " anointed " made his person sacrosanct.[4]

We are, then, not surprised to find that the king played a part in the eschatological speculation of Egypt, Assyria, and Babylonia.[5] " Eschatology," it is true, must not be

[1] Cf. *Myth and Ritual*, cf. esp. pp. 7 ff., 70 ff.

[2] It is possible that we have a trace of this feeling even in the Old Testament, for in 2 Sam. xxi. 17 David's men forbid him to go out to battle with them, in spite of his prowess, for fear that he should " quench the lamp of Israel," i.e. ruin the nation by the loss of his own life.

[3] For a discussion of this subject, with its countless illustrations and ramifications, see Frazer, *The Golden Bough*: " The Dying God," pp. 9–195 (1911).

[4] Cf. 1 Sam. xxiv. 6 (7 in Hebr.), xxvi. 11 ; 2 Sam. i. 14.

[5] Cf. Gressmann, *Der Ursprung der israelitisch-jüdischen Eschatologie*, pp. 250 ff. (1905).

interpreted in too narrow a sense. As Gressmann has insisted,[1] there was no thought of a distant future; what men hoped for was an immediate return of a golden age, in which all wrong should be righted, and all pain and evil give way to happiness and well-being. We find in Egyptian literature, for instance, poems in honour of various kings, in which the singer quoted an ancient prophecy (probably fictitious), and claimed that the monarch he was celebrating was about to fulfil the ancient dream.[2] A parallel may be found in Vergil's adulation of Augustus,[3] and it is a natural mode of expression for a court poet. We may, then, look for similar views in ancient Israel, though they will necessarily be modified by the characteristic political and religious thought of the Hebrew people. More than once we find expressions in certain Psalms which suggest the lengths to which even the Old Testament poet could go. Thus in Ps. ii. 7 ff., the king quotes a divine decree of adoption, which gives him the authority of Yahweh, and a world-wide dominion.[4] Ps. lxxii is a prayer for a monarch who is just ascending the throne, and Ps. cx is a description of the triumph secured for a king by Yahweh.

In passages like these Psalms, however, we seldom have reference to the great and catastrophic events which we usually associate with eschatology. And when we come to consider the characteristic Jewish apocalyptic literature, we find that, in its earlier forms, there is no reference to a human ruler, or even to a human agent of Yahweh, as He recreates the world. A typical apocalypse of this early type is to be found in Isa. xxiv–xxvii, where it is Yahweh alone who wins the great triumph, and whose accession to universal power is celebrated with feasting and with song. In the strict sense of the term, the Messianic hope had a long history before it met and mingled with the stream of eschatology proper, and it is the course of that history which we must endeavour briefly to trace.

The hope of a happy future is a part of the deathless inheritance of humanity. It is but seldom that matters

---

[1] *Der Messias*, p. 2, n. 1 (1929).

[2] For illustrations see Gressmann, *Altorientalische Texte zum Alten Testament*, pp. 46 ff. (1926).

[3] Cf. Aen, VI. 791 ff.

[4] It is extremely difficult to date any Psalms with confidence, but the opinion of modern scholarship tends towards the view that some of the "royal" Psalms belong to the pre-exilic age, at least in their original form, and that they were composed by court poets for special occasions such as the anointing or coronation of a king.

grow to such a pitch of suffering that men believe them to be irremediable, and the worse the state of the people, the stronger becomes the conviction that God will interfere, and the more extravagant the ways in which He will set the world right. At the last extremity men come to hold that the whole universe as we know it will be dissolved, and a new heaven and a new earth created from its shattered fragments. But before this point is reached, there are many stages through which men's hopes and visions pass; most of these have a Messiah of some kind in view.

In the earlier stages, then, of the great hope, men do not contemplate a fundamental change in the established order of things. Society will continue to exist on its present basis, and no far-reaching constitutional revolution is to be expected. The state was naturally organized, for Israel, as a monarchy, and the ideal was that of a perfect king. We have references which may go back as far as the early tenth century, but their date is doubtful and their interpretation uncertain.[1] We find ourselves on safe ground for the first time in Isaiah, and it is to him that we can best carry back the story of the Messianic idea.

In the opening verses of Isa. xxxii we have set before us the prospect of an ideal king, who shall be a refuge and a shelter for all who are in need. It is possible that the original utterance comprises only verses 1–5, for the three following verses are vague in tone, and may well have been appended by a later age. One striking result of the perfect reign is the change in human character. The rash learn prudence, the stammering become fluent, and men cease to compare folly and wisdom. We have also a distinct reference to one of the perennial requirements of Oriental government, insight and honesty in the administration of justice. In the last resort, in ancient Israel, an appeal always lay to the king, and if he had the ability to see who was speaking the truth and who was not, and if he were righteous and well-disposed, then it would follow that true justice would be exercised in all grades of society. The same thought meets us, still more clearly expressed, in the later passage Isa. xi. 1 ff., where[2] it is said that the ideal king "shall not judge after the sight of his eyes, nor reprove after the hearing of his ears." In a society where perjury is the rule and not

---

[1] Gressmann thus includes Gen. xlix. 8–12, and Num. xxiv. 15–19, but his interpretation is not wholly convincing and, in the former case, depends partly on conjectural emendation of the text.

[2] Verse 3.

the exception, it is only circumstantial evidence that can be seriously considered—and that is often manufactured. Hence the perfect judge must have remarkable powers of reaching the truth, and it is not surprising to find this qualification set in the forefront.

In Isa. ix. 6 f. occurs the well-known account of the Wonder-child.[1] He is to be endowed with more than ordinary powers, and is to stand in a special relation to Yahweh. The description is much more developed than that of ch. xxxii. 1 ff., and, perhaps, owes something to the older conceptions of popular and courtly Messianic theory. We shall probably be right in supposing that the prophet had in mind some actual king, perhaps Hezekiah or even Manasseh, and that his words were uttered on the birth of the young prince. We note here that the reign is inaugurated by sweeping triumph over an oppressor, probably, in the first instance, the Assyrians, and the new king is a mighty warrior, and sage in counsel. Other features appear. His dominion is to spread until it is universal, and it is to be of endless duration. So had Egyptian "prophets" spoken in praise of their kings, for the disappearance of the righteous sovereign might well bring about a return of the bad old customs, and failure to leave some portion of the world's surface unsubdued might mean another conquest and another oppression. Naturally, since the kings under whom Isaiah himself lived and worked were of the house of David, the ideal monarch would also be of that stock, or, at least, he would make David's own city the seat and centre of his government. In no small measure the picture here pre-sented served as a model for most of the later Messianic speculation.

Davidic ancestry is asserted in another passage which may be pre-exilic, though it is at least a century later than Isaiah. In Jer. xxiii. 5 f. we have another brief sketch of the coming ideal king, whose reign is to be marked by justice and prosperity for all Israel. Here, for the first time, we have the metaphor of the " Branch," or " shoot " of David. It is possible that the prophet hoped to find his desires fulfilled in Zedekiah, for the coming ruler receives a name which is the reverse of that of the last king of Judah.

---

[1] While the great Immanuel passage (Isa. vii. 14 ff.) attests the prophet's conviction of Yahweh's saving presence in Israel's midst, it cannot be called Messianic in the strict sense, for the promised child is not necessarily royal —indeed is probably a son of Isaiah himself.

If that be so, then the passage will belong to the time of Zedekiah's accession, for his name till that point had been Mattaniah.[1] Though the prophet was to be bitterly disappointed, yet the moment after the shock of Jehoiachin's deportation would be just the situation which would arouse hope. The worst, as it seemed, had happened, and surely now a brighter future must be dawning, a future of which the king's new name appeared symbolic.

From this time onwards Davidic ancestry is one of the normal features of the Messiah.[2] An exilic or early post-exilic passage recalls some of the phraseology of that last mentioned, and may be deliberately reminiscent of it.[3] The metaphor of the "branch" is carried still further; though the tree has now been cut down, yet there remains a hidden vitality in the stump which will send out a fresh shoot and restore the life of the tree. As before, the picture is that of the perfect king, but it includes also features which are new in the prophetic Messianism. There is, indeed, an apocalyptic tinge in its colouring, for, not only have we the perfect judge and the triumphant conqueror, but a new world comes into being. Nature, and not man alone, is affected by the new reign; she is no longer "red in tooth and claw." All the lust, greed, and cruelty of the non-moral world have vanished, the carnivorous animals have ceased to eat flesh, all alike are gentle and amenable to the mildest control, and the very cobra is almost a fit plaything for the babe at the breast. Behind this vision of loveliness and peace on earth there lies a spiritual cause; "the earth shall be full of the knowledge of Yahweh, as the waters cover the sea," and, once more, it is not man alone who has this link with God, but the humbler creation also.

Other passages, coming from the same general period, do not carry us so far. Ezekiel[4] holds that a time will come when all the exiles of Israel will be restored, and Judah and Israel shall be united under the leadership of a single "shepherd." An era of freedom, dominion and prosperity will then ensue, and the new "prince" will be another

[1] 2 Kings xxiv. 17.
[2] We can hardly include in a study of Jewish Messianic hope such a passage as Isa. xlv. 1, where Cyrus is expressly mentioned as the "Messiah."
[3] Isa. xi. 1–9. The passage can hardly be pre-exilic, still less Isaianic, since the word rendered "stem" in the E.V. properly means the stump left in the ground after a tree has been cut down. It could scarcely have been used of David as long as his family sat on the throne of Judah.
[4] Cf. Ezek. xxxiv. 22 ff., xxxvii. 15 ff.

David—or perhaps the original David restored to earth. In the isolated verse, Isa. xi. 10, it is the universality of the Messianic kingdom which is in view, and in Amos ix. 11 f. the power of the coming scion of the restored house of David is to be manifested particularly in the punishment of Edom. We may suspect that we have here a repercussion of the events of the exilic period, during which Edomites pressed into Palestine in numbers. Micah v. 2–4 [1] stresses the eternity and universality of the kingdom, and names Bethlehem as the place whence the Messiah derives his origin. Though the usual interpretation is that the birthplace of the Messiah is intended, the language used may mean no more than that he will be of the house of David. We may also note the late verse Jer. xxxiii. 17, which, again, insists on the eternal duration of the restored dominion of the house of David.

It seems not unlikely that the identification of the coming king with a member of David's family was already current at the close of the exile. Once, at least, within the Old Testament period, the prophetic spirit dared to acclaim as the Messiah a son of David who actually held authority in the land. One of the earliest of the governors of the restored community, appointed by the Persian court, was Zerubbabel, a grandson of Jehoiachin. His personality and his fate have been the subject of a good deal of study and speculation in recent years, but we still cannot say that much is known of him for certain. He is described as the leader of a band of returning exiles,[2] apparently not the first to take advantage of the decree of Cyrus, and he was the builder of the second Temple. There is ground also for the suspicion that he attempted the building of the walls of Jerusalem,[3] but the evidence, though uncertain and confused, suggests that this project was never fully carried out. We have, however, further light on him from the utterances of Haggai and of Zechariah. The book which bears the name of the former closes with a distinctly Messianic passage, in which a complete overthrow of the existing political world-order is contemplated, and Zerubbabel is to be made as a " signet." The word obviously implies some very close association with Yahweh, and it is possible that it was one of the less common terms in the vocabulary of Messianic thought, for we read in Jer. xxii. 24 that, though Jehoiachin were the " signet " on the right hand of Yahweh, he would yet be plucked thence and handed over to Nebuchadrezzar.

[1] Heb. 1–3.   [2] Ezr. ii. 2.   [3] Ezr. v. 3.

It is clear that there is some special significance in the word, and it is not unnatural to suppose that even the Messiahship —not mere kingship, but the highest possible form of kingship—would not save Jehoiachin from his doom.   In Zechariah, however, the Messianic position assigned to Zerubbabel is even clearer than in Haggai.   The prophet takes the old title of " branch," which, as we have seen, was used in this technical sense even before the fall of Jerusalem, and applies it to the Jewish governor.   In ch. iii we have the familiar vision in which Joshua, the high-priest contemporary with Zerubbabel, was arraigned by the Satan before Yahweh, and acquitted.   The judgement of the divine court concludes with the promise : " Behold I will bring forth my servant the branch." [1] Still clearer is the reference in vi. 9 ff. Two crowns of gold are made, to be set on the head of Joshua the high-priest.   It is generally recognized that the text is deficient here (probably deliber- ately mutilated), and that one crown alone was original, and that destined for Zerubbabel. For the passage continues : " Thus speaketh Yahweh of hosts, saying, Behold the man whose name is the branch ; and he shall grow up (literally : shall branch out) out of his place, and he shall build the Temple of the Lord, and he shall bear the glory, and shall sit and rule upon his throne, and a priest shall be upon his throne ; and the counsel of peace shall be between them." [2] The conclusion is inevitable ; the builder of the Temple was to receive royal position, independent of foreign rulers, and was to share the government of the country with the " head of the Church," i.e. with the high-priest.   This civil authority can be none other than Zerubbabel himself, and it is clear that the prophet looked to him for the restoration, not only of the Temple, but also of the independent Jewish state and empire.

It is in the light of this identification of Zerubbabel with the expected Messiah that we must read much of the work of Zechariah.   The task is to be accomplished by super- human means : " Not by might, nor by power, but by my spirit, saith Yahweh of hosts." [3]   Jerusalem itself is to be so safe a place that men shall live in it to great old age, and, at the same time, the streets of the city shall be full of playing children.[4]   The coming prosperity shall at least balance all the affliction that the country has suffered in recent

[1] Zech. iii. 8.   [2] Zech. vi. 12 f.
[3] Zech. iv. 6.   [4] Zech. viii. 4 f.

generations,[1] and the place shall become the religious centre, not only for all Jews, but for every nation on the face of the earth.[2]

We do not know what fate befell Zerubbabel, but it is not unlikely that, in the general settlement which occupied the early years of Darius' reign, he was removed, and may have met with a violent end. But the Messianic hope survived him, and Israel still looked for a deliverer, human indeed, but yet carrying with him the power of Yahweh Himself. There are many passages of exilic and post-exilic date which are sometimes regarded as Messianic, especially, perhaps, the " Servant Songs " in Isa. xl–lv, but it seems probable that they ought not so to be interpreted, and that their Messianic significance is due to later reflection, Jewish and Christian. An exception may be made in the case of Zech. ix. 9–11, where the Messiah appears riding in triumph into Jerusalem, there to inaugurate his universal reign of peace. But, for fuller development of the conception, we must pass on to the last two centuries B.C.

2. THE MESSIAH IN APOCALYPTIC [3]

As we have already seen, the conception of the Messiah, or ideal king, for many centuries maintained an existence independent of eschatology proper. It is necessary to emphasize this point, since in common speech the term " Messianic " is often applied to the ideal state in which the universal convulsions of Apocalyptic always end. We need not doubt that the thought of a Messiah lived long in Israel, or that it played its part in the *tout ensemble* of religious belief, but it was only at a comparatively late stage in pre-Christian Judaism that the two streams of thought were combined.

Apocalyptic is always the product of distress, and reaches its greatest heights only when the situation seems desperate from the human point of view. Then God *must* step in, and, in His own ways, by methods to which man's experience furnishes no parallel, destroy Evil and instal Good in its place. The Persian period of Jewish history, and the first part of the Greek period (during which Palestine was under

---

[1] Zech. viii. 9–15.   [2] Zech. viii. 20 ff.
[3] Only a bare outline of this very large subject can be attempted here. For fuller treatment the reader is referred to special works such as R. H. Charles, *Eschatology, Hebrew, Jewish and Christian* (1899), and W. O. E. Oesterley, *An Introduction to the Books of the Apocrypha*, pp. 95–100 (1936).

Ptolemaic rule), were a time of comparative peace and prosperity, save for such isolated incidents as the invasion of Artaxerxes Ochus. But with the passing of Palestine into the hands of the Seleucids, early in the second century B.C., there came a change.   Greek modes of thought and life became popular, especially in certain quarters; factions arose, the orthodox and the liberal parties drifting ever further into mutual hostility and hatred; and Antiochus IV threw himself with passionate earnestness into the struggle. The age of persecution which ended with the Maccabæan triumph inevitably provided a fresh stimulus to eschatological speculation, and the impulse was sufficiently strong to make Apocalyptic the characteristic form of Jewish religious literature till after the fall of the second Temple in A.D. 70.

But, once more, Apocalyptic could, and did, exist apart from the Messianic hope. There is no mention of a Messiah in the one pre-Maccabæan Apocalypse we have—Enoch xii–xxxvi. An ideal kingdom is established, it is true, but it is God Himself who dwells in the midst of His people.[1] Similarly we find no Messiah in Enoch xci–civ, 1 and 2 Maccabees, or in any of the Apocryphal books except II (IV) Esdras, and even there his figure is absent from the Apocalypse contained in chs. iii–x, which dates from about A.D. 100. He is not mentioned in the Assumption of Moses, the Slavonic Enoch, 4 Maccabees, or in the Apocalypse of Baruch. Wherever, in these books, an ideal kingdom is contemplated, the king is God Himself, conquering and ruling directly, without the aid of any intermediary, human or superhuman.

The one extensive piece of Apocalyptic writing in the Old Testament is the Book of Daniel, and in vii. 13–14 we read of one " like a son of man," i.e. of human form, who appears after the Ancient of Days has won His triumph. He comes on the clouds of heaven, approaches the Ancient of Days, and receives a royal authority which knows no limits of space or time.   While it is sometimes held that he is a personification of Israel as a whole, it is at least possible, even probable, that he is conceived as a superhuman individual, who gathers into his own person all the powers, qualities and functions of the ancient Messiah.

But, for the most part, even when a Messiah appears, he comes as a mere man, though with extraordinary powers and authority. In some of the many varied forms of

[1] Enoch xxv. 2.

Apocalypse he stands curiously apart from the final consummation of eschatological hopes. The old instinct,
which kept asunder the conceptions of an ideal human
king and a finally reconstructed world-order, is still at work,
and there is hardly an instance in the post-Maccabæan
Jewish Apocalyptic where the two are combined,[1] though
there is still room for a Messiah in a spiritual new world
which shall know no end.

We thus find a tendency to develop a doctrine of a
temporary Messiahship, a rule on earth of the ideal king,
as a penultimate stage in the Apocalyptic process. It is
even categorically stated that the Messiah shall die, and that
his departure is the signal for the inauguration of the final
stage.[2] The duration of his reign on earth is fixed at 400
or 1000 years, and even where it is not fixed, it is assumed
that it will come to an end. For Judaism had abandoned
the prophetic hope of an ideal kingdom on earth, and with
it the conception of an everlasting Messianic reign.

Yet often the Messiah plays his part, as a human figure
who is, nevertheless, in a special sense a divine agent. His
character and functions, however, are variously conceived.
Usually, where his ancestry is mentioned, he is of the house
of David, or, at least, of the tribe of Judah, but, in one
instance in the *Testaments of the XII Patriarchs*,[3] he is a
Levite—perhaps a reminiscence of the Maccabæan heroes.
In one passage [4] he comes from the east; both here and in
many other places he appears as a conquering warrior who
destroys the wicked. But, at other times, he is introduced
and enthroned only after the great victory has been won,
and the world lies subject beneath the feet of God.[5]

One independent and original presentation deserves
special mention, that of the *Similitudes of Enoch*.[6] Here
the Messiah is of no human ancestry; he is not even a son
of David. Among the titles applied to him is that of Son
of Man; it would seem that the writer has taken it from the
passage in the Book of Daniel already cited. He comes
as judge of angels and of men, and is possessed in the highest
degree of those qualities which the old prophets had
considered indispensable in the ideal king.

With this one exception, however (though that is most

---

[1] Cf. Charles, *Eschatology: Hebrew, Jewish and Christian*, pp. 200 f.
(1899).
[2] II (IV) *Esdras* vii. 28 f.   [3] *Levi* xviii.   [4] *Sib. Or.* iii. 652–54.
[5] Cf. *Enoch* xc. 38.   [6] *Ethiopic Enoch* xxxvii–lxx.

important), the Messiah plays a secondary part in post-Maccabæan Jewish Apocalyptic. From the first he had been an earthly monarch, and, in spite of his unique capacities and powers, he had never been accorded higher rank. For the age of the apocalyptic writers, the merely human and the merely earthly were inadequate. The world as they knew it had deteriorated past all healing. They may have been remotely and dimly affected by that Greek philosophic idealism which despised all matter, or the sufferings of their present may have sufficed to drive them into a hope of an unearthly future. For, whatever be their motives, that was their ultimate ideal. The prospect of a redeemed Israel had vanished or sunk into the background, and their conception of the world to come was markedly individualistic. Losing all expectation of a restored Israel, they desired a better country, that is, a heavenly.

In such a scheme the traditional figure of the Messiah could have no final place. Like all else about them, he was of the earth, earthy. True, he represented the utmost heights to which this world could attain, but the loftiest physical peaks were still immeasurably lower than that heaven towards which their eyes were turned. The utmost that even a son of David could do was in some measure to prepare the way for the eternal future. He might reign for a space on earth, exhibiting the perfect human character and creating conditions of unalloyed happiness and peace. But that was not enough; these things were but evanescent, and, when they passed, the Messiah must pass with them. It was left to Christian thought to accept, expand, and transfigure the hint dropped in the *Similitudes of Enoch*, and to transfer the Messiah from the realm of this life to that which is eternal in the heavens. Only so could an Apocalyptic writer envisage the dual throne of God and of the Lamb, claim for his Messiah that he should reign for ever and ever, and hail Him King of kings and Lord of lords.

CHAPTER XXXIX

ESCHATOLOGY AND APOCALYPTIC

1. Jewish Eschatology

Eschatological, with its frequently accompanying apocalyptic, thought among the Hebrews goes back to an early period. It centred in the popular idea that a "Day of Yahweh" would come, a day on which the national God would show His might by overcoming the enemies of His people and inaugurate a time of well-being and prosperity for them. This expectation was shattered by Amos (v. 18–20), who brought in an ethical element hitherto absent in eschatological thought. But the way in which Amos refers to the "Day of Yahweh" shows that already in his time the people of Israel were familiar with the idea;[1] indeed, there is much in the prophetical books and elsewhere which makes it clear that the circle of ideas connected with the eschatological outlook goes back to far more ancient times.[2] With the earlier phases of eschatological thought we cannot deal here; but we must recall briefly the main themes of Hebrew eschatology, for it is our purpose to show that Jewish eschatological and apocalyptic ideas as we find them during and after the Persian period have been *added* to by elements taken from the eschatology of Persia. True, this latter is largely the product of earlier pre-Zoroastrian times, too; but Jewish eschatology in its later phases is nevertheless indebted to Persia; and to examine in what directions this was the case is our present task.

Jewish Eschatology as it came down from earlier times comprised (among others to be considered presently) the following themes: The belief that in the "Day of Yahweh" God would intervene in favour of His chosen

---

[1] See p. 235.

[2] The classical works on the subject generally are: Gunkel, *Schöpfung und Chaos in Urzeit und Endzeit* (1895); Gressmann, *Der Ursprung der israelitisch-jüdischen Eschatologie* (1905); A. von Gall, Βασιλέια τοῦ θεοῦ (1926); Bousset, *Die Religion des Judentums*, pp. 202–301 (1926); and see further, Volz, *Die Eschatologie der jüdischen Gemeinde im neutestamentlichen Zeitalter* (1934).

people, and would overthrow the enemies of Israel. There was next the hope of the establishment of a new kingdom ruled over by a Messianic king belonging to the House of David. Further, there was to be the ingathering of the scattered members of the race in their own land, and the conversion of the Gentiles to the belief in Yahweh. These beliefs and hopes had existed in one form or another since the Exile and before; and they were intensified and came to fuller expression whenever the times became dark and perplexing.

Now if the eschatological beliefs of Judaism had had to do with these alone we should not necessarily have grounds for thinking that extraneous influences had been at work. But alongside of these beliefs we find that there are thoughts and expectations of a rather different kind. Thus, it is not for Israel exclusively that the bright future is anticipated. Although in the foreground it is the chosen people who appear, the purview is widened, and the whole world is embraced within this hope. Then, too, there is the expectation of the annihilation of the world in order that the new world of the future may take its place. Again, as regards the present world-order, it is seen to be divided up into different periods, the precise length of each of which is accurately calculated, and at the right time God will intervene in the world's history and bring about this annihilation and the creation of the new world. Further, the judgement upon Israel's enemies became the final judgement of the whole world. And finally, in connection with the end of this world and the new one to come, there appears the belief in the resurrection of the dead, and a world-wide kingdom of God.

We find therefore that with the earlier national Messianic hope there are now combined expectations which are *cosmological* and *universal*. And these new thoughts do not develop organically from the old Messianic prophecies; rather, they are superimposed upon, or else run parallel with, the traditional beliefs. The time-honoured Messianic hopes are not discarded; they continue alongside of these new ideas. It is this mingling of new and old which is one of the causes of the confused and ill-balanced character of the picture of the future presented in Jewish Apocalyptic, wherein we find, for example, hopes concerning this world indiscriminately mixed up with those about the world to come. There

are good grounds for believing that the superimposed
ideas referred to were not indigenous to Israel, but that
they were absorbed by Jewish apocalyptic thinkers, from
extraneous sources.   One of these extraneous sources, and
so far as the present subject is concerned the most important, is to be sought in the religion of ancient Persia,
Iranian religion.   It was pointed out above, p. 312, that
the antecedents of the religion of Persia go back for
centuries before the time of Zoroaster; it is necessary to
bear this in mind, as it applies to much that we meet with
in Iranian apocalyptic belief.

2. Persian Eschatology and Apocalyptic

It is not our purpose to deal with all the marks of
Iranian influence on Jewish Apocalyptic, but we shall
concentrate on those points which are of importance.
As a preliminary, however, we must give in very brief
outline a general *résumé* of Iranian Apocalyptic.

At the base of this lies the dualistic conception of the
irreconcilable antagonism between the highest god, Ahura-
Mazda, who is all-good, and Añgra-Mainyu, the great spirit
of evil.   They are in constant conflict for the possession
of the world and of mankind.   The existence of the world
is to last for a period of 12,000 years.   The first six thousand
years' period is unimportant for our purpose; it is sufficient
to say that it consisted of two eras of three thousand
years each, during the first of which all things were invisible.   We get a reference to this in the *Secrets of Enoch*
xxiv. 4, where God says to Enoch: " For before all were
visible I alone used to go about in the invisible things."
During the second of these two eras Ahura-Mazda created
the material, good world, and the first man.

The second six thousand years are also divided into
two eras ; and it is during both of these that the conflict
between Ahura-Mazda and Añgra-Mainyu takes place.
The first three thousand years of this second great division
of the world's history is the time of the complete ascendancy of Añgra-Mainyu, the evil spirit.   But at the end
of these first three thousand years there appears the
figure of Zarathustra, and with him arises the hope of
better things, though the conflict between the powers of
good and evil continues.   Then, at a certain time, occurs
the miraculous birth of Shaoshyant, of the seed of Zarathustra and the virgin Hvôv : he is to be the saviour of

the world, for his work is to be the gradual improving of mankind until it reaches perfection, when the end of the world will begin to take place. Then the dead will be raised and will be judged. Fire will come down from heaven and will burn up the earth. All men will have to pass through that fire; but some will pass through it easily, and unharmed, " as though through a milky warmth "; while others will suffer fearful torments from it; for the fire will burn up all the dross of iniquity which still clings to them. But ultimately all will be saved. And then Ahura-Mazda will come forth with his angelic hosts for the final conflict against Añgra-Mainyu and his legions of evil spirits. Ahura-Mazda will gain the victory, and the powers of evil will be annihilated. After that there will be inaugurated a life of happiness in a new world, wherein evil and sorrow and pain will find no place.

That is a very brief outline of Iranian Eschatology and Apocalyptic; many details have not been touched on, but what has been indicated includes all that is really fundamental.

We must now compare this with Jewish Apocalyptic; and here we shall restrict ourselves to four subjects, which will, however, be seen to be those of main import- ance, viz. (i) Dualism; (ii) World-Epochs; (iii) the Judge- ment, and the Destruction of the world by fire; (iv) the Resurrection of the dead. And then, finally, we shall refer to one or two other points of interest.

(a) *Dualism.*—Throughout Iranian Eschatology and Apo- calyptic there lies, as we have seen, the fundamental thought of the contrast and conflict between Ahura- Mazda and Añgra-Mainyu. The entire history of man- kind is conditioned by, and is the result of, this perpetual and varying struggle; and the end of the world, with the final judgement, coincides with the triumph of the Lord of good over the powers of evil.

Dualism is foreign to Judaism, so that when dualistic conceptions occur in Jewish apocalyptic writings it is to Persian influence that we must ascribe their presence there. Thus, in a late apocalyptic passage in the book of *Isaiah* we have these mystical words: " And it shall come to pass in that day, that Yahweh shall punish the host of the high ones on high, and the kings of the earth upon the earth. And they shall be gathered together as prisoners into a pit, and shall be shut up in a dungeon,

and after many days they shall be punished. Then the
moon shall be confounded, and the sun shall be put to
shame ; for Yahweh Zebaoth shall reign in mount Zion
and in Jerusalem, and before his ancients there shall be
glory " (xxiv. 21–23). What is here referred to is seen in
a number of passages in the *Book of Enoch*, of which one or
two must be given. In x. 11 ff. it is said : " And the
Lord said unto Michael, Go, bind Semjaza and his
associates . . . bind them fast for seventy generations
in the valleys of the earth, till the day of their judgement
and of their consummation, till the judgement that is
for ever and ever is consummated. . . . Destroy all wrong
from the face of the earth, and let every evil work come
to an end." Again in xci. 15 we read : " There shall be
the great eternal judgement, in which He will execute
vengeance amongst the angels." Similarly in various
other passages of this book, as well as in the *Book of
Jubilees, the Testaments of the Twelve Patriarchs*, the
Secrets of Enoch and the *Assumption of Moses*, books
which contain the floating apocalyptic material of earlier
centuries. In all such passages that which lies behind
the ideas of punishment, vengeance, judgement, etc.,
is the victory of the Lord of good over the powers of evil,
at the head of which stands Satan or the Devil (see
especially *Test. of the xii. Patr.*, Naphthali 8, Issachar 7,
Benjamin 5) ; in other words, we have the same dualistic
conception which, as we have seen, is specifically Iranian.
Particularly noticeable is the fact that the contending
forces are *spiritual* powers.

Now, nobody would for a moment assert that dualistic
conceptions had ever formed part of the prophetic or
official Hebrew religious thought ; and it is certain that
orthodox Judaism would have repudiated them ; so that
when we find that after the Persian period they have
entered into the circle of ideas in Jewish Eschatology,
and that they correspond with what is fundamental in
Iranian belief, the conclusion is irresistible that the former
was influenced here by the latter.[1]

(*b*) *World-epochs.*—This subject, it is true, is not of

---

[1] It is also worth pointing out that Persian dualism was influenced by
the earlier Babylonian Dragon- (*Tiamat*) myth, as one would naturally
expect ; but although this myth appears every now and again throughout
the Old Testament, and must therefore have been quite familiar to Israel,
there is never any hint that Hebrew religion was affected by it, as the
Persian belief was.

much interest, but it is worth a passing notice because it belongs so closely to Iranian thought and has so clearly left its mark on Jewish Apocalyptic. In this latter the idea of world-epochs occurs, for example, in the calculation that the present world-order is to last for six thousand years: this number is strongly reminiscent of Iranian reckoning, and it would easily have lent itself to Jewish adaptation, since here it could be based on the number of days of the Creation, and according to Ps. xc. 4, a thousand years are as one day with God. Another reckoning of the duration of the world was seven thousand years, while in the *Book of Enoch* the time of the world's existence is divided into different periods quite in the Persian style (see xci. 12–17 and xciii).

This idea of world-epochs, again, is not indigenous to Jewish thought; it came from outside into Jewish Apocalyptic, and it would be difficult to say where it could have come from if not from Iranian Apocalyptic.

(c) *The Judgement and the Destruction of the World by Fire.*—Here we come to a subject of greater interest. The two ideas of Judgement and of World-conflagration belong together. To be sure, prophecies of a coming judgement run through the whole of Old Testament prophetic literature; and the special idea of a *World-*judgement, not only that of Israel and its enemies, but of all flesh, the living and the dead, and also of angels, is to be discerned in some of the later writings of the Old Testament (see the book of *Joel*, Isa. xxiv–xxvii and *Daniel*). It is therefore not in the thought of a World-judgement, as such, that there is necessarily any connexion between Iranian and Jewish Apocalyptic. The mark of the influence of the former on the latter is, however, to be seen in the consummation of the Judgement, in the idea of the destruction of the world by *fire*. Reference was made above to the fire which, according to Iranian belief, was to come down from heaven and burn up the earth; the account of this occurs in the *Bundehesh* [1] xxx, where it tells of a fiery stream of molten metal coming down from above and melting mountains and hills; all men, good and bad, have to pass through it. There are indications of the same conception in the earlier *Gathas*,[2]

[1] This work belongs to the later Pahlavi literature; it contains the eschatology of the Parsis, much of which comes from more ancient sources.
[2] The earliest part of the *Avesta*, the Zoroastrian Bible.

which contains the oldest tradition. This is a conception which is peculiar to Iranian Apocalyptic, so that when we find it appearing in the later phases of Jewish Apocalyptic, it is only natural to ascribe its presence here to Iranian influence. One or two illustrations may be given. It is first adumbrated in Zeph. i. 14–18, iii. 8. Other passages are, for example, the following : in the fourth book of the *Sibylline Oracles*, 173 ff., occur these words : " Then fire shall come upon the whole world . . . the whole world shall hear a rumbling and a mighty roar. And he [i.e. God] shall burn the whole earth, and consume the whole race of men, and all the cities and rivers, and the sea. He shall burn everything out, and there shall be sooty dust. . . ." A similar thought lies at the back of Dan. vii. 10 : " A fiery stream issued and came forth from before him : thousand thousands ministered unto him, and ten thousand times ten thousand stood before him : the judgement was set, and the books were opened." The conjunction of the fiery stream with the judgement here is significant. The judgement coming *after* the fiery stream, the point of which is the destruction of all flesh, strikes one as strange ; but in the context of the passage from the *Sibylline Oracles* just quoted, it says that " God will clothe the bones and ashes again in human shape, and re-make men as they were before " ; so that we are evidently meant to understand that the resurrection intervened between the World-conflagration and the Judgement.

Again, in the extraordinary account of the end of the present world-order and of the Judgement given in the *Assumption of Moses*, x. 1–10, it is clearly as a result of the World-conflagration that it is said that " the fountains of waters shall fail, and the rivers shall dry up." Then also, in the many speculative ideas contained in *Enoch* i–xxxvi there is one which conceives of this fire as being kept in a certain place whither Enoch journeys ; for he tells of how he was taken " to the fire of the west, which receives every setting of the sun " ; he comes also " to a river of fire in which the fire flows like water, and discharges itself into the great sea towards the west " (xvii. 4, 5). And once more, in an eschatological passage in the *Psalms of Solomon* xv, the thought of the World-conflagration appears in the words of vers. 6, 7 : " The flame of fire and the wrath against the unrighteous shall not touch him, when it goeth forth from the face of the Lord against sinners."

These passages—and a number of similar ones could be given—all refer to the same event, directly or indirectly. And many authorities, though not all, are agreed that the contents of such bear on them the impress of Iranian influence. And, indeed, so far as this particular subject is concerned, the conception occurs nowhere but in Iranian and in the later Jewish Apocalyptic ; so that the only alternative to Iranian influence is to suppose that it arose independently in the minds of the Jewish Apocalyptists ; this is intrinsically improbable, for according to the traditional Jewish eschatological scheme, the earth was to be the place where the Messianic kingdom would be set up.

This subject has a further interest from the fact that the idea of a World-conflagration was taken over into Christian Apocalyptic ; among other passages in early Christian literature showing this there is the well-known one in 2 Pet. iii. 10 : " . . . The heavenly bodies shall be dissolved with fervent heat, and the earth and the works that are therein shall be burned up." [1]

(d) *The Resurrection.*—Here we come to the most important point of the whole subject, as it is also the most debatable. We have already expressed our conviction that the thought of resurrection was, at any rate, adumbrated in Isa. liii. 12, which we believe to have belonged to the exilic period (see above, p. 308) ; it would therefore seem at first sight to be incongruous to suppose that Jewish belief was indebted to Persia ; but it must be remembered that there are good grounds for the contention that Persian influences were at work for a considerable time before the Babylonian empire came to an end.[2]

In any case, however, we are dealing here with the more developed forms of Jewish Apocalyptic, and it will be

[1] Granting that κατακαήσεται is not the best reading (אBKP Syr^p have εὑρεθήσεται), its occurrence in AL and in one of the Syriac Versions is sufficient witness to the existence of the thought in early Christian circles. It is also worth pointing out that 2 *Clem.* xvi. 3, which is based on this passage, has : καὶ πᾶσα ἡ γῆ ὡς μόλυβδος ἐπὶ πυρὶ τηκόμενος (" . . . melted as lead in fire "). Dr. Edwyn Bevan reminds us (in a private communication) that the Stoics believed in a destruction, or rather absorption, of the Kosmos by fire ; in his opinion this is the more probable source of the Christian belief.

[2] See note on p. 312.

seen that there is every reason for believing in the influence of Persian thought here.

In both Iranian and Jewish Apocalyptic the Resurrection is closely connected with the World-conflagration and the Judgement, and the conjunction of these themes is to be found in Iranian and Jewish Eschatology alone. And further, as Bousset [1] has pointed out, in Jewish Eschatology we have two incongruous ideas side by side ; there is, *in addition* to the Judgement and the general Resurrection of the dead at the last day, retribution on the individual immediately after death, and therefore before the Resurrection. The idea of a twofold retribution in the Hereafter occurs nowhere else but in Iranian Eschatology. The two facts mentioned should be sufficient to prove the indebtedness of Jewish Apocalyptists to Persia. To go further into the question would take us too far afield, and would involve giving a number of quotations from the Apocalyptic literature.[2] We must content ourselves with a reference to Bousset's book (pp. 469–524), and to Böklen's work (to be mentioned below), where the whole subject is most carefully dealt with.

So far, then, we have, in the briefest possible way, drawn attention to four subjects in Jewish Eschatology in which, it is maintained, Persian influence is to be discerned. With the exception of World-epochs these subjects are of far-reaching importance on account of later developments both in Jewish and Christian thought.

3. Some Further Marks of Persian Influence

The subjects dealt with are far from exhausting the marks of Persian influence ; a few others, of less importance, it is true, but not without interest, are worth drawing attention to, as they offer further arguments in favour of our thesis.[3]

(a) In various passages in the *Bundehesh* and in the *Gathas* there are indications that it is the part of Shaoshyant, [4] the great benefactor of the human race, to take

---

[1] *Die Religion des Judentums*, pp. 511 f. (1926).

[2] A few of these will be found below.

[3] For a full presentation of the case for Persian influence one could hardly do better than consult Böklen's *Die Verwandtschaft der jüdisch-christlichen mit der parsischen Eschatologie* (1902).

[4] He is the last (and most important) of other *Shaoshyants* who appeared at earlier periods.

a leading part in the Resurrection of the dead. In Jewish Eschatology it is, as a rule, the Almighty Himself who does this ; but there are exceptions, which are in all probability due to Persian influence. Thus, in *Enoch* li. 1 ff., in a passage dealing with the Resurrection, the central position is taken by the Messiah, the Elect One: " And in those days shall the earth also give back that which hath been entrusted to it, and *She'ol* shall give back that which it hath received, and Hell shall give back that which it owes. For in those days the Elect One shall arise, and he shall choose the righteous and holy from among them ; for the day hath drawn nigh that they should be saved. And the Elect One shall in those days sit upon my throne, and his mouth shall pour forth all the secrets of wisdom and counsel ; for the Lord of Spirits hath given them to him, and hath glorified him." It is clear here that the Elect One (i.e. the Messiah) is thought of as the central figure at the Resurrection ; and this is entirely parallel to that of Shaoshyant in Persian Eschatology.

(*b*) Another, somewhat curious, illustration of Persian influence is connected with some rather *naïve* ideas concerning the nature of the risen body. In *Bundehesh* xxx. 6 it is said that the risen body will be composed of the same elements as those comprised in the formation of man's original, earthly body :

> Bones from the spirit of the earth,
> Blood from water,
> Hairs from the plants,
> Life's vigour from fire.

It must surely be ultimately from this that the fuller description of man's component parts, though not, it is true, in reference to his risen body, given in the *Secrets of Enoch* xxx. 8, was taken :

> His flesh from the earth,
> His blood from the dew,
> His eyes from the sun,
> His bones from stone,
> His intelligence from the swiftness of angels and from cloud,
> His veins and his hair from the grass of the earth,
> His soul from my breath and from the wind.

(*c*) And to give but one other illustration : there was

the strange idea that the possession of immortality would
be retained by partaking of certain food which men will
enjoy after the Resurrection. This food, it is said in
Bundehesh xxx. 25, is the white Haoma, and the fat of
the ox Hadhayaos. This idea of food for the immortals
seems to have been taken over in Jewish Apocalyptic,
though the nature of the food differed. In the difficult
passage, Isa. xxvi. 19, one thing, at any rate, seems clear,
and that is that the dead bodies which shall arise will
partake of the dew of light. It is a far more exalted
conception than the Persian one, but the thought of food
for the risen is the same. According to *Enoch* xxv. 4, 5,
there is in the abode of the risen a tree which has " a
fragrance beyond all fragrance, and its leaves and blooms
and wood wither not for ever ; and its fruit is beautiful,
and resembles the dates of a palm." Similarly, in the
Test. of the xii. Patr., Levi xviii. 10, it is said that the Most
High will open the gates of Paradise, and " shall give to
the saints to eat from the tree of life " ; and in the
Secrets of Enoch viii. 2 ff., the same thought occurs and is
elaborated : " Every tree sweet-flowering, every fruit
ripe, all manner of food perpetually bubbling with all
pleasant perfumes . . . and the tree of life is at that
place " (see also Rev. xxii. 2, 17). These illustrations
will suffice, though there are others which could be given.

What has been said is sufficient to show that Persian
influences have left their mark on Jewish Eschatology.

4. The Jewish Apocalyptists and their Literature

We have emphasized the fact of Persian influence in
Jewish Apocalyptic because, while it is what might be
expected from the nature of the case, it is by no means
always recognized, and indeed is altogether denied by
some writers, though on insufficient grounds.

But to recognize Persian influence in this sphere is not
to deny that there is plenty of individuality and independence of thought among the Jewish Apocalyptists.

The period to which the Jewish Apocalyptic Movement
belongs is roughly from 200 B.C. to A.D. 100, but its roots
and its extraneous engrafted growths go back, as we have
seen, to earlier times.

The nameless teachers and writers of Jewish Apocalyptic
occupied in some respects the position of the prophets

of old ; and this mainly in their denunciation of the
godless, with prophecies of punishment, and in their
words of comfort and encouragement to those seeking to
do what was right, but suffering at the hands of oppressors ;
for these, too, prophecies were uttered, and of a nature
that was calculated to hearten them.

As an illustration of the former the following may be
quoted :

> And when sin and unrighteousness and blasphemy
> And violence in all kinds of deeds increase,
> And apostasy and transgression and uncleanness abound,
> Then shall a great chastisement from heaven come upon all
>   these.
> And the holy Lord will come forth with wrath and chastise-
>   ment,
> To execute judgement upon the earth.
> In those days violence shall be cut off from its roots,
> And the roots of unrighteousness together with deceit,
> And they shall be destroyed from under heaven.
>
> (Enoch xcii. 7, 8.)

On the other side we have words such as these :

> But with the righteous he will make peace,
> And will protect the elect,
> And mercy shall be upon them.
> And they shall belong to God,
> And they shall be prospered,
> And they shall all be blessed.
> And he will help them all,
> And light shall appear unto them,
> And he will make peace with them.
>
> (Enoch i. 8.)

The sense of passages like these occurs very often ; and
thus the main concern of the Apocalyptists was with the
future, with the age that was to come, when all the
inequalities and incongruities of the present age would be
put right. In their pictures of the destruction of the
present world-order the Apocalyptists are fond of lurid
painting, and a supernatural element looms largely.
The frequent occurrence of this theme of world-destruction,
adapted, as we have seen, from Iranian Eschatology,
arises from the fact that the Jewish Apocalyptists regarded
this world, with the majority of mankind, as hopelessly
corrupt ; in their despair of amelioration they became
pessimists ; there was nothing for it but utter annihila-

tion in order that a fresh start might be made, and in a
new world, i.e. the Messianic times.[1]

This leads us to say something of the Messiah as portrayed by the Apocalyptic writers. And here it is
especially necessary to bear in mind that extraneous
elements have been absorbed, and that the varying views
of different writers preclude the possibility of a uniform
picture. Therefore it need not cause surprise if at one
time we find the Messiah spoken of as an ordinary man,
at another as of superhuman nature. Thus, in the *Test.
of the xii. Patr.*, Judah xxiv. 5, it is said : " Then shall the
sceptre of my kingdom shine forth, and from your root
shall arise a stem " ;   the words are purported to have
been uttered by Judah to his sons ; the Messiah is therefore thought of as belonging to the tribe of Judah. On
the other hand, in Dan. vii. 13 the Messiah is clearly
conceived of as superhuman, as appearing on " the clouds
of heaven." The belief in the Messiah's *pre-existence*
obviously assumes his transcendental character ; it is
said, e.g. in the *Apocalypse of Ezra* xiii. 52 : " Just as
one has not the power to search out and to find or to know
what is in the depths of the sea, so can none of those
who are upon the earth see my Son or them that are with
him except in that time in his day " ; here pre-existence
is clearly implied (cp. ver. 26, xiv. 9) ; so, too, in *Enoch*
lxii. 7 :

> For from the beginning the Son of Man was hidden,
> And the Most High preserved him in the presence of his might,
> And revealed him to the elect.

Passages presenting each conception could be greatly
multiplied. When the Messiah appears he will, of course,
come as King (*Psalms of Solomon* [2] xvii. 21, 42 ; cp. *Enoch*
lii. 4). But he will also come as Judge to punish sinners
and destroy the enemies of Israel (*Test. of the xii. Patr.*, Judah
xxiv. 6 ; *Psalms of Solomon* xvii. 22 ff.) ; on the other hand,
he will come as the Saviour of those who " have hated
and despised this world of unrighteousness " (*Enoch*
xlviii. 7).

[1] In the later Jewish literature the woes which are to precede the
Messianic Age are called " the birth-pangs of the Messiah " (*Cheble ha-
Mashiach*) (cp. Mark xiii).

[2] Not to be confused with the *Odes of Solomon*, which are Christian,
and belong to about A.D. 200 or a little earlier; the *Psalms of Solomon*
are Pharisaic, and were written about 50 B.C.

A great deal more is, of course, said about the Messiah, of his close relation to God, of his character, and of his work ; but to deal with all this would take up too much space.

Though the Apocalyptists were dreamers and seers of visions they were fully alive to the claims of practical religion ; and therefore they were loyal to the Law, though not in the rigid way of the strictly orthodox, laying stress rather on the spirit of its observance than in carrying out legal precepts in the letter; herein prophetic influence is plainly discernible.

Reference has been made above to World-epochs as a sign of Persian influence on Jewish Eschatology ; in connexion with this mention must be made of the doctrine of Determinism, which is characteristic of this literature. All things that happen in the world, both as regards its physical changes, as well as the history of nations, has been pre-determined by God ; thus it is said in the *Apocalypse of Ezra* iv. 36, 37 :

> For he hath weighed the age in the balance,
> And by number hath he numbered the seasons;
> Neither will he move nor stir things,
> Till the measure appointed be fulfilled.

But all these things were secrets which could only be made known to certain God-fearing men who possessed the faculty, divinely accorded, of being able to peer into the hidden things of God ; the Apocalyptists believed themselves therefore to be commissioned by God to reveal these secrets to their fellow-creatures. Thus, both as receivers of revelations and as revealers of them to others, they are appropriately called Apocalyptists.

A further mark of prophetic influence may perhaps be seen in the, generally speaking, universalistic attitude of the Apocalyptists ; passages from their works in a contrary sense could be given, but it is true to say that they are inclined to a universalistic rather than to a national particularistic outlook (*Enoch* xlviii. 4; *Test. of the xii. Patr.*, Levi xviii. 4, 5, 9 ; Judah xxiv. 6 ; *Apocalypse of Ezra* xiii. 26, and many other passages). In the main, they embrace the Gentiles equally with those of their own nation in the divine scheme of salvation which they put forth : and the wicked, who are excluded from happiness hereafter, are not restricted to the Gentiles;

the Jews equally with them will suffer punishment according to their deserts.

This leads us, finally, to say a word about the developed ideas concerning the state of the departed. It can hardly occasion surprise to find that the Apocalyptists have differing views as to the sequence of events hereafter ; sometimes it is resurrection, judgement, punishment ; at other times the resurrection comes last ; sometimes it is taught that all will rise, the evil as well as the good ; at other times only the good are thought of as partaking of the resurrection. Then there is also the idea of an intermediate state after death and before the resurrection : the good go to paradise, the evil to a place of torment ; after the allotted time comes the Judgement, followed by eternal bliss or eternal punishment.

It is possible that extraneous influences, Persian and Greek, may have been at work here ; but it does not seem necessarily to have been the case ; for, after all, speculations of this kind would logically have forced themselves upon the mind ; and though there is a good deal to be said in favour of non-Jewish influences here, it is wisest not to dogmatize upon the subject.

There is much else which might be dealt with ; but the more outstanding matters have, we hope, been mentioned.

CHAPTER XL

THE LAW AND ITS DEVELOPMENTS

THIS subject can find a place within the Greek period, for although the process of development began before and continued after it, there can be no doubt that the development was proceeding during this period. Attention has already been drawn to the fact that the beginnings of what came to be the religion of the Law must be sought during the Exile and the period following upon the Return. By 400 B.C., or soon after, the written Law was completed; but even before this time the nature of the Law was such that developments must have begun to arise. By developments we mean, firstly, such things as the addition of new legal precepts necessitated by change of circumstances, the demand for new decisions, directions for cases not contemplated in the written Law, etc.; in a word, all that would be included under the term " Oral Law," which, in course of time, became equally binding with the written Law; secondly, the prominence and central position of the Law, and insistence on the observance of legal *minutiæ*; thirdly, the glorification of the Law; and fourthly, the merit acquired by its observance.

It must be acknowledged that the steps in the process of development cannot be traced. But we can see from various later sources that these developments did take place; and these sources we must briefly examine. They are four in number: (1) some books in the Apocrypha; (2) some events in the history of the Maccabæan rising; (3) the New Testament, more particularly the Synoptic Gospels and some of the Pauline Epistles; (4) the Mishnah.

1. SOME BOOKS OF THE APOCRYPHA

The two books which come into consideration here are the *Wisdom of Ben-Sira* (*Ecclesiasticus*) and the *Book of Tobit*, both pre-Maccabæan, belonging approximately to 200 B.C., or a little later. To deal with the subject

D D

exhaustively is out of the question here ; we shall therefore give just a few illustrations, taking in order the points
of development mentioned above.

It seems probable that Ben-Sira has the Oral Law, to
which as representing the "Sadducæan" attitude he
would object, in mind when, in xxxii. 17, he says :

The man of violence concealeth instruction [so the Syriac Version]
And forceth the Law to suit his necessity.

But more significant is lxv. 5, for here the two terms
Mitzwah (lit. " commandment ") and *Torah* ("Law ")
occur together ; the former, used in the plural, is used of
the details of the Law, and in Rabbinical literature very
often connotes the Oral Law ; so that there are grounds
for the belief that the two terms found together here
refer to the Oral and the Written Law (*Torah*) respectively.[1] This is not contradicted by what was said just
now about Ben-Sira being opposed to the Oral Law ;
for the "Sadducæan" point of view recognized an Oral
Law, but it was of a less rigorous kind than that of the
"Pharisaic" point of view.[2]

Again, in viii. 9 Ben-Sira says :

> Reject not the tradition of the aged,
> Which they heard from their fathers ;
> For thou wilt receive instruction from this,
> And (be able to) answer in time of perplexity.

The reference to the oral tradition, " the tradition of the
fathers," or Oral Law, but in the Sadducæan sense, is
obvious here. Another important illustration, too long
to quote, will be found in xxxix. 1 ff., where the activities
of the Scribe are enumerated.

We have thus ample evidence that the development
represented by the Oral Law had begun to take place
before 200 B.C.

The prominent position occupied by the Law as the
centre of religion, and insistence on its observance,
together with its glorification, may be illustrated by

[1] See the quotation from Maimonides given below, on p. 409.
[2] We use the names " Sadducæan " and " Pharisaic " for convenience'
sake ; as definite parties the Sadducees and Pharisees did not arise until
after the Maccabæan rising ; but the respective points of view represented
by either existed long before.

the way in which it is identified with Wisdom ; here
again Ben-Sira is instructive, e.g., in xix. 20 :

> All wisdom is the fear of the Lord,
> And all wisdom is the fulfilling of the Law.

More pointed still is the passage in which, when speaking
of the things concerning Wisdom, he says : " All these
things are the book of the covenant of God Most High,
the Law which Moses commanded as an heritage for the
assemblies of Jacob " (xxiv. 23 ; cp. also xv. 1).

The prominence of the Law is also emphasized in
Tobit, e.g. in xii. 8, where prayer, almsgiving, and fasting,
especially the second, are strongly insisted upon. The
laws of tithe (i. 7, v. 13), marriage (vi. 12, vii. 13, 14),
honouring parents (iv. 3), keeping the feasts (i. 6, ii. 1),
purifying oneself (ii. 5), as well as others, are all incul-
cated. All this shows the very important position in the
life of the people which the Law held by this time, and,
of course, prior to this time, for such a position could
not have been gained quickly.

In some interesting passages we see that already by
this time the doctrine of merit was recognized ; thus in
Ecclus. iii. 30 it is said :

> A flaming fire doth water quench,
> So doth almsgiving atone for sin (see also xxix. 12).

A rather striking passage occurs in *Tobit* iv. 8–10 :
" . . . If thou have little, be not afraid to give alms
according to that little ; for thou layest up a good treasure
for thyself against the day of necessity ; because alms
delivereth from death, and suffereth not to come into
darkness." So, too, in xii. 9 : " Alms doth deliver from
death, and it shall purge away all sin."

While words such as these do not directly claim merit
and reward for the works of the Law, they point in the
direction for this ; and, as we shall see, in course of time,
this idea became fully developed.

2. Some Events in the History of the Maccabæan Rising

The very fact of the Maccabæan rising is eloquent
testimony of the paramount importance attached to the
Law ; but there are some events connected with the
rising which illustrate this somewhat pointedly.

A piece of indirect evidence is afforded by the strong opposition offered by the orthodox party among the Jews to the Hellenizers among their own people. Stress must be laid upon this, for it was an outcome of the Maccabæan rising and its causes that a great development of Legalism, in a " Pharisaic " direction, took place. What is not always sufficiently grasped is that the causes which ultimately led up to the Maccabæan rising are to be sought prior to the time of Antiochus Epiphanes ; his action in trying to stamp out Judaism in B.C. 168 (i.e. seven years after he came to the throne) was probably due as much to encouragement from Hellenistic Jews as to a personal desire to champion Hellenism. This is not the place to go into any detail regarding the question ; but it cannot be too strongly emphasized that the antagonism aroused by the Hellenistic Jews among the more orthodox had as much to do with the development of Legalism as anything that Antiochus Epiphanes did.

We must begin by quoting again (see p. 341 above) the well-known words from 1 *Macc.* i. 11–15, and then by drawing attention to one or two significant points in the passage :

" In those days came there forth out of Israel transgressors of the Law, and persuaded many, saying, Let us go and make a covenant with the Gentiles that are round about us ; for since we were parted from them many evils have befallen us. And the saying was good in their eyes. And certain of the people were forward herein and went to the king [the advent of Antiochus Epiphanes to the Syrian throne is mentioned in the preceding verse], and he gave them licence to do after the ordinances of the Gentiles. And they built a place of exercise in Jerusalem according to the laws of the Gentiles ; and they made themselves uncircumcized, and forsook the holy covenant, and joined themselves to the Gentiles, and sold themselves to do evil."[1]

The first point to be noted here is that unfaithfulness to Judaism is described as transgression of the Law, so that the Law is practically synonymous with the religion of the Jews. Then, the words " since we parted from them," which refer to the fact that the observance of the Law had been set up as a barrier between the Jews and the Gentiles, illustrates again the central position

---

[1] Cp. Dan. ix. 11; the book of *Daniel* was written about 166 B.C.

assigned to the Law. And, lastly, it will be noticed that the initiative in this movement against the Law is taken by the Jews ; no outside pressure is brought to bear.

It was seven years after this that Antiochus Epiphanes, as an act of vengeance because the orthodox party refused to recognize his nominee to the high-priesthood, ordered a massacre in Jerusalem, which was carried out " by the chief collector of the tribute " (1 *Macc.* i. 30–32). In the citadel, the narrative goes on to say : " They put a sinful nation, transgressors of the Law, and they strengthened themselves therein " (ver. 34) ; obviously, the reference here is to the Hellenistic Jews. The verses which follow must be quoted in full in order to see what the real position of affairs was : it is said in reference to these " transgressors of the Law " that " they stored up arms and victuals, and gathering together the spoils of Jerusalem, they laid them up there ; and they became a sore snare ; and it became a place to lie in wait against the sanctuary, and an evil adversary to Israel continually. And they shed innocent blood on every side of the sanctuary, and defiled the sanctuary. And the inhabitants of Jerusalem fled because of them ; and she became a habitation of strangers, and she became strange to them that were born in her, and her children forsook her. Her sanctuary was laid waste like a wilderness, her feasts were turned into mourning, her Sabbaths into reproach, her honour into contempt." This passage makes it clear that it was these " transgressors of the Law," the Hellenistic Jews, who took the initiative in the anti-Jewish movement ; small wonder that Antiochus Epiphanes with such encouragement should have been eager to take his part.

But what we wish particularly to emphasize is that the Jews, in defence of their Law, had as their primary antagonists men of their own race. It is easy to understand how this would intensify zeal for the Law on the part of the orthodox.

To this indirect evidence for the prominence of the Law some of a more direct character may be added. In 1 *Macc.* ii. 32 ff. it is told of how a number of the loyal Jews were attacked on the Sabbath ; but refusing to break the Sabbath by fighting, they willingly submitted to massacre, both they, their wives, and their children. A similar episode is recounted on the occasion of the capture of Jerusalem by Ptolemy I Soter, in B.C. 321, though not so tragic ; being a Sabbath the orthodox Jews made no resistance, and were carried away captive to Egypt.[1]

A more vigorous championship of the Law is recorded in 1 *Macc.* ii. 42 ff. : " Then were gathered unto them a company of the Chassidim, mighty men of Israel, everyone that offered himself willingly for the Law. . . . And Mattathias and his friends went round about, and pulled down the altars ; and they circumcized by force the children that were uncircumcized, as many as they found in the coasts of Israel. . . . And they rescued the Law out of the hand of the Gentiles. . . ."

This will suffice to show the position which the Law had come to hold towards the middle of the second century B.C.

3. THE NEW TESTAMENT

Religious freedom and political independence were the final results of the Maccabæan struggle. Religious freedom meant the unrestricted sway of the Law. The foremost champions of the Law during this struggle had been the *Chassidim* (1 *Macc.* ii. 42-8) ; when religious freedom had been gained they withdrew from further participation in the struggle, for they were indifferent to the question of political independence (1 *Macc.* vii. 10 ff.). Therefore we hear nothing more of them until the struggle is over. When next they appear, under the high-priesthood of John Hyrcanus (135-104 B.C.), it is with the name of Pharisees ; and they are now no longer supporters of the Maccabæan or Hasmonæan [2] dynasty ; for the High-priest had become much more a political than a religious leader, and consequently lax regarding the Law ; whereas the Pharisees, in conformity with their tradition, made the Law the centre of all their activity. It is, thus, at this time that the Pharisees first appear as a distinct party ; and they are opposed to the High-priestly or Sadducæan party, so-called from the claim of the High-priest to be descended from Zadok the priest (1 Kings i. 26 ff.) ; this was the ruling, and there-

---

[1] Edwyn Bevan, *The Ptolemaic Dynasty*, p. 24 (1927); see also Reinach, *Textes d'auteurs grecs et romains relatifs au Judaïsme*, p. 43 (1895).

[2] Asmonæus, or Hasmonæus, was the name of the ancestor of the family.

fore the aristocratic, party. To the Pharisaic party belonged the Scribes,[1] as was natural enough, for upon them had long devolved the duty of both copying out the Law and explaining it, and from their explanations of the Written Law grew the Oral Law.

The Pharisees had the bulk of the people on their side, and exercised a great influence upon them ; Josephus tells us further that, " they delivered to the people a great many observances by succession from their fathers, which are not written in the Laws of Moses."

Some of the results of this influence and of the development of the Law, here clearly pointed to by Josephus, are dealt with in the New Testament ; to this we must now devote a little attention.

The main tendency in this development was that the observance of legal precepts came to be looked upon as meritorious. The merit acquired by observing the details of the Law's requirements justified a man in the sight of God, and thus constituted a claim for reward. It followed logically that the attainment of salvation was a matter of purely human effort. Belief in divine grace was, of course, not absent ; but the sense of justification felt by a zealous observer of the Law had the effect of obscuring the fact of the initial divine guidance ; and in practice the fulfilment of works of the Law came to be looked upon as the means of salvation.

Much of the teaching of Christ, as well as of St. Paul, is directed against this false estimate of the Law. A few examples must be offered.

The harm done to spiritual religion by observing precepts of the Law for the sake of gaining glory from men (Matt. vi. 1–18) was serious enough ; but the claim of reward from God because of the fulfilment of works of the Law was clearly a more subtle danger ; and the evidence afforded in the New Testament of this development is overwhelming. No more illuminating illustration of the way in which our Lord sought to counteract it could be given than the parable of the Labourers in the Vineyard (Matt. xx. 1–16). The immediate cause of its utterance was St. Peter's words : " Lo, we have left all, and followed thee ; what then shall we have ? " (Matt.

---

[1] " Scribes of the Sadducees " are, however, not unknown entirely, e.g. Josephus, *Antiq.* XIII, x. 6; and the Scribes and High-priests are coupled together both in *Mark* and *Luke* several times, which would seem to point to Sadducæan scribes.

xix. 27). The mental attitude which prompted this was precisely the same as that of the legalist who, having acquired merit by carrying out the precepts of the Law, believed himself entitled to claim a reward from God. Without going into the details of the parable, the significance of its teaching may be briefly pointed out :

The household is entirely independent as regards each individual labourer, and therefore the fact of his seeking them to work in his vineyard is an act of grace on his part. In order to emphasize that it *is* an act of grace he goes out at various hours of the day to offer the advantage of employment to other labourers who would otherwise have nothing to do. " Why stand ye here all the day idle ? They say unto him, Because no man hath hired us." When the time for payment comes and some of the labourers claim more because of their longer hours of work, the householder shows them that their claim is not justified in the words : " Is it not lawful for me to do what I will with mine own ? " The reference is not so much to the amount of wages paid, as to the fact of paying any wages at all, i.e. of taking them into his service ; for it was that which constituted an act of grace on the part of the householder. The claim for more implied a right on account of work done, whereas the possibility of doing any work at all was the result of an act of grace ; and the same applied to all ; hence, " the last shall be first, and the first last."

The same teaching underlies the parable of the Pharisee and the Publican (Luke xviii. 9–14), and is contained in the words, " When ye shall have done all the things that are commanded you, say, we are unprofitable servants ; we have done that which it was our duty to do " (Luke xvii. 10). Further illustrations could, of course, be given.

Similarly St. Paul combats again and again the doctrine of justification by the works of the Law and what this implied ; e.g. : " By the works of the Law shall no flesh be justified in his sight " (Rom. iii. 20) ; " . . . A man is not justified by the works of the Law " (Gal. ii. 16) ; " Not of works, that no man should glory " (Eph. ii. 9) ; and elsewhere.

No doubt this development had begun to take place long previously, but we do not get such pointed evidence both of the development and of its effects as is given in the New Testament.

4. The Mishnah

It will be worth giving here a quotation from the great mediæval teacher Jewish Maimonides (he died in A.D. 1204), for his words represent the Jewish belief regarding the Oral Law from, at the least, the second century B.C. It is taken from the Preface to his work called *Yad ha-chazakah* (" The Strong Hand ") :

" All the commandments which were given to Moses on Sinai were given with their interpretation ; for it is said (Exod. xxiv. 12), ' And I will give thee the tables of stone, and the *Torah* (Law) and the *Mitzwah* (Commandment)' ; *Torah :* that is, the Written Law ; *Mitzwah :* that is, its interpretation. He commanded us to observe the *Torah* in accordance with the *Mitzwah*. And this *Mitzwah* is called the Oral Law. Moses our teacher wrote down the whole Law with his own hand before he died . . . the *Mitzwah*, that is, the interpretation of the Law, he did not write down, but he commanded it to the Elders, and to Joshua, and to the rest of Israel ; for it is written, ' All the words which I have commanded you, these shall ye observe and do ' (Deut. xii. 28). And therefore this is called the ' Oral Law.' "

This is based in the first instance on the opening words of the Mishnah tractate, *Pirqe Abôth* (" the Sections, or ' Sayings,' of the Fathers "), viz. : " Moses received (the) *Torah* from Sinai, and he delivered it to Joshua ; and Joshua (delivered it) to the Elders ; and the Elders (delivered it) to the Prophets ; and the Prophets delivered it to the men of the Great Synagogue." Here *Torah* (" Law "), written without the definite article, includes the entire body of divine laws, both written and oral, i.e. the Pentateuch and what is described, e.g. in Mark vii. 3, as " the tradition of the Elders." The Great Synagogue was, according to Jewish tradition, founded by Ezra ; the basis of the tradition is in all probability the assembly spoken of in Neh. viii–x. It is mentioned here for the first time ; and as neither Philo nor Josephus make any allusion to it, one must regard it as extremely doubtful whether this Great Synagogue ever existed.

The Mishnah is a Hebrew word which comes from the root meaning " to repeat " ; then it is extended to mean " to learn " or " to teach " by repetition ; thus " Mishnah " came to have the sense of teaching by (oral) repetition. In its present form the Mishnah embraces earlier

compilations ; it is due to the work of Rabbi Judah ha-
Nasi, " the Prince," the date being approximately
A.D. 200. In it we are enabled to see the full development
of the Law, though even this great collection of traditional
legal material does not profess to be exhaustive ; for,
as Schechter says, it was compiled " not with the purpose
of providing the nation with a legal code, but with the
intention of furnishing them with a sort of thesaurus,
incorporating such portions of the traditional lore as he
[i.e. Rabbi Judah] considered most important." [1]

This brief survey shows, then, that the Law became the
most important element in Judaism. As compared with
that zenith of Hebrew Religion presented by the teaching
of Deutero-Isaiah this supremacy of the Law cannot but
strike one as having been a religious evolutionary process
in a less exalted direction. But while we feel this to be
the case, justice demands that we should recognize what
was the underlying motive-power in that exaltation of
the Law. It was always taught that it was by means of
the Law that God revealed Himself to His people ; in it
the Divine mind was believed to be reflected, in it the
Divine will was believed to be stated ; therefore the Law
was inseparable from God. This conviction is illustrated
by the following beautiful little parable :

" It is as though a king had an only daughter ; and
one of the kings comes and marries her. He [the latter]
then wants to return to his own country and to take his
wife back with him. Then the king says to him : ' She
whom I have given to thee is my only daughter ; I
cannot bear to be separated from her ; yet I cannot say,
Take her not, for she is thy wife. But show me this
kindness,—wherever thou goest prepare me a chamber
that I may dwell with you, for I cannot bear to be separated from my daughter.' Thus spake the Holy One to
Israel : ' I gave you the *Torah* ; I cannot separate
myself from it ; yet I cannot say to you, Take it not.
But whithersoever ye journey make me a house wherein I
may dwell.' For it is said : ' *And let them make me a
sanctuary, that I may dwell among them* ' (Exod. xxv. 8)." [2]

[1] In Hastings' *Dictionary of the Bible*, v. 61b. To give a real insight into
the way in which the developments of the Law occurred as here presented
would be out of place and beyond the scope of the present volume ; for this
we must refer our readers to some of the tractates translated into English
and published by the S.P.C.K., i.e., *Translations of Early Documents*, Series
III, Rabbinic Texts. See also Danby, *The Mishnah* (1933).
[2] *Shemoth Rabba* 33, quoted by Weber *Jüdische Theologie*, p. 17 (1897).

CHAPTER XLI

CONCLUSION

"THINK not," said Jesus, " that I came to destroy the law or the prophets; I came not to destroy, but to fulfil." [1] His language was familiar, but His meaning unique. To the common mind the fulfilment of the Law implied meticulous observance of its precepts, and the Prophets were fulfilled only with the occurrence of the events which they foretold. Jesus meant that the faith of His people was yet incomplete, and that it was His task to bring it to perfection. The religion of Israel had had a long history, from Moses to the days when a political Apocalyptic was rousing the Jewish spirit to revolt against the imperial power of Rome. But it was still only a part of a larger whole, a preparation for the final revelation of God to man. No Christian, indeed, can fully understand the New Testament apart from the Old, but it is equally true that no Christian can contemplate the Old Testament apart from the New. Every Christian would endorse the view expressed by the writer of the *Epistle to the Hebrews*, when, at the close of his magnificent survey of Israelite spiritual history, he said : " All these, having had witness borne to them through their faith, received not the promise, God having provided some better thing concerning us, that apart from us they should not be made perfect." [2]

Some of the most important elements in the thought of Jesus and His followers were never expressly stated by Him; they were assumed, since they were held in common by Him and by His contemporaries in the Jewish world. Every one of the great religious leaders of humanity had a long heritage which supplied him with a basic system of thought, and each, however startling his own originality, was to a large extent controlled and directed by his spiritual ancestry. Zoroaster was born into a polytheistic world. The Buddha sprang from another polytheism, which was

[1] Matt. v. 17.　　　　[2] Heb. xi. 39, 40.

paradoxically combined with an idealistic pantheism. Socrates inherited the metaphysical speculations of Ionian philosophy. Mohammed lived in an atmosphere charged with Jewish and Christian doctrine. Religion to Confucius meant a rather primitive form of Animism. Jesus was a Jew.

Nowhere else in the world could the founder of a new religion have assumed the unity and the goodness of God. Ethical monotheism was, alike for Jesus and for those to whom He immediately addressed Himself, an obvious platitude; to the rest of the ancient world it was an insoluble paradox. The Greek philosopher might use language suggesting belief in one God, but his sense of personality was weak, and he had hardly abandoned the manifold deities of his contemporaries before he found himself driven to a pantheistic conception of the universe. Men in whom the ethical sense was strong were faced with the contradiction between religion and morality. Confucius declined to commit himself to any positive statement about " the gods," though his deep reverence for tradition impelled him to observe the historic ceremonial. Socrates appeared to his contemporaries to be irreligious, and men like the Buddha, Euripides, and Lucretius found the antithesis between religion and morality insoluble, discarded the gods altogether, and embraced a stark atheism in the interests of purity and righteousness. But Jesus had behind Him that long history of religion whose noblest expression was to be found in the Hebrew prophets, and for Him there was no paradox and no antithesis; He could exhort men to be perfect, as their Father in Heaven was perfect.

Nor was this all. Not only in its general nature did Judaism form a basis for the faith and teaching of Jesus, but also in many of its characteristic features He found truth which needed little more than modification and illustration. In a certain sense He represented the prophetic tradition rather than that of the Scribes and " Lawyers "; Hosea meant more to Him than did Ezra. He held the Law to be a temporal—we may almost say temporary— expression of fundamental principles, and claimed the right to control, or even to supersede, its most sacred provisions, if their observance conflicted with that eternal Will of God which they imperfectly embodied. In the Psalms, too, He found a spiritual life which corresponded to His own experience, and it was not an accident that the cry wrung

from Him by the spiritual agony of His last moments on
the Cross was shaped by the language of Ps. xxii.[1] Yet
there was much, both in the Prophets and in the Psalter,
which he could not have adopted; we cannot imagine Him
using the vindictive language with which they often present
us.

As a Galilean, Jesus was more deeply influenced by the
Pharisaic wing of Judaism than by the Sadducæan. The
worship which had nurtured His young life was that of the
Synagogue, not that of the Temple. The atmosphere about
Him was strongly apocalyptic, and, indeed, Messianic.
A belief in immortality was inevitable, since it sprang out
of the very nature of God. It is worth noting that He
seems to have tended more towards the spiritual type of
the doctrine than to the cruder hope of a material
resurrection. God being what He was, it was unthinkable
that a physical incident like death should be suffered to
destroy, interrupt, or impair His relations with men who
had once experienced their Father's loving companionship.

The extent to which Jesus accepted current theories of
eschatology has been much discussed in recent years.[2] It
is beyond dispute that He freely used apocalyptic language,
but it must be remembered that He had no vocabulary
ready to hand, in which to clothe His new conceptions, and
He had to select that which would be least misleading to
His audience. The first great crisis of His spiritual life
came with His baptism; then, if not earlier, He seems to
have realized that He Himself was the Messiah whose near
approach the Baptist asserted. Yet the relentless logic
which marked all His thought and teaching would not permit
Him to regard Himself as the military and political hero of
a rejuvenated nation. Like all else in the foundations of
true religion, His Messiahship must be spiritual. Further,
it must be one which should meet the forces of materialism,
rampant in every side of life about Him, by permitting
them to do their utmost, and still proving Himself victorious.
None has ever known the full force of temptation save Him
who resisted its fiercest assaults without stumbling or
faltering, and He must allow Evil to exert its utmost power
in order to prove that Good was mightier still. Like Plato,

[1] It may be worth noting that Jesus did not literally *quote* the Psalm.
His words were in the Aramaic language, and He must have been familiar
with the Psalter in Hebrew.
[2] See, especially, Dodd, *The Parables of the Kingdom*, passim (1936).

He realized that perfect righteousness could be manifested only in one who was charged by the whole world about him with the deepest possible iniquity, and shared the experience of the most degraded sinner. Hence He adopted a position which seemed, even to those who knew and loved Him best, the direct antithesis of true Messiahship; not the all-conquering and imperial figure of popular imagination, but the Suffering Servant became His ideal. Lowliness, condemnation and despair, culminating in death itself, were His choice. Only thus could He attest the validity of His spiritual faith, and win His triumph. His condemnation was, in the last resort, the judgement of those who condemned Him, and when He died, the impotence of death was for ever assured—it could not even kill Him.

So novel and paradoxical was His conception of the Messiahship, that Jesus could not at once entrust it even to His own disciples. "Evil spirits" who acclaimed Him were sternly rebuked, and He never publicly admitted His own position till near the end of His career. Those who knew Him best had to discover for themselves that He was the Christ, and only then could He begin to tell them what manner of Christ He was. Even so, they failed to understand Him; their minds were filled with the pomp and circumstance of earthly sovereignty, and it was not till He had actually died that the first glimmering of the true light began to penetrate their spiritual darkness. For a time it seemed that the consummation was but postponed, and the Church was born in the expectation of His speedy return to consummate the age. As years passed, the fuller meaning of His purpose grew on men; the greatest of His followers (though one who never knew Him " after the flesh ") hoped in his earlier days to " meet the Lord in the air," [1] but in the end attained the desire " to depart and be with Christ; for it is very far better." [2]

Yet we shall gravely misunderstand Jesus if we see in Him no more than this. He was the greatest of all exponents of ethical monotheism—we may even say, of a divinely inspired ethic—and He gave to His own people a transcendent conception of the Messiahship. But He went yet further. The supreme aim of human religion is the maintenance of the ideal relation between man and the object of worship. The universal experience of sin necessarily means a universal rupture in that relation, and the ultimate problem of every

[1] 1 Thess. iv. 17.   [2] Phil. i. 23.

religion is its recovery by the sinner, in other words, an Atonement. Understanding God as He did, Jesus could recognize no other ideal than the closest and most intimate fellowship between the human and the divine, an ethical (not a metaphysical) identification between man and his heavenly Father. With His Jewish inheritance it was inevitable that the dominating conception here should be that of a Covenant, the vital unification of two parties originally standing apart. As we have seen, it was under this form that Israel's religion was fundamentally conceived, and the spiritual history of the people from Moses onwards may be described as a record of the Covenant. We have seen how it was inaugurated, how it was repeatedly broken on the human side and restored on the divine, and how it gradually attained to full development and meaning. In Jeremiah [1] we saw the principle that, to be valid, it must be stamped on men's hearts. But Jeremiah failed to offer the world a victim, a medium and a third party, in whose surrendered life an eternal unity between God and man could be achieved. Jesus believed that this function could be discharged only by the Messiah; nothing else that the Christ could do was comparable to the giving of Himself as a ransom for many. Hints, vague or clear according to the perception of the hearer, were dropped during His life-time, and His deepest purpose became unmistakable in His last family gathering with His disciples, when He linked for ever the redemptive Covenant and His own shed blood. He knew that the Messiah alone, and He as the Messiah, could bring man and God into so vital and intimate a union that it should endure eternally, and He chose, obviously and emphatically, a Messianic death as He conceived it. It is in the Cross that Hebrew religion finds its goal; it is there and there only that we see how Jesus came, not to destroy the Law and the Prophets, but to fulfil.

The desperate struggles of the second century B.C. saved the faith that was to culminate in Jesus. But the triumph won by the martyred saints and the victorious warriors of the Maccabæan age tended to enhance the exclusiveness long characteristic of Judaism. The sense of a universal mission is not wholly wanting in the Old Testament (we may cite the *Book of Jonah* as an outstanding illustration), but it is comparatively rare. From the early days of the settlement in Palestine, one of Israel's greatest perils had been that of

[1] Cf. pp. 264 f.

too intimate an association with the nations about her. If her faith were to remain pure, so the greatest of the prophets had insisted, she must keep herself to herself, and rigidly exclude the debasing influence of foreign religion and society. It was only an intensified conviction, and a stern application of this principle that had enabled Judaism, the unique faith of an insignificant people, to survive among the world-movements which ended in the establishment of the Roman Empire. The door was open to proselytes, it is true, and there were periods when converts were comparatively numerous, but Judaism has never been a distinctly missionary religion, and has owed its expansion to natural increase rather than to propagandist activity. Men and women who were attracted by the noble theology and lofty ethics of Judaism were repelled by its meticulous legalism, and numbers preferred to remain as the " devout," but outside the pale of Israel proper.

It was a sound instinct which forbade the Jew to surrender any item of his faith. His charter was the Law, a book containing the known will of God in black and white, and his guides to its observance were the scribes. Until " a prophet should arise " it was not safe to abandon the least jot or tittle of the written word. Once a real breach had been made in the Law, it would be impossible to prevent the whole from crumbling. Hence the earnestness with which the Rabbis " set a hedge about the Law." We may condemn the casuistry of the Scribes, but it is impossible to read the Mishnah without respecting the motives of the men who were responsible for its compilation. At all costs the Law must be observed, for it was the final guide-book dictated by God to man, and if once but the least of its ordinances were disregarded, it would be impossible again to draw the line about it with safety.

But Jesus came, a Prophet, and more than a Prophet, the Messiah. In Him the living power and presence of God were manifested as they were nowhere else. He lived, not by rule, but by the spiritual instinct of one whose communion with God was never broken. Since His day there has been a constant and a growing stream of knowledge of Him and of His purpose. Through these nineteen centuries men have lived in Him, and have found themselves so living in God. The Church was thus able to adopt, even more freely than Jewish liberal thought, any truth she met elsewhere, and to find its highest expression in

Christ. She saw in Him first the risen Messiah, then the crucified Redeemer, and finally the incarnate Word. Now there was no longer any real danger to fear from contact with the outer world. Nor could the abandonment of exact ritual prescriptions and of legal details entail a loss of spiritual life. For, whereas men were forced at first to measure Christ by the Law, as they learned to know Him they realized that they could assess the Law only by Him. " The letter killeth, but the spirit maketh alive," and in Jesus the world has the spirit. In a very real sense the Cross was the liberation of the eternal truth of Judaism from the casing which protected it but limited its range. The God of Jesus and of His followers is indeed the Yahweh of Moses and of Israel, and the story we have tried to trace in the foregoing pages is the record of that long growth and training which culminated in Calvary. Henceforward we can look with confidence and hope to the coming of a time when the kingdom of this world shall become the kingdom of our Lord and of His Christ.

E E

INDEX OF MODERN AUTHORS

Bade, 217
Baethgen, 44, 73
Baikie, 170
Ball, 182
Barton, 13
Battersby Harford, 179
Baudissin, 7, 11, 24, 25, 34, 108, 113
Benzinger, 129
Bertholet, 89
Bevan, 393, 406
Böklen, 394
Bötticher, 77
Bousset, 386, 394
Budde, 134 f., 141, 148, 156
Burckhardt, 26

Charles, 382, 384
Cheyne, 151
Clodd, 4
Codrington, 10
Cook, S. A., 41, 51, 60, 61, 69, 99, 135, 159, 172, 179, 182
Cowley, 177, 219
Curtiss, 24, 26, 35, 44, 132

Dalman, 38
Danby, 410
Davidson, 153
Delitzsch, 245
Dhorme, 51
Dodd, 413
Doughty, 25, 26
Driver, 39, 129, 275
Duhm, 116, 352
Durkheim, 6, 14

Ebeling, 86, 87, 102

Farnell, 7
Frazer, 6, 7, 8, 9, 11, 15, 18, 35, 74, 75, 77, 95, 121, 131 f., 375

Gall, von, 39, 55, 388
Gray, Buchanan, 66, 68, 129, 132, 164, 181, 195, 198
Goblet d'Alviella, 6
Goldziher, 98
Gressmann, 36, 42, 55, 56, 102, 141, 152, 375, 376, 388
Gunkel, 42, 56, 116, 386

Hall, 142, 152
Hartland, 10, 14
Herder, 250
Hilprecht, 271
Hölscher, 99, 137, 166, 297, 342
Hommel, 128, 135
Hooke, 272

Jack, 52, 133, 153, 172
James, 4, 5, 9
Jastrow, 24, 33 f., 51, 63, 69, 72, 74, 75, 83, 85, 86, 99, 108, 110, 116, 120, 245
Jeremias, 24, 43, 83, 85, 86, 88, 99, 101, 102, 245, 274, 326
Jevons, 7, 15, 19 f.
Johnson, 201

Keane, 7
Kennett, 335
Kittel, 43, 179, 197 f., 284, 285
König, 65, 250

Lagrange, 24, 35, 65, 99
Lang, 5
Langdon, 81, 82
Lenormant, 71, 110, 116
Lincoln, 18
Lods, 67, 78, 99, 133, 137, 138
Loisy, 138

Macalister, 94 f, 159
McLennan, 15
McNeile, 28, 151
Marett, 4, 15, 16
Margoliouth, 99, 101
Meinhold, 128
Meissner, 80, 81, 83, 84, 85
Moore, 43

Nicolsky, 73
Niebuhr, 170
Nielsen, 51, 61, 65, 68, 128 f., 131. 135
Nöldeke, 108
Nyberg, 218

Oesterley, 37, 98 f., 101, 111, 130, 219, 325 f., 368, 382
Otto, 163

418

Payne, 8
Ploss, 136

Reinach, 406
Robertson Smith, 9, 15, 23, 25, 30, 34 f., 37 f., 39, 41 f., 47, 60, 62, 63, 64 f., 68, 70, 71, 74, 78, 113, 128, 137, 139, 181
Robinson, T. H., 12, 160, 186, 223
Robinson, Wheeler, 153, 263, 304

Schaeffer, 51
Schechter, 410
Schmidt Hans, 8, 272
Schmidt, W., 5, 16
Schrader, 273
Schürer, 343
Schwally, 100, 250
Sellin, 43, 59, 95 f., 159
Siegfried, 100

Smith, G. Adam, 39, 48
Spencer, 19
Stade, 66, 98 f, 153, 285

Tallquist, 245
Trumbull, 132
Tylor, 9

Vincent, 96, 99
Virolleaud, 56
Volz, 388

Weber, F., 410
Weber, O , 72, 108 f., 120, 128
Welch, 197
Wellhausen, 25, 40, 43, 46, 51, 74, 88, 99, 108, 113, 118, 128, 133
Winckler, 56, 151

Zimmern, 2, 272, 273

INDEX OF BIBLICAL AND POST-BIBLICAL REFERENCES

I. OLD TESTAMENT

Genesis	PAGE	Genesis	PAGE	Genesis	PAGE
i.	225, 371	xxviii. 18	53, 55	xlvii 30	97
i. 1–5	313	xxviii. 19	53	xlix. 8–12	377
ii. 4 ff.	225	xxviii. 20–22	158	xlix. 22	40
iii. 16 *b*	116	xxviii. 20	159	xlix. 24	56
iv.	183	xxviii. 21	159	xlix. 29	97
iv. 7	116	xxx. 27	74	l. 11	37
iv. 10	169	xxxi. 11	55, 105	*Exodus*	
iv. 14	137	xxxi. 13	55	ii. 14	147
iv. 15	137	xxxi. 19	101, 126	ii. 15	147
iv. 23	137	xxxi. 30–35	101	iii.	147
iv. 24	137	xxxi. 30	126	iii. 1 ff.	148
vi. 1–7	251	xxxi. 35	126	iii. 1	44, 147, 149
vi. 4	250	xxxi. 40	167	iii. 2–5	28
viii. 20	182	xxxi. 42	55	iii. 6	152
viii. 21	182	xxxi. 43–54	45	iii. 7	149
xii. 6–8	26	xxxi. 44–48	45	iii. 8	149
xii. 6	100	xxxi. 45	46, 47	iii. 14	153
xiii. 4	330	xxxi. 46	46	iii. 15	126
xiii. 18	27, 100	xxxi. 53	55	iii. 18	152
xiv. 3	121	xxxi. 54	46	iv. 2 ff.	77
xiv. 5	36, 249	xxxii. 2 (Heb. 3)	56	iv. 25 ff.	136
xiv. 7	35, 36	xxxii. 30 (Heb. 31)	40	iv. 25	137
xiv. 13	27	xxxii. 31 (Heb. 32)	53	vi. 3	54, 126
xiv. 18–20	54	xxxv.	126	vii. 11	72, 78
xiv. 24	27	xxxv. 2	56, 126	vii. 22 ff.	78
xv. 21	249	xxxv. 4	27, 56, 100,	viii. 7 (Heb. 3)	78
xvi. 13	54		121, 126	viii. 18 (Heb. 14)	78
xvi. 14	39, 40, 54	xxxv. 5	31	viii. 19 (Heb. 15)	78
xvii. 1–14	136	xxxv. 7	55	ix. 11	78
xviii. 1	27, 100	xxxv. 8	28, 30, 32, 100	xii. 5	129
xviii. 4	27	xxxv. 14	45	xii. 9	131
xx. 3	105	xxxv. 15	45	xii. 23	130
xxi. 22	39	xxxv. 20	100	xii. 46	131
xxi. 23	39	xxxv. 27	27	xiii. 18	141
xxi. 28–30	39	xxxv. 29	97	xv. 25	76
xxi. 30–33	55	xxxvi. 20–30	67	xvii. 8 ff.	77
xxi. 31 *b*	39	xxxvii. 35	246, 248	xvii. 9	77
xxi. 33	27, 39, 55	xxxviii. 12	133	xviii. 1 ff.	44
xxii. 1 ff.	94	xxxviii. 13	133	xviii. 8 ff.	148
xxii. 13	47	xxxviii. 14	38	xviii. 15 ff.	147
xxiii. 1 ff.	100	xxxviii. 18	121	xviii. 24	147
xxiii. 19	27	xxxviii. 21	38	xix. 18	144
xxv. 8	97	xxxviii. 25	121	xx.	158, 162
xxv. 17	97	xli. 8	78	xx. 2–17	162
xxvi. 23 ff.	39, 55	xlii. 38	246, 248	xx. 3–17	168
xxvi. 23–25	27	xliv. 5	74	xx. 4	162
xxvi. 24	39	xliv. 15	74	xx. 8 ff.	134
xxvi. 30	46	xliv. 29	246, 248	xx. 22–xxiii. 33	104
xxvi. 33	39	xliv. 31	246, 248	xx. 24	47, 162, 166
xxviii. 10 ff.	55	xlvi. 1	27	xx. 25	47, 162, 166
xxviii. 11–22	45	xlvi. 3	53	xxi. 6	92

	PAGE		PAGE		PAGE
Exodus		*Numbers*		*Deuteronomy*	
xxi.–xxiii.	158, 256	xv. 5	334	xi. 10–12	226
xxii. 7	29, 92	xv. 38	121	xi. 13–21	132
xxii. 8	29, 92	xvi. 10	322	xi. 30	26 f.
xxii. 18 (Heb. 17)	71	xvi. 18–23	322	xii. 3	59
xxii. 25–27	221	xvi. 20 ff.	247	xii. 20–28	331
xxiii. 12	134	xvi. 29–33	247 f.	xii. 28	409
xxiii. 31	44, 143	xvi. 31–33	247	xiii.	196
xxiv.	156	xvii. 2–11 (Heb. 17–26)		xiii. 12–17	139
xxiv. 12	409		77	xiv. 7–20	70
xxv. 8	410	xx. 1	100, 142	xvi. 1–8	130
xxviii. 33	121	xx. 1 a–13	142	xvi. 1	129, 130
xxix. 38–42	334	xx. 8 ff.	77	xvi. 2	129, 130
xxix. 40	335	xx. 11	77	xvi. 4	131
xxx. 34–38	334	xx. 22	142	xvi. 21	59
xxxi. 12–17	134, 321	xxi.	161, 162	xvii. 16	220
xxxii.	160, 162	xxi. 2	138	xvii. 20	208
xxxiii. 11	164	xxi. 3	138	xviii. 10–14	72
xxxiii. 15	155	xxi. 4–9	161	xviii. 10–12	104
xxxiv.	158, 162, 165	xxi. 4	44, 143	xviii. 10	74, 75
xxxiv. 14–26	162	xxi. 6	111	xviii. 11	74, 106
xxxiv. 17	162	xxi. 8	77, 111	xx. 14	139
xxxiv. 18	165	xxi. 9	38, 77	xxi. 4	40
xxxiv. 21	134	xxi. 16	39	xxii. 12	121
xxxiv. 22	165	xxi. 17	38	xxiii. 17 (Heb. 18)	61
Leviticus		xxi. 18	38	xxiii. 18 (Heb. 19)	61
iv. 5.	335	xxi. 28	58	xxvii.	256
iv. 7	335	xxi. 29	68	xxvii. 5	48
iv. 15–21	335	xxiii.–xxiv.	368	xxvii. 6	48
iv. 16–18	335	xxiii. 14.	45	xxviii.	256
vi. 27 ff.	70	xxiii. 28–30	44	xxix.–xxxiv.	256
x. 1–7	163	xxiv. 15–19	377	xxxii. 13	58
xi.	70, 287	xxiv. 16	54	xxxii. 22	248
xi. 32 ff.	70	xxv. 3	44 f., 58	xxxii. 24	120
xvi.	335	xxvii. 14	142	xxxii. 51	142
xvi. 7–28	114	xxviii. 3–8	334	xxxiii. 16	28
xvi. 29–31	322	xxviii. 3	334	*Joshua*	
xvi. 33	335	xxviii. 11–31	322	iii. 5	139
xvii.–xxvi.		xxxii.	205	iv. 1–14	46
	104, 134, 287, 309	xxxii. 3	57	iv. 6	46
xvii. 7	112	xxxii. 8 ff.	142	iv. 7	46
xvii. 11	131, 156, 335	xxxii. 38	44, 58	iv. 9	46
xvii. 14	131, 156	xxxiv. 11	38	iv. 20	46
xix. 2	287	*Deuteronomy*		v. 2	137
xix. 26	74, 131	i.–v.	256	v. 3	137
xix. 30	134	i. 40	44, 143	v. 5 ff.	136
xx. 6	104	ii. 1	44, 143	vi. 26	183
xx. 22–26	287	ii. 4	142	vii. 1 ff.	139
xx. 27	104, 106	ii. 10	249	vii. 4	263
xxii. 31	287	ii. 11	249	viii. 31	48
xxii. 32	287	ii. 20	249	xi. 14	139
xxiii. 3	134	ii. 21	249	xi. 17	100
Numbers		ii. 34	139	xii. 7	100
v. 17	35	iii. 11	249	xiii. 5	100
x. 29 ff.	44, 147	iii. 31	249	xiii. 12 ff.	249
x. 29	156	iv. 11	144	xv. 6	37, 46
x. 33	44	iv. 12	144	xv. 7	36, 37
xi. 25–29	186	v. 9	292	xv. 11	53
xii. 6	105	v. 12–15	134	xv. 32	38
xiii. 26	142	vi.–xxvi.	256	xv. 34	38
xiii. 33	250	vi. 4–9	132	xv. 37	100
xiv. 25	44, 143	vii. 5	59	xv. 56	53
xiv. 33	142	vii. 16	139	xvii. 7	38
xv. 4	334	viii. 15	112	xvii. 15	249

	PAGE		PAGE		PAGE
Joshua		*I Samuel*		*II Samuel*	
xviii. 16	37	ii. 11–17	184	i. 14	375
xviii. 17	36, 37, 46	iv.	202	v. 3	207
xviii. 19	37	iv. 1	46	v. 23	31
xviii. 21	37	iv. 3	159	v. 24	31
xix. 8	40	v. 1–5	161	vi. 6–8	163
xix. 14	53	v. 1	46	x. 3	38
xix. 21	38	vi. 1 ff.	226	xi. 4	70
xix. 22	48	vi. 7 ff.	161	xii. 19	73
xix. 33	28	vi. 14	47	xiii. 23	133
xix. 37	38	vii. 9	139	xiii. 24	133
xix. 38	53	vii. 12	46	xiv. 7	137
xix. 44	53	viii.	237	xv. 30–32	48
xxiv. 26	28, 30, 45, 47	ix. 16	91	xvii. 17	37
xxiv. 27	28, 45, 47	x. 2	100	xvii. 23	97
xxiv. 32	100	x. 3	30	xx. 8	47
Judges		x. 5	48	xxi. 1–14	137
i. 16	147	x. 6	200	xxi. 14	97
iii. 3	58	x. 17–27	237	xxi. 17	375
iii. 7	59	xii. 2	237	*I Kings*	
iv. 4	29	xii. 2	92	i. 9	37, 46
iv. 5	29	xii. 16–18	75	i. 25	37
iv. 11	28, 156	xiii.	91	i. 26 ff.	406
v.	170	xiii. 10	129	i. 33	40
v. 2	210	xiv.	91	i. 34	40
v. 4	144, 191	xiv. 2	29,30	ii. 6	248
v. 5	144	xiv. 24	139	ii. 9	248
v. 8	92	xiv. 32	131	iii. 4	218
v. 14	205	xiv. 33–35	47	vii. 15	43
v. 15	205	xiv. 41	103	vii. 21	43, 46
v. 16	205	xv. 2	138	ix. 26	143
v. 17	205	xv. 3	94, 138	xi. 7	49
v. 21	40	xv. 22 ff.	139	xi. 33	53
v. 23	155	xv. 23	101	xii. 29	36
vi. 11–24	29	xv. 27	92	xii. 32	36
vi. 11	29	xv. 33	94	xiii. 14	31
vi. 12	29	xvii. 2	31	xv. 10–12	218
vi. 14 ff.	29	xix. 13	100, 101	xv. 13	59
vi. 20	139	xix. 16	101	xvi. 34	183
vi. 26	139	xx. 19	47	xvii. 1	75, 168
vi. 34	193, 200	xxi. 4 ff.	70	xvii. 21	77
vii. 1	38	xxii. 6	29, 31, 48	xvii. 22	77
viii. 18–21	137	xxiv. 7	375	xviii.	48, 175, 213
viii. 24	121	xxv. 2 ff.	48, 133	xviii. 4	40, 209
viii. 33	56	xxv. 8	133	xviii. 19	59
ix. 1 ff.	189	xxv. 36	133	xviii. 26–29	185
ix. 4	56	xxvi. 11	375	xviii. 40	40
ix. 6	29	xxvi. 19	264	xviii. 42–45	75
ix. 37	30, 74	xxvi. 20	37	xix.	191
ix. 45	139	xxviii. 3–25	91, 102	xix. 10	209
ix. 46	56	xxviii. 3	91, 103, 106	xix. 14	209
xi. 16	142	xxviii. 4 ff.	189	xix. 18	209, 214
xi. 31 ff.	94	xxviii. 4	91	xx. 33	74
xiii.	197	xxviii. 6	105	xx. 42	139
xiv. 19	291	xxviii. 7	38, 103, 105	xxi. 17 ff.	213
xv. 18	37	xxviii. 8	106	xxii. 6	200
xv. 19	37	xxviii. 9	92, 106	xxii. 7	202
xvii. 5	101	xxviii. 10	92	xxii. 19–23	222
xviii. 2	38	xxviii. 11	92	xxii. 20	222
xviii. 14	101	xxviii. 12	92	xxii. 21	222, 291
xviii. 17	101	xxviii. 13	53, 100,	xxii. 22	222
xviii. 20	101		127	*II Kings*	
xx. 26	139	xxviii. 15	105	ii. 3	202
xx. 33	30	xxxi. 13	31	ii. 5	202

II Kings	PAGE
ii. 7	202
ii. 8	75
ii. 14	76
ii. 16	291
ii. 19–22	76
iii. 27	94, 183
iv. 23	134, 135
iv. 32–35	77
iv. 38–41	76
v. 17	191
vi. 5–7	76
vi. 18–20	77
ix. 22	72
x. 15	211
x. 29	36
xi. 18	215
xii. 3 (Heb. 4)	218
xii. 16 (Heb. 17)	334
xiii. 14–19	76
xiv. 4	218
xiv. 7	53
xiv. 9	30
xv. 4	218
xvi. 3	94
xvi. 10 ff.	241
xvi. 15	334
xvii. 9	59
xvii. 16	36
xvii. 17	74, 75
xvii. 24–28	191
xviii.	242
xviii. 4	218
xviii. 4–6	242
xix. 34	278
xxi. 1	254
xxi. 6	74, 94, 104, 106
xxi. 7	59
xxiii. 4 ff.	218
xxiii. 4	59
xxiii 5	59
xxiii. 7	59
xxiii. 8	48, 112
xxiii. 10	94
xxiii. 11	271
xxiii. 12	271
xxiii. 24	101, 104, 106
xxiv. 13	278
xxiv. 14–16	276
xxiv. 17	379
xxv. 1–22	277
xxv. 11	277
xxv. 12	277
xxv. 18	277
xxv. 19	277
xxv. 23–26	277
xxv. 25	277
xxv. 26	277

I Chronicles	PAGE
vi. 77 (Heb. 62)	48
viii. 33	199
viii. 34	199
x. 12	31
x. 13	105

I Chronicles	PAGE
x. 14	105
xiv. 7	199
xiv. 15	31
xv. 21	114
xxi. 1	319
xxiii. 31	135

II Chronicles	
ii. 4 (Heb. 3)	135
viii. 13	135
viii. 17	44, 143
xi. 15	112
xx. 2	36
xxxi. 3	135
xxxiii. 6	72, 74, 106
xxxiii. 11	254
xxxvi. 9	276
xxxvi. 10	276
xxxvi. 17–20	277

Ezra	
ii. 2	380
ii. 3 ff.	284
ii. 20 ff.	284
ii. 36 ff.	284
iii. 5	135
v. 3	380
viii. 1 ff.	284
viii. 16 ff.	284
x. 15	321

Nehemiah	
ii. 1	130
ii. 13	37
iii. 12	73
viii.–x.	409
viii. 7	321
viii. 9	333
ix. 14	321
x. 25 (Heb. 26)	73
x. 33 (Heb. 34)	135, 321
x. 37 (Heb. 38)	322
x. 38 (Heb. 39)	322
xi. 16	321
xi. 29	38
xiii. 15–22	321
xiii. 17–21	135

Job	
iii.	348
iii. 11–19	252
iv. 14	56
vi. 12	356
vii. 17	351
vii. 18	351
xiii. 14	256
xiii. 15	350
xvi. 18–21	349
xvii. 13–16	354
xix. 25–27	350, 355 ff.
xxvi. 5	251
xxvi. 6	354
xxviii.	371 f.
xxviii. 22	354
xxxvi. 15	351
xxxvii. 22	279

Job	PAGE
xxxviii. 17	253
xxxix. 18	115
xli. 33 (Heb. 35)	356
xlii. 2 ff.	356
xlii. 5	356
xlii. 6	350

Psalms	
i. 3	40
ii. 7 ff.	376
vi. 5 (Heb. 6)	359
vii.	73
viii. 3 (Heb. 4)	351
viii. 5 (Heb. 6)	53
xi.	339
xix. 7–11 (Heb. 8–12)	322
xxii.	413
xxiii.	87, 339
xxv.	339
xxviii. 1	359
xxix.	155
xxx. 9 (Heb. 10)	359
xxxi. 12 (Heb. 13)	360
xxxv.	73
xxxvi. 6 (Heb. 7)	327
xxxvii.	345, 347
xli. 7 (Heb. 8)	73
xlii.–xliii.	191, 328
xlii. 6 (Heb. 7)	328
xliii. 4	328
xliii. 36	328
xlv. 6 (Heb. 7)	92
l. 8–15	337
li.	339
lviii. 1 (Heb. 2)	92
lviii. 3–9 (Heb. 4–10)	72
lviii. 6 (Heb. 7)	74
lix.	73
lxviii. 7	144
lxviii. 8	144
lxix.	73
lxxii.	376
lxxiii.	363
lxxiii. 2	363
lxxiii. 3–5	363
lxxiii. 12	363
lxxiii. 23–25	364
lxxxi. 3 (Heb. 4)	135
lxxxviii. 4 (Heb. 5)	360
lxxxviii. 5 (Heb. 6)	360
lxxxviii. 10–12 (Heb. 11–13)	361
lxxxviii. 10 (Heb. 11)	251, 252
lxxxviii. 12 (Heb. 13)	359
xc. 4	391
xci.	73
xci. 5	118, 119, 120
xci. 6	119, 120

	PAGE		PAGE		PAGE
Psalms		*Isaiah*		*Isaiah*	
cvi. 28	358	viii. 11	248	xl. 28	300, 307
cvii. 34	139	viii. 19 ff.	240	xli. 4	307
cx.	376	viii. 19		xli. 8–10	301
cxix. 17	323		103, 106, 127, 359	xlii. 1–9	303
cxix. 22	323	ix. 1 ff.	241	xlii. 1–4	303
cxix. 94	323	ix. 6 f.	378	xlii. 1	304, 305, 306,
cxix. 121	323	ix. 13	240		307
cxix. 173	323	x. 1 f.	239	xlii. 2	305
cxxxvii. 1–3	282	x. 5 ff.	241	xlii. 3	305
cxxxvii. 4–6	282	x. 5–19	226	xlii. 4	305
cxxxix. 7–18	362	x. 20 ff.	241	xliii. 10	300, 307
cxxxix. 7–12	361	xi. 1 ff.	241, 377	xliv. 4	40
cxxxix. 13	362	xi. 1–9	379	xliv. 6	307
cxxxix. 14	362	xi. 5	377	xliv. 9	330
cxxxix. 15–18	362 f.	xi. 10	380	xliv. 18	330
cxli.	73	xiii. 1–xiv. 23	309	xliv. 22	301
cxli. 2	334	xiii. 17–19	299	xlv. 1	302, 379
cxlvi. 4	359	xiii. 21	112, 114	xlv. 5–7	300
Proverbs		xiii. 22	114, 115	xlv. 7	313
ii. 18–19	251	xiv. 4–21	368	xlv. 14	302
ii. 19	252	xiv. 9	92, 251	xlv. 18	300
viii.	314, 372	xiv. 10	248, 251	xlv. 20	272
viii. 22	326	xiv. 13	274	xlv. 22	302, 315
viii. 23	326	xiv. 15	354	xlv. 23	302
ix. 18	251	xiv. 29	112	xlvi. 1	273
xv. 11	354	xv. 2	44	xlvi. 10	302
xvi. 10	75	xv. 8	39	xlvi. 11	302
xxi. 16	251	xix. 3	104, 106	xlvii. 9	72, 74
xxvii. 20	354	xxiv.–xxvii.		xlvii. 12	72, 74
xxx. 15	118		355, 376, 391	xlvii. 13	273
Ecclesiastes		xxiv. 21–23	390	xlviii. 11	302
iii. 21	365	xxvi. 14	251	xlviii. 12	307
viii. 10	365	xxvi. 16	73	xlix. 1–13	303
ix. 1–11	354	xxvi. 19	354, 396	xlix. 1–3	307
ix. 1–3	365	xxviii. 2	120	xlix. 1	304
x. 11	72	xxviii. 7 ff.	240	xlix. 3	304, 306
Isaiah		xxviii. 15	247, 248	xlix. 5	304, 306
i. 4–9	262	xxviii. 18	252	xlix. 6	304, 305, 306
i. 10 ff.	231	xxix. 4	103, 106	xlix. 7–9	306
i. 10–17	240, 336	xxix. 8	103	xlix. 7	306
i. 11 ff.	165	xxix. 14	325	xlix. 22	303
i. 11–15	232	xxx. 1 ff.	241	xlix. 23	303
i. 13	135	xxx. 6	112	l. 4 ff.	307
ii. 6	74	xxxi. 1 ff.	241	l. 4–11	303
ii. 8	240	xxxii.	377	l. 4–9	303
iii. 3	73, 74	xxxii. 1 ff.	241, 378	li. 1–3	286
iii. 12	239	xxxii. 1–5	377	li. 6	307
iii. 14	240	xxxiv. 2	139	li. 7	286
iii. 15	239	xxxiv. 3	139	li. 8	307
iii. 16 ff.	240	xxxiv. 5	139	li. 9	272
iii. 20 ff.	121	xxxiv. 6	139	li. 10	272
iii. 20	73, 247, 248	xxxiv. 11–15	117	lii. 13–liii. 12	303, 345
v. 5 ff.	240	xxxiv. 14	112, 117	lii. 13	306
v. 7	239	xxxvii. 6 b	241	lii. 14	305
v. 11 ff.	240	xxxvii. 35	241	lii. 15	306
v. 14	247 f.	xxxviii. 17	354	liii. 2	305
v. 22	240	xxxviii. 18	248	liii. 5	305
v. 23	239	xl.–lv.	299, 345, 382	liii. 4–6	304
vi.	112	xl. 8	300, 307	liii. 4	305
vii. 1 ff.	241	xl. 11	301	liii. 5	306
vii. 3	241	xl. 12–15	300	liii. 6	307
vii. 11	247	xl. 18	53	liii. 8 ff.	353 f.
vii. 14 f.	378	xl. 27 ff.	229	liii. 8–12	352

	PAGE		PAGE		PAGE
Isaiah		**Jeremiah**		**Ezekiel**	
liii. 8	306	xxii. 24	380	viii. 14–17	272
liii. 9	306, 307	xxiii. 1	279	ix. 1–11	292
liii. 11 *a*	346	xxiii. 2	279	ix. 2–11	274
liii. 12	308, 393	xxiii. 5 ff.	378	ix. 9	281
liv. 5	302	xxiii. 11–14	279	x. 1 ff.	292
liv. 13	302	xxiv.	329	x. 4 ff.	295
liv. 14	302	xxiv. 5	278	xi. 1–6	291
lv. 1	323	xxvii. 9	72, 74	xi. 2–11	273
lv. 4	303	xxviii. 1–4	278	xi. 16	284
lv. 5	303	xxix. 1–7	283	xi. 17	296
lv. 13	307	xxix. 8	278	xiii. 11	296
lvi. ff.	323	xxix. 9	278	xiv. 1 ff.	272
lvi.–lxvi.	321	xxxi. 29	338	xiv. 1–11	281
lvi. 1	323	xxxi. 30	338	xiv. 1	284
lvi. 2	321	xxxi. 31–34	265	xiv. 9	222, 263
lvi. 6	321	xxxii.	255	xiv. 11	281
lvii. 3	74	xxxii. 35	59, 94	xiv. 19	296
lviii. 13	321	xxxiii. 17	380	xvi. 29	271
lxii. 4	60	xxxvi. 5	264	xvii. 2	369
lxv. 2–4	105	xl. 7–12	277	xvii. 4	271
lxv. 4	67	xli.–xliv.	277	xviii.	338
lxv. 11	100, 273	xli. 5	203, 334	xviii. 20	292
lxvi. 3	67, 131	xliii. 6	289	xix. 10	40
lxvi. 14	131	xliii. 7	289	xx. 1 ff.	284
lxvi. 17	67, 131	xliv. 8	280	xx. 12–24	286
lxvi. 23	135, 321	xliv. 15–19	280	xx. 33	296
Jeremiah		xliv. 17–19	272	xx. 34	296
ii. 1 ff.	261	xliv. 25	272	xx. 40	296
ii. 2–3	168	xliv. 27	280	xx. 41	296
ii. 16–19	280	xliv. 30	280	xx. 47 (Heb. xxi. 3)	
ii. 20 ff.	261	xlvi. 10	139		296
ii. 23	217	xlviii. 46	68	xx. 48 (Heb. xxi. 4)	
ii. 27	67, 68, 175	xlix. 21	44, 143		296
ii. 28	279	l. 15	139	xxi. 3–5 (Heb. 8–10)	
iii. 6 ff.	261, 262	l. 25	139		296
iv. 30	261	l. 39	114	xxi. 21 (Heb. 26)	
v. 1 ff.	261	lii. 28	276		75, 101, 250
v. 28	261	lii. 29	277	xxi. 22 (Heb. 27)	75
vi. 4	139	lii. 30	277	xxii.	279
vi. 16	285	**Ezekiel**		xxii. 22	296
vi. 20	165, 285, 334	i. 3	271	xxiii. 31–34	296
vii. 4	278	i. 4	273	xxiii. 39	94
vii. 5	261	i. 5 ff.	274	xxiv. 25	353
vii. 9	279	i. 5–10	292	xxv.–xxxii.	296
vii. 12 ff.	262	i. 10	274	xxviii. 8	354
vii. 17–19	279	i. 26–28	290	xxviii. 14	274
vii. 17	272	ii. 2	291	xxviii. 16	274
vii. 18	272, 279	iii. 14	291	xxx. 12	296
vii. 21		iii. 15	273	xxxi. 8	274
	165, 231, 255, 285	iv. 14	294	xxxi. 9	274
vii. 22	285	v. 5–10	279	xxxii. 17–32	252
vii. 31	59, 94	v. 11	279	xxxii. 23	354
viii. 8	257	v. 15–17	296	xxxii. 25	354
viii. 17	72	vi. 3	59	xxxii. 27	93, 250, 253
xvi. 10	279	vi. 4–6	279	xxxii. 28–30	354
xvii. 8	40	vi. 13	279	xxxiii. 21–29	279
xvii. 11	37	vii. 7 ff.	295	xxxiii. 25	131, 279
xviii. 18	325	viii. 1	273, 283	xxxiv. 12	299
xix. 5	59	viii. 2	295	xxxiv. 22 ff.	376
xx. 7 ff.	263	viii. 3	291	xxxiv. 23 ff.	296
xx. 7	222	viii. 9–18	279	xxxiv. 25–27	296
xxii.	262	viii. 10	67	xxxv.	296
xxii. 13	208	viii. 12	281	xxxvi. 16 ff.	293

	PAGE
Ezekiel	
xxxvi 16–30	293
xxxvi. 31	294
xxxvi. 33	296
xxxvi. 34	296
xxxvi. 35	296
xxxvii.	294, 302
xxxvii. 12–14	296
xxxvii 15 ff.	379
xxxvii. 24–26	296
xxxvii. 26–28	296
xxxviii.–xxxix.	295, 297
xxxviii. 18–23	297
xl.–xlviii.	295, 297
xl.	274
xl. 3 f.	291
xlii. 13	295
xliii. 19	295
xliv. 10–27	295
xliv. 17–19	295
xlv. 15	335
xlv. 17	135, 335
xlvi 1	135
xlvi. 2	133
Daniel	
ii. 2	72, 78
vii. 10	392
vii. 13–14	383
vii. 13	398
viii. 11–14	335
ix. 11	404
xi. 31	335
xii. 2	355
xii 11	335
Hosea	
i. 14	215
ii.	60
ii. 5 (Heb. 7)	133, 192
ii. 8 (Heb. 10)	
	192, 196, 217
ii. 11 (Heb. 13)	135
ii. 13 (Heb. 15)	217
ii. 14 f. (Heb. 16 f.)	239
ii. 17 (Heb. 19)	217
iii. 4	101
iv. 2	237
iv. 8	334
iv. 11	240
iv. 14	61
v. 1	48, 238
v. 13	238
vi. 6	165, 231
vii. 3	238
vii. 7	236
vii. 8	238
vii. 11	238
viii. 4	236, 238
viii. 5 ff.	237
viii. 5	36
viii. 6	36
viii. 9–11	238
viii. 10	238
viii. 11 ff.	231

	PAGE
Hosea	
viii. 13	219
ix. 3	219
ix. 6	219, 238
xi. 1–4	237
xi. 2	217
xiii. 2	94, 237
xiii. 10–11	238
xiii. 13 ff.	239
xiii. 14	120 239, 248
Joel	
iii. 9–14	316
Amos	
i. 1	168
i. 2	203
i. 3–15	228
ii. 1–3	229
ii. 1	235
ii. 6	236
ii. 7 b–8	235
ii. 8	221
ii. 9–10	27
ii. 10	159
ii. 11	210
iii. 1–2	229
iv. 1	205
iv. 4 f.	235
iv. 6–11	235
iv. 13	235
v. 4	201
v. 5	39, 218, 235
v. 8	235
v. 18–20	227, 228, 386
v. 18	235
v. 21 ff	165, 235
v. 21–25	336
v. 21–23	231
v. 24	236
v 25	235
v. 26	196, 218
vi 13	238
vii. 9	59, 236
viii. 4	129
viii. 5	129, 135, 236
viii. 6	236
viii. 14	196. 218
ix. 2	247, 248
ix. 3	37
ix. 6	235
ix. 7	227, 235
ix. 11	380
Obadiah	
1–14	309
Jonah	
ii. 5 (Heb. 6)	143
ii. 6 (Heb. 7)	354
Micah	
iii. 5	139
iv. 13	139
v. 2–4 (Heb. 1–3)	380
v. 12 (Heb. 11)	71, 74
vi. 6–8	337
vi. 6	295
vi. 7	285

	PAGE
Nahum	
i. 1 ff.	278
i 1–11	260
iii. 4	72
iii. 16	271
Habakkuk	
i. 12	140
i. 13	266, 344
i. 4	248, 345
ii. 5	247, 248
iii. 7	44
Zephaniah	
i. 5	271
i. 14 ff.	261
i. 14–18	392
ii. 9	139
iii. 3	392
Haggai	
i. 11–15	318
ii. 1–9	306
ii. 4–5	306
ii. 6	317
ii. 7	317
ii. 8	318
ii. 11 ff.	317
ii. 20–23	318
ii. 23	306
Zechariah	
i 19 (Heb. ii. 1)	318
ii. 1–13 (Heb. 5–17)	
	318
iii.	381
iii. 1–2	319
iii. 8	318, 381
iii. 9	318
iv. 6	306, 381
iv. 10	318
iv. 11	306
iv. 14	306
v. 1–4	138, 318
v. 5	318
v. 11	318
vi. 9 ff.	381
vi. 9–15	318
vi. 12	306, 381
vii. 3	286
vii. 5	286
viii. 4	381
viii. 9–15	382
viii. 19	286
viii. 20	382
ix. 7	131
ix. 9–15	382
ix. 9–11	382
ix. 13	155
ix. 14	155
x. 2	101
Malachi	
ii. 11	68
iii. 1–6	318
iii. 5	72
iii. 8–10	322

II. NEW TESTAMENT

	PAGE		PAGE		PAGE
Matthew		*John*		*Colossians*	
v. 17	411	iv. 24	333	ii. 16	129
vi. 1–18	407	*Romans*		*I Thessalonians*	
xvii. 1–8	22	iii. 10	408	iv. 17	414
xix. 27	407 f.	*I Corinthians*		*Hebrews*	
xx. 1–16	407	xv. 55	239	xi. 39	411
Mark		*II Corinthians*		xi. 40	411
vii. 3	409	xii. 2	356	*II Peter*	
ix. 2–8	22	xii. 3	356	iii. 10	393
xiii.	398	*Galatians*		*Revelation*	
Luke		ii. 16	408	v. 8	334
ix. 28–36	22	*Ephesians*		viii. 3	334
xvii. 10	408	ii. 9	408	viii. 4	334
xviii. 9–14	408	*Philippians*		xxii. 2	396
xviii. 31 ff.	353	i. 23	414	xxii. 17	396

III. APOCRYPHA AND PSEUDEPIGRAPHA

	PAGE		PAGE		PAGE
Tobit		*Ecclesiasticus*		*Enoch*	
i. 6	403	xlvi. 12	131	x. 11 ff.	390
i. 7	403	xlix. 10	131	xvii. 4	392
i. 10	282	*I Maccabees*		xvii. 5	392
ii. 1	403	i. 11–15	341, 404	xxv. 4	396
ii. 5	403	i. 30–32	405	xxv. 5	396
iv. 3	403	i. 34	405	xxx. 8	395
iv. 8–10	403	ii. 32 ff.	405	xlviii. 4	399
v. 13	403	ii. 42 ff.	406	xlviii. 7	398
vi. 12	403	ii. 42–48	406	li. 1 ff.	395
vii. 13	403	vii. 10 ff.	406	lii. 4	398
vii. 14	403	*Apocalypse of Ezra*		lxii. 7	398
xii. 8	403	iv. 36	399	xci. 15	390
xii. 9	403	iv. 37	399	xcii. 7	397
Wisdom of Solomon		xiii. 26	398, 399	xcii. 8	397
vii. 22–viii. 1	372	xiii. 52	398	*Psalms of Solomon*	
vii. 25	373	xiv. 9	398	xv.	392
vii. 26	373	*Ascension of Isaiah*		xv. 6	392
Ecclesiasticus		v.	254	xv. 7	392
iii. 30	403	*Assumption of Moses*		xvii. 21	398
viii. 9	402	x. 1–10	392	xvii. 22 ff.	398
xv. 1	403	*Enoch*		xvii. 42	398
xix. 20	403	i.–xxxvi.	392	*Secrets of Enoch*	
xxiv. 23	403	i. 8	397	viii. 2 ff.	396
xxix. 12	403	vi. 7	114	xxiv. 4	388
xxxii. 17	402	ix. 6	114	*Sibylline Oracles*	
xxxix. 1 ff.	402	x. 4–6	114	173 ff.	392
xlvi. 11	131				

TESTAMENTS OF THE TWELVE PATRIARCHS

	PAGE		PAGE		PAGE
Levi		*Judah*		*Naphtali*	
xviii.	384	xxiv. 5	398	viii.	390
xviii. 4	399	xxiv. 6	398, 399		
xviii. 5	399				
xviii. 9	399	*Issachar*		*Benjamin*	
xviii. 10	396	vii.	390	v.	389

INDEX: GENERAL

Aaron, 114, 160, 164
Aaronic priesthood, 163
Aaron's rod, 77, 161
'*Abaddon*, 354
Abel, 169, 183
'*Abib*, 128, 130
Abihu, 163
Abijah, 68
Abimelech, 29, 39, 189
Abomination, a technical term, 70
Abraham, 26, 39, 55, 136, 330
   „ the friend of God, 301
Abrahamic rite, the, 341
Achan, 263
Achikar, Sayings of, 368
   „ Wisdom of, 327
Achor, Valley of, 239
Adapa, 80, 86
Adonijah, 46
Adonis, 34, 40
Adoption of king by Yahweh, 376
Adversity of the righteous, 344 ff.
Ælanitic gulf, 44, 143 f.
After-life, 17 ff., 79 ff., 243 ff.,
     352 ff.
       „ Conflict between official
          teaching and popular
          beliefs on, 248
       „ Final stage of belief in,
          352 ff.
       „ Second stage of belief in,
          243 ff.
Agricultural and pastoral groups,
     205
       „ festivals, 180 f., 198
       „ Palestine, Syncretism
          of, 197, 207
       „ stage in cultural
          development, 60, 165
Agriculture, Hebrews' contact with,
     60, 188
Ahab, 195, 208
       „ Jezebel married to, 209
       „ The court of, 200
Ahaz, 173, 218, 242, 247
Ahaziah, 215
Ahijah, 68, 208, 233
'*Ahu*, 115
Ahura Mazda, 313, 388 f.

Ai, 284
Aijal, 66
Aijalon, 66
'*Ain esh-Shems*, 96
'*Ain Qadis*, 153
Akaba, 142
     „ Gulf of, 143, 147
Aleïon, 51
Alexander, 340
Allatu, 244
'*Allon*, 53
'*Allōn-bakūth*, 28
Aloofness of Jews during the Exile,
     286 f.
Altar, 59
     „ of earth, 48
     „ Primitive, 166
     „ Rock, 197
Alu, 109
'*Aluq*, 118
'*Aluqah*, 118 f.
Amalek, 138
Amanus, Mt., 154
Amarna letters, 59, 244
Amen-em-ope, Teaching of, 326,
     368
Amorites, 27
Amos, 168, 177, 196, 201, 204, 228,
     231 ff., 289, 344
     „ and Hosea, 199, 236
     „ and the abolition of sacrifice,
       336
     „ and the Day of Yahweh,
       227 f., 235, 386
     „ and the northern Sanctu-
       aries, 203
     „ condemns the nations, 228 f.
     „ Condition of Israel during the
       time of, 234
Amulets, 73, 121, 179
Anakim, 249 f.
'*Anan*, 74
Anath, 178, 199, 261
Anathoth, 262, 284
Ancestor, Totem, 65
Ancestor-worship, 19 f., 98 ff.
Ancient of Days, 383
Angel of God, the, 55
     „ of Yahweh, 29, 40

428

Angelology, 314, 319
Angels, 53, 314, 319
Angra-mainyu, 388 f.
Animal-names of clans, 66
    „   „   persons, 66
    „   „   stocks, 63
Animals, forbidden as food, 64, 70
    „   Unclean, 67, 287
Animism, 5 ff., 33 ff., 329
    „   a stage of belief, 5, 7 ff.
Annihilation, Total, 354, 364
Anunnaki, 81, 85, 86 f.
Anthropomorphic demons, 117 ff.
Anthropomorphism, 370 f.
Antioch, 9
Antiochus Epiphanes, 335, 341, 343, 383, 404 f.
Anu, 50, 86
Aphaca, Pool of, 34
Aphek, 46, 202
Apocalyptic, 261, 312, 355, 382 ff., 386 ff.
    „   Christian, 394
    „   ideas, Extraneous, 298, 388
    „   Jewish, Developed forms of, 394
    „   language of Jesus, 413
    „   literature, 376, 396 ff.
    „   movement, 396
    „   Persian, 388 ff.
    „   picture of the Messiah, 382 ff., 398 f.
    „   teaching of Ezekiel, 295 ff.
Apocalyptists, determinism of the, 399
    „   differing views of the, 400
    „   dreamers, 399
    „   mainly concerned with world to come, 397
    „   prophets, 396 f.
    „   revealers, 399
    „   the Jewish, 396 ff.
    „   their universalistic attitude, 399 f.
Apocrypha, 401
Apollo, Sanctuary of, at Delphi, 9, 11
Apostasy, 188 ff., 261
Apprehension of God, 351
Apsu, 326
Apuleius, 185
Arab belief in After-life, 88 ff.
Arabia, Totemism in, 63 ff.
Arabian peninsula the home of the Semites, 3

Arabs as children of their gods, 65
    „   Modern, 25 f.
    „   Moon-worship among, 128
    „   Sacred waters among, 35
Aramæans, Hebrews were, 171
Aramaic, the early language of the Hebrews, 189
Araunah, 197
Archæology, Evidence supplied by, 171 f.
Ardat Lili, 117
Ariel, 103
Ark, 46, 47, 159, 161 f., 194, 202 f., 262
    „   Form of the, 161
    „   Object within the, 161
    „   Sanctuary of the, 202 f.
Arrow, 119
    „   of victory, 76
Arrows, Throwing of, 75
Artaxerxes I, 271
    „   Ochus, 383
Asa, 218
Ascension of Isaiah, the, 254
Ashakku, 109
'Asham, 334
Ashdod, 161, 179
Asher, 127
'Asherah, 43, 59, 175, 178
'Asherat iam, 51
'Asherim, 242
Ashes sprinkled on the head, 99, 196
Ashima(th), 177, 218
'Ashtor-Chemosh, 138
Ashtoreth. *See* Astarte
'Ashtoreth-Karnaim, 36, 178, 249
Ashur, 50, 127, 215, 225
Ashurbanipal, 83, 110, 254
Asia Minor, Mother-goddess of, 178
Asmonæus, 406
Ass, The Golden, 185
Assouan, 280
Assumption of Moses, 383, 392
Assyria and Yahweh, 226
    „   appealed to by Israel, 238
Assyrian cults in Israel, 216
    „   king, Power of, 233
    „   kingdom, End of, 259
    „   protection sought by Jehu, 216
    „   religion, 42
    „   ritual texts, 24
Astarte, 24, 36, 47, 59, 176, 178, 217
    „   of the two horns, 36
Astral deities, 218, 274
Atad, The floor of, 37
Ataroth, 219
Athaliah, 215

Atheistic Jews, 342
Athens, 341
Atonement, 322, 335, 415 f.
    „   Day of, 322, 335 f.
    „   Rabbinical teaching on, 337
    „   Vicarious, 346
Augury, 74
Augustus, 376
Autocracy, Struggle against, 206 ff.
Avesta, 391
Awakeners of the dead, 85
Awe, its place in religion, 4, 5
'Azazel, 113 f.
Azaziah, 114
Azekah, 96
Azriau, 154

Ba'al and 'El, 199
    „   applied to Yahweh, 199, 204
    „   Berith, 56
    „   cult, 279
    „   development from a spirit, 58
    „   enthusiasts, 200
    „   -Gad, 100
    „   -Hermon, 58
    „   Meaning of name, 57
    „   Me'on, 58
    „   of Peor, 45, 58
    „   Prophets of, 185, 213
    „   -religion, 57 ff.
    „   Sidonian, 213
    „   -tamar, 30
    „   -Yahweh, Syncretistic cult of, 231
Ba'alath, 57
    „   -be'er, 40
Ba'alism, 193
    „   Ethic of, 186 f.
Ba'als, 174 f., 190 ff., 237
    „   and Yahweh, 197
    „   worshipped by Israelites, 190 f.
Babylon, 276
    „   Mercantile life of, 271
Babylonia, Jewish exiles in, 283 f.
Babylonian belief in after-life, 79, 243 ff.
    „   beliefs adapted by Ezekiel, 273 f.
    „   cosmology, 252, 326
    „   cult of the dead, 101 ff.
    „   demonology, 275
    „   eschatology, 79, 243 ff., 375 f.
    „   god, Marduk the, 225
    „   gods, Jews tempted to worship, 271 ff.

Babylonian influence on the Jews, 271 ff., 325
    „   mythology, 272 ff.
    „   religion, 24, 42, 272 ff.
    „   " sabbaths," 135
    „   sacrifice, 182
Bamah, Bamoth, 43, 49, 58 f., 179
Balaam's oracles, 368
Balsam trees, 31
Ban, 139
Banu Badr, 65
    „   Hilal, 65
Baptist, John the, 316
Barak, 189
Baruch, Apocalypse of, 383
Be'alim, 57 ff.
Be'eliada, 199
Be'er, 38
    „   'elim, 39
    „   -lahai-roi, 39, 54, 127
Beeroth, 284
Beersheba, 27, 39, 48, 55, 203, 218
Bel, 50, 273
" Beloved," 218, 219
Belief, Three stages of, 4
Belus, 40
Benoth Ya'anah, 115
Ben-Sira, 368, 369 f.
    „   Sadducean attitude of, 365
Bered, 39
Berith, 56
Beth, 36
    „   Ba'al Me'on, 58
    „   Choglah, 37
Bethel, 28, 29, 31, 32, 36, 44, 45, 53, 126, 127, 159, 160, 175, 188, 203 f., 218, 234, 255, 284, 330
Bethel (god), 177
    „   Sacred bulls at, 159, 216
    „   Syncretistic worship of, 223
Beth-hagla, 37
Bethlehem, 205, 284, 380
Bethshean, 189
Bethshemesh, 36, 96
Be'ulah, 60 f.
Beza-'anannum, 28
Bildad, 347 ff.
Bit Humri, 209
Blind, Sight restored to, 77
Blood, 156 f., 255
    „   Atoning efficacy of, 335
    „   Life in the, 131, 157, 335
    „   personified, 169
    „   presented to the deity, 184
    „   -revenge, 137
    „   -ritual of the Passover, 130, 132
    „   smearing, 130, 132
Boaz, 46

Body, elements of the risen, 395
  ,, formed by God, 362 f.
  ,, laceration of, 99
Boghaz-keni, 56
Bohan, 46
Bones, 355
  ,, infants', found at Gezer, 182
  ,, life in the, 131
Book of the Covenant, 134, 158, 256
Bor, 354
Borsippa, 273
Boulé, 340
Branch, a Messianic term, 378
Bread, leavened, 180
Bronze serpent, 77, 111 f., 161, 179
Buddha, 223, 411, 412
Bull at Bethel, 160, 216
  ,, ,, Dan, 216
  ,, cult of, 159 ff, 179, 237
  ,, ,, sexual element in, 204
  ,, sanctuaries, 160
  ,, worship, 159, 204
Bundehesh, 391, 394, 395, 396
Burning bush, 28, 148 f.
  ,, ones, 111
Burnt-offering, 334
  ,, -sacrifice, whole, 181 ff.
Byblos, 43, 61, 153

Cain, 116 f., 183
Caleb, 66
Calf, Golden, 160
Caller, Spring of the, 37
Calvary, 417
Calves, 36
  ,, Spring of the two, 36
Cambyses, 280
Camel, sacred, 64
Canaan, Pre-Israelite inhabitants of, 24
  ,, religion of, 170 ff.
Canaanite cults, 174 ff., 180 ff., 197
  ,, ,, sites of, 170
Canaanites and the Sabbath, 134
Cannibalism, 95
"Captivity" a misleading term, 276
Carchemish, Battle of, 259
Care for the dead, 99
Caria, 11
Carmel, 48, 175, 185, 189, 213
  ,, the southern, 48, 205
"Carriers," 95
Cassiotis, 9
Castaly, 9
Cataclysm, Physical, 146, 317 f.
Cave of Macpelah, 100
Centralization of Sacrifice, 255 f.

Ceremonial, Israelite, 164 ff.
  ,, law, Ezekiel and the, 294 f.
Chabiri, 56
Chakam, 325
Chakam charashim, 74
Changes, social and economic, in eighth century, 233 f.
Chaos personified, 198, 225
Chariots of the sun, 218
"Charismatic" kingship of Saul, 207
Charmer, 74
Charsagkalama, 82
Chassidim, 406
Chattath, 334
Chazazon-tamar, 36
Chebar, 273
Cheble-ham-Mashiach, 398
Chemosh, 49, 68, 137, 157, 183, 218
Cherem, 137 f.
Cherubim, 203, 291 f.
Chesed, 238
Chober chabarim, 74, 121
Choglah, 37
Cimmerians, 260
Circumcision, 136, 286 f., 310
Clan, leadership of the, 167
Clans, named after animals, 66
Cobra, Bronze, at Gezer, 179
Code, Priestly. *See* Priestly Code.
Colonies of Jewish exiles, 283
Commemorations during the Exile, 285
Common law of Israel, 221
  ,, meal between god and worshippers, 183
Communion sacrifice, 183 f.
  ,, service, 331
Communities of religious enthusiasts, 200
Community life in the Exile, 283 f.
Comparative study of religions, 170
Concubinage, 221
Confucius, 223, 412
Conjurors of the dead, 101
Consecrated women, 61
Consultation of the dead, 90 ff.
Continual burnt-offering, 334 f.
Control, 106
Conversion of the Gentiles, 302
Corporate personality, 263
Corruption, 354
Corvée, 208
Cosmology, Babylonian, 326
Coucher, 116
Court-prophets, 202
Covenant, basis of Israelite monarchy, 207

Covenant, Book of the, 104, 129,
        134, 158, 256
    „   feast, 46
    „   New, 265
    „   sacrifices, 133
    „   the, 156 ff., 415
Cow-divinity, 36
Creation, Myth of, 198, 225
    „   Problem of, 370 ff.
Creator, Yahweh the, 225 f., 299 f.
Crescent moon, Sons of the, 65
Cromlech, 46
Crops produced with the aid of the
        deity, 175
Cross, the, 415, 417
Cult-objects excavated, 172
    „   of sacred beings, 99
    „   -prophets, 202
Cults, condemnation of non-Israel-
        ite, 173
Culture, primitive stage of, 4
Cultus in ancient Israel, the, 180 ff.
Cup-marks, 43, 197
Custom, persistence of, 48
Cutting of hair, 99
Cyrus, 299, 302, 379

Dagan, 50
Dagon, 161, 177, 179
Damascus, 177, 216, 233
Dan, cult of, 36, 203, 216, 218
Dance, ecstatic, 185
    „   sacred, 37, 130
Daphne, 9
Darius I, 382
    „   II, 271
Daughters of greed, 115
David, 31, 73, 177, 194, 207 f., 242,
        296, 375
    „   ancestor of the Messiah,
        378 ff., 387
    „   a Yahweh enthusiast, 199
    „   a shepherd, 205
    „   in Bethlehem, 205
David's child, 73
Day of Yahweh, the, 227 f., 235,
    261, 295 f., 318, 386
Dead, awakeners of the, 85, 86
    „   city of the, 245 f.
    „   consultation of the, 90 ff.
    „   cult of the, 19 ff., 101
    „   provision for the, 80 ff., 88 f.
    „   raising of the, 73, 77
    „   sacrifices of the, 358
Death, not the normal human lot,
    18
Deborah, 66
    „   Rebekah's nurse, 28, 100
    „   the prophetess, 29, 189

Deborah, the Song of, 144, 154,
        170, 202, 210
    „   the terebinth of, 30
Decalogue, the 158, 168
Deceit, Divine, 222
Delphi, 9
Demetrius Poliorketes, 340
Democratic spirit in Israel, 206 ff.,
    375
Demonology, 101, 108 ff.
    „   Arabian, 108
    „   Babylonian,   108 ff.,
            275
    „   Jewish, 110 ff.
Demons, authropomorphic, 117 ff.
    „   belief in, a development of
            animistic conceptions,
            111
    „   developing into angels, 113
    „   gods, and goddesses, differ-
            ences between, 12 f.
    „   in serpent form, 110
    „   of pest, 109
    „   of the night, 109, 110
    „   of the threshold, 117
    „   of the waste, 114 f.
    „   theriomorphic, 110, 111 f.
Déné Indians, 95
Departed spirits, Consultation of,
    102 ff.
Deportations of the Jews, 276 ff.
Descent of Ishtar, 85, 245 f.
Desert law, 147
Determinism of the Apocalyptists,
    399
Deutero-Isaiah, adumbration of a
            doctrine of resur-
            rection in, 308
    „   —   „   and the Servant of
            the Lord songs,
            303 ff., 345 f.
    „   „   conception of God
            in, 299 ff., 303
    „   „   teaching of, on re-
            generation, 301 f.
    „   „   teaching of, on uni-
            versalism, 302 f.
Deuteronomic law, 129, 134, 255,
    264, 331
Deuteronomist, the, 106
Deuteronomy, Book of, 255 ff., 310,
        321
    „   „   „   its effect on
                    other por-
                    tions of the
                    O.T., 257 ff.
Dhāt anwāt, 24
Diipolia, 47
Dimetu, 109

Dispersion, Jews of the, 343
Disruption of the kingdom, 202
Divination, 74 f., 166
   ,,   Teraphim used for, 101
Divine deceit, 222
   ,,   government, Justice of, 348
   ,,   justice, 345
   ,,   kingship, 375 f.
   ,,   leadership recognized by Israel, 164
   ,,   transcendence, 318
   ,,   will, Means of ascertaining, 166
Divining rod, 77
Dobaib clan, 64
Dodona, 7, 9
Doleful creatures, 114
Dove, sacred in Syria, 64
Dragon, 272
   ,,   Spring of, 37
Dreams, 105
Drugs, used in magic, 74
Dryden quoted, 291
Dualism, 313, 389 f.
Dying god, 375

Ea, 50, 85, 86, 326
   ,, the god of the deep, 33
Early Judaism, 271 ff.
Ear-rings, 121
Earth-mother, 60
Earthquake, 148
Eastern religion, Jewish contact with, 271 f.
'Eben, 45
   ,, *-bohan*, 46
   ,, *-'ezer*, 46
Ecclesiastes, 364 f., 368
Ecclesiasticus, 365, 368, 370, 401
Economic changes in Israel, 234, 239 f.
Ecstasy, 185, 356
   ,, and prophecy, 200
Edom, 112, 229, 380
   ,, The land of, 143
Edrei, 249
Egel, 66
Eglah, 66
Eglon, 66
Egypt, exodus from, kept in memory, 285
   ,, influence of, 325
   ,, jews in, during the Exile, 280
Egyptian magic, 78
   ,, origin of circumcision, 136
   ,, religion, 176
Eighth century, 216 ff.
Ekimmu, 108, 110

FF

'El, 52 f., 154, 174, 192
   ,, and Ba'al, 51, 192
   ,, nameless, 53
   ,, place-names connected with, 53 ff.
   ,, -religion, 52 ff.
   ,,   ,, ancient, 39
   ,, *-Berith*, 56
   ,, *-Bethel*, 55
   ,, *-'Elyon*, 54, 218
   ,, *-'Olam*, 39, 55
   ,, *-Pachad*, 56
   ,, *-ro'i*, 39, 54 f., 330
   ,, *Shaddai*, 54, 56
'Elah, 31, 53
Elam, 87
   ,, Temple in, 42
Elath, 143
Elders, 169, 283, 409
Eldest son, Offering of, 183
'Elealah, 57
Elect one, 395
Elephantiasis, 356
Elephantiné, Jews of, 172, 177, 195, 196, 219, 280, 327
Eliada, 199
Elihu, 347
Elijah, 75 f., 154, 168, 191, 201 f., 211 ff.
   ,, and Moses, 212
   ,, and the established sanctuaries, 216
   ,, and the prophets of Ba'al, 213
   ,, brings rain, 75
   ,, his work, 211 f.
Elim, 52 ff., (see also *'El*)
   ,, developed from spirits of the animistic stage, 57
Eliphaz, 347 ff.
Elisha, 75 f., 202, 214, 220
   ,, his magical powers, 75 f.
'Eloah, 53, 127
'Elohim, 53, 92, 127
" Elohistic " documents, 134, 141
'Elon Moreh, 26
Elteqeh, 53
Emblems, sacred, 159 ff.
Emim, 249 f.
'En, Names compounded with, 36
   ,, *-'eglaim*, 36
   ,, *-gedi*, 36
   ,, *-hal-Kore*, 37
   ,, *harod*, 38
   ,, *-ha-tannim*, 37, 38
   ,, *-mishpat*, 35, 36
   ,, *-rogel*, 37, 38, 46
   ,, *shemesh*, 36
Endor, witch of, 91, 102 f., 189

Engidu, 84, 102
Enlil, 225, 273
Enoch, Book of, 383
   „   Secrets of, 395
   „   Similitudes of, 384
Epher, 66
'Ephod, 166
Ephron, 66
Epiphanius quoted, 37
Eponym animal, 63, 67
Equinox, Spring, 129
Erech, Priestly school of, 110
Ereshkigal, 108, 244
Eryx, Temple at, 47
E-Sagila, 272
Esarhaddon, Inscription of, 42
Esau, 27
Eschatology, 235, 312, 375, 386 ff.
   „   a corollary of the
           doctrine of creation,
           227
   „   and prophecy, 227
   „   cataclysmic, 227 f.
   „   extraneous influences
           on Jewish, 387
   „   in Ezekiel, 295 ff.
   „   Inconsistencies in
           Jewish, 296, 394
   „   Main themes of He-
           brew, 386 ff.
   „   older than canonical
           prophets, 227 f.
   „   Persian, 386, 388 ff.
   „   popular, 227 f.
Esdraelon, plain of, 188
Eternity of Yahweh, 307 f.
Ethics and religion, 223 ff.
   „   of Ba'alism, 186 ff.
   „   of nomads, 166 ff.
'Etz, 76
Euripides, 223, 412
Evil eye, 73
   „   spirits, 414
Exclusiveness, Jewish, 286 f., 415 f.
Exile, communal life during the,
      283 ff.
   „   development of sacrificial
           system after the, 330 ff.
   „   experience of the, 328
   „   jewish colonies during the, 283
   „   religion during the, 309 f.,
           330 f.
   „   religious freedom during the,
           283
   „   religious teachers during the,
           309
   „   sense of sin quickened by the,
           333
   „   the early years of the, 276 ff.

Exiles, The returned, 284, 316 ff.
Exodus, 141 ff., 152
Exorcism formulas, 83 ff.
Exorcist, 84, 102
Expiation, 334
Eye, Evil, 73
Ezekiel, 259, 279, 281, 283 ff., 289 ff.,
      308, 310, 334, 344
   „   and the ceremonial law,
           294 f.
   „   his doctrine of divine tran-
           scendance, 290 f.
   „   his doctrine of God, 289 ff.
   „   his eschatological-apocalyp-
           tic ideas, 295 ff.
   „   in Exile, 280, 283 f.
   „   Latest record of, 299
   „   on individualism, 292 ff.,
           338
   „   on Messianic times, 296 ff.
   „   „ regeneration, 292 f.
   „   „ repentance, 294
   „   „ superhuman beings,
           291 f.
'Ezel, 47
Ezion-geber, 143
Ezra, 332, 412

False prophets during the Exile,
      278
Familiar spirit, 91
Farmer and nomad, 158, 205 f.
Fast-days abrogated, 286
Fasting, 99, 139, 322, 403
Fat presented to deity, 184
Fate, Book of, 274
Fatherhood of God, 237, 412, 413
Fathers, Tradition of the, 402
Feet, Baring of the, 99
Female demons, 117 ff.
Fertile spots owned by Ba'als, 58
Fertility deities, 60
   „   spirits, 174
Festivals, agricultural, 165, 198
   „   Moon, 128
   „   Passover, 129 ff.
   „   three chief, 165, 180 f.,
           331
Fire, World destroyed by, 391 f.
First-born of animals, 181
   „   of men, 182
Flowing water controlled, 75
Flute, 102
Folklore of Israel, 189
Food for gods burnt on the altar,
      181 f.
   „   forbidden, 287
   „   of immortality, 86, 396
   „   prohibited before battle, 139

Foreign elements in the cultus, 173 f.
Forgiveness, Divine, obtained by sacrifice, 333 ff.
Fortune, God of, 99, 273
Foundation sacrifice, 183
Frau Holde, 118
Fringes, 121
Full moon, 65
Fuller's spring, 38
Future life, Doctrine of the, 99 ff., 243 ff., 352 ff.

Gad (god), 99 f., 177, 273
  ,, (tribe), 205
Gal, 46
Galilee, Sea of, 189
Gallu, 109
Garden of the gods, 274
Garments, Rending of, 99
Gath, 96
Gathas, The, 391, 394
Geba, 48, 282
Gedaliah, 262, 277
Gentiles, converted through Israel, 302 f., 315
Gerousia, 340
Gezer, 43, 93, 170, 171 f., 176, 182, 217
Ghabghab, 43
Gharcad, 25
Ghost of Samuel, 127
Gibeah, 31, 48, 179
Gibeon, 203
Gift sacrifices, 181
Gihon, 40
Gilboa, Mt., 189
Gilead, 205
Gilgal, 46, 203, 218
Gilgamesh, 80, 84, 86, 102
God, Self-revelation of, 300
Gods, Anthropomorphic, 60
  ,, degraded to demons, 113
Go'el, 356
Gog, 297
Golah, 283
Golden Calf, 160
Goshen, 141
Gospels, Synoptic, 401
Graven image, 162, 168
Graves, Sanctity of, 100
Greek cities, 340 f.
  ,, period, 340 ff., 382 f.
  ,, philosophy, 367 f.
Green trees, 59
Gudea, 274
Guilds, Yahwist, 210 f.
Guilt-offering, 334
Gula, 50, 86
Gyges, 297

Habakkuk, 265 f., 344 f.
Hadad-Rimmon, 177
Hadhayaos, 396
Hagar, 54
Haggai, 317, 321, 380 ff.
Hair, Cutting off of the, 99
Hairy ones, 112
Hallochesh, 73
Hammurabi, 50, 189
Haoma, 396
Harp, playing of the, 282
Hasmonæus, 406
Hathor, 176
Hawk, 115
Healing, serpent an emblem of, 35, 38
Heave-offering, 58
Hebrew, pre-Mosaic, dwellers in Palestine, 56
  ,, spoken in pre-Israelite Palestine, 171, 189
Hebrews, Aramæan invaders were, 171
  ,, Epistle to the, 411
Hebron, 27, 188, 205
He-goats, 112
Hellenism, Influence of, on Jews, 340 ff.
Hellenistic Jews, 404 f.
Hepatoscopy, 24
Hephzi-bah, 61
Heracles and Hesione, 8
Hercules, 42
Herem, 177
Hermon, Mt., 328
Herodotus quoted, 42, 136, 260
Hezekiah, 218, 233, 254, 378
  ,, as king, 242
  ,, destroys the bronze serpent, 161
  ,, his reforms, 242
Hiel, 183
Hierapolis, sacred lake at, 34
  ,, ,, hot springs of, 8
  ,, temple of, 42, 69
High places, 43, 58, 179, 187, 218
High-priest, 322
Higr, 109
Hilal, 128
Hilkiah, 256 f.
Hill, worship on a, 58 f., 179
History, Yahweh the Lord of, 226 f.
Hittite civil law, 189
  ,, power, growth of the, 171
Holiness, conception of, 69, 240 f.
  ,, Law of, 104, 134, 287
Holy mountain, 274
  ,, water, 35

Honesty, Prophetic demand for, 236
Hophra, 280
Hor, 161
Horeb, Mt., 147, 152, 154, 160, 192, 203
Hormah, 138
Hosea, 197, 217, 223, 234, 236 ff., 261, 412
   „ and Amos, 236, 237
   „ and the northern sanctuaries, 237
   „ his marriage, 237
Household god, 101, 106
Houses in ancient Palestine, 178
   „ of eastern peasantry, 211
Human sacrifice, 93 f., 182 f.
Humanitarianism, 256
Huna, Rabbi, 120
Hvôv, 388
Hybridism, Religious, 196
Hydromancy, 74
Hyksos, 152
Hypostasis, Wisdom as a, 373
Hyrax Syriacus, 64
Hyrcanus, John, 406

Ideals, Prophetic and Priestly, 323 f.
Idols, 59
Idolaters in Jerusalem, 274
Ilani cha-ab-bi-ri, 56
Images, graven, 162
   „ molten, 162
   „ worship of, 161 f.
Imitative Magic, 76 f., 112, 180
Immanuel, 378
Immortality, Babylonian belief in, 79, 243 ff.
   „ belief in, 17, 308, 357 ff.
   „ popular and official conceptions of, 79 f., 90 ff.
   „ primitive belief in, 79
Incantation, 72 f.
   „ Magic, 76
Incarnation, 417
Incense, 102
   „ offering, 334
Incubation, 105, 221
Indian tribes, N. American, 13
Individual, God and the, 337 f.
Individualism, Ezekiel's teaching on, 292 f.
   „ Jeremiah's teaching on, 263, 292 f., 338
Individualistic Psalms, 339
Infant Sacrifice, 93 f.
Ingathering, Feast of, 165

Intellectualism, 342
Intermediary, Human, 163
Intermediate beings, 291 f., 318 f.
Ionian philosophy, 367 f.
Iranian apocalyptic, 388 ff.
   „ religion, 314
Isaac, Fear of, 55
Isaiah, 234, 239 ff., 247, 254, 289, 378
   „ statesmanship of, 240
   „ vision of, 161
Ishba'al, 199
Ishbosheth, 199
Ishtar, 50, 80, 85, 178, 245 f., 272, 279, 281, 329
Israel and the Ba'als, 190 ff.
   „ and Yahweh, 229 f.
   „ common brotherhood of all in, 206, 208
   „ common law of, 221
   „ democratic spirit of, 206 ff., 375
   „ earliest code of, 189
   „ in Palestine, 188 ff.
   „ limited monarchy in, 206
   „ prosperity of northern, 204
   „ settlements of, east of Jordan, 205 f.
   „ social and economic division of the people of, 205 ff., 220
   „ the king of, 206 ff.
Israels, Two, 205
Istigsam, 75
'Ittim, 106
'Iyyim, 115, 117

" J," Code of, 134
Jabesh, 31, 207
Jabneel, 53, 57
Jachin, 46
Jackal, 115
Jacob, 27, 37, 121, 127, 167
   „ at Bethel, 45, 55
   „ The Mighty one of, 56
Jacob-el, 127
Ja'udi, 154
Jehoiachin, 276, 328, 380
Jehoiakim, 233, 266
Jehu, 214
   „ seeks Assyrian protection, 215
Jeremiah, 68, 168, 217, 259, 261 ff., 277, 280, 283, 289, 345 f., 415
   „ and God, 264
   „ and the law-book, 257, 264
   „ and the New Covenant, 264 f.

Jeremiah, his agony, 263
   „   his letter to the Exiles, 283
   „   his teaching on individualism, 263 f., 292, 338
   „   his vision of the figs, 278
   „   his work, 261 f.
Jericho, 37, 138, 170, 183, 284
Jeroboam I, 36, 112, 203
   „   II, 216, 233
Jerome of Prague, 7
Jerusalem, 37, 170, 179
   „   after the exile, 278
   „   conquest of, 188, 202
   „   cultus at, 203
   „   fall of, 266 f.
   „   idolaters in, 274
   „   inviolability of, 241
   „   sanctity of, 197
Jesus Christ, 407, 411 ff.
Jethro, 147 f., 156
Jewish Apocalyptists, 396 ff.
   „   demonology, 110 ff.
   „   eschatology, 386 ff.
   „   „   Foreign influence on, 387 ff.
   „   exiles, Religious beliefs of the, 278 ff.
   „   Liturgy, Benediction in the, 313
Jews, deportations of the, 276 ff.
   „   hellenistic, 404 f.
   „   in Egypt during the exile, 280
   „   trading habits of the, 271
Jezebel, 72, 173, 209, 212
Jezreel, 53, 57, 189
Jinn, 25, 35, 108 ff., 157, 250
   „   in serpent form, 35
Jiphtachel, 53
Joash, 76, 215
   „   the Abiezrite, 29
Job, Book of, 347 ff., 355 ff.
Johanan, son of Kareah, 277
John the Baptist, 316
Jonadab, son of Rechab, 211, 214
Jonah, Book of, 415
Jonathan, 103, 199
Joqteel, 53
Jose, Rabbi, 120
Joseph, grave of, 100
Joseph-el, 127
Josephus quoted, 132, 152, 407
Joshua, 28, 45, 136, 164, 183, 409
   „   the Bethshemite, 47
   „   the gate of, 112
   „   the High-priest, 318, 381
Josiah, his book begins the history of the Bible, 257, 321

Josiah, his purification of the Temple, 112, 218
   „   reforms of, 104, 196, 218, 254 ff., 321, 331 f.
   „   „   their result not manifest till after the exile, 256
Jotham's parable, 30
Judah, Rabbi, 410
   „   Southern, unsuited for agriculture, 205
Judaism, 337
   „   a book-religion, 313
   „   post-exilic, main foundation of, 320
Judgement, the, 86, 387
Judges, lesson of the, 192 f.
Jupiter (planet), 127, 273
Justice, abuse of, 236
   „   prophetic demand for, 235 f.
Justification through observance of legal precepts, 407

Ka'ba, 64
Kabari, 273
Kadesh, 28, 35, 39, 100, 142
   „   (goddess), 177
   „   -barnea, 153
Kafirs, 9
Kalil, 133
Kappara, 335
Kareah, 277
Kashaph, 71
Kassites, 87
Kedeshoth, 61
Kenites, 147 f., 151, 165
   „   their beliefs compared with those of the Hebrews, 150
Kewan, 177, 196, 218
Khasis of Assam, 11
Kid, Spring of the, 36
King, The perfect, 377
Kingdom, disruption of the, 202
Kinship, common, of all Israelites, 125
   „   physical, between men and animals, 64
Kir, the early home of the Syrians, 227
Kiriath-jearim, 284
Kish (city), 82
   „   (God), 40
Kisheph, 71
Kishon, 40
Knots, 74, 121

Knowledge of Yahweh by the prophets, 223
Kurnugea, 244

Laban, 45, 127, 167
Labartu, 109
Labourers in the vineyard, Parable of, 407 f.
Laceration of the body, 99
Lachash, 72 f.
Lachish, 96, 217
Lamps, Festival of, 25
   „   on graves, 96
Land, Fallow, 181
Lappidoth, 29
Latifundia, 239
Law, 320 ff., 332, 341
   „   a means of salvation, 407
   „   and its developments, 401
   „   central position of the, 402, 404 f.
   „   christ's claims over the, 412
   „   elaboration of the, 287
   „   formulation of the, 309
   „   identified with Wisdom, 314, 403
   „   in the Apocrypha, 401 ff.
   „   of Holiness, 134, 287
   „   of purification, 287
   „   Oral, 320, 401, 402
   „   ordinances of the, affecting daily life, 322
   „   the exaltation of the, 333, 410
   „   the most important element in Judaism, 410
   „   the observance of the, 321
   „   the people of the, 316
   „   the stones of the, 161
   „   the works of the, 403, 408
   „   the written, 320, 401, 402, 409
   „   transgression of the, 404
   „   Yahweh as, 224 f.
   „   -codes, The sabbath in the, 134, 405 f.
Laylah, 118
Leah, 66
Legal precepts, their observance meritorious, 407
Legalism, 322, 404
Le-kapper, 335
Leprosy, 346, 356
Levi, 66, 164
Levites, 295, 322
Levitical prohibitions, 70
Libations, 335
Libnah, 96
Life after death, 17 ff., 79 ff., 243 ff., 264, 350, 352 ff.
  ..   water of, 85

Lilin, a class of demons, 118
Lilith, 117 f., 119
Lilitu, 117
Lilu, 117
Lintel, blood smeared on the, 130
Lithuanians, 7
Liturgies, Jewish, 313
   „   pre-exilic, 201
   „   synagogal, 365
Liver of an animal, 75
Living creatures, The four, 274
   „   water, 33
Lizard clans, 64
Local sanctuaries not condemned by Elijah, 216
Locusts, 64
Logos, the, 373 f.
Loreley, 118
Lot used for oracles, 75, 200 f.
Love, 238 f.
Lucian quoted, 25, 34, 69 f.
Lucretius, 223, 412
Lunar festivities, 128
Lurker, the, 116
Lycia, 11
Lydian kingdom conquered by Cyrus, 299
Lysimachus, 340

Maccabæan rising, 401, 403 ff., 406, 415
Maccabees, Books of the, 383
Machir, 205
Macpelah, Cave of, 100
Macrinus, 63
Magic, 16 f., 71 ff.
   „   among the Hebrews, a survival, 78
   „   Babylonian, 34, 72
   „   brew, 71
   „   condensation of, 72
   „   Egyptian, 78
   „   Imitative, 75 ff.
   „   rod, 77
   „   sympathetic, 180
Magical formula, 77
   „   powers of Elisha, 76 f.
   „   rites, 71
   „   „   the origin of sacrifice, 187
   „   terms, 71 ff.
   „   texts, Babylonian, 33, 72
Magog, 297
Maimonides quoted, 402, 409
Malachi, 317, 321
Mamre, 27
Manasseh, 72, 104, 196, 218, 242, 254, 378
   „   reaction under, 242

Manasseh, reign of, 254
Manes, 127
    „ -oracle, 106
Manifestation at a tree, Divine, 26
Manna, 161
Manoah, 197
Mantle, Magic, 75
Manual acts, 71
Marduk, 50, 86, 198, 225, 272, 275, 281, 329
    „ god of Babylon, 225
    „ Temple of, in Babylon, 33, 272
Marriage laws among nomads, 168 f.
    „ metaphor, 237
Martinique, 146
Masai, 168
Mashal, The, 367 ff.
Materialistic conception of After-life, 362 f.
Materialization, 106
Mattathias, 406
Mazzebah, 23, 45, 59, 175
Mazzeboth, 10, 172
Meal-offering, 334
Mecca, 35
Medes, 254, 299
Medicinal waters, 35
Medium, 101, 102, 127
Megiddo, 43, 170, 189, 217
Mekasheph, 71
Mekashephah, 71
Melanesians, 10
Melek, 218
Melkart, 209, 212, 216
    „ and Yahweh, 213
Memorials, 285 f.
Men changed to animals, 64
Menahem, 238
Menhir, 172
Mein, 100, 273
Me'onenim, Terebinth of, 30
Mephibosheth, 199
Mercantile life of Babylon, 271
Mercenaries, Israelites sold as, 219 f.
Meriba'al, 199
Merodach-baladan, 242
Mesha, 138, 154, 182, 218, 219
Meshalim, 369
Mesopotamia. See Assyria and Babylonia
Mesopotamian literature, 189
Messiah, 305 f., 375 ff., 395, 398
    „ Apocalyptic picture of the, 398
    „ as Judge, 398
    „ " Birth-pangs " of the, 398
    „ Jesus as the, 413 ff.
    „ of the tribe of Judah, 398

Messiah, pre-existence of the, 398
    „ Zerubbabel the, 306, 318
Messianic doctrine begins with Isaiah, 241 f.
    „ era, 318, 323
    „ hope, 320, 375 ff.
    „ ruler called the Shepherd, 296
    „ teaching of Zechariah, 317 ff.
    „ times, 296, 397
Metaphor, sexual, 237
Mezuzah, 132
Micah, 223, 234
Micaiah, 201 f., 222
Michael, 390
Midhbar, 155
Midian, 143, 147, 151
    „ Priest of, 147
Midrash to the Psalms quoted, 120
Migdal-Gad, 100
Migdabel, 53
Mighty one of Jacob, 56
Migrations the work of Yahweh, 226 f.
Mikdash, 59
Miriam, Grave of, 100
Mishnah, 401, 409 ff., 416
Mishpat, 321
Mitzwah, 402, 409
Mizpah, 48, 178, 217
Moab invaded by Israelites, 190
Moabite stone, 138
Mohammed, 412
Molten image, 160, 162
    „ metal poured into water, 162
Monarchy, disappearance of the, 281
    „ establishment of, 195
    „ in Israel based on a covenant, 207 f.
    „ limited in Israel, 206 ff.
Monotheism, 299, 313, 329, 412
    „ not of Babylonian origin, 275
Mont Pelé, 146
Monte Nuovo, 145
Moon, a fertility god, 131
    „ Full, 129
    „ sons of the crescent, 65
    „ sons of the full, 65
    „ worship of the, 128, 132
Moral reform, Impulse to, 223
Morality and sacrifice, 231 f.
Moreh, Terebinth of, 26
Mosaic priesthood, 163
Moses, 111, 125, 140, 146 ff., 151 ff., 156
    a priest, 163

Moses, an Egyptian name, 151
　„　and Elijah, 212
　„　and Jethro, 147 ff.
　„　and the Decalogue, 158
　„　historicity of, 151
　„　inheritance from, 169
　„　magic rod of, 77
　„　possessed of second sight, 186
　„　the task of, 156
　„　uses magic, 76
　„　whole sacrificial system not to be ascribed to, 164
Mot, 51
Mother-goddess of Asia Minor, 179
　„　-sea, 8
Mountain-god, Yahweh a, 154, 225
　„　The holy, 274
Mountains, sacred, 11, 44 f., 48 f.
Mourning customs, 99
Muhammad, 64, 412
　„　and God, 224
Murashu Sons, 271
Murder, nomad law of, 168 f.
Mutterers, 72, 106
Myrtle-tree, 25
Mythology, Babylonian, 272, 273
　„　of Israel, 198, 225

Naaman, 191, 328
Nabi', 194, 207
Nabonidus, 299
Naboth, 210
Nadab, 163
Naqaph, 155
Nahar, 33
Nahum, 260
Nakah, 155
Name taken in vain, 187
Namer, 66
Names, Theophoric, 195, 275
Namtaru, 108, 109, 120
Naples, 145
Naru, the river-god, 33
Narratives in Genesis indebted to a Babylonian prototype, 275
National unity of Israel due to Moses, 125
Nations condemned by Amos, 228 f.
Nature, Yahweh Lord of, 140, 225 f.
Nazirites, 210 f.
Nebi'im, 210 f., 222
　„　contrasted with the canonical prophets, 222 f.
Nebo 44, 50, 219, 273, 284, 330
Nebopolassar, 259
Nebuchadrezzar, 72, 272, 276
Necho, 255, 259

Necromancy, 21 ff., 71, 84, 90 ff., 98 ff., 240
　„　Babylonian, 101 f.
Negeb, 154
Nehemiah, 134, 321
Nehushtan, 177
Nephilim, 250
Nereids, 8
Nergal, 86, 102, 120, 177, 244, 274
New covenant, 265
New-moon festivals, 128 f.
New-moons and sabbaths, 128 f., 134 ff., 322
New Testament, 401, 406 ff.
New Year's Day, 272
Nichesh, 74
Niçibin, 109
Night-terror, 109, 118, 119
Nikal, 177
Nikunau, 11
Nimra, 66
Ninakhakuddu, 33
Ninazu, 85
Nineveh, 72, 233, 259, 260, 282
Ninib, 274
Nippur, 273
　„　excavations in, 271
　„　Jewish names on tablets from, 271
Nisan, 130
Noah, 80, 86
Nomad and farmer, 220
　„　his poverty, 166
　„　his religion, 3, 57, 125 ff., 140 ff.
　„　traditions of, 223 f.
Nomads and moon-festivals, 128
　„　ethical standards high among, 168
　„　law of murder among, 168 f.
　„　marriage laws of, 168 f.
Noph, 277
Numen, Possession by, 48, 185
Numina, 330
　„　venerated in Palestine, 174
" Numinous," 163
Nuzb, 43
Nymphs, 8

Oath, 187
'Ob, 91 f, 105 f.
Observance of legal precepts gives justification, 407
'Ochim, 114
Odes of Solomon, 398
Offerings in early Israel, 164 ff.
　„　of firstfruits, 58

Og, 249
Oil poured on sacred pillar, 43, 44
„ The offering of, 335
'Olah, 182
Older tribal members, Respect for, 169
Olives, Mount of, 48
Omar, Mosque of, 203
Omens, 74
Omnipotence of Yahweh, 224, 301
Omri, 209
„ end of the house of, 214
Ophel, 203
Ophrah, 29, 66
Oracle by lot, 75
„ -giving springs, 9
„ -terebinth, 27, 29
Oren, 66
Orthodoxy and the quest of truth, 347
Ostrich, 115
Owl, 89

Pahlavi literature, 391
Palestine, 176
„ conquest of, 188 f.
Palmetum, sanctuary at the, 35
Paphos, 11
„ temple of, 42
Parable of the Labourers in the Vineyard, 407
Particularism, 315 ff.
Partridge, 37
„ spring, 37
Passover, 129 ff., 132, 158, 165
„ a night celebration, 129
„ a spring festival, 130 f.
„ blood ritual of the, 132
„ explanations of the, 130
„ prohibitions regarding the, 131
„ sacrificial meal at the, 129
„ sacrificial victim at the, 129, 131
Pastoral and agricultural groups, 158, 205 ff.
Pathah-Moab, 284
Pathros, 277, 280
Paul, St., 239, 338, 401, 407, 408
Peer Gynt, 118
Pelé, Mont, 146
Peniel, River spirit of, 127, 330
Penuel, 53
Pe'or, 44, 45
Perfect king, 377
Perjury, 187
Perseus and Andromeda, 8
Persian eschatology, 388 ff.

Persian influence on Jewish belief, 308, 312 ff., 334
„ period, 382 f.
Persians, dualism of the, 314
Personal animal names, 66
„ names, formation of with Yahweh not found in Genesis, 56
„ religion, 263 f., 293
„ responsibility, 293
Personality, 336
„ corporate, 263
Personification of Wisdom, 372
Persons, sacred, 163 ff., 184 ff.
Peruvians, ancient, 8
Pesach, 130
Pestilence, 119, 120
Petra, 89
Phallic symbols, 41
Pharisee and publican, 408
Pharisees, 365, 402, 406, 413
Philistines, 31, 91, 176, 189, 194, 207, 227, 286
„ early home of the, 227
„ invasions of Palestine by the, 176
Philo of Alexandria, 342 f., 373, 409
„ Byblius quoted, 24
Philosophical speculation, 366, 372 ff.
Philosophy, Hebrew, 267, 370 ff.
„ Semites have no gift for, 366
Phœnicians, 51 f., 135, 136, 177, 208
„ holy places of the, 34, 42
Pietism, 320, 328 ff.
Piety, disinterested, 351
Pillars at entrance to temples, 42
„ sacred, 30, 42, 44, 55
Pirqe Abôth, 409
Pisgah, 44, 45
Pit, 354
Planets, the seven, 274, 292
Plato, 373, 413
Pliny quoted, 7
Pole, sacred, 43, 59
Polydæmonism, 11, 174
Polygamy, 221
Polytheism among the Hebrews, 50 ff., 177 ff., 196, 220
„ as a stage in religious development, 12 f.
Pomegranate tree, 30
Popana, 47
Porphyry quoted, 6
Positivism, 342
Possession by a numen, 185

Prayer, 403
" an accompaniment of sacrifice, 330 f.
Pre-animistic stage in religion, 4 ff.
Prerogative and privilege, 208
Priest and prophet, 257
" " " in the Exile, 286
Priesthood, 184 ff.
" Aaronic, 163
" development of, 322
" during the exile, duties of the, 288
" early, 163
" Mosaic, 163 f.
Priestly Code, 28, 105, 134, 287, 295, 313, 321, 334
" " priests and Levites in the, 295
Priests, apartments of the, 179
Problem of suffering and the Book of Job, 347
Procession, ritual, 37
Production of crops aided by deity, 180
Prohibited food, 287
Prophecy and eschatology, 227 f.
" ecstatic, 200, 222 f.
" spontaneity of, 201
Prophetic revolution, 213 ff.
" teaching on sacrifice, 165, 231
Prophets attached to sanctuaries, 201
" attitude of, to foreign politics, 238, 240 f.
" canonical, 222 f.
" denounce syncretism, 217 f.
" eighth century, 233 ff.
" identified God with goodness, 223
" in Babylon, 329
" sacrosanct, 213
" seventh century, 259 ff.
" teaching of the, 223 ff.
Proportion, Sense of, 351
Prosperity of the wicked, 265 f., 327, 345
Proverbs, Book of, 327, 368 f.
Prussians, Ancient, 7
Psalms, 286, 412
" doctrine of immortality in, 357 ff.
" individualistic, 339
" of Solomon, 392 f., 398
" of the post-exilic period, 337
" revision and adaptation of, 358

Ptolemy I, Soter, 340, 406
Punic votive tablet, 42
Punishment, Divine, 230
Puzzuoli, 145
Pyre festival, 25

Qasam, 74
Qesem, 74
Qeteb, 120
Queen of heaven, 199, 279, 280
Questioner of the dead, 102
Qor'an, 132, 224

Rabbis, teaching of the, 337
Rabitzu, 116
Race, solidarity of the, 338
Rachel, 66, 126
" grave of, 100
Ragab, 128
Rahab, 272
Rain brought by Elijah, 75
" "Inspirited," 75
" -making, 75
Ramah, 29, 179, 284
Ramoth Gilead, 222
Ras Shamra, 51 f., 59, 127, 153 f., 172, 177
Reason, 373
Rechabites, 210, 211
Reconciliation effected by sacrifice, 335
Red Sea, 141, 142 f.
Reed Sea, 142
Reform, moral impulse to, 223
" of Hezekiah, 242
" " Josiah 254 ff.
Regeneration, 293 ff., 301 f., 310
" of Nature in the Messianic age, 379
Rehoboam, 208
Religion and ethics, choice between, 220 f., 223
" during the Exile, 271 ff.
" " " " Freedom of, 283
" of Palestinian Jews retrograde during the Exile, 278 f.
Religious beliefs and practices, Roots of, 4
" " of Jewish exiles, 278
" observances during the Exile, 284 ff.
Remnant, doctrine of the, 241 f.
Rending of garments, 99
Repha'im, 100, 249 ff.
" a mythical race of giants, 249 ff.

Repha'im, the dead, 251 ff.
Resheph, 177
Responsibility, Individual, 292 f., 337 ff.
Resurrection, belief in the, 308, 393 f.
   „   doctrine of the, adumbrated, 355
   „   general, 355
   „   of the dead, 355
Retribution, doctrine of, 230
   „   twofold in the Hereafter, 394
Reuben, 205
Reuel, 156
Revenant, 105
Rewards, doctrine of, 323
Righteous, ambiguity of the term, 348
   „   God is ethically, 223, 287
   „   suffering of the, 308 f., 311, 344 ff.
Risen body, constitution of, 363, 395
Ritual, Babylonian, 290
   „   early Israelite, 164 ff.
   „   elaboration of, 335
   „   not demanded by Yahweh, 231 f.
   „   of sacrifice, 183
   „   prescriptions in their present form post-exilic, 198
   „   primarily sacrificial, 164
River-spirit, 127
Robetz, 116
Rock, water from the, 77
   „   -altar, 197
Rocks, sacred, 41 ff.
Rod, divining, 77
   „   magic, 77
   „   of Aaron, 77, 161
Rustling in the tree-tops, 31

Sabbath(s), 133, 134 ff., 158, 165, 168, 310, 321
   „   and New-moons, 136, 322
   „   Babylonian, 135
   „   first mention of, in O.T., 134
   „   gatherings on the, 286, 310
   „   laws of the, 134
   „   not originally a rest-day, 134
   „   observance of, not from Babylonia, 135
   „   origin of, unknown to Hebrews, 135

Sabbath(s) originated in nomadic times, 136
   „   refusal to break the, 235, 405 f.
   „   rest, 134, 288, 321
Sackcloth, wearing of, 99
Sacred dance, 37, 130
   „   dues, 322
   „   emblems, 159 ff.
   „   persons, 163 ff., 184 ff.
   „   „   representing a deity, 43
   „   springs, 35 ff.
   „   stone among pre-Islamic Arabs, 43
   „   „   as witness, 45 f.
   „   „   smeared with blood, 43
   „   stones in Palestine to-day, 44
   „   trees, 6 ff., 23 ff.
   „   „   Babylonian belief in, 24
   „   waters, 33 ff.
Sacrifice(s), abolition of, not taught by Amos, 336
   „   absence of, 336
   „   accompanied by prayer, 330
   „   and morality, 231 f.
   „   and worship, 336
   „   centralization of, 255, 331
   „   communion, 183
   „   covenant, 133
   „   for the dead, 358
   „   gift, 181 f.
   „   human, 93 f., 182 f.
   „   infant, 93 f.
   „   nature of, 181
   „   of Totem animal, 64
   „   offered before a campaign, 139
   „   originally magical rites, 181
   „   prophetic teaching on, 231 f.
   „   to the dead, 88
Sacrificial meal at Passover, 129
   „   system, 181 ff.
   „   „   and the Temple, 333 ff.
   „   „   development of the, 333 ff.
   „   victim, 58
Sad 'El, 51
Sadducees, 364 f., 402, 406, 413
Sages, 327
Sa'ir, Se'irim, 12, 112 f., 114, 117

Sakkuth, 177, 196, 218
Salt, sowing with, 139
  „ used in magic, 76
Salvation through Law, 407
Samaria, 36, 170, 234, 238
Samuel brings rain, 75
  „ ghost of, 91, 127
Sanctity of life among members of a
    tribe, 168 f.
Sanctuaries adapted to Yahwism,
    197
  „ in ancient Palestine,
    178 f.
  „ on elevated spots, 58 f.
Sanctuary, 58
Sarah, Grave of, 100
Saraph, Seraphim, 12, 111 f.
Satan, 114, 319, 347, 381, 390
Saturn, 46
Satyrs, 112 f.
Saul, 30, 31, 91, 103, 105, 161, 189,
    194, 199, 207
  „ a Yahweh enthusiast, 199
  „ burying of bones of, 31
Scapegoat, 114
Scepticism, 342
Scribes, 332, 367, 402, 407, 412, 416
  „ and Pharisees, 365
Scripture, first appearance of, 257
Scythians, 254, 260
Sea of Weeds, 143
Second commandment, 168
Seer, 185
Seir, the Horonite, 67
Seleucus, 340
Self-righteousness, 322
Semites, original home of the, 3
Semitic mind, 366
Semjaza, 390
Sennacherib, 233, 254
Sense of proportion, 351
  „ sin, 275, 279, 322, 333
Seraiah, 277
Serpent(s), bronze, 77, 111 f., 242
  „ emblem of healing, 38
  „ fiery, 111
  „ incarnation of demons,
    110
Servant of the Lord, character of
    the, 304 ff.
  „ „ „ Messiah, 305
    ff.
  „ „ „ prophet, 305
  „ „ „ songs, 303
    ff., 345 f.,
    352 f., 382
  „ „ „ the nation
    personi-
    fied, 304

Servant of the Lord, vicarious,
    suffering
    of the, 306
  „ „ „ vocation of
    the, 304
Seven planets, 274, 292
  „ sacred number, 39
  „ sages, 367 f.
  „ wells, 39
Seveneh, 280
Sexual element in bull cult, 204
  „ irregularities abhorrent to
    Israel, 221
  „ „ characteristic
    of Ba'alism,
    187
  „ metaphor, 237
Shaalbim, 66
Shabbethai, 321
Shachath, 354
Sha'ilu, 102
Shaman, 22
Shamash, 50, 86, 177
Shaoshyant, 388, 394, 395
Shapattu, 135
Sharon, 46
Sheaf, cutting of the first, 180
Sheba, 39
Shechem, 26, 27, 28, 29, 45, 100,
    126, 170
Shedim, 120, 121
Sheep-shearing, Feast of, 133
Shema', 132
Shemoneh 'Esreh, 365
Shemoth Rabba quoted, 410
She'ol, 57, 120, 246 ff., 267, 275, 308,
    352, 354, 358 ff., 395
  „ belief in, incompatible with
    Yahweh wor-
    ship, 360
  „ „ the second stage
    in the doctrine
    of immortality,
    253
  „ conception of, displaced
    older beliefs, 358
  „ earliest mention of, in eighth
    century literature, 248
  „ Hebrew conception of, 358 ff.
  „ official teaching on, 246 ff.
  „ seldom mentioned in pre-
    exilic writings, 246 ff.
Sheshbazzar, 275
Shiloh, 194
  „ Destruction of, 202
Shobal, 66
Shubililuiuma, 171
Sibylline oracles, 392
Sickness due to demons, 119 f.

Siddharta (Buddha), 223
Siddim, Vale of, 121
Sidon, alliance with, 209
  „   Ba'al of, 209 ff.
Sight given to the blind, 77
Sihon, 68
Silver cup, Joseph's, 74
Simeon, 66
Simone Porzio, 146
Sin (god), 50, 177
Sin couching at the door, 116
  „ -offering, 114, 334
  „ prophetic idea of, 230
  „ rabbinical teaching on, 407
  „ sense of, 275, 279, 322, 333
Sinai, 44, 143 ff., 154, 192
  „ a volcano, 143 f.
  „ location of, 143
  „ revelation at, 285
  „ Yahweh's dwelling-place, 328
Sinaitic peninsula, 143
Sisera, 155, 193
Sites on hill-tops, 179
Sky-god, 60
Slaughter of domestic animals in-
    volved sacrifice, 183
Slavonic Enoch, 383
Smith clan, 156
Smiths, 165
Snake, Bronze, 159, 161, 162, 179,
    203
Social orders existing side by side,
    Two, 205 ff., 223 f.
Socrates, 412
Soil, how it became fruitful, 60
Solidarity of the race, 292, 338
Solomon, 40, 173, 195, 208, 364
  „ Odes of, 398
  „ Psalms of, 392, 398
  „ Temple of, 161, 203
Soothsayers' terebinth, 30
Sorcerers, 72
Southern Judah unsuited for agri-
    culture, 205
Spectre, 101
Spirits, 6
  „ evil, at night-time, 118 ff.,
      132
  „ of the dead, 83 f.
Spiritual powers, contending, 390
  „ worship, 333
Spring equinox, 129
  „ festival, 128
  „   „   Passover, a, 130
Spring of decision, 35
  „   „ the caller, 37
  „   „   „ dragon, 37
  „   „   „ kid, 36
  „   „   „ partridge, 37

Spring of the sun, 36
  „   „   „ two calves, 36
  „   oracle-giving, 9
  „   seat of spirits, 36
Standing stone, 30, 41 f.
Stars, influence of, on men's lives,
    273
Stoicism, 373
Stone(s), animistic ideas concern-
    ing, 9 ff.
  „ anointing of, 11, 42
  „ -circle, 46
  „ -heap, Sacred, 41
  „ mark of spirit on, 10
  „ of covering, 46
  „   „ help, 46
  „ sacred, 9 ff., 41 ff., 161 ff.
  „ sanctuaries, 42
  „ twelve, as a memorial,
      46
Storm, Yahweh in, 155
Streams, 8 ff.
Suffering, mystery of, 265 f., 350
  „ of the righteous, 308 f.
  „ problem of, 265 f., 344 ff.
  „ strengthening of char-
        acter through, 351
  „ vicarious, 306, 346
Sumerian god Enlil, 225
  „ religion, 244
  „ tombs, 81 f.
Sun, spring of the, 36
  „ -stroke, 119
  „ -worship, 36, 218, 279
Sutekh, 177
Swearing, well of, 39
Syene, 280
Sympathetic magic, 180
Synagogue, 332
  „ Great, 409
  „ liturgy, 286, 365
  „ origin of, 256
  „ -worship traditionally
        founded by Ezra, 332
Syncretism, 196 f., 204
  „ of agricultural Pales-
        tine, 206, 220
Syncretistic worship, 281
Synoptic Gospels, 401
Syrens, 115
Syria, holy waters in, 34
Syrians from Kir, 227

Taanach, 43, 59, 95, 170
  „ pillars found on the site
        of, 43
Tabernacle, 162
Taboo, 15 f., 49, 67, 69 ff., 139, 220,
    263, 287

Taboo, explained, 69
Tabor, 30, 48
Tacitus quoted, 48
Tahpanhes, 277
Tamarisk, 31, 39, 55
Tame, 70
Tamid, 334 f.
Tammuz, 80, 85, 102, 177, 272
„   weeping for, 28
„   -worship, 279
Tannhäuser, 118
Tannim, 115
Tarahumares, 9
Tarifa, 100
Tarpu, 101
Taunt-song, 368
Tehom Rabbah, 272, 327
Tekoa, 234
Tel-abib, 273
Tell Duweir, 96
„   -el-Amarna age, 189
„   „   „   letters, 170 f., 244
„   „   -Mutesellim, 96
„   „   -Nasbeh, 178, 217
„   „   -Obeid, 81
„   -es-Safi, 96
„   -Sandahannah, 96
„   -Taanach, 59
„   -*Ta'anek*, 59
„   -Zakariya, 96
Temple and the sacrificial system, 333 ff.
„   inviolability of, 278
„   Jewish, in Elephantiné, 280
„   Josiah's purification of the, 218, 254 f.
„   of Solomon, 161, 203
„   rebuilding of the, 317, 318
„   repairs in the, 254 f.
„   services, Substitute for, during the exile, 285
„   the, 332, 365
Temples near sacred waters, 34
Terah, 127
Teraphim, 75, 100 f., 106, 126
„   a remnant of ancestor worship, 100
„   used for divination, 101
Terebinth valley, 31
Terebinths, well of the, 39
Theocratic government, 318
Theocritus, 180
Theophoric names, 275
Threshold demon, 117
Thummim, 103, 166
Tiamat, 198, 272, 390
Tiglath-pileser, 154, 219, 233
Time-periods, 387
Tithes, 181

Tobit, 401 f., 403
Tombs, deposits in, 80 ff., 94
„   food in, 80 ff.
Torah, 337, 402, 409 f.
Totem, 13
„   -ancestor, 68, 98
„   -animal, 63 ff.
Totemism, 13 ff., 49, 62 ff., 98, 183
Tradition of the fathers, 401
„   „   „   „   Respect for the, 169
Traditions retained, ancient, 205
Transcendence, Divine, 290 f.
Tree(s) animated by a spirit, 6 ff.
„   green, 59
„   Hebrew fables of, 30
„   held to be living beings, 6
„   oracular, 24, 25
„   Phœnician worship of, 24
„   possessed by spirits, 24
„   sacred, 23 ff.
„   -sanctuary, 24
„   -tops, rustling in the, 29
„   voice of a, 25
Trembling, well of, 38
Trespass-offering, 334
Tribal names, 99 f.
Tribes of same blood as animals, 63
„   and their gods, 137, 157
Tupper, Martin, 368
Tyre, 42

Uganda, Natives of, 7
Ugarit, 172
Unclean, 69, 70
„   animals, 287
Underworld according to Babylonian belief, Divine beings in the, 244
Uniqueness of Hebrew religion, 150, 157
Universalism, 302 f., 310, 315, 415 ff.
„   of the Apocalyptists, 387
„   teaching of, 302 f.
Unleavened bread, Feast of, 165, 180
Ur, 80, 82
'Urim, 91, 103
„   and *Thummim*, 166
Ut-napishtim, 80, 86
Utukku, 108, 110
Uzzah, 163
Uzziah, 216

Vegetation-god, 180
„   revival of, 131
Vergil, 376

Vicarious atonement, 346
   ,,   suffering, 306, 346
Victim, sacrificial, 59
Victory, Arrow of, 76
Vine, 211
Vineyard, Parable of the labourers in the, 407 f.
Vision of God, 350, 356, 357
Visions of Zechariah, 318
Volcano(es), 44, 154
   ,,   Mount Sinai a, 143 f.

Wailing, 99
Wanika, 9
War among Semites, 155
   ,, to consecrate, 139
Water deities among Babylonians, 33
   ,, from the rock, 77
   ,, living, 33
   ,, of life, 85
   ,, running, 8, 40
   ,, -witches, 33
Waters, medicinal, 35
   ,, sacred, 33 ff.
Wealthy class, Growth of, 233 f.
Weeks, Feast of, 165
Well(s), mistress of the, 40
   ,, of seven, 39
   ,, ,, swearing, 39
   ,, ,, terebinths, 39
   ,, ,, trembling, 38
   ,, oracles at holy, 38
   ,, sacred, 38 f.
Were-wolf, 64
Whisperer, 72 f., 106
Wilderness, Yahweh God of the, 155
Will of God made known, 163
Wine-offering, 334
Wisdom, 314, 320, 325 ff., 366 ff.
   ,, a hypostasis, 373
   ,, Ea, the Lord of, 326
   ,, existed before Creation, 326
   ,, Hebrew conception of, 325
   ,, in its fuller meaning, 370 ff.
   ,, -literature of Hebrews influenced by Babylonian and Egyptian thought, 325
   ,, of Ben-Sira, 365, 368
   ,, of Solomon, 372
   ,, personified, 372 ff.
   ,, the house of, in the Deep, 326
   ,, the vehicle of the divine message, 372
Wizard(s), 103
Women, consecrated, 61

Wonder, its place in religion, 4, 5
Wonder-child, 378
Wool given by deity, 133
Word, 370
Works, doctrine of, 324, 407
World, Creation of the, 371 ff.
   ,, destroyed by fire, 391 ff.
   ,, -epochs, 390 f.
   ,, -judgement, 391 ff.
   ,, -order, end of the present, 392, 397
   ,, -problems, 370 ff.
Worship, 320, 328 ff.
   ,, and sacrifice, 331
   ,, Canaanite objects of, 174ff.
   ,, centralization of, 255
   ,, non-sacrificial, 285, 336 f.
   ,, of Israel, 330 ff.
   ,, ,, Popular, 195
   ,, recognized objects of, 127
   ,, spiritual, 337
   ,, syncretistic, 279

Yah, 153
Yahu, 280
Yahweh, 153 ff., 195
   ,, a fertility God, 197
   ,, a fire God, 155
   ,, a Kenite God, 150, 156
   ,, a moral being, 228, 344
   ,, a mountain 'El, 154
   ,, ,, God, 225
   ,, a warrior, 155
   ,, a wilderness God, 155, 192
   ,, and Assyria, 226
   ,, and Israel, 149 f., 156, 226 f., 229 f., 236, 237, 241
   ,, and Melkart, 212 f.
   ,, and the Ba'als, 197
   ,, angel of, 29, 40
   ,, approach to, 164
   ,, as Law, 224 f., 235
   ,, beginning of the worship of, 136, 140 ff.
   ,, conception of, in the prophets, 222
   ,, ,, spiritualized, 307 f.
   ,, early exiles faith in, 278
   ,, has no dealings with the dead, 360 f.
   ,, in She'ol, 361
   ,, indistinguishable from the Ba'als save by His name, 200, 204
   ,, Land of, 191, 195
   ,, Lord of History, 226 f., 235, 329

Yahweh, Lord of nature, 140, 225 f., 235, 329
 ,, Lord of universal morality, 228, 329
 ,, makes no ritual demands, 231 f.
 ,, marriage of, 199
 ,, meaning of the name, 153
 ,, not found in personal names in *Genesis*, 56
 ,, omnipotence of, 224
 ,, origin of belief in, 149 f.
 ,, revelation of, 150
 ,, sanctuaries of, 197 f.
 ,, supremacy of, 344
 ,, the Creator-hero, 225, 235
 ,, the Day of, 228, 235, 261, 296, 386
 ,, the Everlasting, 307 f.
 ,, the God of all mankind, 338
 ,, the God of nature, 140
 ,, the God of the Hebrews, 146 ff., 159
 ,, the holiness of, 240 ff.
 ,, the knowledge of, 225
 ,, the Lord of the end of things, 227 f.
 ,, the name on Babylonian inscriptions, 153, 275
 ,, universality of, 328 ff.
 ,, with the exiles, 329
 ,, worship of, an unifying force, 193
 ,, worshipped before becoming the God of Israel, 149, 155 f.
 ,, worshipped in form of bull, 209
Yahwism, sanctuaries adapted to, 197 f.

Yahwist guilds, 210 f.
 ,, principles, Declension from, 206
 ,, revival, 205 ff.
Yam-Suph, 143, 148
Yav, 153
Yeno, 153
Yidde'oni, 106
Yo, 153
Yo-elath, 153
Yom-tob, 133

Zadok, 406
 ,, sons of, 295
Zamzam, The well, 35
Zamzummim, 249 f.
Zarathustra, 312, 388
Zebach, 133
Zechariah, 317 f., 321, 381 ff.
 ,, visions of, 317
Zedek, 177
Zedekiah, 378
Zemer, 133
Zephaniah, 259, 260 f.
Zerubbabel, 275, 306, 317
 ,, the Messiah, 306, 317, 380 ff.
Zeus, 7
Zion, Mt., 103, 154
Ziyyim, 114, 117
Zocheleth, 46
Zon, 133
Zophar, 347 ff.
Zor'ah, 197
Zoroaster, 312 f., 388, 411
Zoroastrian Bible, 391
Zoroastrianism, 312, 366
 ,, a book-religion, 314
 ,, and Judaism, parallels between, 312 ff.
Zuhal, 46
Zuzim, 250

*Printed in Great Britain by Richard Clay (The Chaucer Press), Ltd.,
Bungay, Suffolk*